The elements in order of atomic number

Atomic molar masses (in g/mol) are listed with five or fewer significant figures. For elements with no stable isotopes, the integer atomic mass number of the most common isotope is listed.

name	symbol	Z	Molar mass	name	symbol	Z	Molar mass
Hydrogen	H	1	1.0079	Iodine	I	53	126.90
Helium	He	2	4.0026	Xenon	Xe	54	131.29
Lithium	Li	3	6.941	Cesium	Cs	55	132.91
Beryllium	Be	4	9.0122	Barium	Ba	56	137.33
Boron	B	5	10.811	Lanthanum	La	57	138.91
Carbon	C	6	12.011	Cerium	Ce	58	140.12
Nitrogen	N	7	14.007	Praseodymium	Pr	59	140.91
Oxygen	O	8	15.999	Neodymium	Nd	60	144.24
Fluorine	F	9	18.998	Promethium	Pm	61	147
Neon	Ne	10	20.180	Samarium	Sm	62	150.36
Sodium	Na	11	22.990	Europium	Eu	63	151.96
Magnesium	Mg	12	24.305	Gadolinium	Gd	64	157.25
Aluminum	Al	13	26.982	Terbium	Tb	65	158.93
Silicon	Si	14	28.086	Dysprosium	Dy	66	162.50
Phosphorus	P	15	30.974	Holmium	Ho	67	164.93
Sulfur	S	16	32.066	Erbium	Er	68	167.26
Chlorine	Cl	17	35.453	Thulium	Tm	69	168.93
Argon	Ar	18	39.948	Ytterbium	Yb	70	173.04
Potassium	K	19	39.098	Lutetium	Lu	71	174.97
Calcium	Ca	20	40.078	Hafnium	Hf	72	178.49
Scandium	Sc	21	44.956	Tantalum	Ta	73	180.95
Titanium	Ti	22	47.867	Tungsten	W	74	183.84
Vanadium	V	23	50.942	Rhenium	Re	75	186.21
Chromium	Cr	24	51.996	Osmium	Os	76	190.23
Manganese	Mn	25	54.938	Iridium	Ir	77	192.22
Iron	Fe	26	55.845	Platinum	Pt	78	195.08
Cobalt	Co	27	58.933	Gold	Au	79	196.97
Nickel	Ni	28	58.693	Mercury	Hg	80	200.59
Copper	Cu	29	63.546	Thallium	Tl	81	204.38
Zinc	Zn	30	65.39	Lead	Pb	82	207.2
Gallium	Ga	31	69.723	Bismuth	Bi	83	208.98
Germanium	Ge	32	72.61	Polonium	Po	84	210
Arsenic	As	33	74.922	Astatine	At	85	210
Selenium	Se	34	78.96	Radon	Rn	86	222
Bromine	Br	35	79.904	Francium	Fr	87	223
Krypton	Kr	36	83.80	Radium	Ra	88	226
Rubidium	Rb	37	85.468	Actinium	Ac	89	227
Strontium	Sr	38	87.62	Thorium	Th	90	232
Yttrium	Y	39	88.906	Protactinium	Pa	91	231
Zirconium	Zr	40	91.224	Uranium	U	92	238
Niobium	Nb	41	92.906	Neptunium	Np	93	237
Molybdenum	Mo	42	95.94	Plutonium	Pu	94	239
Technetium	Tc	43	99	Americium	Am	95	241
Ruthenium	Ru	44	101.07	Curium	Cm	96	244
Rhodium	Rh	45	102.91	Berkelium	Bk	97	249
Palladium	Pd	46	106.42	Californium	Cf	98	252
Silver	Ag	47	107.87	Einsteinium	Es	99	252
Cadmium	Cd	48	112.41	Fermium	Fm	100	257
Indium	In	49	114.82	Mendelevium	Md	101	258
Tin	Sn	50	118.71	Nobelium	No	102	259
Antimony	Sb	51	121.76	Lawrencium	Lr	103	262
Tellurium	Te	52	127.60				

CHEMBOOK

A textbook of general chemistry

R.J.C.Brown Ph.D., F.C.I.C.

The Campus Bookstore · Clark Hall at Queen's University Kingston, Ontario · Canada
www.campusbookstore.com

Introduction

Chemistry is so rich and diverse a subject that learning the established facts and theories of the science requires a long period of study. A university course in general chemistry can only cover a small part of the whole subject, but provides a broad basis of chemical knowledge for further studies of chemistry and other sciences.

The textbook for a course in general chemistry should provide an up-to-date view of the subject, and should be a reliable source of relevant information in a readily understandable form. The objective in writing this textbook has been to present appropriate material in clear language. These statements sound obvious, but introductory courses in chemistry serve a wide variety of students, with many different backgrounds and plans for the future, and the objective is difficult to achieve in practice.

This book is written primarily with Canadian students in mind. A typical Canadian high school background in chemistry is assumed, and the book covers much of the material usually covered in first year university courses. There are specific references to Canadian chemical industry, so students may learn something of the place of chemistry in the national economy.

The choice of topics in the book is fairly conventional, and reference to other books may be helpful in dealing with points that may seem unclear. Use of calculus is avoided until the chapter on chemical kinetics, where calculus is essential. An effort has been made to emphasize the connections between different parts of the book so that, by the end of the course, the student can see the different parts of the story in relation to each other.

This book uses Système International, or SI, units consistently and with few compromises. For years I have tried to find a satisfactory way of combining systematic units with traditional units, and I have concluded that confusion among students increases with every compromise. The use of a consistent and logical set of units avoids difficulties for students who need to make any except the simplest calculations. The conversion of data from other units to SI units is rarely a problem.

Amid the rising cost of university education, the cost of textbooks is significant for many students. The production of this book is an attempt to address this issue by using new technology and new approaches to publishing. Every effort has been made to provide students with an interesting and useful book at low cost.

For the 2000 printing, the entire text has been revised, chapters 6 and 11 have been changed considerably, and a chapter on organic chemistry has been added. These changes should improve the book, but there is a price for progress: new errors or misprints may have crept in as the revisions were made. Corrections will be published as soon as possible. A book of solutions to all the problems will be published this year, in response to popular demand.

R.J.C.Brown
Queen's University
July 2000

email: brownrjc@chem.queensu.ca

Acknowledgements

This book could not have been written and produced without a great deal of help from friends and colleagues, and I am grateful to all those who have supported the project. Many people have made constructive comments on the manuscript, and have helped in a variety of other ways. Credit for the good features of this book is to be shared widely, but responsibility for errors and omissions is entirely mine.

CHEMBOOK is a development of an earlier book, "Chemistry for Science and Engineering", by W.G.Breck, J.D.McCowan and myself, published by McGraw-Hill Ryerson Limited in 1981 and (in a second edition) 1988. I wish to acknowledge here the earlier collaboration with those co-authors, from which many good ideas were developed.

Colleagues at Queen's University who have helped me in various ways are: Professors M.C.Baird, W.E.Baker, A.D.Becke, R. Stephen Brown, R. Stan Brown, E.Buncel, N.Cann, R.D.Gordon, G.W.Hay, B.K.Hunter, M.Koether, R.P.Lemieux, J.D.McCowan, M.Mombourquette, J.A.Page, V.H.Smith, J.A.Stone, H.S.Tilk, S.Wang, D.M.Wardlaw, R.A.Whitney. Others who have helped are Lewyn Li (a former student at Queen's), Professors R.F.C.Brown of Monash University in Melbourne, G.Erskine of John Abbott C.E.G.E.P. in Montreal, L. Norrby of University of Stockholm, M.A.White of Dalhousie University in Halifax, and Dr. E. Hollingshead of Kingston. A number of students and teaching assistants who used the book provided very valuable comments and pointed out errors. I have received advice on software from M. Mombourquette, K.Umanetz and M.Oosten. My wife Kaaren designed the cover of the book and provided advice and support in all sorts of ways.

Every effort has been made to secure permission to reproduce copyright material, and I thank the following organizations, which have granted permission.

CRC Press Inc., Boca Raton, Florida, USA, for a number of tables of data, which are identified in the text, from the 77th Edition of CRC Handbook of Chemistry and Physics.

American Institute of Physics, for the majority of the listings of thermochemical data in Appendix 1, which are drawn from the NBS (now the National Institute of Standards and Technology) Tables of thermochemical data.

Thermodynamics Research Centre, Texas A&M University, College Station Texas, USA, for some entries in the thermochemical tables in Appendix 1.

THERMOCHEM GMBH: Thermodynamik und Prozesstechnik, 52080 Aachen, Germany, for some entries in the thermochemical tables in Appendix 1.

American Chemical Society, for data on US industrial production in Table 4-1.

Statistics Canada information is used with the permission of the Minister of Industry, as Minister responsible for Statistics Canada. Information on the availability of the wide range of data from Statistics Canada can be obtained from Statistics Canada's Regional offices, its World Wide Web site at http://www.statcan.ca, and its toll-free access number 1-800-263-1136. (Tables 4-1, 9-2, 9-3 and 9-4).

I thank the following organizations, which supplied photographs or drawings.

Alcan Aluminum Ltée, Montreal, Quebec for Figures 17-9 and 10; Ballard Power Systems for Figure 17-6; Dr H.Horton for Figure 3-3; Inco Limited, Toronto, Ontario for Figure 4-1; Dr. H-P. Loock for Figure 5-4; Merck Frosst Centre for Therapeutic Research for Figure 19-1; Miller Western Forest Products Ltd for Figure 2-2; Department of Mining Engineering, Queen's University, for Figure 9-1; Steacie Institute for Molecular Sciences, Chalk River, for Figure 12-1.

Finally, I wish to express my appreciation to the many Queen's University chemistry students who have been patient listeners, willing learners and good friends over many years.

R.J.C.Brown
Queen's University, July 2000

TABLE OF CONTENTS

1 Review of Fundamentals

Objectives

After reading this chapter, the student should be able to do the following:

♦ Describe the fundamental structure of matter in terms of atoms, molecules, and ions.

♦ Write and interpret chemical formulae.

♦ Define the mole and molar mass of atoms and molecules.

♦ Specify the composition of a mixture.

♦ Specify the composition and concentration of a solution.

♦ Use numbers and units to report and record results of measurements and calculations.

♦ Choose the appropriate number of significant figures and decimal places in a number.

1-1 What is chemistry?

Chemistry is the science that deals with the nature and composition of matter, and with the structure, properties and transformations of substances. It consists of a body of knowledge and information collected systematically through experiment and observation of the material world in which we live.

What does that knowledge consist of? For each substance studied, chemistry is concerned with its chemical properties (e.g. the chemical reactions it takes part in), its physical properties, and the structure of the molecules or ions of which it is made.

Chemistry overlaps with other sciences such as physics, which is also concerned with the properties and structure of matter, and biology, parts of which are concerned with the chemical basis of life. Chemistry finds practical application in many of the health sciences and applied sciences. Some of the relationships between chemistry and related subjects are shown in Figure 1-1. Despite the clear distinctions between sciences indicated in Figure 1-1, it should be remembered that the boundaries of chemistry are indistinct, and it merges seamlessly into other subjects such as biochemistry, biology, engineering and physics.

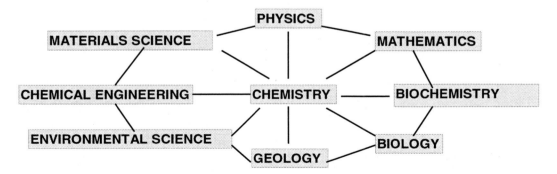

Figure 1-1 The relationships between chemistry and some of the other sciences which contribute to, and depend upon, chemistry. Although chemistry is placed at the centre of the diagram, it is only one part of a complex web of interrelated "pure" and "applied" sciences.

Production of food, fuel, construction materials, automobiles, pharmaceutical drugs, plastics and rubber, and household materials all involve chemistry to some extent, and without some knowledge of chemistry, production and use of these materials would be impossible, or inefficient, or dangerous. Many environmental problems have been recognized only when the techniques of analytical chemistry have been used. In facing and correcting environmental problems, chemistry nearly always plays a central role.

Many students study introductory chemistry at university. Of these, some intend to become professional chemists, while others study chemistry either because it is necessary for the study of other subjects, or simply because of interest. Regardless of the ultimate objective, every student can get pleasure and benefit from a chemistry course. Chemistry consists of a rich collection of scientific knowledge about the world we live in, so rich in fact that more information about chemistry has been accumulated than about any other science. Chemistry has many applications in everyday life, and chemical research continues to expand both basic understanding and the application of new knowledge to practical problems.

1-2 The essentials of chemistry in just ten points

What are the essential ideas of chemistry? Is it possible to summarize in a few points those ideas and facts which form the central core of chemical thinking and chemical practice? Following is a list of ten essential facts and ideas which underlie all of chemistry.

1. All matter is formed from fundamental substances called elements. An element cannot be broken down into other substances by chemical means. Only about a hundred elements are known.

2. A compound consists of several elements combined together in fixed proportions.

3. In a chemical reaction, the reacting substances change into other substances.

4. A chemical reaction may be slow or fast. Many reactions reach a condition of equilibrium if enough time is allowed.

5. Matter is composed of atoms, which are exceedingly small. An atom consists of a positively charged nucleus and a number of negatively charged electrons. The nuclear charge of any atom is an integer multiple of the nuclear charge of a hydrogen atom, and the integer is the atomic number of that atom. All the atoms of a given element have the same atomic number.

6. The periodic table is a systematic list of the elements in order of atomic number. The table displays similarities and trends in the physical and chemical properties of the elements.

7. A molecule consists of atoms joined together by chemical bonds. An ion is an atom or molecule that is electrically charged because it has lost or gained electrons.

8. Chemical bonds are formed by the sharing of electrons between the atoms, or by the transfer of electrons from one atom to another to form ions.

9. Quantum theory provides an explanation of the structure of atoms and molecules, the periodicity of the properties of the elements, and the formation of chemical bonds.

10. The chemical properties of a compound are related to the shape of the molecules, and to the spatial distribution of the electrons within the molecules or ions.

The first two points are discussed in Chapter 1. The third and fourth points are discussed in Chapter 2, but chemical equilibrium is discussed at greater length in Chapters 13 to 17, and the rate of chemical reactions in Chapter 18. The fifth point is discussed in Chapters 1 and 10, and the sixth point is discussed in Chapter 3. The last four points are discussed in Chapters 10, 11 and 12.

There are other important aspects of chemistry that are not included in this list. However, any list has to come to an end somewhere, and ten points seems like a good place to stop. After reaching the end of the book, students may wish to make up their own personal lists of the most important aspects of chemistry.

1-3 Atoms and Molecules

For a chemist, the building blocks of matter are **atoms**. Atoms are not the most fundamental particles of matter, but they provide a reliable basis for understanding what happens in chemical reactions because reactions do not create or destroy them. Chemical reactions change the way the atoms are connected together, but there must be the same number of atoms of each element after the reaction as there were before. It is therefore not necessary to know what atoms are made of in order to describe, at an elementary level, what happens in a reaction. At a deeper level, knowledge of the internal structure of atoms helps understand how atoms join together to form molecules, and the way in which chemical reactions take place.

An atom consists of two kinds of very small particles: the **nucleus**, which has a positive electric charge, and a number of **electrons** that are negatively charged and much lighter than the nucleus. The ultimate particles that make up the nucleus, and the forces that control them, are not usually considered in chemistry because chemical processes are not sufficiently energetic to affect the nucleus of any atom. The nucleus of the lightest atom, hydrogen, is called a **proton**. In every other atom the electric charge on the nucleus is an exact integer multiple of the charge on a proton. This integer is called the **atomic number**, which is designated by the symbol Z. An electron carries a negative electric charge equal in magnitude to the positive charge on a proton. In an electrically neutral atom the number of electrons is equal to the atomic number of the nucleus, and the electric charge on the atom as a whole is zero. An atom that has gained or lost one or more electrons is called an **ion**; positively charged ions are called **cations** and negatively charged ions are called **anions**. Ions have quite different properties from the atoms from which they are derived, but the atoms are not destroyed when they are converted to ions and can be recovered by chemical means.

Electrons in atoms and molecules fall under three main influences: the electrostatic attraction of the negatively charged electrons to the positive nuclei, the electrostatic repulsion between the like-charged electrons, and a quantum effect called the exclusion principle. The laws governing the motion of the electrons are those of quantum mechanics rather than those of classical Newtonian mechanics that are familiar in everyday life, and chemical phenomena are almost entirely governed, at a fundamental level, by quantum mechanics.

The mass of the nucleus is much larger than the mass of the electrons, and constitutes more than 99.95 % of the total mass of the atom, the remainder being the mass of the electrons. The relative masses of atoms can be determined by an instrument known as a **mass spectrometer** in which the atoms are converted into ions and passed in a beam through a vacuum under the influence of electric and magnetic fields. Ions of different masses follow different paths, from which the relative masses of different atoms can be calculated. Using a mass spectrometer, it has been shown that for any atom, the ratio of its mass to the mass of a hydrogen atom is very close to an integer. This integer is called the **mass number**, A, for that particular atom. We shall have more to say about atomic masses later in this chapter.

A nucleus can be considered to consist of **protons** and **neutrons** held together by strong nuclear forces. A proton is the nucleus of a hydrogen atom with $Z = 1$ and $A = 1$, while a neutron has no charge and a mass slightly greater than that of a proton. Protons and neutrons are known as **nucleons**, and the number of nucleons in the nucleus is equal to the mass number A. Within a nucleus, the number of protons is Z and the number of neutrons is $(A–Z)$. For most nuclei, the mass number A is a bit more than twice the atomic number Z, so there are more neutrons than protons in the nucleus. Nuclei with a particular value of Z belong to a single **element**.

A nucleus with particular values of A and Z is called a **nuclide**. The notation used to identify a nuclide is the chemical symbol that corresponds to the element with the atomic number Z, together with the mass number A written as a superscript prefix. For example the nuclide with $Z = 6$ and $A = 12$ is identified by the symbol ^{12}C since the element carbon has atomic number 6. In chemistry, the same notation is used to represent the entire atom, not just the nucleus. Two nuclides or atoms with the same atomic number Z but different mass number A are called **isotopes**. Isotopes have equal nuclear charges, and the electrons in atoms that are isotopes behave in almost exactly the same way, which leads to almost identical chemical properties. Examples are the two isotopes of carbon, ^{12}C and ^{13}C.

Most of the nuclides found in nature are stable and do not "decay" or change to other nuclides by spontaneous nuclear processes. Those that are unstable are called **radioactive** and, over a period of time, change spontaneously to other nuclides by a variety of processes, usually with the emission of a high energy particle and radiation. The radioactive nuclides formed by nuclear processes in the early history of the universe, or in nuclear processes in stars, have mostly decayed over the very long time period of geological history.

Some elements are found in nature with only one stable nuclide, while for others, several stable isotopes are found. The fraction of the total number of atoms found in the form of a particular isotope is called the **natural abundance** of that isotope, and is usually constant from one natural sample to another. Natural abundances are often expressed as a percentage. Table 1-1 lists some stable nuclides, with their atomic numbers and mass numbers, and natural abundances.

Table 1-1 Some nuclides and their properties

Element	Symbol	Atomic no. Z	Mass no. A	Natural Abundance (%)
hydrogen	^{1}H	1	1	99.985
hydrogen	^{2}H	1	2	0.015
carbon	^{12}C	6	12	98.90
carbon	^{13}C	6	13	1.10
sodium	^{23}Na	11	23	100.00
chlorine	^{35}Cl	17	35	75.77
chlorine	^{37}Cl	17	37	24.23

A **molecule** is a collection of atoms firmly bound together to form a single entity which has characteristic chemical properties. Much of the subject of chemistry is the study of molecules, how to make them, and how they react. A molecule can be described by giving the number of atoms of each element present in the molecule and the way they are joined together. The atoms are joined together by **chemical bonds**, consisting of some of the electrons in the atoms. Traditionally, a chemical bond is described as a pair of electrons shared between the two atoms, and there is much evidence supporting this concept. However, some well-established chemical bonds do not conform to the electron pair picture and require an extension of the traditional description of a chemical bond.

In compounds of the lighter elements it is possible to distinguish between **single, double and triple bonds** consisting of one, two or three pairs of electrons respectively. The total number of bonds formed by an atom in a molecule is called the **valence** of the atom, and often has the same value in a number of different molecules: for example, the usual valence of carbon is four.

Ions may contain more than one atom joined together by chemical bonds. Such ions are called **molecular ions** or **polyatomic ions**, and they have characteristic chemical properties, just like uncharged molecules.

It is sometimes convenient to refer to a particular type of atom, molecule, or ion, as a **species**. This word, taken from biology, implies that the members of a species are the same in all their important properties.

1-4 Elements, compounds and mixtures

Every substance can be classified as an element, a compound or a mixture. Before the discovery of atoms, definitions were based upon what was known at the time about chemical reactions.

An **element** cannot be broken down into other stable chemical substances by chemical means. For example, when limestone is heated strongly, a gas is given off leaving a white solid that reacts with water, so limestone is not an element. When an electric current is passed through water to which certain salts have been added, bubbles of a gas are formed at one electrode, and bubbles of a different gas are formed at the other electrode. The two gases can be recombined in a vigorous, even explosive, chemical reaction, the product of which is a liquid having the same properties as the original water. The two gases produced by the electric current are in some sense constituents of water, and water is not an element. On the other hand, iron has never been decomposed by chemical means, and is recognised as an element.

These criteria for defining the concept of an element are of historical interest, but the modern definition is phrased in terms of atomic structure. An element is a substance in which all the atoms have the same atomic number, or nuclear charge, Z. The element carbon, for instance, contains only atoms with $Z = 6$. Iron sulfide, a mineral which looks like gold, is not an element because it contains two kinds of atom, iron with $Z = 26$ and sulfur with $Z = 16$.

Modern experimental techniques allow identification of the atomic numbers of the atoms contained in a given sample. In the technique known as X-ray fluorescence, for example, a sample of an element, when placed in a beam of high energy electrons or radiation, emits characteristic X-ray radiation which serves to identify the atomic number of that element. If the sample is a compound or mixture containing more than one element, then the characteristic radiation of each element present will be observed, from which the elements can be identified.

A **compound** is a substance containing more than one element, with well-defined physical and chemical properties that differ from those of the elements contained in the compound. In most compounds, the elements are combined in fixed proportions by mass, and the ratio of masses of the elements present is a basic property of the compound. This is called the **law of definite**

proportions; it can be traced back to the ideas of John Dalton published in 1806. For example, in any sample of water the ratio of the mass of oxygen to the mass of hydrogen is 7.94:1.

Figure 1-2 The water molecule consists of two atoms of hydrogen and one atom of oxygen. A molecule containing any other combination of atoms is not a water molecule. Molecular compounds obey the law of definite proportions because all molecules of a given compound are composed of the same numbers of the same atoms joined together in the same way.

A compound in which the characteristic unit is a molecule is called a **molecular compound**. The chemical and physical properties of the compound are a reflection of the properties of the molecules themselves. The molecules of a particular compound are identical, although large molecules may be flexible and able to change shape without forming a new compound. If the molecules of a compound are broken up or changed in some essential way by a chemical reaction, the compound itself is changed.

Ionic compounds consist of ions, which are electrically charged atoms or molecules. Monatomic ions contain a single atom, and polyatomic or molecular ions contain more than one atom. The relative numbers of ions in an ionic compound are in ratio of simple integers determined by the charges on the ions because the compound must be electrically neutral. For example sodium chloride, $NaCl$, contains equal numbers of positive sodium ions Na^+ and negative chloride ions Cl^-, while sodium sulfate, Na_2SO_4, consists of sodium ions Na^+ and doubly charged negative sulfate ions SO_4^{2-} in the ratio 2:1. Pure ionic compounds, when in the solid state, form crystals in which the ions are arranged in a regular array or lattice, such as that illustrated in Figure 1-3.

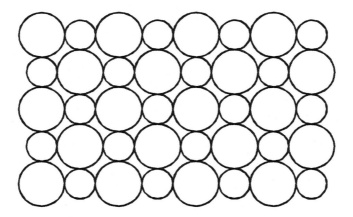

Figure 1-3 Ionic compounds obey the law of definite proportions because the compound must be electrically neutral. A crystal of an ionic compound such as sodium chloride, $NaCl$, contains equal numbers of positive sodium ions Na^+ and negative chloride ions Cl^-. In a crystal of pure sodium chloride, the ions are arranged in a regular lattice. In this diagram showing one plane of ions in an $NaCl$ crystal, the small circles represent sodium ions and the large circles represent chloride ions.

When two or more substances, whether elements or compounds, are mixed together without any chemical reaction occurring, the resulting material is called a **mixture**. A mixture is called **heterogeneous** if the substances in the mixture retain their separate physical and chemical characteristics so that different parts of the sample have different properties. An example is sand mixed with iron filings, in which the mixture retains the properties of both substances, and the two components can be separated by purely physical means: the iron can be separated from the sand with a magnet.

A mixture is called **homogeneous** if it is uniform in its properties even when examined on a fine scale, for instance with a microscope. A homogeneous mixture is usually called a **solution**. An example is a solution of table salt, sodium chloride NaCl, in water. The law of definite proportions does not apply to solutions because solutions are mixtures, not compounds. Sodium chloride can be dissolved in water in any amount (up to a certain limit), and the properties of the solution vary smoothly with the amount dissolved. Examination of a fully mixed solution using a microscope or similar instrument would show no variation in the properties of the solution from one place to another.

Virtually all substances encountered in daily life are mixtures, and the **purity** of the substances used in chemical experiments must be considered. Impurities can be present as either heterogeneous mixtures or as solutions. A substance from a reputable chemical supplier can be assumed to consist almost entirely of the material named on the label, with only small amounts of other substances present as impurities up to some limit that is often stated on the label. For industrial or general laboratory uses, some impurities may not be of any consequence and may be tolerated since high purity chemicals are usually expensive. The assessment of purity and identification of impurities is the business of the analytical chemist.

1-5 Chemical symbols and formulae

A listing of the elements in order of atomic number, together with their symbols, is printed inside the front cover of the book, and in Table 1-8 later in this chapter.

The names of the elements are derived from a variety of sources, of which some are ancient, but many are recent; many of the names of recently discovered elements are based on the places where the source minerals were located or the names of the people who first isolated and identified them. Standard names for most of the elements have been decided by international agreement.

The names of some of the elements, or their spelling, are not universally agreed upon. This book uses the international spelling "sulfur", rather than the older British spelling "sulphur", for element no. 16. The international spelling was adopted in most of the British chemical literature some time ago. At the moment, the usual spelling used in Canada is "sulphur", but it seems pointless to retain this spelling which is no longer used in either Britain or the United States.

The ending "-ium" in the name of an element generally indicates that the element is a metal. The international spelling of the name of element no. 13 is "aluminium", but "aluminum" is used almost universally throughout North America, and we follow this practice. Similarly, we will use the American spelling "cesium" rather than the international spelling "caesium" for element no. 55.

In chemical notation, the elements, and atoms of the elements, are indicated by symbols formed from the letters of the alphabet. For most elements, the chemical symbol consists of the first one or two letters of the English or Latin name of the element. Examples of chemical symbols derived in this way are O for oxygen, N for nitrogen, H for hydrogen, Au for gold *(aurum)*, and Cu for copper *(cuprum)*.

In studying or reading about chemistry, it is helpful to be familiar with the names and symbols for as many elements as possible. As a beginning, students should memorize the names and symbols of the first twenty elements. The names of many of those elements are familiar, and the symbols are all closely related to the names. In addition, knowing the order of the elements is useful, and this is best achieved using the **periodic table** of the elements. The periodic table of the elements is printed inside the cover of this book, and will be discussed in more detail in Chapter 3.

The atoms that make up a compound are specified using a **chemical formula**, which lists the relative numbers of atoms of each element present. The number of atoms of each element is written as a subscript on the symbol for that element. For example calcium carbonate has the formula $CaCO_3$ indicating that the elements calcium, carbon and oxygen are present in the relative proportions (by number) of 1:1:3.

The purpose of a formula is to summarise information about the compound at an appropriate level of detail. For some purposes a simple formula such as the one quoted is adequate, while for other purposes a detailed drawing showing the relative arrangement of the atoms in space is required. The main types of chemical formulae are the following.

An **empirical formula** shows the relative numbers of atoms of each element present, usually expressed as the simplest set of whole numbers.

A **molecular formula** shows the actual numbers of atoms of each element present in a single molecule of the compound. This type of formula can be used only for substances consisting of molecules.

A **structural formula** shows how the atoms are joined by chemical bonds, with chemical bonds indicated by lines drawn between the symbols for atoms. In addition, a structural formula may indicate details of the relative positions of the atoms in space.

Some examples of these three types of chemical formula are shown in Table 1-2, in which it will be seen that a structural formula can represent a variety of features. The spatial arrangement of atoms, the angles between chemical bonds, and the distinction between single bonds and double bonds can all be represented in a structural formula. It is sometimes important that the structure drawn on paper show certain subtle details of molecular structure which require more sophisticated conventions than are shown here. More will be said about molecular structure in later chapters.

Table 1-2 Examples of different types of chemical formula for molecular substances

Substance	*empirical formula*	*molecular formula*	*structural formula*
hydrogen	H	H_2	H—H
water	H_2O	H_2O	 O H H
hydrogen peroxide	HO	H_2O_2	H O-O H H
methane	CH_4	CH_4	$H-\overset{H}{\underset{H}{C}}-H$
ethane	CH_3	C_2H_6	$H-\overset{H}{\underset{H}{C}}-\overset{H}{\underset{H}{C}}-H$
ethene (ethylene)	CH_2	C_2H_4	$\overset{H}{\underset{H}{{}}}C=C\overset{H}{\underset{H}{{}}}$

1-6 The states of matter

Matter usually exists either as a **solid**, a **liquid**, or a **gas**. These different forms of matter are called the **states of matter** and can be distinguished on the basis of four physical properties: the density, the compressibility, the rigidity and the ability to expand to fill the volume available. The **density** is the mass per unit volume of the substance, and the **compressibility** measures how much the density (or volume) changes for a given change in pressure.

The characteristics of the three ordinary states of matter are as follows. A gas has low density and is easily compressed; for example air can be compressed into a smaller volume using a bicycle pump operated by hand. A gas expands to fill the space available, and will escape into the atmosphere if it is not confined to a closed vessel. Liquids and solids have high density, and are almost incompressible, which means that the volume changes only slightly even if the pressure is increased considerably. Liquids and solids in a container retain their volume regardless of the size of the container. Solids differ from liquids in that they are rigid and do not change their shape readily under external forces, whereas liquids and gases change their shape to that of the container. These properties are summarised in Table 1-3 and illustrated in Figure 1-4.

This classification is based upon the ordinary properties of matter, but other categories are based upon the arrangement of the atoms or molecules, particularly in the case of solids. Glass, for example, is a solid by the rules of Table 1-3, yet the arrangement of the atoms in glass is more like that of a liquid, which influences the properties of glass.

Table 1-3 The distinguishing properties of solids, liquids and gases

Property	Gas	Liquid	Solid
density:	low	high	high
compressibility:	high	low	low
retains shape?	no	no	yes
expands to fill space?	yes	no	no

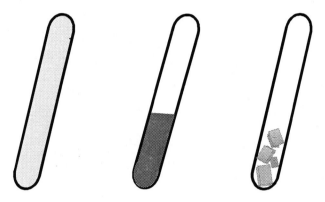

Figure 1-4 Three sealed tubes containing respectively some gas, some liquid, and some crystals of a solid. The gas fills the entire container, the liquid adjusts its shape to that of the container but retains its volume, and the solid retains both its volume and shape.

1-7 Units and measurements

Like other sciences, chemistry deals with measurements and quantitative observations of physical quantities. It is not sufficient to report that a sample is "heavy" or that the volume of a solution is "large". Numerical values are nearly always needed if scientific work is to have much value.

The magnitude of a physical quantity is expressed using a **number** and **a unit** and both parts are required (except for quantities that have no units). To say that the mass of a sample is 25 without giving any units is meaningless, since this statement might be interpreted variously to mean that the mass is 25 grams, 25 kilograms or 25 pounds. The combination of number and unit may be regarded as a mathematical product of a number and its units: quantity = numerical value × units. A length of 5 metres is 5 times the unit length of 1 metre. More complex units are constructed as products or quotients of the basic units. The unit for speed is metre per second, which is written as a formal division of units, metre/second or metre second^{-1}.

When a symbol is used to represent a quantity, the symbol represents the units as well as the magnitude. If the mass of an object is represented by the symbol m, we can write an equation such as $m = 25$ gram to state that the object weighs 25 gram. An equivalent statement would be m/gram = 25; this may seem an odd way to give the mass, but this notation is often used in labelling the rows or columns of a table, or the axes of a graph. Examples can be found in many tables and graphs throughout the book.

Units can be modified by multiplication by a factor, usually a power of 10. A length of 0.0020 metre can be written 2.0×10^{-3} metre, and the factor of 10^{-3} can be taken either as multiplying the number, or as multiplying the units to convert metre into millimetre. This length can also be written as 2.0 millimetres, the prefix *milli* indicating multiplication by the factor 10^{-3}. The standard prefixes for multiplying units by powers of 10 are shown in Table 1-4.

There is often a choice of units to use, and even a choice of systems of units, but it is usually best to work within a single consistent system of units. The International Union of Pure and Applied Chemistry, IUPAC for short, has adopted a system of units, called "Le Système Internationale d'Unités" or SI for short, which is always acceptable in chemistry, although some older units are still used. Deciding which of the older units ought to be retained, and which discarded, is difficult, and students must be prepared to be flexible in dealing with units when reading books (particularly older books) or journals. In this book, SI units will be used for most purposes.

Table 1-4 Prefixes and the corresponding factors

Prefix	Symbol	Factor	Prefix	Symbol	Factor
deca	da	10	deci	d	10^{-1}
hecta	h	10^{2}	centi	c	10^{-2}
kilo	k	10^{3}	milli	m	10^{-3}
mega	M	10^{6}	micro	μ	10^{-6}
giga	G	10^{9}	nano	n	10^{-9}
tera	T	10^{12}	pico	p	10^{-12}
peta	P	10^{15}	femto	f	10^{-15}
exa	E	10^{18}	atto	a	10^{-18}

There are six fundamental quantities that are of importance in making measurements in chemistry: length, mass, time, electric current, temperature, and amount of substance. Formal definitions of the units for these quantities are to be found in the Handbook of Chemistry and Physics, or in publications of the International Union of Pure and Applied Chemistry. The definitions of the fundamental units are based on the most reliable and reproducible standards that are available, while maintaining consistency with previous definitions. Other quantities such as force, pressure, concentration and electric charge are defined in terms of the basic quantities, using the laws of physics or chemistry.

The basic units of SI and the standard abbreviations are summarised in Table 1-5. The unit of length, the **metre**, used to be defined as the length between lines engraved on a particular bar of metal, chosen as a close approximation to a ten-millionth of the distance between the equator and the North Pole. The metre is now defined in terms of the wavelength of a particular spectral line emitted by excited krypton atoms. The unit of mass is the **kilogram**, defined by the mass of a particular standard of mass maintained in Paris; this historical definition has been maintained. The unit of time is the **second**, which used to be defined in terms of the time required for the earth to rotate on its axis. The second is now defined in terms of the period (i.e. the time per cycle) of oscillations of the radiation emitted by cesium atoms under certain conditions. The unit of electric current is the **ampere**, which is defined in terms of the electromagnetic force between wires carrying an electric current. Temperature is measured in units of **kelvin**, and is based on the temperature of a mixture of ice and water in contact with water vapour.

Table 1-5 Basic SI quantities, symbols and units

Quantity and symbol	SI Unit	Abbreviation
length	metre	m
mass	kilogram	kg
time	second	s
electric current	ampere	A
temperature	kelvin	K
amount of substance	mole	mol

For chemistry, perhaps the most important of the basic quantities is the **amount of substance**. This quantity is a measure of the number of atoms or molecules in a sample. Since atoms are so small, the numbers involved are unimaginably large, so the amount of substance is measured as a multiple of the number of atoms contained in a well-defined and characterised sample. The unit of amount of substance is the **mole**, which is discussed further in section 1-9.

All the other quantities of physics and chemistry are derived from these basic quantities, and the units used are derived in a corresponding way. Table 1-6 lists some derived quantities used in chemistry, and their SI units. Table 1-7 lists some non-SI units that are in common use. Of these, some are useful, but others are redundant and will not be used in this book.

The names of some units are derived from the names of the scientists who first investigated the related phenomena. By convention, the first letter of the name of the unit is not capitalized when it is spelled out in full, but is capitalized in the abbreviation.

When substituting quantities in equations, the units are part of the calculation. This can be very helpful, for if all quantities in an equation are substituted in their basic SI units, the numerical result of the calculation will be expressed in the appropriate SI units. Consider the calculation of a pressure using the ideal gas equation:

$$P = \frac{nRT}{V}$$

where R is the gas constant with units $J\ K^{-1}\ mol^{-1}$, n is the amount of gas (in moles), T is the temperature (in kelvin) and V is the volume (in cubic metres).

Recalling that a joule is the same as a newton metre, the units of the right hand side are:

$$\frac{mol \times J\ K^{-1}\ mol^{-1} \times K}{m^3} = \frac{J}{m^3} = \frac{N\ m}{m^3} = N\ m^{-2} = Pa$$

Table 1-6 SI units for derived quantities

Quantity	SI unit	Abbreviation and equivalent units
velocity or speed	metre/second	$m\ s^{-1}$
acceleration	metre/second^2	$m\ s^{-2}$
force = mass×acceleration	newton	$N = kg\ m\ s^{-2}$
pressure = force/area	pascal	$Pa = N\ m^{-2} = kg\ m^{-1}\ s^{-2}$
volume = length^3	cubic metre	m^3
density = mass/volume	kilogram/metre^3	$kg\ m^{-3}$
concentration = amount/volume	mole/metre^3	$mol\ m^{-3}$
energy = work = force×distance	joule	$J = N\ m = kg\ m^2\ s^{-2} = Pa\ m^3$
power = energy/time	watt	$W = J\ s^{-1}$
electric charge = current×time	coulomb	$C = A\ s$
electric potential = energy/charge	volt	$V = J\ C^{-1}$

Table 1-7 Some commonly used non-SI units

Quantity	Unit	Abbreviation and equivalent basic units
volume	litre	$L = 10^{-3}\ m^3 = dm^3$
mass	tonne	$t = 10^3\ kg$
pressure	bar	$bar = 10^5\ Pa$
pressure	atmosphere	$atm = 101325\ Pa$ *exactly*
pressure	torr	$Torr = (101325 / 760)\ Pa$
length	ångstrom	$\text{Å} = 10^{-10}\ m$
energy	calorie	$cal = 4.184\ J$ *exactly*
energy	electron volt	$eV = 1.6021773 \times 10^{-19}\ J$
mass	atomic mass unit, or dalton	$amu = 1.6605402 \times 10^{-27}\ kg$
electric charge	elementary charge	$e = 1.6021773 \times 10^{-19}\ C$

1-8 Two basic measurements: mass and volume.

The **mass** of an object is a measure of its mechanical inertia and is proportional to the amount of matter in an object. Mass is the primary measurement for determining how much matter takes part in chemical reactions. The **weight** of an object is the force of gravity on that object. In common language the distinction between mass and weight is often blurred or ignored, but in science the distinction is important. Mass and weight are totally different quantities, and have different units: kilogram for mass and newton for weight. The weight of an object is the product mg of the mass m and the acceleration due to gravity, g. The value of g is approximately 9.80 m/s^2, and varies from place to place on the earth's surface by about 0.5 % of its value.

The basic unit of mass is, slightly illogically, not the gram but the kilogram, and is defined as the mass of a particular piece of metal that has been agreed upon as the international prototype kilogram. The kilogram is rather a large unit and many experiments involve masses of a few grams rather than kilograms. For very large masses the tonne, defined as 10^3 kg, may be used.

Mass is measured using a **balance**. Several sorts of balance are in common use in chemical laboratories. In older balances, the sample is placed in a pan suspended from one end of a lever supported on an almost frictionless bearing. Pieces of metal from a set of standard masses are added to a second pan at the other end of the lever until the lever "balances". Then the weight (i.e. the force of gravity) of the sample must be equal to the total weight of the pieces of metal added to the other pan, and hence the masses must be equal too. Many different types of balance working on this principle have been used over the years. In recent times a new type of electronic single pan balance has almost completely superseded mechanical balances. The weight, i.e. the force of gravity, of a sample placed on the pan is "balanced" against an electromagnetic force caused by an electric current, as shown in Figure 1-5; the current is measured and used to calculate and display in digital form the mass of the sample. Balances of this type must be calibrated from time to time using an accurate standard mass.

When a liquid or powdered sample is to be weighed, it is placed in a **weighing bottle** made of inert plastic or glass. This protects the balance pan from damage and avoids contamination or loss of the sample. Electronic balances usually have a "tare" button to set the display to zero with the empty weighing bottle on the pan; after this is done the mass displayed for the bottle plus sample is the mass of the sample alone.

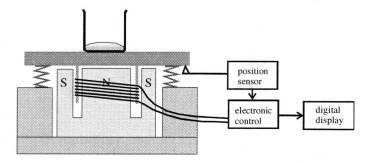

Figure 1-5 The working parts of an electronic single pan balance. Current passing through the coil within the magnet generates an electromagnetic force which balances the weight of the sample and container.

The **volume** of an object is a measure of its bulk, or the space it occupies. The basic SI unit of volume, the **cubic metre**, is very large and in laboratory work the cubic decimetre and the cubic centimetre are more convenient. The **cubic decimetre**, abbreviated dm^3 and equal to 10^{-3} m^3, is also known as the **litre** for which the abbreviation is L; the **cubic centimetre**, abbreviated cm^3 and equal to 10^{-6} m^3, is also known as the millilitre. The litre and its subdivisions are very commonly used, and the conversion factors should be memorized:

1 litre $= 1 L = 1$ cubic decimetre $= 10^{-3}$ cubic metre

1 millilitre $= 1$ mL $= 1$ cubic centimetre $= 10^{-6}$ cubic metre

In this book, we will generally use litres and millilitres as the volume units when dealing with liquids, and cubic decimetres and cubic centimetres when dealing with gases. The litre is legally established in Canada for commercial use, and is in everyday use for measuring gasoline, milk, soft drinks. However, certain calculations, particularly for gases, are most easily understood by expressing volumes in cubic metres.

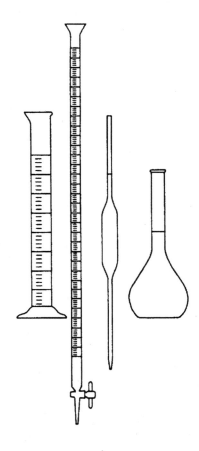

Figure 1-6 Various instruments for measuring volume: measuring cylinder, buret, pipet, and volumetric flask.

Various devices are used in the laboratory for measuring the volume of a liquid sample, and some of these are shown in Figure 1-6. Approximate measurements can be made with a graduated **measuring cylinder**. The volume of liquid delivered in a titration is measured by running the solution from a **buret**, a long glass tube of constant cross-section equipped with a stop-cock and graduated in volume units along its length. Samples of fixed and known volume can be delivered to another container using a **pipet**. Automatic push-button pipets are commercially available and are now widely used. A **volumetric flask** is used to dissolve solutes in water or other solvents to make a solution of known total volume. Pipets and volumetric flasks carry a single calibration mark on the narrow neck, so as to define the volume of liquid precisely.

The **density** of a substance is the mass of the substance per unit volume. The density of a sample is given by the equation:

$$\text{density} = \frac{\text{mass}}{\text{volume}} \qquad \text{or in symbols,} \qquad \rho = \frac{m}{V} \qquad (1\text{-}1)$$

where ρ is the density, m is the mass of the sample and V is its volume. The density is a characteristic of the substance, and does not depend on the size of the sample.

The volume of a container can be measured by weighing it first when empty and then when filled with a liquid of known density; the mass of the liquid is equal to the difference of the two masses, and the volume is calculated from the mass and density.

Example 1-1 A flask has a mass of 35.245 g when empty and 98.326 g when filled with water of density 0.9971 g/mL. Calculate the volume of the flask.

The density is related to the mass m divided by the volume V by the equation:

$$\text{density} = \frac{\text{mass}}{\text{volume}}.$$

On rearranging this equation, it follows that the volume is:

$$\text{volume} = \frac{\text{mass}}{\text{density}} = \frac{(98.326 - 35.245)\,\text{g}}{0.9971\,\text{g/mL}} = 63.26\,\text{mL}$$

1-9 Amount of substance: the mole

In chemical reactions, atoms are neither destroyed nor created. Another way to say this is that atoms are *conserved*. The result of a reaction is that atoms are rearranged so that the **reactants** (which are the substances that react) are converted into the **products** of the reaction. The molecules or ions of the reactants disappear, to be replaced by those of the products, but in this process the atoms themselves are preserved. The number of atoms of every element present after the reaction has finished (and indeed during the reaction) must be the same as the number of atoms of those elements present before the reaction, remembering that in some reactions, atoms are converted to ions (or *vice versa*). Further, electric charge must be conserved and cannot be created or destroyed in any chemical reaction, because electrons cannot be created or destroyed. Thus the principles of "accounting" in chemical reactions are based upon counting of atoms, and perhaps also of electrons.

Different atoms have different masses. Originally, atomic and molecular masses were measured as multiples of the mass of a hydrogen atom, which was taken to have unit mass. This procedure proved to be unsatisfactory and has been modified several times. The mass of a single atom is now expressed in terms of the **atomic mass unit** (abbreviation: amu); another name for the atomic mass unit is the **dalton** (abbreviation: Da).

The atomic mass unit is defined as exactly 1/12 of the mass of a ^{12}C atom:

$$1\,\text{amu} = \tfrac{1}{12} \times \text{mass of a } ^{12}C \text{ atom}$$

In other words, an atom of ^{12}C has been assigned a mass of exactly 12 amu.

The mass of an atom can be expressed in amu as follows:

$$\text{mass of atom in amu} = \frac{\text{mass of atom}}{\text{mass of }^{12}\text{C atom}} \times 12 \, \text{amu} \tag{1-2}$$

Atomic and molecular masses are sometimes given without units and called **atomic weights** and **molecular weights**. These are simply the ratio of the mass of the atom or molecule to $1/12$ of the mass of a ^{12}C atom.

The **amount of substance** in a sample is a measure of the number of atoms or molecules contained in the sample. The fundamental unit used to measure the amount of substance is called the **mole**, for which the abbreviation is mol. The mole is defined as the amount of substance that contains the same number of elementary entities as there are atoms in exactly 12 grams of chemically and isotopically pure ^{12}C. This enormous number is called the **Avogadro constant** N_A and is related fundamentally to the mass of an atom of ^{12}C by the following formula:

$$
\begin{aligned}
N_A &= \text{number of atoms per mole} \\
&= \text{number of atoms in exactly 12 gram of }^{12}\text{C} \\
&= \frac{12 \, \text{gram}}{\text{mass of one atom of }^{12}C \text{ in grams}}
\end{aligned}
$$

The Avogadro constant has been measured in many different experiments, and the presently accepted value is:

$$N_A = 6.022137(4) \times 10^{23} \, \text{mol}^{-1} \approx 6.0221 \times 10^{23} \, \text{mol}^{-1}$$

The Avogadro constant is also known as the Avogadro number, and its value may be given without the units of mol^{-1}.

The amount of any elementary entity (such as an atom, a molecule, an electron, etc) can be measured in units of moles. A mole of iron atoms contains Avogadro's number of iron atoms. A mole of nitrogen molecules contains Avogadro's number of nitrogen molecules. A mole of hydrogen ions contains Avogadro's number of hydrogen ions. It is important to specify the elementary entity that is being "counted" whenever there is the possibility of confusion. For example, one mole of chlorine molecules, Cl_2, contains two moles of chlorine atoms, Cl, since each molecule contains two atoms. One mole of sodium chloride NaCl contains one mole of sodium ions Na^+ and one mole of chloride ions Cl^-.

The mass of one mole of a specified atom or other elementary entity is called the **molar mass** and is usually quoted in units of grams per mole, or g mol^{-1}. The molar mass M of an atom is the mass of Avogadro's number of the specified atoms:

$$M = \text{mass of one atom} \times N_A \tag{1-3}$$

The molar mass of isotopically pure ^{12}C is exactly $12 \, \text{g mol}^{-1}$. The molar mass of any other atom is proportional to the mass of a single atom, and hence

$$\text{molar mass} = \frac{\text{mass of atom}}{\text{mass of }^{12}\text{C atom}} \times 12 \, \text{g mol}^{-1} \tag{1-4}$$

Comparing equations (1-2) and 1-4), it follows that the molar mass of an atom in g mol^{-1} is *numerically* equal to atomic mass in amu. The use of molar masses (in g mol^{-1}) rather than atomic masses (in amu) is recommended for most calculations.

The molar mass of a particular element as it is found in nature is the weighted average of the molar masses of the various isotopes of the element that are present. For example, the molar mass of naturally-occurring carbon is $12.011 \, \text{g mol}^{-1}$, because one mole of carbon contains N_A

carbon atoms, of which most (98.90 %) are ^{12}C but a small fraction (1.10 %) are the heavier isotope ^{13}C. The molar masses and abundances for the stable nuclides of several elements are given in Table 1-8. It should be noted that, if there is more than one stable nuclide for an element, the molar mass of the element is less accurately known than the molar masses of the individual isotopes, because of variations and uncertainties in the abundances. This does not apply to an element with only one stable nuclide, such as sodium.

None of the molar masses of the elements is an exact integer. This is because no nuclide of any element has a mass that is an exact integer, except for ^{12}C. However, even in the case of carbon, there are two isotopes and the molar mass of natural carbon is a weighted average of the two molar masses.

Example 1-2 Calculate the average atomic mass of carbon from the masses of the nuclides and their natural abundances given in Table 1-8.

There are two isotopes, ^{12}C and ^{13}C, with masses 12 amu exactly and 13.003 354 83 amu, and abundance fractions 0.99985 and 0.00015 respectively. Hence the average atomic mass of carbon is:

$$M = 12 \times 0.9890 + 13.00335483 \times 0.0110 = 12.011 \, \text{amu}$$

Table 1-9 lists the molar masses of the elements in order of their atomic number, and the table is also printed inside the front cover of the book. The molar mass values have been limited to no more than five significant figures (see section 1-13 for a discussion of significant figures). These values are accurate enough for most ordinary calculations, but more accurate numbers available in the CRC Handbook of Chemistry and Physics if they are needed.

Table 1-8 Molar masses of some elements

Element	Isotope	Isotopic molar mass in g/mol	Natural Abundance %	Molar mass of the element in g/mol
hydrogen	^{1}H	1.007 825 03	99.985	1.0079
	^{2}H	2.014 101 78	0.015	
carbon	^{12}C	12 exactly	98.90	12.011
	^{13}C	13.003 354 83	1.10	
sodium	^{23}Na	22.989 767 7	100.	22.989 767 7
chlorine	^{35}Cl	34.968 852 72	75.77	35.4527
	^{37}Cl	36.965 902 6	24.23	

Table 1-9 The elements and their molar masses in g mol⁻¹.
Atomic masses are listed with five or fewer significant figures. For elements with no stable isotopes, the integer atomic mass number of the most common isotope is listed.

name	symbol	Z	Molar mass	name	symbol	Z	Molar mass
Hydrogen	H	1	1.0079	Iodine	I	53	126.90
Helium	He	2	4.0026	Xenon	Xe	54	131.29
Lithium	Li	3	6.941	Cesium	Cs	55	132.91
Beryllium	Be	4	9.0122	Barium	Ba	56	137.33
Boron	B	5	10.811	Lanthanum	La	57	138.91
Carbon	C	6	12.011	Cerium	Ce	58	140.12
Nitrogen	N	7	14.007	Praseodymium	Pr	59	140.91
Oxygen	O	8	15.999	Neodymium	Nd	60	144.24
Fluorine	F	9	18.998	Promethium	Pm	61	147
Neon	Ne	10	20.180	Samarium	Sm	62	150.36
Sodium	Na	11	22.990	Europium	Eu	63	151.96
Magnesium	Mg	12	24.305	Gadolinium	Gd	64	157.25
Aluminum	Al	13	26.982	Terbium	Tb	65	158.93
Silicon	Si	14	28.086	Dysprosium	Dy	66	162.50
Phosphorus	P	15	30.974	Holmium	Ho	67	164.93
Sulfur	S	16	32.066	Erbium	Er	68	167.26
Chlorine	Cl	17	35.453	Thulium	Tm	69	168.93
Argon	Ar	18	39.948	Ytterbium	Yb	70	173.04
Potassium	K	19	39.098	Lutetium	Lu	71	174.97
Calcium	Ca	20	40.078	Hafnium	Hf	72	178.49
Scandium	Sc	21	44.956	Tantalum	Ta	73	180.95
Titanium	Ti	22	47.867	Tungsten	W	74	183.84
Vanadium	V	23	50.942	Rhenium	Re	75	186.21
Chromium	Cr	24	51.996	Osmium	Os	76	190.23
Manganese	Mn	25	54.938	Iridium	Ir	77	192.22
Iron	Fe	26	55.845	Platinum	Pt	78	195.08
Cobalt	Co	27	58.933	Gold	Au	79	196.97
Nickel	Ni	28	58.693	Mercury	Hg	80	200.59
Copper	Cu	29	63.546	Thallium	Tl	81	204.38
Zinc	Zn	30	65.39	Lead	Pb	82	207.2
Gallium	Ga	31	69.723	Bismuth	Bi	83	208.98
Germanium	Ge	32	72.61	Polonium	Po	84	210
Arsenic	As	33	74.922	Astatine	At	85	210
Selenium	Se	34	78.96	Radon	Rn	86	222
Bromine	Br	35	79.904	Francium	Fr	87	223
Krypton	Kr	36	83.80	Radium	Ra	88	226
Rubidium	Rb	37	85.468	Actinium	Ac	89	227
Strontium	Sr	38	87.62	Thorium	Th	90	232
Yttrium	Y	39	88.906	Protactinium	Pa	91	231
Zirconium	Zr	40	91.224	Uranium	U	92	238
Niobium	Nb	41	92.906	Neptunium	Np	93	237
Molybdenum	Mo	42	95.94	Plutonium	Pu	94	239
Technetium	Tc	43	99	Americium	Am	95	241
Ruthenium	Ru	44	101.07	Curium	Cm	96	244
Rhodium	Rh	45	102.91	Berkelium	Bk	97	249
Palladium	Pd	46	106.42	Californium	Cf	98	252
Silver	Ag	47	107.87	Einsteinium	Es	99	252
Cadmium	Cd	48	112.41	Fermium	Fm	100	257
Indium	In	49	114.82	Mendelevium	Md	101	258
Tin	Sn	50	118.71	Nobelium	No	102	259
Antimony	Sb	51	121.76	Lawrencium	Lr	103	262
Tellurium	Te	52	127.60				

The mass of a molecule is the sum of the masses of the atoms which are bonded together to form the molecule. Hence the molar mass of a molecule is the sum of the molar masses of the atoms which form the molecule.

For a sample of a pure substance, the mass is related to the amount of substance and the molar mass by the following equation:

$$\text{mass of sample} = \text{amount of substance} \times \text{molar mass}$$

or in symbols, $m = nM$ (1-5a)

where m is the mass of the sample, n is the amount of substance and M is the molar mass. Usually, m is expressed in grams, n in moles, and M in grams per mole. The amount of substance in the sample can be calculated by rearranging this equation:

$$n = \frac{m}{M} .$$ (1-5b)

Many substances consist of ions rather than molecules, an example being sodium chloride with the empirical formula NaCl. The molar mass based on the empirical formula is called the **formula molar mass**, regardless of whether the substance is composed of ions or molecules.

The following examples illustrate calculations related to molar masses.

Example 1-3 Calculate the molar mass of H_2 from data in Table 1-8.

The molar mass of H is 1.0079 g mol^{-1}, so the mass of one mole of H atoms is 1.0079 g. Each hydrogen molecule contain 2 hydrogen atoms, so 1 mole of H_2 molecules contains 2 moles of H atoms. The molar mass of H_2 is 2×1.0079 = 2.0158 g mol^{-1}.

Example 1-4 Calculate the molar mass of methane, CH_4.

Reading the molar masses of C and H from the table,

$$\text{molar mass of } CH_4 = 12.011 \text{ g mol}^{-1} + 4 \times (1.0079 \text{ g mol}^{-1}) = 16.043 \text{ g mol}^{-1}$$

Example 1-5 Calculate the amount of CH_4 in 42.0 g of methane.

The molar mass of methane is $M = 16.043$ g mol^{-1} , and the mass of methane is $m = 42.0$ g, so the amount of methane is given by $n = m/M$:

$$\text{amount of methane } = \frac{42.0g}{16.043 \text{ g mol}^{-1}} = 2.62 \text{ mol}$$

Example 1-6 What is the mass of 0.7852 mol of carbon dioxide, CO_2?

The molar mass of CO_2 is $M = 12.011$ g mol^{-1} + 2 × (15.999 g mol^{-1}) = 44.009 g mol^{-1}. The mass of CO_2 is given by the equation $m=nM$:   mass = 0.7852 mol × 44.009 g mol^{-1} = 34.56 g.

1-10 The law of definite proportions

Each compound has a characteristic **composition by mass**, which is specified by stating the fractional contribution of each element to the total mass of a sample of the compound. The **law of definite proportions** states that the composition by mass of a compound is fixed and is the same for any pure sample of that compound regardless of how big the sample is. The law of definite proportions results from the fixed ratios of the numbers of atoms of each element in a compound, and the constant mass of each type of atom. For example, in water there are two hydrogen atoms for every oxygen atom, and the masses of the atoms of these two elements are constant, and hence oxygen contributes a constant fraction of the mass of any sample of water.

The **fraction by mass** of each element in a compound is the mass of that element present in a sample divided by the total mass of the sample. The fraction by mass is often expressed as a percentage. The fractions by mass of all the elements in a compound must add up to 1 (or 100 % if expressed as a percentage).

The fraction by mass of an element in a compound can be calculated from the molecular or empirical formula of the compound, and the molar masses of the elements present.

Example 1-7 What is the fraction by mass of oxygen in CO_2?

It is convenient to consider a sample containing one mole of CO_2. This sample has a mass of 44.009 g, from our calculation above, and the mass of oxygen is 2 mol ×15.999 g mol^{-1} = 31.998 g. Hence the fraction by mass of oxygen is 31.998/44.009 = 0.72708.

From the composition by mass of a compound, it is possible to determine the empirical formula of the compound. This is the basis for the long-established method of determining empirical formulae, and is demonstrated in the following example. However, it is not possible to find out the molecular formula of a compound knowing only the composition by mass; determination of the molecular formula requires further information, such as the molar mass of the compound.

Example 1-8 A compound containing only carbon and hydrogen is analyzed and found to contain 85.63 % carbon and 14.37 % hydrogen by mass. What is the empirical formula of this compound?

Consider a sample of exactly 100 grams of this compound. This sample contains 85.63 grams of carbon, and so the number of moles of carbon atoms = 85.63 g / 12.011g mol^{-1} = 7.129 mol.

The sample contains (100 – 85.63) grams = 14.37 grams of hydrogen, and so the number of moles of hydrogen atoms = 14.37 g / 1.0079 g mol^{-1} = 14.26 mol.

The ratio of the number of carbon atoms to the number of hydrogen atoms is equal to the ratio of the number of moles, which is 14.26/7.128 = 2.0003. This ratio is very close to 2, so we conclude that the empirical formula is CH_2.

The information given in the question is not sufficient to determine the molecular formula of this compound, which may be C_2H_4 or C_3H_6 or some higher multiple of the empirical formula; in order to distinguish between these possibilities, more information, such as the molar mass, is needed.

1-11 Concentration of solutions

A solution is a homogeneous mixture of two or more substances. When one substance is present in much larger amount than the others, and controls the physical form of the solution, that substance is called the **solvent** and the other substances dissolved in the solvent are called **solutes**. Solutions in which water is the solvent are called **aqueous** solutions; a solute in aqueous solution is often identified by the letters *aq* in brackets, to distinguish it from the pure solid, liquid or some other state.

The **concentration** of a solute in a solution is the amount, or the mass, of the solute per unit volume of solution. Concentration is used whenever the solution is being measured by volume.

The **molar concentration**, $c(A)$, of a solute A in a solution is the amount $n(A)$ of the solute (in moles) divided by the volume V of the solution:

$$\text{molar concentration of A} = c(A) = \frac{\text{amount of solute A}}{\text{volume of solution}} = \frac{n(A)}{V} \qquad (1\text{-}6)$$

Any appropriate units may be used for the molar concentration $c(A)$, but the **molarity** of a solute in solution is specifically the molar concentration expressed in moles per litre. A solution with a concentration of 1.0 mol/L may be referred to as a 1.0 molar solution, abbreviated as 1.0 M.

The **mass concentration** of a solute A in a solution is the mass $m(A)$ of the solute divided by the volume V of the solution:

$$\text{mass concentration of A} = \frac{\text{mass of solute A}}{\text{volume of solution}} = \frac{m(A)}{V} \qquad (1\text{-}7)$$

If the volume of a sample of a solution is measured, using either a pipet or a buret, and the concentration of the solute is known then the amount of solute in the solution can be calculated from equation (1-6). Conversely, if a known amount of solute is dissolved in solvent and the solution is made up to known volume (in a volumetric flask, for instance) then the concentration of the solution can be calculated. It is important to note that, in calculations with concentration, the volume used is the volume of the solution after it has been mixed, not the volume of the pure solvent used to make up the solution.

Table 1-10 summarizes these definitions of concentration.

Table 1-10 Measures of concentration in liquid solutions.

The solutes are represented by A, B,..., and the solvent by S.

Measure	symbol	Definition	Usual units
molar concentration, or molarity	$c(A)$	$\dfrac{n(A)}{V}$	mol L^{-1} (or M)
mass concentration		$\dfrac{m(A)}{V}$	g L^{-1}

Example 1-9 A sample of 25.43 g of sucrose, $C_{12}H_{22}O_{11}$, is dissolved in water, and the solution is made up to a volume of 250.0 mL in a volumetric flask. Calculate the concentration of sucrose.

Molar mass of sucrose is 342.29 g/mol, so $n(\text{sucrose}) = \dfrac{m(\text{sucrose})}{M(\text{sucrose})} = \dfrac{25.43\,\text{g}}{342.29\,\text{g mol}^{-1}} = 0.07429\,\text{mol}$

The volume of the solution is 0.2500 L. Hence concentration of sucrose is:

$$\text{concentration} = \frac{n(\text{sucrose})}{V(\text{solution})} = \frac{0.07429\,\text{mol}}{0.2500\,\text{L}} = 0.2972\,\text{mol/L}$$

Example 1-10 What amount of sodium hydroxide, NaOH, is contained in a 35.2 mL of a 0.255 M solution?

Volume of the solution is 35.2 mL or 0.0352 L. From the definition of concentration, the amount of sodium hydroxide is:

$n(\text{NaOH}) = \text{concentration of NaOH} \times \text{volume} = 0.255\,\text{mol/L} \times 0.0352\,\text{L} = 0.00898\,\text{mol} = 8.98\,\text{mmol}$

Some substances, when dissolved in water, dissociate into ions, partially or completely. These substances are called **electrolytes**, and the solutions conduct electricity through the motion of the electrically charged ions. The concentration of an electrolyte can be expressed as the amount of a specified formula per unit volume. Thus we can speak of a 1 M NaCl solution, which contains 1 mole of the formula NaCl per litre, even though this substance exists in solution in the form of sodium ions, Na^+, and chloride ions, Cl^- rather than as NaCl molecules. Electrolytes that are not fully ionized require separate consideration and will be discussed in later chapters. Care must be taken where there is a possibility of confusion over the meaning of concentration, particularly in the case of electrolytes that are partially dissociated.

1-12 The composition of solutions and mixtures

A **mixture** of substances may be a solid, a liquid or a gas, and may be either homogeneous or heterogeneous, as discussed in Section 1-4. A solution is a homogeneous mixture.

We can specify the **composition** of a solution or mixture by using the relative amount of each substance present. This can be done using either the mass fraction or the mole fraction of each substance. The composition of a liquid solution is sometimes expressed by a quantity called the molality.

The **mass fraction** of a substance in a solution or mixture is the mass of that substance present divided by the total mass of the solution. If a solution contains substances A, B, etc, then the mass fraction of each substance is the mass of that substance present divided by the total mass of all substances present. For example, the mass fraction $w(A)$ of substance A is given by the equation:

$$\text{mass fraction of A} = w(A) = \frac{\text{mass of A}}{\text{total mass of mixture}} = \frac{m(A)}{m(A) + m(B) + \dots} \tag{1-8}$$

The mass fractions of all the substances present in a solution (including the solvent) must add up to one:

$$w(A) + w(B) + \ldots = 1 \qquad (1\text{-}9)$$

In a mixture, the proportions of the various substances present may be varied, and the mass fraction of a substance in a mixture varies with the composition of the mixture. On the other hand, the fraction by mass of an element in a compound is fixed, as discussed in section 1-10.

The **mole fraction**, $x(A)$, of a substance in a solution or mixture is defined in a similar fashion. If a solution contains an amount $n(A)$ of substance A, an amount $n(B)$ of substance B, and so on, then the mole fraction of each substance is the amount of that substance present divided by the total amount of all substances present. For example, the mole fraction $x(A)$ of substance A is given by the equation:

$$\text{mole fraction of A} = x(A) = \frac{\text{amount of A}}{\text{total amount of all substances}} = \frac{n(A)}{n(A) + n(B) + \ldots}$$

The mole fractions of all the substances present in a solution (including the solvent) must add up to one:

$$x(A) + x(B) + \ldots = 1 \qquad (1\text{-}10)$$

The composition of a liquid solution is sometimes expressed in terms of the molality of each solute in the solution. The **molality** of a solute A in a solution is the amount $n(A)$ of the solute (in moles) divided by the mass of the *solvent* S in kilograms:

$$\text{molality of A} = \frac{\text{amount of solute A}}{\text{mass of solvent S}} = \frac{n(A)}{m(S)} \qquad (1\text{-}11)$$

In a dilute aqueous solution the molality is approximately equal, numerically, to the molarity (or molar concentration) since a litre of solution contains about a kilogram of water. However it must be remembered that the molality measures composition while molarity measures concentration; the two quantities are different in nature, have different units, and are used in different situations. The composition of a solution does not change with temperature, whereas the concentration does change because of thermal expansion. For this reason, the molality is useful when the temperature of the solution is likely to change.

Table 1-11 summarizes these definitions of composition.

Table 1-11 Measures of composition of solutions and mixtures

The substances in the mixtures are represented by A, B,...The mass of each substance is indicated by m and the amount of substance by n.

Measure	Symbol	Definition	Units
mass fraction	w(A)	$\dfrac{m(A)}{m(A)+m(B)+...}$	none*
mole fraction	x(A)	$\dfrac{n(A)}{n(A)+n(B)+...}$	none*
molality	**	$\dfrac{n(A)}{m(S)}$	mol kg^{-1}

* More precisely, the units of mass fraction are kilogram of solute per kilogram of solution, and those of mole fraction are moles of solute per mole of solution, but it is usual to omit the units for these two quantities.

** It is tempting to use the symbol m for molality, but this is omitted here because of the possibility of confusion with the symbol for mass. When molality is used in an equation, a suitable unambiguous symbol can be chosen according to the circumstances.

Example 1-11 10.00 grams of sodium chloride NaCl is mixed with 10.00 grams of barium chloride $BaCl_2$. Calculate the mass fraction and the mole fraction of NaCl in the mixture.

The mass fraction of NaCl can be calculated directly from the definition:

$$w(NaCl) = \frac{10.00\,g}{10.00\,g + 10.00\,g} = 0.5000$$

To calculate the mole fraction, it is necessary to calculate the amount of each salt present. The molar masses are 58.443 g/mol for NaCl and 208.24 g/mol for $BaCl_2$. Hence:

$$n(NaCl) = \frac{10.00\,g}{58.443\,g/mol} = 0.1711\,mol$$

$$n(BaCl_2) = \frac{10.00\,g}{208.24\,g/mol} = 0.04802\,mol$$

Hence mole fraction is: $x(NaCl) = \dfrac{0.1711\,mol}{0.1711\,mol + 0.04802\,mol} = 0.7808$

Notice that the values of the mass fraction and the mole fraction differ considerably in this case.

Example 1-12 10.0 g of NaCl is dissolved in 250.0 g of water. Calculate the composition of the solution, expressed as (a) mass fraction, (b) mole fraction and (c) molality.

(a) Total mass of solution is 250.0 + 10.0 = 260.0 g, so mass fraction is $w(NaCl)$ = 10.0 g/260.0 g = 0.0385.

(b) Molar mass of NaCl = 58.443 g/mol, so $n(NaCl)$ =10.0 g/58.44 g mol^{-1} = 0.171 mol.

Molar mass of H_2O = 18.015 g/mol, so $n(H_2O)$ = 250.0 g/18.015 g mol^{-1} = 13.88 mol.

Total amount of solution is $n(NaCl) + n(H_2O)$ = 0.171 mol + 13.88 mol = 14.05 mol.

Hence mole fraction is $x(NaCl)$ = 0.171 mol/14.05 mol = 0.0122.

(c) Molality is $b(NaCl)$ = 0.171mol/0.2500 kg = 0.684 mol/kg.

If only a very small amount of a substance is present in a mixture, then the mass fraction and mole fraction may be multiplied by 10^6 to express these quantities as parts per million (ppm) by mass or by mole. They may also be multiplied by 10^9 to express them as parts per billion (ppb). This convention is often used in dealing with environmental chemistry. Some difficulty is sometimes caused if it is not stated whether the fraction is measured by mass or by mole. In atmospheric chemistry, the composition is usually quoted on a per volume basis, which is almost the same as a mole fraction, and for trace substances this is indicated by "ppmv" or "ppbv".

Example 1-13 Lead is found to be present in water from a certain source at the level of 2.0 ppm by mass. What mass of lead is contained in 3.0 litres of this water?

From the definition of mass fraction, we know: $\dfrac{m(Pb)}{m(Pb) + m(H_2O)} = 2.0 \times 10^{-6}$.

Rearranging this equation: $m(Pb) = \dfrac{2.0 \times 10^{-6}}{1 - 2.0 \times 10^{-6}} \times m(H_2O) \approx 2.0 \times 10^{-6} \times m(H_2O)$

The mass of 3.0 dm^3 of water is approximately 3.0 kg, since the density of water is close to 1.0 g/mL, or 1.0 kg/L, and so:

$m(Pb) = 2.0 \times 10^{-6} \times 3.0 \times 10^3$ g $= 6.0 \times 10^{-3}$ g , or 6.0 mg.

1-13 Errors of measurement

The result of a measurement is always subject to uncertainties because of limitations of the equipment used and the skill of the observer. In making measurements, it is usually assumed that there is a single "correct" value of the quantity being measured, and that a skilled observer would obtain this "correct" value exactly if an error-free measurement could be carried out. In practice, all measurements are affected by errors and this must be kept in mind whenever experimental data is being used.

We will discuss four sources of error: the limit of reading of the instrument used for the measurement, systematic error, random error, and sampling error.

The **limit of reading** is the smallest change in a quantity that can be reliably detected on the scale of the instrument being used. It is usually determined by the size of the smallest subdivision of the scale used for the reading. For instance, a typical buret used in an undergraduate laboratory is graduated in 0.1 mL subdivisions, and with care and practice it is possible to read the level of the liquid to within one fifth of one of these subdivisions, or 0.02 mL. The limit of reading of this buret is therefore 0.02 mL. The reading corresponding to the meniscus of the liquid in the buret should therefore be read to the nearest even integer in the second decimal place. For example, the volume might be read as 35.46 mL, but not 35.45 or 35.47 mL. The uncertainty associated with this single reading is therefore half of this, or ±0.01 mL.

The volume of liquid delivered from a buret is determined by taking readings of the height of the liquid before and after delivery, and subtracting one reading from the other. The total uncertainty in the volume delivered, due to the limit of reading, is therefore twice the uncertainty of a single reading, a total of ±0.02 mL. The only way to reduce this uncertainty is to use some other instrument or technique for making the measurement.

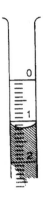

Figure 1-7 The position of the bottom of the meniscus, or curved surface, of the liquid in a buret can (with care) be read to a fifth of the smallest division, or about 0.02 mL.

When a measurement is made on an instrument with a digital readout, the limit of reading is ±1 unit in the last digit of the readout. Analytical balances, which are used for routine weighing of small samples, usually indicate the mass in grams on a digital readout with four decimal places. For instance, the mass of a sample in a small plastic container may be indicated as 3.1467 g. The limit of reading for the balance is ±0.0001 g or ±0.1 mg. The result of the weighing can be quoted as 3.1467±0.0001 g, or as 3.1467(1) g where the uncertainty in brackets refers to the last figure quoted.

Systematic error results from errors in the equipment used to make measurements or errors in experimental procedure. Systematic errors affect the result of a measurement the same way every time the measurement is made. If, for example, the calibration marks on a buret are incorrectly engraved on the glass, then the measure of the volume of solution delivered from that buret will be wrong every time it is used. If, in carrying out a titration, the wrong indicator is used to detect the equivalence point, then the results of repeated titrations will be systematically wrong even if the calibration of the buret is perfect.

Detection of systematic errors is usually very difficult. Repetition of the experiment is not effective for this purpose. Careful calibration of instruments, testing of methods by measuring known standards, replacement of equipment, and comparison of results on the same samples determined in independent laboratories by different people are all techniques which help to reveal systematic error. The most convincing test for systematic error is to repeat a measurement using a different method, or using different equipment, followed by comparison of the two separate results.

Random errors in a measurement are caused by uncontrolled factors in the experiment which affect the result. In every repetition of the experiment, changes in these factors change the numerical result of the measurement. Random errors are readily detected by repetition of a measurement.

Given a set of results of repeated measurements, statistical methods are used to calculate the best estimate of the "true" value of the quantity being measured, and an estimate of the uncertainty in this estimate due to random error. The best estimate of the true value is usually taken to be the **mean** or **average** of the results of repeated measurements, and the uncertainty in the mean is indicated by the **sample standard deviation**. For a series of measurements $x_1, x_2, ...x_n$ the mean and standard deviation are calculated from the following formulae:

Mean:
$$<x> = \frac{1}{n}(x_1 + x_2 + ...x_n) = \frac{1}{n}\sum_{i=1}^{n} x_i \qquad (1\text{-}12)$$

Sample standard deviation:
$$s = \sqrt{\frac{1}{n-1}\sum_{i=1}^{n}(x_i - <x>)^2} \qquad (1\text{-}13)$$

In the second formula, the division by n–1 rather than n comes about because one number, the mean, has already been calculated from the set of n measurements. There are several techniques for doing the calculations conveniently, and many hand calculators and computer spreadsheets have built-in functions for the mean and standard deviation.

Example 1-14 Five measurements of the mass, in grams, of a particular object gave the results 3.4589, 3.4583, 3.4586, 3.4588, 3.4586. Calculate the mean and standard deviation of the mass.

Mean = (3.4589+3.4583+3.4586+3.4588+3.4586)/5 = 3.4586 g.

Sample standard deviation = $\sqrt{\frac{1}{4}(0.0003^2 + 0.0003^2 + 0.0000 + 0.0002^2 + 0.0000)} = 0.0002$ g.

The mass is 3.4586 ± 0.0002 g. This can also be written 3.4586(2) g.

In environmental chemistry or in biological work, the variations in repeated measurements are often due to real fluctuations in samples taken from different locations, or at different times, or from different individual animals. These variations are random but are not "errors" because they would be present even if there were no errors at all in the measurement technique. We are not concerned here with this source of variability in results.

Sampling error can occur when measurements are made on small samples which are thought to be representative of a much larger body of material. In analytical and environmental chemistry it is common to take samples for chemical analysis, either because the object is too big to analyze in its entirety, or because the analytical procedure destroys the sample.

It is impractical, for instance, to measure the mass of copper per tonne of ore produced in a mine by analyzing the entire output of the mine. Instead, the analytical chemist takes many small samples at random from the mine output, and mixes them carefully to form a "gross sample". From the gross sample, several small samples are taken for analysis. The results are then averaged to determine the average copper content of the ore produced at the mine. If the gross sample is not truly representative of the mine output, then the estimate of the copper content is unreliable no matter how many analyses are made or how accurate the analytical method may be. Such errors are called sampling errors, and strenuous efforts are made to minimize them in analytical chemistry. Similar errors can also occur in the laboratory. If a solution is not properly mixed, the concentration will vary from place to place and if samples of the solution are used in titrations, erratic results will be obtained.

As a result of one or more of these four sources of error, each experimental quantity has an associated **uncertainty** or **probable error.** The **precision** of a quantity is an estimate of the total uncertainty due to random error, sampling error and the limit of reading. The **accuracy** of a quantity includes any systematic errors as well as the other three sources of error, and measures the possible discrepancy between the measured quantity and the "true" value, if the latter is known. It is quite possible for an experiment to produce a very precise result that is inaccurate due to systematic error. High precision means that repeated measurements are in good agreement with each other. High accuracy implies not only high precision, but also low systematic error.

1-14 Decimal places and significant figures

Most of the numbers used in calculations are approximations to the quantities they represent and carry with them an uncertainty or probable error, as discussed in the last section. Each number should be written in a way that is consistent with the probable error: it should specify the magnitude of the quantity correctly, but without implying a greater level of precision than is justified. This is achieved by writing the number using the correct number of digits. In this section we discuss the rules to be followed in doing this.

In a number written in decimal format, the number of digits to the right of the decimal point is the number of **decimal places.** For example the numbers 1.234, 12.345, 123456.789, 0.012, and 0.001 all have three decimal places although they have different magnitudes and some are much more accurately specified than others. Changing the units of a number, or expressing it in scientific notation with a power of 10, changes the number of decimal places: a mass of 1234.5 g can be expressed as 1.2345 kg, or as 1.2345×10^3 g ; the number of decimal places changes, but the meaning of the number with its associated units is exactly the same in all three formats.

In a decimal number, the **significance** of the digits decreases from left to right. The number of **significant figures** is the number of digits used to specify the size of the number, apart from leading or trailing zeroes that serve only to indicate the place of the decimal point. For example the following numbers all have four significant digits: 1.234, 0.001234, 0.01230, 0.01034. The leading, or left-hand, zeroes in the last three numbers do not count as significant figures, since they are present only to place the decimal point. Trailing zeroes to the right of the decimal point are treated as significant figures: the numbers 0.1000, 0.1200, 0.1230 and 0.1234 all have four significant figures. Trailing zeroes to the left of the decimal point are ambiguous however, and large numbers should be written in scientific notation since they may otherwise cause difficulty for the reader. For example, in the number 1234000 it is not clear whether the three trailing zeroes are significant (i.e. show that the magnitude is 1234000 and not 1234001 or 123399) or are there merely to locate the decimal point. If this number is written as 1.234×10^6 then it is clear that there are four significant figures since the function of indicating the location of the decimal point is separately indicated by the appropriate power of 10. If a number ends with a zero, then a decimal point can be used at the end to indicate that all figures are significant: for example, the number 100. has three significant figures.

The number of digits used in recording an experimental measurement should be chosen so that the last digit at the right-hand end of the number is equivalent to the first non-zero digit of the estimated experimental error. For example, if a mass has an uncertainty of ±0.0002 g then the first non-zero digit of the uncertainty is in the fourth decimal place, and it would be appropriate to record the mass with four decimal places. If this rule is followed, the uncertainty in the last figure quoted would not be greater than 9, nor less than 1.

An alternate rule used in some scientific journals is that the number of figures quoted in reporting a result should be such that the uncertainty does not exceed 19 in the last decimal place. This called the "rule of 19". The purpose is to avoid losing a significant figure when the uncertainty exceeds 9 in the last place, but not by very much. However the "rule of 9" given in the previous paragraph is simpler to apply.

In reading an instrument with a digital readout, all digits displayed should be recorded. For example, if an analytical balance reading to four decimal places shows a mass of 10.1234 g, then all six digits should be recorded. If the reading happens to have a zero in the last place, 10.1230 g for example, then the zero should be recorded just as it would be if it were some other integer. Whether it is zero or not, the final digit is treated as a significant digit.

When numbers based upon experiment are used in a calculation, care must be taken that the result of the calculation is expressed to the appropriate number of significant figures or decimal places. The rules for doing this are as follows:

(a) When numbers are added or subtracted, the answer should be quoted with a number of decimal places equal to the smallest number of decimal places among the numbers being combined.

(b) When numbers are multiplied or divided, the answer should be quoted with a number of significant figures equal to the smallest number of significant figures among the numbers being combined.

(c) When the number of figures in a calculated result is to be reduced by dropping digits off the right hand end, the result should be **rounded off**.

Rounding off is carried out as follows. Digits are removed from the right-hand end of the number, leaving the desired number of significant figures; an adjustment may be needed in the digits retained. For instance 1.234567 is rounded to three significant figures by dropping the digits 4567, and leaving 1.23. If the left-hand digit being dropped (which is 4 in the case quoted) is less than 5, then no change is made in the digits that are retained. If the left-hand digit being dropped is 6 or more, then the last retained digit is increased by one. If the left-hand digit being dropped is 5, then the last retained digit is unaltered if it is even, but is increased by one if it is odd.

The rule for rounding off a 5 seems a little odd, but it avoids the bias that results from always rounding upwards. Some examples of rounding off to give three significant figures are as follows:

1.234 → 1.23   1.238 → 1.24   1.235 → 1.24   1.245 → 1.24.

Example 1-15 A weighing bottle containing a powder has mass of 13.7895 g and after some of the powder is removed, the mass is 13.2950 g. What mass of powder was removed?

The mass removed is the difference, 13.7895 − 13.2950 = 0.4945 g. Notice that there are only four significant figures in the result, even though each weighing was carried out with an accuracy of six significant figures.

Example 1-16 The sample of powder described in the last example was heated, and the mass was found to be reduced to 0.3695 g. What is the ratio of masses after and before heating?

The ratio is $0.3695/0.4945 = 0.7472194$. Since each of the masses in the ratio has four significant figures, this must be rounded to four significant figures: 0.7472.

The molar masses of the elements listed in Table 1-9 have been rounded off where necessary, to no more than five significant figures. In addition, the tabulated values of the fundamental constants have also been rounded off to five significant figures in order to make them more convenient to use. Very few calculations in chemistry require more than five significant figures. If more accurate values are needed, the student may consult the CRC Handbook of Chemistry and Physics or similar publications of reference data.

Chemical calculations often require several steps, and the question often arises whether or not to round off the intermediate results at each stage. Generally speaking, it is not necessary to round off the intermediate stages of a calculation, but the number of significant figures used in the final answer should be consistent with the least accurate stage of the calculation. When using an electronic calculator, the intermediate results are often retained in the calculator and can be used for the next step of the calculation. If some of the intermediate results are to be written down as the problem is worked out on paper, at least one more figure than is needed should be recorded, to avoid accumulating round-off errors through the calculation.

For the purpose of comparing two quantities, it is sometimes sufficient to use the ratio with only one significant figure. If the ratio is less than about $\sqrt{10} \cong 3.2$ the two quantities are of the same **order of magnitude.** If the ratio is roughly 10 (i.e. between $\sqrt{10}$ and $10\sqrt{10}$) then the two quantities differ by one order of magnitude, and so on. For instance, the density of copper is 8.93 times that of water, to three significant figures, and so is an order of magnitude greater than the density of water and four orders of magnitude greater than the density of the atmosphere, which is 1.2×10^{-3} g/mL.

Key concepts of this chapter

Chemistry is the science of matter, and deals with the structure, the properties and transformations of substances. Within the context of chemistry, atoms are the fundamental building block of matter, but in many substances the atoms are bonded together as molecules or ions. An element is a substance that cannot be broken down into other substances by chemical means. Every atom of an element has the same charge on its nucleus. Compounds contain more than one element in fixed proportions, and have well-defined chemical and physical properties. Elements are represented by symbols, which are combined to represent compounds by chemical formulae.

The magnitude of a physical quantity is represented by a number and units. The units used are usually combinations of the fundamental units (length, mass, time, electric current, temperature, and amount of substance). Prefixes are used to indicate powers of 10, so as to avoid very large and very small numbers.

Concentration of a substance in solution is measured in terms of mass concentration, and molar concentration or molarity. The composition of mixtures and solutions is measured in terms of mass fraction, mole fraction or molality.

Experimental measurements are never completely free of error and uncertainty, and should be quoted with the appropriate number of significant figures. The precision of a quantity indicates the uncertainty due to random error, sampling error and the limit of reading. The accuracy of a quantity includes systematic error in addition to the other sources of error.

Review Questions

1. What is the difference between an element and a compound?

2. What is the difference between a compound and a solution?

3. What are the two main particles from which an atom is formed?

4. What is the characteristic feature of an ion?

5. Give the names and symbols for the ten lightest elements, in the correct order.

6. What are the three normal states of matter?

7. What instrument would you use to measure a mass?

8. What is a buret used for?

9. What is a pipet used for?

10. Define a mole of substance.

11. Define an atomic mass unit.

12. Why are none of the molar masses of the elements an exact integer?

13. Define the mass fraction of a substance in a solution.

14. Define the mole fraction of a substance in a solution.

15. Is molarity a measure of composition, or of concentration?

16. What is the difference between systematic error and random error?

17. What is the difference between precision and accuracy?

Problems

1. Classify each of the following common substances as a heterogeneous mixture, a solution or a pure compound: table salt, gasoline, maple syrup, wet sand, distilled water, sea water, soda water, reinforced concrete, air, sugar.

2. Write the abbreviations for nanogram, picosecond, kilojoule, millimole, kilopascal, kilonewton.

3. Write the abbreviations for megawatt, kilogram, nanometre, gigajoule, cubic decimetre.

4. Write the full name of the abbreviated units: km, cm, mg, μs, MPa, MJ, N.

5. Express (a) a length of 32.4 cm in mm and km; (b) a length of 0.12 nm in cm and m; (c) a mass of 12.346 g in kg and in t; (d) a volume of 0.250 dm^3 in litres and in cm^3.

6. What is the volume of 25.0 g of liquid of density 0.896 g/mL? [27.9 mL]

7. What is the mass of 2.0 litre of oil of density 0.89 g/mL? [1.78 kg]

8. What is the amount (in moles) of water in exactly one litre of water, if the density is 0.998 g/mL? [55.4 mol]

9. An empty volumetric flask weighs 120.62 g, and when filled with 25.00 mL of liquid, the total mass is 150.75 g. What is the density of the liquid? [1.205 g/mL]

10. What is the mass of air inside a room of dimensions 3.00 m × 4.00 m × 3.00 m, if the density of air is 1.16 g dm^{-3}? [41.8 kg]

11. Calculate the mass of 2.58 mol of pure iron. [144. g]

12. How many electrons are there in each of the following atoms: Na, Fe, C, Ti, Hg, Kr?

13. How many electrons are there in each of the following ions: K^+, Cl^-, Ca^{2+}, Cr^{3+}, O^{2-}?

14. How many electrons are there in each of the following ions: OH^-, H_3O^+, SO_4^{2-}, NO_3^-?

15. How many neutrons and protons are there in each of the following nuclides: ^{16}O, ^{26}Mg, ^{75}As, ^{233}U, ^{197}Au, ^2H, ^{15}N?

16. What is the composition by mass of each of the following compounds: H_2O, CH_3Cl, C_6H_6, $C_7H_4Br_3NO_2$?

17. Calculate the molar mass of each of the following substances: sulfur dioxide SO_2, butane C_4H_{10}, buckminsterfullerene C_{60}, carbon tetrachloride CCl_4, propanol C_3H_7OH, ammonia NH_3, calcium carbonate $CaCO_3$. Be careful of significant figures.

18. Calculate the fraction by mass of carbon in each of the following substances: methane CH_4, butane C_4H_{10}, carbon tetrachloride CCl_4, propanol C_3H_7OH.

19. Chlorofluorocarbons, or CFCs, were used formerly for operating refrigerators and air conditioners, but are now known to interfere with the ozone layer in the upper atmosphere. They are compounds containing carbon, chlorine and fluorine atoms. A particular CFC has the following composition by mass: 10.0 % C, 58.6 % Cl, 31.4 % F. Determine the empirical formula for this compound, and suggest a molecular formula assuming that the molecule contains only one or two carbon atoms.

20. A chlorofluorocarbon has the following composition by mass: 11.5 % C, 33.9 % Cl, 54.6 % F. Determine the empirical formula for this compound, and suggest a molecular formula assuming that the molecule contains only one or two carbon atoms.

21. A compound has the following composition by mass 74.03 % C, 17.27 % N and 8.70 % H. Determine the empirical formula of the compound.

22. A compound of the elements M and A with the formula M_2A_3 contains 61.0 % M by mass. A second compound of the same two elements has the formula MA_2. What is the percentage by mass of the element M in the second compound.   [54.0 %]

23. A sample of a compound known to contain only carbon, hydrogen and oxygen was burned in excess oxygen. The mass of the sample was originally 0.707 g and the products of the combustion were 1.606 g of carbon dioxide CO_2 and 0.659 g of water H_2O. What is the empirical formula of the compound?

24. Arrange the following samples in order of increasing number of atoms: (a) 4.0 g of hydrogen gas H_2, (b) 1.0 mol of oxygen gas O_2, (c) 30.0 g of water H_2O, (d) 300.0 g of uranium metal U, (e) 32.0 g of sulfur dioxide SO_2.

25. How many molecules are there in 1.0 µg of sulfur dioxide SO_2?   [$9.4×10^{+15}$]

26. Sodium chloride NaCl has a density of 2.16 g cm^{-3}. How many sodium ions are there in a crystal which is a cube with each edge 0.50 mm long?   [$2.8×10^{18}$]

27. If Glauber's salt $Na_2SO_4.10H_2O$ is heated carefully, water is driven off leaving sodium sulfate Na_2SO_4. What fraction of the original mass of Glauber's salt is left if all the water is removed?   [0.4409]

28. Dry air has a composition by mole of 78.084 % N_2, 20.946 % O_2, 0.934 % Ar and 0.036 % CO_2. What is its composition by mass?

29. What mass of sodium chloride NaCl is contained in 25.43 mL of a solution containing 15.0 g/L of NaCl?   [0.381 g]

30. How many moles of hydrochloric acid HCl are contained in 27.3 mL of a 0.237 M solution?   [6.47 mmol]

31. 10.0 g of sodium chloride NaCl is dissolved in water to make a solution of total volume 100.0 mL. What is the molar concentration of NaCl in the solution?   [1.71 M]

32. 20.0 g of ammonium sulfate $(NH_4)_2SO_4$ is dissolved in water to make a solution of total volume 100.0 mL. What is the molar concentration of ammonium ions NH_4^+ in the solution?

                    [3.03 M]

33. If a person eats 450 g of food containing 0.15 ppm by mass of mercury, what is the total mass of mercury eaten? How many moles of mercury is this?   [68 µg, 0.34 µmol]

34. 10.0 g of sucrose $C_{12}H_{22}O_{11}$ is dissolved in 100.0 g of water. Calculate the mass fraction, the mole fraction, and the molality of sucrose in the solution.   [0.0909, 0.00523, 0.292 mol/kg]

35. A 10.00 % by mass solution of sodium chloride NaCl in water has a density of 1.06879 g/mL at 25 °C. What is the molality of NaCl? What is the molarity of NaCl?

                    [1.901 mol/kg, 1.829 mol/L]

36. The solution described in Problem 35 is heated to 40 °C, and as a result of thermal expansion the density drops to 1.06238 g/mL. Calculate the molality and molarity of the solution at this temperature.   [1.901 mol/kg, 1.818 mol/L]

37. There are two isotopes of chlorine, ^{35}Cl with a natural abundance of 75.77 % and molar mass 34.968853 g/mol, and ^{37}Cl with a natural abundance of 24.23 % and a molar mass of 36.965903 g/mol. Calculate the average molar mass of chlorine from these data, using the appropriate number of significant figures.   [35.45 g/mol]

38. A student measured the mass of a weighing bottle several times, obtaining the results 24.5784 g, 24.5786 g, 24.5786 g, 24.5785 g, 24.5782 g, 24.5788 g. What is the best estimate of the true mass of the weighing bottle based on these measurements? What is the uncertainty in this value, as measured by the sample standard deviation? [24.5785(2) g]

39. How many significant figures are there in each of the following masses: 0.00038 g; 3.8×10^{-4} g; 3.8×10^{-6} g; 3.80×10^{-4} g; 0.38000 g? [2,2,2,3,5]

40. The mass of a weighing bottle plus sample is 18.6392 grams, and after some material is transferred to another container, the mass of the bottle plus the remaining sample is 18.0092 g. What is the mass of the material transferred? How many significant figures are there in the result? [0.6300 g, 4]

41. A volumetric flask contains 100.03 mL of a liquid with a density of 2.33 g/mL. What is the mass of the liquid? [233. g]

2 Chemical compounds and chemical reactions

Objectives

After reading this chapter, the student should be able to do the following:

♦ Name a compound given its chemical formula.

♦ Write a chemical formula given the name of a compound.

♦ Write balanced chemical equations to describe reactions.

♦ Make stoichiometric calculations based upon balanced chemical equations.

♦ List the common types of chemical reaction.

♦ Determine the oxidation numbers of elements in compounds.

♦ Identify acid-base reactions based on proton transfer.

♦ Identify reduction-oxidation reactions.

Related topics to review:

Elements, atomic structure, and molar mass in Chapter 1.

Related topics to look forward to:

Discussion of chemical equilibrium in Chapters 13, 14 and 15, and of electrochemistry in Chapter 17.

2-1 Nomenclature: The names of inorganic compounds

In the previous chapter, the names and symbols for the elements were introduced. We begin this chapter with a discussion of the names of chemical compounds. The system of naming chemical compounds is called **chemical nomenclature**.

A chemical name is not just a translation of the formula, element by element, into words. Certain names are used to identify groups of atoms that are joined together by chemical bonds and react chemically as a single unit. For instance, the compound with formula Na_2SO_4 is called sodium sulfate. The name tells us that the compound contains sodium ions and a group of atoms called the sulfate ion consisting of one sulfur atom and four oxygen atoms. In many reactions of this compound, the sulfate ion retains its identity, and imparts its characteristic properties to the compound.

Each compound has a unique chemical formula, and it is essential that each compound also have a name that corresponds uniquely to the chemical formula. Many common compounds have traditional names, which have been used for many years, and are still used regularly. Examples are common salt (sodium chloride NaCl) and caustic soda (sodium hydroxide NaOH). However, so many compounds are now known that it is impractical to give each a special name, and so a systematic procedure for naming compounds has been adopted. While the systematic names avoid confusion, they are sometimes inelegant or clumsy, so chemists often use the traditional names when dealing with common compounds or when referring repeatedly to a complicated molecule. Students should learn to recognize both names for simple compounds.

The study of compounds of carbon with other non-metals is called **organic chemistry**. The study of compounds of all the other elements (plus a few compounds of carbon) is known as **inorganic chemistry**. In this section, we give an introduction to the names of inorganic compounds, sufficient to allow the student to deal with many simple compounds. The next section deals with organic compounds. These two introductory sections on chemical nomenclature are far from complete, but the student's knowledge of how to read and write names for chemical compounds will grow as a result of studying topics such as oxidation numbers, electronegativity and molecular structure in later chapters.

A set of practical rules for naming an inorganic compound from its formula is as follows. Compounds can be classified according to how many different elements they contain. A compound containing only two elements is called a **binary compound**. Binary compounds can usually be named by following these rules:

1. The formula is read from left to right.

2. The name of the first element is used unchanged.

3. The name of the second element is derived from the name of the second element by combining the root of the name with the ending "-ide". For example, oxygen becomes oxide, chlorine becomes chloride, and so on.

4. The two names are then combined.

Example 2-1 Write the name for the compound with formula LiCl.

Reading from the left, the first element is Li, which is lithium. The second element is Cl, chlorine, and this name is modified by combining "chlor-" with "-ide", making "chloride". Hence the name is lithium chloride.

Prefixes such as "di-" meaning two and "tri-" meaning three, are often added to the name of the second element, and sometimes to the first element as well.

Example 2-2 Write the name for the compound with formula Na_2S.

Reading from the left, the first element is Na, which is sodium. The second element is S, sulfur, and this name is modified by combining "sulf-" with "-ide", making "sulfide". Since there are two sodium atoms for every sulfur atom, the systematic name is disodium sulfide. However, there is only one binary compound of sodium and sulfur, so omitting the prefix "di-" causes no ambiguity. The usual name of this compound is sodium sulfide.

Example 2-3 Write the name for the compound with formula BF_3.

Reading from the left, the first element is B, which is boron. The second element is F, fluorine, and this name is modified by combining "fluor-" with "-ide", making "fluoride". The formula indicates that there are three fluorine atoms to each boron atom, so the name is boron trifluoride.

If one element in the formula of a binary compound is hydrogen and the other is a metal, then the compound is named as a hydride, according to the above rules. However, if the other element is a non-metal there is usually a common name, which is nearly always used. For example, H_2O is always called **water**, CH_4 is always called **methane**, and NH_3 is always called **ammonia**. These binary compounds of hydrogen with non-metals may be described as **molecular hydrides** or **covalent hydrides**, to distinguish them from the **ionic hydrides** of metals, such as lithium hydride LiH.

If hydrogen is the first element in the formula, it is usually an indication that the compound is an **acid**, and the name usually used for the compound is that of the acid. For example, the compound HCl may be called hydrogen chloride when it is pure, following the above rules, but when dissolved in water HCl is known as hydrochloric acid. Table 2-1 lists some of the common acids and their names. According to the simplest definition, an acid is a substance that forms positively charged **hydrogen ions**, H^+, when dissolved in water. When ionized, the acid also forms one or more negatively charged ions, and the names of these ions are derived from the names of the acids from which they are formed. The names and formulae (including electric charge) of the ions are listed in Table 2-1. Water is included in the table, together with the corresponding negative ions, the hydroxide ion OH^- and the oxide ion O^{2-}.

Table 2-1 Some acids and the negative ions derived from them

Acids		Negative ions	
H_2O	water	OH^-	hydroxide
		O^{2-}	oxide
HF	hydrofluoric acid	F^-	fluoride
HCl	hydrochloric acid	Cl^-	chloride
HBr	hydrobromic acid	Br^-	bromide
HI	hydriodic acid	I^-	iodide
H_2S	hydrogen sulfide	S^{2-}	sulfide
HNO_3	nitric acid	NO_3^-	nitrate
HNO_2	nitrous acid	NO_2^-	nitrite
H_2SO_4	sulfuric acid	SO_4^{2-}	sulfate
H_2SO_3	sulfurous acid	SO_3^{2-}	sulfite
H_2CO_3	carbonic acid	CO_3^{2-}	carbonate
H_3PO_4	phosphoric acid	PO_4^{3-}	phosphate
HClO	hypochlorous acid	ClO^-	hypochlorite
$HClO_2$	chlorous acid	ClO_2^-	chlorite
$HClO_3$	chloric acid	ClO_3^-	chlorate
$HClO_4$	perchloric acid	ClO_4^-	perchlorate

Many compounds containing three elements are related to acids, and named by reference to the names of acids, using the following rules.

1. The formula is read from left to right.

2. The name of the first element is used unchanged.

3. The next two elements are examined. In many cases they correspond to one of the negative ions derived from an acid. The name for this ion is used to represent this group of atoms collectively

4. The two names are then combined.

Example 2-4 Write the name for the compound with formula $CaCO_3$.

Reading from the left, the first element is Ca, which is calcium. The next two elements are C, carbon, and O, oxygen, in the ratio of 1:3. This combination is found in Table 2-1 and is named carbonate. Hence the name of the compound is calcium carbonate.

Example 2-5 Write the name for the compound with formula NaClO.

Reading from the left, the first element is Na, sodium. The next two elements are Cl, chlorine, and O, oxygen, in the ratio of 1:1. This combination is found in Table 2-1 and is named hypochlorite. Hence the name of the compound is sodium hypochlorite.

Some acids, such as sulfuric acid H_2SO_4 and carbonic acid H_2CO_3, contain two hydrogen atoms which can be ionized. These acids can form compounds in which either one or two hydrogen atoms are replaced by other atoms. These compounds are named by adding the word "hydrogen" in front of the name of the negative ion, or (in an older notation) by adding the prefix "bi-" to the name of the negative ion.

Example 2-6 Write two names for the compound with formula $NaHCO_3$.

Reading from the left, the first element is Na, sodium, and the second element is H, hydrogen. At the end of the formula we recognize C, carbon, and O, oxygen, in the ratio of 1:3. This combination is found in Table 2-1 and is named carbonate. Hence the systematic name is sodium hydrogen carbonate. The traditional name is sodium bicarbonate.

In naming compounds and writing formulae, ions play an important part. Table 2-2 lists some common positive ions that are found in combination with the negative ions from Table 2-1. Some elements form several positive ions with different charges. In such cases, different names are used to distinguish between them. The distinction will be explored further later in this chapter under the heading of oxidation number, which in the present context is simply equal to the charge on the ion but is indicated by a Roman numeral placed in brackets after the name or symbol for the element.

Example 2-7 Write the name of $CuSO_4$.

The first element is Cu, copper. The elements S, sulfur, and O, oxygen, are present in the ratio 1:4, and constitute the sulfate ion, SO_4^{2-}. Thus the compound can be named copper sulfate. But Table 2-2 shows that copper forms two ions, the copper (I) ion, Cu^+, and the copper(II) ion Cu^{2+}. Because of there is one copper ion per sulfate ion, and the sulfate ion carries a charge of –2, the copper ion must carry a charge of +2. Hence the copper is in the form of the copper(II) ion, and the name of the compound is copper(II) sulfate. An alternative name is cupric sulfate.

Table 2-2 Common positive ions

Positive ions	
H^+	hydrogen
Na^+	sodium
K^+	potassium
Mg^{2+}	magnesium
Ca^{2+}	calcium
Cu^+	copper(I) or cuprous
Cu^{2+}	copper(II) or cupric
Al^{3+}	aluminum
Fe^{2+}	iron(II) or ferrous
Fe^{3+}	iron(III) or ferric
NH_4^+	ammonium

The reverse problem, of writing a formula corresponding to the name of a compound, can be addressed by the following rules, which apply primarily to ionic compounds.

1. The name of the compound is read from left to right, as usual. Many names of inorganic compounds consist of two words.

2. The first symbol of the formula is that for the first element named, except for names beginning with "ammonium", which contain the ion NH_4^+.

3. If the second word in the name ends in "-ide", then it refers to a single element, which can be identified from the beginning of the word. If the second word ends in "-ate" or "-ite", then it refers to a polyatomic negative ion containing oxygen in addition to the element identified by the beginning of this word. If the name is not familiar, it is best to refer to Table 2-2 (or a more extensive listing) to determine the formula.

4. The ratio of the numbers of atoms of each element is then set to correspond to the charges on the ions, which can be found in Tables 2-1 and 2-2.

5. If the substance named is an acid, the first symbol is H for hydrogen, and the other symbol or symbols serve to identify the acid. If the name is not familiar, then it is best to refer to Table 2-2 (or a more extensive listing) to determine the formula.

Example 2-8 Write the formula of sodium oxide.

The first symbol is Na, for sodium. The beginning of the second word "oxide" identifies the element oxygen, O. The relative number of atoms of sodium and oxygen is determined by the need to balance the charge of –2 on the oxide ion with two sodium ions each having a charge of +1. Hence the formula is Na_2O.

Example 2-9 Write the formula of potassium chlorate.

The first symbol is K, for potassium. The second word in the name, chlorate, indicates that the negative ion contains chlorine and oxygen. Reference to Tables 2-1 and 2-2 shows that the potassium ion has a charge of +1, and chlorate ion has formula ClO_3^-. Hence the formula is $KClO_3$.

Example 2-10 Write the formula of potassium dihydrogen phosphate.

The first symbol is K, for potassium. The second word is hydrogen, and the prefix "di-" indicates that two hydrogen atoms are present. The third word in the name, phosphate, indicates that the negative ion contains phosphorus and oxygen. Reference to Tables 2-1 and 2-2 shows that the potassium ion has a charge of +1, and phosphate ion has formula PO_4^{3-}. Hence the formula is KH_2PO_4.

2-2 Nomenclature: the names of organic compounds

The chemistry of carbon-containing compounds is called **organic chemistry**. In the early days of chemistry, a distinction was drawn between compounds derived from living matter, which were called organic compounds, and inorganic compounds obtained from minerals and other non-living sources. But in time it was realized that the compounds that had been classified as "organic" could be synthesized from inorganic carbon-containing substances. Nowadays, the defining feature of organic compounds is the presence of carbon, rather than their origin in plants and animals.

Living matter consists largely of carbon compounds, and so organic chemistry is of particular relevance to biology and the medical sciences. Many organic compounds have been isolated from natural sources, some of which have been in use for thousands of years for food or drink or as natural cures for diseases. But many more organic compounds that are not found in nature have been synthesized in chemical laboratories, and have become the basis for much of our present chemical and pharmaceutical industry.

There are more known compounds of carbon than of all the other elements added together. This is because carbon atoms can form chemical bonds to other carbon atoms to form extended chains and rings, as well as forming bonds to the atoms of other elements, especially hydrogen, nitrogen and oxygen.

The naming and classification of organic compounds can be confusing initially because there are both the traditional and systematic names in common use. Traditional names are used for compounds that have been known for a long time, and are often derived from associations with natural products. For example, acetic acid is found in vinegar, for which the Latin name is *acetum*.

Only a relatively small number of compounds have traditional names, however, and a systematic procedure for naming compounds has been adopted by the International Union of Pure and Applied Chemistry (IUPAC). The IUPAC system of names can deal with very complex molecules, but traditional names are still used for common compounds. In this book, both IUPAC and traditional names are used where appropriate.

Compounds containing only hydrogen in addition to carbon are called **hydrocarbons**, which includes **alkanes** containing only C–C single bonds, **alkenes** containing C=C double bonds, and **alkynes** containing C≡C triple bonds.

Alkanes, which are also known as **saturated hydrocarbons**, have molecular formulae C_nH_{2n+2} where n is an integer. The alkanes are named as follows:

CH_4	methane	C_6H_{14}	hexane
C_2H_6	ethane	C_7H_{16}	heptane
C_3H_8	propane	C_8H_{18}	octane
C_4H_{10}	butane	C_9H_{20}	nonane
C_5H_{12}	pentane	$C_{10}H_{22}$	decane

The structures of some of these are shown below:

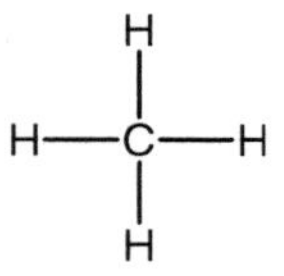

methane 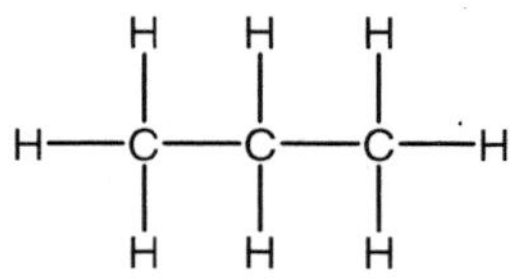   propane 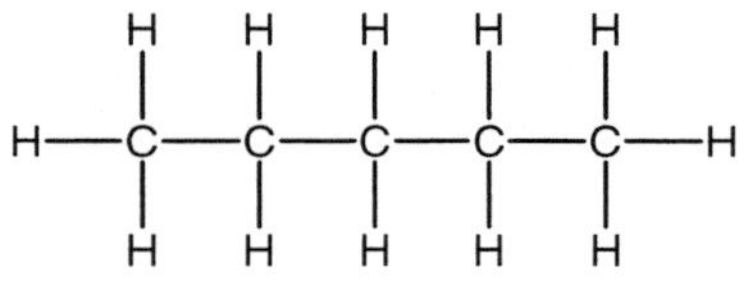   pentane

The key feature of alkanes is the presence of chains of carbon atoms linked together by single bonds. Alkanes such as those shown above are called **straight chain alkanes**, because there is a single chain of carbon atoms which is not branched. It is important to note that a drawing of an alkane structure on paper does not give a good idea of the three-dimensional shape of the molecule, or the relative directions of the bonds. The important thing is the way the carbon atoms are bonded together, not the layout of symbols on paper. For example, the following are all acceptable formulae for pentane:

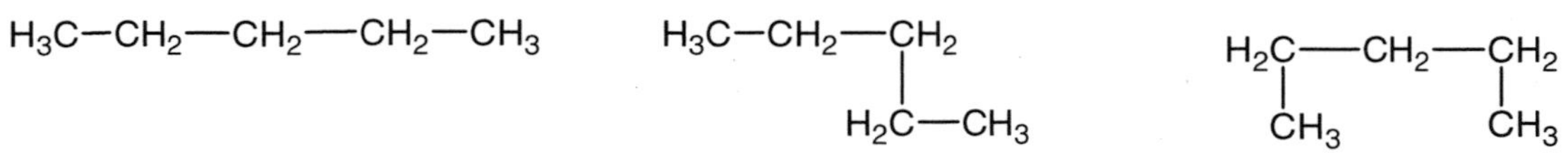

A straight chain alkane may be given a prefix, "n-" to emphasize that it is the "normal" straight chain isomer. For example, the name n-butane may be used rather than just butane. The reason for this is as follows.

For alkanes C_nH_{2n+2} with four or more carbon atoms, there are several **structural isomers** with the same molecular formula. Each structural isomer is a different compound, with unique chemical and physical properties. There are two structural isomers with the molecular formula C_4H_{10}, namely butane and methylpropane:

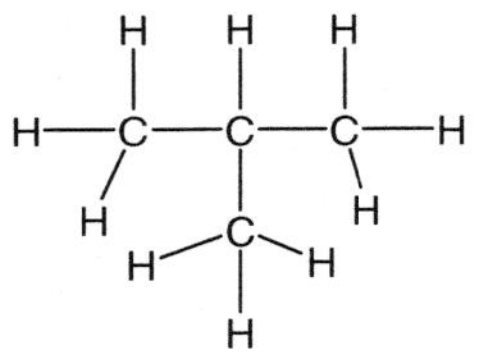

methylpropane 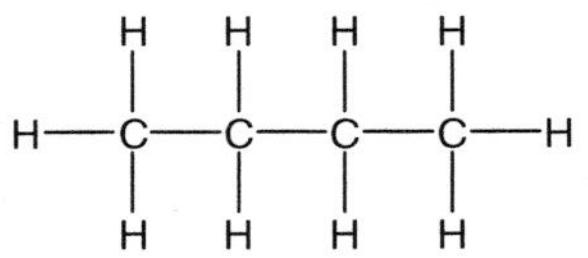   butane

Each of these molecules has four carbon atoms and ten hydrogen atoms, joined together by single bonds. The difference between them lies in the way the chain of carbon atoms is bonded together in each molecule. This can be seen more clearly if the two formulae are written in the following way:

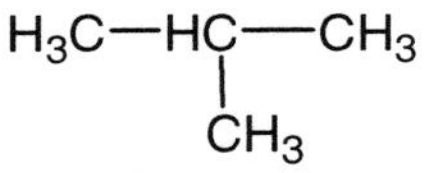

The number of possible alkane isomers with formula C_nH_{2n+2} increases very rapidly for larger values of n. There are 3 structural isomers of C_5H_{10}, 75 isomers of $C_{10}H_{22}$, 4347 isomers of $C_{15}H_{32}$ and 366 319 isomers of $C_{20}H_{42}$. For this reason, careful specification of a compound by name or structure is often required.

Alkenes are hydrocarbons in which there is a double bond between carbon atoms. Alkenes contain fewer hydrogen atoms than the alkane with the same of number of carbon atoms, and for this reason are described as **unsaturated hydrocarbons.** The simplest alkenes are ethene, with formula C_2H_4 and propene, C_3H_6, which have the following structures:

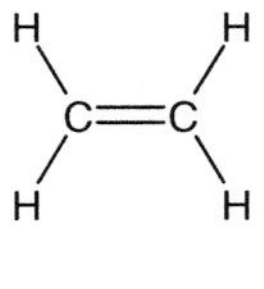

ethene   propene

ethylene   propylene

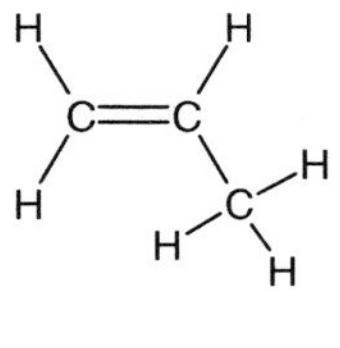

The names of the alkenes are based upon the names of the alkanes with the same number of carbon atoms. Many chemists use older nomenclature, particularly in industry: alkenes are called olefins, ethene is called ethylene, and propene is called propylene.

Alkynes are unsaturated hydrocarbons in which there is a triple bond between carbon atoms. The simplest alkene is ethyne, which is also called acetylene. Ethyne has the formula C_2H_2 and the following structure:

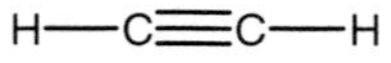

$$H \!-\! C \!\equiv\! C \!-\! H$$

ethyne

acetylene

Special names are used to identify characteristic groups of atoms that are found in many different molecules. For example, within the methane molecule CH_4 we can see a group of atoms CH_3, called a **methyl** group, that consists of all the atoms of methane except for one hydrogen atom. The methyl group has already been encountered in the compound methylpropane, an isomer of butane. Similarly, within the ethane molecule C_2H_6 we can see a group of atoms C_2H_5 that is called an **ethyl** group which consists of all the atoms of ethane except for one hydrogen atom. The next member of the series is the propyl group C_3H_7. In general, an **alkyl** group is part of an alkane molecule from which a hydrogen atom is excluded. The name of an alkyl group is formed from the name of the corresponding alkane by replacing the ending "-ane" by "-yl". Three alkyl groups are illustrated in the following structures.

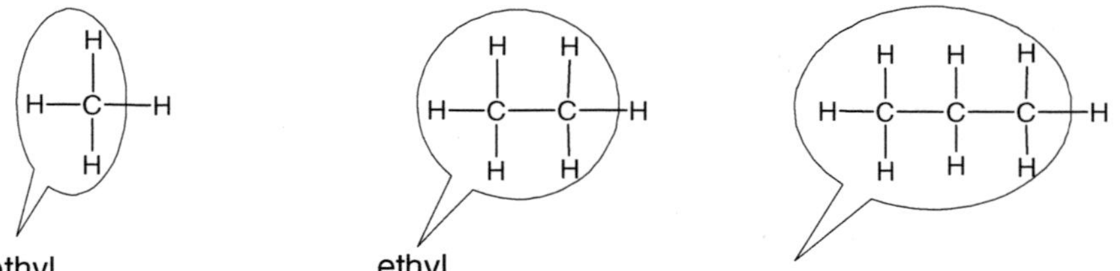

methyl   ethyl   propyl

The procedure for naming branched chain alkanes is based upon the length of the longest chain of carbon-carbon bonds. Consider for example the molecule with the following structure:

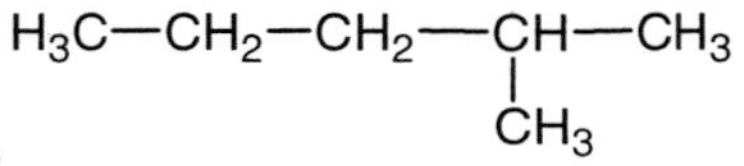

$$H_3C\!-\!CH_2\!-\!CH_2\!-\!CH\!-\!CH_3$$
$$|$$
$$CH_3$$

The longest chain of carbon atoms in the molecule contains five atoms, and hence the **parent name** for the molecule is pentane. A methyl group occupies the place of one hydrogen atom along the chain of five carbon atoms, and so the prefix "methyl" is added: methylpentane. In order to specify *which* hydrogen atom has been replaced, the carbon atoms of the main chain are numbered beginning at the end of the chain that is closest to the methyl group. Since the methyl group is bonded to the second carbon atom from the end, the compound is named 2-methylpentane.

When there are two identical substituents, the prefix "di-" is added; if three, the prefix "tri-" is used.

Example 2-11 Draw a structural formula for 2,2-dimethylpropane.

The molecule is derived from propane, and therefore the longest chain contains three carbon atoms. The prefix "dimethyl-" indicates that there are two methyl groups that replace hydrogen atoms, and the numbers "2,2-" mean that the methyl groups are bonded to the second carbon atom from one end of the main chain of carbon atoms. The structure is therefore as follows:

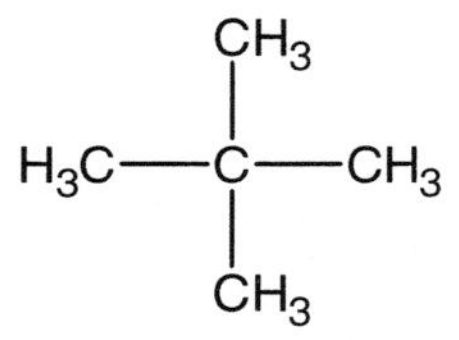

$$
\begin{array}{c}
\quad\quad CH_3 \\
\quad\quad | \\
H_3C - C - CH_3 \\
\quad\quad | \\
\quad\quad CH_3
\end{array}
$$

The molecular formula is C_5H_{12}. An older name for this compound is neopentane.

_____

Example 2-12 The "octane" rating of gasoline is based on its behaviour as a fuel in an internal combustion engine. The comparison is made relative to the behaviour of a particular compound, 2,2,4-trimethylpentane, which is an isomer of octane. Draw a structural formula for this molecule.

_____

We read from the end of the name, where we find the parent name "pentane", showing that the longest chain of carbon atoms contains five atoms. The prefix "trimethyl" indicates that three methyl groups, CH_3, have been substituted for hydrogen atoms, and the numbers "2,2,4-" specify their locations along the chain. Two methyl groups are bonded to the second carbon atom from one end of the chain, and the third is bonded to the fourth carbon atom from the same end. The structure is therefore the following:

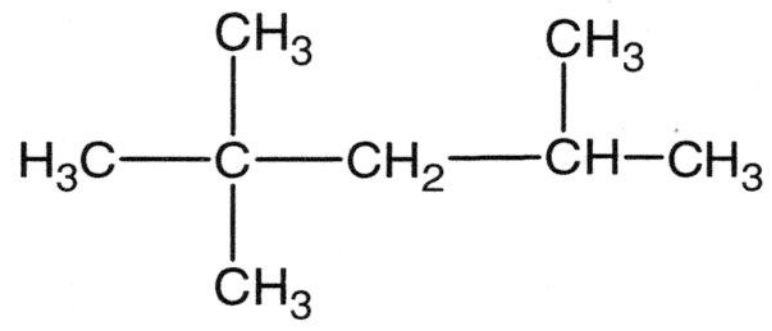

$$
\begin{array}{c}
\quad\quad CH_3 \quad\quad\quad CH_3 \\
\quad\quad | \quad\quad\quad\quad\quad | \\
H_3C - C - CH_2 - CH - CH_3 \\
\quad\quad | \\
\quad\quad CH_3
\end{array}
$$

_____

Example 2-13 Name the compound with the following structure:

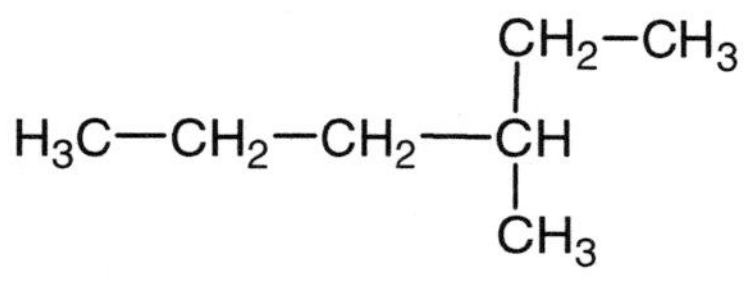

$$
\begin{array}{c}
\quad\quad\quad\quad\quad\quad CH_2 - CH_3 \\
\quad\quad\quad\quad\quad\quad\quad | \\
H_3C - CH_2 - CH_2 - CH \\
\quad\quad\quad\quad\quad\quad\quad | \\
\quad\quad\quad\quad\quad\quad CH_3
\end{array}
$$

_____

The substance is a hydrocarbon, and the first step is to identify the longest chain of carbon atoms in the molecule. There are two chains, one containing five carbon atoms and the other six carbon atoms. Choosing the longer chain, the parent name is hexane. In addition to the hexane chain, there is a methyl group located on the third atom from the right hand end of the chain as it is written, so the compound is 3-methylhexane.

_____

Notice that in identifying the length of the chains present in a hydrocarbon, it does not matter how the symbols for the carbon atoms are arranged on paper. The important thing is how the carbon atoms are bonded together.

A hydrocarbon of special importance is **benzene**, C_6H_6, for it forms the basis for a large group of compounds called **aromatic** compounds. The molecule of benzene contains a ring of carbon atoms with alternating single and double bonds. There are many compounds derived from benzene by substitution of other groups of atoms for the hydrogen atoms around the ring.

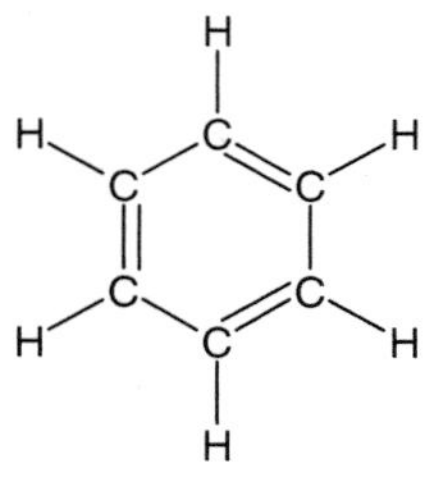

benzene

In addition to the structure based on a framework of carbon atoms, a molecule may contain **functional groups** of atoms that take part in characteristic reactions and often determine the chemical characteristics of a particular compound. For example **carboxylic acids** contain the group –COOH. The structures of some simple carboxylic acids, together with their traditional and IUPAC names are shown below. Two names are given for each acid, the traditional name (above), and the formal IUPAC name (below). The IUPAC name is derived from the name of the alkane with the same number of carbon atoms as the acid.

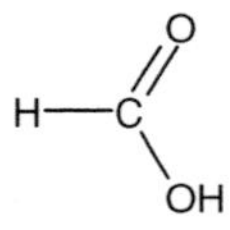

formic acid

methanoic acid

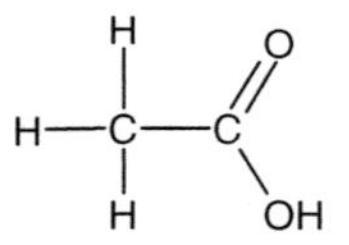

acetic acid

ethanoic acid

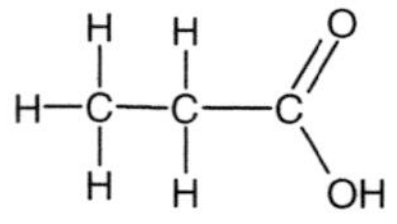

propionic acid

propanoic acid

Amines are organic bases that are derived from ammonia NH_3 by substituting organic groups in place of hydrogen atoms. In methylamine, which has the formula CH_3NH_2, a methyl group CH_3 replaces one hydrogen atom,. Other amines are named using the name of the alkyl group: examples are ethylamine, $C_2H_5NH_2$, and propylamine $C_3H_7NH_2$. In trimethylamine, with formula $(CH_3)_3N$, three methyl groups replace three hydrogen atoms.

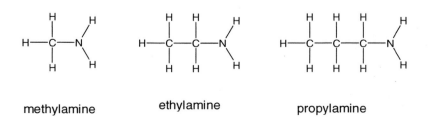

methylamine

ethylamine

propylamine

Alkyl halides are derivatives of alkanes, with one or more hydrogen atoms replaced by halogen atoms, such as fluorine or chlorine. Examples are chloromethane, CH_3Cl, and bromoethane, C_2H_5Br. Alternate names for these compounds are methyl chloride and ethyl bromide.

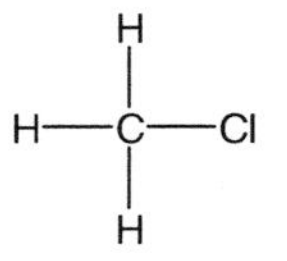

chloromethane

methyl chloride

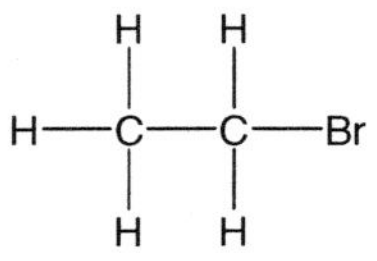

bromoethane

ethyl bromide

An **alcohol** contains the group –OH bonded to a carbon atom in place of a hydrogen atom. Alcohols derived from the alkanes are named by removing the "–e" from the end of the name of the alkane and adding the suffix "-ol", or else using the name of the alkyl group in front of the word "alcohol". Examples are methanol or methyl alcohol, CH_3OH, and ethanol or ethyl alcohol, C_2H_5OH.

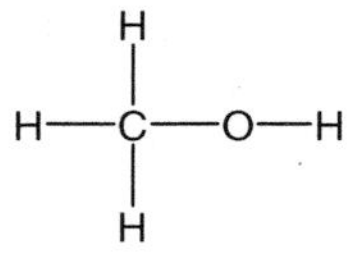

methanol

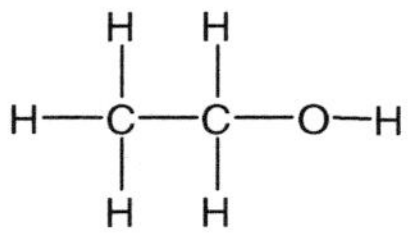

ethanol

2-3 Chemical equations

Chemical reactions are processes in which matter changes from one chemical form to another through the rearrangement of atoms. Chemical reactions are described on paper by means of **chemical equations**. A chemical **equation** specifies the compounds that take part in the reaction and distinguishes between the **reactants**, or starting materials, and the **products**, which are the substances produced by the reaction. The formulae of the reactants are shown on the left side of the reaction, and an arrow indicates the direction of the reaction which produces the products, the formulae of which are written on the right hand side. For example, the combustion of carbon in air to form carbon dioxide can be represented by the equation:

$$C + O_2 \rightarrow CO_2.$$

In a chemical reaction the number of atoms of each element present is not altered and no element is converted into another element. This fact, mentioned in Chapter 1, can be summarized as a basic principle of chemical processes:

"In a chemical reaction, atoms of each element involved are neither created nor destroyed."

This principle may be called principle of conservation of atoms. Chemical equations are nearly always written so as to be consistent with the conservation of atoms. The amounts of the various substances that take part in a chemical reaction are controlled by this principle, and the study of the relationships between these amounts is called **stoichiometry**.

When hydrogen reacts with oxygen to produce water, the reaction can be described by the following equation:

$$H_2 + O_2 \rightarrow H_2O$$

This equation lists the reactants and products properly, but is not consistent with the principle of conservation of atoms. Two atoms of oxygen are indicated on the left-hand side but only one on the right-hand side, which seems to indicate that an oxygen atom disappears in the reaction. In chemical reactions, atoms do not appear or disappear. A chemical equation is described as **balanced** if it contains equal numbers of atoms of every element on the two sides of the equation. The reaction can be balanced by indicating that two molecules of hydrogen react for every one molecule of oxygen, producing two molecules of water:

$$2\,H_2 + O_2 \rightarrow 2\,H_2O.$$

The need to balance chemical equations is easily seen by looking at a diagram of the molecules involved in this reaction, shown in Figure 2-1.

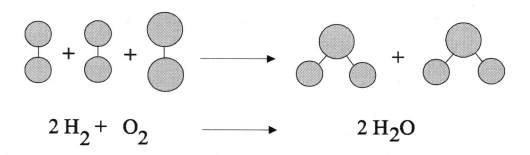

Figure 2-1 The reaction between two molecules of hydrogen, H_2, and one molecule of oxygen, O_2. The number of atoms of each element must be the same on both sides of the equation: in this case four hydrogen atoms and two oxygen atoms are shown. The equation written in terms of chemical symbols must reflect the fact that the chemical reaction does not create or destroy atoms.

The ratio of the numbers of molecules of hydrogen and oxygen is determined by the principle of conservation of atoms. Division or multiplication of all the coefficients by the same number does not change this condition; if the coefficients in the last equation are divided by two, the number of atoms of each element on both sides of the equation are still equal:

$$H_2 + \tfrac{1}{2}\,O_2 \rightarrow H_2O$$

The number appearing in front of the formula of each substance appearing in a chemical equation is called the **stoichiometric coefficient**. In a balanced chemical equation the stoichiometric coefficients must indicate equal numbers of atoms of every element on the two sides of the equation, and through this requirement they determine the relative amounts, measured in moles, of each substance consumed or produced in the reaction. For example the last reaction shows that one mole of water is formed from one mole of hydrogen and half a mole of oxygen.

In cases where ions are involved, the chemical equation must be written so as to be consistent with the principle of conservation of electric charge:

"In a chemical reaction, electric charge is neither created nor destroyed."

If ions are involved in the reaction, the amount of electric charge must be the same on both sides of the equation. An example is:

$$Cu + 2\,Ag^+ \rightarrow Cu^{2+} + 2\,Ag$$

In this case the ratio of the numbers of atoms of copper and silver is determined by the principle of conservation of charge.

Chemical equations should always be balanced. Many chemical equations can be balanced by eye, looking at each element in turn. It is best to begin with those elements that appear in only one reactant and one product.

Example 2-14 Write a balanced equation for the reaction of butane, C_4H_{10} with oxygen to form carbon dioxide and water.

The unbalanced reaction summarizing the reactants and products is:

$$C_4H_{10} + O_2 \rightarrow CO_2 + H_2O$$

We start with carbon. In order to balance the carbon, four moles of CO_2 are required for every mole of C_4H_{10}. A partially balanced reaction showing this can be written as follows:

$$C_4H_{10} + O_2 \rightarrow 4\,CO_2 + H_2O$$

We then deal with hydrogen. In order to balance the hydrogen, five moles of H_2O are required for every mole of C_4H_{10}. This is shown in the next equation, which is still only partially balanced:

$$C_4H_{10} + O_2 \rightarrow 4\,CO_2 + 5\,H_2O$$

The only element remaining to be balanced is oxygen. The right-hand side of the equation contains a total of 13 moles of O atoms, and so 6½ moles of O_2 molecules are required. The fully balanced equation is:

$$C_4H_{10} + 6\tfrac{1}{2}\,O_2 \rightarrow 4\,CO_2 + 5\,H_2O$$

This approach is adequate for balancing simple chemical equations, but for more complicated chemical equations a systematic procedure is helpful. The following method can be used for any equation, and will be illustrated first for the equation that was balanced in Example 2-1. Later in this chapter, this method will be used for balancing reduction-oxidation reactions, which are not always easy to balance.

The first step is to write an unbalanced chemical equation, assuming that the stoichiometric coefficient of the first compound is one, and the others are written as unknowns $a, b, c\ldots$ The equation is written with vertical lines to keep the calculations tidy. Every element involved in the reaction is listed on a separate line in the middle column under the arrow. Under each compound, the total number of atoms of each element is listed; this is the product of the number of atoms of that element in the formula, multiplied by the stoichiometric coefficient. The total number of atoms of each element in the reactants is written in the left hand column, and the total number of atoms of each element in the products is written in the right hand column. Because atoms must be conserved in the chemical reaction, the entries in the two columns of totals must be equal for every element.

totals	$C_4H_{10} + a\,O_2$		$\rightarrow$		$b\,CO_2 + c\,H_2O$		totals
4	4	0	C		b	0	b
10	10	0	H		0	$2c$	$2c$
$2a$	0	$2a$	O		$2b$	c	$2b + c$

Equating the totals for each element leads to a set of equations, which can be solved simultaneously. From the C line, $b = 4$. From the H line, $c = 5$. From the O line, $2a = 2b+c$; substituting the previously determined values of b and c it follows that $a = 6\frac{1}{2}$. These are the same as the results found in Example 2-1.

This formal method of balancing equations may seem unnecessarily complicated, but in more difficult cases, the method has advantages. This is illustrated in the following example.

Example 2-15   Balance the following equation: $NaIO_3 + SO_2 + H_2O \rightarrow I_2 + Na_2SO_4 + H_2SO_4$.

The table for this equation is:

totals	$NaIO_3 + a\,SO_2 + b\,H_2O$			$\rightarrow$		$c\,I_2 + d\,Na_2SO_4 + e\,H_2SO_4$			totals
1	1	0	0	Na		0	$2d$	0	$2d$
1	1	0	0	I		$2c$	0	0	$2c$
$3 + 2a + b$	3	$2a$	b	O		0	$4d$	$4e$	$4d + 4e$
a	0	a	0	S		0	d	e	$d + e$
$2b$	0	0	$2b$	H		0	0	$2e$	$2e$

From the Na line, $d = \frac{1}{2}$. From the I line, $c = \frac{1}{2}$. From the H line, $b = e$. Substituting these values into the other two lines gives two equations in two unknowns:

$1 + 2a = 3b$

$a = \frac{1}{2} + b$

Substituting the second equation into the first gives $b = 2$, and hence $e = 2$ and $a = 2\frac{1}{2}$. Hence the balanced reaction is:

$$NaIO_3 + 2\tfrac{1}{2}\,SO_2 + 2\,H_2O \rightarrow \tfrac{1}{2}\,I_2 + \tfrac{1}{2}\,Na_2SO_4 + 2\,H_2SO_4$$

or
$$2\,NaIO_3 + 5\,SO_2 + 4\,H_2O \rightarrow I_2 + Na_2SO_4 + 4\,H_2SO_4$$

2-4 Mass relationships in chemical reactions

The stoichiometric coefficients in a chemical equation govern the mass relationships as well as the mole relationships, since each substance has its own molar mass. This is the principle of stoichiometric calculations, and the following examples demonstrate the methods used.

Example 2-16 What mass of oxygen is required to burn 1.000 gram of carbon to form carbon dioxide?

From the equation $C + O_2 \rightarrow CO_2$, we see that the amount of moles of O_2 required is equal to the amount of carbon which reacts. The amount of carbon contained in 1.000 gram of carbon is:

$$\text{amount of carbon} = 1.000 \text{ g}/12.011 \text{ g mol}^{-1}$$

$$= 0.08326 \text{ mol}$$

The molar mass of O_2 is $2 \times 15.999 = 31.998$ g mol^{-1}.

Hence mass of oxygen = 0.08326 mol $\times 31.998$ g mol^{-1} = 2.664 g

Example 2-17 Sodium iodate, $NaIO_3$, reacts with sulphur dioxide to produce iodine, as follows:

$$2 \text{ NaIO}_3 + 5 \text{ SO}_2 + 4 \text{ H}_2\text{O} \rightarrow \text{I}_2 + \text{Na}_2\text{SO}_4 + 4 \text{ H}_2\text{SO}_4$$

What is the mass of SO_2 required to react with 100.0 grams of sodium iodate, and what mass of iodine is produced?

The molar mass of $NaIO_3$ is 197.89 g mol^{-1}, and so:

$$\text{amount of NaIO}_3 = \frac{100.0 \text{ g}}{197.89 \text{ g mol}^{-1}} = 0.5053 \text{ mol}$$

From the stoichiometric coefficients of the balanced equation, 5 moles of SO_2 are required for every 2 moles of $NaIO_3$, and so:

$$\text{amount of SO}_2 \text{ required} = (5/2) \times 0.5053 \text{ mol} = 1.263 \text{ mol}.$$

The molar mass of SO_2 is 64.064 g mol^{-1}, so mass of SO_2 required = 1.263 mol $\times$ 64.064 g mol^{-1} = 80.91 g.

Again, from the balanced chemical equation, 1 mole of I_2 is produced from 2 moles of $NaIO_3$, and so

amount of I_2 produced = $(1/2) \times 0.5053$ mol = 0.2526 mol.

The molar mass of I_2 is 253.80 g mol^{-1}, so mass of I_2 produced = 0.2526 mol $\times$ 253.80 g mol^{-1} = 64.11 g

Example 2-18 When heated strongly, calcium carbonate decomposes to calcium oxide and carbon dioxide gas. What is the ratio of the mass of calcium oxide to the mass of calcium carbonate from which it is produced?

The balanced equation for the decomposition is $CaCO_3 \rightarrow CaO + CO_2$

Since one mole of the carbonate yields one mole of the oxide,

$$\frac{\text{mass of oxide}}{\text{mass of carbonate}} = \frac{\text{molar mass of CaO}}{\text{molar mass of CaCO}_3} = \frac{56.077 \text{ g mol}^{-1}}{100.09 \text{ g mol}^{-1}} = 0.5603$$

Example 2-19 Chlorine, Cl_2, and caustic soda, NaOH, are produced industrially by electrolysis of a solution of sodium chloride. The overall reaction is summarized by the equation:

$$2\,NaCl + 2\,H_2O \rightarrow 2\,NaOH + Cl_2 + H_2$$

In 1994, Canadian production of chlorine was 1.13 million tonnes. Estimate the corresponding production of caustic soda for that year.

Two moles of NaOH are produced for every one mole of Cl_2 and so

$$\frac{\text{mass of NaOH produced}}{\text{mass of } Cl_2 \text{ produced}} = \frac{2\,\text{mol NaOH} \times 39.997\,\text{g mol}^{-1}}{1\,\text{mol } Cl_2 \times 70.906\,\text{g mol}^{-1}} = 1.128$$

This ratio can be applied to the entire output for the year, and so:

mass of NaOH produced $= 1.128 \times$ mass of Cl_2 produced

$$= 1.128 \times 1.13 \times 10^6 \text{ tonne}$$

$$= 1.27 \times 10^6 \text{ tonne}$$

2-5 Chemical equilibrium and chemical kinetics

In a chemical reaction, the reactants are converted to the products of the reaction. The reaction is finished when there are no more changes in the amounts of the reactants and products present. Some reactions, once started, continue to run until one or more of the reactants is almost entirely used up. Such a reaction is said to "go to completion." At the other extreme are reactions in which only a very small part of the reactants is converted to products, no matter how much time is allowed for the reaction to take place. Between these extremes are reactions in which a sizeable fraction, but not all, of the reactants is converted to products. In all cases, when a reaction has run its course, it reaches a condition of **equilibrium,** in which no further changes in the amounts of reactants and products take place.

After a reaction reaches equilibrium, the reaction which converts reactants to products continues to take place. But the **reverse reaction,** which converts the products back into reactants, now runs at the same rate so that there is no longer any *net* change in the amounts or concentrations of the substances present. The existence of the two reactions taking place simultaneously in opposite directions is indicated by a double arrow, whenever it is necessary to show the presence of chemical equilibrium. For example, the equilibrium between dinitrogen tetroxide, N_2O_4, and nitrogen dioxide, NO_2, is shown as follows:

$$N_2O_4 \rightleftharpoons 2\,NO_2$$

If, when a chemical system comes to equilibrium, hardly any reaction has taken place and the concentrations of reactants are large compared with the concentrations of products, then we say that the "position of equilibrium" lies to the left, favouring reactants. If, on the other hand, the concentrations of products are large, and at least one of the reactants has almost disappeared, then the position of equilibrium lies to the right. In the extreme, when only a small trace of the reactants remains, it is sometimes said that the reaction "goes to completion"; this statement is not strictly true because the reactants never completely disappear, but it is a useful approximation for some purposes.

For a given reaction the position of equilibrium usually changes with conditions such as temperature, pressure or the initial concentrations of the reactants. The change induced in a system at equilibrium by a change in conditions can often be predicted qualitatively from **Le Chatelier's principle.** This principle, which was proposed by Henry Louis Le Chatelier, states that when a system at equilibrium is subjected to a change of external conditions, the system shifts its position of equilibrium in a direction that tends to reduce the effect of the change.

For example, increasing the temperature of an equilibrium mixture shifts the position of equilibrium in the direction that absorbs heat. In a reaction involving gases, compressing the system into a smaller volume shifts the position of equilibrium in the direction that decreases the total number of moles of gas present, if possible. Dilution of a solution containing various solutes in equilibrium shifts the position of equilibrium in the direction that increases the total number of moles of solutes present, if possible. These aspects of chemical equilibrium will be treated quantitatively in later chapters.

After the reactants are mixed, a chemical reaction takes time to reach equilibrium, and the time required is a measure of the **rate of the reaction**. A reaction that reaches equilibrium within a fraction of a second after the reactants are mixed is described as a fast reaction. For a slow reaction, a much longer period of time, measured in minutes or hours, may pass before equilibrium is reached.

The rate of a chemical reaction can be increased by several means. In many cases increased concentrations or pressures of reactants result in an increased rate of reaction. The rate of a reaction increases as the temperature of the reaction is increased. In some reactions, adding a **catalyst** to the reaction mixture increases the rate of the reaction. A catalyst is a substance that increases the rate of a reaction without itself being used up as the reaction proceeds. The presence of a catalyst does not change the composition of the reacting mixture when equilibrium is reached.

The study of the rates of chemical reactions is called **chemical kinetics.** Kinetic studies of a chemical reaction can often give information about how the reaction takes place. For a reaction which is to be carried out industrially, kinetic studies help in the choice of reaction conditions such as temperature and pressure when designing the process to be as economical as possible.

2-6 Decomposition and synthesis

Decomposition is a reaction is which a single compound breaks up into two or more simpler compounds or elements. Many compounds decompose if heated. If one of the products is a gas which is removed from the site of the reaction, then the reaction proceeds to completion. If the decomposition products are prevented from escaping, then an equilibrium develops between reactant and the decomposition products.

Metal carbonates decompose when heated to yield carbon dioxide and the oxide of the metal. The temperature required for decomposition varies with the metal; for the important case of calcium carbonate a temperature near 1000 °C is suitable.

$$CaCO_3(s) \rightarrow CaO(s) + CO_2(g)$$

The physical state of each substance may be stated as part of the reaction by means of a symbol in brackets: (s) means solid, (ℓ) means liquid, and (g) means gas. For ions or molecules in aqueous solution, i.e. dissolved in water, the symbol (aq) is used.

Oxygen gas can be prepared in the laboratory by decomposition of potassium chlorate, $KClO_3$, in the presence of manganese dioxide, MnO_2, at a temperature of about 270 °C:

$$2\ KClO_3(s) \rightarrow 2\ KCl(s) + 3\ O_2(g)$$

The MnO_2 acts as catalyst, which allows the decomposition to take place at a lower temperature and in a more controlled manner than would otherwise occur. The catalyst does not appear in the balanced equation.

Dinitrogen tetroxide, N_2O_4, is a light brown gas or volatile liquid at room temperature. As the temperature rises, this substance decomposes to nitrogen dioxide, NO_2, which has a much darker brown colour:

$$N_2O_4(g) \rightleftharpoons 2\ NO_2(g)$$

At temperatures not too far from room temperature, the reaction comes to equilibrium with substantial concentrations of both substances present. A bulb containing a mixture of these two gases changes its colour from light brown at low temperature to a much darker brown at high temperature, due to the shift in the position of this equilibrium. At higher temperatures, the position of equilibrium is shifted towards the right-hand side of the equation. In other words, decomposition is favoured by an increase in temperature.

The reverse of decomposition is a reaction in which two compounds or elements combine to form a single compound. Such a reaction may be called **synthesis** although the meaning of this word has been extended to mean any process for making a substance by chemical reactions, instead of extracting it from plants or other natural sources. Examples of synthesis are the formation of carbon dioxide by combustion of carbon:

$$C(s) + O_2(g) \rightarrow CO_2(g)$$

and the manufacture of ammonia, NH_3, from the elements nitrogen and hydrogen:

$$N_2(g) + 3\ H_2(g) \rightleftharpoons 2\ NH_3(g)$$

This reaction is a famous example of the application of chemical theory and experimentation to industrial production, and will be considered in more detail in Chapter 4. In choosing conditions for the efficient and economical production of ammonia, the position of the chemical equilibrium, the rate of reaction, and the use of a suitable catalyst are all important.

In a synthesis reaction, suitable amounts of the reactants must be mixed before the reaction is initiated. If the reaction proceeds to completion, it usually happens that one of the reactants is completely used up before the other, and the other reactants are present in excess. When one of the reactants has been completely consumed by the reaction, the reaction comes to a stop. The compound which first disappears is called the **limiting reagent**, for it is this reagent which limits the amount of product which is formed. If none of the reactants is present in excess, then the reactants form a **stoichiometric mixture**, the composition of which is determined by stoichiometric coefficients of the various reactants in the balanced equation.

Example 2-20 2.00 grams of hydrogen H_2 and 75.00 grams of iodine I_2 are reacted together to produce hydrogen iodide, HI. Which reactant is the limiting reagent, and what is the maximum mass of hydrogen iodide which could be produced, assuming that the reaction were to go to completion?

The balanced reaction is $H_2 + I_2 \rightarrow 2\ HI$. The amounts of hydrogen and iodine initially available are:

$$n(H_2) = \frac{2.00\,g}{2.0158\,g\,mol^{-1}} = 0.992\,mol \text{ and } n(I_2) = \frac{75.00\,g}{253.80\,g\,mol^{-1}} = 0.2955\,mol\,.$$

Since one mole of iodine reacts with 1 mole of hydrogen, there is more than enough hydrogen to react with the iodine, and so iodine is the limiting reagent. Hence the maximum amount of HI which can be produced is 2× 0.2955 mol, and the maximum mass is:

$$\text{mass} = 2 \times 0.2955 \text{ mol} \times 127.91 \text{ g mol}^{-1} = 75.60 \text{ g.}$$

_____

2-7 Precipitation reactions

When salts are dissolved in water, they dissociate into ions. If the result of mixing solutions containing two salts is merely a solution containing all the ions formed by the two salts, then there is no chemical reaction. For example, when solutions of sodium chloride and potassium bromide are mixed, the result is a solution which contains the four ions Na^+, K^+, Cl^-, Br^-. No chemical reaction takes place since no new substance is formed.

However, if a solid substance separates from solution by combination of ions or molecules present in the solution, that solid is called a **precipitate** and the reaction is called a **precipitation reaction**; the ions and molecules involved are removed from the solution. In a precipitation reaction, two pairs of ions exchange partners to form a new salt. Reactions in which ions or atoms exchange partners are called **metathesis reactions**.

For example, if a solution of silver nitrate containing Ag^+ and NO_3^- ions is mixed with a solution of potassium chloride containing K^+ and Cl^- ions, then a white precipitate of solid silver chloride is formed. The reaction can be represented by the following equation:

$$AgNO_3(aq) + KCl(aq) \rightarrow AgCl(s) + KNO_3(aq)$$

In this equation, the designation (aq) indicates a substance in aqueous solution, i.e. a substance dissolved in water, while (s) indicates a precipitate of a substance that has very low solubility.

The K^+ and NO_3^- ions do not play any significant part in the reaction shown above and could be replaced by any of a number of other ions in solution without changing the result of the reaction, which is the formation of the precipitate of insoluble silver chloride. They are sometimes described as **spectator** ions. The net ionic equation, from which the spectator ions have been omitted, expresses the essential part of the reaction:

$$Ag^+(aq) + Cl^-(aq) \rightarrow AgCl(s)$$

If an excess of KCl solution is added to a solution of $AgNO_3$, then essentially all of the Ag^+ ions are removed from solution as a precipitate of AgCl. The Ag^+ ions are the limiting reactant, and the solution remaining contains all the K^+ ions, all the NO_3^- ions, and the excess Cl^- ions.

_____

Example 2-21   A 15.0 mL sample of 0.100 M solution of potassium hydroxide, KOH, is added to 40.0 mL of 0.0150 M ferrous chloride, $FeCl_2$, resulting in the precipitation of insoluble ferrous hydroxide, $Fe(OH)_2$. Determine which ions are present in significant concentrations in the remaining solution, and calculate the concentration of each of them.

_____

The equation for the precipitation reaction is

$$2 \text{ KOH}(aq) + FeCl_2(aq) \rightarrow Fe(OH)_2(s) + 2 \text{ KCl}(aq)$$

The process can also be described by the net ionic reaction

$$2 \text{ OH}^-(aq) + Fe^{2+} \rightarrow Fe(OH)_2(s)$$

The amount of OH^- added = 15.0×10^{-3} L $\times$ 0.100 mol/L = 1.50×10^{-3} mol

The amount of Fe^{2+} added = 40.0×10^{-3} L $\times$ 0.0150 mol/L = 0.600×10^{-3} mol

The amount of Cl^- added = $2 \times 0.600 \times 10^{-3}$ mol = 1.200×10^{-3} mol

The calculation of the amount of Cl^- includes the factor 2 because the formula unit $FeCl_2$ contains two chlorine atoms per iron atom.

All of the Fe^{2+} present initally, namely 0.600×10^{-3} mol, will be precipitated provided that the amount of OH^- added is at least 1.200×10^{-3} mol. This is in fact the case. The actual amount of OH^- added exceeds the amount required by 0.30×10^{-3} mol. Hence all of the Fe^{2+} is precipitated and forms 0.600×10^{-3} mol of solid $Fe(OH)_2$.

The total volume of the solution after mixing is 55.0 mL or 0.055 L, and so the concentrations of the ions remaining in solution are:

$$[K^+] = 1.50 \times 10^{-3} \text{ mol}/0.055 \text{ L} = 0.0273 \text{ mol/L}$$

$$[Cl^-] = 1.20 \times 10^{-3} \text{ mol}/0.055 \text{ L} = 0.0218 \text{ mol/L}$$

$$[OH^-] = 0.30 \times 10^{-3} \text{ mol}/0.055 \text{ L} = 0.0055 \text{ mol/L}$$

————————

Prediction of the outcome of a reaction that is controlled by precipitation depends on knowing the solubility of various salts. When a solid is placed in contact with a liquid, some or all of the solid dissolves and a solution is formed. The maximum concentration of the solution that can be reached is called the **solubility** of the solid in the liquid. A solid for which the solubility is very small is sometimes described as "sparingly soluble", or "insoluble", although no substance is totally insoluble.

For many purposes it is helpful to know which salts or groups of salts have such low solubilities that they can be expected to precipitate from aqueous solution when the proper combination of ions is present.

Table 2-3 summarizes information on the solubility of salts, which can be used in predicting whether a precipitate can be expected to form. This table summarizes a mass of data in a few qualitative rules for the purpose of helping the student develop a sense of which salts are likely to be soluble, and which are likely to form precipitates. Exceptions to the rules are not hard to find. Data for specific salts can be found in comprehensive tables of solubility and are discussed further in Chapter 15.

Table 2-3 A Brief Table of Solubility of Salts

Highly soluble salts:

Most nitrates NO_3^-, nitrites NO_2^-, chlorates ClO_3^-, perchlorates ClO_4^- and acetates CH_3COO^-

Many salts of sodium Na^+, potassium K^+, and ammonium NH_4^+

Sparingly soluble or "insoluble" salts:

Most sulfides S^{2-}, except Na_2S and K_2S. Some sulfides dissolve in an acidic solution.

Chlorides Cl^-, bromides Br^- and iodides I^- of Ag^+ and Hg_2^{2+}

Sulphates SO_4^{2-} of Ba^{2+}, Pb^{2+}, Bi^{3+}, Sn^{2+}, Sn^{4+}, Sb^{3+} and Hg_2^{2+}.

Most carbonates CO_3^{2-}, phosphates PO_4^{3-} and oxalates $C_2O_4^{2-}$ are sparingly soluble, but dissolve in an acidic solution.

2-8 Acid-base reactions

In the simplest view of acid-base reactions, an acid reacts with a base to produce a salt and water. The reaction between hydrochloric acid and sodium hydroxide produces sodium chloride and water:

$$HCl + NaOH \rightarrow NaCl + H_2O$$

$$acid + \quad base \quad \rightarrow \quad salt + water$$

Such an equation is good enough for calculations of the stoichiometry of a reaction between an acid and a base, but for many purposes a closer examination of acid-base reactions is required.

In aqueous solution, the chemistry of acid-base reactions is based upon hydrogen ions. The hydrogen ion is unique in chemistry, and its exact nature in aqueous solution is not easy to describe. A hydrogen atom H consists of a proton and a single electron, while a hydrogen ion H^+ is just a proton without any electrons at all. Since it has no electrons of its own, the proton interacts with the electrons on neighbouring water molecules, and a chemical bond is formed between the proton and the oxygen atom of a water molecule. Hence the hydrogen ion exists in solution as the **hydronium ion** H_3O^+. Even this is not the complete picture, for other water molecules are attached to the ion more loosely. In writing chemical equations, the hydrogen ion in aqueous solution can be represented either as the hydronium ion H_3O^+, or more simply as $H^+(aq)$, depending on the circumstances.

In the theory of acids and bases proposed by the Swedish chemist Svente Arrhenius, an acid produces hydrogen ions $H^+(aq)$ when dissolved in water, and a base produces hydroxide ions $OH^-(aq)$. In the Arrhenius theory, the reaction between an acid and a base is a reaction between hydrogen ions and hydroxide ions to produce water:

$$H^+(aq) + OH^-(aq) \rightarrow H_2O(\ell)$$

Experiments with weak acids and bases led to further development of thinking about these reactions. In the proton-transfer theory proposed independently by the Danish chemist Johannes Brønsted and the English chemist Thomas Lowry, the essence of an acid-base reaction is the transfer of a hydrogen ion H^+ between the acid and the base. The **acid** is the **proton donor** and the **base** is the **proton acceptor**. In the following discussion this idea is applied to both strong and weak acids and bases.

(i) Strong acids and bases

An acid that is completely ionized in aqueous solution to yield hydrogen ions is a **strong acid**. The process of ionization can be represented either as a simple dissociation to yield a hydrogen ion and a chloride ion:

$$HCl(aq) \rightarrow H^+(aq) + Cl^-(aq)$$

or as the transfer of a proton to a solvent water molecule:

$$HCl(aq) + H_2O(\ell) \rightarrow H_3O^+(aq) + Cl^-(aq).$$

Metal hydroxides such as sodium hydroxide are strong electrolytes and are completely ionized in aqueous solution:

$$NaOH(aq) \rightarrow Na^+(aq) + OH^-(aq)$$

They are generally called **strong bases**. The hydroxide ion is a base because it is able to accept a proton to form a water molecule. The reaction between a strong acid and a strong base can be described by the following net ionic reaction:

$$H^+(aq) + OH^-(aq) \rightarrow H_2O(\ell).$$

In the reaction between hydrochloric acid and sodium hydroxide, the Na^+ and Cl^- ions are spectator ions. In the solution remaining after the reaction these ions constitute a solution of sodium chloride. Table 2-4 lists some common strong acids and bases that the student may encounter in the laboratory. It should be noted that the strength of an acid or base is not the same as the concentration. The concentration measures how much acid or base is present per unit volume of solution, whereas the strength of an acid or base refers to the extent of ionization, strong acids and bases being almost completely ionized.

Table 2-4 Common Strong Acids and Bases in Aqueous Solution

Strong acids	Strong bases
hydrochloric acid HCl	sodium hydroxide NaOH
nitric acid HNO_3	potassium hydroxide KOH
sulfuric acid H_2SO_4 (first H^+)	calcium hydroxide $Ca(OH)_2$

Example 2-22 A 23.4 mL sample of 0.214 M NaOH is mixed with 25.0 mL of 0.104 M HCl. Determine which ions are present in significant concentration after mixing, and calculate the concentration of each of them.

Both NaOH and HCl are strong electrolytes and are completely dissociated in solution. The amounts of Na^+ and OH^- added are each 23.4×10^{-3} L $\times$ 0.214 mol/L = 5.01×10^{-3} mol, and the amounts of H^+ and Cl^- added are each 25.0×10^{-3} L $\times$ 0.104 mol/L = 2.60×10^{-3} mol. The net ionic reaction is $H^+(aq) + OH^-(aq) \rightarrow H_2O$. The hydroxide ion is in excess, and the hydrogen ion is therefore the limiting reagent. After the hydrogen ions and the hydroxide ions react to form water, the hydrogen ion concentration is close to zero, and the amount of OH^- remaining in solution is $(5.01 - 2.60) \times 10^{-3}$ mol $= 2.41 \times 10^{-3}$ mol. The volume of the solution is 48.4 mL, or 48.4×10^{-3} L, and hence the concentrations of the major ions present in solution are:

$[Na^+] = 5.01 \times 10^{-3}$ mol $/ 48.4 \times 10^{-3}$ L $= 0.104$ mol/L.

$[Cl^-] = 2.60 \times 10^{-3}$ mol $/ 48.4 \times 10^{-3}$ L $= 0.0537$ mol/L.

$[OH^-] = 2.41 \times 10^{-3}$ mol $/ 48.4 \times 10^{-3}$ L $= 0.0498$ mol/L.

(ii) Water and aqueous solutions

An aqueous solution of an electrolyte conducts electricity because the ions are free to move through the solution carrying electric charge. In water containing dissolved salts, acids or bases, the current is carried mostly by the ions. Water that has been purified carefully to remove electrolytes also conducts electricity slightly due to the presence of ions produced by proton transfer between water molecules:

$$H_2O + H_2O \rightleftharpoons H_3O^+ + OH^-$$

One of the water molecules acts as an acid in donating a proton to the other molecule, which acts as a base. As indicated by the double arrow, the water molecules and the ions are in equilibrium. Ionization of pure water yields equal concentrations of hydrogen ions and hydroxide ions, and so a solution containing equal concentrations of hydrogen ions and hydroxide ions is described as **neutral.** If the hydrogen ion concentration in a solution is greater than the hydroxide ion concentration, then the solution is **acidic,** and if the hydroxide ion concentration is greater than the hydrogen ion concentration, the solution is **basic.** If an acid is added to water, then transfer of protons from the acid to the solvent increases the concentration of H_3O^+ ions, and the solution becomes acidic. If a base is added to water, then the concentration of OH^- ions is increased by ionization of the base and the solution becomes basic.

(iii) Weak acids and bases

Most acids are not strong acids. Acetic acid, CH_3COOH, has the structure:

$$H_3C - C \overset{\displaystyle O}{\underset{\displaystyle OH}{\big<}}$$

The acidic properties of acetic acid are associated with the hydrogen atom in the –COOH group. Acetic acid ionizes in aqueous solution to yield the acetate ion and a hydronium ion:

$$CH_3COOH(aq) + H_2O \rightleftharpoons H_3O^+ + CH_3COO^-(aq)$$
$$\text{acetic acid} \qquad\qquad\qquad \text{acetate}$$

Acetic acid is a weak acid and a weak electrolyte because in an aqueous solution (except at very low concentration), only a small fraction of the acetic acid molecules is ionized by proton transfer to the solvent. The ionization equilibrium for weak acids will be discussed in detail in a later chapter. Acetic acid is typical of a large class of **carboxylic acids** containing the **carboxyl** group, –COOH. Some examples of carboxylic acids are listed in Table 2–5. Carboxylic acids are weak acids.

Table 2-5 Some Weak Acids

Inorganic acids		Carboxylic acids	
nitrous acid	HNO_2	formic acid	$HCOOH$
hydrofluoric acid	HF	acetic acid	CH_3COOH
hypochlorous acid	$HOCl$	propanoic acid	C_2H_5COOH
carbonic acid	H_2CO_3	benzoic acid	C_6H_5COOH
phosphoric acid	H_3PO_4	phthalic acid	$1,2\text{-}C_6H_4(COOH)_2$

Many bases do not contain any hydroxide ions, and are weak electrolytes. Ammonia, NH_3, does not contain the hydroxide ion, but when ammonia is dissolved in water, protons are transferred from water to ammonia, and the concentration of OH^- increases:

$$NH_3(aq) + H_2O \rightleftharpoons NH_4^+(aq) + OH^-(aq)$$

The NH_4^+ ion is the ammonium ion. The nitrogen atom in the ammonia molecule is the atom which is responsible for the basic properties of ammonia, and in a later chapter it will be seen that this is related to the presence of a "lone pair" of electrons on the nitrogen atom.

The $-NH_2$ group is called the **amino** group. Compounds containing this group, called **amines**, are similar to ammonia and are weak bases. An example is methylamine, CH_3NH_2. Structural formulae for ammonia and methylamine, including the lone pairs of electrons on the nitrogen atom, are shown below:

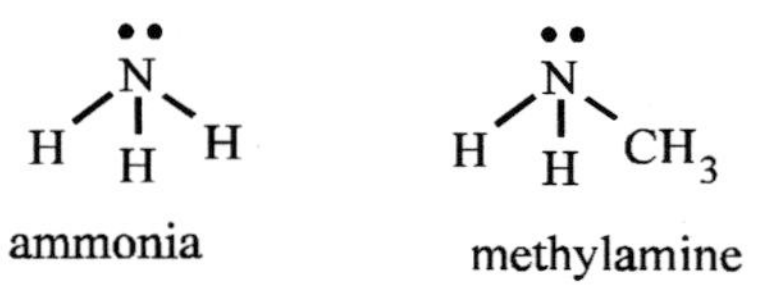

ammonia   methylamine

The majority of weak bases are organic molecules containing nitrogen. Some examples are listed in Table 2-6.

Table 2-6 Some Weak bases

ammonia	NH_3
methylamine	CH_3NH_2
ethylamine	$C_2H_5NH_2$
trimethylamine	$(CH_3)_3N$

(iv) Conjugate acids and bases

In the Brønsted-Lowry theory, the ionization of a weak acid is regarded as the transfer of a proton from the acid molecule to a water molecule:

$$CH_3COOH(aq) + H_2O \rightleftharpoons CH_3COO^-(aq) + H_3O^+(aq)$$

If this equation is read from right to left (rather than left to right), it can be seen that the acetate ion can accept a proton. By accepting a proton the acetate ion acts as a base.

In support of this idea, it is found that when a salt of acetic acid, such as sodium acetate, is dissolved in water, hydroxide ions are formed in small concentration and the solution is slightly basic. The reason for this is as follows. The dissolved salt dissociates completely into sodium ions and acetate ions:

$$CH_3COONa(aq) \rightarrow CH_3COO^-(aq) + Na^+(aq)$$

The acetate ions establish the following proton transfer equilibrium, and so cause the solution to become basic:

$$CH_3COO^-(aq) + H_2O \rightleftharpoons CH_3COOH(aq) + OH^-(aq)$$

An anion that is derived from an acid by loss of a proton is the **conjugate base** to the acid. An acid that is derived from a base by addition of a proton is the **conjugate acid** to the base. Thus, acetate ion is the conjugate base to acetic acid, and acetic acid is the conjugate acid to acetate ion. Together they form a conjugate acid-base pair.

Similarly, ammonium ion NH_4^+ is the conjugate acid to ammonia NH_3 because it can be obtained by addition of a proton to ammonia. In the following base ionization reaction, a water molecule supplies the proton:

$$NH_3(aq) + H_2O \rightleftharpoons NH_4^+(aq) + OH^-(aq)$$

A solution of an ammonium salt such as ammonium chloride is slightly acidic. The dissolved salt dissociates into ions in solution:

$$NH_4Cl(aq) \rightarrow NH_4^+(aq) + Cl^-(aq).$$

The ammonium ions establish the following proton transfer equilibrium, and so cause the solution to become acidic:

$$NH_4^+(aq) + H_2O \rightleftharpoons NH_3(aq) + H_3O^+(aq)$$

Thus ammonium ion and ammonia together form a conjugate acid-base pair.

The relative strengths of acid and its conjugate base are not independent. The stronger the acid, the weaker is the conjugate base. This relationship will be demonstrated in Chapter 14.

(v) Amphiprotic compounds

Some compounds have both acidic and basic properties, and can either accept or donate a proton depending upon circumstances. These substances are called **amphiprotic** since they can act both as a proton donor (an acid) and a proton acceptor (a base).

The simplest examples are the salts of acids with two acidic protons such as carbonic acid H_2CO_3. If one acidic proton has been replaced by a sodium ion, the resulting salt has the formula $NaHCO_3$ and is called sodium hydrogen carbonate or sodium bicarbonate. The bicarbonate ion HCO_3^- in solution can react either as a weak acid:

$$HCO_3^-(aq) + H_2O \rightleftharpoons CO_3^{2-}(aq) + H_3O^+(aq)$$

or as a weak base:

$$HCO_3^-(aq) + H_2O \rightleftharpoons H_2CO_3(aq) + OH^-(aq)$$

(vi) Acid-base titrations

Concentrations of solutions of acids and bases are usually determined in the laboratory by carrying out a **titration**. A known amount of one reactant (for instance, the acid) in solution is placed in a conical flask, and a solution of the other reactant (the base) is added from a buret.

The **equivalence point** of the acid-base reaction is reached when the amount (in moles) of the base added from the buret is equal to the amount (in moles) of the acid placed in the flask. The equivalence point can be detected by adding a small amount of an **indicator** to the solution in the conical flask. An indicator is a water-soluble dye that has conjugate acid and base forms and can exchange hydrogen ions in solution. The acidic form of the dye absorbs light differently from the conjugate base form, and so the colour of the dye in solution depends on the hydrogen ion concentration in the solution, $[H^+]$. The solution changes from one colour to the other at a particular value of $[H^+]$ that is characteristic of the indicator used.

Different indicators change colour at different values of hydrogen ion concentration. For example, methyl red is red in strongly acidic solution, and yellow in neutral or basic solution; litmus is red in acidic solution, and blue in basic solution; phenolphthalein is colourless in acidic or neutral solution and red in strongly basic solution. It is important to choose the right indicator for a titration if accurate results are to be obtained.

When the equivalence point is reached, the product of the reaction is in effect a solution of the salt of the acid and the base. For example, a titration of hydrochloric acid with sodium hydroxide produces a solution of sodium chloride:

$$HCl(aq) + NaOH(aq) \rightarrow Na^+(aq) + Cl^-(aq) + H_2O(\ell)$$

If both acid and base are strong, as in this case, then the solution at the equivalence point is neutral. However, if a weak acid is titrated with a strong base, then at the equivalence point the solution will be slightly basic. For example, in a titration of acetic acid with sodium hydroxide, the solution at the equivalence point contains sodium acetate, and is slightly basic because the acetate ion is a weak base. Phenolphthalein is an appropriate indicator for this titration.

On the other hand, if a strong acid is titrated with a weak base, then at the equivalence point the solution will be acidic. The indicator used for such a titration should change colour in slightly acidic solution; a suitable indicator would be either methyl orange and methyl red.

In any titration involving either a weak acid or a weak base, the accuracy of the result depends upon choosing an appropriate indicator.

Example 2-23 A 25.0 mL sample of a solution of sodium hydroxide of unknown concentration is titrated with 0.2240 M hydrochloric acid. The equivalence point is reached when 36.4 mL of the acid has been added. What was the concentration of the sodium hydroxide?

The titration reaction is: $\quad HCl + NaOH \rightarrow NaCl + H_2O$.

Amount of HCl added $= 36.4 \times 10^{-3} \, L \times 0.224 \, mol/L \ = 8.15 \times 10^{-3}$ mol

Since the titration was carried to the equivalence point, and since one mole of HCl reacts with one mole of NaOH, the amount of NaOH was also 8.15×10^{-3} mol, and this was contained in a volume of 25.0 mL.

Hence $[NaOH] = 8.15 \times 10^{-3}$ mol $/ \, 25.0 \times 10^{-3} \, L = 0.326$ mol/L $= 0.326$ M.

2-9 Reduction-oxidation reactions

Originally, the word "oxidation" meant a reaction involving the element oxygen, such as the following:

$$C + O_2 \rightarrow CO_2$$

$$CH_4 + 2\,O_2 \rightarrow CO_2 + 2\,H_2O$$

$$2\,Fe + O_2 \rightarrow 2\,FeO$$

$$4\,Al + 3\,O_2 \rightarrow 2\,Al_2O_3$$

In all of these reactions, the first reactant is **oxidized** and the oxygen is **reduced**. Such reactions are called **redox reactions**, a convenient contraction of the words describing the two processes. In a redox reaction, reduction and oxidation take place together: one substance is reduced, and another substance is oxidized.

The definitions of oxidation and reduction include many more reactions than just those involving oxygen. The concepts of oxidation and reduction depend on the idea of transfer of electrons from one molecule to another. The transfer of electrons results in changes in the **oxidation numbers** or oxidation states of atoms involved in the process. In iron oxide, FeO, for instance, the atoms of iron and oxygen are in the form of the ions Fe^{2+} and O^{2-} respectively. The iron atom has been oxidized by the loss of two electrons and is assigned an oxidation number of +2. Similarly the oxygen atom, which was reduced in the reaction between iron and oxygen, has gained two electrons and is assigned an oxidation number –2. In any reaction in which two electrons are removed from an Fe atom to form Fe^{2+}, iron is oxidized:

$$Fe + S \rightarrow FeS$$

$$Fe + Cl_2 \rightarrow FeCl_2$$

In the first reaction, sulphur is reduced to sulphide ion S^{2-}. In the second reaction, chlorine is reduced to chloride ion Cl^-.

The idea of oxidation and reduction also applies to the reactions in which no ions are formed. For example, in the combustion reaction between carbon and oxygen, which is shown above, carbon is oxidized and oxygen is reduced, although neither of the reactants nor the product, carbon dioxide, are ionic substances. In such cases, the concept of oxidation number helps in recognizing whether or not a reaction involves a reduction-oxidation process.

Table 2-7 Some oxidizing and reducing agents used in the laboratory

Oxidizing agents	Reducing agents
potassium permanganate $KMnO_4$	sodium bisulfite $NaHSO_3$
potassium dichromate $K_2Cr_2O_7$	zinc metal Zn
hydrogen peroxide H_2O_2	hydrogen peroxide H_2O_2
sodium hypochlorite NaClO	sodium borohydride $NaBH_4$
nitric acid HNO_3	hydrogen gas H_2
perchloric acid $HClO_4$	stannous chloride $SnCl_2$

Redox reactions are often carried out in the laboratory and Table 2-7 lists some common oxidizing and reducing reagents which the student may encounter. **Oxidizing agents** are compounds which are able to oxidize many other compounds, and **reducing agents** are compounds which can reduce many other compounds. Some compounds can react as a reducing agent or oxidizing agent, depending upon conditions; an example in Table 2-7 is hydrogen peroxide.

Figure 2-2 The manufacture of pulp from wood chips is one of the largest industries in Canada. Opened in 1992, Millar Western's state-of-the-art chlorine-free bleached chemi-thermomechanical pulp mill at Meadow Lake, Saskatchewan, was the world's first zero-liquid-effluent-discharge pulp mill. All of the wastewater from the mill is treated and recycled. During processing, the pulp is bleached by treatment with an oxidizing agent, and in this mill hydrogen peroxide is used instead of chlorine based bleach. *Photograph courtesy of Millar Western Forest Products Ltd.*

(i) Oxidation number

The state of oxidation of each atom in a molecule, called the **oxidation number** or **oxidation state**, can be calculated from a set of rules based upon the distribution of bonding electrons among the atoms of a molecule according the electronegativity of the atoms bonded together. The electronegativity of an element measures the power of an atom of that element to attract electrons within a molecule, and will be discussed in Chapter 11. Electronegativity values for some elements are listed in Table 11-6.

The determination of oxidation numbers is based on the assumption that all the electrons in a chemical bond are assigned to the more electronegative of the two atoms bonded together. Oxidation numbers do not necessarily reflect the actual distribution of electrons within a molecule, but are useful for analyzing redox reactions.

The oxidation number of an atom within a molecule is determined by the following set of rules. The basis for the rules will be better understood after the concepts of electronegativity and Lewis structures have been discussed in a later chapter. Each rule takes precedence over those that follow it.

Chapter 2

1. *For an element that is not chemically combined with any other element, the oxidation number is zero.*

2. *The sum of the oxidation numbers of the atoms in a molecule or ion is equal to the charge on the molecule or ion.*

3. *Fluorine has an oxidation number of –1 in all its compounds.*

4. *Oxygen has an oxidation number –2 in most of its compounds, but –1 in peroxides, which are compounds in which there is an O–O bond.*

5. *Hydrogen has an oxidation number of +1 in most of its compounds with non-metals, and –1 in alkali metal hydrides such as NaH.*

6. *The halogens chlorine, bromine and iodine have oxidation numbers of –1, except when bonded to oxygen or a lighter halogen.*

The application of these rules is illustrated in the following examples.

(a) Oxidation numbers are zero in metallic iron, Fe; in oxygen gas, O_2; and in ozone, O_3.

(b) In SO_4^{2-}, the sum of the oxidation numbers is –2, by rule 2; by rule 4, the oxidation number for each of the four O atoms is –2 and so the oxidation number of S is +6.

(c) In the molecule hydrogen fluoride HF, F has oxidation number of –1 by rule 3, and so by rule 2 the oxidation number of H is +1.

(d) In methane, CH_4, H has oxidation number +1 by rule 5, and so C has oxidation number –4.

(e) In CO_2, O has oxidation number –2 and so C has oxidation number +4.

(f) In formaldehyde CH_2O, C has oxidation number 0.

(g) In chlorine trifluoride ClF_3, oxidation number of F is –1 by rule 3, and so that of Cl is +3.

(h) In the perchlorate ion ClO_4^-, rules 2 and 4 give Cl an oxidation number of +7.

(i) In hydrogen peroxide, H_2O_2, oxidation numbers are –1 for O by rule 4, and +1 for H.

(j) In H_2O oxidation number of H is + 1, but in lithium hydride LiH, oxidation number of H is –1, by rule 5.

Oxidation numbers can be designated by Roman numerals written in brackets or as a superscript like an ionic charge. For instance Fe(II) and Fe^{II} refer to the +2 oxidation state of iron in ferrous sulfate, also called iron(II) sulfate, with formula $FeSO_4$.

(ii) Balancing redox equations

The technique for balancing equations that was described in Section 2-1 can be applied to redox equations, and this was done in Example 2-2. However, there are some features of redox equations that require special consideration.

First, redox equations often involve ions, and it is necessary to take account of the conservation of electric charge as well as the conservation of atoms of each element. This is done by adding a line labelled "charge" to the table that is used in the calculations. Second, water and either hydrogen ions or hydroxide ions are often involved. These features are illustrated in the following discussion.

When potassium permanganate, $KMnO_4$, reacts with ferrous nitrate, $Fe(NO_3)_2$ in acidic aqueous solution, the permanganate ion MnO_4^- is reduced to Mn^{2+}, and the ferrous ion Fe^{2+} is oxidized to ferric ion Fe^{3+}. The oxidation numbers for Mn and Fe are listed under the symbols for these elements in the following unbalanced net ionic equation for the reaction:

$$MnO_4^- + Fe^{2+} \rightarrow Mn^{2+} + Fe^{3+}$$

$$+7 \qquad +2 \qquad +2 \qquad +3$$

The oxidation number for Mn decreases by 5, and that for Fe increases by 1.

In the equation shown above, oxygen occurs on the left-hand side of the reaction (in the permanganate ion) but not on the right. This can be accounted for if water is produced in the reaction. But production of water requires hydrogen atoms, and so in acidic solution, hydrogen ions must be added to the left-hand side of the equation. Hence a more complete equation for the reaction is:

$$MnO_4^- + Fe^{2+} + H^+ \rightarrow Mn^{2+} + Fe^{3+} + H_2O$$

This equation is still not balanced. Balancing the equation is then carried out by the previously described method, with an extra line added to the table to account for the charges on ions. The extra line is labelled "charge", and is otherwise handled in the same way as the lines used in accounting for the elements.

Example 2-24 Balance the equation for the reaction between permanganate ion and ferrous ion in acidic aqueous solution:

$$MnO_4^- + Fe^{2+} + H^+ \rightarrow Mn^{2+} + Fe^{3+} + H_2O$$

The table for the calculations is as follows.

totals	\multicolumn{3}{c}{$MnO_4^- + a\ Fe^{2+} + b\ H^+$}	$\rightarrow$	\multicolumn{3}{c}{$c\ Mn^{2+} + d\ Fe^{3+} + e\ H_2O$}	totals
1	1	0	0	Mn	c	0	0	c
4	4	0	0	O	0	0	e	e
a	0	a	0	Fe	0	d	0	d
b	0	0	b	H	0	0	$2e$	$2e$
$-1 + 2a + b$	-1	$+2a$	$+b$	charge	$+2c$	$+3d$	0	$+ 2c + 3d$

From the Mn line, $c = 1$.

From the O line, $e = 4$.

From the H line, $b = 2e = 8$.

From the Fe line, $a = d$.

From the charge line, $-1 + 2a + b = +2c + 3d$. Substituting the values that have already been determined, this equation becomes $7 + 2a = 2 + 3a$, from which $a = 5$.

Since $d = a$, then $d = 5$.

Hence the balanced equation is:

$$MnO_4^- + 5\ Fe^{2+} + 8\ H^+ \rightarrow Mn^{2+} + 5\ Fe^{3+} + 4\ H_2O$$

_____

Often the water, and either hydrogen ions or hydroxide ions, are omitted from the unbalanced equation used to describe a redox reaction, and it is necessary to add them to the equation before setting out the table.

_____

Example 2-25 Balance the following reaction in acid solution:

$$Pb(s) + PbO_2(s) + SO_4^{2-}(aq) \rightarrow PbSO_4(s)$$

_____

In this reaction, Pb is oxidized to $PbSO_4$, and PbO_2 is reduced, also to $PbSO_4$. Hydrogen ions and water molecules are involved in the reaction, and if we add water on the right-hand side and hydrogen ions on the left-hand side, the table appears as follows.

	$Pb + a\ PbO_2 + b\ SO_4^{2-} + c\ H^+$				$\rightarrow$	$d\ PbSO_4 + e\ H_2O$		
totals								totals
$1+a$	1	a	0	0	Pb	d	0	d
$2a + 4b$	0	$2a$	$4b$	0	O	$4d$	e	$4d + e$
b	0	0	b	0	S	d	0	d
c	0	0	0	c	H	0	$2e$	$2e$
$-2b + c$	0	0	$-2b$	$+c$	charge	0	0	0

Finding the best way to solve these equations can be a bit of a puzzle; in this case it is best to start at the bottom line.

From the charge line, $-2b + c = 0$, so $c = 2b$.

From the H line, $c = 2e$. From these two results, $b = e$.

From the S line, $b = d$. Hence b, d and e are all equal.

From the O line, $2a + 4b = 4d + e$; combining this with the previous results, it follows that $2a = b$.

From the Pb line, $1+a = d = 2a$; hence $a = 1$. Working back, $b = d = e = 2$ and $c = 4$.

The balanced equation is therefore:

$$Pb(s) + PbO_2(s) + 2\ SO_4^{2-}(aq) + 4\ H^+(aq) \rightarrow 2\ PbSO_4(s) + 2\ H_2O(\ell)$$

_____

Sometimes it is not clear to which side of the equation the water molecules and hydrogen ions should be added. In the last example, a guess was made (water was placed on the right, hydrogen ion on the left), which turned out to be correct. But if a molecule or ion is inadvertently placed on the wrong side of the equation, the only consequence is that the calculations will result in a negative value of the corresponding stoichiometric coefficient. The correct balanced equation is obtained by transposing the molecule or ion to the other side of the chemical equation. This is illustrated below in Example 2-26.

The two examples above deal with reactions taking place in acidic solution. Hydrogen ions take part in both reactions. For many redox reactions, the outcome of the reaction depends on whether the solution is acidic or basic, since in basic solution different ions or molecules may take part in the reaction. When balancing redox reactions in basic solution, balancing of hydrogen and oxygen atoms involves water and hydroxide ions rather than hydrogen ions.

Example 2-26 Balance the following reaction in basic solution :

$$CrO_4^{2-}(aq) + Zn(s) \rightarrow Cr(OH)_3(s) + Zn(OH)_4^{2-}(aq)$$

Since the reaction takes place in basic solution, it is necessary to add H_2O and OH^- to the equation. If we add water on the right-hand side and hydroxide ions on the left-hand side, the table appears as follows.

totals	CrO_4^{2-}	+a Zn	+ b OH^-	$\rightarrow$		c $Cr(OH)_3$	+ d $Zn(OH)_4^{2-}$	+ e H_2O	totals
1	1	0	0	Cr		c	0	0	c
4 + b	4	0	b	O		3c	4d	e	3c+4d+e
a	0	a	0	Zn		0	d	0	d
b	0	0	b	H		3c	4d	2e	3c+4d+2e
–2 – b	–2	0	–b	charge		0	–2d	0	-2d

From the Cr line, $c = 1$.

From the O line, $4 + b = 3c+4d+e$.

From the H line, $b = 3c+4d+2e$. Subtracting one equation from the other, we find $e = -4$. Substituting the above values back into the H line, we find $b = 4d - 5$.

From the charge line, $-2 - b = -2d$. Adding this to the previous equation gives $d = 1.5$, and then substitution back gives $b = 1$.

From the Zn line, $a = d = 1.5$.

Hence the balanced equation is:

$$CrO_4^{2-}(aq) + 1.5\ Zn(s) + OH^-(aq) \rightarrow + Cr(OH)_3(s) + 1.5\ Zn(OH)_4^{2-}(aq) - 4\ H_2O(\ell)$$

If the water is transposed to the left-hand side, the final result is:

$$CrO_4^{2-}(aq) + 1.5\ Zn(s) + OH^-(aq) + 4\ H_2O(\ell) \rightarrow Cr(OH)_3(s) + 1.5\ Zn(OH)_4^{2-}(aq)$$

Redox reactions may be separated into two "half-reactions" which show explicitly the loss of electrons upon oxidation, and the gain of electrons upon reduction. For example in the reaction between permangate and ferrous ion, which was discussed in Example 2-24, the oxidation process is $Fe^{2+} \rightarrow Fe^{3+}$. To balance this half-reaction, it is only necessary to add an electron:

$$Fe^{2+} \rightarrow Fe^{3+} + e^-.$$

The reduction process is $MnO_4^- \rightarrow Mn^{2+}$. This is balanced (in acid solution) by adding electrons, hydrogen ions and water, using the following table.

totals	$MnO_4^- + a\,H^+ + b\,e^-$			$\rightarrow$	$c\,Mn^{2+} + d\,H_2O$		totals
1	1	0	0	Mn	c	0	c
4	4	0	0	O	0	d	d
a	0	a	0	H	0	$2d$	$2d$
$-1+a-b$	-1	$+a$	$-b$	charge	$+2c$	0	$2c$

From the Mn line, $c = 1$.

From the O line, $d = 4$.

From the H line, $a = 2d = 8$.

From the charge line, $2c = -1+a-b$, from which $b = 5$.

Hence the balanced reduction half-reaction is:

$$MnO_4^-(aq) + 8\,H^+(aq) + 5\,e^- \rightarrow Mn^{2+} + 4\,H_2O(\ell).$$

Notice that the five electrons correspond to the change of five in the oxidation number. If the oxidation half-reaction is multiplied by 5 and added to the reduction half-reaction, the overall reaction is obtained, as in Example 2-10.

In a reduction half-reaction, the electrons appear on the left-hand side of the equation, and in oxidation half-reactions, the electrons appear on the right hand side of the equation.

Half-reactions are useful because, for some reactions, the oxidation and reduction processes can be carried out separately at metal electrodes. This is the basis for the subject known as **electrochemistry**. The simplest experiments of this nature are those involving electrolysis.

(iii) Electrolysis reactions

Many redox reactions can be carried out by the process known as **electrolysis,** in which an electric current is passed through a solution or a molten electrolyte, and a redox reaction occurs as a result of electron transfer driven by the external source of current. In electrolysis, the electrons taking part in the half-reactions are transported through wires, and the half-reactions take place on the surfaces of two electrodes.

In any electrochemical cell, the electrode at which oxidation takes place is called the **anode,** and the electrode at which reduction takes place is called the **cathode.** In an electrolysis cell, the cathode is connected to the negative terminal of the external source of current and supplies electrons for the reduction process. The anode is connected to the positive terminal of the external source of current, and removes electrons in the oxidation process.

Positively charged ions are attracted to the cathode and are called **cations.** Negatively charged ions are attracted to the anode and are called **anions.**

When water is electrolysed using non-reactive platinum electrodes to carry the current into solution, the products of the reaction are hydrogen gas and oxygen gas. This electrolysis is most easily carried out if an inert salt such as sodium sulphate is added to the water to carry the electric current through the solution. The gases can be collected separately as shown in Figure 2-1. The equation describing the observed decomposition, and the two half-reactions are:

$$2 H_2O(\ell) \rightarrow 2 H_2(g) + O_2(g)$$

reduction at the cathode: $2 H_2O(\ell) + 2e^- \rightarrow H_2(g) + 2 OH^-(aq)$

oxidation at the anode: $H_2O(\ell) \rightarrow \frac{1}{2} O_2(g) + 2 H^+(aq) + 2e^-$

The overall reaction obtained by combining these two half-reactions is:

$$3 H_2O(\ell) \rightarrow H_2(g) + \frac{1}{2} O_2(g) + 2 H^+(aq) + 2 OH^-(aq)$$

This equation represents not only the decomposition of water into its elements but also the ionization of water. If the solution is given time to mix, the ions produced will recombine to produce water and the solution will be neutral. But during the process, it can be shown using suitable acid-base indicators that the solution near the cathode (where hydrogen gas is produced) is basic, and the solution near the anode (where oxygen gas is produced) is acidic.

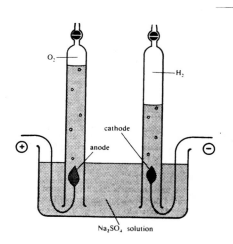

Figure 2-3 Electrolysis of water. Electrons are supplied from the negative terminal of the external source of current, and cause reduction of water to hydrogen gas at the right hand electrode, the cathode. Electrons leave the solution at the anode, where water is oxidized to oxygen gas, and return to the positive terminal of the external source. The dissolved electrolyte, Na_2SO_4, does not take part in the processes at the electrodes, but the Na^+ and SO_4^{2-} ions transport the electric current through the solution.

Other electrolytic reactions may occur in aqueous solutions containing ions that are oxidized or reduced more readily than water. Copper plating consists of the reduction of $Cu^{2+}(aq)$ ions to copper metal, which is deposited on the cathode. Chlorine gas and sodium hydroxide are produced by electrolysis of a solution of NaCl; chloride ions Cl^- are oxidized at the anode to give chlorine gas, while at the cathode, water is reduced yielding hydrogen gas and hydroxide ions. These and other examples of electrolysis will be discussed in later chapters. Electrolysis is the basis for several important Canadian industries because large amounts of hydroelectric power are available in this country.

The amount of chemical reaction produced by electrolysis depends on the amount of electrical charge that passes through the cell and the number of electrons exchanged in the reaction. For instance, to deposit one mole of silver from solution by electrolysis requires one mole of electrons:

$$Ag^+(aq) + e^- \rightarrow Ag(s)$$

Two moles of electrons are needed to deposit one mole of copper:

$$Cu^{2+}(aq) + 2e^- \rightarrow Cu(s).$$

The amount of electrical charge carried by one mole of electrons is called the **faraday** (abbreviation F), after the English scientist Michael Faraday. This amount of charge is also called the **Faraday constant** and is designated by the symbol F. The value of the Faraday constant (to five significant figures) is:

$$F = 96\ 485 \text{ coulomb/mole.}$$

_____

Example 2-27 What mass of copper is deposited at the cathode by the passage of a current of 1.56 amperes for 500. seconds through a solution of $CuSO_4$?

_____

Since electric charge Q is the product of electric current I and time t, and an ampere is a current of one coulomb per second, the charge passing through the cell is:

$$Q = 1.56 \text{ ampere} \times 500. \text{ second} = 780. \text{ coulomb.}$$

The amount of electrons is the charge divided by the Faraday constant:

$$n = \frac{Q}{F} = \frac{780.\,\text{coulomb}}{96485\,\text{coulomb/mole}} = 8.08 \times 10^{-3} \text{ mole}$$

Two electrons are required to reduce each Cu^{2+} ion so the amount of Cu deposited = $(1/2) \times 8.08 \times 10^{-3}$ mole or 4.04×10^{-3} mole, and the mass of Cu deposited = 4.04×10^{-3} mole $\times$ 63.546 gram/mole = 0.257 gram.

_____

Example 2-28   Aluminum is produced by electrolytic reduction of the ion Al^{3+} in a molten mixture of Al_2O_3 and Na_3AlF6. A machine produces 600. aluminum beverage cans per minute, each of which has a mass of 20.0 g. What current would be required for the reduction process to supply aluminum metal for the cans by reduction in a single electrolytic cell (or in a set of cells operating in parallel)?

_____

The cans are produced at a rate of 600. cans per minute, or 10.0 cans per second. The metal must be produced at the rate of 10.0 cans/second $\times$ 20.0 gram/can, or 200. g/s. The molar mass of Al is 26.982 g/mol, so the rate at which aluminum must be produced is:

$$\text{production rate} = \frac{200.\,\text{g/s}}{26.982 \text{ g/mol}} = 7.41 \text{ mol/s}.$$

Since the aluminum ions are triply charged, three moles of electrons are required per ion, and hence 3×7.41 moles of electrons per second are required for the reduction process, and so the electric current required is:

$$\text{current} = 3 \times 7.41 \text{ mol/s} \times 96485 \text{ C/mol} = 2.14 \times 10^6 \text{ ampere}$$

since an ampere is one coulomb per second. The current required in the actual industrial process would be somewhat higher because of non-electrolytic conduction and subsidiary reactions in the cells.

_____

Key concepts

The system of naming chemical compounds is called **chemical nomenclature**. For inorganic compounds, the nomenclature is largely based on the names of the elements, and common ions. For compounds of carbon, also known as organic compounds, the nomenclature is based on the names of certain parent compounds, and the names of common functional groups of atoms.

Chemical reactions are represented by chemical equations, which must be balanced so as to be consistent with the conservation of atoms and electric charge. Balancing some equations is easy but for other equations a systematic procedure can be used.

Chemical reactions can be classified into several general categories: decomposition, synthesis, precipitation, acid-base, and reduction-oxidation. Decomposition is a reaction in which a compound is broken down into simpler compounds, or elements. Synthesis is a reaction in which simpler compounds are combined to form more complex compounds. Precipitation takes place when a solution contains ions that combine to form a sparingly soluble salt, which separates from the solution as a solid.

In an acid-base reaction, a hydrogen ion is transferred from the acid to the base. When an acid ionizes in water, the hydrogen ion is attached to a water molecule to form the hydronium ion. When a base ionizes in solution, a hydrogen ion is transferred from a water molecule to the base, leaving a hydroxide ion. When a hydrogen ion leaves an acid, the part of the acid molecule that remains is a base, which is conjugate to the acid. Acids and bases are classified as strong or weak, depending on the degree of ionization.

In a reduction-oxidation reaction, one or more electrons is transferred from one reactant to another. The reactant that loses an electron is oxidized, and the reactant that gains the electron is reduced. The oxidation numbers of the atoms involved give a measure of the state of oxidation. Redox reactions can be carried by electrolysis of solutions.

Review Questions

1. What is the name of the system used for naming chemical compounds?

2. What is the difference between an organic and an inorganic compound?

3. What two principles govern the procedure for balancing equations?

4. What is an acid? What is a base?

5. What is the relationship between an acid and its conjugate base?

6. What is transferred in an acid-base reaction?

7. What is transferred in a reduction-oxidation reaction?

Problems

1. Balance the following equations:

    (a) $C_2H_5OH + O_2 \rightarrow CO_2 + H_2O$

    (b) $BCl_3 + H_2O \rightarrow B(OH)_3 + HCl$

    (c) $NiS + O_2 \rightarrow NiO + SO_2$

    (d) $NH_4VO_3 \rightarrow V_2O_5 + NH_3 + H_2O$

    (e) $N_2O_5 + H_2O \rightarrow HNO_3$

    (f) $Ca_3(PO_4)_2 + SiO_2 + C \rightarrow P_4 + CaSiO_3 + CO$

Chapter 2

2. Methane burns with oxygen according to the equation

$$CH_4 + 2\,O_2 \rightarrow CO_2 + 2\,H_2O$$

How many moles of O_2 are required per mole of CH_4? How many kilograms of oxygen are required per kilogram of CH_4? [2; 3.99]

3. A sample of a mixture of barium salts and sodium salts was completely dissolved in nitric acid. Upon adding dilute sulphuric acid to the solution, virtually all of the barium was precipitated as white $BaSO_4$, which was filtered, dried and weighed. If the mass of the original sample was 0.2270 g, and the mass of the precipitate was 0.0235 g, calculate the mass fraction of barium in the mixture. [0.0609]

4. Equal masses of sodium metal and water are reacted to form hydrogen gas, H_2, and sodium hydroxide, NaOH. Write a balanced equation for the reaction. Which of the reactants is in excess if the reaction goes to completion? What fraction of that reactant remains unreacted?

[H_2O, 0.216]

5. Baking powder is a mixture of sodium bicarbonate and an acid. When dissolved in water, carbon dioxide gas is released. Some examples of the reactions which are used in different powders are shown below:

$$KH_2PO_4 + NaHCO_3 \rightarrow CO_2 + KNaHPO_4 + H_2O$$

$$Na_2Al_2(SO_4)_4 + 6\,NaHCO_3 \rightarrow 6\,CO_2 + 4\,Na_2SO_4 + 2\,Al(OH)_3$$

If each of the powders represented by these reactions consists of a stoichiometric mixture, calculate the amount of CO_2 (in moles) which would be released by 1.00 gram of baking powder in each case.

[4.54×10^{-3} mol, 6.07×10^{-3} mol]

6. For the following reactions in acidic aqueous solution, write balanced half-reactions for the oxidation and reduction processes, and balanced equations for the full reactions.

(a) $Fe^{2+} + O_2 \rightarrow Fe^{3+}$

(b) $H_2O_2 + Sn^{2+} \rightarrow Sn^{4+} + H_2O$

(c) $H_2O_2 \rightarrow H_2O + O_2$

(d) $SbCl_4^- + SO_4^{2-} + Cl^- \rightarrow SbCl_6^- + H_2SO_3$

(e) $PbS + H_2O_2 \rightarrow PbSO_4 + H_2O$

(f) $Mn^{2+} + BiO_3^- \rightarrow MnO_4^- + Bi^{3+}$

(g) $NO + NO_3^- \rightarrow N_2O_4$

(h) $CS(NH_2)_2 + BrO_3^- \rightarrow CO(NH_2)_2 + SO_4^{2-} + Br^-$

7. For the following reactions in basic aqueous solution, write balanced half-reactions for the oxidation and reduction processes, and balanced equations for the full reactions.

(a) $C_2H_4 + MnO_4^- \rightarrow CH_3COO^- + MnO_2$

(b) $ClO^- \rightarrow ClO_3^- + Cl^-$

(c) $Al(s) + NO_3^- \rightarrow Al(OH)_4^- + NH_3$

(d) $Bi(OH)_3 + Sn(OH)_4^{2-} \rightarrow Bi + Sn(OH)_6^{2-}$

(e) $MnO_4^- + CN^- \rightarrow MnO_2 + CNO^-$

(f) $S + HO_2^- \rightarrow SO_4^{2-} + OH^-$

8. A sample of seawater is titrated with an aqueous solution of silver nitrate, taking advantage of the reaction in which silver ion reacts with chloride ion to precipitate insoluble silver chloride. What is the concentration of chloride ion in the seawater, if it takes 19.7 mL of 0.100 M $AgNO_3$ solution to precipitate all of the chloride ion from a 10.0 mL sample of seawater? What mass of silver chloride is precipitated?

[0. 197 mol/L; 0.282 g]

9. A sample of a mixture of KBr and NaBr weighing 0.5605 g was treated with aqueous $AgNO_3$, and all the bromide ion was precipitated in the form of insoluble AgBr; the precipitate, when dried, weighed 0.9702 g. What was the mass fraction of KBr in the original sample?

[0.380]

10. Determine the oxidation number of phosphorus in each of the following molecules and ions: H_3PO_4, HPO_3^{2-}, PH_3, PCl_4^+, PCl_5, PCl_6^-

11. Determine the oxidation number of chromium in each of the following molecules and ions: $Cr_2O_7^{2-}$, CrO_4^{2-}, $CrOCl_3$, $Cr_2Cl_9^{3-}$.

12. Heating potassium chlorate, $KClO_3$, causes it to decompose, yielding potassium chloride, KCl, and oxygen, O_2. If a sample of 15.35 g of $KClO_3$ is decomposed, what mass of KCl remains after the reaction, and how many moles of oxygen gas are produced?

[9.34 g, 0. 1878 mol]

13. 10.0 mL of a 0.054 M solution of Na_2CO_3 is added to 20.0 mL of a 0.120 M solution of $CaCl_2$, and a precipitate of $CaCO_3$ is formed. Identify the major ions remaining in solution and calculate the concentration of each of them. [Ca^{2+} 0.062 M, Na^+ 0.036 M, Cl^- 0.16 M]

14. What volume of a 0.563 M solution of NaOH is required to react completely with 10.0 mL of a 0.255 M solution of HNO_3? [4.53 mL]

15. What volume of a 0.563 M solution of NaOH is required to react completely with 10.0 mL of a 0.255 M solution of acetic acid, CH_3COOH? [4.53 mL]

16. What volume of a 0.563 M solution of NaOH is required to react completely with 10.0 mL of a 0.255 M solution of sulphuric acid, H_2SO_4? [9.06 mL]

17. What is the conjugate base for each of the following acids?

(a) HCl   (b) H_2SO_4 (c) NH_4^+ (d) CH_3COOH (e) H_2O.

18. What is the conjugate acid for each of the following bases?

(a) $C_6H_5COO^-$ (b) SO_3^{2-} (c) CH_3NH_2 (d) H_2O

19. What mass of zinc metal is deposited by electrolytic reduction of a solution containing Zn^{2+} if a current of 100. amperes is passed through a solution for a period of 10. hours? [1.22 kg]

20. Which of the following substances, when added to water, would produce an acidic solution? And which a basic solution? Ammonia, NH_3 ; sodium carbonate, Na_2CO_3; hydrobromic acid, HBr; ammonium chloride, NH_4Cl; sodium acetate, CH_3COONa; methylamine, CH_3NH_2.

21. Determine the oxidation number of S in sodium thiosulphate $Na_2S_2O_3$ and in sodium tetrathionate $Na_2S_4O_6$.

22. Draw structural formulae for all three isomers of C_5H_{10} and name the compounds.

23. Write down the oxidation number of carbon in each of the following compounds:
    (a) CH_3Cl (b) HCOOH   (c) CCl_2F_2 (d) CH_3NH_2.

24. When metallic sodium is placed in water, gaseous hydrogen is evolved and the solution becomes very basic. Write a balanced equation to describe this reaction. If 1.00 g of sodium is reacted with 1.00 L of water, what is the resulting concentration of hydroxide ion OH^-? [0.0435 mol/L]

25. A 1.596 gram sample of an oxide of iron was found to contain 72.4 % by weight of iron. What is the empirical formula of the oxide? [Fe_3O_4]

26. How many moles of butanoic acid C_3H_7COOH are there in a 25.62 g sample of pure butanoic acid? [0.2908 mol]

27. What is the maximum mass of calcium nitrate $Ca(NO_3)_2$ that could be prepared by the reaction of 18.9 g of nitric acid, HNO_3, with 7.40 g of calcium hydroxide $Ca(OH)_2$? [16.4 g]

28. Write a balanced equation for the oxidation of iodine, I_2 , to iodate ion, IO_3^-, by hydrogen peroxide H_2O_2 which is reduced to water. The reaction takes place in acid solution.

29. Consider the following substances, NH_3 , NaOH, HNO_3 , HNO_2 , CH_4, $Ca(NO_3)_2$ and list all those that: (a) are strong electrolytes in aqueous solution; (b) are weak bases in aqueous solution; (c) contain nitrogen in oxidation state +5 (d) would form a solid precipitate when reacted with sulfate ion in aqueous solution.

30. A compound containing only the elements C, H and Cl is known to be 56.7 % Cl by weight. A 0.1056 g sample of the compound is burned in excess oxygen, producing 0.1487 g of $CO_2(g)$ and 0.0457 g of $H_2O(\ell)$. Find the empirical formula of the compound. [C_2H_3Cl]

31. 50.0 mL of 0.100 M lead nitrate $Pb(NO_3)_2$ is added to a solution containing 0.596 g of potassium chloride KCl, and a precipitate of solid lead chloride $PbCl_2(s)$ is formed. Write a net balanced ionic equation for the reaction and calculate the mass of the precipitate if the reaction goes to completion. [1.11 g]

32. A very concentrated solution of sulfuric acid H_2SO_4 has a density of 1.84 g/mL and contains 96.0 % sulfuric acid by weight. What is the concentration of acid in the solution?

    [18.0 mol/L]

33. When a particular hydrocarbon is burned in air, 5.00 moles of the hydrocarbon forms 5.00 moles of CO_2 and 2.00 moles of H_2O. What are the empirical and the molecular formulae of the hydrocarbon?

34. In acidic solution the permanganate ion MnO_4^- reacts with the oxalate ion $C_2O_4^{2-}$ to form Mn^{2+} and CO_2. Write a balanced equation for the reaction.

35. A 3.460 g sample of sodium metal exposed to air reacts with oxygen to produce solid sodium oxide. Write a balanced equation to describe this reaction, and calculate what mass of sodium oxide is produced. The oxide produced is then dissolved in water to produce a basic solution. Write a balanced equation to describe this reaction and calculate what volume of 0.512 M hydrochloric acid HCl would be required to neutralize the basic solution. [4.664 g, 294 mL]

36. 500. mL of a 0.600 M solution of silver nitrate $AgNO_3$ is mixed with 500. mL of a solution of 0.550 M potassium chromate K_2CrO_4 solution, and a bright yellow precipitate of sparingly soluble silver chromate $Ag_2CrO_4(s)$ is formed. Write a balanced equation to describe the reaction, and calculate the mass of solid silver chromate which would be formed if the reaction goes to completion. [49.8 g]

37. In the following reaction, which species is the reducing agent?

$$3 \text{ Cu(s)} + 6 \text{ H}^+\text{(aq)} + 2 \text{ HNO}_3\text{(aq)} \rightarrow 3 \text{ Cu}^{2+}\text{(aq)} + 2 \text{ NO(g)} + 4 \text{ H}_2\text{O}(\ell)$$

38. Common sugar, or sucrose, has the molecular formula $C_{12}H_{22}O_{11}$. What is the mole fraction of sugar in a solution made by dissolving 10.0 g of sucrose in 200. g of water.   [2.62×10^{-3}]

39. In a 0.05 M solution of sodium chloride NaCl in water, which one of the following has a numerical value closest to 0.05?   mole fraction of NaCl;   mass fraction of NaCl;   mass percent of NaCl;   molality of NaCl.

40. Give the molecular formula and draw the structural formula for each of the following alkanes: 2-methylbutane, 2,3-dimethylbutane, 3-ethylhexane.

41. Give the molecular formula and draw the structural formula for each of the following alkyl chlorides: 2-chloropropane, 1,2-dichloroethane, 1,3-dichloropropane, propyl chloride, dichloromethane.

42. Name the following compounds:

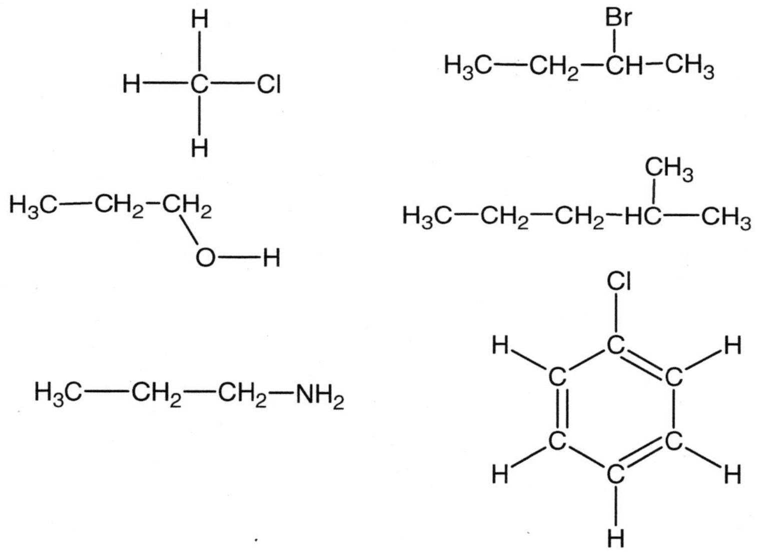

3 Elements and the Periodic Table

Objectives

After reading this chapter, the student should be able to do the following:

♦ Use the periodic table as a source of information about the elements.

♦ Give the name and chemical symbol for the elements of the first three rows of the periodic table.

♦ Define the two systems of numbering the groups of the periodic table.

♦ Name the most important categories of elements.

♦ Correlate the common oxidation numbers of an element with its group number.

Related topics to review:

Elements in Chapter 1. Nomenclature of inorganic compounds, and types of reaction in Chapter 2.

Related topics to look forward to:

Atomic structure in Chapter 10.

3-1 Historical introduction

Although millions of chemical compounds are known, the composition of all of them can be described in terms of less than a hundred elements. The idea of elements as the basic building blocks of matter was put forward in its modern form by John Dalton in 1806, and was supported by many chemical experiments. The final proof of the nature of the elements came with the discovery of the structure of atoms and the study of their characteristic X-rays in the early part of the twentieth century. In addition to the elements found in nature, about a dozen other elements have been manufactured by nuclear transformations. Table 1-8 contains a list of the names and symbols of the elements in order of atomic number, and in this chapter we describe how the physical and chemical properties of the elements change systematically and periodically with atomic number.

In 1869 the Russian chemist Dmitry Mendeleev published a table of the elements which showed that the chemical and physical properties of the elements are not random but displayed regular similarities. He was not the first to try to systematize the known facts about elements but his work has been recognized as the most important. His table of the elements helped understand the chemical properties of the elements and the relationships between the properties of different elements. In addition to summarizing the chemistry of the known elements, he predicted the discovery of specific "new" elements and, by comparison with the neighbouring elements in his table, predicted their chemical and physical properties. Within Mendeleev's own lifetime, several of these elements were discovered, and their properties were found to be very close to his predictions. This ensured acceptance of his theory that the properties of the elements show regular and periodic progressions in their properties. The modern **periodic table** has been developed directly from that of Mendeleev.

In early studies of periodicity, the elements were listed in order of their atomic molar mass, and this led to several difficulties. First, the molar masses were not known with confidence;

inaccurate measurements caused some errors, and in some cases a change in the assumed valence of an element changed its molar mass by a factor of two or three. Secondly, many elements were not known at the time, and naturally it was not known how many elements remained to be discovered. The properties of the known elements suggested that gaps had to be left if the assumed periodicity of the elements was to be recognizable; it was these gaps which led to the discovery of some of the new elements referred to above. Thirdly, an increase of nuclear charge does not always lead to an increase in the average molar mass of samples found in nature. It is the nuclear charge and the number of electrons which determine the chemical properties of an element and its place in the periodic table, not the atomic mass. Thus in some instances the order of elements in the periodic table does not correspond to increasing molar mass; not until the atomic numbers of the elements were established was it possible to put the elements in their proper order.

Table 3-1 The Periodic Table of the Elements

1	2	3	4	5	6	7	8	9	10	11	12	13	14	15	16	17	18
1A	2A	3B	4B	5B	6B	7B	8B	8B	8B	1B	2B	3A	4A	5A	6A	7A	8A
1 **H**																	2 **He**
3 **Li**	4 **Be**											5 **B**	6 **C**	7 **N**	8 **O**	9 **F**	10 **Ne**
11 **Na**	12 **Mg**											13 **Al**	14 **Si**	15 **P**	16 **S**	17 **Cl**	18 **Ar**
19 **K**	20 **Ca**	21 **Sc**	22 **Ti**	23 **V**	24 **Cr**	25 **Mn**	26 **Fe**	27 **Co**	28 **Ni**	29 **Cu**	30 **Zn**	31 **Ga**	32 **Ge**	33 **As**	34 **Se**	35 **Br**	36 **Kr**
37 **Rb**	38 **Sr**	39 **Y**	40 **Zr**	41 **Nb**	42 **Mo**	43 **Tc**	44 **Ru**	45 **Rh**	46 **Pd**	47 **Ag**	48 **Cd**	49 **In**	50 **Sn**	51 **Sb**	52 **Te**	53 **I**	54 **Xe**
55 **Cs**	56 **Ba**	57 **La**	72 **Hf**	73 **Ta**	74 **W**	75 **Re**	76 **Os**	77 **Ir**	78 **Pt**	79 **Au**	80 **Hg**	81 **Tl**	82 **Pb**	83 **Bi**	84 **Po**	85 **At**	86 **Rn**
87 **Fr**	88 **Ra**	89 **Ac**															

Row 6:

58 **Ce**	59 **Pr**	60 **Nd**	61 **Pm**	62 **Sm**	63 **Eu**	64 **Gd**	65 **Tb**	66 **Dy**	67 **Ho**	68 **Er**	69 **Tm**	70 **Yb**	71 **Lu**
90 **Th**	91 **Pa**	92 **U**	93 **Np**	94 **Pu**	95 **Am**	96 **Cu**	97 **Bk**	98 **Cf**	99 **Es**	100 **Fm**	101 **Md**	102 **No**	103 **Lr**

3-2 The periodic table

Several forms of the periodic table are in common use, but we will focus on the most widely used form of the table, shown in Table 3-1. The elements are arranged in seven rows and eighteen columns, and each cell of the table contains the chemical symbol and other information for a single element. The names of the elements are to be found in Table 1-8 on page 15.

The columns of the table are identified by **group numbers** running from 1 to 18. An older system of identifying the groups using numbers and the letters A and B is also shown. In that system, the groups are numbered from 1 to 8 twice, the elements in the central part of the table are given a letter B, and elements in columns 8, 9 and 10 are gathered together in a single group, 8B. This system has been in use for a long time and is still widely used, but the new scheme is simpler. The group numbers 11 to 18 in the new system are related to the old group numbers by the addition of ten.

The rows of the table are numbered from 1 to 7. The first row contains only two elements, hydrogen and helium, the second and third rows contain 8 elements, and the fourth and fifth rows contain 18 elements. The sixth and seventh rows contain 32 elements, and of these 14 are listed in a separate block because the table becomes too wide to print or read easily if all 32 elements were placed on one line.

The number of elements found in nature is limited by the instability of the nuclei of the heavier elements. The seventh row contains many radioactive elements, some of which are not found in nature because they decay by nuclear processes in a very short time; the chemistry of these elements is known only through study of man-made samples.

Very recently, in 1999, reports were published claiming that several new heavy elements have been produced in particle accelerators, specifically elements with atomic numbers 114, 116 and 118. If confirmed, these observations support the prediction by nuclear physicists that some elements with high atomic number would have relatively long lifetimes if they could be produced. The periodic table can be used to predict some aspects of the chemistry of these elements.

Table 3-2 The metals, semi-metals and non-metals.

The non-metals are shaded in dark grey and the metals are in white. The elements shaded in light grey are semi-metals.

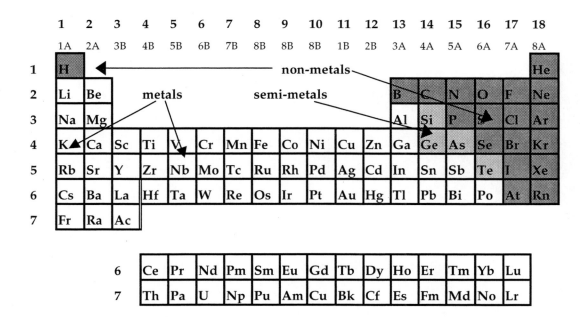

There are two kinds of relationships between the properties of the elements. **Vertical similarities** are those between elements in the same column or group of the periodic table. Vertical similarities are found mostly for properties which are closely related to the electronic structure of the atoms since, as we will see in Chapter 10, elements in the same group have similar electronic configurations of the outermost shell of electrons. For example, the group 14 elements carbon, silicon, germanium, tin and lead all show a valence of four.

Diagonal similarities are those between properties which change from one row to another as well as changing across each row. An example is the metallic character of the elements, to be discussed shortly, and many other examples will be found in the appropriate places throughout the book.

The second row elements, from lithium to neon, represent in many ways the prototype, or paradigm, for the elements of the subsequent rows. Many properties of the heavier elements can be deduced by analogy with those of the more familiar elements of the second row by judicious use of known vertical and diagonal similarities. However, the second row elements are also non-typical in many ways. For example, carbon atoms readily form bonds to other carbon atoms and hydrogen atoms, leading to the whole field of organic chemistry, but the corresponding compounds of silicon are quite different in their chemical properties and instead the characteristic chemistry of silicon is that of silicon-oxygen bonds and mineral silicates. Another difference is that the second row elements form double and triple bonds, which are not common among the elements of the subsequent rows.

The elements can be classified into various categories according to their chemical and physical properties. The classification into metals and non-metals is shown in Table 3-2 and gives a good example of diagonal similarities and trends.

Table 3-3 The names of the common categories of elements

Metals are good electrical conductors. Their surfaces are shiny when clean, but almost all metals corrode when they are exposed to the atmosphere and to moisture. At room temperature, all metals are solids except for mercury, Hg, which is a liquid. Pure metals are malleable, which means that hammering changes the shape of a piece of metal, particularly at high temperature. This behaviour is in contrast to some other solids, which are brittle and break into many pieces when hammered. In combination with other elements, metals form positive ions and take positive oxidation numbers.

Non-metals are found in all three states of matter, solid, liquid and gas. Solid non-metals are electrical insulators and are found in a great variety of crystal forms. In binary chemical compounds with metals, non-metals form negative ions such as chloride Cl^-, oxide O^{2-} and sulfide S^{2-}, but positive oxidation numbers are found in polyatomic anions such as sulfate SO_4^{2-}, nitrate NO_3^- and phosphate PO_4^{3-}. The non-metals are at the right hand side of the table, and are divided from the metals by a diagonal boundary running from boron in the second row down to the bottom right hand corner. Hydrogen is also a non-metal but is placed in group 1 which separates it from the other non-metals; this is because it is logical to place the first element in the first group, but also because hydrogen readily forms positive ions H^+ like the metals of group 1. However under other circumstances hydrogen forms the hydride ion H^- like the negative ions of the non-metals of group 17 such as fluorine and chlorine.

There is a gradation of properties between metals and non-metals, and the distinction between the two groups of elements is not absolutely sharp. Several elements lie on the boundary between the metals and the non-metals, and have both metallic and non-metallic characteristics. Among these elements, which are called **semi-metals**, are the semi-conducting elements silicon and germanium, which are so important in the electronics industry.

Special names are given to some categories of elements. The elements of groups 1, 2, and 12 to 18 (primarily those with the letter A in the older group numbers) are called the **main group elements** or the **representative elements**, and the elements of groups 3 to 11 are called the **transition metals**. The group 12 elements zinc, cadmium and mercury are not transition metals, since none of them forms any compound in which the d-shell (to be discussed in Chapter 10) of the metal atom is unfilled. Some groups of representative elements are given special names, as shown in Table 3-3. On the left hand side of the table are the **alkali metals** (group 1) and the **alkaline earth metals** (group 2). Among the non-metals on the right hand side of the table, the group 18 elements are all gases and are either inert chemically or form only a few compounds, and so they are known as the **noble gases**. Group 17 elements are called the **halogens**, meaning "salt-formers", and the group 16 elements are the **chalcogens**, meaning "chalk-formers".

There is a separate block of elements shown below the main part of the table. The elements of the upper row (elements 58 to 71) are called **lanthanides** because they follow the element lanthanum (element 57), and the elements of the lower row (elements 90 and up) are called the **actinides** because they follow the element actinium (element 89).

3-3 The elements in the earth's crust

The earth's crust, the sea and the atmosphere are the only sources of matter available to us, apart from meteorites and a few samples brought back from the moon, and curiosity leads us to ask which elements are most abundant in our environment. The atmosphere consists almost entirely of oxygen and nitrogen (see table 5-1), and the water in the lakes and oceans consists of hydrogen and oxygen, plus small amounts of other elements in solution.

The rocks and minerals of the earth's crust contain all the naturally occurring elements in varying amounts. The most abundant elements in the earth's crust are oxygen (46 % by mass) and silicon (28 % by mass). Many different types of rock are silicates containing the SiO_4 group of atoms. The next most abundant elements are aluminum (8.2 % by mass) and iron (5.6 %), which are important metals for construction purposes.

Many metals occur in a wide variety of rocks and minerals, although they are recoverable economically only from certain ores.

How were all these the elements made, and what determined their relative abundances? Answering this complicated question requires study of nuclear physics, astrophysics, cosmology, and geology, rather than chemistry. Chemistry and mineralogy help to understand the properties and chemical reactions of the minerals, from which many of the elements are obtained in pure form.

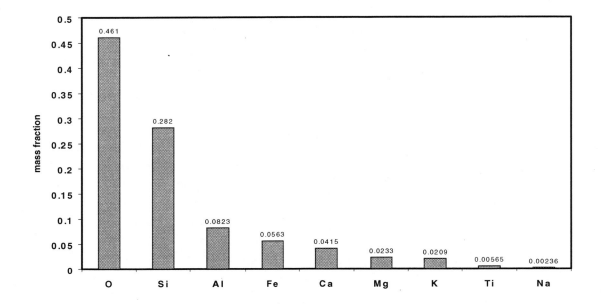

Figure 3-1 The mass fractions of the most abundant elements of the earth's crust.

3-4 Physical properties of the elements

The elements are found in all three states. The gaseous elements are all non-metals: hydrogen, nitrogen, oxygen, fluorine, chlorine, plus the noble gases of group 18. Two elements are liquids under ambient conditions: bromine and mercury. All the other elements are solids.

Some solid elements are found in more than one form under ordinary conditions, notably boron, carbon, sulfur and phosphorus. The different forms are called **allotropes**. Different allotropes of an element have different crystal structures, and the atoms are arranged differently in relation to each other, often as a result of different chemical bonding between the atoms. As a result, two allotropes have different physical properties, and may have different chemical reactivities, even though they contain the same atoms.

As an example, consider the case of carbon. Carbon has three allotropes, of which two, diamond and graphite, have been known for a very long time, while the third allotrope, called buckminsterfullerene, was discovered in the 1980s. The structures of these forms of carbon are shown in Figure 3-2.

Diamond is a very hard, transparent crystalline solid which is an almost perfect electrical insulator; each carbon atom in diamond is bonded to four other carbon atoms in a three-dimensional structure of single bonds.

Graphite is a soft black solid which is a good electrical conductor. It consists of layers of carbon atoms bonded to form hexagonal six-sided rings in a two-dimensional structure; the layers are held together by only relatively weak forces and slide over each other easily; for this reason, graphite is used as a lubricant. Figure 3-3 shows the structure of the surface of a graphite crystal, as seen in a very high resolution microscope.

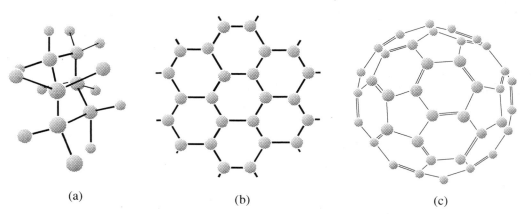

(a)   (b)   (c)

Figure 3-2 The three allotropes of carbon. (a) In diamond each carbon atom is bonded to four nearest neighbours by single bonds in a three dimensional structure. (b) In graphite, each carbon atom is bonded to three nearest neighbours to form a two dimensional hexagonal layer in which all the atoms lie in one plane. The bonds are intermediate in character between single and double bonds. (c) In buckminsterfullerene, each carbon atom is bonded to three other carbon atoms to form a spherical molecule containing 60 carbon atoms. Note that some of the bonds are shown as double bonds and some as single bonds. The bonds form pentagons and hexagons like the panels of a soccer ball.

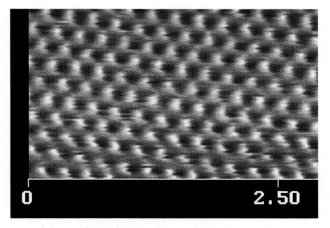

Figure 3-3 An image of the surface of a graphite crystal taken with a scanning tunnelling microscope. Each dark spot corresponds to the centre of a ring of carbon atoms shown in Figure 3-2 (b). Notice that each dark spot is surrounded by a hexagon of six other dark spots. The distance scale along the bottom is in units of nanometres. *Photograph courtesy of Prof. H.Horton, Queen's University.*

Buckminsterfullerene is a molecular solid consisting of spherical molecules of formula C_{60}. The 60 carbon atoms are bonded together with a pattern of chemical bonds similar to the hexagonal (six-sided) and pentagonal (five-sided) panels of a soccer ball; the spherical molecules are packed together to form the crystal. There are other similar molecules containing only carbon atoms, such as C_{70}, forming different but very closely related allotropes.

Many physical properties of the elements are strongly correlated with position in the periodic table. An example is the volume occupied by one mole of the substance, called the **molar volume** V_m. The molar volume of a pure substance can be calculated from the following equation:

$$V_m = \frac{M}{\rho}$$

where V_m is the molar volume, M is the molar mass and ρ is the density. This equation is based upon equation (1-1) in section 1-8. Figure 3-4 shows a graph of molar volume (in cm^3/mol) of the elements versus atomic number. The molar volume of an element reflects the size of the atoms: if the atoms are large, the molar volume is large, and vice-versa.

The peaks in the graph of molar volume occur at the alkali metals, except for the second row element lithium. The repeated minima in the graph at atomic numbers around 26, 43 and 76 correspond to the transition metals. The trend in molar volumes of the lanthanides, numbers 58 to 71 is a smooth decrease in volume apart from an anomaly for europium, number 63. This smooth decrease is called the **lanthanide contraction.**

A graph similar to this was used by the German chemist Lothar Meyer when investigating periodicity of the properties of the elements at about the same time as Mendeleev.

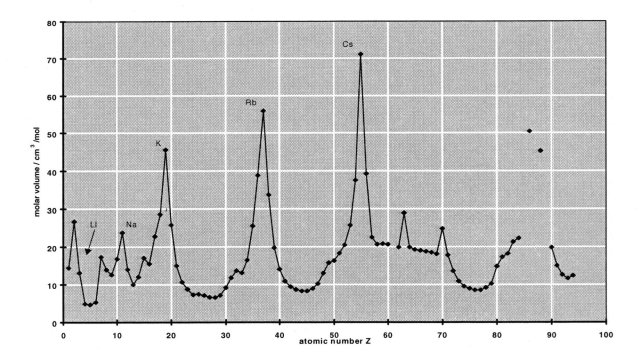

Figure 3-4 The molar volumes of the elements in the solid state plotted as a function of atomic number. The molar volume is given in units of cm^3/mol.

3-5 Chemical properties: oxidation numbers and valence

Most compounds can be broadly classified as **ionic** or **molecular**, although there is a gradation of properties between the two categories and it is not always easy to decide whether or not a given compound is ionic or molecular.

Compounds formed from two non-metals, including the enormous number of organic carbon-containing compounds, are generally molecular rather than ionic. Such compounds usually have low melting points and boiling points.

Compounds of metals with non-metals are generally ionic since metals tend to form positive ions (cations) while non-metals tend to form negative ions (anions). Ionic compounds typically have high melting points and are not volatile. There are, however, some molecular compounds in which metals form covalent bonds to non-metals.

When two metals combine chemically, they may form either (1) a compound with fixed proportions of the elements, or (2) a solid solution with variable composition. Compounds or mixtures of metals are often referred to as **alloys**.

The definition and method of determining **oxidation number** was discussed in Chapter 2, and here we note that there are systematic trends in the oxidation numbers which are found for the elements. For non-metals, the negative oxidation numbers are usually determined simply by the group number. The halogens (group 17) have oxidation numbers of –1 in the halides of metals, and the chalcogens such as oxygen (group 16) normally have oxidation numbers of –2.

For positive oxidation numbers, the maximum oxidation number for an element is equal to the group number for groups 1 to 8 (i.e. the metals at the left hand side of the table) , and the group number minus 10 for groups 13 and above (mostly the non-metals). The transition metals and many non-metals are typically found in a variety of oxidation states, but the maximum oxidation number for an element never exceeds its group number.

Example 3-1 Determine the maximum oxidation numbers of vanadium , manganese and sulfur, and predict the formula of the oxide of each element in which the maximum oxidation number is found.

Vanadium, atomic number 23, lies in group 5, and so the maximum oxidation number is +5. The highest oxide of vanadium has formula V_2O_5.

Manganese, atomic number 25, lies in group 7, and so the maximum oxidation number is +7. The highest oxide of manganese is Mn_2O_7.

Sulfur, atomic number 16, lies in group 16, and so the maximum oxidation number is +6. The highest oxide of sulfur is SO_3.

The **valence** of an element is a measure of its "combining power" in forming compounds with other elements. The **normal valence** of an element is defined as the number of hydrogen atoms that combine with one atom of that element in simple typical compounds. Valence is always a positive number, unlike the oxidation number. The normal valences of the representative elements are closely related to their position in the periodic table, as shown in Table 3-4. The normal valences of the representative elements increase from 1 up to 4 across the first four groups, and then decrease again, reaching zero at the right hand side of the table.

Table 3-4 The hydrogen compounds and normal valences of the representative elements.

Group:	1	2	13	14	15	16	17	18
Row 2:	LiH	BeH_2	B_2H_6	CH_4	NH_3	H_2O	HF	none
Row 3:	NaH	MgH_2	AlH_3	SiH_4	PH_3	H_2S	HCl	none
Row 4:	KH	CaH_2	GaH_3	GeH_4	AsH_3	H_2Se	HBr	none
Normal valence:	1	2	3	4	3	2	1	0

In drawing a structural formula for a molecule, a line is drawn for each valence of an atom. A bond has two ends, and the structures of molecules are usually determined by the need to "satisfy" the normal valences of the atoms bonded together. A single bond is represented by a single line between the symbols for the atoms; examples are found in the structural formulae shown in Table 1-2. Where necessary, two or three lines are drawn to show double or triple bonds, which may be required to satisfy the valences of the atoms bonded together. Examples are oxygen, O=O, nitrogen N≡N and carbon dioxide, CO_2, with structural formula O=C=O.

Non-metals form some compounds in which the valence is larger than the normal value. This is usually found in compounds with oxygen or the halogens, in which the oxidation number of the non-metal is positive. In these cases, the valence is equal to the oxidation number, in most cases. For example, two chlorides of phosphorus are known: phosphorus trichloride PCl_3, and phosphorus pentachloride PCl_5. The valence of phosphorus is 3 in the first compound, and 5 in the second.

Example 3-2 Draw structural formulae for molecules of phosphorus trichloride PCl_3 and phosphorus pentachloride PCl_5.

In both PCl_3 and PCl_5 chlorine has valence 1. Phosphorus has a valence of 3 in PCl_3 and 5 in PCl_5. The structural formulae for these compounds are:

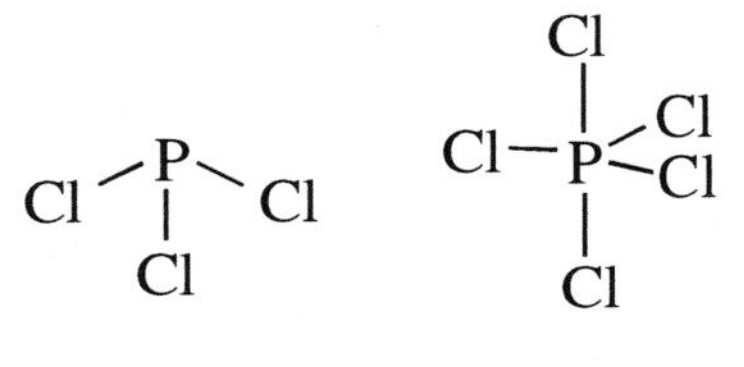

The structures of these molecules are drawn to suggest the relative positions of the atoms. The shapes of molecules such as these will be discussed in Chapter 11.

Example 3-3 Draw a structural formula for formaldehyde CH_2O.

The oxidation number of carbon is 0, but the valence is 4; the valence of oxygen is 2. The following structural formula with a double bond between carbon and oxygen satisfies these valences:

$$\begin{matrix} H \searrow \\ \\ H \nearrow \end{matrix} C = O$$

Example 3-4 Write a structural formula for hydrogen peroxide H_2O_2.

Since hydrogen has an oxidation number of +1, its valence is 1, while the valence of oxygen is 2. These valences are satisfied by the following structural formula in which there is a single bond between the oxygen atoms:

$$\begin{matrix} H \searrow \\ O - O \\ \searrow \\ H \end{matrix}$$

The structure is drawn to suggest the angles between the bonds in the molecule. Notice that the valence of each oxygen atom is 2, but the oxidation number is –1 since the molecule is a peroxide.

The valences of the main group metals are determined by the charges on the ions which they form in simple compounds, which is +1 for group 1 metals (alkali metals), +2 for group 2 metals (alkaline earth metals), and +3 (or sometimes +1) for the group 13 metals.

Example 3-5 Determine the formula for aluminum(III) oxide.

In this compound, oxygen has an oxidation number of –2, and the aluminum(III) ion has oxidation number +3. If the formula is written Al_xO_y, the sum of the oxidation numbers is $+3x-2y$. Since the sum of the oxidation numbers must be zero, it follows that $y/x = 3/2$. Hence the formula is Al_2O_3.

Nearly every element reacts with oxygen to form an **oxide**. The chemical nature of the oxides of the elements varies systematically across the periodic table. The oxides of the metals are characteristically basic. When reacted with water, for instance the oxides of the alkali and alkaline earth metals form basic hydroxides:

$$Na_2O + H_2O \rightarrow 2\,NaOH(aq)$$

$$CaO + H_2O \rightarrow Ca(OH)_2(s)$$

Although calcium hydroxide is only slightly soluble in water, it reacts with acids to give salts, which is the typical reaction of a base.

The oxides of the non-metals are characteristically acidic in nature and when dissolved in water yield acidic solutions:

$$SO_3(g) + H_2O \rightarrow H_2SO_4(aq)$$

$$3\,NO_2(g) + H_2O(l) \rightarrow 2\,HNO_3(aq) + NO(g)$$

The shift from the basic oxides of the alkali metals to the acidic oxides of non-metals across the periodic table is gradual, and the oxides and hydroxides of many metals react both as acids and as bases under appropriate circumstances. For instance, a precipitate of aluminum hydroxide $Al(OH)_3$ dissolves in both acids and bases due to the following reactions:

$$Al(OH)_3(s) + 3\,H^+(aq) \rightarrow Al^{3+}(aq) + 3\,H_2O$$

$$Al(OH)_3(s) + OH^-(aq) \rightarrow Al(OH)_4^-(aq)$$

In the first reaction, $Al(OH)_3(s)$ reacts as a base, and in the second it reacts as an acid.

Key concepts

The periodic table is helpful in developing familiarity with the elements and their properties, and in understanding the nature of their compounds and reactions.

There are similarities and progressions in the chemical and physical properties of the elements, which are correlated with atomic number. The periodic table is a way of listing the elements in order of atomic number so as to illustrate the periodicity in properties, the groups of elements with similar properties, and gradations of properties within groups.

The columns of the table are numbered from 1 to 18 in the modern classification. Elements within each column show many similarities to each other and are called groups. The rows are numbered from 1 to 7, and correspond to different shells in the electronic structure of the atoms.

Elements are classified in several different ways. There are the metals, semi-metals and non-metals. Another classification is into the main group elements, the transition metals, and the lanthanides and actinides. The main groups elements are further subdivided into individual columns: the alkali metals (group 1), the alkaline earth metals (group 2), the chalcogens (group 16), the halogens (group 17) and the noble gases (group 18).

The normal valence of an element is defined as the number of hydrogen atoms that combine with one atom of the element in simple compounds. The normal valence of an element is simply related to its group number in the periodic table. The valence of an element in some compounds may differ from the normal valence. Molecular structures are drawn with lines to represent bonds, and the number and nature of the bonds is determined by the need to "satisfy" the valences of all the atoms.

Further reading

R.T.Sanderson, *Chemical Periodicity* (Reinhold, 1960). A older compendium of descriptive chemistry of elements and simple compounds based on the periodic table.

R.J.Puddephatt and P.K.Monaghan, *The Periodic Table of the Elements* (Oxford Chemistry Series, 1986). A small and readable book on the periodic table.

N.N.Greenwood and A.Earnshaw, *Chemistry of the Elements* (Pergamon Press, 1984). A general reference textbook on inorganic chemistry.

Problems

1. Examine a periodic table and find elements for which the molar mass does not increase smoothly with atomic number.

2. Name two alkali metals, two halogens, two chalcogens, four transition metals, two noble gases.

3. Determine the formulae of the oxides in which the following elements achieve their highest oxidation numbers: boron, phosphorus, antimony, molybdenum, zirconium, tin.

4. In the following polyatomic ions, the first atom in the formula has its highest oxidation number: MnO_4^{n-}, $Cr_2O_7^{n-}$, NO_3^{n-}, CO_3^{n-}, VO_4^{n-}. Determine the charge on each ion, i.e. the value of n.

5. Which metallic elements would you expect to float on water? You may base your answer on the data in Figure 3-4.

6. Draw structures for molecules with the following formulae: CH_4O, CH_5N, $C_2H_4O_2$, C_3H_6, $C_3H_6O_2$, C_3H_8O, C_3H_9N. Make sure that your structures satisfy the normal valences of hydrogen, oxygen, nitrogen and carbon.

7. (a) The density of the radioactive element francium, number 87, is apparently not known and is omitted from the graph in Figure 3-4. From the molar mass suggested in the periodic table, Table 3-1, and the molar volume data summarized in Figure 3-4, estimate the density of francium. [2.5 g cm^{-3}]

8. What is the formulae of francium hydroxide and francium sulfate?

9. To represent the bonding of carbon atoms in graphite, draw an extended sheet of carbon atoms bonded together in hexagons as shown in Figure 3-2 (b). Fill in double bonds so that each carbon atom has its proper valence of four. Is there more than one way of doing this? Can you count how many different ways there are?

10. Notice that in the structure of buckminsterfullerene Figure 3-2 (c), some of the bonds between carbon atoms are shown as single bonds and some are shown as double bonds. Is it possible to draw the double and single bonds in different positions in the molecules? Describe in words the location of the double bonds relative to the pentagons and hexagons. Would you expect the hexagons to be regular, that is with all bond lengths and bond angles equal? What about the pentagons?

11. Nine elements are listed in the diagram in Figure 3-1. What is the total mass fraction of all the other elements of the periodic table in the rocks of the earth's crust? [0.025]

12. The carbon-carbon bond length in graphite, as measured by X-ray diffraction, is 0.142 nanometres. From the image of graphite shown in Figure 3-3 and the distance scale given, measure the carbon-carbon bond length in graphite using a ruler. Hint: measure the distance between the centres of the dark spots, and use the structure in Figure 3-2 to interpret this distance in terms of the carbon-carbon bond length.

13. Consider the newly reported elements with atomic numbers 114, 116 and 118. To what groups of the periodic table would these elements belong?

4 The Chemical Industry

Objectives

After reading this chapter, the student should be able to do the following:

♦ Name some of the important products of the chemical industry.

♦ Identify raw materials from which important chemicals are manufactured.

♦ Illustrate Le Chatelier's principle using industrial examples.

♦ Describe the use of catalysts in industrial processes.

Related topics to review:

Nomenclature, stoichiometry and types of reaction in Chapter 2.

Related topics to look forward to:

Fuels in Chapter 9. Gas phase equilibrium in Chapter 13. Electrochemistry in Chapter 17. Kinetics in Chapter 18.

4-1 The chemical industry

People living in an industrial society consume a lot of goods and services. In the production of these goods and services, which is "industry," and in their sale and distribution, which is "commerce," chemistry has a significant part to play. The chemical industry itself is a large one, with annual sales in Canada of approximately $25 billion dollars, and is too diverse and large a subject for detailed study at this point. However a discussion of some of the reactions and processes used in the chemical industry serve well to illustrate points in elementary chemistry, as well as indicating the importance of chemistry in an industrial society.

Many other industries depend on chemistry or chemical technology. The mineral processing industry and the petroleum industry both use many chemical techniques in processing huge amounts of raw materials into valuable products used by other industries and consumers. The pharmaceutical industry depends upon sophisticated organic chemistry to produce drugs and medical supplies. The polymer, or plastics, industry is based on chemistry, but is a consumer rather than a producer of chemicals, and the same can be said for the paper industry. Chemistry is involved in the production of explosives and propellants for the military forces and the mining industry. Industrial activities often affect the natural environment adversely, and chemistry plays a central role in identifying and treating environmental problems.

There are two main subdivisions of the chemical manufacturing industry: the **heavy chemical** industry, which produces chemicals in very large amounts, and the **fine chemical** industry, which produces chemicals in much smaller amounts, but in higher states of purity. The chemical industry in Canada constitutes about 7% of all manufacturing in terms of the value of goods shipped. Chemical exports from Canada exceed chemical imports, so the industry makes a positive contribution to the balance of trade. Table 4-1 contains figures for the annual North American production in 1997 of some of the more important chemicals that are produced on a large scale.

In this chapter we discuss the processes used in producing several important chemicals. The purpose of doing this is, first, to learn something about how chemicals are produced industrially, and second, to provide practical examples of the reactions that were discussed in Chapter 2.

Table 4-1 North American production of some heavy chemicals in 1997

Units: 10^6 tonnes (Mt)

Inorganic chemicals	Canada	U.S.	Organic chemicals	Canada	U.S.
Sulfuric Acid H_2SO_4	4.10	43.4	Ethylene C_2H_4	3.27	23.2
Ammonia NH_3	4.78	17.4	Propylene C_3H_6	0.86	12.5
Chlorine Cl_2	1.04	11.8	Ethylene dichloride $C_2H_4Cl_2$	n/a	11.9
Sodium hydroxide $NaOH$	1.08	10.3	Urea $(NH_2)_2CO$	3.47	7.05
Nitric acid HNO_3	1.01	8.24	Benzene C_6H_6	0.72	1.06
Ammonium nitrate NH_4NO_3	0.98	7.50			

n/a = not available.

Canadian data adapted from "Industrial Chemicals and Synthetic Resins", Statistics Canada Catalogue No. 46-002, December 1997, page 2. U.S. data reprinted with permission from Chemical and Engineering News, 29 June 1998, volume 76, no. 26, pp 43,44.

4-2 Sulfuric acid

Sulfuric acid is produced in immense quantities and is used in a wide variety of other industries. Some industries, such as the phosphate fertiliser industry, use sulfuric acid in very large quantities. Other industries use it in small amounts, but nevertheless depend upon a ready supply at low cost.

The raw material for sulfuric acid manufacture is the element sulfur, which is derived from three sources. Sulfur occurs in the form of mineral deposits of the pure element; the major North American deposits are on the Gulf coast of the United States. Sulfur is also found in the form of the smelly and poisonous gas hydrogen sulfide, H_2S, in some natural gas wells. Natural gas consists mostly of methane, CH_4. Natural gas contaminated with H_2S is described as "sour," and the H_2S must be removed before the gas is distributed for use as a fuel. Large amounts of sulfur are produced in Alberta from this source.

Minerals containing sulfides of metals such as nickel and copper are the third source of sulfur. When sulfide minerals are heated in contact with oxygen, the gases from the furnaces contain sulfur dioxide, SO_2, which in former times was vented to the atmosphere and caused environmental damage through "acid rain." As part of the effort to control this source of pollution, the SO_2 is now largely removed from the furnace gases and either sold in liquid form or converted at once to sulfuric acid. A large fraction of the sulfuric acid made in Canada is made directly or indirectly from metal sulfides.

There are three major steps in the manufacturing process: the production of sulfur dioxide, SO_2; the conversion of SO_2 to sulfur trioxide, SO_3; and the reaction of SO_3 with water to give sulfuric acid, H_2SO_4. Starting from either sulfur, hydrogen sulfide or a sulfide ore, SO_2 is produced by reaction with oxygen in reactions such as the following:

$$S(s) + O_2(g) \rightarrow SO_2(g)$$

$$2 H_2S(g) + 3 O_2(g) \rightarrow 2 SO_2(g) + 2 H_2O(g)$$

$$2 Cu_2S(s) + 3 O_2(g) \rightarrow 2 Cu_2O(s) + 2 SO_2(g)$$

The first two of these reactions produce a large amount of heat, which is used for the production of steam for use elsewhere in the plant.

Figure 4-1 A view of the Inco sulfuric acid plant at Sudbury, Ontario. The plant has a rated capacity of 2900 tonnes of sulfuric acid per day. The size of the pipes can be judged from the size of the man standing in the doorway at the right of the picture. *(Photograph courtesy of Inco Limited.)*

The oxidation of SO_2 to SO_3 is an example of chemical equilibrium in a mixture of gases:

$$SO_2\,(g) + \tfrac{1}{2}\,O_2\,(g) \rightleftharpoons SO_3(g)$$

The reaction goes almost to completion at low temperatures, but under these conditions the reaction takes place too slowly for the process to be economical. The reaction proceeds faster at a higher temperature but because the reaction as written produces heat, the position of equilibrium shifts to the left at higher temperature, reducing the yield of SO_3. This is in accord with Le Chatelier's principle, discussed in section 2-5. The equilibrium can be shifted back to the right by raising the pressure of the reacting mixture. The reaction can also be speeded up by passing the reaction mixture over a catalyst, which increases the rate of the reaction without altering the position of the equilibrium. Use of a catalyst to increase the rate of the reaction means that the temperature can be kept lower for the same rate of reaction, and the position of equilibrium is more favourable to the production of SO_3.

The choice of operating conditions must be a compromise between the requirements of high speed of reaction and favourable position of the chemical equilibrium. The reaction produces enough heat to raise the temperature of the reacting mixture above the optimum, and the temperature of the reacting mixture is controlled by heat exchangers which remove this heat.

The final step in the manufacture is the reaction of SO_3 with water,

$$SO_3(g) + H_2O(\ell) \rightarrow H_2SO_4(aq)$$

There are practical difficulties in carrying out this apparently simple step. If the SO_3 is brought into contact with water, a mist of sulfuric acid solution is formed which is impossible to handle. This can be avoided by dissolving the SO_3 in either pure H_2SO_4, to form a solution called **oleum**, or in a very concentrated (98%) aqueous solution of H_2SO_4, which can be subsequently diluted.

The prime use for H_2SO_4 is in the production of phosphate fertilizers. Phosphate rock is the largest primary source of phosphorus and consists mostly of calcium phosphate $Ca_3(PO_4)_2$. This salt is insoluble in water, and, in order to make the phosphate ion available for use in the soil by plants, it must be converted to a salt which is soluble in water. Addition of sulfuric acid to phosphate rock results in several chemical reactions, but in simple terms the following reaction takes place, forming hydrated calcium dihydrogen phosphate (which is soluble in water) and hydrated calcium sulfate:

$$Ca_3(PO_4)_2(s) + 2H_2SO_4(aq) + 5\ H_2O(\lambda) \rightarrow Ca(H_2PO_4)_2.H_2O(s) + 2CaSO_4.2H_2O(s)$$

This is the main reaction in the conversion of phosphate rock to superphosphate, an important fertilizer. Superphosphate production accounts for more than half of the total annual production of sulfuric acid, and consequently production of sulfuric acid is closely related to the state of the fertilizer industry, and hence to the state of agricultural markets of the world.

4-3 Ammonia

The production of ammonia, NH_3, nitric acid, HNO_3, and related chemicals is known collectively as the **nitrogen industry**. Ammonia is used for the production of agricultural nitrogenous fertilizer and of explosives. Before the development of the synthetic ammonia process early in the twentieth century, compounds of nitrogen were derived mostly from the salt sodium nitrate, $NaNO_3$, which is found as a mineral on the west coast of South America.

The production of nitrogen compounds for use as explosives and fertilizers using nitrogen in the air was an important objective for the chemical industry in the nineteenth century. In 1914, when the first World War began, Germany was cut off from supplies of nitrate minerals from South America and would have quickly run out of explosives without a synthetic source of nitrogen-containing compounds. The German chemist F. Haber had been studying the synthesis of ammonia from nitrogen and hydrogen, and his work had reached the stage where a practical large scale process for ammonia production could be developed. Within a short time a large plant was installed using the Haber process, and then the production of explosives and nitrogenous fertilizers could proceed without a supply of mineral nitrates. The use of the Haber process extended worldwide after the war ended, and the nitrogen industry is now entirely based upon the synthetic production of ammonia.

There are two main parts to the ammonia synthesis process. First, a mixture of nitrogen and hydrogen must be prepared from natural gas and air and the second step is the synthesis of ammonia from its elements. Ammonia plants in Canada are situated primarily in Alberta, close to the source of natural gas which is the major raw material.

Hydrogen is obtained from methane and steam in a two-stage process. In the first stage methane reacts with steam in the presence of a catalyst to produce carbon monoxide and hydrogen:

$$CH_4(g) + H_2O(g) \rightarrow CO(g) + 3\ H_2(g)$$

This reaction is called **steam reforming** of the hydrocarbon. Carbon monoxide is a reducing agent, and it reacts further with steam to produce more hydrogen:

$$CO(g) + H_2O(g) \rightarrow CO_2(g) + H_2(g).$$

This reaction is called **shift conversion**. The overall reaction between steam and methane is the sum of the two steps.

$$CH_4(g) + 2 H_2O(g) \rightarrow CO_2(g) + 4 H_2(g).$$

Nitrogen is obtained by adding air to the mixture. Oxygen from the air reacts with methane left over from the previous stages to produce more CO_2 and water:

$$CH_4(g) + 2 O_2(g) \rightarrow CO_2(g) + 2 H_2O(g)$$

Nitrogen does not react and remains in the gas stream. Carbon dioxide, which is acidic, is removed from the gas stream by reaction with a solution of a base such as potassium carbonate,

$$CO_2(g) + H_2O(\ell) + K_2CO_3(s) \rightarrow 2 KHCO_3(aq)$$

and water is removed by condensation. After this treatment the gas stream contains only nitrogen and hydrogen, and by adjustment of the proportions of steam, methane and air, the proportions of hydrogen and nitrogen can be adjusted to the 3:1 ratio needed for ammonia synthesis. Such a gas mixture is called **synthesis gas**.

Starting from a mixture of nitrogen and hydrogen, the synthesis of ammonia is chemically simple, but sophisticated technology is required to put it into practice because of the need for high temperature, high pressure and a catalyst. The reaction is:

$$N_2(g) + 3 H_2(g) \rightleftharpoons 2 NH_3(g)$$

When nitrogen, hydrogen and ammonia are in equilibrium at low temperatures, the position of equilibrium lies far to the right, favouring the formation of ammonia from its elements. However, at low temperatures the reaction is too slow for the process to be practical. Raising the temperature accelerates the reaction. But because the reaction generates heat, a higher temperature moves the position of equilibrium to the left, in accordance with Le Chatelier's principle. At temperatures high enough for the reaction to be reasonably fast, the equilibrium mixture contains very little ammonia. A practical process for ammonia production depends upon two more features.

First, according to Le Chatelier's principle, the production of ammonia is favoured by compressing the gas mixture to high pressure, since the reaction reduces the amount of gas from 4 moles on the left to 2 moles on the right. Ammonia production requires compression of large amounts of gas to high pressures – up to 1000 times atmospheric pressure in some plants. Second, catalysts have been developed which make the reaction fast enough to be economical without using extremes of temperature and pressure. The choice of temperature, pressure and catalyst for the synthesis reaction is made on the basis of minimizing the cost of the final product.

Ammonia is sometimes used directly as fertilizer. However, large amounts of ammonia are converted to other compounds for fertilizer and for other uses. The first stage of the conversion is the manufacture of nitric acid.

4-4 Nitric acid

Nitric acid, HNO_3, is manufactured from ammonia by the **Ostwald** process. The first step is the oxidation of ammonia in the presence of a catalyst to produce nitric oxide, NO, which is then further oxidized to nitrogen dioxide, NO_2:

$$4 NH_3(g) + 5 O_2(g) \rightarrow 4 NO(g) + 6 H_2O(g)$$

$$NO(g) + \tfrac{1}{2} O_2(g) \rightarrow NO_2(g).$$

In the final stage, NO_2 gas reacts with water:

$$3\ NO_2(g) + H_2O(\ell) \rightarrow 2\ HNO_3(aq) + NO(g)$$

This is a disproportionation reaction in which the oxidation number of N changes from +4 in NO_2 to two different values, +5 in HNO_3 and +2 in nitric oxide NO. The nitric oxide NO produced in the last reaction is recycled to the preceding oxidation step to produce more NO_2.

From ammonia (which is a base) and nitric acid, a variety of ammonium salts and nitrate salts can be manufactured. Ammonium salts are made by reaction of ammonia with the appropriate acid. For example, ammonium sulfate is produced in large amounts using sulfuric acid:

$$2\ NH_3(g) + H_2SO_4(aq) \rightarrow (NH_4)_2SO_4(aq).$$

Nitrate salts are made by reaction of nitric acid with the appropriate base:

$$K_2CO_3(aq) + 2\ HNO_3(aq) \rightarrow 2\ KNO_3(aq) + CO_2(g) + H_2O(\ell)$$

The largest production of salts of this type is of ammonium nitrate itself:

$$NH_3(aq) + HNO_3(aq) \rightarrow NH_4NO_3(aq)$$

Ammonium nitrate is widely used as a fertilizer for supplying nitrogen to the soil, and as such it is commonly handled in very large amounts. It is also a powerful explosive. When heated or given a sudden shock it can decompose explosively with the release of energy and the formation of a large volume of gas. This combination of properties has led to some immense accidental explosions of fertilizer in ships and storage facilities, as well as a number of terrorist explosions.

4-5 Limestone products: lime and soda ash

Limestone is a common type of rock composed largely of calcium and magnesium carbonates. It is used as a building material itself, for the manufacture of cement, and as the raw material for the manufacture of two important heavy chemicals. When limestone (which we can regard as pure $CaCO_3$) is heated above about 900°C it decomposes to give CO_2 and calcium oxide, CaO, a process called **calcination**:

$$CaCO_3(s) \rightarrow CaO(s) + CO_2(g)$$

Calcium oxide is commonly called **quicklime**, or simply **lime**. Quicklime reacts vigorously with water to produce calcium hydroxide, $Ca(OH)_2$, which is called **slaked lime**. Both forms of lime are sold and used in the building industry for making mortar, and in many other parts of the chemical industry. Slaked lime is sometimes used in the form of a suspension of fine particles of precipitated calcium hydroxide in water, called "milk of lime".

Limestone is also the starting point for the **Solvay** process for manufacturing the important industrial chemical sodium carbonate, Na_2CO_3, commonly called **soda ash**. The overall chemical reaction is:

$$CaCO_3(s) + 2\ NaCl(aq) \rightarrow Na_2CO_3(s) + CaCl_2(aq).$$

Despite the apparent simplicity of the reaction shown above, there are several steps to the process. Limestone is calcined to CO_2 and CaO, which is converted to slaked lime $Ca(OH)_2$ as described above. A concentrated solution of common salt, NaCl, is treated with ammonia and carbon dioxide, and sodium bicarbonate, $NaHCO_3$, precipitates from the solution. The net reaction can be represented by the following equation:

$$NH_3(g) + CO_2(g) + Na^+(aq) + H_2O(\ell) \rightarrow NaHCO_3(s) + NH_4^+(aq)$$

The sodium bicarbonate is filtered off, and heated to produce sodium carbonate, or soda ash:

$$2\,NaHCO_3(s) \rightarrow Na_2CO_3(s) + H_2O(\ell) + CO_2(g)$$

There are two steps in which materials are recycled. Firstly, the carbon dioxide produced in the last step is recovered and dissolved in more brine in the preceding step. Secondly, the solution containing NH_4^+, which remains after the sodium bicarbonate is precipitated, is treated with the basic slaked lime produced from the calcined limestone. The resulting acid-base reaction converts the ammonium ion to ammonia:

$$2\,NH_4^+(aq) + Ca(OH)_2(s) \rightarrow 2\,NH_3(g) + Ca^{2+}(aq) + 2\,H_2O(\ell)$$

The ammonia used in the process is all recovered in the last step and recycled.

Soda ash is used industrially as a base, and large amounts are used to manufacture soap and glass. In the U.S., soda ash is presently obtained from mineral sources, but the Solvay process is still used in other parts of the world since mineral sources of soda ash are limited compared with the available supplies of raw materials for the Solvay process.

4-6 The electrolytic chlorine-alkali industry

Chlorine, Cl_2, and caustic soda or sodium hydroxide, NaOH, are produced simultaneously by the electrolysis of a solution of NaCl. The process is summarized in the following chemical equation:

$$NaCl(aq) + H_2O(\ell) \rightarrow NaOH(aq) + \tfrac{1}{2}\,H_2(g) + \tfrac{1}{2}\,Cl_2(g).$$

The process requires a cheap and reliable source of electrical energy, and so most of the factories are situated near large hydroelectric power generators.

There are three main types of electrolytic cell in use. In the **diaphragm cell**, the anode and cathode are on opposite sides of a porous barrier, which keeps the products separate. At the anode, chloride ions are oxidized to chlorine gas:

$$Cl^-(aq) \rightarrow \tfrac{1}{2}\,Cl_2(g) + e^-$$

At the cathode, water is reduced to hydrogen gas, and hydroxide ions are produced:

$$H_2O(\ell) + e^- \rightarrow \tfrac{1}{2}\,H_2(g) + OH^-(aq)$$

Gaseous chlorine and hydrogen bubble out of the solution at the anode and cathode respectively. Sodium ions, hydroxide ions and some chloride ions remain in the solution in the cathode compartment. When this solution is evaporated, NaCl precipitates, leaving a solution of caustic soda. Solid caustic soda is isolated by further evaporation. In the **membrane cell**, an ion-exchange membrane is used in place of the porous barrier and apart from some details of operation, the chemistry of this cell is similar to that of the diaphragm cell.

The second type of electrolytic cell is the **mercury cell** in which the cathode is made of liquid mercury metal, but the overall reaction is the same as in the diaphragm cell. Until fairly recently, substantial quantities of mercury were released into rivers each year because of careless operation of mercury cells. Although this source of mercury pollution has been almost entirely eliminated, mercury which has already been released to the environment may remain as a hazard to people and wildlife for a long time to come.

Chlorine and caustic soda are both used in a wide variety of industrial chemical operations, as well as in the plastics, soap and paper industries. Since they are produced simultaneously, the markets for these substances are closely linked together. The hydrogen produced as a by-product is used for making ammonia and other chemicals.

Chapter 4

4-7 Ethylene

Oil refineries handle vast amounts of petroleum, which consists mostly of hydrocarbons. Petroleum is processed into fuels, lubricants and solvents, which are usually not refined to a state of high chemical purity. However the petrochemical industry uses materials derived from petroleum for the manufacture of a variety of pure chemicals. Ethylene, C_2H_4, is the starting point for much of this industry.

Petroleum consists mostly of alkanes, i.e. saturated hydrocarbons in which all the carbon-carbon bonds are single bonds. Alkenes, also known as olefins, are hydrocarbons containing double bonds; the simplest alkene is ethene, with formula $H_2C=CH_2$. In industry, ethene is commonly known by its older name, ethylene. Alkenes are not found in significant concentrations in petroleum or natural gas, and must be manufactured.

Ethylene is produced by **cracking** or **pyrolysis** reactions starting from the alkanes ethane and propane, which are obtained from natural gas. The ethane or propane is passed at high speed through a very hot tube, and ethylene is formed by decomposition of ethane and propane at high temperature:

$$H_3C–CH_3(g) \quad \rightarrow \quad H_2C=CH_2(g) \quad + \quad H_2(g)$$

$$H_3C–CH_2–CH_3(g) \quad \rightarrow \quad H_2C=CH_2(g) \quad + \quad CH_4(g)$$

Propylene is also produced from propane in the following reaction:

$$H_3C–CH_2–CH_3(g) \quad \rightarrow \quad H_2C=CH–CH_3(g) \quad + \quad H_2(g)$$

The ethylene is separated from the reaction mixture by distillation.

As part of the process of refining and upgrading of petroleum to produce gasoline, cracking reactions are also carried out on longer chain alkanes, C_5 and up, in order to convert them to shorter chain alkanes. These reactions produce olefins as well, and so oil refineries produce large amounts of ethylene and propylene.

The largest use for ethylene is the production of the polymer called polyethylene. This is formed from ethylene at high pressure in the presence of a catalyst. The double bonds in the unsaturated hydrocarbon molecules are rearranged to form single bonds between the carbon atoms in very long chains:

$$.... + H_2C=CH_2 + H_2C=CH_2 + ... \rightarrow \quad .... – CH_2 – CH_2 – CH_2 – CH_2 – .....$$

Many petrochemicals are produced from ethylene. One example is ethylene glycol, used for antifreeze in automobile cooling systems. The first step in its manufacture is the controlled oxidation of ethylene. Ethylene, like other hydrocarbons, burns in air to form carbon dioxide and water. However, if ethylene and oxygen are reacted at low temperature in the presence of a suitable catalyst, the cyclic compound ethylene oxide is formed instead:

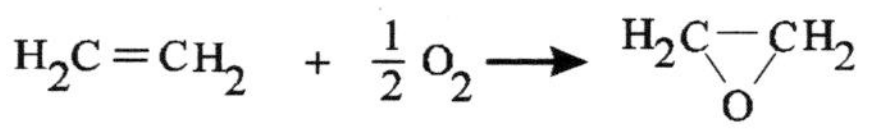

$$H_2C=CH_2 \quad + \quad \tfrac{1}{2}O_2 \longrightarrow \quad H_2C\overset{}{\underset{O}{-}}CH_2$$

Ethylene oxide is a very versatile "intermediate," which can be used to make a number of other products. To make ethylene glycol, $(CH_2OH)_2$, it is reacted with water:

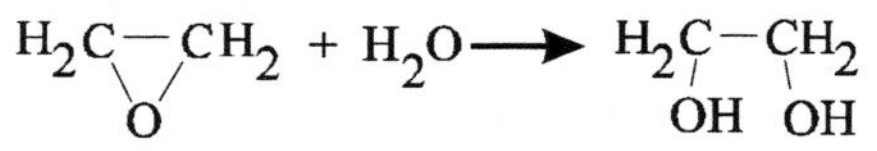

$$H_2C\overset{}{\underset{O}{-}}CH_2 + H_2O \longrightarrow H_2C\underset{OH}{-}\,CH_2 \atop OH$$

Ethylene glycol is used as antifreeze in automobile engines because a concentrated solution of ethylene glycol in water has a much lower freezing point than pure water and can be used as a liquid coolant for car and truck engines operating in cold climates.

Ethyl alcohol or ethanol, C_2H_5OH, is used for many industrial purposes in addition to its use in beverages. It is produced in large amounts by fermentation of sucrose and starch, but it is also manufactured from ethylene by reaction with steam in the presence of a catalyst:

$$C_2H_4(g) + H_2O(g) \rightarrow C_2H_5OH(g)$$

4-8 Catalysis

In several discussions of industrial chemical processes in this chapter, the use of a catalyst was mentioned. A catalyst is a substance that increases the rate of approach to equilibrium of a chemical reaction without itself being substantially consumed in the reaction. A catalyst does not alter the position of a chemical reaction but increases the rate of the reaction leading towards equilibrium. Catalysts are important in industrial processes for several reasons. First, and most obviously, if a reaction is faster then a greater amount of product can be obtained per unit time for a given size of reactor. In some cases the reaction in the absence of a catalyst is so slow that, in effect, it does not take place at all. Secondly, for a reaction in which a lower temperature changes the equilibrium so as to favour the products, use of a catalyst allows the reaction to be run at a lower temperature so as to obtain more of the product of the reaction without reducing the speed of the reaction. Thirdly, several different reactions may be possible starting from the reactants. If this is the case, then the use of a suitable catalyst may make one reaction much faster than all the other reactions. In this way, the reaction leading to a single desired product can be selected from the competing reactions.

There are two broad categories of catalyst. A **heterogeneous** catalyst is in a different physical state from the reaction mixture, usually the solid state. Transition metals in the form of fine powders are commonly used as catalysts: nickel, palladium, platinum, iron, copper. The powdered metals may also be "supported" on the surface of another solid or porous material which does not itself take part in the catalytic process. Many metal oxides are also active as catalysts; examples are Cr_2O_3, V_2O_5 and mixed oxides of iron and molybdenum. The treatment and surface condition of a solid catalyst are important in controlling its effectiveness, and the details of the preparation of commercially important catalysts are often not published. Solid catalysts are thought to work by inducing structural changes in the reactant molecules that are temporarily attached to the surface, making the molecules more reactive.

A **homogeneous** catalyst is a substance dissolved in the reacting mixture. Some reactions are catalysed by acids, some by bases, and some by compounds of the transition metals. In biological systems, **enzymes** accelerate specific reactions and provide the selectivity that is needed to perform specific biological functions.

The specific mechanisms by which homogeneous catalysts work vary enormously, but the process can be summarized in general by the following general reaction scheme. A reactant molecule R combines with a catalyst molecule C to form a "complex" RC in which R and C are temporarily bonded together:

$$R + C \rightarrow RC$$

The molecule RC then decomposes to form the product P plus the original catalyst C:

$$RC \rightarrow P + C$$

The catalyst C is regenerated in the second reaction, and can then take part in the first reaction again. In this way, the catalyst is not used up as the reaction proceeds, and hence a small amount of catalyst can convert a much larger amount of reactant into the product. The structure of the molecule RC depends of course on the specific reactant R and the catalyst C.

These reactions can be combined to show more clearly how the catalyst is recycled:

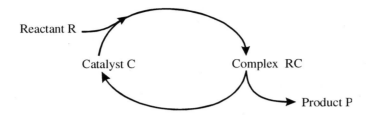

Catalysis is the subject of very active research, partly because of its commercial importance, but also because it provides insight into the actual processes by which chemical reactions take place.

Key concepts

The chemical industry is an important part of the modern economy, and provides many examples of useful and interesting applications of chemistry. The heavy chemical industry produces both inorganic and organic chemical compounds in very large quantities, usually for use in other industries. Many of the reactions are simple, but some knowledge of the chemical reactions involved in producing each compound is helpful in understanding the economic, geographical and historical aspects of the chemical industry.

Catalysts are substances that make reactions go faster, and are of great importance in chemical industry because they make processes more efficient.

Further Reading

Several books giving broad surveys of the chemical industry are listed below.

Chemical Process Industries, by R.N. Shreve and J.A. Brink. 5th edition. McGraw-Hill, 1984.

Riegel's Handbook of Industrial Chemistry. J.A.Kent, editor. Van Nostrand, 1992.

Industrial Organic Chemicals in Perspective. Part I. H.A.Witkoff and B.G.Reuben. John Wiley, 1980.

Industrial Organic Chemicals in Perspective. Part II. H.A.Witkoff and B.G.Reuben. Kreiger, 1991.

Accounts of current trends in the chemical industry are to be found in magazines such as "Chemical and Engineering News" published in the U.S., "Chemistry and Industry" and "Chemistry in Britain" published in the United Kingdom, and "Canadian Chemical News." Statistics on Canadian production and related data are published regularly in government publications such as Statistics Canada Report 46-002. Information is also available from the Canadian Chemical Producers Association. (www.ccpa.ca)

Problems

1. What mass of sulfur is used in producing one million (1.0x10⁶) tonnes of sulfuric acid? [0.33 Mt]

2. Which raw material is used both in the manufacture of ammonia and the manufacture of ethylene?

3. Which raw material is used both in the manufacture of sodium carbonate by the Solvay process and the manufacture of chlorine by the electrolytic process.

4. Consider an ammonia synthesis plant which produces 1.2 kilotonne/day and operates for 284 days per year. Calculate the following quantities for one year. Assume that air has a composition of 80. % N_2 and 20. % O_2 by mole.

    (a) The amount and the mass of NH_3 produced.   [2.00×10^{10} mol, 341 kt]

    (b) The amount and the mass of N_2 which must be prepared.   [1.00×10^{10} mol, 280 kt]

    (c) The amount and the mass of CH_4 consumed in N_2 production.   [0.125×10^{10} mol, 20.0 kt]

    (d) The amount and the mass of H_2 which must be prepared.   [3.00×10^{10} mol, 60.5 kt]

    (e) The amount and the mass of CH_4 consumed in H_2 production.   [0.75×10^{10} mol, 120. kt]

5. A chlorine plant produces 20. kilotonnes of chlorine per annum in electrolytic diaphragm cells, as described in Section 4-6.

    (a) Calculate the average current in the electrolytic cells, assuming that there are no losses.

       [1.7 MA]

    (b) Calculate the mass of sodium hydroxide which is produced per annum.   [23 kt]

    (c) Calculate the mass of hydrogen that is produced per annum.   [0.57 kt]

    (d) Calculate the mass of ammonia that could be produced per annum from the hydrogen generated in the plant, and compare with the output of the plant that was described in Question 3.   [3.2 kt]

6. The following are some of the reactions that may take place when sulfides of copper, iron and nickel are treated with oxygen at high temperature. In each case, determine the oxidation numbers of all elements and determine which are reduced and which oxidized in each reaction.

$$CuS + \tfrac{1}{2} O_2 \rightarrow \tfrac{1}{2} Cu_2S + \tfrac{1}{2} SO_2$$

$$Cu_2S + 3/2\, O_2 \rightarrow Cu_2O + SO_2$$

$$FeS_2 + O_2 \rightarrow FeS + SO_2$$

$$FeS + 3/2\, O_2 \rightarrow FeO + SO_2$$

$$Ni_3S_2 + 7/2\, O_2 \rightarrow 3\, NiO + 2\, SO_2$$

7. What mass of ethylene is required to produce a kilogram of ethylene glycol?   [0.455 kg]

8. A sample of polyethylene is found to have an average molar mass of 2.0×10^5 g mol^{-1}. How many carbon atoms and how many hydrogen atoms are there in each molecule, on average? You may assume that the empirical formula of the polymer is CH_2.

    [1.4×10^4 C atoms, 2.8×10^4 H atoms]

9. Draw a structural formula for part of a molecule of polypropylene.

10. Locate recent data for production of several chemicals not listed in Table 4-1, in the Government Documents section of the library. Find the appropriate issue of Chemical and Engineering News, published in June of each year, to find data on the same chemicals in the U.S., Europe and Japan.

Chapter 4

5   Gases

Objectives

After reading this chapter, the student should be able to do the following:

♦   State the laws of Boyle, Charles and Avogadro.

♦   Make calculations of the bulk properties of gases using the ideal gas equation.

♦   Define partial pressures in a mixture of gases, and state Dalton's law.

♦   Interpret the gas laws in terms of molecular motion.

♦   Make calculations of the bulk properties of gases using van der Waals equation.

Related topics to review:

States of matter in Chapter 1.

Related topics to look forward to:

Relationship between the states of matter in Chapter 7. Gas phase equilibrium in Chapter 13. Thermodynamics of gases in Chapter 16.

5-1 The nature of gases

The three states of matter are gas, liquid and solid. As compared with the other states of matter, a **gas** has low density, is easily compressed, and expands to fill all the space available. Many substances are found in the gaseous state under ordinary or ambient conditions. Among the elements, all the elements of Group 18 (He, Ne, Ar, Kr and Xe) and the light non-metals hydrogen, oxygen, nitrogen, fluorine and chlorine are gases. Many compounds with low molar mass are gases, some examples being CO_2, CO, SO_2, NH_3, CH_4 and other light hydrocarbons; a notable exception is H_2O, which is a liquid at room temperature.

Air is the most familiar gas because we are surrounded by it and breath it constantly. It is a mixture consisting mostly of nitrogen, which is chemically fairly inert, and oxygen, which plays an essential role in providing energy in animals through oxidation processes. The composition of dry air is given in Table 5-1 as the volume fraction, which (as we will see later in this chapter) is equivalent to the mole fraction.

Table 5-1   The composition of dry air by volume

Major gases	% by volume	Minor gases	ppm by volume
N_2	78.084	CO_2	360
O_2	20.946	Ne	18
Ar	0.934	He	5
		CH_4	2

All gases condense to form a liquid or a solid when cooled, and liquids with a free surface evaporate to some extent to form a vapour. For instance, air in the atmosphere always contains a certain amount of water vapour, and the data in Table 5-1 refer to air from which the water vapour has been removed. The word **vapour** usually means a gas that is easily condensed by cooling. In the present chapter, we discuss the properties of gases in which the temperature is not too low and the pressure not too high. In Chapter 7 we will discuss the phenomenon of condensation and deviations from simple "ideal" gas behaviour induced by extremes of temperature and pressure.

A **vacuum** is a space from which almost all gas has been removed by pumping out air and other gases. Vacuum technology is used in producing television tubes and semiconductors, and in many experiments in chemistry and physics. In the chemical industry, many processes involve gases and require the use of large pumps, compressors and pipes, as we saw in Chapter 4.

A completely closed container is required for storage of a gas, or for maintaining a vacuum. The storage vessel must not have any leaks and must be strong enough to resist any pressure difference between the inside and the outside. For samples of gas at ordinary pressures, glass bulbs or tubes can be used. Gases can also be stored at high pressure in steel cylinders equipped with valves and connections for attachment to other apparatus. Many gases are sold commercially in such cylinders and are used in laboratory work.

In the laboratory, gas samples can be collected, and the volume measured, by displacement of water under an inverted tube. An example of the procedure was seen in Figure 2-3. In that experiment, gases evolved in electrolysis are collected under inverted burets, which were initially filled with water. Gases collected in this way are contaminated by water vapour, and some of the gas is lost if it is soluble in water; this procedure is therefore not suitable for accurate work.

Gas samples can also be collected in metal or glass bulbs and syringes such as those shown in Figure 5-1. A bulb with a single stopcock connection can be used if the bulb is first evacuated with a vacuum pump and then connected to the source of gas. A sample of a gas can be collected bulb with a double connection by allowing the gas to flow through the bulb, sweeping out the air or other gas that initially occupied the bulb. This procedure avoids the need for a vacuum pump. Gas samples can be collected or delivered using a syringe, which is a cylinder equipped with a sliding piston.

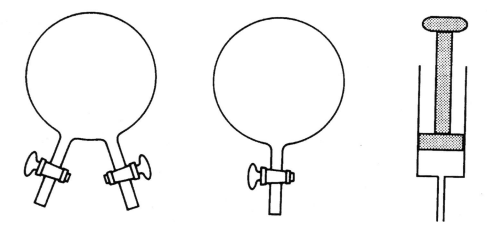

Figure 5-1 Two types of bulb and a syringe used for collecting samples of gases.

Like any other form of matter, the mass of a sample of gas contained in a suitable vessel can be weighed by difference. A precise balance is needed, for gases have such low density that the mass of the gas is much less than the mass of the bulb. Corrections for the buoyancy of the bulb in air should be considered in weighing a gas sample; such corrections can be safely ignored when weighing solid or liquid samples. When the bulb is filled with air at atmospheric pressure (whether the stopcock is open or not), the measured mass of the bulb is equal to the mass of the glass or metal of the bulb. But if the bulb is evacuated when it is weighed, the measured mass is less than the mass of the bulb by the mass of the air originally in the bulb. Another way to say this is that the measured mass of the evacuated bulb is reduced by a buoyancy correction equal to the mass of air displaced by the entire volume of the sealed bulb.

In order to determine the density of a sample of gas inside a bulb, it is necessary to know the volume of the bulb. This is easily measured by weighing the bulb both empty and when filled with water, for which the density is accurately known.

_____.

Example 5-1 A bulb has a mass of 178.510 g when open to the atmosphere, 178.252 g when evacuated and sealed, and 178.349 g when filled with CO_2 gas. What is the mass of the air in the bulb initially and the mass of the CO_2 sample?

_____

When the air in the bulb is pumped out, the mass decreases by 178.510 – 178.252 = 0.258 g and this is the mass of air in the bulb when it is open to the atmosphere. When the sample of CO_2 is transferred to the evacuated bulb the mass increases by 178.349 – 178.252 = 0.097 g, and this is the mass of the CO_2.

_____

Example 5-2 The bulb described in the last example has a mass of 398.3 g when filled with water with a density of 0.9982 g cm^{-3}. What is the internal volume of the bulb, and the density of the CO_2 sample?

_____

The water fills the bulb, and so the volume of the water is equal to the internal volume of the bulb.

The mass of water = 398.3 – 178.252 = 220.0 g, so the internal volume of the bulb is:

$$V = \frac{220.0\,\text{g}}{0.9982\,\text{g cm}^{-3}} = 220.4\,\text{cm}^3.$$

Hence the density of the CO_2 sample $= \dfrac{0.097\,\text{g}}{220.4\,\text{cm}^3} = 4.4 \times 10^{-4}\,\text{g cm}^{-3}.$

_____

5-2 Volume and Pressure

Although the S.I. unit of volume is the cubic metre, the volume units most commonly used in chemistry are the litre (exactly 10^{-3} m^3) and the millilitre (exactly 10^{-6} m^3). These are the units used for solution chemistry throughout this book. However, for the calculations involving gases it is best to use the S.I. unit, the cubic metre, or its subdivisions.

The appropriate subdivisions are the cubic decimetre, dm^3, which is the same as a litre, and the cubic centimetre, cm^3, which is the same as a millilitre. The conversion factors to the cubic metre are easy to work out:

$$1 \text{ dm}^3 = (10^{-1} \text{ m})^3 = 10^{-3} \text{ m}^3$$
$$1 \text{ cm}^3 = (10^{-2} \text{ m})^3 = 10^{-6} \text{ m}^3$$

We will use cubic decimetres and cubic centimetres when dealing with gases.

A gas exerts a force on its surroundings. This is familiar to anyone who has pumped up a bicycle tire with a hand pump: a good deal of force must be exerted on the pump handle attached to the piston, in order to overcome the force of the gas on the piston. The force of the gas on the piston depends on the size of the piston. The force increases in proportion to the area of the piston, and so the condition of the gas is described, not by the force on the piston, but by the force divided by the area of the piston. The force per unit area is the **pressure** of the gas on the piston.

The fundamental S.I. unit of pressure is the newton per square metre, which is given the special name **pascal,** abbreviated Pa. The pascal named for the French physicist Blaise Pascal who carried out experiments on the pressure of the atmosphere.

In terms of the basic units, the pascal is equal to $\text{kg m s}^{-2} \times \text{m}^{-2} = \text{kg m}^{-1}\text{s}^{-2}$.

Throughout this book, we will almost always express pressures in pascals, in order to simplify calculations. However several other units are often used for measuring pressure. The definitions of these secondary units are summarized in Table 5-2. The **atmosphere** was originally defined in terms of a barometer height of 760 mm of mercury under specific conditions, but is now defined as exactly 101325 pascal, a value that is equivalent to the original definition. The **torr** is defined as 1/760 of an atmosphere, and is very close to the hydrostatic pressure exerted by a height of 1 mm of mercury; it is named for the Italian physicist Evangelista Torricelli. The **bar** is defined as exactly 100 000 pascal; it is a little smaller than the atmosphere and is a convenient unit to use for some purposes.

The pressure of air in the atmosphere near sea level is usually about one atmosphere, but can fall as low as 0.97 atmosphere during bad weather and can rise as high as 1.03 atmosphere in fine weather. Atmospheric pressure decreases systematically with height above sea-level.

A pressure of 100 000 pascals, or 1 bar, has been adopted as the **standard pressure,** designated as $P°$, and is used for tabulation of thermodynamic data.

Table 5-2 Secondary Units of Pressure

Unit	Definition
atmosphere	101 325 pascals
bar	100 000 pascals
torr	1/760 atmosphere = 133.32 pascal

Gas pressure can be measured in various ways. In a **manometer,** the pressure of a gas is balanced against the hydrostatic pressure of a liquid caused by the effect of gravity on the liquid. Because gases usually have such low densities, the effect of gravity on gas pressure in laboratory samples is negligible. Several forms of manometer are shown in Figure 5-2. A differential manometer, shown in Figure 5-2(a), is used for measuring the pressure *difference* between two vessels, or between one vessel and the atmosphere. A single ended manometer is shown in Figure 5-2(b); one side is evacuated and so is at zero pressure, so this manometer can be used to measure the absolute pressure at the other side. The **barometer**, shown in Figure 5-2(c), is a special form of single ended manometer used to measure the pressure of the atmosphere.

In any manometer, the pressure (or pressure difference) is determined by measuring the height difference between the two sides of the liquid column, and calculating the corresponding hydrostatic pressure difference due to gravity. The hydrostatic pressure difference in a manometer P is:

$$P = \rho g h \qquad (5\text{-}1)$$

where h is the height difference, g is the acceleration due to gravity, and ρ is the density of the liquid. Mercury is often used for manometers since it is a liquid with a high density, $\rho = 13.546$ g cm^{-3} at 20°C. Small pressure differences can be measured using a manometer filled with a low density liquid such as water.

Pressures can be quoted as an equivalent height of mercury (or some other liquid), but this practice has two disadvantages. First, the value of the gravitational acceleration, g, varies from place to place on the surface of the earth, and second, the density of mercury varies with temperature. These can contribute systematic errors of as much as 0.5 per cent, not large but easily measurable. For accurate work, pressures in mm of mercury should be converted to torr by applying corrections for temperature and acceleration due to gravity.

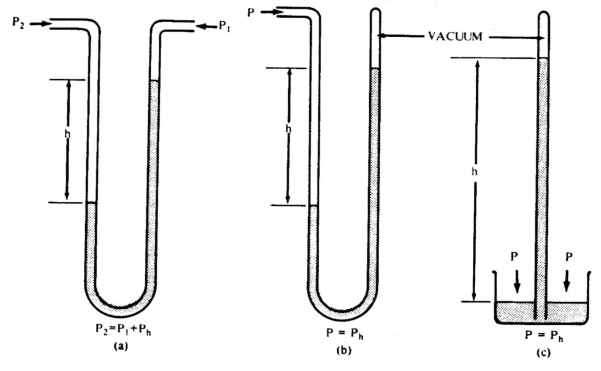

Figure 5-2   Three different types of manometer. (a)   A differential manometer; (b) a single ended manometer; (c) a barometer used for measuring atmospheric pressure.

Example 5-3 Calculate the pressure corresponding to 76.00 cm Hg, at a temperature at which the density of mercury is 13.59508 g cm^{-3} and at a place where the acceleration due to gravity is 9.80665 m s^{-2}.

———

Converting the density and height into fundamental units, ρ = 13.59508×10^3 kg m^{-3}, and h = 0.7600 m.

From the above formula, P = 13.59508×10^3 kg m^{-3} × 9.80665 m s^{-1} × 0.7600 m

$$= 1.01325×10^5 \text{ kg m}^{-1} \text{ s}^{-2}$$

$$= 101.325 \text{ kPa.}$$

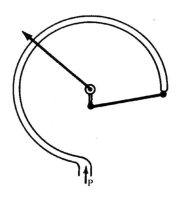

Figure 5-3 A Bourdon gauge consists of a bent tube containing the fluid at pressure. The end of the tube is mechanically linked to a pointer, which rotates as the tube straightens out.

There are many devices for measuring pressure that are more practical than a manometer. Figure 5-3 shows a **Bourdon gauge**, in which the gas is contained in a bent tube linked mechanically to a pointer. The difference in pressure between the inside and the outside of the tube causes the tube to straighten out a little, causing the pointer to move.

There are several types of pressure gauge which operate electrically and can be read by a computer. In a **pressure transducer**, the pressure-induced distortion of a thin silicon wafer attached to the end of a tube is measured electrically. Low pressures in a vacuum system can be measured with an **ionization gauge** in which the gas is ionized and its electrical properties are measured. For accurate measurements, these gauges must be calibrated against a manometer or other absolute pressure gauge.

Figure 5-4   A high vacuum system which operates at pressures as low as 10^{-7} Pa. The equipment is designed for experiments on the behaviour of molecules bombarded by intense laser light. The pressure is measured with the ionization gauge at the top of the apparatus on the right hand side. In the middle is a large hand-operated valve, which can close off part of the equipment. The experimental chamber is at the left, and can be seen through the glass window. The vacuum pumps are out of sight underneath the vacuum chamber. *Photograph courtesy of Prof. H-P. Loock, Queen's University.*

5-3 Temperature and its measurement

The behaviour of gases depends on temperature, and in this section we consider how temperature is defined and measured. **Temperature** is a measure of the hotness or coldness of things and is familiar from everyday experience. In winter, snow falls, lakes freeze and we feel "cold" when we go outside. In summer, lakes contain water warm enough for swimming, and in the sunshine we feel "hot". The qualities of hotness and coldness are transferable from one object to another. A piece of metal placed in a fire becomes hot, and if the metal is then placed in a pan of water, the water becomes hot. If the metal is cooled in snow, instead, and then placed in a pan of water, the water becomes cold.

Two objects that are equally hot or cold have the same temperature. When two objects are left in contact with each other for a period of time but are thermally insulated from the outside world, they come to thermal equilibrium with each other, and have the same temperature.

It is important to recognize that temperature and heat are two different things. Temperature measures a quality or condition of an object, whereas heat is a form of energy, as we will see in the next chapter. We do not need to know what heat is in order to be able to define and measure temperature.

Unlike volume or mass, temperature cannot be measured directly. Usually temperature is measured with a device called a **thermometer**, which can be placed in contact with another object. The temperature of the thermometer indicated by the thermometer is, by inference, also the temperature of the object.

Various properties of materials vary with temperature and can be used to devise thermometers and temperature scales. For most materials the volume of a sample increases with increasing temperature, a property known as thermal expansion. Other properties change, too, but we will focus on thermal expansion and the way it is used to build a thermometer and to define a temperature scale. Figure 5-5 shows the familiar mercury-in-glass thermometer, with a bulb containing mercury attached to a narrow capillary tube. The space above the mercury is a vacuum. An increase of temperature causes an increase in the height of the column of mercury as the mercury expands along the capillary tube.

A temperature scale can be defined using two fixed points, that is two temperatures that are easily and reliably reproduced. This is similar to the definition of a length scale using a ruler with two fixed marks, one at each end. Historically, zero degrees on the Celsius scale (0°C) is defined as the **ice point**, the temperature of a mixture of ice and water at a pressure of one atmosphere. One hundred degrees, 100°C, is defined as the **steam point**, the temperature of steam in contact with boiling water at a pressure of one atmosphere. These definitions are no longer used for the most accurate work, but are accurate enough for most purposes.

Figure 5-5

A mercury-in-glass thermometer.

A mercury-in-glass thermometer is calibrated by placing it first in an ice-water mixture and marking the height of the mercury column corresponding to 0 degrees, and then placing it in a bath of steam generated by boiling water and marking the height of the mercury column corresponding to 100 degrees. The distance between these two marks is then divided into 100 equal distances, each corresponding to one degree Celsius.

Other thermometers could be devised using the linear expansion of an iron rod, or the thermal expansion of air, or the electrical resistance of a piece of platinum wire. But to start with, we will assume that temperatures are measured using the familiar mercury-in-glass thermometer calibrated in degrees Celsius.

5-4 Expansion and compression of gases: Boyle's law

The volume of a sample of gas varies with temperature and pressure. In addition, of course, the volume is proportional to the mass of the sample. The relationships between volume, temperature, pressure and mass have been studied over a long period of time and are summarized in three well-known "laws" called the **gas laws**. All gases obey these laws as long as the pressure is not too high; deviations from the gas laws will be discussed later in this chapter.

The English physicists Robert Boyle and Robert Hooke investigated the relationship between volume and pressure of a gas in the seventeenth century. **Boyle's law** states that for a fixed mass of gas at constant temperature, the product of pressure and volume is constant:

$$PV = \text{constant} \quad \text{at constant temperature} \tag{5-2}$$

For a particular sample of gas at a fixed temperature, it follows that for two different conditions identified by the subscripts 1 and 2, the pressures and volumes are related by the equation:

$$P_1V_1 = P_2V_2 . \tag{5-3}$$

A graph of pressure *versus* volume at constant temperature is a hyperbola, as shown in Figure 5-6. Each graph corresponds to a particular temperature, which is the same for all points on the graph; such graphs referring to conditions of constant temperature are called **isotherms**.

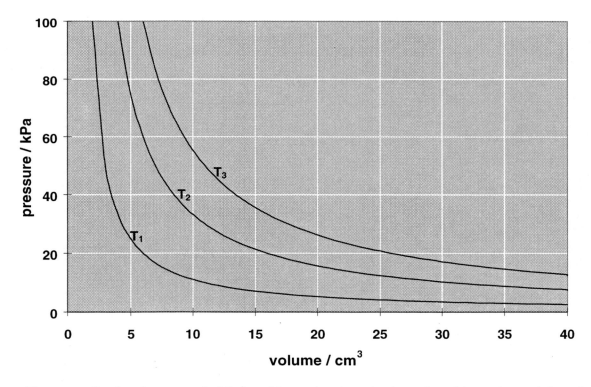

Figure 5-6 Graphs of pressure (in kilopascals) as a function of volume (in cubic centimetres) for a fixed mass of gas at three different temperatures, indicated by T_1, T_2 and T_3. The shape of each curve is a hyperbola, described by the equation PV = constant.

It follows from Boyle's law that the pressure of a gas is proportional to the inverse of the volume:

$$P \propto \frac{1}{V} \qquad \text{at constant temperature and mass} \qquad (5\text{-}4)$$

The density of a material is the mass per unit volume: from equation (1-1), $\rho = m/V$ where ρ is the density, m is the mass and V is the volume. It is clear that for a fixed mass of gas the density is inversely proportional to the volume. Combining this with Boyle's law, we see that at constant temperature, the pressure of a gas is proportional to its density:

$$P \propto \rho \qquad \text{at constant temperature} \qquad (5\text{-}5)$$

Example 5-6   A tank has a volume of 2.34 m^3 and holds air at a pressure of 70.0 kPa. What would be the volume of this sample of air if it were measured at a pressure of 100.0 kPa at the same temperature?

Since the temperature and amount of air are constant, $P_1 V_1 = P_2 V_2$ and the volume at a pressure of 100. kPa would be:

$$V = 2.34 \text{ m}^3 \times \frac{70.0 \text{ kPa}}{100.0 \text{ kPa}} = 1.64 \text{ m}^3$$

Example 5-7   Air has a density of 0.00139 g cm^{-3} at a temperature of –20 °C and at sea-level where the pressure is 101.3 kPa. What would be the density of air at the same temperature at the top of Mount Everest, where the pressure is only 31 % of its value at sea level?

Since the density of a gas is proportional to pressure, the density is:

$$\rho = 0.00139 \text{ g cm}^{-3} \times 0.31 = 4.3 \times 10^{-4} \text{ g cm}^{-3}$$

5-5 Thermal expansion of gases: Charles' law

If held at constant pressure, gases expand with increasing temperature. The thermal expansion of gases was first investigated by Jacques-Alexandre-César Charles, but the first published account was given by Joseph Louis Gay-Lussac, who had improved the earlier experiments.

If the temperature is measured with a mercury-in-glass thermometer, it is found by experiment that for air, and for many other gases, the volume of a sample maintained at constant pressure varies linearly with temperature. Figure 5-6 shows a graph of temperature dependence, at constant pressure, of the ratio V/V_o, where V is the volume of a sample of gas and V_o is its volume V_0 at 0°C. The graph is based upon measurements for gases such as air at atmospheric pressure. The straight line graph of V/V_o *versus* t in Figure 5-7 is described by the following linear equation:

$$\frac{V}{V_0} = 1 + at \qquad \text{at constant pressure} \qquad (5\text{-}6)$$

where t is the temperature of the gas in degrees Celsius and a is a constant. This statement is called **Charles' law,** or **Gay-Lussac's law.**

It is remarkable that for almost all gases at atmospheric (or lower) pressure the value of the constant a in the above equation has almost the same value. The value of a varies slightly with pressure and with the chemical composition of the gas, but if the pressure is low enough, the constant a in equation (5-6) has exactly the same value for all gases regardless of the chemical nature of the gas:

$$a = 0.0036610 \ °C^{-1}$$

Hence a temperature scale based upon the thermal expansion of gases at low pressure is in some sense a universal scale which is not linked to the properties of any specific substance such as mercury. This temperature scale is called the **ideal gas temperature scale.**

The point at which the extrapolation of the straight line graph in Figure 5-7 crosses the temperature axis is clearly a special temperature, for it is the temperature at which the gas would have zero volume if condensation did not occur. Since $1/a = 1/0.0036610 = 273.15°C$, equation (5-6) can be written:

$$V = V_0(1 + at) = aV_0\left[\frac{1}{a} + t\right] = aV_0(273.15 + t) \qquad \text{at constant pressure}$$

The volume of the gas would become zero at $-273.15°C$, and a more advanced discussion using the theory of thermodynamics shows that no lower temperature is possible for any substance, whether a gas or not. Hence this temperature is the **absolute zero** of temperature.

The **absolute temperature** is defined by shifting the origin of the temperature scale to absolute zero. The absolute temperature T is related to the Celsius temperature by the equation:

$$T = t + 273.15. \tag{5-7}$$

The unit for absolute temperature is the **kelvin,** with abbreviation K, as discussed in Chapter 1; it is named after the Irish physicist William Thomson, better known as Lord Kelvin. One kelvin is the same size as one degree on the Celsius scale; the difference between the two scales is only a change of origin.

The volume of a fixed amount of gas at constant pressure is proportional to the absolute temperature:

$$V = V_o \frac{T}{273.15} \qquad \text{at constant pressure}$$

As long as the pressure is constant, V/T is constant for a given sample of gas. For any two conditions of a sample of gas maintained at constant pressure,

$$\frac{V_1}{T_1} = \frac{V_2}{T_2} \qquad \text{at constant pressure} \tag{5-8}$$

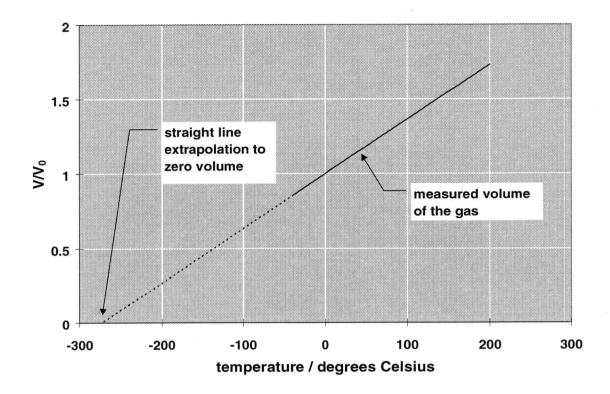

Figure 5-7 The volume of a sample of gas at constant pressure, plotted as a function of temperature as measured by a mercury thermometer. The volume is expressed as the ratio V/V_0, where V_0 is the volume of the gas at 0 °C. The full line represents measurements above about –40 °C, and the dotted line is the linear extrapolation of these measurements to lower temperatures.

Example 5-8 A sample of gas occupies 2.50 dm^3 at atmospheric pressure and a temperature of 0.0 °C. What would be the volume, at the same pressure, if the temperature were raised to 100.0 °C?

The two absolute temperatures involved are 273.15 K and 373.15 K, and so the new volume is:

$$V = 2.50 \text{ dm}^3 \times \frac{373.15 \text{ K}}{273.15 \text{ K}} = 3.42 \text{ dm}^3$$

Example 5-9 The density of air at 25 °C and at atmospheric pressure is 0.00118 g cm^{-3}. What is the density of air at a temperature of 300.°C, and the same pressure?

The mass of the sample of air is: $m = \rho V = 0.00118 \text{ g cm}^{-3} \times 1 \text{ cm}^3 = 0.00118 \text{ g}$.

The two absolute temperatures involved are 298 K and 573 K. Consider a sample of one cm^3 of air at the lower temperature. By Charles' law, the volume at the higher temperature is:

$$V = 1\,cm^3 \times \frac{573\,K}{298\,K} = 1.92\,cm^3$$

The density of air at the higher temperature is therefore:

$$\rho = \frac{m}{V} = \frac{0.00118\,g}{1.92\,cm^3} = 0.000614\,g\,cm^{-3}$$

5-6 Avogadro's principle

As a result of studies of chemical reactions between gases, the Italian physicist Amedeo Avogadro proposed in 1811 that equal volumes of different gases under the same conditions of temperature and pressure, contain equal numbers of molecules. Despite some changes in our understanding of elements, valence and atomic weights since the original experiments, the theory has survived and remains a fundamental principle of chemistry. **Avogadro's principle** can be restated in slightly different language as follows: at the same temperature and pressure, equal volumes of different gases contain equal amounts (measured in moles) of each gas.

It follows that, at the same temperature and pressure, the ratio of masses of equal volumes of two gases is equal to the ratio of the molar masses of the two gases. The ratio of densities of two gases at the same temperature and pressure is equal to the ratio of the molar masses. Figure 5-8 shows the densities of a number of gases plotted as a function of molar mass at equal temperatures and pressures. The graph is a straight line, and shows that the density of a gas at fixed temperature and pressure is proportional to its molar mass.

Example 5-10 From the graph in Figure 5-8, estimate the density of argon at a pressure of 101.3 kPa and a temperature of 0 °C.

The molar mass of argon is 39.9 g mol^{-1}, so reading from the graph, the density is estimated to be 1.9 g/L or 0.0019 g cm^{-3}.

5-7 The ideal gas equation

A gas that obeys the gas laws of Boyle, Charles and Avogadro over a wide range of conditions is called an **ideal gas**, and The equation expressing these laws is called the **ideal gas equation,** or the **ideal gas law**.

We can summarize the three laws as follows:

From Boyle's law, we know that $V \propto 1/P$ at constant T and n.

From Charles' law, we know that $V \propto T$ at constant P and n.

From Avogadro's Principle, we know that $V \propto n$ at constant P and T.

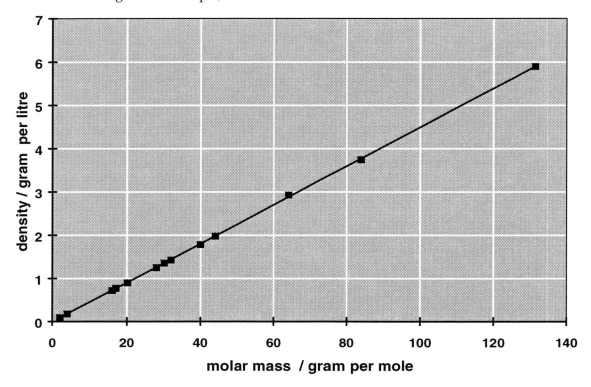

Figure 5-8 The density, in g/dm³, of some gases at a pressure of 101.325 kPa and a temperature of 0 °C, plotted as a function of molar mass in g/mol, ranging from hydrogen H_2 with M = 2 g/mol, up to xenon Xe with M = 131 g/mol.

If all three laws are considered together, then $V \propto nT/P$. The constant of proportionality is a universal constant, called the **gas constant** and denoted by the symbol R, which does not depend at all on the nature of the gas. With the constant of proportionality written explicitly, the **ideal gas equation** is:

$$PV = nRT \qquad (5\text{-}9)$$

The value of R can be calculated from the well-known fact that one mole of gas occupies a volume of 22.414 litre, or 22.414 dm³, at a temperature of 273.15 K (i.e. 0.00°C), and a pressure of 101.325 kPa (i.e. one atmosphere). These conditions are sometimes called **"standard temperature and pressure** or "STP", but should not be confused with the standard pressure $P° = 100.$ kPa defined earlier in this chapter. Inserting these values into the equation and solving for R we find:

$$R = \frac{101325 \, \text{N m}^{-2} \times 0.022414 \, \text{m}^3}{1 \, \text{mol} \times 273.15 \, \text{K}} = 8.3145 \, \text{N m K}^{-1} \, \text{mol}^{-1} = 8.3145 \, \text{J K}^{-1} \, \text{mol}^{-1}$$

In this calculation we have used the fact that the joule (J) is equal to a newton metre.

Care must be taken with units in using the ideal gas equation, as with any other equation. The gas constant is often quoted and used in other units, but this practice causes more trouble than it saves and will be avoided here. With pressures in pascals, volumes in cubic metres, temperatures in kelvin, and amount of substance in moles, the units are always consistent and numerical errors are avoided. The final result of a calculation can be converted to other units if desired. As a final note, the gas constant is used in a variety of calculations which do not involve gases at all, such as electrochemistry in solution, where the use of units for R other than $J\ K^{-1}\ mol^{-1}$ can easily lead to error and confusion.

The concentration of a gas is $c = n/V$, and so the ideal gas equation can be written as follows:

$$P = cRT \tag{5-10}$$

Sometimes it is convenient to work with this equation, since it contains the simple statement that pressure is proportional to concentration at fixed temperature. Like the density ρ, concentration is an intensive variable which does not depend on how much gas there is.

The concentration of a gas can be written in terms of its density and molar mass:

$$c = \frac{n}{V} = \frac{m}{MV} = \frac{\rho}{M}$$

Hence another form of the ideal gas equation is:

$$P = \frac{\rho RT}{M} \tag{5-11}$$

Example 5-11 What is the pressure of 1.00 g of nitrogen gas N_2 in a volume of 1.20 dm^3 at a temperature of 20.2 °C?

Since the molar mass of N_2 is 28.014 g/mol, $n=1.00/28.014 = 0.0357$ mol. The volume is $V = 1.20\times10^{-3}\ m^3$, and the temperature is $T = 273.2 + 20.2\ K = 293.4$ K. Hence:

$$P = \frac{0.0357\ mol \times 8.3145\ J\ K^{-1}\ mol^{-1} \times 293.4\ K}{1.20\times10^{-3}\ m^3} = 7.26\times10^4\ N\ m^{-2} = 72.6\ kPa$$

Example 5-12 What is the volume of 0.184 mol of oxygen gas O_2 at 98.0 kPa and 23.0°C?

Volume is: $V = \dfrac{0.184\ mol \times 8.3145\ J\ K^{-1}\ mol^{-1} \times (23.0+273.2)\ K}{98.0\times10^3\ Pa} = 4.62\times10^{-3}\ m^3 = 4.62\ dm^3$

Example 5-13 The vapour of an organic compound is found to have a density of 4.73 $g\ dm^{-3}$ at 100°C and 100.0 kPa. Assuming that the vapour is an ideal gas, calculate the molar mass of the compound.

Consider a volume of 1.00 dm^3 of the vapour. Under the conditions stated, the amount of the compound contained in this volume is:

$$n = \frac{PV}{RT} = \frac{1.000 \times 10^5 \text{ Pa} \times 1.00 \times 10^{-3} \text{ m}^3}{8.3145 \text{ J K}^{-1} \text{ mol}^{-1} \times 373.2 \text{ K}} = 0.03223 \text{ mol}$$

But from the density, the mass of this amount of gas is 4.73 g.

Hence the molar mass is 4.73 g/0.03223 mol = 147 g/mol.

_____

5-8 Mixtures of gases: Dalton's law

It is often necessary to deal with gases consisting of a mixture of two or more different substances. Air, for example is a mixture of oxygen and nitrogen and small amounts of other gases. In a gas mixture, each gas usually behaves independently of the other gases in the mixture, unless a chemical reaction takes place.

A pressure gauge such as a manometer or a Bourdon gauge measures the total pressure P of a gas mixture. The composition of a gas mixture can be specified using the mole fractions $y(A)$, $y(B)$, ... of the various compounds which are present in the mixture, and the **partial pressure** of each compound present is defined as the product of the mole fraction and the total pressure:

$$p(A) = y(A)P, \quad p(B) = y(B)P, \text{ etc.} \tag{5-12}$$

The partial pressure of each gas is proportional to its mole fraction in the mixture. Since the sum of the mole fractions of all the gases present is unity, i.e. $y(A) + y(B) + ... = 1$, the sum of the partial pressures is equal to the total pressure:

$$p(A) + p(B) + ... = P \tag{5-13}$$

Suppose we have a mixture of gases A, B,... which obeys the ideal gas law. The total amount (in moles) of gas in the mixture, n, is the sum of the amounts of the individual gases, $n(A)$, $n(B)$, etc:

$$n = n(A) + n(B) + ...$$

According to the definitions of partial pressure and mole fraction, the partial pressure of one gas in the mixture, say the substance A, is:

$$p(A) = y(A)P = \frac{n(A)}{n}P$$

The preceding definitions and equations are valid whether or not the gases in the mixture are ideal or not. If the gas mixture is ideal, then the ideal gas equation $PV=nRT$ is obeyed, and hence $P/n = RT/V$. Substituting this in the previous equation, we find:

$$p(A) = \frac{n(A)RT}{V} \tag{5-14}$$

According to this equation, the partial pressure of a gas in the mixture is equal to the pressure which that gas would exert if it alone were present in the volume V at temperature T, assuming ideal behaviour. This is known as **Dalton's law of partial pressures**.

Many gas mixtures obey Dalton's law of partial pressures to a good approximation. However, even if a particular mixture of gases does not obey Dalton's law, the definition of partial pressure given in equation (5-12) is still used. Consequently the sum of the partial pressures is always equal to the total pressure, as stated in equation (5-13).

Example 5-14   A mixture of 8.00 g of methane CH_4 and 9.00 g of ethane C_2H_6 is stored at a total pressure of 500. kPa. What is the partial pressure of each component?

The molar mass of CH_4 is 16.043 g/mol, so $n(CH_4) = 8.00/16.043 = 0.499$ mol. The molar mass of C_2H_6 is 30.069 g/mol, so $n(C_2H_6) = 9.00/30.069 = 0.299$ mol. The total amount of gas = 0.499 + 0.299 = 0.798 mol. Hence the mole fractions of the gases are:

$$y(CH_4) = 0.499/0.798 = 0.625$$

and $\qquad y(C_2H_6) = 0.299/0.798 = 0.325$

The partial pressures are:

$$p(CH_4) = 0.625 \times 500.\ kPa = 312.5\ kPa$$

and $\qquad p(C_2H_6) = 0.325 \times 500.\ kPa = 162.5\ kPa.$

Example 5-15   A tank of volume 2.00 dm^3 containing oxygen at a pressure of 100. kPa is connected to a tank of volume 0.10 dm^3 containing helium at the same temperature and a pressure of 3.00 Mpa. The gases are allowed to mix. What are the partial pressures and the total pressure after mixing, assuming the gases are ideal and the temperature is held constant?

By Dalton's law, the two gases behave independently. When the tanks are connected, the volume available to the oxygen increases from 2.00 dm^3 to 2.10 dm^3, and so the partial pressure of oxygen is:

$$p(O_2) = \frac{2.00\ dm^3}{2.10\ dm^3} \times 100.\ kPa = 95.2\ kPa$$

Similarly, the volume available to the helium increases from 0.10 dm^3 to 2.10 dm^3, and the partial pressure of helium is:

$$p(He) = \frac{0.10\ dm^3}{2.10\ dm^3} \times 3000.\ kPa = 142.8\ kPa$$

The total pressure is $P = 95.2 + 142.8 = 238$ kPa.

5-9 The kinetic theory of gases

There is a simple model for a gas which, when combined with the ideal gas equation $PV = nRT$, gives useful insight into the motion of molecules in a gas and the meaning of temperature. The model is called the **kinetic theory of gases**. The theory is based on the assumption that a gas consists of a huge number of molecules, which are in a state of constant motion, flying about and colliding with the walls of the container and with each other. Newton's laws of motion govern the motion of each molecule.

The kinetic theory of gases originated in the work of James Clerk Maxwell and Ludwig Boltzmann in about 1860, and is one of a number of theories that relate the **macroscopic**, or visible, properties of matter to the **microscopic** world of atoms and molecules. Because a gas contains an enormous number of molecules, the connection between macroscopic and microscopic properties must be made using the methods of statistics. We are not able to follow the motion of so many molecules, and it is not profitable to try to do so. We are interested in only a few quantities like pressure and temperature and it would not be helpful to calculate enormous lists of the positions and velocities of individual molecules. The key assumption of the kinetic theory is that the pressure of a gas is a statistical average of the forces due to the collisions of the molecules with the walls of the container.

Gases have low density and are easily compressed, as compared with liquids and solids. In liquids and solids the molecules are in close contact with each other and are held together by the forces between the molecules. In a gas, the density is low and, on average, each molecule in a gas is well separated from other molecules. Hence, for most of the time, the forces between molecules are weak, and by Newton's law of motion, the molecules travel in straight lines with constant speed. From time to time, molecules collide with each other or with the walls of the container, and these collisions, like the collisions between balls on a billiard table, cause sudden changes in direction and speed. The measured pressure of the gas is due to the collisions of the gas molecules with the walls of the container.

In the following discussion, we derive the relationship between the bulk properties of a gas and the kinetic energy of motion of the molecules. Then, by means of the ideal gas equation, the kinetic energy is related to the temperature of the gas.

We assume that the gas consists of an enormous number of identical molecules. The shape of each molecule is not important but can be assumed to be a sphere with a well-defined diameter, like a billiard ball. The only time there is a force on a molecule is during a collision with another molecule or with a wall of the container. Collisions with other molecules can be ignored as long as the diameter of the molecules is small compared with the average distance between the molecules. In the present discussion, we ignore collisions between molecules altogether, and assume that each molecule moves around inside the container independently of all other molecules, as shown in Figure 5-9.

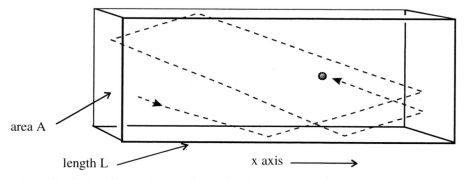

Figure 5-9 The dashed line indicates the path of a single molecule in a gas inside a rectangular container. The molecule bounces off each wall like light reflected from a mirror.

Consider the motion of a single molecule as it bounces off the walls of the container. We assume that the box has rectangular faces, with ends of area A separated by a length L and we define the x-axis as the direction along the length of the box. We assume that the walls are perfectly smooth and flat, and that the molecules collide elastically with the walls, like a billiard ball (without spin) colliding with the cushions of a good billiard table or light reflected from a mirror. In an elastic collision with the walls, the direction of motion of the molecule changes but its speed is constant.

The velocity of the molecule is a vector quantity, with component v_x along the x-axis and components v_y and v_z along the directions at right angles to the x-axis. The speed of the molecule, v, is related to the three components of the velocity by the following equation based upon the theorem of Pythagoras:

$$v^2 = v_x^2 + v_y^2 + v_z^2$$

Newton's law of motion states that *force = mass × acceleration*. Since acceleration is the rate of change of velocity, and momentum is *mass × velocity*, force can be expressed as follows:

force = rate of change of momentum.

Like velocity, force and momentum are vector quantities and each has three components corresponding to the x, y and z directions. The x-component of the momentum of a molecule is the product mv_x of the mass m of the molecule and the x-component of its velocity, v_x. The x component of the momentum of the molecule changes only when there is a force on the molecule in the x direction. This occurs only when the molecule strikes one of the two end walls, which are perpendicular to the x-axis. The four side walls are parallel to the x-axis, and when the molecule collides with these walls, the force on the molecule is at right angles to the x-axis. Hence in these collisions the x component of the velocity does not change.

Between the collisions with the end walls, the molecule moves backwards and forwards with a constant x component of velocity. Since the molecule has to travel twice the length of the container between collisions with the right hand wall, the number of collisions per second with that wall is $v_x/2L$.

At each collision with the right hand wall, the x component of velocity is exactly reversed, since the collisions are assumed to be elastic collisions: the x component of momentum changes from $+mv_x$ to $-mv_x$. Hence the total change of momentum in each collision is $2mv_x$.

For this one molecule, the total change of momentum per second due to its collisions at the right hand wall is the product of the number of collisions per second and the momentum change at each collision:

$$\text{momentum change per second at the right hand wall} = \frac{v_x}{2L} \times 2mv_x = \frac{mv_x^2}{L}$$

Since force equals the rate of change of momentum, this last quantity is the force on the wall due to the repeated collisions of this one molecule. The pressure p due to this one molecule is this force divided by the area of the right hand wall, A:

$$\text{pressure due to one molecule} = \frac{\text{force}}{\text{area}} = \frac{mv_x^2}{L} \times \frac{1}{A}$$

In the denominator, the product of the length L of the box and the area A of the end wall is the volume V of the box: $V = LA$. Hence:

$$\text{pressure in x direction due to one molecule} = \frac{mv_x^2}{V}.$$

By considering the motion of this molecule in each of the y and z directions, we can show by a similar calculation that:

$$\text{pressure in y direction due to one molecule} = \frac{m v_y^2}{V}$$

$$\text{and: pressure in z direction due to one molecule} = \frac{m v_z^2}{V}.$$

The total pressure of the gas is the same in any direction, and the contribution of this molecule to the total pressure is the average of the pressures in the x, y and z directions. Adding the last three equations together and dividing by three, we find that the pressure due to one molecule is:

$$\text{pressure due to one molecule} = \frac{m}{3V}(v_x^2 + v_y^2 + v_z^2) = \frac{m}{3V}v^2$$

This equation applies to each molecule in the gas. We now add together the equations for all the molecules in the container. The sum of the pressures p for each individual molecule is the total pressure P, as measured by a manometer or other pressure gauge. If the N molecules have identical masses and their speeds are $v_1, v_2,...v_N$, then:

$$\text{pressure due to all molecules} = P = \frac{m}{3V}(v_1^2 + v_2^2 + v_3^2 + ... + v_N^2)$$

Multiplying both sides of this equation by the volume V, we find:

$$PV = \tfrac{1}{3}m(v_1^2 + v_2^2 + v_3^2 + ... + v_N^2)$$

The molecules do not all have the same speed, of course, but we can call on a statistical quantity, the mean squared speed of the molecules:

$$< v^2 > = \frac{1}{N}(v_1^2 + v_2^2 + ... + v_N^2)$$

where the angular brackets <..> are used to indicate an average, or mean value, of the quantity inside the brackets, and N is the number of molecules in the gas. The sum of the squares of the speeds of the individual molecules in the previous formula can be replaced by the mean squared speed:

$$PV = \tfrac{1}{3}Nm < v^2 > \tag{5-15}$$

The motion of a molecule through space is described as **translation**, and the associated energy is called translational kinetic energy, to distinguish it from other kinds of molecular energy, which will be discussed in later chapters.

Since the translational kinetic energy of a molecule is $\varepsilon = \tfrac{1}{2}mv^2$, we can write:

$$PV = \tfrac{2}{3}N < \varepsilon > = \tfrac{2}{3} \times \text{total translational kinetic energy} \tag{5-16}$$

Hence the product PV is related to the total translational kinetic energy of the molecules.

We can now interpret this result in terms of Boyle's law: if the temperature is constant, then the product PV is constant. In other words, PV is a function only of the temperature. It follows from equation (5-16) that the total translational kinetic energy of the molecules is also a function only of the temperature. Charles' law now allows us to determine what that function is. For one mole of gas, $PV = RT$, and so:

$$\text{total translational kinetic energy per mole} = \tfrac{3}{2}PV = \tfrac{3}{2}RT \tag{5-17}$$

It is helpful to recall that the product of pressure and volume has the units of energy, since

$$N\ m^{-2} \times m^{3} = N\ m = joule.$$

Example 5-16 What is the increase in the translational kinetic energy of the molecules in one mole of oxygen gas when the temperature increases by 1 kelvin? Assume that oxygen is an ideal gas. Repeat your calculation for nitrogen gas.

The translational kinetic energy increases by the amount $(3/2)R \times \Delta T = 1.5 \times 8.3245 \times 1 = 12.47$ J.

The calculation does not depend on knowing the chemical composition of the gas, so the result would be the same for any ideal gas.

Finally, Avogadro's hypothesis states that equal volumes of different gases at the same temperature and pressure contain the same number of molecules, N. Hence PV/N is the same for the two gases, and by equation (5-14) the average translational kinetic energy of the molecules $<\varepsilon>$ is the same for two gases at the same temperature, even though they may have different molar masses and be quite different chemically. This is an example of the **principle of equipartition of energy,** which applies in several fields of physics and chemistry.

5-10 Molecular motion in gases

The results of kinetic theory can be used to calculate how fast, on average, the molecules in a gas are travelling. Because of collisions between the molecules, the speed of a given molecule changes many times a second, but the average speed of molecules in the gas is constant as long as the temperature is constant.

The mean (or average) translational kinetic energy of a molecule in the gas is the total translational kinetic energy of a mole of molecules divided by Avogadro's number. Hence, from equation (5.17) in the previous section,

$$< \text{translational kinetic energy} >= \frac{1}{2} m < v^{2} >= \frac{3}{2} \frac{RT}{N_A}$$

where the angular brackets indicate the mean of the quantity inside, and N_A is Avogadro's number. From the second equality, we can calculate the mean squared speed of the molecule:

$$< v^{2} >= \frac{3RT}{N_a m} = \frac{3RT}{M}$$

Note that $N_a m$, is equal to the molar mass, M. If we take the square root of the mean squared speed, we obtain the **root mean squared speed**, which is the most easily calculated estimate of how fast the molecules in a gas are moving:

$$v_{rms} = \sqrt{< v^{2} >} = \sqrt{\frac{3RT}{M}} \quad (5\text{-}18)$$

The simple average speed of the molecules is about 8 per cent smaller than the "rms" speed, but considerably more calculation is required to demonstrate this.

Example 5-17 What is the root mean squared speed of an oxygen molecule at room temperature, 300 K.

_____

Substituting the values $T = 300.$ K and $M = 0.03199$ kg/mol in the last formula,

$$v_{rms} = \sqrt{\frac{3 \times 8.3145 \times 300.}{0.031998}} = 484 \text{ m s}^{-1}$$

It is very important that the molar mass be given in kg/mol, not g/mol, in order to obtain the correct result.

_____

The rms speed of a molecule in a gas is determined by its molar mass and the temperature of the gas. At the same temperature, molecules of different molar mass have different average speeds. Heavier molecules move more slowly than lighter molecules because the rms speed of a molecule is inversely proportional to the square root of its molar mass.

When a gas at low pressure is allowed to escape through a very small hole into a vacuum, the process is called **effusion.** The rate of effusion of a gas is proportional to the mean speed of the molecules, and therefore varies inversely with the square root of the molar mass of the molecules. This effect is used in the separation of the two isotopes of uranium, ^{235}U and ^{238}U. Uranium hexafluoride, UF_6, forms a vapour at room temperature. Fluorine has only one naturally occurring isotope, ^{19}F, so there are two isotopically distinct molecules $^{235}U^{19}F_6$ and $^{238}U^{19}F_6$. The molar masses of these molecules are 349 g/mol and 352 g/mol respectively. The lighter molecules move faster and pass through the tiny holes in the barrier more rapidly than the heavy molecules, so the gas passing through the barrier is slightly enriched in the lighter isotope of uranium. The enrichment factor is equal to the square root of the ratio of molar masses of the two molecules, 1.0043. Because this is so close to unity, and the abundance of ^{235}U in natural uranium is only 0.7 per cent, many stages of enrichment are required to reach a substantial degree of separation of the two isotopes. During the Second World War, an enormous plant in Oak Ridge, Tennessee was built to produce enriched uranium for use in nuclear weapons.

At any instant, some molecules in a gas are moving fast, and some are moving slowly. Because of collisions, the speed of a given molecule fluctuates constantly. Hence it is impossible to say what the speed of a given molecule is at a given moment. The best that can be done is to give a statistical distribution of molecular speeds, which is called the **Maxwell distribution**. The average speed of a molecule, which we have calculated above, is the average over this distribution. Figure 5-10 shows the distribution of speeds of oxygen molecules at a temperature of 300 K.

It can be seen that the distribution is peaked at about 400 m/s, which is a little less than the root mean squared speed of 484 m/s which was calculated for oxygen at this temperature in Example 5-17. Most molecules in the gas move at speeds reasonably close to the rms speed, but a few molecules move very much slower, and a few very much faster, than the rms speed. The fast molecules at the upper end of the distribution are particularly important because they are the ones with sufficient kinetic energy to take part in chemical reactions.

For different temperatures and different gases, the distribution keeps the same form. If the temperature is increased, or the molecules are lighter, the distribution is stretched out to higher speeds. If the temperature is lower, or the molecules are heavier, the distribution is confined to a smaller range of speeds.

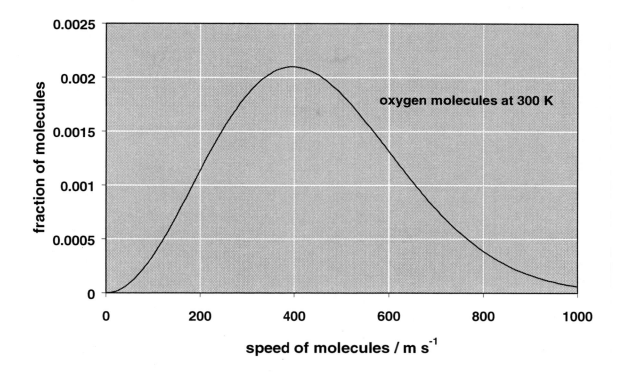

Figure 5-10 The distribution of molecular speeds in oxygen at 300 K. The area under the curve is numerically equal to 1.00, so the fraction of molecules in a given range of speeds can be estimated from the area under the corresponding part of the curve. In Example 5-17, it was shown that the rms speed for oxygen molecules at 300 K is 484 m/s, a value which lies just to the right of the peak.

5-11 The van der Waals equation

Ideal gases are those that obey the ideal gas equation, $PV = nRT$, even when compressed to high density or cooled to low temperature. All gases obey this equation well at low densities and moderate temperatures, but no gas obeys it exactly under all conditions. The reason for this is that molecules exert forces on each other when they get close together. In the kinetic theory of gases, which was discussed in the previous section, collisions between molecules were ignored. It was assumed that the forces between the molecules are sufficiently weak that the molecules move almost independently of each other.

When a gas is condensed to the solid or liquid state, the molecules are held together by the intermolecular forces. The same forces also act between molecules in the gaseous state, and lead to deviations from the ideal gas equation under some conditions. As two molecules approach each other, there is a weak attractive force that draws the molecules together. When the molecules collide, there is a repulsive force as they bounce off each other and move apart again. Figure 5-11 shows the forces between two molecules as they approach each other and collide. Thus both attractive and repulsive forces operate when molecules get close together, and both types of force influence the properties of a gas under certain conditions.

Intermolecular forces affect the pressure of a gas both at high density, when the molecules are close together, and at low temperature, when the molecules have low kinetic energy. Under some conditions, the actual pressure of a gas is higher than expected from the ideal gas equation, and under other conditions, the actual pressure is lower than the ideal value.

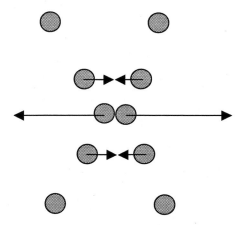

Figure 5-11 A collision between two molecules, one coming from the upper left and the other coming from the upper right of the diagram. The arrows show the forces between molecules as they approach each other and collide. At the top, the molecules are far enough apart that there are no forces. As they get closer together (middle), there are weak attractive forces (shown by the arrows) that pull the molecules together. At the moment of collision (bottom), there are strong repulsive forces that push the molecules apart. At the bottom of the diagram the two molecules move apart again after the collison

In 1873, the Dutch physicist Johannes van der Waals proposed an equation that described the properties of real gases to a good approximation. Since that time, other more accurate equations have been devised, but the **van der Waals equation** is adequate for many purposes.

The van der Waals equation is:

$$\left(P+\frac{n^2a}{V^2}\right)(V-nb)=nRT \tag{5-19a}$$

The equation can also be written:
$$\left(P+\frac{a}{V_m^2}\right)(V_m-b)=RT \tag{5-19b}$$

where $V_m = V/n$ is the molar volume of the gas.

The van der Waals equation is similar in structure to the ideal gas equation. The left-hand side contains two factors, one for pressure and the other for volume, and the product of these two factors is equal to nRT. Each factor on the left-hand side contains an additional term. The quantities a and b are parameters which depend upon the chemical nature of the gas. Table 5-2 lists values of the van der Waals a and b parameters for some gases.

The separate effects of these corrections on the pressure can be seen by rearranging the van der Waals equation to show the pressure explicitly:

$$P=\frac{RT}{V_m-b}-\frac{a}{V_m^2}$$

The term a/V_m^2 takes account of the weak attractive forces that act when molecules approach each other, and are close together but not actually in collision. The attractive forces tend to keep the molecules together briefly. The two molecules interact with each other over a finite period of time, and during this period they act to some extent as if they were a single molecule. This reduces the effective number of particles in the gas, and hence reduces the pressure. The number of collisions taking place at any time is proportional to the square of the concentration of molecules in the gas, $(n/V)^2 = 1/V_m^2$ and hence this term in the van der Waals equation is proportional to $1/V_m^2$.

The term b in the volume factor takes account of the strong repulsive forces that push the molecules apart when they collide. The repulsive forces prevent two molecules occupying them same space. Like a billiard ball, a molecule is not infinitely small and occupies a definite volume. Hence the volume that is accessible to a particular molecule is the total volume of the container minus that volume which is inaccessible due to the presence of the other molecules. Further analysis shows that the van der Waals b parameter is four times the volume of a single molecule, multiplied by Avogadro's number. If the molecule is assumed to be sphereical, the radius calculated from the b parameter is called the **van der Waals radius** of the molecule.

The attractive forces represented by the last term a/V_m^2 decrease the pressure, while the repulsive forces represented by the term b in the denominator increase the pressure. Thus these two terms act in opposite ways, and under some conditions they cancel out and the gas is almost ideal. This is the situation for air at around room temperature.

Consider the trends in the van der Waals parameters for the series of compounds CH_4, CH_3Cl, $CHCl_3$ and CCl_4. Both the a and b parameters increase with the number of chlorine atoms which replace hydrogen atoms. A chlorine atom is larger than a hydrogen atom, and replacement of a hydrogen atom by a chlorine atom increases the size of the molecule, and hence increases the b parameter. A chlorine atom also has more electrons than a hydrogen atom, and this increases the attractive forces between molecules when they are close together.

Table 5-2 van der Waals parameters

Substance	a Pa m^6 mol^{-2}	b 10^{-6} m^3 mol^{-1}	Substance	a Pa m^6 mol^{-2}	b 10^{-6} m^3 mol^{-1}
Elements			**Hydrocarbons**		
He	0.0035	23.8	CH_4 methane	0.230	43.0
H_2	0.0245	26.5	C_3H_8 propane	0.939	90.4
N_2	0.137	38.7	C_4H_{10} n-butane	1.393	116.8
O_2	0.138	31.9	**Halocarbons**		
Oxides			CH_3Cl	0.7566	64.8
CO	0.147	39.5	$CHCl_3$	1.534	101.9
CO_2	0.366	42.9	CCl_4	2.001	128.1
Hydrides			**Alcohols**		
NH_3	0.423	37.1	CH_3OH methanol	0.947	65.8
H_2O	0.554	30.5	C_2H_5OH ethanol	1.256	87.1

Example 5-18 What is the pressure in a tube containing 1.000 mole of nitrogen gas in a volume of 127.0 cm³ at a temperature of 133.2 K? Use the van der Waals equation and compare your result with that obtained from the ideal gas equation and with the observed pressure of 4.13 Mpa.

The molar volume of the gas, 127.0 cm³/mol, is very small, so the gas is highly compressed and it is necessary to take account of deviations from the ideal gas equation.

The van der Waals parameters for nitrogen are $a = 0.137$ Pa m⁶ mol⁻² and $b = 38.7 \cdot 10^{-6}$ m³ mol⁻¹. The molar volume is $V_m = 127.0$ cm³ mol⁻¹ $= 127.0 \times 10^{-6}$ m³ mol⁻¹. Hence the pressure calculated from the van der Waals equation is:

$$P = \frac{8.3145\, \text{J K}^{-1}\, \text{mol}^{-1} \times 133.2\, \text{K}}{(127.0 - 38.7) \times 10^{-6}\, \text{m}^3\, \text{mol}^{-1}} - \frac{0.137\, \text{Pa m}^6\, \text{mol}^{-2}}{(127.0 \times 10^6\, \text{m}^3\, \text{mol}^{-1})^2} = 4.05\, \text{MPa}$$

The units in this equation should be carefully studied. The calculated pressure is in reasonable agreement with the observed pressure of 4.13 Mpa.

For comparison, the pressure calculated from the ideal gas equation is much higher, and clearly disagrees with experiment:

$$P = \frac{8.3145\, \text{J K}^{-1}\, \text{mol}^{-1} \times 133.2\, \text{K}}{127.0 \times 10^{-6}\, \text{m}^3\, \text{mol}^{-1}} = 8.72\, \text{MPa}$$

Key concepts

Gases have low density, are easily compressed, and expand to fill the whole space available. They exert a pressure on the walls of the container, which depends on the volume of the gas, its temperature, and the amount of gas present.

Temperature is a measure of the hotness or coldness of things, and is measured with a thermometer. The most familiar thermometer is based on thermal expansion of mercury, and can be used to define the Celsius temperature scale. The absolute or Kelvin temperature scale is based upon the thermal expansion of gases.

As long as the pressure is not too high, all gases follow Boyle's law, Charles' law and Avogadro's principle, and these laws can be summarized in a single equation, the ideal gas equation. The ideal gas equation contains a universal constant called the gas constant, which can be used for calculations on all gases regardless of chemical composition.

In a mixture of gases, the partial pressure of each gas is the product of the total pressure and the mole fraction of that gas in the mixture.

The pressure of a gas can be understood using the kinetic theory, in which molecules are assumed to move about randomly at high speed and collide with the walls of the container. Analysis of the motion of the molecules in conjunction with the gas laws shows that the mean speed of the molecules can be calculated from the temperature of the gas. The analysis gives an interpretation of the energy of the gas.

When gases are compressed to high pressure, they deviate from the ideal gas equation. The van der Waals equation gives a reasonably good description of how each gas deviates, using two parameters that depend upon the chemical nature of the gas.

Review questions

1. What are the three defining properties of a gas?

2. What is the name of the S.I. unit for pressure and its definition in terms of fundamental units?

3. Name three devices for measuring pressure.

4. Name the device used to measure temperature.

5. State Boyle's law.

6. State Charles' law.

7. State Avogadro's principle.

8. What is the relationship between Celsius temperature and absolute temperature?

9. Define partial pressure in a mixture of gases.

10. What is the ideal gas equation?

11. What is the van der Waals equation? When would you use it?

Problems

1. A bottle of soft drink contains a small amount of gas above the liquid at a pressure of 150 kPa. If the pressure of the atmosphere is 98 kPa, and the inside diameter of the neck of the bottle is 15 mm, calculate the net force on the bottle cap. [9.2 N]

2. A bulb has a mass of 126.453 g when evacuated, 204.937 g when filled with water of density 0.9975 g/cm^3, and 127.297 g when filled with a sample of a gaseous compound. What is the density of the gas? [0.0107 g/cm^3]

3. A sample of gas is compressed to 1/3 of its original volume, and the temperature is increased from 15°C to 145°C. Calculate the ratio of the final pressure to the initial pressure. [4.35]

4. The volume of a sample of gas is reduced to 1/4 of its original volume and the temperature is increased from 15°C to 80°C. Calculate the ratio of the final density to the initial density.[4]

5. In a diesel engine, air is heated by rapid compression. Suppose that air is taken into the cylinder at a pressure of 95 kPa and 27°C and compressed into 1/10 of its original volume. After compression the pressure of the air is measured to be 2500 kPa. Calculate the temperature of the compressed air. [790 K]

6. Calculate the hydrostatic pressure at a depth of 10. metres under water, assuming the density of water is 1.00 g/cm^3 and the acceleration due to gravity is 9.8 m/s. [98 kPa]

7. One of the oxides of nitrogen is a gas with density 1.41 g/dm^3 at a temperature of 127°C and a pressure of 101 kPa. What is the molecular formula of the compound? [NO_2]

8. A gaseous compound has the following composition by weight: 74.03 % C, 17.27 % N and 8.70 % H. The gas has density 0.98 g/dm³ at a temperature of 400. K and a pressure of 40.0 kPa. What is the empirical formula, the molar mass, and molecular formula of the compound? [81.5 g/mol, C_5H_7N]

9. Calcium hydride, CaH_2, reacts with water to produce calcium hydroxide $Ca(OH)_2$, and hydrogen gas. Write a balanced equation for the reaction. Calculate the volume of hydrogen gas, measured at a pressure of 100. kPa and a temperature of 298 K, which would be produced by the reaction of 27.3 g of CaH_2 with excess water. [32.1 dm³]

10. Calcium carbide CaC_2 reacts with water to produce acetylene gas, C_2H_2. What volume of acetylene is produced by the reaction of 10.0 g of calcium carbide, with excess water? The gas is to be measured at a pressure of 100. kPa and a temperature of 27°C. [3.89 dm³]

11. Consider two identical bulbs, containing gas at equal temperatures and equal pressures. One bulb contains pure gaseous phosphine, PH_3, and the other pure gaseous hydrogen sulfide, H_2S. Assuming the gases are ideal, which bulb weighs more? Which bulb contains more molecules? Which tank contains more atoms?

12. Calculate the amount, in moles, of oxygen contained in a normal breath of air of volume 0. 50 dm³ at 20°C and 100. kPa. The mole fraction of oxygen in air is 0.21. [4.3×10^{-3} mol]

13. The mole fraction of CO_2 (expressed as a percentage) is 0.036 % in normal air, and about 4 % in exhaled air. If a person breathes 10. dm³ of air per minute, what mass of CO_2 is being produced per minute? [0.7 g]

14. Calculate the density of air at 20.°C and 100. kPa from the ideal gas equation. The mole fractions of the predominant gases are 0.78 N_2, 0.21 O_2, and 0.01 Ar. [1.19 g/dm³]

15. Calculate the density of methane at 20.°C and 250. kPa. [1.64 g/dm³]

16. A long-distance pipeline across Canada has an average diameter of 0.7 m and extends for a distance of 4000 km. If the average pressure in the pipeline is 300. kPa and the average temperature is −10°C in winter, calculate the amount of gas (in moles) contained in the pipeline. [2.1×10^8 mol]

17. A very good vacuum system is able to maintain a pressure as low as 10^{-10} Torr inside a vessel. How many molecules of residual gas are present in 1 cm³ at this pressure and room temperature? [3×10^6 molecules/cm³]

18. A bulb with a volume of 0.508 dm³ contains 42.1 mg of helium. If the pressure is 98.2 kPa, calculate the temperature of the bulb. [570 K]

19. Two bulbs, A and B, are connected by a length of thin flexible tubing with a valve, as shown in the diagram. As long as the valve is open the pressure is the same in both bulbs. Bulb A has a volume of 1.20 dm³, bulb B has a volume of 0.80 dm³, and the volume of the tubing can be neglected. The two bulbs contain a total of 0.10 mole of helium gas between them.

    (a) Calculate the pressure when the valve is open and the temperature of both bulbs is 300. K. [125 kPa]

    (b) If bulb B is cooled to a temperature of 100 K while the valve is still open and bulb A remains at 300K, calculate the pressure in the system. [69 kPa]

    (c) The valve is now closed and bulb B is returned to a temperature of 300 K. Calculate the pressure in each bulb. [A, 69 kPa; B, 208 kPa]

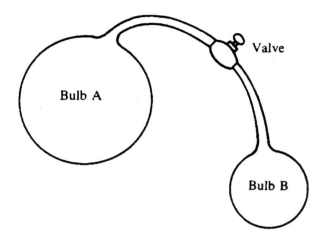

Bulb A

Valve

Bulb B

20. A sample of 100. cm^3 of oxygen at a pressure of 750. torr is mixed with 200. cm^3 of nitrogen at a pressure of 500 torr, and the mixture is transferred to a vessel of volume 150 cm^3; the temperatures of all gases are the same throughout the process. Calculate the total pressure and the partial pressure of each gas after mixing. [1167 torr, 500 torr O_2, 667 torr N_2]

21. Ammonium nitrite, NH_4NO_2, decomposes when heated to give nitrogen gas and water vapour. Write a balanced equation to show the reaction. What volume of nitrogen gas, measured at 300. K and 100. kPa, would be produced by decomposition of 8.0 g of ammonium nitrite? [3.1 dm^3]

22. What volume of hydrogen gas, measured at 300. K and 100. kPa, is produced by the electrolytic decomposition of water, if a current of one ampere flows through the electrolytic cell for one second? [0.129 cm^3]

23. Calculate the root mean squared speed of a molecule of (a) helium, (b) hydrogen, and (c) carbon dioxide at a temperature of 300. K. [1.37 km/s, 1.93 km/s, 0.412 km/s]

24. A gas mixture contains hydrogen, carbon monoxide, carbon dioxide, and water molecules. Calculate the ratio of the root mean squared speeds of the two species of molecule which are (on average) the fastest and slowest. [4.67]

25. The time required for a given volume of nitrogen to effuse through a tiny hole is 35 seconds. Calculate the molar mass of a gas which requires 50 s for the same volume of gas to effuse through the same hole under the same conditions. [57 g/mol]

26. Calculate the total kinetic energy of translation of each of (a) one mole of nitrogen molecules and (b) one mole of methane molecules, at a temperature of 25.°C. [3.72 kJ, 3.72 kJ]

27. 64.0 g of gaseous ethane, C_2H_6, is placed in a 33.0 dm^3 bulb at 27.0°C. (a) What is the pressure of the gas? (b) Strong ultraviolet light is shone on the gas, and 56.2% of the ethane molecules are converted to ethyne (acetylene), C_2H_2, and hydrogen H_2. Write a balanced equation to show the decomposition reaction. (c) Calculate the pressure in the bulb after the decomposition, assuming that the temperature is still 27°C. [161 kPa, 342 kPa]

28. In normal operation a mass spectrometer is pumped down to a very low pressure of 2.5×10^{-4} Pa. Calculate the number of air molecules per cubic centimetre in the remaining gas if the temperature is 24°C. [6×10^{10} molecules/cm^3]

29. A 1.000 g sample of a pure gaseous hydrocarbon was burned in excess oxygen and produced 3.142 g of CO_2 and 1.268 g of H_2O. What is the empirical formula of the compound? [CH_2]

30. A 0.500 g sample of the pure gaseous hydrocarbon described in question 29 has a volume of 437 cm^3 at a pressure of 50.7 kPa and a temperature of 25.0°C. What is the molecular formula of the compound? [C$_4$H$_8$]

31. Air bags are now being fitted as safety equipment in cars. Many such airbags are inflated with nitrogen gas, N$_2$, generated by the rapid reaction of sodium azide, NaN$_3$(s), and iron oxide Fe$_2$O$_3$(s). The products of the reaction are sodium oxide, metallic iron, and gaseous nitrogen. Write a balanced equation for the reaction, and calculate the mass of sodium azide required to provide 75.0 dm^3 of gas at 25°C and a pressure of 120. kPa. [157 g]

32. Calculate the pressure of oxygen at a molar volume of 24.00 dm^3/mol and a temperature of 25.0°C using the ideal gas equation and the van der Waals equation. [103.3 kPa, 103.2 kPa]

33. Calculate the pressure of methane at a molar volume of 1.00 dm^3/mol and a temperature of 25.0°C using the ideal gas equation, and the van der Waals equation. [2.48 MPa, 2.36 MPa]

34. Carbon dioxide vapour in equilibrium with the liquid carbon dioxide at a temperature of 20.0°C has a molar volume of 227 cm^3/mol. Calculate the pressure of the gas under these conditions using the ideal gas equation, and the van der Waals equation. Compare your results with the experimental pressure, 5.73 MPa. [10.7 MPa, 6.15 MPa]

35. Use the relationship between the van der Waals b coefficient and the volume of the molecules to estimate the van der Waals radius of a methane molecule from data in Table 5-2. [0.16 nm]

6 Thermochemistry

Objectives

After reading this chapter, the student should be able to do the following:

♦ Define adiabatic and isothermal processes.

♦ Define the relationship between heat, work and energy.

♦ State the first law of thermodynamics.

♦ Define enthalpy change in terms of heat and work at constant pressure.

♦ Define enthalpy change of reaction, and enthalpy change of formation.

♦ Use tabulated data to calculate enthalpy change of reaction.

♦ Define heat capacity.

♦ Describe how a calorimeter is used to measure enthalpy change of reaction.

♦ Define internal energy change in terms of heat and total work.

Related topics to review:

Properties of gases in Chapter 5.

Related topics to look forward to:

Molecular structure and bond energies in Chapter 11. Thermodynamics and chemical equilibrium in Chapter 16.

6-1 Chemical reactions and energy

Nobody who has been close to a big fire in a dry forest, or watched a welder cutting steel with an oxyacetylene torch, or felt the heat from a barbecue can help but wonder what makes the flames which vaporize and melt and scorch. A big explosion can leave a great hole in the ground or a broken and twisted building, even though the explosion itself lasts only a fraction of a second. The dramatic effects of fires and explosions are caused by the energy released in chemical reactions. These and other manifestations of chemical energy are of great interest, both for practical applications and for the information they can give about chemical reactions. The study of energy in chemistry is called **thermochemistry**, and is part of a much larger subject called **thermodynamics**.

In many chemical reactions, the temperature of the reacting mixture changes. Burning a fuel like propane produces a very hot flame, and mixing sulfuric acid with water produces a warm solution. The opposite effect, a large drop in temperature caused by a chemical reaction, is not so common, but is found in some cases. Some reactions proceed only at high temperature and with a large input of energy. Although the temperature change caused by a chemical reaction is easy to detect and measure, it is the energy involved in the reaction, rather than the temperature change, which is important. The temperature change in a reaction depends on how the reaction is carried out, but the energy of a chemical reaction is always the same for a particular reaction. In this chapter we develop the concept of energy, and the techniques for calculating and measuring the energy of a chemical reaction.

6-2 Processes

In thermochemistry, a **process** is defined as a chemical event of interest, such as a reaction, the mixing of substances to form a solution, or physical changes such as melting or boiling. A process may be an experiment in the laboratory, a large-scale reaction in a large industrial plant, or an event in the natural environment. A process may be an actual experiment, or a "thought experiment" which we discuss in order to demonstrate a principle or carry out a calculation. In some cases we consider processes in which the changes are very small, in order to simplify the calculations.

The substances and things directly involved in a process are called the **system.** There may be some choice in how the system is defined, but the definition should be a practical one. For example, in considering a chemical reaction, the system must include all the substances that take part in, or influence, the reaction.

If a solution takes part in a reaction, both the solvent and the solutes should be included as part of the system. It is not practical to consider the solute molecules (or ions) separately from the solvent molecules because there are very energetic interactions between them, which are not directly under the control of the experimenter.

The **surroundings** are defined as everything outside the system. The system and its surroundings make up the entire universe. However it is usually sufficient, when considering small scale chemical experiments, to consider only the immediate neighbourhood of the system as the surroundings. Thermochemical experiments are designed so that the only part of the surroundings that matters is the equipment in which the experiment takes place. In considering large scale processes such as the operation of an electric generating station, or photosynthesis in a forest, a much broader view is needed, and in such cases the surroundings include the whole natural environment, including the atmosphere, the earth, lakes and oceans and so on. In such cases it is sometimes helpful to use the word **environment** in place of surroundings. This changes the emphasis slightly but helps to clarify the implications of thermodynamics for environmental science.

Chemical experiments are nearly always carried out in some kind of **container,** which serves to define the system and control the process. The container should be chemically inert so that it does not take part in any reactions. Since by definition the container *contains* the system, it must be in physical contact with the system. For calculations the container may be included either as part of the system, or as part of the surroundings, and so it is often not mentioned explicitly.

The **state** of a system is specified by its temperature and pressure (or volume), and the amounts, chemical composition and state of aggregation of all substances present. In specifying a state, it is assumed that the system is in internal equilibrium and that the temperature and pressure are uniform throughout the system.

6-3 Thermal insulation: adiabatic and isothermal processes

Consider the following experiments. Take a tube containing hot water at a temperature of about 60°C in a room at a temperature of about 20°C and measure the temperature of the water as a function of time; Figure 6-1 shows a sketch of the equipment. The temperature of the water decreases as time goes on, and after some minutes, the temperature approaches room temperature. A graph of temperature as a function of time is shown in Figure 6-2. Now heat the water again, but this time insulate the tube with foam plastic or fibre **insulation**; with the insulation in place the temperature drifts down over a much longer period of time, perhaps an hour or more, depending on how much insulation is used.

The best insulation is to be found in a **Dewar flask**, consisting of a double-walled container with a vacuum between walls made of silvered glass or thin metal sheet. The Dewar flask is also known as a vacuum flask, or by its commercial name, Thermos flask. If the water, after being heated again, is transferred to a Dewar flask, the time required for cooling could be a day rather than an hour.

There is no specific time at which the cooling process is finished, but we can estimate the approximate thermal drift time-scale in each experiment by the time required for about 50% of the total temperature change to occur. The graphs in Figure 6-2 show that the thermal drift time-scale is about 10 minutes for the tube without insulation, an hour for the insulated tube, and many hours for the Dewar flask.

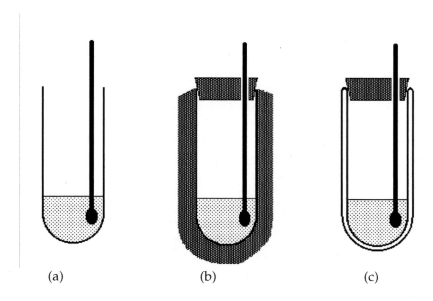

(a)   (b)   (c)

Figure 6-1   Three temperature drift experiments in which the system is contained in a round bottomed tube and the temperature is monitored with a thermometer. There are three conditions of insulation: (a) the tube is not insulated, (b) the tube is insulated with foam plastic or fibre, and (c) the system is contained in a Dewar flask consisting of a double walled vessel with a vacuum between the walls.

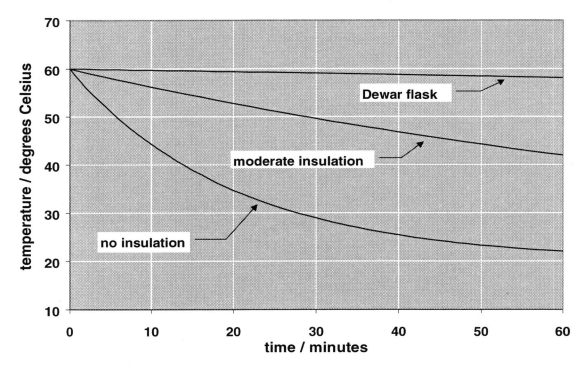

Figure 6-2 Graphs of temperature versus time for some hot water cooling from 60°C towards room temperature of 20°C, with three different levels of insulation as shown in Figure 6-1. The system in the Dewar flask is described as nearly adiabatic because the thermal drift timescale is many hours, which is much longer than the time required to complete most chemical experiments.

The quality of the insulation can be judged by the thermal drift time-scale. For the best possible insulation, the thermal drift time-scale can be made almost infinitely long. This can be achieved by placing the system in a Dewar flask inside yet another container, which is maintained at the same temperature as the outside of the Dewar flask using electronic controls.

Now consider a chemical reaction or other process that takes place in a well-insulated beaker or a Dewar flask. If the process is a fast one and is finished in a time much less than the thermal drift time-scale, then the process is said to be **nearly adiabatic.** For fast reactions, such as acid-base reactions in solution, nearly adiabatic conditions can be achieved with simple paper or foam plastic insulation, and a Dewar flask provides satisfactory adiabatic conditions for most experiments. **True adiabatic** conditions can be obtained by making the thermal drift time-scale infinitely long as described in the last paragraph, and this is done for the most precise measurements.

Some processes are extremely fast, and such processes are nearly adiabatic even though there may be no insulation at all. Explosive reactions take only milliseconds, and in flames the molecules of fuel and oxygen travel through the reaction zone in a very short time. In both explosions and flames the actual reaction processes are almost adiabatic, although the heat of reaction is transferred to the environment as the hot reaction products disperse.

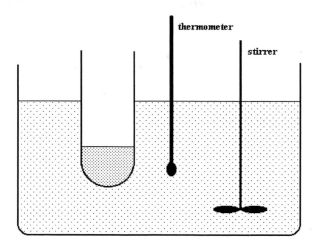

Figure 6-3 In this apparatus the system contained in the round-bottomed tube is immersed in a large tank of water. The water is stirred continuously and there is very good thermal contact between the system and the water, which keeps the temperature of the sample constant through any process such as a chemical reaction in the system. These conditions are called isothermal because the temperature is constant.

In some experiments it is necessary to keep the temperature of the system constant. A process carried out at constant temperature is described as **isothermal**. A simple way to achieve almost isothermal conditions is to place the system and its container in a large tank of water, which is constantly stirred, as shown in Figure 6-3. If the tank of water is much larger than the chemical system, the temperature of the water will remain nearly constant regardless of any chemical reaction in the system, and in turn this maintains the temperature of the system nearly constant. For very accurate work, the temperature of the water can be held exactly constant using an electronic temperature control.

6-4 Work

The fundamental definition of work is related to force and distance. The work done is the product of the force and the distance moved:

$$work = force \times distance\ moved. \tag{6-1}$$

The units of work are newton × metre, or joule (See Table 1-5). It is important to note that in order for work to be done, there must be both a force and a displacement. If you hold up a heavy weight at a constant height, you are not doing any work on the weight, although you may feel tired after a while because of physiological processes taking place in your muscles!

Four types of work are commonly encountered in chemistry: mechanical work, electrical work, photochemical work and atmospheric work.

Mechanical work derived from a chemical reaction is done in internal combustion engines: the fuel burns in the cylinders and the hot gases expand and drive the pistons, which are mechanically linked to a rotating shaft. When the point of application of a force moves, work is done.

Electrical work is done whenever an electric charge passes through a potential difference, whether as a result of an electrochemical process in a battery or electrolytic cell, or an electric current passing through a resistor. Flashlight "batteries" and electrolysis cells are examples of chemical devices that produce or absorb electrical work. The amount of electrical work done is the product of the electric charge and the potential difference:

$$work = electric\ charge \times potential\ difference = Q{\times}E \qquad (6\text{-}2)$$

where Q is the electric charge in coulombs and E is the potential difference in volts.

Example 6-1   A current of 500. amperes passes through an industrial electrolysis cell at a potential difference of 3.50 volts. How much work is done per second?

The charge passing per second is 500. coulomb/second, and so:

work done per second $= +500.$ coulomb/second $\times 3.50$ volts

$$= +1.75{\times}10^3 \text{ joules/second or } 1.75 \text{ kilowatt.}$$

Photochemical work is done when light is absorbed or emitted by a system. This process takes place at the molecular level, and is governed by the laws of quantum mechanics, about which we will say more in Chapter 10. The process of photosynthesis in plants depends upon the conversion of the energy of light into chemical energy through photochemical work.

Atmospheric work may be done when a chemical reaction is carried out in a beaker or flask that is open to the atmosphere. If a chemical reaction gives off or absorbs a gas, the volume of the reacting system changes. As a result of the change in the volume, work is done due to the forces exerted by the atmosphere; we call this work the **atmospheric work**. We will show how to calculate atmospheric work later in this chapter.

Throughout this book, the symbol w designates the total work done in a process and includes electrical, mechanical, photochemical and atmospheric work. The symbol w' designates the total mechanical, electrical and photochemical work, while w_{atmos} designates the atmospheric work. These quantities are related by the following equation:

$$w = w' + w_{atmos} \qquad (6\text{-}3)$$

Work can be done either on, or by, the system, and we distinguish between these two possibilities by giving an algebraic sign to the work. Work done *on* the system is given a positive sign; for example, when electric current is driven through an electrolysis cell, work is being done on the electrolysis cell and w' is positive. Work done *by* the system *on* the surroundings is negative; for example, when a battery drives an electric current through a motor, the battery is doing work, and the work w' is negative.

6-5 Energy and heat

Energy is defined as the ability to do work. In a purely mechanical system, the total energy is the sum of the potential energy and the kinetic energy. When work is done on such a system, the increase in the total energy is equal to the work done. For example, in the sport of curling, the player throws a rock across the horizontal ice surface, and the work done accelerating the rock increases the kinetic energy of the rock moving across the ice. If, instead, the player were to carry the rock up a hill, the work done against the force of gravity increases the potential energy of the rock. In both cases, doing work on the rock increases its energy.

In thermodynamics, we must expand our ideas of energy to include heat. The line of reasoning is as follows. At the end of the 18th century, Count Rumford observed that the a barrel of a cannon became hot while machining was in progress, even though the barrel was nowhere near a fire. The metal continued to get hotter as long as machining continued, roughly in proportion to the mechanical effort expended. The temperature increase was caused by the work that was done during machining, not by the flow of heat.

A similar experiment can be carried out with a bicycle pump. If the piston is pushed in quickly, the air inside the pump gets hot, and you can feel the pump itself get hot. The air inside the pump gets hot because of the work done on it.

These observations allow us to deduce the nature of heat. In the early days of thermodynamics, it was thought that heat was an actual fluid, and that temperature changes could only be caused by a flow of heat. This idea is wrong. The experiments described above show that work can produce a temperature change even when no heat flows. The same change of temperature can be produced by a flow of heat, and since work is a form of energy, heat must be a form of energy too.

Heat flows whenever there is a difference of temperature, and the direction of flow is always from hot to cold. The decrease of the temperature of the water illustrated in Figures 6-1 and 6-2 is due to the flow of heat from the hot water to the cooler surroundings. The effect of insulation is to slow down the flow of heat. In everyday language, "heat" is sometimes used where "temperature" is meant, but the two are not the same and care should be taken to avoid confusion. Heat is a form of energy, while temperature is the quality of hotness or coldness.

The nature of energy in a thermodynamic system was investigated quantitatively by James Joule in a famous series of experiments carried out around 1840. When work was done on a well-insulated tank of water, the temperature of the water increased. Electrical or mechanical work was done in several ways: by stirring the water with a paddle, by rubbing pieces of metal together, by compressing a gas, and by passing electric current through a resistor. Since the insulation reduced the flow of heat during the experiment to almost zero, the change in the energy of the water was equal to the work done.

Joule showed that, to produce a given change of temperature in the insulated tank of water, the same amount of work was required regardless of how the work was done. For a given initial temperature and a given final temperature, the change in the energy of the water was always the same. Hence the energy of the water was always the same at a particular temperature.

The energy of a system can change either through the action of heat or work. The amount of heat involved in a process is measured by the amount of work required to produce the same change of temperature in the same system when it is well insulated.

The symbol q is used to designate the amount of heat that is transferred to the system in a process. If heat flows into the system, then q is positive, and if heat flows out of the system then q is negative. Heat q is measured in units of joules, since it is defined in terms of an amount of work.

The **first law of thermodynamics** summarizes these conclusions and extends them to all systems:

The energy of a system in a particular state of temperature, pressure and chemical composition is always the same. The change in the energy of a system in a process is equal to the sum of the heat and work transferred to the system.

There are two parts to the law. The first sentence declares that the energy is a **state function**, which depends only on the state of the system. The second sentence declares the equivalence of heat and work in producing a change in energy.

6-6 Thermal energy and chemical energy

Energy can pass between a system and its surroundings either as heat or as work, and the change in the energy of the system is the sum of the heat and work that flow into the system. The terms "heat" and "work" are used to describe how energy passes between system and surroundings.

The energy contained within a system cannot be classified as heat or work, but nevertheless it can be divided into several different categories. For our purposes, the two most important types of energy are the chemical energy and the thermal energy. The relationships between these quantities are shown in Figure 6-4.

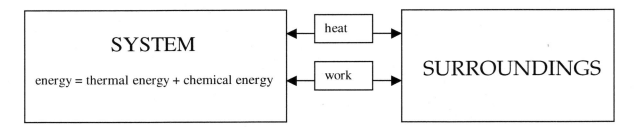

Figure 6-4 The energy within a system consists of the thermal energy and the chemical energy. Energy may flow between the system and its surroundings either in the form of heat of work, and the total change in the energy of the system is the sum of the heat and the work.

The **chemical energy** of a system is stored in its chemical bonds, or in the case of ionic substances, the electrostatic interactions between the ions. The chemical energy of a system depends on its chemical composition, and when a chemical reaction takes place, the energy associated with the chemical bonds changes as the reactants are converted to products and the composition of the system changes.

The **thermal energy** consists of the kinetic energy of molecular motion, and the energy of interaction between molecules, but does not involve the chemical bonds within each molecule. In the previous chapter we discussed the kinetic energy of random motion of molecules in a gas. In liquids and solids the molecules also move rapidly, although they do not move around as much as in gases. Within each molecule, the atoms vibrate around their average positions, and the vibrations store kinetic and potential energy. In liquids and solids, molecules are held together by attractive forces, and potential energy is stored as a result of these forces. These forms of energy all vary with temperature, and so together are classified as thermal energy.

When energy is transferred to a system without causing a chemical reaction, the energy is stored in the form of thermal energy and the result is an increase in the temperature. This is true whether the energy is transferred as heat or work.

If the temperature is held constant during a chemical reaction, the thermal energy of the system does not change very much, if at all, and the energy change in the reaction is due almost entirely to the change in the chemical energy alone. In calculating and measuring the energy of chemical reactions, we assume that the temperature of the reacting system does not change.

Many chemical effects are the result of conversion of energy from one form to another. For example, combustion of a hydrocarbon fuel in air releases large amounts of energy. The energy of combustion comes from rearrangement of the chemical bonds in the molecules of the hydrocarbon and the oxygen, as they are converted into carbon dioxide and water. In a flame, the chemical energy is released rapidly and converted directly into thermal energy, and hence the reaction products are hot. As the hot reaction products rise out of the flame, heat is lost to the surroundings and they cool down. The ultimate source of the heat is the chemical energy.

6-7 Energy and Enthalpy

If the external pressure on a system is constant, then the energy of the system is most conveniently measured by a quantity called the **enthalpy**. Enthalpy is a word derived from the Greek word meaning *to heat*, but (now that we recognise the equivalence of heat and work) includes work as well. The symbol H is always used to represent the enthalpy. The Greek letter Δ (delta) in front of a symbol indicates the change in the corresponding quantity, so ΔH is the enthalpy change due to a process.

Since the tank of water in Joule's experiments was open to the atmosphere, the external pressure was constant, and the conclusion drawn from those experiments, namely the first law of thermodynamics, is best stated in terms of the enthalpy: the enthalpy of a system depends only on its state.

The enthalpy change due to a process is equal to the difference between the enthalpy of the final state H_f and the enthalpy of the initial state H_i:

$$\Delta H = H_f - H_i \tag{6-4}$$

For an adiabatic process in an insulated system at constant external pressure, the heat transferred, q, is zero and the enthalpy change is equal to the electrical or mechanical work done:

$$\Delta H = w' \qquad \text{for an adiabatic process at constant pressure} \tag{6-5}$$

If the system is not insulated, then heat can be transferred between the system and its surroundings during the process, and causes a change in the enthalpy. The change in the enthalpy of a system due to a process at constant pressure is equal to the sum of the heat q_P transferred to the system and the mechanical, electrical or photochemical work w' done on the system during the process:

$$\Delta H = q_P + w' \qquad \text{at constant pressure} \tag{6-6}$$

Equation (6-6) is a mathematical statement that follows from the first law of thermodynamics.

In a process in which there is no mechanical, electrical or photochemical work done on the system, then $w' = 0$ and the change in enthalpy is equal to the heat transferred to the system:

$$\Delta H = q_P \qquad \text{at constant pressure} \tag{6-7}$$

Different processes that start from a particular initial state and end at a particular final state may involve different amounts of heat q_P and work w', but the sum $q_P + w'$ is the same for all such processes. The sum $q_P + w'$ is a state function, but the heat q_P and the work w' are not. Various possible processes with the same initial and final states, but different values of q_P and w', are shown in Figure 6-5.

When a process returns the system to exactly the same condition that it was in before the process, the process is called **cyclic**. Because the enthalpy is a state function, the change in enthalpy ΔH is zero for any cyclic process. Cyclic processes might seem to be of little importance, but they play an important role in calculations and discussions in thermodynamics, and form the basis for understanding heat engines and heat pumps, used in refrigerators and air conditioners.

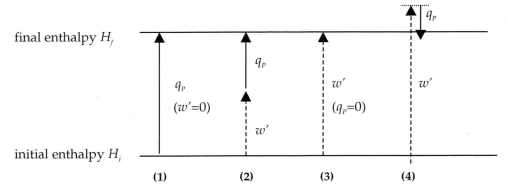

Figure 6-5 Four different processes which change a system at constant pressure from an initial state with enthalpy H_i to a final state with enthalpy H_f by different paths. The process might, for example, be a change in the temperature of some water. The change in the enthalpy is the same for all four processes because the same initial and final states are involved. For each process, the amount of heat q_P is indicated by a full arrow, and the amount of mechanical, electrical or photochemical work w' by a dashed arrow. In process (1) heat is added, but no work is done. In process (3), no heat is added, but work is done, perhaps by stirring the water. In process (2), both heat and work are involved. In process (4) more work is done than is necessary, and some heat actually leaves the water.

6-8 Enthalpy change of a chemical reaction

The energy involved in a chemical reaction is nearly always expressed in terms of the enthalpy change, because most chemical reactions are open to the atmosphere, which provides a constant external pressure.

The **enthalpy change of reaction** is the change of enthalpy ΔH for a chemical reaction when the temperature is held constant. This means that, if the reacting mixture gets hot, heat must be allowed to escape so that the temperature returns to its initial value. If, on the other hand, the reacting mixture gets cold, heat must be added to the system to return it to the initial temperature.

For an **exothermic reaction**, the enthalpy change of reaction ΔH is negative, and for an **endothermic reaction** the enthalpy change of reaction ΔH is positive.

The enthalpy change of reaction is sometimes referred to as the heat of reaction. However, in an electrochemical cell the amount of heat produced or absorbed in a reaction is not equal to the enthalpy change of reaction if electrical work is done. Hence it is best to refer to the enthalpy change of reaction rather than heat of reaction.

The enthalpy change of a reaction depends on how much material actually reacts. The amount of reaction taking place can be specified in terms of the **amount of reaction**. The amount of reaction is measured in units of moles, and refers to a specific statement of the equation for the reaction.

One mole of reaction means that the amount (in moles) of each substance taking part is equal to the stoichiometric coefficient in the balanced equation. For example, one mole of the reaction

$$N_2 + 3\,H_2 \rightarrow 2\,NH_3$$

means that 1 mole of N_2 reacts with 3 moles of H_2 to yield 2 moles of NH_3.

The enthalpy change of a chemical reaction is quoted *per mole of reaction* according to the balanced chemical equation. The chemical equation should always accompany the ΔH value. The enthalpy change of a chemical reaction is usually quoted with units of kilojoule per mole (of reaction).

When tabulating data, it is necessary to adopt agreed upon standard conditions for the substances involved. The **standard state** of a substance is defined as the pure substance in the specified state (i.e. solid, liquid or gas) at the standard pressure $P°$, at any specified temperature. Other aspects of the standard state will be discussed in the appropriate places. If all the substances taking part in a reaction are in their standard states, the enthalpy change of reaction is called the **standard enthalpy change of reaction**.

It follows from the first law that when chemical equations are added, the enthalpy changes can be added. This is called **Hess' law**, and was discovered through studies of chemical reactions, independently of Joule's experiments. Much of the rest of this chapter consists of applications of Hess' law.

Hess' law is often used to obtain data for reactions that are difficult to measure directly. Consider the combustion of carbon to give carbon dioxide, for which the enthalpy change is:

$$C(s) + O_2(g) \rightarrow CO_2(g) \qquad \Delta H° = -393.5 \text{ kJ/mol} \qquad \text{(i)}$$

This reaction can be carried out in two steps. The first step is the partial oxidation of carbon to carbon monoxide, and the enthalpy change for this reaction is denoted by the unknown x:

$$C(s) + \tfrac{1}{2} O_2(g) \rightarrow CO(g) \qquad \Delta H° = x \qquad \text{(ii)}$$

Because this reaction in practice always leads to a mixture of CO and CO_2 a direct measurement of the enthalpy change of reaction is not possible. However if pure CO is isolated from the reaction products and reacted with more oxygen to form CO_2, the standard enthalpy change can be measured:

$$CO(g) + \tfrac{1}{2} O_2(g) \rightarrow CO_2(g) \qquad \Delta H° = -283.0 \text{ kJ/mol} \qquad \text{(iii)}$$

Equations (ii) and (iii) add up to give the overall equation (i) for the complete oxidation of carbon, and the standard enthalpy changes for these two reactions add up to the standard enthalpy change for the complete oxidation. Hence, for the reaction (i), the standard enthalpy change of reaction can be expressed in two ways:

$$\Delta H° = x + (-283.0) = -393.5 \text{ kJ/mol},$$

The standard enthalpy change of oxidation of C(s) to give CO(g) is therefore:

$$x = (-393.5) - (-283.0) = -110.5 \text{ kJ/mol}.$$

Example 6-2 The standard enthalpy changes of reaction for the two steps in the production of hydrogen from methane and steam as described in Chapter 4 are as follows:

$$CH_4(g) + H_2O(g) \rightarrow CO(g) + 3 H_2(g) \qquad \Delta H° = +206.1 \text{ kJ/mol}$$

$$CO(g) + H_2O(g) \rightarrow CO_2(g) + H_2(g) \qquad \Delta H° = -41.2 \text{ kJ/mol}$$

Calculate the standard enthalpy change for the overall reaction, assuming complete oxidation of carbon monoxide CO.

If the CO produced in the first reaction is entirely converted to CO_2 in the second reaction, the equation for the overall process is obtained by adding the two equations together:

$$CH_4(g) + 2\ H_2O(g) \rightarrow CO_2(g) + 4\ H_2(g)$$

The standard enthalpy change of the overall reaction is the sum of the standard enthalpy changes for the individual reactions:

$$\Delta H° = (+206.1) + (-41.2) = +164.9 \text{ kJ/mol}$$

Example 6-3 Given the standard enthalpy change of reaction for each of the following reactions, calculate the standard enthalpy change of oxidation of sulfur to $SO_3(g)$.

$$S(s) + O_2(g) \rightarrow SO_2(g) \qquad \Delta H° = -296.83 \text{ kJ/mol}$$

$$2\ SO_2(g) + O_2(g) \rightarrow 2\ SO_3(g) \qquad \Delta H° = -197.78 \text{ kJ/mol}$$

Before these equations can be added together, the second equation must be divided by 2 in order for the SO_2 to cancel when it is added to the first:

$$SO_2(g) + ½\ O_2(g) \rightarrow SO_3(g) \qquad \Delta H° = (-197.78)/2 = -98.89 \text{ kJ/mol}$$

Adding this equation to the first equation above, we get:

$$S(s) + 3/2\ O_2(g) \rightarrow SO_3(g) \qquad \Delta H° = (-296.83) + (-98.89) = -395.72 \text{ kJ/mol}$$

In visualizing the energy relationship in a chemical reaction, a diagram is often useful. The enthalpy of the products of a reaction relative to the enthalpy of the reactants can be indicated by writing the chemical reaction as a diagram, in which a vertical displacement on the paper indicates the direction of the enthalpy change of reaction. In an exothermic reaction, in which the enthalpy change of reaction is negative, the enthalpy of the products is lower than the enthalpy of the reactants. This is illustrated in Figure 6-7. Most of the diagrams in the rest of this chapter follow this convention.

Although they are unfavourable energetically, endothermic reactions may take place as long as the enthalpy change of reaction is supplied, usually in the form of heat. For instance, many substances decompose when heated although the decomposition reactions are endothermic. The thermal decomposition of calcium carbonate was discussed in section 4-5.

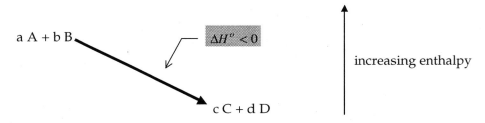

Figure 6-6 The standard enthalpy change of reaction may be indicated by displacing the products vertically from the reactants. This shows an exothermic reaction in which the standard enthalpy change of reaction is negative. For an endothermic reaction, in which the enthalpy change of reaction is positive, the enthalpy of the products is higher than the enthalpy of the reactants, and the products would be shown higher than the reactants.

6-9 Standard enthalpy change of formation

For any compound, we can write a reaction in which the compound is formed from the elements. Some examples are as follows:

$$C(s) + 2\,H_2(g) \rightarrow CH_4(g)$$

$$Ca(s) + C(s) + 3/2\,O_2(g) \rightarrow CaCO_3(s)$$

$$2\,C(s) + 3\,H_2(g) + \tfrac{1}{2}\,O_2(g) \rightarrow C_2H_5OH(\ell)$$

In each of these equations, the reactants are elements in their standard states and the product is a single compound in its standard state. Such reactions can be summarized as:

elements $\rightarrow$ compound

The standard enthalpy change of this reaction is called the **standard enthalpy change of formation** of the compound. Although it is unusual for a compound to be formed directly from elements in a single reaction, the standard enthalpy change of formation can be calculated from data for other related reactions using Hess' law.

The standard enthalpy change of formation is designated by the symbol $\Delta H_f^{\,\circ}$ and is always quoted per mole of the compound. Appendix 1 contains a table of standard enthalpy changes of formation for elements and compounds at a temperature of $25\,^\circ C$.

The standard enthalpy change of formation of an element in its standard state is zero, since the chemical equation

element $\rightarrow$ *element*

shows that nothing happens. If an element occurs in more than one allotrope, the standard state is usually chosen to be the most stable allotrope; the one exception is phosphorus for which white phosphorus is chosen as the standard state although it is not the most stable allotrope.

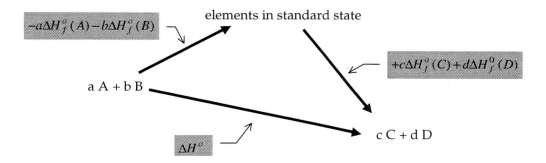

Figure 6-7 Any chemical reaction can, in principle at least, be carried out by the alternate path of decomposing the reactants into elements in their standard states and then reacting the elements to form the products. The standard enthalpy changes of these steps are shown for a general reaction aA + bB → cC + dD in terms of the standard enthalpy changes of formation of all the substances involved. The vertical displacement represents the standard enthalpy change for the isothermal reaction, and the drawing shows an exothermic reaction.

Chapter 6

From a table of ΔH_f° values it is possible to calculate the standard enthalpy change of reaction for a large number of chemical reactions at the temperature specified in the table, using Hess' law. Any reaction can be carried out, in principle, by a reaction in which the reactants are converted into elements in their standard state, followed by reaction of the elements to give the products. These reactions and the corresponding standard enthalpy changes are shown in Figure 6-7.

Figure 6-7 shows that the standard enthalpy change of the reaction is the sum of the standard enthalpy changes of the two steps involving the elements:

$$aA \quad + \quad bB \quad \rightarrow \quad cC \quad + \quad dD$$

$$\Delta H^0 = -a\Delta H_f^o(A) - b\Delta H_f^o(B) + c\Delta H_f^o(C) + d\Delta H_f^o(D) \tag{6-8}$$

It is convenient to lay out the calculation with the stoichiometric coefficient and ΔH_f° value under each substance involved in the reaction, with negative signs for the reactants and positive signs for the products. The stoichiometric coefficients a, b, c, and d do not have units, but represent the relative numbers of molecules of each substance that takes part in the reaction. The following examples show how this equation is used.

Example 6-4 Calculate the standard enthalpy change for the decomposition reaction reaction $CaCO_3(s) \rightarrow CaO(s) + CO_2(g)$ at 25°C using data from Appendix I.

Reading from Appendix I, the standard enthalpy changes of formation are found to be:

$\Delta H_f^\circ(CaCO_3) = -1206.92$ kJ/mol,

$\Delta H_f^\circ(CaO) = -635.09$ kJ/mol,

$\Delta H_f^\circ(CO_2) = -393.509$ kJ/mol.

The calculation can be laid out by writing the standard enthalpy changes of formation under each substance taking part in the reaction, as follows:

$$CaCO_3(s) \quad \rightarrow \quad CaO(s) \quad + \quad CO_2(g)$$

$$\Delta H^\circ = -(-1206.92) + (-635.09) + (-393.509) = +178.32 \text{ kJ/mol}$$

The reaction is strongly endothermic. Notice that negative signs precede the term for the reactant, and that parentheses are used liberally to avoid errors with the signs.

Example 6-5 Calculate ΔH° for the following reaction at 25°C:

$4 NH_3(g) + 5 O_2(g) \rightarrow 4 NO(g) + 6 H_2O(g)$

The standard enthalpy changes of formation (in the gas state) are:

$\Delta H_f^\circ(NH_3) = -46.11$ kJ/mol,

$\Delta H_f^\circ(O_2) = 0$ kJ/mol,

$\Delta H_f^\circ(NO) = +90.25$ kJ/mol,

$\Delta H_f^\circ(H_2O) = -241.818$ kJ/mol

The chemical equation and standard enthalpy change of reaction are as follows:

$$4\,NH_3(g) \;+\; 5\,O_2(g) \;\rightarrow\; 4\,NO(g) \;+\; 6\,H_2O(g)$$

$$\Delta H^\circ = -\,4\times(-46.11) \;-\;5\times(0) \;+\;4\times(+90.25)\;+\;6\times(-241.818)\;=\;-905.47\;kJ/mol$$

Note that the standard enthalpy change of formation of the element oxygen is zero.

Many organic compounds burn readily in oxygen, and the **standard enthalpy change of combustion** can be measured accurately in a calorimeter. The standard enthalpy change of formation of the compound is readily calculated from the standard enthalpy change of combustion as long as the products of the reaction are known.

Example 6-6   The standard enthalpy change of combustion of hexane, $C_6H_{14}(\ell)$ to give liquid water and carbon dioxide gas is –4163.1 kJ/mol. Calculate the standard enthalpy change of formation of $C_6H_{14}(\ell)$.

The standard enthalpy changes of formation of CO_2 and $H_2O(\ell)$ are:

$\Delta H_f^\circ\,(CO_2) = -393.509$ kJ/mol,

$\Delta H_f^\circ(H_2O(\ell)) = -285.830$ kJ/mol.

Let x be the standard enthalpy change of formation of liquid hexane. The equation for the combustion reaction is:

$$C_6H_{14}(\ell) + 9\tfrac{1}{2}\,O_2(g) \;\rightarrow\; 6\,CO_2(g) + 7\,H_2O(\ell)$$

The standard enthalpy change of combustion can therefore be written:

$$\Delta H = \; -x - 9\tfrac{1}{2}\times(0) \;+6\times(-393.905) + 7\times(-285.830)\;=\;-4163.1\;kJ/mol$$

Solving this equation yields $x = -201.1$ kJ/mol, and so the standard enthalpy change of formation of hexane is –201.1 kJ/mol.

6-10 Reactions in solution

The standard enthalpy change for a reaction in solution can be calculated by the same method as for other reactions. Appendix 1 lists the standard enthalpy changes of formation of some solutes in aqueous solution. A solute dissolved in water is designated by the symbol (aq) (together with a concentration if appropriate), meaning a solute in aqueous solution. The standard state of solutes in solution is defined as a hypothetical solution that has a concentration c° of 1.000 M but has the same properties as a very dilute solution. The reason for this rather artificial definition is that it simplifies certain more advanced measurements and calculations on concentrated solutions. In most of our work we will assume that the difference between the hypothetical solution and the real solution is not important, at least until the basic ideas are established.

In the case of electrolytes that dissociate into ions in solution, another difficulty arises because it is not possible to have a solution containing only one type of ion with no ions of opposite charge. The convention has been adopted that in aqueous solution the standard enthalpy change of formation of the aqueous hydrogen ion $H^+(aq)$ is equal to zero exactly. Having assigned this value, measured standard enthalpy changes for actual chemical reactions are then used to calculate standard enthalpy changes of formation for other ions.

Chapter 6

The standard enthalpy change of the process of dissolving a solute in water is called the **standard enthalpy change of solution**.

_____

Example 6-7   Calculate the standard enthalpy change of solution of sodium chloride in water from standard enthalpy changes of formation.

_____

The equation for dissolving NaCl in water to form a solution containing the fully ionized salt is:

$$NaCl(s) \rightarrow Na^+(aq) + Cl^-(aq)$$

Taking the standard enthalpy changes of formation for these species from Appendix 1,

$$\Delta H^\circ = -(-411.153) + (-240.12) + (-167.159) = +3.87 \text{ kJ/mol}$$

_____

It is notable that the process of dissolving a salt such as NaCl in water does not involve very much energy. The energy of interaction between the ions in the crystal is called the **lattice energy**. The energy of interaction between ions in solution and the surrounding water molecules is called the **solvation energy**. Both the lattice energy and the solvation energy are large, but because they are nearly equal, the enthalpy change of solution is small in most cases, and may be either positive or negative depending upon the solute.

In many processes in solution, the solvent does not explicitly take part in the reaction as written, and is not included in the calculations. However, if the solvent takes part in the reaction it must be included, as in the following example.

_____

Example 6-8 Calculate the standard enthalpy change of neutralization of a strong acid with a strong base.

_____

The net ionic reaction between a strong acid and a strong base is represented by the equation:

$$H^+(aq) + OH^-(aq) \rightarrow H_2O(\ell)$$

Reading the enthalpy changes of formation from Appendix1 the standard enthalpy change is:

$$\Delta H^\circ = -(0) - (-229.994) + (-285.830) = -55.836 \text{ kJ/mol}$$

_____

Example 6-9   Calculate the standard enthalpy change of ionization of acetic acid in aqueous solution.

_____

The ionization reaction is represented by the equation:

$$CH_3COOH(aq) \rightarrow CH_3COO^-(aq) + H^+(aq)$$

and the standard enthalpy change for this process is:

$$\Delta H^\circ = -(-485.76) + (-486.01) + (0) = -0.25 \text{ kJ/mol}$$

The standard enthalpy change of ionization of acetic acid is close to zero, and this also is true for other carboxylic acids, i.e. acids containing the group –COOH. Since the enthalpy change of ionization is negative, though very small, the ionization process is favourable energetically.

Acetic acid is a weak acid and dissociates only slightly in most solutions. The above calculation gives the enthalpy change per mole of acid that actually ionizes.

Example 6-10 Calculate the standard enthalpy change of solution of pure liquid sulfuric acid in water, assuming that the solution contains H^+ ions and bisulfate ions, HSO_4^-.

The process of forming the specified solution and the standard enthalpy change are:

$$H_2SO_4(\ell) \rightarrow H^+(aq) + HSO_4^-(aq)$$

$$\Delta H^\circ = -(-813.989) + (0) + (-887.34) = -73.35 \text{ kJ/mol}$$

This shows that mixing sulfuric acid with water is an exothermic reaction. If a small amount of water is added to concentrated sulfuric acid, the energy released may be sufficient to boil the water and cause dangerous splashing of the hot corrosive liquid. Hence, in mixing acid with water, the acid should always be added to the water so the water is in excess and can absorb the energy released without boiling.

Example 6-11 Calculate the standard enthalpy change for the reaction between zinc metal and a strong acid in solution.

The reaction and the standard enthalpy change are:

$$Zn(s) + 2 H^+(aq) \rightarrow Zn^{2+}(aq) + H_2(g),$$

$$\Delta H^\circ = -(0) - 2\times(0) + (-153.89) + (0) = -153.89 \text{ kJ/mol.}$$

Note that the standard enthalpy changes of formation are zero for the metal, for hydrogen ions, and for hydrogen gas are all zero. This is also a strongly exothermic reaction.

6-11 Heat capacity

If heat is added to a system in which there is no chemical reaction, and no physical change such as melting or evaporation, the temperature of the system increases. The heat required to increase the temperature per unit temperature change is the **heat capacity** of the system; if heat q causes a temperature change ΔT then the heat capacity C is:

$$C = \frac{q}{\Delta T}$$

Heat capacity may refer to an entire system, or to a fixed amount of a specified substance. The heat capacity per mole of a specified substance is called the **molar heat capacity** with units $J \text{ K}^{-1} \text{mol}^{-1}$. It should be noted that the molar heat capacity has the same units as the gas constant. The heat capacity per gram is called the **specific heat capacity, or specific heat**, and has units $J \text{ K}^{-1} \text{g}^{-1}$.

Chapter 6

The above definition is not complete, however, since heat is not a state function, and the amount of heat required for a given change of temperature depends other conditions. If the pressure is kept constant and there is no electrical or mechanical work, then $q_P = \Delta H$ by equation (6-7) and the **heat capacity at constant pressure** is:

$$C_P = \frac{q_P}{\Delta T} = \frac{\Delta H}{\Delta T} \qquad (6\text{-}9)$$

Appendix 1 contains values of $C_p{}^\circ$ for many substances in their standard state at 25°C.

It is instructive to compare the standard heat capacities at constant pressure for various substances listed in Appendix I. . Generally, the heat capacity of gases increases with the molar mass and complexity of the molecules. The heat capacities of the monatomic gases such as He and Ne are all close to 20.786 J K^{-1} mol^{-1}. The heat capacities of gases consisting of diatomic molecules such as oxygen O_2 and carbon monoxide CO are larger than for monatomic gases, and the heat capacities of polyatomic molecules such as carbon dioxide CO_2 and sulfur trioxide SO_3 are larger still. This is because the energies associated with the rotational motion of these molecules and the vibrations of the atoms within the molecules contribute to the thermal energy.

The heat capacity of a substance is larger in the liquid state than in either the gaseous or solid states. As an example, for ice at 0°C $C_p = 37.8$ J K^{-1} mol^{-1}, for liquid water at 25°C $C_p = 75.3$ J K^{-1} mol^{-1}, and for water vapour at 25°C $C_p = 33.6$ J K^{-1} mol^{-1}.

Example 6-12 Calculate ΔH° and q when 10.0 g of water is heated from 20.0°C to 30.0°C at constant pressure.

Amount of water = 10.0 g/18.0 g mol^{-1} = 0.556 mol. From Appendix I, the molar heat capacity of water at constant pressure is $C_p = 75.29$ J K^{-1} mol^{-1}, the temperature change is $\Delta T = 10.0$ K, and so:

$$\Delta H^\circ = q_P = nC_p{}^\circ \Delta T = 0.556 \text{ mol} \times 75.29 \text{ J K}^{-1} \text{ mol}^{-1} \times 10.0 \text{ K} = 419 \text{ J}.$$

6-12 Calorimetry

Enthalpy changes are measured experimentally using a **calorimeter**, an instrument in which chemical reactions take place under adiabatic conditions. A simple calorimeter used for measurements on reactions in solution consists of a Dewar flask or other well-insulated container, a means for mixing the reactants, and a theometer for measuring the temperature.

The reactants are first placed in the calorimeter but kept separate; the temperature of the system is measured at regular time intervals, and after it has become constant at the initial temperature T_i, the reactants are mixed and the reaction begins. Because the reaction takes place under adiabatic conditions, the temperature changes to the final temperature T_f. Once the temperature has stabilized, the temperature change $T_f - T_i$ caused by the chemical reaction is determined. The change of temperature through the experiment is shown in Figure 6-10.

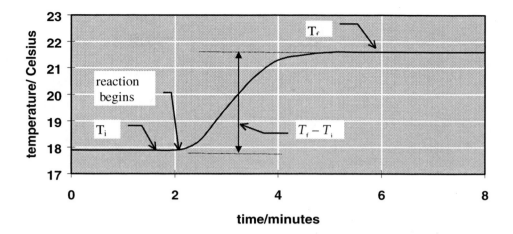

Figure 6-9 Graph of temperature *versus* time in a calorimeter experiment. In practice, there is usually a slow drift of the temperature before and after the reaction takes place, which is taken into account by linear extrapolation to the centre of the reaction period.

The calculation of the heat of reaction is carried out as follows. The system is defined as the chemical system inside the container plus the part of the calorimeter that is in contact with the sample. During the actual reaction, the good insulation prevents exchange of heat between the system and the surroundings, so $q = 0$. Because the process takes place at constant pressure, the enthalpy change for the system during the actual reaction is $\Delta H_1 = q_p = 0$. The actual reaction that takes place can be represented as follows:

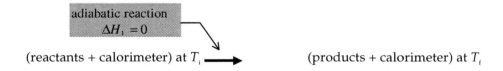

The enthalpy change of reaction is the enthalpy change for the *isothermal* reaction in which the products are at the same temperature as the reactants. Hence it is necessary to calculate the

enthalpy change ΔH_2 required to return the products to the initial temperature T_1, as shown in Figure 6-10. ΔH_2 can be calculated from the heat capacity of the reaction products plus the calorimeter:

$$\Delta H_2 = (C_{calorimeter} + C_{products}) \times (T_i - T_f)$$

where $C_{calorimeter}$ is the heat capacity of the calorimeter, and $C_{products}$ is the heat capacity of the products of the reaction. The enthalpy change of the isothermal reaction is then the sum of the enthalpy changes for the adiabatic reaction and the temperature adjustment step, $\Delta H = \Delta H_1 + \Delta H_2$, which is just ΔH_2 since ΔH_1 is zero.

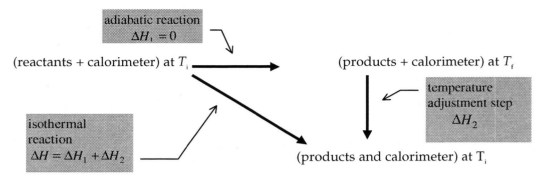

Figure 6-10 The calculation of the enthalpy change of reaction ΔH from the temperature change caused by the reaction taking place under adiabatic conditions. In this diagram, vertical displacement indicates changes in enthalpy. The arrow at the top indicates the actual reaction (which is adiabatic), the vertical arrow indicates the (hypothetical) step in which the products are returned to the initial temperature, and the diagonal arrow indicates the isothermal reaction for which the enthalpy change is to be calculated.

In the isothermal reaction in Figure 6-10, the calorimeter does not change temperature, so the enthalpy change is the standard enthalpy change for the chemical reaction:

$$\Delta H^o = (C_{calorimeter} + C_{products}) \times (T_i - T_f) \tag{6-10}$$

The heat capacities of the products and the calorimeter can be determined by a calibration experiment; usually the calorimeter makes only a small contribution to the total heat capacity. Notice that if the temperature increases in the first (adiabatic) step, then $T_f > T_i$, the standard enthalpy change of reaction is negative and the reaction is exothermic.

The other common form of chemical calorimeter is the **bomb calorimeter**, which is used for very energetic reactions such as combustion reactions. The reaction is carried out inside a strong vessel (the "bomb") which is immersed in a well-insulated tank of water. The bomb initially contains the fuel plus pure oxygen at high pressure, and in this highly oxidising atmosphere the combustion reaction proceeds rapidly to completion once it is started electrically. Heat is transferred from the hot combustion products to the bomb, the water and other parts of the calorimeter, causing the temperature to rise. The analysis of the bomb calorimeter experiment is discussed in books on physical chemistry.

6-13 The internal energy

For some purposes, it is necessary to calculate the total energy change in a process, including the work done by the atmosphere when the volume of the system changes. This can be done by adding the atmospheric work to the enthalpy change calculated by the methods outlined earlier in this chapter.

The atmospheric work in a constant pressure process is designated by the symbol w_{atmos}. We recall here equation (6-3), which states that the total work done in a process, w, is the sum of the mechanical, electrical, photochemical work w' and atmospheric work w_{atmos}:

$$w = w' + w_{atmos}$$

The atmospheric work for a process carried out in contact with the atmosphere can be calculated as follows. Consider some gas contained in a cylinder sealed with a piston, as shown in Figure

6-11. The piston has area A and can move without friction. The piston serves to separate the system inside the cylinder from the atmosphere outside the cylinder, but moves so that the pressure inside is equal to the pressure of the atmosphere outside. If the atmospheric pressure is P_{atmos} then the force of the atmosphere on the outside of the piston is $A \times P_{atmos}$.

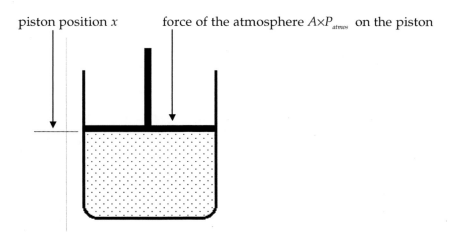

piston position x force of the atmosphere $A \times P_{atmos}$ on the piston

Figure 6-11 A sample of gas contained in a cylinder fitted with a piston which can move without friction. . The gas inside the cylinder is at atmospheric pressure. The piston has area A and its position is measured by the distance x measured from some fixed position. The atmosphere at pressure P_{atmos} exerts a force $A \times P_{atmos}$ on the outside face of the piston, and when the piston moves, atmospheric work is done.

Suppose that some process taking place inside the cylinder causes the volume to change by moving the piston. If the piston moves down by a distance Δx, then the volume changes by an amount $\Delta V = -A \times \Delta x$. The atmospheric work is the product of the force and the distance through which it travels:

$$w_{atmos} = (P_{atmos} \times A) \times \Delta x = P_{atmos} \times (A \times \Delta x) = -P_{atmos} \Delta V \qquad (6\text{-}11)$$

Notice that when the system is compressed into a smaller volume, ΔV is negative so the negative sign makes w_{atmos} positive; this is consistent with the intuition that work must be done on a system to compress it.

Example 6-13 A sample of gas is compressed from 6.20 dm^3 to 2.48 dm^3 by the atmosphere at a pressure of 99.0 kPa. Calculate the atmospheric work.

The external pressure due to the atmosphere and the volume change are:

$$P_{atmos} = 99.0 \times 10^3 \text{ Pa} = 99.0 \times 10^3 \text{ N m}^{-2}$$

$$\Delta V = (2.48 - 6.20)\ \text{dm}^3 = -3.72\ \text{dm}^3 = -3.72 \times 10^{-3}\ \text{m}^3$$

Hence

$$w_{atmos} = -99.0 \times 10^3\ \text{N m}^{-2} \times (-3.72 \times 10^{-3}\ \text{m}^3) = +368\ \text{N m} = +368\ \text{J}$$

When a chemical reaction that absorbs or generates a gas takes place at a constant external pressure P_{atmos}, the volume changes and atmospheric work is done. The amount of work done on the system is $-P_{atmos}\Delta V$, and while this may be small, it is not zero and must be taken into account in accurate calculations of the internal energy change. If the amount of gas changes by Δn_g moles at pressure P_{atmos}, and if the gas is assumed to be ideal so that $PV=nRT$, then the atmospheric work due to the change in the amount of gas is:

$$w_{atmos} = -P_{atmos}\Delta V = -\Delta n_g RT \tag{6-12}$$

The calculation is illustrated in the following example.

Example 6-14 1.00 mole of $SO_2(g)$ is oxidized to $SO_3(g)$ by reaction with $O_2(g)$ at a constant external pressure and a temperature of 500. K. Calculate w_{atmos} for the process.

The balanced equation is:

$$SO_2(g) + \tfrac{1}{2}O_2(g) \rightarrow SO_3(g),$$

so the change in the number of moles of gas is $\Delta n_g = -0.5$ mole per mole of reaction. Hence by equation (6-12) the work done is:

$$w_{atmos} = -\Delta n_g RT = -(-0.5\ \text{mol}) \times 8.3145\ \text{J K}^{-1}\ \text{mol}^{-1} \times 500.\ \text{K} = +2.08\ \text{kJ}.$$

Since the number of moles of gas decreases in the reaction, the volume of the system decreases, and the work done by the atmosphere on the system w is positive.

In any process, the sum of the heat gained plus the total work done on the system is the change in the **internal energy** of the system. The total work w includes the mechanical, electrical and photochemical work, w', and the atmospheric work w_{atmos}. The internal energy is the total energy of the system, since it includes all forms of work including the atmospheric work due to changes in the volume of the system. The internal energy will be denoted by the symbol U, although some books use E. The change in the internal energy in a process is expressed by the following equation:

$$\Delta U = q + w' + w_{atmos} = q + w \tag{6-13}$$

For a process at constant pressure, $q+w' = \Delta H$ and the atmospheric work is $w_{atmos} = -P\Delta V$, and hence this equation can be rewritten:

$$\Delta U = q + w' + w_{atmos} = \Delta H - P\Delta V$$

The general relationship between the internal energy and the enthalpy of a system is expressed by the following equation:

$$U = H - PV \quad \text{or} \quad H = U + PV \tag{6-14}$$

This equation can be applied to any process, whether at constant pressure or not, but the internal energy is mostly used when dealing with processes at constant volume. For a process at constant volume, there is no atmospheric work and no mechanical work, and the change in internal energy is given by:

$$\Delta U = q_V + w' \quad \text{at constant volume.}$$

where w' represents only electrical and photochemical work. If $w' = 0$ then:

$$\Delta U = q_V \quad \text{at constant volume.} \tag{6-15}$$

This equation shows that when a chemical reaction takes place at constant volume, the internal energy change is equal to the heat of the process. This equation is used in the analysis of the bomb calorimeter.

The heat capacity of a gas or liquid measured at constant volume C_V is smaller than the heat capacity at constant pressure C_P. From the definition of heat capacity in Section 6-11 we see that:

$$C_V = \frac{q_V}{\Delta T} = \frac{\Delta U}{\Delta T} \tag{6-16}$$

For one mole of an ideal gas, the difference between the two heat capacities (per mole) is equal to the gas constant:

$$C_P - C_V = R. \tag{6-17}$$

where R is the gas constant. This can be shown by the following simple (though not rigorous) method. From the relationship between the enthalpy and the internal energy, equation (6-14), we see that for one mole of gas, $H - U = PV_m = RT$ (where V_m is the molar volume), and so if the temperature of one mole of ideal gas is changed by ΔT, then:

$$\Delta H - \Delta U = \Delta(RT) = R\Delta T$$

Dividing by ΔT we obtain the result: $\quad \dfrac{\Delta H}{\Delta T} - \dfrac{\Delta U}{\Delta T} = C_P - C_V = R$

Liquids are much more diverse in their properties. The difference between the two heat capacities, $C_P - C_V$, can be as small as zero, but for some liquids $C_P - C_V$ is even larger than for gases. As examples, for liquid water at 25°C, $C_P - C_V = 0.075R$, and for liquid benzene, $C_P - C_V = 5.1 R$.

For monatomic gases such as the noble gases of Group 18, Appendix I shows that the experimental value of C_P is 20.786 J/K/mol. Hence by equation (6-17) above, the heat capacity at constant volume is obtained by subtracting the gas constant: $C_V = 20.786 - 8.3145 = 12.472$ J/K/mol.

In Section 5-9 of the previous chapter we showed in equation (5-17) that the total translational energy per mole of the molecules in a gas is $1.5RT$. For monatomic molecules, the kinetic energy of translation is the only form of thermal energy in the gas, and can be identified with the thermodynamic internal energy: $U = 1.5RT$. Hence from equation (6-16), $C_V = 1.5R = 12.472$ J/K/mol for a monatomic gas. Thus the heat capacity for monatomic gases calculated from kinetic theory agrees with the experimental data in Appendix I to high accuracy.

For gases in which the molecules contain more than one atom, the heat capacity is larger than for monatomic gases because thermal energy can be stored in the molecules as vibrational and rotational energy.

Final note: Many books state the first law of thermodynamics in terms of the internal energy, and introduce the enthalpy subsequently. The present discussion is simpler for the purposes of chemistry, yet is firmly based historically on Joule's experiments on a system in contact with the atmosphere.

Chapter 6

Key concepts

Thermochemistry is the study of the energy involved in chemical reactions. Thermochemistry is part of the larger subject of thermodynamics, which is the study of heat, work, and processes such as chemical reactions.

In thermodynamics, the system is defined as the substances and things directly involved in a process, and everything apart from the system forms the surroundings. Adiabatic and isothermal processes are defined by comparing the time required for the process with the time required for a significant drift in temperature. In an adiabatic process, the heat transferred is zero.

Work is done when a force moves through a distance, or an electric charge moves through a potential difference. Energy is the ability to do work. Heat is a form of energy that flows when there is a temperature difference. The change in the energy of a system is the sum of the work done and the heat transferred to the system from the surroundings. The energy of a substance can be divided into chemical energy, associated with the chemical bonds of the molecules, and thermal energy, associated with the thermal motion and vibration of the molecules.

The change in the energy of a system due to transfer of heat and/or electrical and mechanical work during a process at constant external pressure is expressed in terms of the change in the enthalpy. The first law of thermodynamics states that the enthalpy of a system depends only on its state. If a chemical reaction is carried out at constant pressure, and no work is done, the enthalpy change of the reaction is equal to the heat of the reaction. When reactions are combined, the enthalpy changes of the reactions can be added. This is known as Hess's law.

The enthalpy change of formation of a compound is the enthalpy change of a reaction in which the compound is formed from the elements. The standard state is a specified condition of the substance at a stated pressure. The enthalpy change of formation is the basic data of thermochemistry.

Heat capacity is the heat required to increase the temperature of a system by one kelvin. The numerical value of the heat capacity depends on whether the system is held at constant volume or constant pressure.

A calorimeter is an instrument for measuring the heat of reaction.

The internal energy is related to the enthalpy by including the atmospheric work done when the system changes its volume. The change in internal energy in a process is the sum of the heat, and all the work transferred to the system from the surroundings

Review questions

1. What is the difference between temperature and heat?

2. Define an isothermal process.

3. Define an adiabatic process, making use of the concepts of time and temperature.

4. Define an adiabatic process, making use of the concept of heat.

5. Describe the construction of a Dewar flask. What are Dewar flasks used for in domestic life? What are Dewar flasks used for in the laboratory?

6. Define work. What are the units of work?

7. Define energy. What are the units of energy?

8. What is the necessary condition for heat to be transferred from one place to another?

9. Why is enthalpy rather than internal energy used in most calculations of thermochemistry?

10. What is the difference between thermal energy and heat?

11. What is the sign of the enthalpy change of reaction for an endothermic reaction?

12. Give a concise statement of Hess' law of thermochemistry.

13. What is the usual standard state for a gaseous substance?

14. What is the usual standard state for a liquid substance?

15. What is the usual standard state for a solid substance?

16. What is the usual standard state for a solute in solution?

17. Define the standard enthalpy change of formation for a compound.

18. Why is the enthalpy change of formation of an element in its standard state equal to zero?

19. The enthalpy change of formation of magnesium carbonate $MgCO_3(s)$ is –1095.8 kJ/mol. Write a chemical equation for the reaction to which this information refers. Is it possible to carry out this reaction directly?

Problems

1. If the standard enthalpy change $\Delta H°$ for the reaction $SO_2(g) + \frac{1}{2} O_2(g) \rightarrow SO_3(g)$ is –98.9 kJ/mol, what is the standard enthalpy change for each of the following reactions?

   (a) $2 SO_2(g) + O_2(g) \rightarrow 2 SO_3(g)$ [–197.8 kJ/mol]

   (b) $SO_3(g) \rightarrow SO_2(g) + \frac{1}{2} O_2(g)$ [+98.9 kJ/mol]

2. Calculate $\Delta H°$ for the dehydrogenation of ethane, $C_2H_6(g) \rightarrow C_2H_4(g) + H_2(g)$, from the following data:

   $$C_2H_4(g) + 3 O_2(g) \rightarrow 2 CO_2(g) + 2 H_2O(\ell) \qquad \Delta H° = -1411.0 \text{ kJ/mol}$$

   $$C_2H_6(g) + 3\frac{1}{2} O_2(g) \rightarrow 2 CO_2(g) + 3 H_2O(\ell) \qquad \Delta H° = -1559.9 \text{ kJ/mol}$$

   $$H_2(g) + \frac{1}{2} O_2(g) \rightarrow H_2O(\ell) \qquad \Delta H° = -285.8 \text{ kJ/mol} \quad [+136.9 \text{ kJ/mol}]$$

3. Calculate $\Delta H°$ at 25°C for combustion of buckminsterfullerene, $C_{60}(s)$, per mole of carbon atoms, and compare the result with that for graphite, C(s, graphite). [–432.3 kJ/mol]

Chapter 6

4. Stearin, with formula $C_{57}H_{110}O_6$, is a typical fat and its oxidation is an important source of energy in the body. The standard enthalpy change of combustion of stearin in oxygen to give carbon dioxide and liquid water is –37.7 MJ mol^{-1}. Write a balanced equation for the combustion reaction and calculate the standard enthalpy change of formation of stearin. [–450 kJ/mol]

5. Use data from the thermochemical tables to calculate $\Delta H°$ per mole for each of the following processes at 25°C.

    (a) $CaCO_3(s) \rightarrow CaO(s) + CO_2(g)$ [+178.32 kJ/mol]

    (b) $CaO(s) + H_2O(\ell) \rightarrow Ca(OH)_2(s)$ [–65.17 kJ/mol]

6. Use data from the thermochemical tables to calculate $\Delta H°$ for each of the following reactions at 25°C.

    (a) $CH_4(g) + \frac{1}{2} O_2(g) \rightarrow CH_3OH(\ell)$ [–163.85 kJ/mol]

    (b) $CH_4(g) + Cl_2(g) \rightarrow CH_3Cl(g) + HCl(g)$ [–98.33 kJ/mol]

7. Calculate the heat of combustion per gram of ethane, $C_2H_6(g)$, and propane, C_3H_8, in air at 25°C and compare your results with those given in Table 9-1.

8. Calculate the standard enthalpy change at 25°C for dissociation of each of the following gas molecules into atoms: H_2, F_2, Cl_2, Br_2, I_2, O_2, N_2. Note in the standard state, Br_2 is a liquid and I_2 is a solid, while all the other substances are gases.

    [+435.9, +158.0, 243.4, +192.9, +151.2, +498.3, +945.4 kJ/mol]

9. Calculate the standard enthalpy change at 25°C for dissociation of each of the following gas molecules into atoms: HF, HCl , NO.   [+568.1, +432.0, +631.6 kJ/mol]

10. Calculate the enthalpy change at 25°C for the neutralization of acetic acid by sodium hydroxide in aqueous solution, as described by the net ionic equation

    $CH_3COOH(aq) + OH^-(aq) \rightarrow CH_3COO^-(aq) + H_2O(\lambda)$.   [–56.09 kJ/mol]

11. Calculate the enthalpy change at 25°C for neutralization of aqueous ammonia $NH_3(aq)$, a weak base, with hydrochloric acid. The net ionic equation is $NH_3(aq) + H^+(aq) \rightarrow NH_4^+(aq)$.

    [–52.22 kJ/mol]

12. Calculate the enthalpy change at 25°C for the reaction between $SO_2(g)$ and $H_2S(g)$ to give elemental sulfur, a reaction used in the purification of "sour" natural gas:

    $SO_2(g) + 2 H_2S(g) \rightarrow 3 S(s) + 2 H_2O(\ell)$ [–233.57 kJ/mol]

13. Calculate the enthalpy change of solution of (a) sodium chloride NaCl (b) potassium chloride KCl and (c) lithium chloride LiCl, in water at 25°C.

    [+3.87 kJ/mol, +17.21 kJ/mol, –37.04 kJ/mol]

14. Calculate the standard enthalpy change at 25°C for the steam reforming and shift conversion reactions described in Chapter 4:

    $CH_4(g) + H_2O(g) \rightarrow CO(g) + 3 H_2(g)$ [+206.10 kJ/mol]

    $CO(g) + H_2O(g) \rightarrow CO_2(g) + H_2(g)$ [–41.17 kJ/mol]

15. When heated and compressed to a high pressure, nitric oxide NO reacts to form nitrous oxide N_2O and nitrogen dioxide NO_2. Using standard enthalpy changes of formation calculate $\Delta H°$ for the reaction: $3 NO(g) \rightarrow N_2O(g) + NO_2(g)$ [–155.52 kJ/mol]

16. Using standard enthalpy changes of formation calculate $\Delta H°$ at 25°C for the following reaction. The reaction takes place only at high temperature since it is strongly endothermic.

$$MgCO_3(s) \rightarrow MgO(s) + CO_2(g) \qquad\qquad [+100.6 \text{ kJ/mol}]$$

17. Using standard enthalpy changes of formation calculate $\Delta H°$ for the reaction:

$$Fe_2O_3(s) + 1.5 \, C(s) \rightarrow 2 \, Fe(s) + 1.5 \, CO_2(g)$$

This reaction is the basis for the high temperature reduction of iron oxide to metallic iron. The reaction is carried out at high temperature in a blast furnace, and produces liquid iron rather than solid iron, but this does not change the result greatly.
    [+233.9 kJ/mol]

18. Using standard enthalpy changes of formation calculate $\Delta H°$ for the reaction between nickel metal and carbon monoxide to form nickel tetracarbonyl: $Ni(s) + 4 \, CO(g) \rightarrow Ni(CO)_4(g)$. This reaction is the basis for the purification of nickel metal. The reaction proceeds to the right at about 50°C, but at higher temperatures the reaction reverses to form pure metallic nickel. The boiling point of $Ni(CO)_4$ is 43°C. [−160.81 kJ/mol]

19. Calculate the standard enthalpy change of solution of NaOH(s):

$$NaOH(s) \rightarrow Na^+(aq) + OH^-(aq). \qquad\qquad [−44.51 \text{ kJ/mol}]$$

20. Calculate the standard enthalpy change of solution of KOH(s):

$$KOH(s) \rightarrow K^+(aq) + OH^-(aq). \qquad\qquad [−57.61 \text{ kJ/mol}]$$

21. Calculate the standard enthalpy change at 25°C for the "water gas" reaction between solid carbon and steam. The reaction is $C(s) + H_2O(g) \rightarrow CO(g) + H_2(g)$. The products of the reaction are two combustible gases, and is used as an industrial fuel.   [+131.29 kJ/mol]

22. Water gas is an equimolar mixture of carbon monoxide and hydrogen which is produced by the reaction between carbon and steam. Water gas burns when mixed with oxygen. Write equations to show the combustion processes, and calculate the enthalpy change of combustion for one mole of the mixture. Assume that the water is produced as steam, $H_2O(g)$. [−262.40 kJ/mol]

23. Calculate the standard enthalpy of reaction for the vigorous reaction between "phosphorus pentoxide" P_4O_{10} and excess water. The reaction can be represented by the equation:

$$P_4O_{10}(s) + 6 \, H_2O(\ell) \rightarrow 4 \, H_3PO_4(aq). \qquad\qquad [−454.38 \text{ kJ/mol}]$$

24. Calculate the standard enthalpy change of solution of hydrogen sulfide H_2S.   [−19.1 kJ/mol]

25. Calculate $\Delta H°$ for the combustion of one cubic metre of natural gas, measured at a pressure of 100. kPa and a temperature of 15°C. Take natural gas to be pure methane.   [−37.1 MJ]

26. The alkali metals such as potassium react vigorously with water to produce hydrogen gas and a solution of the metal hydroxide. Calculate $\Delta H°$ for the reaction:

$$2 \, K(s) + 2 \, H_2O(\ell) \rightarrow H_2(g) + 2 \, K^+(aq) + 2 \, OH^-(aq). \qquad [−393.09 \text{ kJ/mol}]$$

27. Draw an equation for the isomerization of cyclopropane C_3H_6 to propene C_3H_6 using structural formulae. Calculate $\Delta H°$ for the reaction. Is the reaction endothermic or exothermic? [−32.80 kJ/mol]

28. Calcium oxide reacts vigorously with water to form calcium hydroxide. Calculate $\Delta H°$ for the reaction: $CaO(s) + H_2O(\ell) \rightarrow Ca(OH)_2(s)$. [−65.17 kJ/mol]

Chapter 6

29. Magnesium oxide reacts with carbon dioxide to form magnesium carbonate. Calculate $\Delta H°$ for the reaction: $MgO(s) + CO_2(g) \rightarrow MgCO_3(s)$. [−100.6 kJ/mol]

30. Calcium fluoride is a sparingly soluble salt. Calculate $\Delta H°$ for the reaction in which calcium fluoride is precipitated from solution: $Ca^{2+}(aq) + 2\ F^-(aq) \rightarrow CaF_2(s)$. [−11.5 kJ/mol]

31. Calculate $\Delta H°$ for the neutralization of formic acid HCOOH by sodium hydroxide in aqueous solution. [−55.96 kJ/mol]

32. A sample of 135.0 grams of water at 21.5°C is placed in a Dewar flask equipped with an electric heater, and an electric current passing through the heater releases 5500. joules of energy. Calculate the final temperature of the water, assuming that the heat capacity of the water is constant and equal to the value given in Appendix 1, and that the heat capacity of the Dewar flask and heater is 125 J/K. [29.5°C]

33. A sample of 98 gram of pure sulfuric acid is dissolved in 2.0 kg of water in an insulated vessel at 15°C, and the temperature rises rapidly because of the process of forming the solution. The reaction is summarized in the equation: $H_2SO_4(\ell) \rightarrow H^+(aq) + HSO_4^-(aq)$. Estimate the temperature change, assuming that the heat capacity of the solution is 4.0 J K^{-1} g^{-1} and the heat capacity of the tank is 300 J K^{-1}. [+8.4°C]

34. A sample of 100.0 mL of 0.95 M hydrochloric acid, HCl, is added to 100.0 mL of 0.85 M NaOH in an insulated beaker. Both solutions are initially brought to a temperature of 22.0°C, and the final temperature after the reaction is 26.9°C. The mass of the beaker is 106.3 grams and the heat capacity of the glass is 0.753 J K^{-1} g^{-1}. The solutions can be assumed to have a heat capacity of 4.18 J K^{-1} g^{-1}, and a density of 1.02 g/mL. Calculate the enthalpy change of neutralization per mole. [−54 kJ/mol]

35. Electrolysis of water yields hydrogen and oxygen gases. If these are generated in contact with the atmosphere at a pressure of 100. kPa and a temperature of 20.°C, calculate the atmospheric work w_{atmos} when 1.00 mole of water is electrolysed. [−3.65 kJ]

36. Calculate $\Delta U°$ at 25°C for the reaction $N_2(g) + 3\ H_2(g) \rightarrow 2\ NH_3(g)$. [−87.26 kJ/mol]

7 Solids, Liquids and Gases

Objectives

After reading this chapter, the student should be able to do the following:

♦ Describe the processes of melting, freezing, boiling, condensation, evaporation, sublimation.

♦ Describe the relationship between the solid, liquid and gaseous states of matter.

♦ Define the critical point and the triple point.

♦ Describe the properties of supercritical fluids.

Related topics to review:

States of matter in Chapter 1. Properties of gases in Chapter 5. Thermochemistry in Chapter 6

Related topics to look forward to:

Properties of solutions in Chapter 8.

7-1 Intermolecular forces and the states of matter

The three states of matter are the solid state, the liquid state and the gaseous state. Their characteristic properties were described in section 1-6, and are summarized again here. Gases have low density but are easy to compress into a smaller volume, while liquids have high densities and are almost incompressible. Gases expand to fill the whole space available to them, while a liquid does not. Solids are also dense and almost incompressible, but in contrast to liquids, solids retain their shape. In a liquid the relative positions of the molecules are not fixed so the liquid can change its shape easily, while the molecules in a solid stay close to strictly defined positions relative to each other.

As compared to gases, the characteristic properties of solids and liquids vary from one substance to another. The forces between molecules in a gas during collisions have little effect on the properties of the gas at low or moderate pressure and under these conditions all gases obey the ideal gas equation of state to a good approximation. But in liquids and solids, the molecules are in almost continuous contact with each other and intermolecular forces determine many properties of substances in the liquid and solid states.

A particular state of a substance is often referred to as a **phase** of that substance. A phase is a state of a substance with characteristic physical properties. Obviously the solid, liquid and gas states are different phases, but there is more to it than that. Some substances form more than one crystalline form, and these are classified as different phases because they have different symmetry, density and other physical properties. Some substances form phases called **liquid crystals** that are intermediate between the solid and liquid phases in the way the molecules are arranged. Some substances form a **glass** phase that is like a solid in its mechanical properties, but like a liquid in the arrangement of the atoms or molecules.

In this chapter we discuss **changes of phase**, such as melting or boiling, and **phase diagrams** which describe the relationships between phases. The liquid and solid phases will be referred to together as **condensed phases** because of their high density relative to the gas phase.

Chapter 7

Compared with those of a gas, the properties of a liquid are much more dependent on the chemical nature of the substance and there is no "ideal liquid" equation which applies to all liquids as there is for gases. For example, the properties of water are quite different from the properties of almost every other liquid, due to the particular properties of water molecules, whereas water vapour is not much different in its properties from other substances in the gaseous state. Nevertheless, liquids have many properties in common and general rules about their behaviour have been formulated.

When cooled, a gas **condenses** to form either a liquid or a solid. When heated, a liquid **evaporates** to form a gas or vapour. A liquid **freezes** to a solid when it is cooled, and a solid usually **melts** when it is heated. A solid may also evaporate to give a vapour directly without the formation of a liquid; this process is called **sublimation**.

The words "vapour" and "gas" are a potential source of confusion. Firstly, the everyday use of "gas" as an abbreviation for gasoline is very confusing and should be disregarded completely in the present discussion: the conventional fuel used in cars and trucks is a liquid, not a gas. Secondly, the word "vapour" is often used for the gaseous form of a substance that is normally found as a liquid, such as water (or gasoline!), or a gas that is close to condensation. A **saturated vapour** means a vapour in contact with the liquid. The word **fluid**, meaning a substance that can flow, is used to refer to both gases and liquids.

7-2 Vapour pressure of liquids

We start our study of the various phases of matter by studying the vapour pressure of liquids. Every liquid has a tendency to evaporate to form vapour. If the space above the liquid is enclosed, the liquid continues to evaporate until the pressure of the vapour reaches a limiting value called the **vapour pressure** which is characteristic of the liquid and the temperature.

The vapour pressure of a liquid can be measured using apparatus such as that shown in Figure 7-1. The liquid is contained in a bulb equipped with a valve and connection to a vacuum pump,

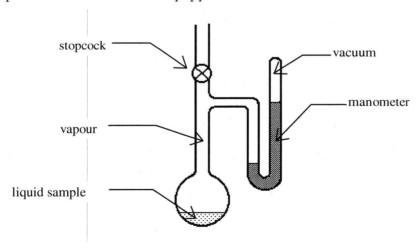

Figure 7-1 Apparatus for measuring the vapour pressure of a liquid. The space above the liquid must be evacuated before starting measurements, which may require that the liquid be frozen during the pumping process. The temperature of the liquid must be controlled with a thermostat, which is not shown. The manometer indicates the pressure of vapour in equilibrium with the liquid.

and a manometer or other pressure-measuring device. After evacuation of the space above the liquid, the valve is closed and some liquid evaporates to form vapour. The pressure of the vapour is measured using the manometer.

The **vapour pressure** of a liquid is the pressure of the vapour in equilibrium with a liquid. The symbol $P*$ will be used to designate the vapour pressure. The vapour pressure of a chemically pure liquid is a characteristic property of that substance and is a sensitive function of temperature. The graphs in Figure 7-2 show the variation with temperature of the vapour pressure of three liquids, water, pentane and benzene. For each liquid, the vapour pressure is low at low temperature but rises with increasing slope as the temperature increases. At high temperature, the vapour pressure exceeds atmospheric pressure.

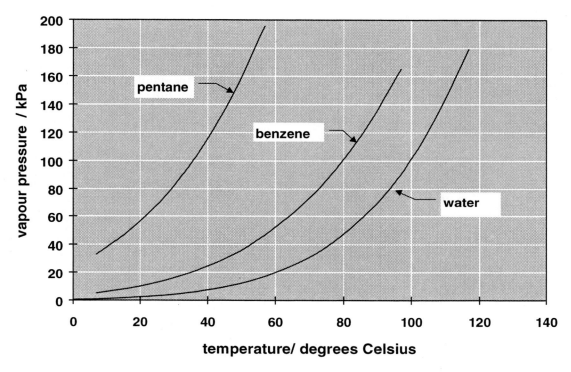

Figure 7-2 The vapour pressure $P*$ plotted against temperature, in degrees Celsius, for three liquids. The vapour pressure of water at 100°C is 101.3 kPa. Pentane, C_5H_{12}, and benzene, C_6H_6, have higher vapour pressures, and are more volatile, than water.

All the vapour pressure graphs shown in Figure 7-2 have the same general shape, and indeed the temperature dependence of vapour pressure is similar for all liquids. In the last section of this chapter, we will discuss the mathematical function that describes the temperature dependence of vapour pressure of liquids. Up to that point, the discussion will be largely descriptive.

The evaporation of a liquid to form vapour can be regarded in two different ways. The first approach is to consider the rate at which molecules are transferred between the liquid and the vapour, which may be called the **kinetic approach**. The intermolecular forces tend to hold the molecules together in the liquid. At any temperature, some molecules in the liquid have sufficient thermal energy that they are able to overcome the intermolecular forces and escape into the vapour phase. At the same time, some molecules in the vapour collide with the surface of the liquid (as discussed in connection with the kinetic theory of gases, in Section 5-9) and are re-absorbed. When the liquid and vapour are at equilibrium, the rate at which molecules from the vapour are absorbed by the liquid must be equal to the rate of leaving, and this balance between the two rates determines the pressure of the vapour at equilibrium. If the temperature of the liquid is increased, the molecules in the liquid become more energetic, the rate of leaving increases, and so the rate of absorption must increase in the new equilibrium situation, which in turn requires that the vapour pressure increase.

The second approach, based upon concepts of equilibrium and called the **thermodynamic approach**, is to consider the balance between the tendency for molecules to decrease their energy and the opposing tendency for molecules to increase their disorder. The energy of a molecule is lowest when it is close to other molecules, because of the intermolecular forces of attraction. Hence the energy of a set of molecules is lowest when they are all gathered close together to form a liquid, with no vapour. The average energy holding each molecule to all the other molecules of the liquid is equal to the enthalpy of vaporization per molecule.

However if all the molecules stay close together to form only a liquid, a large volume of space is left empty. In Figure 7-3, for instance, the whole space above the liquid would contain no molecules at all, regardless of the temperature. This is a highly unlikely situation, for in all thermodynamic systems there is a tendency for the molecules to maximize their disorder consistent with energy limitations. Hence there is always some evaporation and always some vapour in equilibrium with the liquid. If the temperature is increased, then more energy is available and the balance shifts towards a higher vapour pressure.

The heat required to evaporate a certain amount of liquid (usually either one gram or one mole) at a fixed temperature is called the **heat of vaporization**. Since the heat is absorbed at fixed external pressure, the heat of vaporization is the **enthalpy change of vaporization**.

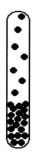

Figure 7-3 An exaggerated view of molecules in a sealed tube containing both liquid (at the bottom) and vapour (at the top). The two phases are separated by the liquid surface, called the meniscus.

7-3 Boiling

When a pure liquid is heated in an open vessel such as a beaker or a kettle, the temperature of the liquid rises. Eventually boiling begins, with bubbling from the bottom of the vessel and the temperature becomes constant. Further addition of heat continues the boiling and converts more liquid to vapour, but does not change the temperature of the liquid. The essential feature of boiling, as distinct from merely evaporation, is that the liquid is open to the atmosphere, which allows the vapour to escape as bubbles when the vapour pressure reaches atmospheric pressure.

The **boiling point** of a liquid is the temperature at which boiling takes place when the liquid is heated continuously in contact with the atmosphere. At the boiling point, the vapour pressure of the liquid is equal to the pressure of the atmosphere. The boiling point varies significantly with the pressure of the atmosphere, which in turns varies with the weather. Most tables of boiling points list the boiling point at a pressure of 101.325 kPa (i.e. one atmosphere).

When a vapour at atmospheric pressure is cooled, the vapour starts to condense to the liquid state when the temperature reaches the boiling point of the liquid. In other words, for a fixed pressure, boiling and condensation take place at the same temperature.

It is possible to **superheat** a liquid to a temperature above the boiling point; this sometimes happens when water is heated in glass vessels with very smooth surfaces and can lead to explosive boiling, which is dangerous. For this reason it is usual to add a few pieces of inert ceramic called **boiling chips** which promote the formation of bubbles and prevent the temperature from rising above the boiling point. It is also possible to **supercool** a vapour below the boiling point under certain conditions.

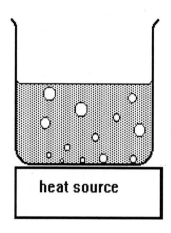

Figure 7-4 A liquid boiling in a beaker. Heat enters the liquid from the heat source at the bottom, which may be either an electric heater or a Bunsen burner. Bubbles form on the bottom of the beaker.

The heat required to boil a certain amount of liquid (usually either one gram or one mole) is called the **latent heat of boiling**, since the heat is absorbed without change of temperature while the boiling is taking place. The latent heat of boiling is the enthalpy change of vaporization at the boiling point.

Boiling takes place when the vapour pressure of the liquid being heated is equal to atmospheric pressure. Consider what happens when water is boiled. To induce boiling, heat is usually applied to the bottom of a container of water. When a bubble is formed, the gas inside consists mostly of water vapour together with some oxygen and nitrogen from air dissolved in the water. The bubble is under the external pressure of the atmosphere plus contributions from the hydrostatic pressure of the liquid above it and the surface tension. If the gas pressure inside the bubble is larger than the external pressure, then the bubble will expand and rise to the surface of the liquid, otherwise it will collapse and disappear. In the reverse process of condensation, there are no complications caused by bubbles by superheating of the liquid, and the vapour condenses to the liquid at the true boiling point. For this reason, the boiling point is best measured by placing a thermometer in the vapour just above the boiling liquid, since this measures the temperature at which the vapour pressure of the liquid is equal to the pressure of the atmosphere.

Chapter 7

The dependence of the boiling point temperature on pressure can be read from the graphs such as those in Figures 7-2. Because it varies with pressure, the boiling point temperature varies with weather conditions and height above sea level. The boiling point is traditionally quoted at a pressure of 101.325 kPa (one atmosphere) even though a standard state pressure of 100.000 kPa has been adopted for other thermodynamic data.

Table 7-1 lists the boiling point T_b and latent heat of boiling ΔH_b for some elements and compounds. Note that if you calculate the enthalpy change of vaporization from data in Appendix I by the methods of thermochemistry, the result will differ somewhat from the latent heat of boiling listed in Table 7-1. This is because the enthalpy change of formation data in Appendix I refer to a temperature of 25°C, not the boiling point.

Example 7-1 Calculate the enthalpy change of vaporization at 25°C for water from data in Appendix I, and compare your result with the enthalpy change of vaporization at the boiling point of 100°C listed in Table 7-1.

For the process $$H_2O(\ell) \rightarrow H_2O(g)$$

$$\Delta H° = -(-285.830) + (-241.818) = 44.012 \text{ kJ/mol.}$$

This result is about 10% larger than the enthalpy change of vaporization at the boiling point (i.e. the latent heat of boiling) of water listed in Table 7-1.

Table 7-1 Boiling point and latent heat of boiling for some liquids

Data is for atmospheric pressure of 101.325 kPa.

Substance	T_b K	ΔH_b kJ/mol	$\Delta H_b/T_b$ J/K/mol	Substance	T_b K	ΔH_b kJ/mol	$\Delta H_b/T_b$ J/K/mol
Elements				**Hydrocarbons**			
He	4.22	0.0829	19.6	CH_4	111.6	8.19	73.4
H_2	20.28	0.898	44.2	C_2H_6	184.5	14.69	79.6
N_2	77.36	5.57	72.0	C_3H_8	231.0	19.04	82.4
O_2	90.20	6.82	75.6	C_4H_{10} n-butane	272.6	22.44	82.3
F_2	85.0	6.62	77.8	C_6H_{14} n-hexane	341.8	28.85	84.4
Ne	27.1	1.71	63.1	**Halocarbons**			
Oxides				CH_2Cl_2	313	28.06	89.6
CO	81.6	6.04	74.0	$CHCl_3$	334.3	29.24	87.5
SO_2	263.1	24.94	94.7	CCl_4	349.9	29.82	85.2
				CF_2Cl_2	243.3	20.9	85.9
Hydrides							
NH_3	293	28.7	97.9	**Alcohols**			
H_2O	373.15	40.65	108.9	CH_3OH methanol	337.7	35.21	104.3
HF	239.82	23.33	97.3	C_2H_5OH ethanol	351.3	38.56	109.8

Reprinted with permission from CRC Handbook of Chemistry and Physics, 77th edition. Copyright CRC Press, Boca Raton, Florida, U.S.A.

The boiling points of related compounds usually show systematic trends that can be correlated with molecular structure. Figure 7-5 shows the boiling points of three such series of compounds, the straight chain n-alkanes with formulae C_nH_{2n+2}, and two sets of derivatives, the alkyl chlorides $C_nH_{2n+1}Cl$ and the alcohols $C_nH_{2n+1}OH$. The graphs show smooth increases of the boiling point with chain length within each series.

The boiling points of a series of similar compounds across the rows of the periodic table reflect the periodicity of properties of the elements. An example can be seen in the boiling points of the molecular hydrides of the elements of groups 14 to 17 of the periodic table plus the noble gases. The molecular hydrides of the second row elements are methane CH_4, ammonia NH_3, water H_2O, hydrogen fluoride HF; the noble gas neon Ne is relevant because although it is not a hydride it has the same number of electrons as the other molecules. There are corresponding sets of compounds of the third, fourth and fifth rows of the table. The boiling points of these four sets of compounds XH_n are plotted *versus* the group number of the element X in Figure 7-6.

Figure 7-6 shows that, among the molecular hydrides of each row of the periodic table, the highest boiling points are found for the Group 16 compounds, (H_2O, H_2S, H_2Se and H_2Te). However the second row molecular hydrides show this effect to a much greater extent than the others, and clearly ammonia, water and hydrogen fluoride have high boiling points compared with the molecular hydrides of the corresponding elements in subsequent rows. This is usually ascribed to a phenomenon called **hydrogen bonding** which is found to occur in molecules containing hydrogen atoms bonded to nitrogen, oxygen, fluorine and other electronegative elements. Hydrogen bonding will be discussed further in Chapter 11.

It is a good thing that water is hydrogen bonded, for if it were not, the boiling point would be expected to be about 180 K (or –90°C), on the basis of the trends shown in Figure 7-6. If that were the case, life as we know it would be impossible, because the water on earth would be a vapour instead of a liquid. Ammonia is interesting because although it is usually thought of as a hydrogen bonded liquid on the basis of evidence such as its boiling point, other studies throw doubt on whether ammonia molecules can form hydrogen bonds to other ammonia molecules; the matter is the subject of current research.

Hydrogen bonding also affects the boiling points of alcohols. This can be seen in the data in Table 7-1 and Figure 7-5. Methanol CH_3OH boils at 338 K whereas ethane C_2H_6 has almost the same molar mass but boils at 185 K, and chloromethane CH_3Cl, with a significantly higher molar mass than methanol, boils at 249 K. This pattern is repeated for longer chain alcohols which all have high boiling points compared with the corresponding alcohols and alkyl chlorides.

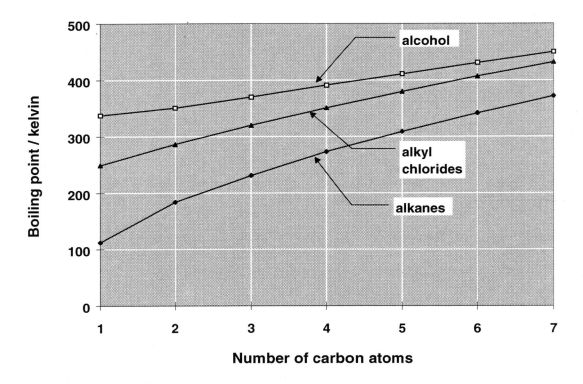

Figure 7-5 The boiling points of three series of organic compounds, the n-alkanes C_nH_{2n+2}, the straight chain alkyl chlorides $C_nH_{2n+1}Cl$ and alcohols $C_nH_{2n+1}OH$, plotted against the number, n, of carbon atoms in the molecules. Boiling points generally increase with molar mass for a series of similar molecules.

The fourth column of Table 7-1 shows that for many liquids the enthalpy of vaporization divided by the boiling point has a characteristic value:

$$\frac{\Delta H_b}{T_b} \approx 75 \text{ to } 85 \text{ J K}^{-1} \text{ mol}^{-1} \tag{7-1}$$

Frederick Trouton discovered this in 1884 while he was still an undergraduate, and so the rule is called **Trouton's rule**. It will be seen in a later chapter that the left-hand side of the equation is a measure of the change in the **entropy**, which is related to the disorder of the molecules. Trouton's rule suggests that, for many substances, evaporation of a liquid at the boiling point results in roughly the same change in molecular disorder.

Table 7-1 shows that there are exceptions to Trouton's rule, notably liquids with very low boiling points such as hydrogen and helium, and hydrogen-bonded liquids such as water and alcohols.

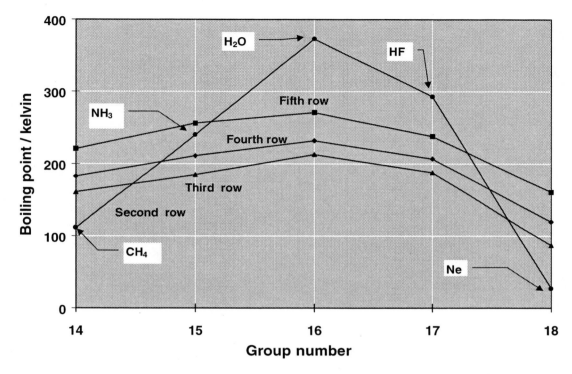

Figure 7-6 Periodicity in the boiling points of the molecular hydrides XH_n of representative elements X, plus the noble gases. The boiling points are plotted as a function of the group number of the element X. Each row of the periodic is plotted as a separate graph.

7-4 Melting and freezing

When a solid **melts**, it changes from the solid state to the liquid state. When a liquid **freezes**, it changes from the liquid state to the solid state. A pure liquid freezes at a particular temperature called the **freezing point**. A pure solid melts at a particular temperature called the **melting point**, which is usually the same as the freezing point. The melting point is affected only very slightly by changes in atmospheric pressure, though later in this chapter we will distinguish between the melting point and the triple point.

A pure solid melts at constant temperature. The heat required to melt the solid is absorbed without any change of temperature, and so is called the **latent heat of melting**. Since the external pressure is constant, the latent heat of melting is the enthalpy change of melting. The latent heat of melting is, in most cases, much smaller than the latent heat of vaporization, since the molecules do not separate from each other on melting.

In principle, a pure liquid freezes at the same temperature as the solid melts, but under certain conditions it is possible to lower the temperature of a liquid below the freezing point without any solid forming. This happens more easily if the liquid is free of dust and the container does not have scratches on the inner surfaces. This phenomenon is called **supercooling**. Supercooled liquids can sometimes be held for long periods of time at temperatures several degrees or more below the freezing point, but freezing can be initiated by addition of a small "seed" crystal of the substance, by scratching the side of the container, or by lowering the temperature further.

Chapter 7

Some supercooled liquids become so viscous that they take on the properties of a solid without passing through a sharply defined freezing point. Such solids are called **glasses** because of their similarity to ordinary glass, which is used to make laboratory "glassware" and windows.

Table 7-2 Melting point temperature and enthalpy change of melting for some solids

Substance	T_m K	ΔH_m kJ/mol	$\Delta H_m/T_m$ J/K/mol	Substance	T_m K	ΔH_m kJ/mol	$\Delta H_m/T_m$ J/K/mol
Elements				**Hydrocarbons**			
H_2	13.9	0.12	8.6	CH_4 methane	90.7	0.94	10.4
N_2	63.2	0.71	11.2	C_2H_6 ethane	90.4	2.86	31.6
O_2	54.4	0.44	8.1	C_3H_8 propane	85.6	3.53	41.3
F_2	53.54	0.51	9.53	C_4H_{10} n-butane	135.0	4.66	34.5
Ne	24.6	0.34	13.8	C_6H_{14} n-hexane	177.9	13.08	73.5
Oxides				C_6H_6 benzene	278.7	9.95	35.7
CO	68.2	0.83	12.2	$C_6H_5CH_3$ toluene	178.2	6.85	38.4
SO_2	197.6	7.40	37.4	**Halocarbons**			
Hydrides				CH_2Cl_2	178.0	6.00	33.7
NH_3 ammonia	195.4	5.66	29.0	$CHCl_3$	209.4	8.80	42.0
H_2O water	273.2	6.01	22.0	CCl_4	250.2	3.28	13.1
HF	189.8	4.58	24.1	**Alcohols**			
Ionic crystals				CH_3OH methanol	175.5	3.18	18.1
NaCl	800.7	28.16	35.2	C_2H_5OH ethanol	159.1	5.02	31.6
CaO	2927	59.00	20.2	C_3H_7OH 1-propanol	147.0	5.20	35.3
Al_2O_3	2327	111.1	47.7	C_3H_7OH 2-propanol	183.7	5.37	29.2

Reprinted with permission from CRC Handbook of Chemistry and Physics, 77th edition. Copyright CRC Press, Boca Raton, Florida, U.S.A.

Table 7-2 lists the melting points of a number of substances. Trends in the data are not as consistent as for boiling point data, but melting points tend to be high for substances with high molar mass.

High melting point is often associated with high molecular symmetry. This empirical rule was discovered by the English chemist Thomas Carnelley in 1882. In some cases, high symmetry allows molecules to pack together more efficiently. In other cases, highly symmetrical molecules are partially disordered in the crystalline state, which leads to higher melting point. Examples that illustrate the rule are methane as compared with propane; benzene as compared with toluene; carbon tetrachloride as compared with trichloromethane; methanol as compared with ethanol; 2-propanol as compared with 1-propanol.

Most ionic crystals have higher melting points than molecular crystals, reflecting the high electrostatic energy that holds the ions together in the crystal. Oxides of divalent and trivalent metals in particular have very high melting points and are used to construct furnaces and other devices that must operate at high temperature. Despite these generalities, some ionic crystals with very unsymmetrical organic anions have melting points below room temperature, and are finding uses as liquid solvents at room temperature.

The melting points of metals are a periodic property, with the highest melting points found for the transition metals in the bottom row of groups 5 to 10, such as tungsten, rhenium and osmium. These metals are used in high temperature technology for heaters and other electrical devices. Mercury, with a melting point of 234.2 K, is notable as a metal that is liquid at room temperature.

Melting points are hardly affected by pressure. For almost all substances the melting point increases slightly upon application of high pressure, but there are a few exceptions, of which ice is the most famous. High pressure decreases the melting point of a substance if the density of the solid phase is less than the density of the liquid. Ice is less dense than water, which is easy to remember because ice floats in water: remember the collision of the Titanic with a floating iceberg. Application of a pressure of 100. MPa (about 1000 times atmospheric pressure) decreases the melting point of ice from 0.0 °C to –9.0°C.

It is sometimes said that the weight of a person on an ice skate is enough to melt ice, and the water produced lubricates the skate and allows almost frictionless motion. However, the pressure on the ice due to the weight of a person on a skate blade is roughly 10 MPa, which would lower the melting point to approximately –1°C, not enough to explain how we can skate at much lower temperatures. A more likely explanation is the presence of a film of water on the surface of ice, a phenomenon known as surface melting.

7-5 Sublimation and the triple point

If a liquid is cooled sufficiently in the absence of air, in an apparatus such as that shown in Figure 7-1, it freezes to a solid at a temperature slightly different from the freezing point. The temperature at which a pure liquid freezes in contact only with its own vapour is called the **triple point** temperature, since at this temperature three phases or states of the substance are simultaneously present. For most substances the triple point and freezing point temperatures are almost equal.

The conversion of a solid directly to a vapour without formation of a liquid is called **sublimation**. The vapour pressures of solids are usually small compared with those of liquids, though this is not always the case. Table 7-3 lists the temperature and pressure at the triple point, and the enthalpy of sublimation, for some compounds. For most substances the triple point pressure is much less than atmospheric pressure, but carbon dioxide is a notable exception.

The enthalpy of sublimation ΔH_s should be equal to the sum of the enthalpies of vaporization and melting, by the first law of thermodynamics since the transformation from solid to vapour can be achieved by either of the following paths:

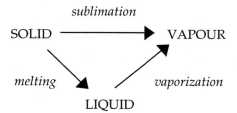

Hence we expect that $\Delta H_s = \Delta H_m + \Delta H_v$ but this relationship is obeyed exactly only when all the enthalpies involved are evaluated at the triple point.

Table 7-3 The triple point and enthalpy of sublimation for some solids

Substance	T_t K	P_t kPa	ΔH_{sub} kJ/mol	Substance	T_t K	P_t kPa	ΔH_{sub} kJ/mol
Elements				**Hydrocarbons**			
Ar	83.81	68.8	7.7	CH_4 methane	90.69	11.70	9.7
Xe	161.4	81.7	15.4	**Fluorides**			
Oxides				SiF_4	186.3	220.8	26.1
CO	68.13	15.4	7.7	SF_6	223.1	232.7	23.3
CO_2	216.58	518.0	26.0				
Hydrides							
NH_3 ammonia	195.4	6.12	30.8				
H_2O water	273.16	0.61166	51.1				

Reprinted with permission from CRC Handbook of Chemistry and Physics, 77th edition. Copyright CRC Press, Boca Raton, Florida, U.S.A.

Carbon dioxide is the best known example of sublimation. The triple point pressure is 518.0 kPa, or more than five times atmospheric pressure. Under atmospheric pressure solid carbon dioxide CO_2 evaporates at a temperature of about –80°C by sublimation without forming a liquid. For this reason, solid CO_2 is convenient to use as a refrigerant because it does not make a mess by melting. Another example of sublimation is to be found on cold sunny days in late winter when snow and ice disappear by sublimation under the intense sunlight at temperatures well below the freezing point of water. Sublimation is used industrially for the preparation of dried foods and other materials by **freeze-drying**. In this process, heat is supplied at a carefully controlled rate, sufficient to supply the latent heat of sublimation without raising the temperature to the point at which liquid water is formed by melting.

The temperature of triple point of pure water is the fixed point used to calibrate the absolute, or Kelvin, temperature scale, and has been assigned a value 273.16 K. The temperature of the triple point is 0.01 kelvin higher than the melting point.

7-6 The critical point

When a liquid in equilibrium with its vapour is heated in a closed vessel such as that shown in Figure 7-3, extraordinary changes are found to occur near a particular temperature. Figure 7-2 shows that the vapour pressure rises steeply with temperature. From the ideal gas equation, the molar volume of the vapour is:

$$\frac{V}{n} = \frac{RT}{P}$$

Since the pressure increases much faster than the temperature, the molar volume of the vapour in equilibrium with the liquid decreases as the temperature increases. At the same time, the molar volume of the liquid increases slightly as a result of thermal expansion. Figure 7-7 shows these changes on a pressure-volume diagram for the case of water. The right hand side of the curve (the full line) shows how the vapour pressure rises and the molar volume decreases as the temperature increases. The left-hand side the curve (the dotted line) shows the slight increase of the molar volume of the liquid as the temperature rises.

At higher and higher temperatures, the molar volumes of the liquid and gas phases approach each other, and eventually the curves bend over and join at a point on the graph called the **critical point,** labelled C in Figure 7-7. At this temperature, the differences between the molar volumes of the liquid and vapour phases disappear and the two parts of the curve join together smoothly. Above the critical temperature the meniscus or surface which divides the liquid from the vapour (shown in Figure 7-3) disappears and the distinction between the two phases cannot be seen.

The critical point is characterized by the **critical temperature, critical pressure** and **critical molar volume**. Table 7-4 contains a list of these quantities for a number of substances.

The last two columns of Table 7-4 demonstrate two useful empirical rules. The second last column shows that at the critical point, PV/RT has about the same value for many substances:

$$\frac{P_c V_c}{RT_c} \approx 0.25 \pm 0.04 ,\qquad (7\text{-}2)$$

whereas for an ideal gas $PV/RT = 1$. The last column shows that the ratio of the boiling point to the critical temperature has about the same value for many substances:

$$\frac{T_b}{T_c} \approx 0.6 \pm 0.04 .\qquad (7\text{-}3)$$

Table 7-4 Critical point data for some substances

Substance	T_c / K	P_c / MPa	V_c / cm^3 mol^{-1}	$P_c V_c/RT_c$	T_b/T_c
Elements					
He	5.19	0.227	57	0.30	0.81
H$_2$	32.97	1.293	65	0.31	0.62
N$_2$	126.21	3.39	90	0.29	0.61
O$_2$	154.59	5.043	73	0.29	0.58
Oxides					
CO	132.91	3.499	93	0.29	0.61
CO$_2$	304.14	7.375	94	0.27	–
SO$_2$	430.8	7.884	122	0.27	0.61
Hydrides					
NH$_3$ ammonia	405.5	11.35	72	0.24	0.59
H$_2$O water	647.14	22.06	56	0.23	0.58
Hydrocarbons					
CH$_4$ methane	190.56	4.599	98.6	0.29	0.59
C$_2$H$_6$ ethane	305.32	4.872	145.5	0.28	0.60
C$_3$H$_8$ propane	369.83	4.248	200	0.28	0.62
C$_4$H$_{10}$ n-butane	425.12	3.796	255	0.27	0.64
C$_6$H$_6$ benzene	562.05	4.895	256	0.27	0.63
Halocarbons					
CF$_2$Cl$_2$	384.95	4.136	217	0.28	0.63
CF$_4$	227.6	3.74	140	0.28	0.64
CCl$_4$	556.6	4.516	276	0.27	0.63
Alcohols					
CH$_3$OH methanol	512.5	8.084	117	0.22	0.66
C$_2$H$_5$OH ethanol	514.0	6.137	168	0.24	0.68

Chapter 7

Consider a partially filled tube, such as that shown in Figure 7-3, containing some liquid and some vapour. The average molar volume of the whole system is smaller than the molar volume of the vapour, but larger than the molar volume of the liquid. If plotted in Figure 7-7, the point representing the average molar volume must lie between the two sides of the curve. Hence the entire region under the curve in Figure 7-7 defines the conditions of temperature, pressure and molar volume under which both liquid and vapour phases can co-exist. The region to the right of the full line, labelled "vapour" in the diagram, defines conditions under which the sample exists as a single vapour or gas phase. The region to the left of the dotted line, labelled liquid, defines conditions under which the sample exists as a single liquid phase.

At temperatures above the critical temperature, the liquid state no longer exists. If a gas is compressed at a temperature above the critical temperature, the molar volume decreases smoothly to liquid-like values without any sudden condensation to a liquid occurring. A gas that is compressed to a pressure above the critical pressure, at a temperature above the critical temperature, is called a **supercritical fluid**.

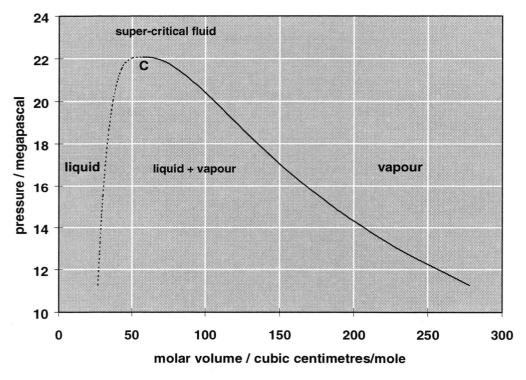

Figure 7-7 Graph showing the pressure-volume properties of liquid water (dotted line) and water vapour (full line) in equilibrium at high temperature and high pressure. The molar volumes of the liquid and vapour in equilibrium at any pressure can be found by drawing a horizontal line between the liquid and vapour branches of the curve. At pressure-volume conditions between the two branches of the curve, both liquid and vapour are present. The critical point is indicated by the letter C, and at higher pressures, water forms a supercritical fluid.

7-7 The complete phase diagram

We can now assemble what we have learnt into a single diagram called a **phase diagram**, which shows the relationships between the various phases and processes. Figures 7-8 and 7-9 show the phase diagram for water. The diagram is shown in two different stages of magnification, because the pressure range covered is too large to represent on a single diagram.

There are three lines corresponding to the three processes of evaporation of a liquid, melting of a solid, and sublimation (or evaporation) of a solid. Figure 7-8 extends up to just above the critical point conditions. The liquid-vapour evaporation line repeats the curve of vapour pressure first encountered in Figure 7-2. The solid-liquid melting line is almost vertical. Figure 7-9 gives a more detailed view of the diagram up to pressures a little above atmospheric pressure. Melting and boiling take place at atmospheric pressure under the conditions indicated by the letters M and B on the corresponding lines in Figure 7-9. Melting of water under its own vapour pressure takes place at the triple point, which is indicated by the letter T.

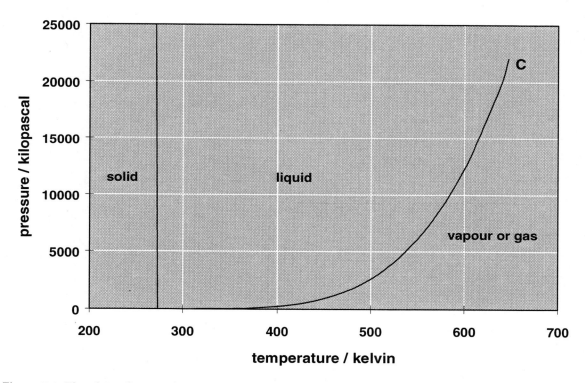

Figure 7-8 The phase diagram for water including the critical point. The line separating the gas and liquid regions of the diagram is the same curve as that shown for water in Figure 7-2, and comes to an end at the critical point, marked C. The supercritical range of temperature and pressure lies above and to the right of the critical point C.

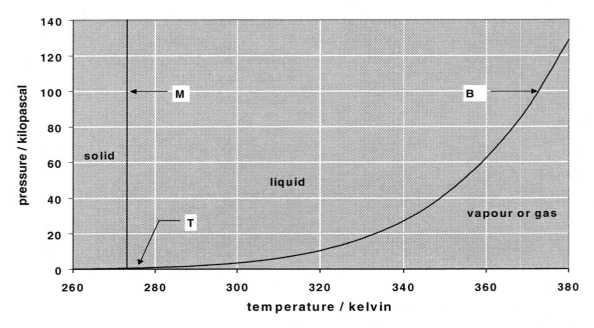

Figure 7-9 The low pressure part of the phase diagram for water. The boiling point, where the vapour pressure of the liquid reaches 101.3 kPa, is marked B. The melting point at 101.3 kPa is marked M. The triple point where ice, water and water vapour are in equilibrium in the absence of air is marked T.

7-8 The van der Waals equation and the critical point

The van der Waals equation of state was introduced in section 5-11 as a way of describing how real gases deviate from the ideal gas equation of state under certain conditions, because the molecules of the gas exert forces on each other when they are close together. The van der Waals equation also gives a description of the phenomena related to the critical point and the relationship between the gaseous state and the liquid state. In describing the properties of gases close to the critical point, the van der Waals equation is not the most accurate equation that can be used, but it is a fairly simple equation which gives an adequate description of the nature of the critical point.

The van der Waals equation stated in terms of molar volume is:

$$\left(P + \frac{a}{V_m^2}\right)(V_m - b) = RT$$

where $V_m = V/n$ is the molar volume of the gas. At a fixed temperature, the van der waals equation can be used to calculate the pressure as a function of molar volume. Such curves are called **isotherms**.

Figure 7-10 shows pressure-volume isotherms for water vapour in the super-critical region calculated from the van der Waals equation. At the highest temperature shown, 740 K, the isotherm looks very similar to a Boyle's law isotherm, but as the temperature is lowered towards the critical temperature of 647 K, an inflection appears in the isotherms. Near the critical point, the pressure-volume isotherms become almost horizontal, indicating that the volume of the fluid can be changed over a substantial range by a small change of pressure. Under these conditions the gas is best described as a **supercritical fluid.**

A supercritical fluid has the property that its density can be changed without much change in pressure. Supercritical fluids can be used as solvents, as long as they are kept under pressure.

Changing the density of a supercritical fluid changes its properties as a solvent, so the solubility of another substance in the fluid can be controlled by small changes of pressure. Carbon dioxide is particularly useful because it is fairly inert chemically and has a critical temperature just above room temperature. Supercritical carbon dioxide is used to dissolve caffeine from coffee beans in the manufacture of decaffeineated coffee, as a solvent for recovering petroleum in the oil industry, and for chemical analysis.

The temperature, pressure and molar volume at the critical point can be calculated from the van der Waals equation. Table 5-2 lists values of the van der Waals parameters a and b for a number of gases, which were calculated for each substance so as to give agreement between the predicted and observed critical point data. The equations relating the van der Waals parameters to the observed critical pressure and temperature are:

$$a = \frac{27R^2 T_c^2}{64 P_c} \qquad\qquad b = \frac{RT_c}{8P_c} \tag{7-4}$$

The van der Waals equation predicts that, regardless of the values of a and b, the critical pressure, temperature and volume are related by the following equation:

$$\frac{P_c V_c}{RT_c} = \frac{3}{8} = 0.375 \tag{7-5}$$

For comparison, $PV/RT = 1$ for an ideal gas, and the observed values of $P_c V_c/RT_c$ for real gases (listed in Table 7-4) lie mostly in the range 0.25 to 0.30.

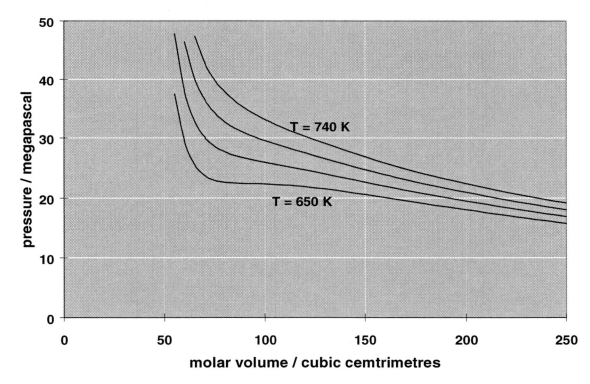

Figure 7-10. The pressure-volume isotherms for water calculated from the van der Waals equation in the vicinity of the critical point. The four temperatures are 650 K, 680 K, 710 K and 740 K. The critical point is close to the almost flat section of the lowest curve. The shape of these isotherms may be compared with those shown in Figure 5-5 for an ideal gas.

Chapter 7

7-9 Temperature dependence of vapour pressure: calculations

We now return to re-consider the temperature dependence of the vapour pressure P^*. The graphs shown in Figure 7-2 all have the same shape, to a good approximation, and can all be described by the same equation with parameters which vary from one substance to another. Plotting the same data in a different way reveals the form of this function. Two changes are required in the way the data are plotted. First, the logarithm of the vapour pressure rather than the pressure itself is plotted on the vertical axis; secondly, the inverse of the absolute temperature (in kelvin) is plotted on the horizontal axis. The same data as in Figure 7-2 are plotted this way in Figure 7-11: the natural logarithm of the vapour pressure P^* in units of kilopascal is plotted against the inverse of the absolute temperature in kelvin.

The graphs in Figure 7-11 require some thought to interpret. Since the quantity plotted along the horizontal axis is the inverse of the absolute temperature in kelvin, the scale is not linear in temperature. In addition, high temperatures are to the left of the graph and low temperatures to the right. The vertical scale is labelled "ln(P^*/kPa)", which means the natural logarithm of the numerical value of the vapour pressure in units of kilopascal. The boiling points of the liquid is found where at the point on the graph where ln(P^*/kPa) = ln(101.3) = 4.62.

The graph of the logarithm of vapour pressure as a function of inverse absolute temperature is called a **van't Hoff** plot, following the work of the Dutch scientist Jacobus van't Hoff, who investigated the effects of temperature on chemical equilibrium and on the rates of chemical reactions. We will meet similar graphs when dealing with the temperature dependence of equilibrium constants.

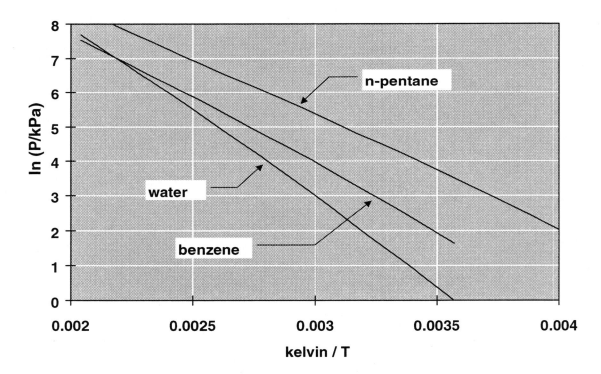

Figure 7-11 The natural logarithm of the vapour pressure P^* in kilopascal, ln(P^*/kPa), plotted as a function of the inverse of the absolute temperature in kelvin. Note that kelvin/T is the same as $1/(T/\text{kelvin})$. This graph shows the same information as Figure 7-2, but in a different format. Note that the high temperature end of the horizontal axis is at the left.

The straight line graphs show that for each substance $\ln(P^*/\text{kPa})$ is a linear function of $1/T$ and can be represented satisfactorily by the equation:

$$\ln\left(\frac{P^*}{\text{kPa}}\right) = a\left(\frac{1}{T}\right) + b$$

where the slope a and intercept b are constants for a particular substance. The slope a in this equation is related to the enthalpy of vaporization by the formula:

$$a = -\frac{\Delta H_{vap}}{R}$$

where R is the gas constant and ΔH_{vap} is the enthalpy change of vaporization. Liquids with a high latent heat of vaporization have a steep negative slope of their van't Hoff plots of vapour pressure.

Combining the last two equations, we obtain:

$$\ln\left(\frac{P^*}{\text{kPa}}\right) = -\frac{\Delta H_{vap}}{R}\left(\frac{1}{T}\right) + b \tag{7-6}$$

It follows from this equation that, for two temperatures T_1 and T_2, the two vapour pressures P_1 and P_2 are related by the equation:

$$\ln\left(\frac{P_2^*}{P_1^*}\right) = -\frac{\Delta H_{vap}}{R}\left(\frac{1}{T_2} - \frac{1}{T_1}\right) \tag{7-7}$$

This equation is called the **Clausius-Clapeyron equation**. When substituting values in this equation, the two vapour pressures can be expressed in any pressure units, as long as the same units are used for both P_1^* and P_2^*.

The ratio of the vapour pressures at two different temperatures depends only on the enthalpy of vaporization and so a good way of measuring the enthalpy change of vaporization of a liquid is to measure the vapour pressure at several different temperatures.

Example 7-2 The vapour pressure of mercury is 0.25 Pa at 25°C and 1.7 Pa at 50°C. Calculate the enthalpy of vaporization of mercury.

The two temperatures must first be converted to absolute temperatures: 298.15 K and 323.15 K. Substituting into equation (7-7), we get the equation:

$$\ln\left(\frac{1.7\ \text{Pa}}{0.25\ \text{Pa}}\right) = -\frac{\Delta H_{vap}}{8.314\ \text{J K}^{-1}\ \text{mol}^{-1}}\left(\frac{1}{323.15\ \text{K}} - \frac{1}{298.15\ \text{K}}\right)$$

from which the enthalpy can be calculated:

$$\Delta H_{vap} = 61.4\ \text{kJ / mol}.$$

This result may be compared with the enthalpy calculated from thermochemical data in Appendix 1, which gives the ΔH_f° of Hg(g) as 61.3 kJ/mol.

Chapter 7

Example 7-3 If the vapour pressure of water at 25°C is 3.17 kPa, calculate the vapour pressure at 35°C using data from thermochemical tables.

_____

From the heats of formation of water in the gas and liquid states, the enthalpy of vaporization is:

$$\Delta H_{vap} = \Delta H_f^\circ(H_2O(g)) - \Delta H_f^\circ(H_2O(l)) = (-241.81) - (-285.83) = 44.02 \text{ kJ/mol}$$

Using this value in equation (7-7),

$$\ln\left(\frac{P^*}{3.17 \text{ kPa}}\right) = -\frac{44.02 \times 10^3 \text{ J mol}^{-1}}{8.314 \text{ J / K mol}^{-1}}\left(\frac{1}{308.15} - \frac{1}{298.15}\right) = +0.5673$$

and hence:

$$P^* = 3.17 \times \exp(+0.5673) = 5.641 \text{ kPa}$$

_____

Key concepts

The three states of matter are the solid state, the liquid state and the gaseous (or vapour) state. Matter transforms from one state to another by melting, freezing, evaporation, sublimation or condensation.

The vapour pressure of a liquid depends on the temperature of the liquid. The temperature at which the vapour pressure is equal to atmospheric pressure is the boiling point. Trouton's rule gives a general relationship between the latent heat of boiling and the boiling point temperature.

The temperature at which a solid melts in contact with the atmosphere is the melting point. The triple point is the temperature at which solid, liquid and vapour phases are equal, and may be slightly different from the melting point.

The critical point is the temperature and pressure at which the distinction between the liquid and vapour phases disappears. At higher temperatures and pressures a supercritical fluid is formed. Near the critical point the supercritical fluid deviates considerably from the ideal gas equation. The van der Waals equation accounts for the existence of the critical point, and describes the properties of supercritical fluids reasonably well. The parameters for the van der Waals equation can be calculated from the critical temperature and critical pressure.

The relationships between the solid, liquid and gaseous states of matter, and the special points such as the triple point and critical point, can be represented on a pressure-temperature graph called a phase diagram. The temperature dependence of the vapour pressure of a liquid (or solid) can be calculated from the latent heat of vaporization, using the Clausius-Clapeyron equation.

Review Questions

1.   Define the vapour pressure of a liquid.

2.   Define the melting point and boiling point.

3.   Why do some liquids smell?

4.   Why do some solids smell?

5.   What is latent heat?

6. Define the triple point.

7. What is the difference between the triple point and the melting point?

8. What is the difference between sublimation and boiling?

9. What is the opposite of evaporation?

10. Can evaporation occur at a temperature other than the boiling point?

11. Describe qualitatively how vapour pressure varies with temperature.

12. Describe the critical point.

13. Explain how you might be able to convert a vapour to a liquid without ever having a meniscus, or surface separating the two phases.

14. What is the usual approximate relationship between critical temperature and boiling point?

Problems

1. Pentane, C_5H_{12}, boils at 309 K. Estimate the critical temperature using information from Table 7-4. [475 K]

2. Which straight-chain hydrocarbon has a critical temperature closest to that of carbon dioxide?

3. Estimate the boiling point of pentane from the graph in Figure 7-2 and compare your result with the information in Table 7-1 and Figure 7-5.

4. Which of the substances listed in Table 7-3, besides carbon dioxide, is not found in the liquid state at atmospheric pressure?

5. Choose two substances which are listed in both Tables 7-4 and 7-5. Calculate the van der Waals parameters from the critical point data in Table 7-4 and compare your results with the data in Table 7-5.

6. Make a sketch of the phase diagram of carbon dioxide using data from the tables in this chapter. Identify the triple point and the critical point, and explain why no boiling point or melting point data is listed in the tables.

7. Using the data for carbon dioxide in Table 7-3 and the van't Hoff equation, estimate the temperature of "dry ice", i.e. solid carbon dioxide in equilibrium with its vapour at a pressure of 100 kPa. [194 K]

8. On a trip through the Himalayas, a mountain climbing team reaches a height of 5000 metres above sea level , where the atmospheric pressure is 54.0 kilopascals. There they sit down and boil some water. Use the Clausius-Clapeyron equation to estimate the temperature of the water under these conditions. [83°C]

9. At what temperature is the vapour pressure of ethanol equal to 33 kPa? Use data from Table 7-1. [324 K]

10. By how much does the boiling point temperature of water change if atmospheric pressure changes by 1.0 kPa? [0.28 K]

11. Difluorodichloromethane, CF_2Cl_2, is used as a refrigerant in many older domestic refrigerators which were built before the use of chlorofluorocarbons was banned because of concern over the "ozone layer" in the upper atmosphere. What mass of CF_2Cl_2 must be evaporated in order to absorb 100. kilojoule of latent heat? Use data from Table 7-1. [0.578 kg]

12. A standard commercial tank of propane, such as those supplied for gas barbecues, has a volume of 23 litres, and contains 9.0 kilogram of propane when "filled".

    (a) Calculate the average molar volume of the propane in the tank and compare your result with the critical molar volume listed in Table 7-2. [113 cm³/mol]

    (b) Hence show that at 25°C the propane is largely in the liquid state, by comparing the average molar volume with the critical volume.

    (c) Use the Clausius-Clapeyron equation and the boiling point data from Table 7-1 to calculate the pressure in the tank at a temperature of 30.0°C. [1.07 MPa]

    (d) After half the propane has been used for cooking hamburgers, calculate the pressure in the tank at the same temperature? [1.07 MPa]

    (e) Estimate the pressure you would expect if the temperature of a tank containing 9.0 kg of propane increased to 100°C. Use the van der Waals equation with parameters taken from Table 5-2. What would be the likely result if this happened? [61 Mpa]

13. Calculate the enthalpy of vaporization at 25°C for $CH_3OH(\ell)$ and $C_2H_5OH(\ell)$ from enthalpy of formation data in Appendix 1, and compare your result with the data in Table 7-1. [38.00 kJ/mol, 42.59 kJ/mol]

14. Calculate the enthalpy of sublimation at 25°C for $I_2(s)$, C(graphite), and $SbCl_3(s)$ from enthalpy of formation data in Appendix 1. [62.438 kJ/mol, 716.682 kJ/mol, 68.4 kJ/mol]

15. Gases prepared in the laboratory are often collected "over water", and are consequently mixed with saturated water vapour. Figure 2-2 shows the apparatus being used to collect hydrogen and oxygen generated by electrolysis. A student collects 653.4 cm³ of hydrogen saturated with water vapour at a temperature of 16.8°C, at which temperature the vapour pressure of water is 1.919 kPa. The pressure of the gas is carefully adjusted to be equal to the atmospheric pressure of 99.52 kPa at the time of the experiment. Calculate the number of moles of H_2 gas in the sample. What percentage error would result from ignoring the presence of the water vapour? [0.02645 mol, 2 %]

16. Taking into account that the oxygen and hydrogen in the electrolysis experiment shown in Figure 2-2 are both saturated with water vapour, would you expect that the ratio of the volumes of the gases collected would be greater than 2.000, exactly 2.000, or less than 2.000? Assume that the pressure of each gas is adjusted to be equal to the pressure of the atmosphere.

17. Using a data from Table 7-2, construct a graph of melting point of the second row molecular hydrides XH_n similar to Figure 7-6, and show that the trend in melting point is similar to that for boiling point.

8 Liquid Solutions

Objectives

After reading this chapter, the student should be able to do the following:

♦ Define properties of ideal solutions using Raoult's law.

♦ Sketch vapour pressure and boiling point diagrams for ideal solutions.

♦ Explain simple distillation and fractional distillation.

♦ Define zeotropic and azeotropic solutions.

♦ Draw boiling point diagrams for azeotropic solutions.

♦ Sketch freezing point diagrams for solutions.

♦ Describe the solubility of gases in liquids using Henry's law.

♦ Define and calculate colligative properties of dilute solutions.

Related topics to review:

Composition of solutions in Chapter 1. Properties of liquids in Chapters 1 and 7.

Related topics to look forward to:

Solubility equilibrium in Chapter 15. Thermodynamics of equilibrium in Chapter 16.

8-1 Solutions

A solution is a homogeneous mixture of two or more substances, in which the substances present are mixed together in a single phase of uniform properties. The composition of a solution is not fixed, and the properties of a solution vary continuously as the composition is varied. For example, the density of a solution of sucrose (sugar) in water increases with the amount of sucrose dissolved, and the colour of a dye solution gets more intense as more dye is dissolved.

A solution can be a solid, a liquid or a gas. Solid solutions are rare, except for some metallic alloys. Gaseous solutions are simply mixtures of gases, such as air, and were discussed in Chapter 5. In dealing with gaseous solutions, the most important concepts are partial pressures and Dalton's law.

In this chapter we discuss liquid solutions, which are used so commonly in chemistry. Important properties of liquid solutions are the vapour pressure, boiling point, melting point, limits to solubility, and the so-called colligative properties.

If one compound is present in a liquid solution in a much larger amount than other substances, then it is called the **solvent**. The other substances dissolved in the solvent are called **solutes**. When water is the solvent, the solution is called an **aqueous solution**. The composition of solutions can be described by measures such as mole fraction, mass fraction, molality or molar concentration, as described in Chapter 1.

8-2 Liquid-vapour equilibrium of solutions: ideal solutions

We begin by considering the liquid-vapour equilibrium of a liquid solution formed by mixing several pure substances. A solution has a vapour pressure, just like a pure liquid, and the vapour pressure varies with the composition of the solution as well as the temperature. The vapour that evaporates from a liquid solution contains some of each substance that is present in the solution, but the composition of the vapour is usually different from that of the liquid solution. This is because the substances forming the liquid solution are not equally volatile, and in addition may interact with each other in the solution.

The relationships between the vapour pressure of the solution, the composition of the solution, and the composition of the vapour in equilibrium with the solution, can be complicated. We start our study with the simplest case, that of so-called **ideal solutions**.

Consider a solution containing two chemically similar, volatile liquids. As a specific example, we will take a mixture of two straight-chain hydrocarbons, hexane C_6H_{14} and heptane C_7H_{16}. The vapour pressure of the solution can be measured using apparatus such as that shown in Figure 7-1. The composition of the liquid and the composition of the vapour can be determined separately using an appropriate method of chemical analysis. Compositions will be expressed as the mole fraction of hexane.

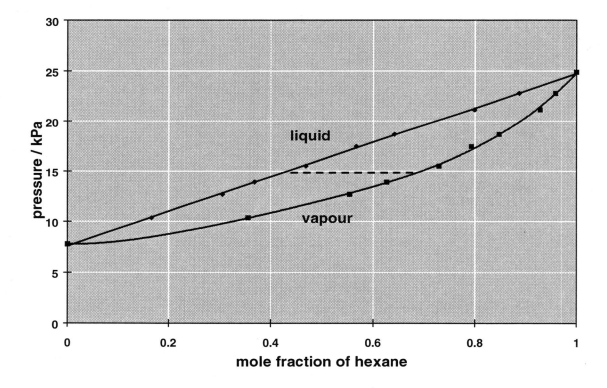

Figure 8-1 The vapour pressure of mixtures of hexane and heptane at 30°C, plotted *versus* mole fraction of hexane in both the liquid and vapour phases. The points represent experimental data on the compositions of the liquid and vapour phases that are in equilibrium at various temperatures. The upper curve gives the vapour pressure as a function of composition of the liquid; the lower curve gives the vapour pressure as a function of composition of the vapour. The horizontal dotted line is a tie line, and shows the composition of the vapour in equilibrium with a liquid of a particular composition.

Figure 8-1 shows experimental data on the vapour pressure of hexane-heptane solutions at a temperature of 30°C. There are two graphs of the vapour pressure, plotted as a function both of the composition of the liquid and the composition of the vapour. The straight line graph marked "liquid" is a graph of the vapour pressure *versus* the mole fraction of hexane in the liquid phase, and the curved graph marked "vapour" is a graph of the vapour pressure *versus* the mole fraction of hexane in the vapour phase.

When seeing this graph for the first time it might be thought that, because there are two graphs on the diagram, there must be two vapour pressures, but this is not the case. There is only one vapour pressure for a given solution at a given temperature. One graph shows the vapour pressure of the solution as a function of the composition of the liquid phase, the other shows the vapour pressure of the solution as a function of the composition of the vapour phase.

From the two graphs, we can discover the relationship between the compositions of the two phases, as well as the vapour pressure. Given the composition of the liquid phase, we read the vapour pressure from the liquid line; we can then read the composition of the vapour phase by drawing a horizontal line called a **tie line** from the liquid curve to the vapour curve at the level of the vapour pressure. The dotted horizontal line in Figure 8-1 is a tie line.

Example 8-1 What is the vapour pressure of a liquid mixture of hexane and heptane in which the mole fraction of hexane is 0.42, and what is the composition of the vapour in equilibrium with the liquid?

Reading from the "liquid" line in Figure 8-1, the vapour pressure of a solution with a liquid mole fraction of 0.42 is 15 kPa. The mole fraction of hexane in the vapour phase is read from the intersection of the 15 kPa tie line with the "vapour" curve, giving the value 0.70. Notice that the mole fraction of hexane in the vapour is higher than in the liquid. This is because hexane has a higher vapour pressure and is more volatile than heptane.

In the graph of vapour pressure as a function of composition in Figure 8-1, the "liquid" line is straight. This shows that the vapour pressure of the solution is a linear function of the composition of the liquid phase expressed as a mole fraction. The theory used to explain this behaviour is called **Raoult's law**, which states that the partial pressure of each compound is proportional to its mole fraction in the liquid.

Expressing Raoult's law algebraically is not difficult but requires some care over notation. We will use letters A and B to represent the two compounds present in an ideal solution, hexane and heptane in the present example. The mole fractions in the liquid state will be designated by $x(A)$ and $x(B)$, and the vapour pressures of the two pure compounds at the temperature of the solution will be designated by $P^*(A)$ and $P^*(B)$. The partial pressures of the two compounds in the vapour are $p(A)$ and $p(B)$ and are smaller than the vapour pressures of the pure compounds. According to Raoult's law, the partial pressure of each compound in the vapour is the vapour pressure of the pure compound multiplied by the mole fraction of that compound in the liquid state:

$$p(A) = x(A)P^*(A) \quad \text{and} \quad p(B) = x(B)P^*(B) \tag{8-1}$$

Chapter 8

The total vapour pressure of the solution, *P*(solution)*, is the sum of the partial pressures of the two components:

$$P^*(solution) = p(A) + p(B)$$

Substituting equations (8-1) for the two partial pressures, the vapour pressure of the solution can be expressed in terms of the composition of the liquid:

$$P^*(solution) = x(A)P^*(A) + x(B)P^*(B) \tag{8-2}$$

Since the sum of the mole fractions must be 1, $x(B) = 1 - x(A)$ and this equation can be written in a slightly different form:

$$P^*(solution) = P^*(B) + x(A)\left(P^*(A) - P^*(B)\right)$$

Hence the vapour pressure of an ideal solution is a linear function of the composition mole fraction of one compound in the liquid phase. This is shown in Figure 8-2.

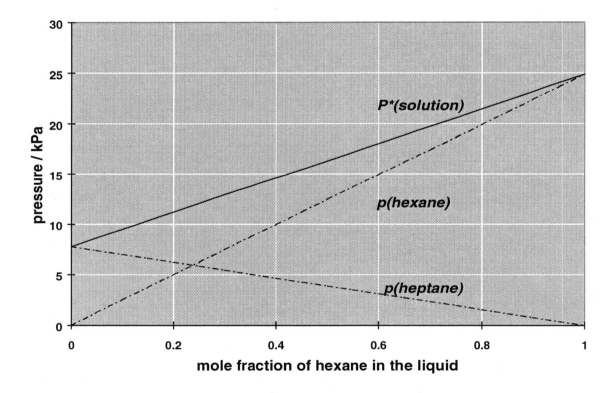

Figure 8-2 The partial pressures *p(hexane)* and *p(heptane)* (dotted lines) and the total vapour pressure *P*(solution)* (full line) of a solution of hexane and heptane, calculated using Raoult's law for ideal solutions.

Solutions that obey Raoult's law are called **ideal,** and provide a benchmark with which the behaviour of other solutions may be compared. Mixtures of hexane and heptane are ideal solutions. Most ideal solutions are formed from compounds that are similar in their chemical and physical properties. Table 8-1 lists some mixtures that form ideal solutions.

Table 8-1 Some examples of ideal and nearly ideal solutions

Pairs of alkanes with similar molar masses, e.g. n-hexane C_6H_{14} and n-heptane C_7H_{16}.

Pairs of halogenated alkanes, e.g. trichloromethane $CHCl_3$ and dichloromethane CH_2Cl_2.

Benzene C_6H_6 and toluene $C_6H_5CH_3$.

Methanol CH_3OH and ethanol C_2H_5OH.

Methanol CH_3OH and water H_2O.

The composition of the vapour phase in equilibrium with a solution can be calculated from the partial pressures using the definition of partial pressure given in equation (5-11). The mole fraction of a substance in the vapour is the ratio of its partial pressure to the total pressure. Hence the mole fractions $y(A)$ and $y(B)$ of the two substances in the vapour are given by the following equations:

$$y(A) = \frac{p(A)}{p(A) + p(B)} \qquad y(B) = \frac{p(B)}{p(A) + p(B)} \qquad (8\text{-}3)$$

In these equations, the partial pressures $p(A)$ and $p(B)$ can be calculated from Raoult's law using equations (8-1), and hence the composition of the vapour can be calculated from the composition of the liquid. The calculations are illustrated in Example 8-2.

By this means, it is possible to construct the graph of vapour pressure *versus* the composition of the vapour phase, and this is shown for hexane-heptane mixtures in Figure 8-3. Comparison of the calculated graphs in Figure 8-3 with those in Figure 8-1 shows that Raoult's law accounts for the experimental data very well.

Example 8-2 The vapour pressures of pure hexane and heptane at 30°C are 24.9 kPa and 7.75 kPa respectively. Calculate the vapour pressure of a solution containing a mole fraction of 0.42 hexane, and the composition of the vapour phase in equilibrium with the liquid.

The partial pressures of hexane and heptane are:

$$p(hex) = x(hex) \times P^*(hex) = 0.42 \times 24.9 \text{ kPa} = 10.4 \text{ kPa}$$

$$p(hep) = x(hep) \times P^*(hep) = 0.58 \times 7.75 \text{ kPa} = 4.5 \text{ kPa}$$

The total vapour pressure is $P^* = 10.4 + 4.5 = 14.9 \text{ kPa}$, and the mole fraction of hexane in the vapour phase is $y(hex) = \dfrac{10.4}{14.9} = 0.70$. These figures are in good agreement with the numbers estimated in Example 8-1 from the graphs in Figure 8-1.

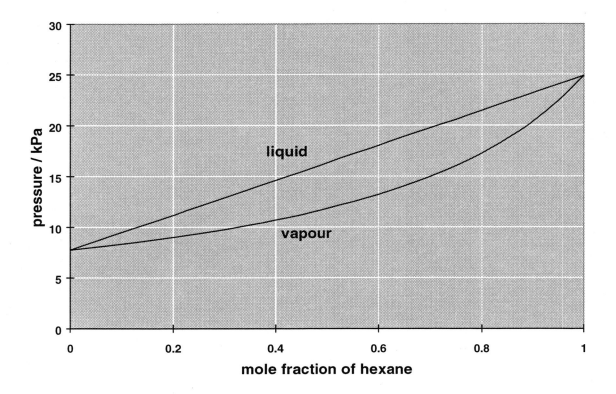

Figure 8-3 The vapour pressure diagram for hexane-heptane solutions at 30°C calculated from Raoult's law. This may be compared with the experimental data shown in Figure 8-1.

8-3 Boiling point diagrams

When heated, a liquid boils when its vapour pressure reaches atmospheric pressure. This is true for liquid solutions, as well as for the pure liquids discussed in Chapter 7. There are two effects to be considered when discussing the boiling of solutions. First, the boiling point of a solution depends upon its composition, because the vapour pressure depends on composition. Second, the composition of the vapour produced is different from the composition of the boiling liquid.

Figure 8-4 shows the boiling point of mixtures of hexane and heptane as a function of composition. The diagram shows two graphs, one (labelled "liquid") showing the boiling point as a function of composition of the liquid phase , and the other (labelled "vapour") showing the boiling point as a function of the composition of the vapour phase. These graphs are similar to those in Figure 8-1 and 8-3. The composition of the vapour that is boiled off from a solution can be read from the "vapour" graph by drawing a horizontal tie line at the boiling point of the solution.

Example 8-3 What is the boiling point of a liquid mixture of hexane and heptane in which the mole fraction of hexane is 0.42, and what is the composition of the vapour produced?

Reading from the "liquid" line in Figure 8-4, the boiling point of a solution with a liquid mole fraction of 0.42 is 84°C. Reading from the intersection of the 84°C line with the "vapour" curve, the mole fraction of hexane in the vapour phase is 0.63.

Note that the composition of the vapour produced by boiling this liquid at 84°C is different from the composition of the vapour in equilibrium with the same liquid at 30°C (see Examples 8-1 and 8-2).

Several points should be noted about the temperature-composition diagram (Figure 8-4) when comparing it with the pressure-composition diagram (Figure 8-1). First, neither of the graphs in the temperature-composition diagram is a straight line even though the solution is ideal. This is not surprizing because vapour pressure is not a linear function of temperature (see Figure 7-2). Second, the liquid line lies below the vapour line; this is easy to remember since the solution is a liquid at low temperature, and a vapour at high temperature. The graphs come together at the two sides of the graph, at the boiling point of each pure substance.

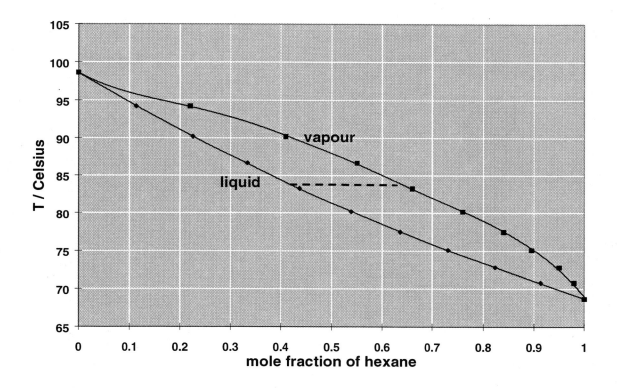

Figure 8-4 The boiling point temperature of a solution of hexane and heptane plotted as a function of the mole fraction of hexane in both the liquid and vapour phases. The horizontal dotted line is a tie line.

8-4 Distillation

If the vapour produced by boiling a liquid is passed into a cool tube, it condenses. The vapour condenses on the surface of the tube, and can be separated from the boiling liquid. The liquid resulting from condensation has the same composition as that of the vapour, which is different from that of the original liquid. The process of boiling and condensation is called **distillation**, and the condensed vapour is called the **condensate** or **distillate**. Distillation can often be used to purify mixtures of volatile liquids, using apparatus such as that shown in Figure 8-5.

The composition of the distillate can be calculated from the boiling point diagram, as described above. For instance, if a solution of hexane and heptane with a mole fraction of hexane of 0.42 is distilled, the mole fraction of hexane in the initial condensate will be 0.63, as calculated in Example 8-3. In the distillate, the mole fraction of the more volatile, lower-boiling compound (hexane in this case) is higher than in the original liquid.

As distillation continues, the composition of the liquid remaining in the round-bottomed flask changes. Because the vapour produced is richer in the more volatile compound than the liquid from which it was produced, the liquid remaining must be richer in the less volatile compound. Hence after some of the liquid has been distilled off, the boiling point of the remaining liquid is higher than it was initially, and as the distillation proceeds, the boiling point gradually drifts to higher temperatures and the mole fraction of the higher boiling point compound gradually increases.

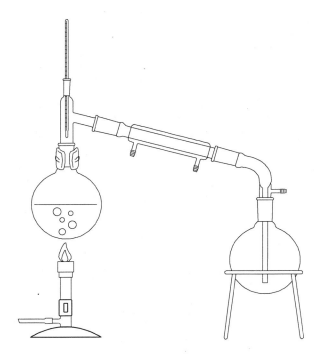

Figure 8-5 Apparatus for carrying out a distillation. The vapour from the boiling solution in the left-hand flask passes up the neck of the flask and into the condenser. The condenser is cooled by a flow of water through the outer jacket. The vapour condenses on the cool walls of the condenser, and the condensate runs down the inner tube and drips into the right-hand flask. For clarity, the diagram shows a bunsen burner as the source of heat, but a snug-fitting electric heater is commonly used for safety reasons.

In the process called **fractional distillation**, some of the distillate produced initially is distilled a second time. The first distillate is richer in the lower boiling point compound, and the second distillate will be richer still. The path of the two stages of distillation is shown by the arrows on Figure 8-6 starting at a hexane mole fraction of 0.42. It can be seen that in two stages of distillation, the mole fraction of hexane increases to 0.82, and a few more stages would produce almost pure hexane from the mixture.

If the two compounds in a solution can be separated by repeated distillation, the solution is called **zeotropic**. Ideal solutions are zeotropic; the composition of the vapour phase differs from that of the liquid phase, and so the two compounds can be separated by distillation.

Special fractional distillation columns have been designed to carry out many stages of fractional distillation in a single operation. Fractional distillation is used in industry to isolate almost pure compounds from zeotropic solutions, and to process the complex mixtures of hydrocarbons found in crude petroleum into commercial fuels.

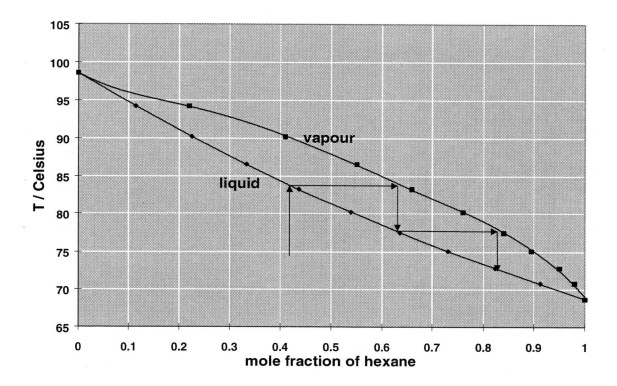

Figure 8-6 The path followed in a two-stage fractional distillation of a solution of hexane and heptane. As a specific example, the mole fraction of hexane in the initial solution is assumed to be 0.42. The liquid and vapour curves are the same as those shown in Figure 8-4.

8-5 Azeotropes

Most pairs of liquids do not form ideal solutions and we turn now to consider how the properties of these solutions deviate from the ideal properties described by Raoult's law. The most important deviation from ideality is the formation of **azeotropes**, or **azeotropic solutions**. The word "azeotropic" means "not zeotropic", and is used to describe solutions that cannot be separated into their components by distillation.

In an ideal solution which obeys Raoult's law, the vapour pressure and the boiling point are monotonic functions of the composition of the liquid; in other words, there is no maximum or minimum in either the vapour pressure-composition graphs or the temperature-composition graphs. However, if there are strong **negative** deviations from Raoult's law, there is a minimum in the vapour pressure-composition diagram, and a **maximum** in the boiling point-composition diagram. A solution with composition corresponding to the maximum boiling point is called a **maximum-boiling azeotrope.** It is helpful to recall that a reduction in vapour pressure causes an increase in the boiling point of the solution since boiling takes place only when the vapour pressure reaches atmospheric pressure.

The opposite case is that of **positive** deviations from Raoult's law, with a maximum in the vapour pressure-composition diagram and a **minimum** in the boiling point-composition diagram. A solution with composition corresponding to the minimum boiling point is called a **minimum-boiling azeotrope.**

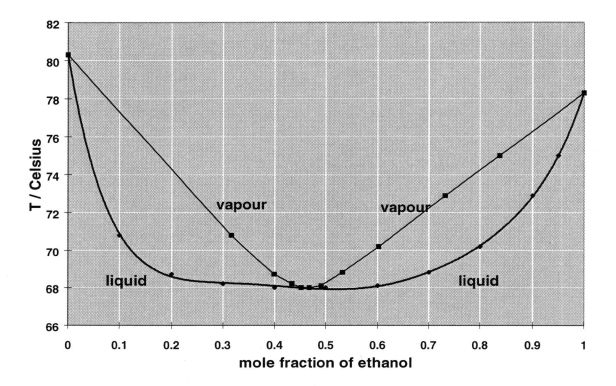

Figure 8-7 The boiling point diagram for a minimum-boiling azeotropic system, benzene and ethanol. The graph of boiling point *versus* vapour composition has a smooth rounded minimum and touches the graph *versus* liquid composition at the azeotropic composition.

Figure 8-7 shows a boiling point diagram for mixtures of ethanol C_2H_5OH and benzene C_6H_6, which form a positive deviation, minimum boiling azeotrope. At a mole fraction *x(ethanol)* = 0.46, the boiling point reaches a minimum of 68.0°C, which is well below the boiling points of the two compounds, 80.3°C and 78.3°C.

At the composition corresponding to the minimum boiling point, *x(ethanol)* = 0.46, the composition of the vapour is the same as that of the liquid. Boiling the azeotropic solution produces a vapour with the same composition as the liquid, so no amount of distillation can separate the two compounds from a solution with this particular composition. For solutions with other compositions, fractional distillation leads to the azeotropic composition. This can be seen by the same construction as that shown in Figure 8-6

Minimum boiling azeotropes are found when the attractive forces between *unlike* molecules are weaker than the attractive forces between *like* molecules. This can be thought of as a net repulsion between unlike molecules. The partial pressures of both compounds in the vapour are larger than would be predicted by Raoult's law, and the larger vapour pressure reduces the boiling point of the solution compared with what would be expected for an ideal solution.

Some solutions possess a maximum in their boiling point diagrams, though this is less common than minimum boiling azeotropes. Maximum boiling azeotropes are found when the attractive forces between *unlike* molecules are stronger than the attractive forces between *like* molecules. This can be thought of as a net attraction between unlike molecules. The partial pressures of both compounds in the vapour are smaller than would be predicted by Raoult's law, and the smaller vapour pressure increases the boiling point of the solution compared with what would be expected for an ideal solution. The boiling point-composition diagrams in such cases are similar to Figure 8-7 except that the curves pass through a maximum rather than a minimum..

Tables 8-2 and 8-3 list the composition and boiling point of some azeotropic solutions.

Table 8-2 Some positive deviation, minimum boiling azeotropes

Liquid A		Liquid B		Azeotrope	
compound	T_b / °C	compound	T_b / °C	T_b / °C	x_A
C_2H_5OH ethanol 78.3		H_2O water	100.0	78.17	0.90
C_2H_5OH ethanol 78.3		C_6H_6 benzene	80.1	67.9	0.440
CH_3OH methanol		CCl_4 carbon tetrachloride 76.8		55.7	0.554
C_6H_{14} n-hexane 69.0		$(CH_3)_2CO$ acetone		49.8	0.319

Reprinted with permission from CRC Handbook of Chemistry and Physics, 77th edition. Copyright CRC Press, Boca Raton Florida.

Table 8-3 Some negative deviation, maximum boiling azeotropes

Liquid A		Liquid B		Azeotrope	
compound	T_b / °C	compound	T_b / °C	T_b / °C	x_A
$CHCl_3$ chloroform		$(CH_3)_2CO$ acetone 56.5		64.4	0.634
HCl hydrogen chloride −85		H_2O water	100.	108.6	0.111
HCOOH formic acid 100.8		H_2O water	100.	107.2	0.573

Reprinted with permission from CRC Handbook of Chemistry and Physics, 77th edition. Copyright CRC Press, Boca Raton Florida.

Chapter 8

8-6 Freezing of solutions

When cooled sufficiently, a solution freezes, and the nature of the solid that separates from the solution depends on the composition of the solution. In most cases, the solid that separates from a liquid solution is a pure substance, since solid solutions are rare.

We start by studying one specific solution from which we can identify several important phenomena that are common to a great many solutions.

Figure 8-8 shows a temperature-composition diagram for aqueous solutions of acetic acid, the acid found in vinegar. Pure water freezes at 0°C and pure acetic acid at +16.6°C; pure solid acetic acid is sometimes called glacial acetic acid because it looks like ice. These two points can be identified in Figure 8-8 at the extreme left and right hand sides of the diagram. The upper part of the diagram indicates that at room temperature, acetic acid and water can be mixed in any proportions in a liquid solution. Towards the left side of the diagram, the solution would be described as a solution of acetic acid in water, and on the right it would be more accurate to think of a solution of water in acetic acid. In the middle, the distinction between solute and solvent loses its meaning.

When an aqueous solution of acetic acid is cooled and frozen, the solid which first separates may be either pure ice or pure acetic acid. The curve starting from the left hand side shows that up to a mole fraction $x(acetic\ acid) = 0.31$, the freezing point of the solution is lower than that of pure water. The solid which separates the solution on freezing is pure ice.

The curve starting from the right hand side shows that for a mole fraction of acetic acid greater than 0.31, the freezing point of the solution is lower than that of pure acetic acid. The solid which separates from these solutions on freezing is pure acetic acid.

The region of the diagram above the two curves indicates the conditions of temperature and composition under which solutions of acetic acid and water can exist entirely in the liquid state. The two triangular regions under the slightly curved freezing point curves correspond to conditions of temperature and composition under which there is a solid phase present as well as the liquid solution. Tie lines can be drawn across these regions to indicate the compositions of phases that are in equilibrium at a particular temperature.

The lowering of the freezing point of a solvent by the addition of a solute is typical of solutions where freezing produces pure solid solvent. This is normal behaviour. At the edges of the temperature-composition diagram, where the mole fraction is not too high, the lowering of the freezing point is proportional to the amount of solute added; the constant of proportionality is characteristic of the solvent. Towards the middle of the freezing point diagram, the two freezing point curves intersect at a point called the **eutectic point**. For acetic acid - water solutions, the eutectic point is at a temperature of –26.7°C and a mole fraction of acetic acid equal to 0.31. The eutectic temperature is the lowest temperature at which an acetic acid/water solution can exist in the liquid state.

The freezing point diagram can be used to predict the course of events when the temperature of a solution is lowered from the liquid region down to below the eutectic temperature. For example, consider a solution with a mole fraction of 0.05 acetic acid; the concentration of this solution is about 3 mol/L. If this solution is cooled from room temperature, the graph in Figure 8-8 indicates that freezing would start at a temperature of –5°C, and that pure ice would crystallize from the solution; all the acetic acid in solution remains in solution.

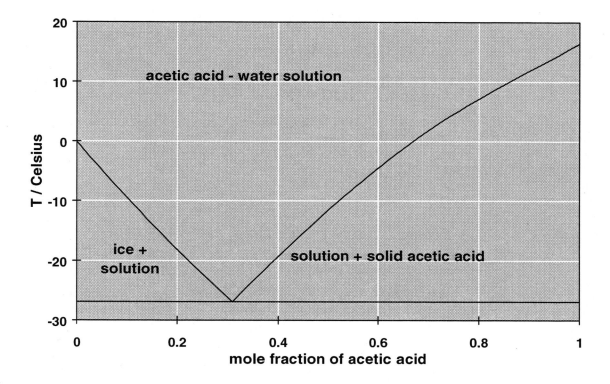

Figure 8-8 The freezing point diagram for solutions of acetic acid in water. The two sloping lines are graphs of the freezing point as a function of the composition of the solution, and beside each graph is an indication of the nature of the solid that separates out when the solution is cooled. The point where the two graphs intersect is the eutectic point.

As the temperature is lowered further, more ice crystallizes from the solution and the mole fraction of the acetic acid in the solution increases because water is being removed from the solution. As the temperature and composition change, the corresponding point on the diagram "slides down" the freezing point line towards the eutectic point. When the eutectic point is reached at a temperature of –26.7°C, pure solid acetic acid starts to crystallize as well as ice. The temperature then remains fixed at the eutectic temperature until all the liquid is converted to the two separate pure solids, ice and solid acetic acid.

Hence an aqueous solution of acetic acid freezes over a temperature range extending from a little below 0°C down to the eutectic temperature of –26.7°C. A pure liquid freezes at a fixed temperature, but a solution freezes over a significant range.

In many cases, a molten mixture of two high melting point salts remains liquid at temperatures well below the melting points of both of the pure salts, if the composition of the mixture is close to the eutectic composition. This technique is used in industrial electrolysis of salts and other ionic solids, to reduce the temperature required for electrolysis. An example the electrolytic refining of aluminum metal, which is discussed in Chapter 17.

Metals also form alloys with low melting points because of the existence of the eutectic point. An example is the lead/tin solder used for electronics.

A pure solid, when heated, melts to a liquid at a single sharp temperature, but a mixture of solids usually melts over a temperature range beginning around the eutectic temperature for the mixture. The process is the reverse of what we considered above, but since the two solids are insoluble in each other in the solid state, the mechanism of melting of mixtures is not obvious. One explanation of mixed melting is that at temperatures not too far below the melting point, molecules on the surface of a crystallite are mobile like the molecules in a liquid, a phenomenon called surface melting. In a mixture of two powders, mobile molecules at the points of contact between the crystallites of the two different substances mix sufficiently that a liquid solution is formed in bulk when the temperatures is above the eutectic temperature.

The study of mixed melting points is an important qualitative test of purity which is used in organic chemistry: a solid which melts sharply is probably a pure solid, while a solid which melts gradually over a range of temperatures is probably impure. Further, a pure unknown solid with a sharp melting point may sometimes be identified by mixing it with a known solid: if the mixture melts sharply, the two solids are probably identical, otherwise they are different compounds.

For some solutions the freezing process is more complicated and involves the formation of compounds between the two substances in the solution. One example of this is the formation of hydrates of salts in the solid state. An example is $CuSO_4.5H_2O(s)$, the common blue form of copper sulfate crystals. This leads to more complicated freezing point diagrams.

The lowering of the freezing point of solutions by solutes is very important in the operation of liquid cooled car and truck engines. It is necessary for the engine coolant to remain liquid at temperatures down to $-30°C$ or even lower in cold climates, and this is achieved by using a solution of an **antifreeze** rather than pure water for the coolant. The usual antifreeze is 1,2-dihydroxyethane, often called ethylene glycol, $(CH_2OH)_2$, which was discussed in Section 4-7 and has the following structure:

$$
\begin{array}{c}
H \\
| \\
H-C-O-H \\
| \\
H-C-O-H \\
| \\
H
\end{array}
$$

1,2-hydroxyethane, or ethylene glycol

The addition of ethylene glycol to the cooling water of an automobile engine achieves two things. Firstly, the onset of freezing of the solution occurs at a much lower temperature than $0°C$. Secondly, freezing takes place gradually over a range of temperatures down to the eutectic temperature of about $-50°C$. Together, these features protect the radiator and engine from damage that would be caused by the expansion of water when it freezes under winter conditions. Ethylene glycol has a boiling point of $197°C$, so is much less volatile than water. Any evaporation from the coolant during the summer consists primarily of water vapour.

A second application of low freezing point solutions is in windshield washer fluid. This consists of a water-methanol solution. Methanol is cheaper to produce and less damaging to the environment than ethylene glycol, and the aqueous methanol solution has a very low eutectic temperature of about $-100°C$. The fact that methanol is more volatile than water does not matter for this application.

8-7 Solubility

Consider, with the help of Figure 8-8, the addition of acetic acid to water at a temperature of 10°C. The added acid dissolves to form a solution, but if enough acid is added the mole fraction of acid reaches the right hand curve at a mole fraction of about 0.85. At that stage no further acid can be dissolved in the liquid phase, and any further acid that is added simply lies on the bottom of the saturated solution, as a separate solid phase. The solution is described as a **saturated solution**, and the concentration of acetic acid in the saturated solution is the **solubility** of acetic acid in water at the specified temperature (10°C in this case). The situation can be represented by a horizontal tie line joining the curve for saturated solution to the right hand side of the diagram (which corresponds to pure acetic acid) at the specified temperature.

A temperature-composition diagram is useful for representing the temperature dependence of solubility of a salt, and the position of the eutectic point. For many salts the diagram is similar to Figure 8-8. For example, Figure 8-9 shows freezing point and solubility data for aqueous solutions of potassium chloride KCl. The left-hand curve EF shows the freezing point of the solution as a function of composition. The right hand curve ES shows how the solubility of KCl in water changes with temperature. The solubility of KCl increases with temperature, but for some other salts the solubility decreases with temperature. This diagram can be used to understand the following practical applications.

In order to melt ice and snow during winter, it is standard practice to spread salt on roads and sidewalks. Both sodium chloride NaCl and calcium chloride $CaCl_2$ are used for this purpose. Ice and snow on a roadway are always mixed with a little water, and when excess crystalline salt is added, some of it dissolves in the water and forms a concentrated (or even saturated) solution. But a solution in contact with ice near 0°C must have a low salt concentration; in the case of KCl this is indicated by the left-hand curve EF in Figure 8-9. The only way to reduce the concentration of salt in the solution is for some of the ice to melt; water formed by melting the ice is added to the solution and reduces the concentration of salt.

Hence around each crystal of salt, ice is converted to a puddle of salt solution. Snow is converted to a slushy mixture of snow, salt crystals and salt solution. However, having solved the problem of melting ice at low temperatures, the salt solution causes major corrosion problems for steel car bodies and reinforcement bars in concrete road structures.

The traditional freezing mixture used in making ice cream at home is a mixture of crushed ice and common salt, NaCl. The freezing mixture is usually contained in an insulated bucket. Addition of salt to crushed ice lowers the temperature to well below 0°C, and this can be explained as follows.

Crushed ice always contains a little water, and when excess salt is added, some of the salt dissolves in the water and forms a concentrated solution. We showed in Example 6-7 that this is an endothermic process, by several kilojoules per mole of NaCl.

But a solution in contact with ice near 0°C has a low concentration, as we pointed out when discussing the use of salt on roads. The only way to achieve a low concentration is to dilute the concentrated solution of salt by melting some ice to form water. This is an endothermic process to the extent of 6 kilojoules per mole of ice, according to Table 7-2.

Hence two endothermic processes take place: salt dissolves in water to form a concentrated solution, and ice melts in order to dilute the solution. Consequently, under the nearly adiabatic conditions inside the insulated bucket, the temperature of the mixture drops. As long as there is some ice and some crystalline salt present, the temperature of the mixture remains well below 0°C, and can be as low as the eutectic temperature of –21°C.

A simplified explanation of the drop in temperature is that the salt melts some of the ice, and the latent heat of melting has to be supplied by the ice itself.

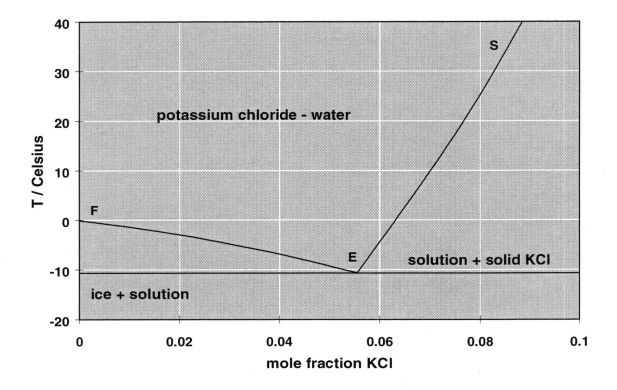

Figure 8-9 The freezing point / solubility diagram for aqueous potassium chloride solutions. The point F is the freezing point of pure water, and E is the eutectic point. The curve EF shows the lowered freezing point of dilute solutions, and the curve ES shows the solubility of KCl in water as a function of temperature. The eutectic temperature is –10.7°C at a mole fraction of 0.055.

8-8 Solubility of gases in liquids

Gases dissolve to some extent in liquids, and the amount dissolved depends not only on the chemical nature of the solvent and of the gas, but also on the temperature and the partial pressure of the gas. William Henry showed by experiment that the solubility of the gas is proportional to its pressure, as long as the pressure is not too high. This is called **Henry's law** and is usually written:

$$p(B) = x(B)K_H \tag{8-4}$$

where $p(B)$ is the partial pressure of the solute gas B in contact with the liquid solvent A, $x(B)$ is the mole fraction of the solute B in the liquid solution. K_H is called the Henry's law constant for that particular gaseous solute and liquid solvent, and has units of pressure.

Henry's law, equation (8-4), may be compared with Raoult's law, equation (8-1). The difference between the two equations is that in Henry's law, the Henry's law constant K_H replaces the vapour pressure of the solute $P^*(B)$. Notice that for, a given partial pressure of the gas, a large value of K_H corresponds to a small solubility.

The Henry's law "constant" K_H is constant for a particular combination of gaseous solute and liquid solvent at a particular temperature, but varies with the temperature of the solution. Table 8-4 gives some K_H values for various gases dissolved in water, at three temperatures.

In every case in Table 8-4 K_H increases with temperature, showing that the solubilities of these gases decrease with increasing temperature. The formation of the solution from the gas and liquid solvent can be represented by a chemical equation, such as:

$$CH_4(g) \rightleftharpoons CH_4(aq)$$

It is known from experiment that the equilibrium shifts to the left with increasing temperature. Applying Le Chatelier's principle, we conclude that the reaction as written is exothermic and the enthalpy change of solution is negative. Thus the formation of the solution is energetically favourable, even though these gases are not very soluble; the reason for this is related to the entropy change of solution and will be discussed further in Chapter 16.

Table 8-4 Henry's law parameter for gases dissolved in water

K_H / GPa at three temperatures

Solute	15°C	25°C	35°C
H_2	6.71	7.18	7.50
O_2	3.67	4.42	5.11
N_2	7.31	8.56	9.68
CO_2	0.123	0.165	0.211
H_2S	0.0434	0.0548	0.0671
CH_4	3.24	3.97	4.65
C_4H_{10}	3.09	4.52	6.16

Reprinted with permission from CRC Handbook of Chemistry and Physics, 77th edition. Copyright CRC Press, Boca Raton Florida.

Example 8-4   Calculate the mole fraction and molar concentration of atmospheric oxygen O_2 in water at a temperature of 25°C given the Henry's law constant is K_H = 4.42 GPa at this temperature and the partial pressure of oxygen in the atmosphere is 21 kPa.

The mole fraction of oxygen is: $x(O_2) = \dfrac{21 \times 10^3 \text{ Pa}}{4.42 \times 10^9 \text{ Pa}} = 4.8 \times 10^{-6}$

For oxygen dissolved in otherwise pure water, the mole fraction can be written:

$$x(O_2) = \frac{n(O_2)}{n(O_2) + n(H_2O)} = 4.8 \times 10^{-6}$$

In 1.0 litre of water, containing 55.5 moles of water and a very small amount of oxygen, this equation becomes:

$$\frac{n(O_2)}{n(O_2) + 55.5} = 4.8 \times 10^{-6}$$

Since the mole fraction is very small, the amount of oxygen dissolved is $55.5 \times 4.8 \times 10^{-6}$ = 2.6×10^{-4} moles, to a very good approximation. The molar concentration of O_2 in water is therefore 2.6×10^{-4} mol/L.

8-9 Dilute solutions of non-volatile solutes: colligative properties

In this section we consider the special case of dilute solutions of non-volatile solutes. Such solutions are similar in their physical properties to the pure solvent, but there are small differences between the properties of the solution and those of the pure solvent. There are four important and useful properties of solutions which depend only on the amount (in moles) of solute dissolved, but not the chemical nature of the solute. These four so-called **colligative properties** are the lowering of the vapour pressure, the elevation of the boiling point, the lowering of the melting point, and the osmotic pressure. In this section we discuss each of them in turn.

All four colligative properties can be used to determine the molar mass of a solute in solution.

(i) The lowering of the vapour pressure

A non-volatile solute has a very low vapour pressure, and so for practical purposes the vapour above the solution is composed entirely of the solvent. The vapour pressure of the solution is therefore equal to the vapour pressure of the solvent in the solution.

In dilute solutions, the vapour pressure of the solvent obeys Raoult's law, even if the solution does not meet the requirements of an ideal solution as defined in section 8-2. In a dilute solution, most of the solvent molecules are surrounded completely by other solvent molecules, and the partial pressure of the solvent is reduced in proportion to its mole fraction in the liquid, just as in an ideal solution.

Since the solvent (which we designate as compound A) obeys Raoult's law, the vapour pressure of the solution $P^*(solution)$ is:

$$P^*(solution) = p(A) = x(A)P^*(A)$$

Since the mole fraction of solvent x_A is less than one, the vapour pressure of the solution $P^*(solution)$ is less than the vapour pressure of the pure solvent $P^*(A)$. The **vapour pressure lowering** is the difference between the vapour pressures of the pure solvent and the solution:

$$\Delta P^* = P^*(A) - P^*(solution) = P^*(A)\{1 - x(A)\}$$

From the definition of mole fraction, $x(A) + x(solutes) = 1$, where $x(solutes)$ is the total mole fraction of all solutes. This equation can be rearranged to give $1-x(A) = x(solutes)$ and hence the vapour pressure lowering is:

$$\Delta P^* = P^*(A)x(solutes) \tag{8-5}$$

Example 8-5 Calculate the vapour pressure lowering of a solution containing 10.0 g of sucrose $C_{12}H_{22}O_{11}$ in 100.0 g of water at 25. °C. The vapour pressure of water is 3.17 kPa at this temperature.

The molar mass of sucrose $C_{12}H_{22}O_{11}$ is 342.30 g mol^{-1}, so the amounts of sucrose and water in the solution are:

$$n(\text{sucrose}) = \frac{10.0\,g}{342.30\,g/mol} = 0.02921\,mol$$

$$n(\text{water}) = \frac{100.0\,g}{18.015\,g/mol} = 5.551\,mol$$

The mole fraction of sucrose in the solution is:

$$x = \frac{0.02921\,mol}{(0.02921 + 5.551)\,mol} = 5.23 \times 10^{-3}$$

Hence the vapour pressure lowering is: $\quad \Delta P^* = 5.23 \times 10^{-3} \times 3.17\,kPa = 16.6\,Pa$

In this section, the mole fraction of the solutes, *x(solutes)* is the total mole fraction of all solutes present. If a solute is an electrolyte such as sodium chloride, which dissociates into several ions, the anions and cations act independently to reduce the vapour pressure. In calculating *x(solutes)* the number of moles of solutes present is larger than the number of moles of the undissociated electrolyte by a factor equal to the number of ions produced. This is demonstrated by the following example, which is based on actual measurements of vapour pressures.

Example 8-6 The measured vapour pressure of a solution of 0.50 mol potassium chloride KCl dissolved in 1.000 kg water is lowered by 1.63 kPa at a temperature of 100. °C relative to pure water, which has a vapour pressure of 101.325 kPa at this temperature. Calculate *x(solutes)* and compare with *x(KCl)*.

From equation (8-5), $x(\text{solutes}) = \dfrac{\Delta P^*}{P^*(\text{water})} = \dfrac{1.63\,kPa}{101.325\,kPa} = 1.61 \times 10^{-2}$

A mass of 1.000 kg of water contains (1000./18.015) = 55.51 mol of water. Hence the mole fraction of KCl in the solution is $x_{KCl} = 0.50/(0.50+55.51) = 8.9 \times 10^{-3}$. Hence the total mole fraction of solutes is larger than the mole fraction of KCl by the ratio $1.61 \times 10^{-2}/8.9 \times 10^{-3} = 1.8$.

This value is close to the value of 2.0 expected if the potassium ions K^+ and chloride ions Cl^- acted as separate solutes. The discrepancy between 1.8 and 2.0 indicates that the ions do not act completely independently.

(ii) The elevation of the boiling point

As a result of the lowering of vapour pressure by non-volatile solutes, the boiling point of the solution is higher than that of the pure solvent. This is because a higher temperature is needed to bring the reduced vapour pressure of the solution up to atmospheric pressure. The difference between the boiling point of the solution and that of the pure solvent is called the **boiling point elevation** ΔT_b:

$$\Delta T_b = T_b(\text{solution}) - T_b(\text{solvent})$$

The relationship between the boiling point elevation and composition of the solution is usually expressed in terms of molality m rather than mole fraction. For a dilute solution, the boiling point elevation is proportional to the total molality of all the solutes in the solution, $m(solutes)$:

$$\Delta T_b = K_b m(solutes) \qquad (8\text{-}6)$$

where K_b is a constant called the molal boiling point constant, and has a characteristic value for each solvent.

(iii) The depression of the freezing point

The freezing point of a solution is, in most cases, lower than that of the pure solvent. This can be seen from phase diagrams such as Figures 8-8 and 8-9, in which the left-hand end of each graph shows the freezing point of the solution as a function of mole fraction. For dilute solutions (i.e. for small mole fraction of solute) the curve is only slightly curved, so the freezing point is reduced by an amount proportional to the mole fraction of the solute.

The difference between the freezing point of the pure solvent and that of the solution is called the **freezing point depression** ΔT_f:

$$\Delta T_f = T_f(solvent) - T_f(solution)$$

The relationship between the freezing point depression and composition of the solution is usually expressed in terms of molality m rather than mole fraction. For a dilute solution, the freezing point depression is proportional to the total molality of all the solutes in the solution, $m(solutes)$:

$$\Delta T_f = K_f m(solutes) \qquad (8\text{-}7)$$

where K_f is a constant called the molal freezing point constant, and has a characteristic value for each solvent.

Table 8-5 Molal boiling point and freezing point constants for various solvents

Solvent	T_b / °C	K_b / °C mol^{-1} kg	T_f / °C	K_f / °C mol^{-1} kg
H_2O water	100.0	0.512	0.0	1.86
C_6H_6 benzene	80.1	2.53	5.5	4.90
CCl_4 carbon tetrachloride	76.7	5.03	−23.	30.

Reprinted with permission from CRC Handbook of Chemistry and Physics, 77th edition. Copyright CRC Press, Boca Raton, Florida, U.S.A.

Example 8-7 A solution contains 0.025 moles of naphthalene in 85.0 g of benzene. At 25°C benzene has a vapour pressure of 12.7 kPa; naphthalene has a vapour pressure of 0.011 kPa and so can be treated as non-volatile for the present purpose. Calculate the vapour pressure lowering, the boiling point elevation, and the freezing point depression of the solution.

First we calculate the mole fraction of naphthalene in the solution. The molar mass of benzene is 78.113 g mol^{-1}, so the amount of benzene is 85.0g / 78.113 g mol^{-1} = 1.088 mol. Hence the mole fraction is:

$$x(naph) = \frac{0.025}{1.088 + 0.025} = 0.022$$

Hence the vapour pressure lowering is $\Delta P^* = 0.022 \times 12.7 = 0.28 \text{ kPa}$.

The molality of napthalene is $m(naph) = \dfrac{0.025 \text{ mol naphthalene}}{0.0850 \text{ kg benzene}} = 0.294 \text{ mol kg}^{-1}$

The boiling point elevation can be calculated using the molal boiling point elevation constant for benzene from Table 8-5:

$$\Delta T_b = 2.53 \text{ °C mol}^{-1} \text{ kg} \times 0.294 \text{ mol kg}^{-1} = 0.74 \text{ °C} .$$

The freezing point depression can be calculated using the molal freezing point lowering constant for benzene from Table 8-5:

$$\Delta T_f = 4.90 \text{ °C mol}^{-1} \text{ kg} \times 0.294 \text{ mol kg}^{-1} = 1.44\text{°C} .$$

Example 8-8 A solution contains 7.25 g of an unknown non-volatile solute dissolved in 100.0 g of benzene. The boiling point is found to be 0.76°C higher than the boiling point of pure benzene. What is the molar mass of the unknown solute?

The boiling point elevation constant for benzene is 2.53 °C mol^{-1} kg, and the boiling point elevation is 0.76°C, so the molality of the solution is:

$$m = \frac{\Delta T_b}{K_b} = \frac{0.76^o\text{C}}{2.53^o\text{C mol}^{-1} \text{ kg}} = 0.30 \text{ mol kg}^{-1}$$

Mass of solvent is 0.1000 kg, so amount of solute present in solution is 0.1000 kg × 0.30 mol kg^{-1} = 0.030 mol. Hence molar mass is 7.25 g / 0.030 mol = 242 g/mol.

(iv) Osmotic pressure

Certain membranes allow solvent molecules to pass through them, but not solute molecules and ions. For example, the walls of cells in living organisms allow water to pass but not large biological molecules or ionic solutes. Such membranes are called **semi-permeable.**

A semi-permeable membrane is selective in allowing passage to some molecules but not others. The mechanism for this selectivity is not known in all cases. Some membranes contain holes that are so small that polymer molecules cannot fit through, but yet are large enough to allow solvent molecules to pass through. In some cases, solute ions are prevented from passing through the holes in the membrane by surface effects.

Regardless of the mechanism that distinguishes between the solvent and solute, what is important is that membrane permits only the solvent, and not the solute, to pass through. When solution and pure solvent are placed in contact with each other through a semi-permeable membrane, solvent molecules are found to pass through the membrane into the solution. The direction of flow is such as to dilute the solution. This process is called **osmosis**.

The flow can be reduced and even reversed by applying pressure to the solution but not to the pure solvent. The pressure required to reduce the osmotic flow to zero is called the **osmotic pressure** and is designated by the Greek letter π. An apparatus for measuring osmotic pressure is shown in Figure 8-10.

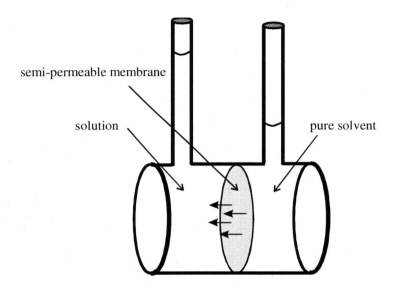

semi-permeable membrane

solution

pure solvent

Figure 8-10 Apparatus for measuring osmotic pressure. The solution is separated from pure solvent by a semi-permeable membrane that allows the solvent to pass through but not the solute. Solvent passes into the solution, as shown by the full-headed arrows. The pressure on the solution side of the membrane builds up until it is sufficient to stop further flow of solvent; the pressure required to stop the flow is called the osmotic pressure of the solution.

The osmotic pressure of a solution is proportional to the concentration of solutes, and can be calculated from an equation that has the same form as the ideal gas equation:

$$\pi V = n_{solutes} RT \tag{8-8}$$

where V is the volume of the solution containing $n_{solutes}$ moles of solutes at temperature T and R is the gas constant.

The similarity of the osmotic pressure equation to the ideal gas equation suggests that motion of the solute molecules causes the osmotic pressure directly, but this is not the case. Rather, it is the flow of solvent molecules into the solution that causes the pressure difference. The theory of osmotic pressure is therefore quite different from the kinetic theory of gas pressure discussed in section 5-9.

Osmotic pressure is important in controlling the transfer of water through biological membranes such as cell walls. Measurements of osmotic pressure of polymer solutions are commonly used for determining average molar mass for polymers.

Example 8-9 Calculate the osmotic pressure of a 0.10 M solution of sucrose in water at 20℃.

A volume of 1.00 L $=1.00\times10^{-3}$ m³ of solution contains n = 0.10 mol of solute, and so:

$$\pi = \frac{0.10\,\text{mol}\times8.314\,\text{J K}^{-1}\,\text{mol}^{-1}\times293\,\text{K}}{1.0\times10^{-3}\,\text{m}^3} = 2.44\times10^5\,\text{Pa} = 244\,\text{kPa}$$

This pressure is several times higher than atmospheric pressure.

Example 8-10 1.50 g of a polymer is dissolved in enough water to make 85.0 mL of solution. The osmotic pressure is 375 Pa. Calculate the average molar mass of the polymer.

The osmotic pressure is 375 Pa and the volume is 85.0×10^{-6} m³. From the equation for osmotic pressure, the number of moles of solute is:

$$n = \frac{375\,\text{Pa}\times85.0\times10^{-6}\,\text{m}^3}{8.314\,\text{J K}^{-1}\,\text{mol}^{-1}\times298\,\text{K}} = 1.29\times10^{-5}\,\text{mol}$$

Hence the molar mass of the polymer is:

$$M = \frac{1.50\,\text{g}}{1.29\times10^{-5}\,\text{mol}} = 1.16\times10^5\,\text{g mol}^{-1}$$

Key concepts

The vapour in equilibrium with a solution formed by mixing volatile liquids is a mixture of the vapours of the individual components. For an ideal solution containing two chemically similar liquids, Raoult's law states that the partial pressure of each substance in the vapour is proportional to the mole fraction of that substance in the liquid. The relationship between the vapour pressure of the solution and its composition can be expressed using a pressure-composition diagram. The relationship between the boiling point of the solution and its composition can be expressed using a temperature-composition diagram.

Distillation is a process of evaporation and condensation, which can be used to separate volatile liquids. Solutions that can be separated by distillation are called zeotropic solutions. For many solutions, the boiling point is a maximum or a minimum at a particular composition; solutions with that particular composition cannot be separated by distillation and are called azeotropic.

When a solution is frozen, the freezing point of the solution is (nearly always) lower than that of the pure liquid. A solution freezes over a range of temperatures, instead of freezing sharply at a particular temperature. The eutectic temperature is the lowest temperature at which the solution remains a liquid. A mixture of crystals of different substances melts over a range of temperatures.

The solubility of a solid in a liquid is the concentration of the saturated solution. Solubility varies with temperature. The solubility of a gas in a liquid is proportional to the partial pressure of the gas.

For solutions of non-volatile solutes, the vapour pressure is lower, the boiling point is higher, and the freezing point is lower, than for the pure solvent. When a solution is separated from the pure solvent by a semi-permeable membrane through which the solvent but not the solutes can pass, a pressure difference called the osmotic pressure develops across the membrane. These effects are proportional to the total amount of solutes dissolved.

Review Questions

1. Define partial pressure in a mixture of gases.

2. State Raoult's law.

3. State Henry's law.

4. If two liquid compounds form ideal solutions when mixed, which compound has the higher mole fraction ion the vapour phase?

5. In a vapour pressure diagram (i.e. a graph of vapour pressure versus the compositions of both vapour and liquid phases), which line lies higher, the vapour line or the liquid line?

6. In a boiling point diagram (i.e. a graph of boiling point versus the compositions of both vapour and liquid phases), which line lies higher, the vapour line or the liquid line?

7. Make a sketch of the boiling point diagram for a pair of liquids that form a minimum boiling azeotrope.

8. Make a sketch of the boiling point diagram for a pair of liquids that form a maximum boiling azeotrope.

9. Define a eutectic point.

10. Define the molal boiling point elevation constant and molal freezing point depression constant.

11. Define osmotic pressure.

Problems

1. At a temperature of 75°C, the vapour pressure of water is 38.6 kPa and that of methanol is 151 kPa. Sketch the pressure-composition diagram approximately to scale for mixtures of methanol and water, assuming that they form ideal solutions.

2. The boiling point of n-pentane is 36.1°C, and that of n-hexane is 68.6°C. Sketch the temperature-composition diagram approximately to scale for mixtures of n-pentane and n-hexane, assuming that they form ideal solutions.

3. Use the graphs shown in Figure 8-1 to estimate the mole fraction of hexane in the vapour in equilibrium with a liquid mixture of hexane and heptane in which the temperature is 30°C and the mole fraction of hexane is 0.20.   [0.42]

4. Use Raoult's law to calculate the partial pressures of hexane and heptane and the mole fraction of hexane in the vapour phase, in equilibrium with a liquid mixture in which the mole fraction of hexane is 0.20. Compare your result with your answer for Problem 8-3. At 30°C, the vapour pressures are 24.9 kPa for hexane and 7.75 kPa for heptane.

[5.0 kPa, 6.2 kPa, 0.45]

5. A liquid mixture of hexane and hexane boils at a temperature of 85°C. Use the graphs in Figure 8-4 to estimate the mole fraction of hexane in the liquid and vapour phases respectively. [0.38, 0.60]

6. A liquid mixture of hexane and heptane is distilled in a fractional distillation apparatus that can achieve three stages of successive distillation. If the mole fraction of hexane in the liquid is initially 0.20, what is the composition and boiling point of the distillate? Use the boiling point diagram shown in Figure 8-6 for your estimates [0.81, 73°C]

7. A liquid mixture of benzene and ethanol is distilled in a fractional distillation apparatus that can achieve two stages of successive distillation. The temperature-composition diagram is shown in Figure 8-7. If the mole fraction of ethanol in the liquid is initially 0.10, what is the composition and boiling point of the distillate? [0.42, 68°C]

8. An aqueous solution of acetic acid in which the mole fraction of acid is 0.20 is cooled. At what temperature does the first solid crystallize from solution, and what is the composition of that solid? The temperature-composition diagram is shown in Figure 8-8. [–18°C, ice]

9. A student wishes to separate pure acetic acid from aqueous solution by cooling the solution. What is the minimum mole fraction of acetic acid required for this separation to be possible? The temperature-composition diagram is shown in Figure 8-8. [0.3]

10. An aqueous solution of hydrochloric acid, with mole fraction 0.05, is boiled gently in a beaker. It is observed that the temperature gradually increases as the boiling continues, and eventually approaches 108°C. Explain this observation using information from Table 8-3, and estimate the composition of the solution at a late stage in the boiling.

11. What is the solubility of potassium chloride in water at 25°C, expressed as a mole fraction? The temperature-composition diagram is shown in Figure 8-9. [0.08]

12. An aqueous solution containing a mole fraction of 0.060 of potassium chloride is cooled. At what temperature does the first solid appear and what is its composition? If cooling is continued, what is the lowest temperature at which some liquid is present, and what is the composition of that liquid? ? The temperature-composition diagram is shown in Figure 8-9.

    [–5°C, KCl, –10.7°C, x(KCl) = 0.055]

13. Chlorobenzene, C_6H_5Cl, and bromobenzene, C_6H_5Br, form ideal solutions. At 137°C, chlorobenzene has a vapour pressure of 115.1 kPa and bromobenzene has a vapour pressure of 60.4 kPa. Calculate the composition of a solution that has a vapour pressure of 100.0 kPa at this temperature, and the composition of the vapour in equilibrium with the liquid, expressed as mole fraction of chlorobenzene. [0.724, 0.833]

14. Calculate the mole fraction and molar concentration of oxygen from the atmosphere in water at 35°C using Henry's law. The partial pressure of oxygen in the atmosphere is 21 kPa. [4.1×10^{-6}, 2.3×10^{-4} M]

15. Gaseous hydrogen sulfide, H_2S, is bubbled through water at atmospheric pressure (about 100 kPa) at a temperature of 15°C. What is the mole fraction and the molarity of H_2S in the solution? [2.3×10^{-3}, 0.13 M]

16. Methane from a leak in a natural gas pipeline bubbles through water at atmospheric pressure (about 100 kPa) at a temperature of 15°C. What is the mole fraction and the molarity of methane dissolved in the water? [3.1×10^{-5}, 1.7×10^{-3} M]

17. What is the ratio of mole fractions of nitrogen and oxygen in air? What is the ratio of mole fractions of oxygen and nitrogen dissolved in water saturated with air at 25°C? [3.728, 1.92]

18. From the data in Table 8-3, sketch a boiling point-composition diagram for solutions of formic acid in water. Show some tie lines between phases that are in equilibrium, and identify those regions of the diagram which are inaccessible. What would be the composition of the final distillate produced by fractional distillation of an aqueous solution of formic acid in which the mole fraction of the acid is 0.2?

19. A solution is prepared containing 2.50 g of anthracene $C_{14}H_{10}$ in 80.0 g of benzene C_6H_6 at a temperature of 25.0°C. The vapour pressure of anthracene is very low compared with that of benzene. Estimate the vapour pressure lowering, relative to the vapour pressure of pure benzene at this temperature, which is 12.7 kPa.   [171 Pa]

20. Calculate the freezing point (in degrees Celsius) of a 0.35 mol kg^{-1} aqueous solution of potassium chloride. Recall that potassium chloride is an electrolyte.   [–0.36°C]

21. A solution is prepared containing 2.50 g of anthracene $C_{14}H_{10}$ in 80.0 g of benzene C_6H_6. Calculate the boiling point elevation and the boiling point of this this solution. You may refer to Table 7-1 to find the boiling point of benzene.   [0.44 K, 353.5 K]

22. 3.255 g of an organic substance of unknown molar mass is dissolved in 120. g of benzene. The boiling point of the solution is 0.25°C higher than that of pure benzene. What is the molar mass of the solute? Assume that the solute does not dissociate into ions.   [274 g/mol]

23. A solution of polystyrene in benzene has a mass concentration of 8.0 g/L. The solution is found to have an osmotic pressure of 890 Pa at 25. °C. Calculate the average molar mass of the polystyrene.   [22×10^3 g mol^{-1}]

24. Calculate the osmotic pressure of a 0.10 M aqueous solution of sodium chloride at a temperature of 37°C. Recall that sodium chloride is an electrolyte.   [520 kPa]

9 Fuels and Explosives

Objectives

After reading this chapter, the student should be able to do the following:

♦ List and describe commercial fuels.

♦ Relate the properties of commercial fuels to thermochemistry and the gas laws.

♦ Discuss environmental problems related to the energy industry.

♦ List and describe commercial explosives.

Related topics to review:

Properties of gases in Chapter 5. Thermochemistry in Chapter 6.

Related topics to look forward to:

Chemical kinetics in Chapter 18.

9-1 Primary and secondary sources of energy

The provision and the distribution of energy are essential services in an industrial economy. Productivity in a factory or on a farm is so increased by the application of energy that it is impossible to compete in the market place without using machinery that uses energy. Increased energy usage has been the key factor in the great industrial expansion of the nineteenth and twentieth centuries.

To obtain energy in a form that can be distributed economically and used conveniently, energy from a primary energy source in nature must be converted or processed into a secondary source which can be used by the consumer. The most important primary sources are petroleum, natural gas, coal, uranium and falling water, and of these the first three, the fossil fuels, produce energy when they are burned. Energy obtained from nuclear fission of uranium is a significant though controversial primary source, and in specific places or applications solar, geothermal, wind and tidal power sources have been developed.

The main secondary sources of energy are electricity and commercial hydrocarbon fuels. The bulk of electric power is produced in generators coupled to turbines driven either by hot gases produced directly by combustion, by steam generated by combustion of fossil fuels or nuclear reactors, or by falling water. The main commercial fuels derived from petroleum are gasoline, diesel fuel, fuel oil and natural gas. Galvanic cells, better known as batteries, are a useful secondary source of energy.

9-2 Heat of combustion of fuels

The combustion of fuels provides the largest fraction of the primary energy used in most industrialized countries, and hydroelectric, nuclear, solar and wind sources provide most of the remainder. The chemistry of fuels is therefore a matter of general interest, which for the most part can be easily understood using the principles discussed in the previous chapters.

Coal, petroleum and natural gas all contain carbon and hydrogen as the major elements present, and the main products of combustion are carbon dioxide and water. The **enthalpy change of**

combustion or **heat of combustion** of a fuel, $\Delta H°_{comb}$, is the enthalpy change for complete combustion of the fuel in oxygen, with liquid water and carbon dioxide as the products. The heat of combustion is usually tabulated at 25°C under standard conditions. The heat of combustion is measured in a bomb calorimeter, as discussed in Chapter 6. Some values for pure substances occurring in fuels are given in Table 9-1, and are a reliable indication of the energy that can be obtained in an actual furnace from a given fuel. In the table, water is assumed to be in the liquid form, and if (as is usual) water leaves a furnace in the form of vapour, an adjustment for the latent heat of vaporisation must be included in calculations.

The table shows that, although the molar heat of combustion of saturated hydrocarbons C_nH_{2n+2} varies from one compound to another, the heat of combustion per unit mass is about –48 kJ/g for all the compounds in this class. This fact is useful in understanding the properties of commercial fuels and will be discussed further in a later chapter dealing with the properties of chemical bonds.

Commercial fuels are typically mixtures of many compounds. Their heats of combustion and volatility depend on their composition and so the heat of combustion is best quoted per unit mass rather than per mole.

Table 9-1 Standard heat of combustion and boiling point of pure fuels at 25°C and 100 kPa.

Water produced in combustion is assumed to be a liquid.

Substance	State	Heat of combustion		Boiling point
		kJ mol^{-1}	kJ g^{-1}	°C
C carbon	s	–393.5	–32.7	–
H$_2$ hydrogen	g	–285.8	–141.8	–253
CH$_4$ methane	g	–890.3	–55.5	–161
C$_3$H$_8$ propane	g	–2220.0	–50.3	–42
C$_8$H$_{18}$ octane	ℓ	–5470.7	–47.9	+125
C$_2$H$_2$ acetylene	g	–1229.6	–49.9	–84
CH$_3$OH methanol	ℓ	–726.6	–22.6	65
C$_2$H$_5$OH ethanol	ℓ	–1366.9	–29.7	79

9-3 Commercial fuels

(a) Solid fuels

World consumption of coal is of the order of 1000 million tonnes per year and accounts for about a quarter of the total energy consumed; total annual Canadian production is 75 million tonnes per year. Coal is classified into four **ranks** on the basis of the moisture content, the content of volatile organic compounds, and the content of carbon. The four ranks in order of decreasing "quality" are anthracite, bituminous coal, sub-bituminous coal and lignite. The commercial value of coal is affected by its sulfur content, since sulfur dioxide released to the environment from burning coal causes "acid rain" and is a serious pollution problem. Although coal is a good fuel for furnaces, it cannot be used to run internal combustion engines, and so processes have been developed for production of liquid fuels from coal in times of military crisis when petroleum supplies are inadequate or inaccessible.

Table 9-2 Heat of combustion and Canadian production of various types of coal

Type of coal	Heat of combustion $kJ\ g^{-1}$	Annual Canadian production* 10^6 tonnes/year
Anthracite	−30	–
Bituminous	−29	38.6
Sub-bituminous	−19	25.6
Lignite	−15	10.7

*1995. Statistics Canada, Coal and Coke Statistics, Catalogue No. 45-002-XPB, December 1995, page 6.

Although its major use is as a fuel, coal is also used to manufacture a variety of chemical products. When heated in the absence of air, coal decomposes to yield **coal gas**, **coal tar** and **coke**. Coal gas is a fuel containing methane, carbon monoxide (which makes it poisonous) and hydrogen, but has now been replaced by natural gas as a domestic fuel in most places. Coke is a solid and is used as a fuel in blast furnaces for smelting iron ore. Coal tar is a complex mixture from which compounds such as benzene, toluene, naphthalene and anthracene (named for the coal from which it is derived) can be recovered. The structures of these **aromatic** compounds, which contain one or more ring of carbon atoms as part of their structure, are shown below.

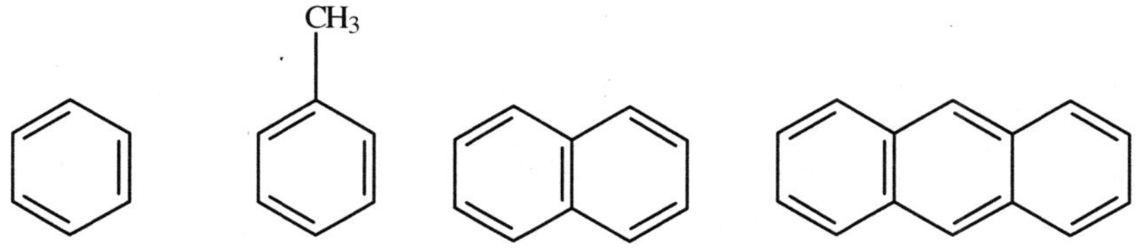

benzene   toluene   naphthalene   anthracene

In the convention used in these drawings, the ring carbon atoms located at the vertices of the hexagons are not explicitly indicated, and it is understood that a hydrogen atom is bonded to each ring carbon atom unless another atom is explicitly indicated.

Coal is formed from vegetation that has been compressed and altered over long periods of time. As the coal ages over thousands of years, the trend is toward elimination of hydrogen and water, giving molecules with many benzene rings joined together as in anthracene. Progressively, from the young lignite to the old anthracites, compounds of increasing molar mass are formed, with more and more rings fused together.

The global reserves of coal are enormous, at least an order of magnitude greater than the known reserves of crude oil. All of the major industrial countries except Japan have large domestic supplies, and coal is certain to remain an important fuel source despite environmental problems.

(b) Liquid fuels

Liquid fuels are predominantly mixtures of hydrocarbons of formula C_nH_{2n+2}, with n between 5 and 20. Hydrocarbon fuels are produced by refining crude petroleum pumped out of the ground and have become essential commodities in an economy dependent on cars and trucks driven by internal combustion engines. Propane (n=3) and butane (n=4) are gases at normal temperature and pressure but can be condensed easily by compression. Described as liquefied petroleum gases, or L.P.G., they can be stored in small tanks as liquids under pressure, and when released they evaporate and burn efficiently as gases. The refining of petroleum into commercial fuels is an immense industry, one of the cornerstones of the modern economy. In 1995 the total volume of refined petroleum products sold in Canada was 84 million cubic metres, or 84 trillion litres.

Crude petroleum varies in composition depending on the geographical source. However the composition of each type of industrial fuel is fairly narrowly defined by standards and regulations, so the heat of combustion of refined petroleum products such as gasoline and fuel oil does not vary much. Table 9-3 lists the saturated hydrocarbons found in common fuels and typical figures for the heat of combustion per gram. The data show that variations in composition of hydrocarbon fuels do not affect the heat of combustion per gram appreciably.

Table 9-3 Heat of combustion and Canadian sales of liquid fuels

| Fuel | Heat of combustion | | Annual Canadian sales* |
	kJ g^{-1}	kJ/mL	10^6 m^3/year
Heavy fuel oil	–45	–42	6.6
Light fuel oil C_{12}–C_{20}	–47	–42	5.4
Diesel fuel C_{12}–C_{20}	–47	–39	19.2
Gasoline C_4–C_{12}	–48	–35	35.0
L.P.G. C_3–C_4	–50	–27	2.2

* 1995. Statistics Canada, Refined Petroleum Products, Catalogue No. 45-004-XPB, December 1995, page 78.

A key step in the refining process consists of partially separating the different chemical constituents of petroleum by distillation. The mixture of light hydrocarbons that is obtained by distillation is called **straight run gasoline** and consists mainly of straight chain hydrocarbons. Gasoline containing only straight chain hydrocarbons is found to produce explosive burning called **knocking** in high-compression engines, which can be avoided by addition of branched hydrocarbons. Addition of the compound tetramethyl lead, $Pb(CH_3)_4$, to prevent knocking has been discontinued because of the danger of lead poisoning, and essentially all gasoline sold in North America now is unleaded.

The tendency of a gasoline to cause knocking is measured by its **octane number**: the higher the octane number the lower the tendency towards knocking. The name arises from the observation some decades ago that a particular branched eight-carbon compound, 2,2,4-trimethylpentane (also called iso-octane), was the best fuel then known for avoiding knocking. The octane number for a gasoline is measured by its performance compared with that of a mixture of 2,2,4-trimethylpentane with heptane. Structures for these compounds are shown below.

$$CH_3-CH_2-CH_2-CH_2-CH_2-CH_2-CH_3$$

heptane

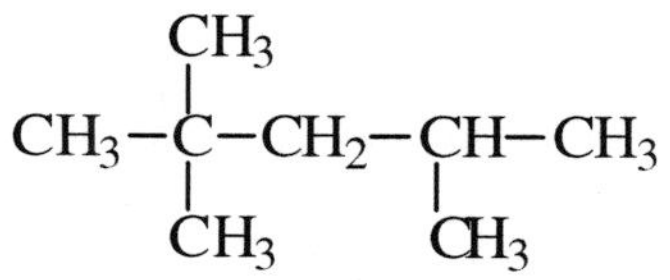

$$CH_3-\underset{\underset{CH_3}{|}}{\overset{\overset{CH_3}{|}}{C}}-CH_2-\underset{\underset{CH_3}{|}}{CH}-CH_3$$

2,2,4-trimethylpentane
(isooctane)

For instance 90 octane gasoline is equivalent in its performance to a mixture of 90% isooctane and 10% heptane. High octane gasoline must contain a large proportion of various branched hydrocarbons in addition to isooctane. Thus a second important part of the refining process is the **catalytic cracking** or **reforming** in which the high molar mass hydrocarbons decompose into smaller branched molecules when heated over appropriate catalysts. Typically hydrocarbons in the C_{11} to C_{16} range are split into a mixture of alkenes and alkanes in the C_3 to C_5 range, which then combine to form branched alkanes in the C_7 to C_{10} range. The alkenes produced in the cracking reactions contribute further to smooth combustion.

Ethanol, C_2H_5OH, and methanol, CH_3OH, are of interest as fuels where liquid hydrocarbons are in short supply. They have been mixed with gasoline to produce "gasohol" to decrease dependence on imported oil. Alcohols can be produced readily from vegetation and hence are a renewable energy source but their heats of combustion are considerably lower than those of the hydrocarbons (see Table 9-1).

(c) Gas fuels

Throughout Europe and North America, natural gas from gas or oil wells is an important fuel. It is mainly methane, but typically includes some ethane, propane and butane. Canada is a major producer of natural gas by world standards and exports about half of its total production to the United States.

Natural gas is familiar as a fuel for domestic heating furnaces and hot water systems. It is a preferred fuel for boilers in large electric generating stations since it produces less carbon dioxide per unit energy than liquid hydrocarbon fuels or coal. For such purposes, natural gas is supplied by fixed pipeline. For special applications, vehicles running on natural gas have been developed, and have environmental advantages when used in urban areas, so further developments can be expected.

Table 9-4 Heat of combustion and Canadian production of natural gas.

The volume of natural gas is quoted at a temperature of 15°C and a pressure of 101.325 kPa.

Fuel	Heat of combustion		Canadian production*
	kJ g^{-1}	MJ m^{-3}	m^3/year
Natural gas	–55	–37	138×10^9

* 1995. Statistics Canada, Gas Utilities, Catalogue No. 55-002-XPB, December 1995, page 7.

Natural gas is prepared for market in three stages. First, "sour" natural gas is contaminated with hydrogen sulfide, H_2S, which is foul-smelling and poisonous and must be removed before the gas is used. Hydrogen sulfide is a weak acid, and is removed by passing the gas through a solution of a base such as ethanolamine:

$$HOCH_2CH_2NH_2(aq) + H_2S(g) \rightarrow HOCH_2CH_2NH_3^+(aq) + HS^-(aq)$$

This reaction can be reversed subsequently by heating the solution. The H_2S gas driven off by heating is then oxidized to SO_2 for conversion to sulfuric acid as described in Section 4-2, or to elemental sulfur by the following reaction:

$$2\, H_2S(g) + SO_2(g) \rightarrow 3\, S(s) + 2\, H_2O(\ell)$$

Secondly, butane and propane are removed by condensation for sale separately as L.P.G. Thirdly, ethane is separated from the methane by distillation to provide a feedstock for the petrochemical industry, as described in Section 4-7.

For some time the use of hydrogen as a fuel gas has been proposed as an important secondary source of energy in the future, partly because combustion of hydrogen yields only water as the main product. In considering these arguments, it should be kept in mind that there are no primary sources of hydrogen to be found in nature, and when used as a fuel it can only serve, like electricity, to distribute or store energy that has been derived from some other primary source. However, for specialized applications such as the main rocket boosters on the space shuttle, the reaction between hydrogen and oxygen is a good way to release a lot of energy quickly. Fuel cells running on hydrogen are being tested as a power source for vehicles at the present time, and are discussed further in Chapter 17.

9-4 Environmental problems associated with fuels

All major industrial activity causes environmental problems, and the problems associated with the production and consumption of fossil fuels for energy generation are some of the most difficult to deal with. Other primary sources of energy also cause problems. Hydroelectric generators use no fuel but require large dams, which flood river valleys permanently. Nuclear-powered generators use only small amounts of fuel, but the spent fuel is highly radioactive and the political and engineering problems of long term disposal have not been resolved. Wind powered generators are noisy and unsightly, and cannot provide enough electric power. None of these "environmentally friendly" energy sources is able to power trucks and cars. Fossil fuels will therefore continue to be used in enormous amounts for the foreseeable future, and the associated environmental problems cannot be approached effectively without some chemical knowledge. The chemically related environmental problems caused by fuel usage can be classified under the following headings: acid rain, nitrogen oxides, and global warming.

Acid rain is caused largely by sulfur dioxide produced by the combustion of fuels containing sulfur, and by smelters used to process sulfide ores of nickel and other metals. The sulfur content of coal is typically 0.3 to 3.0% by mass, and sometimes much more. When the coal is burned, this sulfur is oxidized to SO_2, which passes into the atmosphere with the other "stack gases". The SO_2 is oxidized in the atmosphere to SO_3 and combines with water in the atmosphere to form sulfuric acid. This acid is returned to the earth's surface as acid rain.

Acid rain damages forests and fish populations in freshwater lakes. It causes rapid deterioration of buildings and sculpture made of marble or limestone as the surface layer of calcium carbonate is converted to calcium sulfate through following reaction:

$$CaCO_3(s) + H_2SO_4(aq) + H_2O \rightarrow CaSO_4.2H_2O(s) + CO_2(g)$$

Although hydrated calcium sulfate is shown as a solid in the equation above, it is slightly soluble and affected surfaces wash away slowly. Many European antiquities that have survived from medieval or even from Greek and Roman times have deteriorated rapidly in the twentieth century.

The removal of sulfur from oil and coal is possible but adds to their cost. Another approach is to remove the SO_2 from the stack gases. Indeed SO_2 recovered from stack gases from smelters can be used for the manufacture of sulfuric acid and this is done at nickel smelters in Ontario and the zinc smelter at Trail in British Columbia. In gases from coal-fired furnaces, however, SO_2 is only a small fraction of the total gas produced and is therefore more difficult and expensive to remove.

Nitrogen forms several oxides, most notably nitric oxide NO and nitrogen dioxide, NO_2, which are known collectively by the general formula NO_x. These oxides are acidic and make a minor contribution to acid rain, but there are other more complex problems caused by oxides of nitrogen. Nitric oxide is formed in the combustion of fuels in air at high temperatures, most importantly in automobile engines and in thermal generating stations. Nitric oxide is oxidized by any of a number of molecules in the atmosphere, one of which is ozone, O_3:

$$NO + O_3 \rightarrow NO_2 + O_2$$

In sunlight, nitrogen dioxide decomposes to produce nitric oxide and a highly reactive oxygen atom:

$$NO_2 + light \rightarrow NO + O$$

Reactions that are induced by light, such as this one, are called **photochemical** reactions. Some of the oxygen atoms produced by the last reaction in turn react with molecular oxygen to form ozone:

$$O + O_2 \rightarrow O_3$$

Other oxygen atoms react with hydrocarbon vapours in the air to form organic peroxides, which cause eye irritation and other health problems. Concentrations of NO_x in the atmosphere are normally low, but concentrations are higher near sources such as heavy car traffic or industrial furnaces. Hydrocarbons are always present in the air in cities due to evaporation of gasoline released by leaks in fuel tank lids, spillage at filling stations and unburned fuel in exhaust gases. The combination of nitrogen oxides NO_x, ozone, gasoline vapours and sunlight lead to formation of so-called **photochemical smog**. The smog begins to form early each day and reaches a peak in the early afternoon. The solution to the problem lies in reducing the emissions of NO_x and fuel vapour to the atmosphere, and reducing usage of cars by car pooling and improving public transport systems. New cars are now fitted with catalytic converters in the exhaust system and spring-loaded flaps in the filling pipe of the fuel tank, in response to regulations introduced in California where photochemical smog is a serious problem.

Long term trends in the average climate of the world suggest that at the present time the average temperature of the surface of the earth is slowly increasing, an effect called **global warming**. Dramatic changes in the environment, such as melting of polar icecaps, may follow as a consequence. Further, it is thought that this increase is caused by the release of carbon dioxide into the atmosphere by combustion of fossil fuels. The evidence for both these statements is somewhat controversial, but research and discussion continue very actively.

Carbon dioxide is a normal and essential component of the atmosphere. Carbon dioxide is produced by animals as they breath, and by vegetation as it decays or burns. It is removed from the atmosphere by photosynthesis processes in plants, which convert CO_2 to carbohydrates such as cellulose, and by the formation of carbonate deposits in the sea. During the past two centuries, combustion of fuels has greatly increased the amount of CO_2 entering the atmosphere while the clearing of forests, particularly of fast growing tropical forests, has reduced the rate at which CO_2 is removed. In pre-industrial times (the 18th century, for instance) the atmosphere contained about 280 ppm by volume of CO_2, according to measurements on air trapped in bubbles in ice; at present (mid-1990's) it contains about 360 ppm and this value is increasing at the rate of 1.6 ppm per year. The increase might seem to be of little consequence, rather good for plant life in fact, were it not for another role which CO_2 plays in the atmosphere.

Light from the sun consists of visible light, ultraviolet light and infrared light; these are differentiated by their wavelength, and are discussed further in the next chapter. Short-wavelength visible and ultraviolet light that is absorbed at the surface of the earth is re-radiated as long-wavelength infrared light. Carbon dioxide in the air absorbs some of this infrared radiation because of its internal vibrational motion, and helps to retain the energy in the atmosphere. The more such absorption occurs, the higher the overall temperature of the earth. Gases whose molecules can act in this way are called **greenhouse gases**, some examples being water, ozone and methane in addition to carbon dioxide. The effect on the world's climate is far from trivial. It is estimated that the average temperature of the surface of the earth would be – 17°C, as compared to the actual value of +15°C, were it not for trapping of radiation by this mechanism. It is further estimated that the average temperature would increase by about 3°C if the CO_2 concentration in the atmosphere doubled from its pre-industrial level. The reader can estimate when this might happen, assuming the present trends continue, from the numbers given in the last paragraph.

Although the build-up of CO_2 is a demonstrated fact, the extent to which this will cause a change in the climate is disputed. Carbon dioxide is not the only greenhouse gas that traps heat. The need to take action is also disputed, partly because computer models of the world climate have not been proven to be reliable, and partly because if action is to be taken, capital expenditures in new non-polluting energy technology will be very expensive. Efforts to reduce the rate of emission of CO_2 have not been effective in stopping the growth of CO_2 levels because nations cannot act individually if they are to remain competitive, and in any case actions by individual companies, or even whole countries, are not likely to be effective. Only a major shift in world opinion will result in effective action, if action is indeed needed. Optimists think that increased levels of CO_2 and other greenhouse gases will not cause any problems and may not be caused by human activity in any case, while pessimists think that it is already too late to avoid serious climatic change.

9-5 Explosives

The main characteristics of an explosive reaction are the sudden release of a large amount of energy, the formation of a large volume of gas, and the initiation of a shock wave. Since the reaction is so fast, it takes place under almost adiabatic conditions and the energy released causes a sudden rise in temperature and expansion of the gases generated in the decomposition reaction, causing the shock wave. Explosions are very destructive, and are used in mining, excavation, and military operations. Apart from nuclear weapons, explosives are unstable chemical substances or mixtures which undergo very rapid exothermic reactions in which a large amount of gas is produced from a small amount of solid. Explosions can be understood in terms of thermochemistry and the properties of gases.

Almost all explosives are compounds of nitrogen, manufactured from nitric acid or nitrate salts. It is for this reason that the Haber process for producing synthetic ammonia and the Ostwald process for producing nitric acid are of strategic importance.

The energy released per gram of explosive is rather small compared with the energy released in the combustion of the same mass of fuel, but the *rate* of energy release in an explosion is very much greater than in combustion. The volume of gas produced per gram of explosive is also very large.

The oldest known explosive is a mixture of sodium nitrate, sulfur and carbon called **black powder** or **gunpowder.** The explosion reaction can be represented by the following equation:

$$2NaNO_3(s) + S(s) + 3C(s) \rightarrow Na_2S(s) + N_2(g) + 3CO_2(g)$$

This reaction is highly exothermic, and produces a large volume of gas entirely from solids.

Ammonium nitrate decomposes explosively when shocked or heated:

$$NH_4NO_3(s) \rightarrow N_2(g) + 2 H_2O(g) + \frac{1}{2} O_2(g)$$

The solid salt decomposes yielding only gaseous products; the water is in the form of a gas because of the high temperature produced in the explosion. Ammonium nitrate is also used as a fertilizer and it is common practice to store large amounts of ammonium nitrate fertilizer and to transport it in bulk. Careless handling has on occasion caused immense explosions in warehouses or ships containing thousands of tonnes of ammonium nitrate. It is easily available in large quantities from fertilizer suppliers. The most famous recent ammonium nitrate explosion was the Oklahoma City bombing in 1995.

Figure 9-1 An explosion of one tonne of pure ammonium nitrate. *(Reproduced with permission from Ph.D. thesis of Dr. A. King, "Shock Characteristics of Ammonium Nitrate". Department of Mining Engineering, Queen's University. 1979)*

One of the products of the explosive decomposition of ammonium nitrate is half a mole of molecular oxygen per mole of salt. This oxygen can be used to oxidize a suitable fuel mixed with the salt, which leads to a great increase in the amount of energy released, and hence the power of the explosion. Aluminum powder has been used for this purpose since the heat of formation of Al_2O_3 is so strongly exothermic. Ammonium nitrate mixed with fuel oil has largely replaced dynamite in the mining industry.

Lead azide, $Pb(N_3)_2$ is a sensitive explosive which decomposes explosively to give nitrogen gas and metallic lead. Metal azides are used as detonators for setting off explosions of other less sensitive explosives, and as a source of gas in "air bags" which fill rapidly to prevent injury in car crashes. If the car decelerates suddenly due to a collision, explosive decomposition of sodium azide is triggered and the airbag fills rapidly with nitrogen, preventing the occupant of the seat from hitting the dashboard or steering wheel.

There are many organic explosives, which typically contain the nitro group, $-NO_2$. Two examples are nitroglycerine and trinitrotoluene, with the following structures.

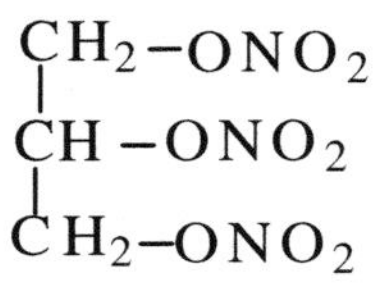

$$CH_2-ONO_2$$
$$CH-ONO_2$$
$$CH_2-ONO_2$$

nitroglycerine

(glyceryl trinitrate)

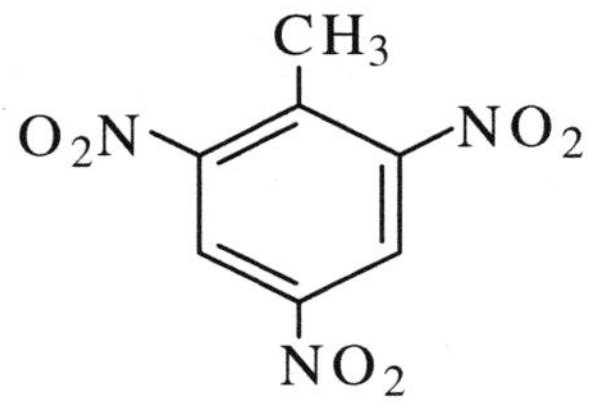

TNT

(2,4,6-trinitrotoluene)

Nitroglycerine is an oily liquid that is uncontrollably explosive unless diluted with some inert material as, for example, when mixed with fine clay to make the industrial explosive dynamite. In this form it is much less sensitive. Dynamite was the first of the modern industrial explosives, and the profits from its invention by Alfred Nobel are used to finance the annual Nobel prizes in science and other fields. 2,4,6-trinitrotoluene, commonly known as TNT, is typical of a class of explosive compounds in which nitro groups replace hydrogen atoms around a benzene ring. The products of the explosive reactions include CO_2, CO, C_2H_2 and N_2; the decomposition cannot be represented by a single chemical equation.

Another type of explosion can occur with fuels which normally burn smoothly but can become explosive when mixed with air in certain proportions. Hydrogen gas and gasoline vapour are notoriously dangerous in this regard, and have caused many explosions and fires. Wheat dust in grain elevators and finely powdered coal dust have been known to explode unexpectedly. Coal dust is believed to have contributed to the explosion in the Westray coal mine in Nova Scotia in 1992.

The technology of explosives is very complex, since all manufacturing, handling and storage operations are hazardous. No explosive should be made or handled except in accordance with established practice.

Table 9-5 Properties of Explosives

Name	Composition	Heat of explosion $kJ\ g^{-1}$
Black powder	$NaNO_3$, S, C	–2.6
Ammonium nitrate	NH_4NO_3	–1.6
Lead azide	$Pb(N_3)_2$	–1.6
Nitroglycerine	$C_3H_5(ONO_2)_3$	–6.4
Trinitrotoluene	$C_6H_2(NO_2)_3CH_3$	–2.7

9-6 Energy supplies in the future

During the last quarter of the twentieth century, the supply of energy in the industrialized countries has become a matter of public debate, and the phrase "the energy crisis" was coined to describe the confusion surrounding this debate. Prior to this period, energy supplies were so firmly within the control of the main user nations that their availability and low price was regarded as assured. This is no longer the situation, particularly in regard to petroleum.

We have seen in this chapter that the major part of the world's energy comes from three primary sources – coal, petroleum and natural gas – which are found as geological deposits in various parts of the world. At one time, coal was the most important primary source of energy. It was burned in fireplaces for heating, and in the furnaces of boilers to make steam to drive factories, locomotives, steamships and electric generating stations. This was a satisfactory situation politically because the industrial countries of Europe and North America had ample supplies of coal within their boundaries, and so were not dependent on imports from foreign countries for their energy supplies. Gradually, however, coal was replaced as a primary source by the liquid and gaseous hydrocarbon fuels. Oil and natural gas are more convenient fuels than coal, and the development of the internal combustion engine changed the transportation industry from a coal-using to a petroleum-using industry. The introduction of the cheap and popular private automobile ensured the rapid growth of the consumption of petroleum for transportation. Despite the rapid increase in oil consumption, the prices of hydrocarbon fuels remained low, as long as supplies remained plentiful and ownership lay with the user countries.

During the twentieth century, the economic life of industrial countries became dependent on cheap, abundant liquid hydrocarbons. Demand doubled every ten years for several decades. However, the realization grew that geological deposits of hydrocarbons are limited in extent, and that the rate of consumption is now higher than the rate of discovery. The supply of energy has become a major item of international trade and politics, particularly as the United States and the U.S.S.R. become increasingly less able to meet their requirements from their own domestic sources. Since Japan and most European nations have long been major importers, and the demand for petroleum is increasing in other Asian countries, the oil trade has become much more volatile than it was prior to 1972.

Examination of the pattern of energy sources in different countries shows that each, naturally, exploits its own resources. Hydroelectricity is important in Canada and Norway; natural gas in Canada, the Netherlands and the United States; and coal in Germany and the United Kingdom. Nevertheless, petroleum is the largest single energy source in every industrial country, always providing over 40% of the national energy supply and, in countries with few native sources, as much as 90%.

How these patterns will change in the twenty-first century is difficult to predict. One strategy favours keeping existing technology as unchanged as possible, and finding alternative sources of liquid hydrocarbons, such as tar sands and heavy oils in Canada, oil shales in the United States, and liquid hydrocarbons manufactured from coal. An alternative strategy is based on the belief that the present widespread use of gasoline and diesel engines is the product of an over-abundance of inexpensive liquid hydrocarbons, and that a new generation of vehicles and other equipment using different secondary sources should be developed. These other sources include electricity, stored probably in a new generation of rechargeable batteries; methanol, which is a renewable source which can be manufactured from vegetation; and hydrogen, produced from coal and steam or from electrolysis of water using nuclear power. Solar energy is being utilized increasingly, in both active and passive ways. Wind generation of electricity is being actively developed in several countries, and wave energy has been examined in the United Kingdom. Many of these sources tend to be suited to a more decentralized system of energy production than has been appropriate in the past. Research and development into these and other possibilities is a major challenge to science and technology. Those systems that become established must, of course, be reliable technically, but environmental protection, national security and economics must also be considered.

In energy, as in many things, the course which nations follow will be determined as much by political considerations as by technical, environmental or market considerations. The sudden increase in petroleum prices by a factor of about ten in the 1970s arose not from any significant increase in the cost of production but from a realization in the producing countries that the resource they were selling was a finite one. In many cases it was their only large resource, and they naturally decided to obtain as high a price as they could. They formed a reasonably effective cartel, which was able to use the disruption of supplies caused by instability in the Middle East to escalate prices rapidly. The time and investment required to produce alternative patterns of usage in the consuming countries are so large that there was little alternative but to pay the price for some time. Market considerations do have importance in the long run, however. High petroleum prices have permitted recovery of large amounts of otherwise uneconomic oil in the United States. The development of the expensive offshore oil in the North Sea has put the United Kingdom among the top ten oil producing nations in the world and oil discovered in Bass Strait now supplies more than half of Australia's requirements. All of these new sources increased the supply at the same time as high costs were reducing the demand. Smaller, more fuel-efficient cars became much more common, particularly in Canada and the United States. Moreover, considerable substitution of coal and natural gas in place of oil has taken place, especially in domestic heating and industrial heating. Coal production has increased markedly in Australia and South Africa, and to a considerable extent in the United States and Canada. Demand for electricity has levelled off in many areas, partly from market forces but also from public acceptance of the need to avoid waste and to conserve energy resources.

Overlying all considerations of fuel supply is the issue of conservation. There is every reason to believe that most industrial countries could reduce their consumption without reducing their living standards. In particular, each resident of Canada and the United States uses approximately 70% and 90% more energy, respectively, than residents of such prosperous countries as Australia, Denmark, France, Germany and Sweden. Analysis of usage figures shows that this arises from such sources as inefficient transportation, especially the use of automobiles to move single persons. While variations in climate and transportation distances complicate national comparisons, there seems to be little doubt that Canada and the United States could maintain and improve their standard of living while reducing their per capita consumption of energy. Moreover, almost every study, whether from industry or government sources, has indicated that the cheapest way of bringing supply and demand together is to reduce demand.

It is difficult to know the extent to which environmental considerations will influence our future. Generally speaking, the environment benefits from a strategy of reducing demand rather than expanding supplies. Supply expansion carries at least the risk, and in some cases the certainty, of substantial environmental damage. Building dams floods large areas, and expanding the use of nuclear power creates problems of storing spent fuel. In Section 9-4 we noted several ways in which the combustion of carbon-containing fuels damages the atmosphere; burning more fuel helps to maintain the rate of increase in the concentration of carbon dioxide in the atmosphere, with possible consequences for the global climate. Again, decreasing consumption has substantial advantages over increasing supplies.

The eventual decisions on energy sources for the twenty-first century and beyond will arise from a period of major research and development. The outcome may well vary from country to country, just as present patterns differ from country to country. These differences reflect cultural and geographical factors, as well as availability of primary sources. The Scandinavian countries and Canada require much energy for heating buildings. Canada and the United States use a large fraction of their total for transportation, partly because distances within these countries are great and partly because there is much travel by automobile and aircraft, both of which are inefficient when energy per passenger kilometre is considered. The large petroleum and petrochemical industry of the Netherlands, which has grown there for geographic and commercial reasons, makes that country a major user of petroleum simply because of the requirements for operating the refineries themselves. In many countries in Asia the standard of living is improving rapidly, and with that improvement comes increased use of energy. Over the period 1985-95, energy usage increased by 53% in China, 77% in India, 98% in Indonesia, 183% in both Malaysia and South Korea; in the same period energy usage in the U.S. grew by only 19%. In 1995 consumption of energy in China was 0.40 times the consumption in U.S., and 1.7 times the consumption in Japan.

These few illustrations are included to demonstrate the close relationship between the details of energy consumption in a country and the culture and commerce of that country. Any abrupt change, such as a disruption of the traditional energy sources, is capable of creating deep social unrest. The widespread economic recession that followed the petroleum price increase in the late seventies and early eighties is evidence of this.

Early in the year 2000, there were sharp increases in the Canadian prices of gasoline and diesel fuel, due primarily to an increase in the international price of crude petroleum from about US\$12 to US\$32 per barrel. The increased cost of fuel is having serious effects on the transportation industry, and there have been protest demonstrations by truck drivers on Parliament Hill in Ottawa, and elsewhere. There may be further repercussions in other parts of the economy, since Canada is a large country with cold winters. These events, which are still developing as this book goes to press, are a reminder of our dependence on reliable sources of energy.

When discussing the economic and environmental aspects of the energy market, it is obviously helpful to know something about thermochemistry and the chemical nature of the fuels we depend on.

Further reading

The following reports on the energy industry are published regularly by Statistics Canada and are available in libraries: 45-004-XPB Refined petroleum products; 57-001-XPB Electric Power statistics; 55-002-XPB Gas Utilities; 45-002-XPB Coal and Coke Statistics. 57-601-XPB Energy Statistics handbook.

There are many popular books on issues related to energy, an example being *Fuel and Energy* by J.H. Harker and J.R. Backhurst. Academic Press, 1981.

The following references are helpful in connection with environmental aspects of energy.

Our Common Future. World Commission on Environment and Development. Oxford 1987.

Climate Change. Report of the Intergovernmental Panel on Climate Change. Cambridge, 1990.

Global Warming. S.H.Schneider. Vintage Books, 1990.

The American Geophysical Union publishes much information about the global climate and may be contacted through the Internet at: www.agu.org/homepage.html.

Key concepts

The main source of industrial energy is the combustion of fuels. The main solid duel is coal. The main liquid fuels are hydrocarbons derived from petroleum. The main gaseous fuel is methane. The heat of combustion of hydrocarbon fuels per gram is about the same regardless of composition.

Explosives are unstable substances or mixtures that decompose rapidly, releasing energy and producing large volumes of gas. Most explosives are compounds containing nitrogen.

The combustion of fuels on a large scale causes various environmental problems, particularly acid rain and an increase in the carbon dioxide concentration in the atmosphere, which is possibly related to global warming. The future of energy usage depends on the balance between supply and demand, which are affected by economic and commercial factors, international politics, environmental problems, and government policy.

Problems

1. Write balanced equations for combustion of the following fuels: CH_4 ,C_3H_8, C_8H_{18}, C_2H_2, C_2H_5OH.

2. Using the data listed in Appendix 1, calculate the heat of combustion, per mole and per gram, for the fuels in Problem 1 and compare your answers with the data in Table 9-1.

3. A sample of natural gas, known to contain only methane and ethane, was burned under controlled conditions, and was found to produce 15.80 g of water, and 410.0 kJ of heat. What was the composition of the gas, expressed as mole fraction of ethane? [0.221]

4. A small tank has a capacity of 2.0 litres, and has been constructed to hold a pressure of 0.70 MPa. Calculate ΔH, in megajoules, for the combustion of one tank of each of the following fuels:

   (a) methane at a pressure of 0.70 MPa and 25°C, assumed to be an ideal gas. [–0.50 MJ]

   (b) propane at a pressure of 0.70 MPa and 25°C, assumed to be an ideal gas. [–1.25 MJ]

   (c) motor gasoline of density 0.740 g/mL. [–70. MJ]

5. Suppose the 2.0 litre tank in Problem 4 was filled with trinitrotoluene, with a density of 1.65 g/mL. Calculate the total heat of explosion from Table 9-5. [–8.9 MJ]

6. Calculate the total heat of combustion available from the fuel in each of the following cases. Use data from Table 9-5.

   (a) household storage tank containing 900 litres of light fuel oil. [–38 GJ]

   (b) a car fuel tank containing 50 L of gasoline. [–1.8 GJ]

   (c) a hiker's fuel cartridge containing 250 g of butane. [–12 MJ]

   (d) a motor camper's fuel supply of 4.5 kg of propane. [–230 MJ]

   (e) a can containing 300 g ethanol. [–8.9 MJ]

7. Mixing a modest amount of fuel oil with ammonium nitrate greatly increases the power of the explosion. (a) Estimate the mass of fuel oil per gram of ammonium nitrate that will react stoichiometrically with the oxygen produced in the explosion. (b) Estimate the factor by which the energy released is increased by the oxidation of the fuel oil. Since fuel oil consists primarily of long chain hydrocarbons, its empirical formula may be taken to be CH_2 and the products of oxidation should be taken to be CO_2 and $H_2O(g)$.

   [0.058 g fuel oil per g of ammonium nitrate; 2.7]

8. If methane reacts stoichiometrically with the oxygen in air, what is the ratio of the volume of air to that of methane if both gases are at the same temperature and pressure. Take the mole fraction of oxygen in air to be 0.21. [9.5]

9. Write a balanced equation for decomposition of sodium azide, NaN_3, to yield nitrogen gas and sodium metal. What volume of nitrogen gas, measured at 25°C and 100. kPa, is released from one gram of sodium azide? [0.57L]

10. Write a balanced equation for the decomposition of nitroglycerine to yield carbon dioxide, water, nitrogen and oxygen.

11. Try to write a balanced equation for the decomposition of trinitrotoluene to yield nitrogen and other products. Show that there is not enough oxygen in nitroglycerine to oxidize all the carbon and hydogen to carbon dioxide and water.

12. How much electrical energy, measured in kilowatt-hours, is equal to the enthalpy change of combustion of one cubic metre of natural gas?   [10.3 kW h]

13. In March 2000, typical retail costs (including taxes) of various energy sources were as follows: gasoline, 70 cents/litre; heating oil, 55 cents/litre; natural gas, 31 cents/cubic metre; electricity, 9 cents/kilowatt-hour. Use these figures to estimate the cost per gigajoule of energy in from each of these sources. Which of these energy sources is the most economical, based on these figures?

10 Atomic Structure

Objectives

After reading this chapter, the student should be able to do the following:

♦ Describe the structure of atoms in terms of the nucleus and electrons.

♦ Describe some of the experiments which demonstrate the quantum nature of light and matter.

♦ Describe the otical spectra of atoms.

♦ Relate optical spectra to the valence shell of electrons in atoms.

♦ Relate X-ray spectra to the inner shells of electrons in atoms.

♦ List the quantum numbers for electrons in atoms, and state the rules governing them.

♦ Write down electronic configurations of atoms using the periodic table.

♦ Define ionization energy and electron affinity of atoms.

Related topics to review:

Atoms and elements in Chapter 1. Periodicity in Chapter 3.

Related topics to look forward to:

Structure of molecules in Chapter 11. Quantum theory in Chapter 12.

10-1 Atoms and quantum theory

The idea of a fundamental particle of matter dates back to Greek philosophy, but it was not until 1803 that John Dalton gave the idea the status of a scientific principle based firmly upon experimental evidence. Dalton's theory of the atomic structure of matter stated that atoms are the fundamental and indivisible particles of the chemical elements. With certain limitations, this statement is still valid as a chemical principle; for instance, it provides the basis for stoichiometric calculations and for explaining the difference between elements and compounds. But we now know that an atom has an internal structure, namely a nucleus and some electrons, and that the electronic structure of each type of atom determines the chemical properties of the corresponding element.

The structure of atoms was discovered in a series of experimental and theoretical studies beginning around the beginning of the twentieth century. Although much of that work is classified as physics, some knowledge of it is essential to understanding modern chemistry.

Atoms are so small that the conventional measuring equipment in an elementary laboratory cannot be used in any simple way to measure the diameter of a single atom and so most measurements on atoms are therefore made by indirect methods. Upon reflection, this is not surprizing since the instrument used (a microscope, for instance) is itself made of atoms; atoms must be much smaller than the finest divisions of the scale of distance, or otherwise the atomic nature of atoms would have been obvious long ago. The physical reality of atoms and molecules was proven in about 1907 when the constant random motion of very small particles (such as grains of pollen) in water, which can be seen using an ordinary microscope, were shown to be caused by molecular collisions. Shortly thereafter, the atomic structure of matter was demonstrated by diffraction of X-rays from crystals.

It is not possible to understand the internal structure of atoms and molecules without knowing something about **quantum mechanics**. Soon after the discovery of the internal structure of atoms it was realized that the **classical mechanics**, based on Newton's laws of motion and Maxwell's laws of electromagnetism, is inadequate for describing the behaviour of electrons and other very small particles behave. A **particle** is a very small object which has mass, and possibly carries an electric charge; a moving particle has momentum and kinetic energy, and an electrically charged particle may have potential energy as a result of electric fields. In classical mechanics, the future motion of a particle is completely determined by the forces acting upon it, and both the position and momentum can be calculated or measured simultaneously without any limitation on precision. This turns out to be impossible for the particles that make up atoms, and only quantum mechanics can give a proper account of the structure of atoms and molecules. The form of quantum mechanics used most commonly in chemistry is called **wave mechanics**.

A **wave** is an oscillatory motion that propagates through space. Examples of waves are waves on the surface of water, sound waves carried by variations in the density of air, and light waves, carried through space by oscillating electric and magnetic fields. Waves extend over a region of space, and by their very nature cannot be localized to a point. The characteristics and motion of a wave are determined by the properties of the medium through which the wave is travelling; for instance the path of a beam of light waves is bent when the wave travels from one medium to another, as in a prism.

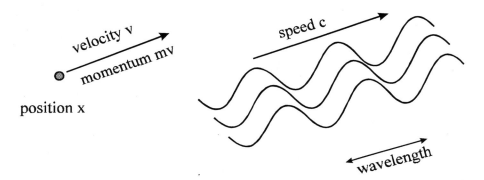

Figure 10-1 A particle is a very small object located at a point in space. A wave consists of a series of wave fronts moving through space with a characteristic velocity, wavelength and frequency.

A feature of quantum theory is the **wave-particle duality**, the statement that very small objects may behave sometimes as particles and sometimes as waves. What we call electrons were first characterized as particles, and their charge and mass were measured around the beginning of the twentieth century. However serious difficulties were encountered in applying classical mechanics to the behaviour of electrons when confined inside an atom. These difficulties were resolved by treating the electron as though it were in some sense a wave. It was found that certain experimental facts, which were inconsistent with classical mechanics, could be explained in a natural way using the appropriate mathematical equation that governs the electron wave. The new quantum theory, proposed in 1925 and developed rapidly in the following years, is fundamental to all contemporary understanding of chemical bonding and the properties of atoms and molecules.

The quantum theory leads to new conceptual difficulties. Since a wave cannot be localized to a point, neither can an electron when its behaviour is wave-like, and so the position of the electron is uncertain to some extent. Similarly, the momentum or velocity of an electron cannot be specified precisely. Instead, the wave gives us information about the probability distribution for the position and momentum of the electron. Furthermore, increasing the precision in measuring the position of an electron is found to decrease the precision of the momentum; this principle is called the **uncertainty principle**. Energy may be very precisely defined, and in fact only certain energy levels are permitted for electrons confined in atoms or molecules; such states or energy levels are said to be **quantized**.

In the classical theory of physics, light is described as an electromagnetic wave, but under certain conditions light may behave like a stream of particles called **photons**. This is another example of wave-particle duality. Photons differ from electrons in that they have no mass and are readily created or destroyed when light is absorbed or emitted by atoms or molecules; electrons cannot be created or destroyed without involving a much larger amount of energy than is found in chemical reactions. Light is involved in chemistry in two common ways. First, some reactions take place only in the presence of light, and are called **photochemical reactions**. Second, the study of light emitted or absorbed by atoms and molecules is the most important source of information about atomic and molecular structure. This area of chemistry and physics is called **spectroscopy**.

10-2 The electron and the nucleus as particles

The charge and the mass of the electron were measured in a series of experiments carried out at the beginning of the twentieth century. In the first experiment, performed in 1897, the English physicist J.J.Thomson made an apparatus to generate a beam of electrons (called *cathode rays* at that time) passing through a vacuum, similar to what is used in a modern television picture tube or cathode ray tube. He measured the deflection of the beam caused by electric and magnetic fields applied at right angles to the beam, and by applying the ordinary laws of classical mechanics determined a value of the ratio e/m of the electric charge e to the mass m of the electron.

In a second experiment carried out at about the same time, the American physicist Robert A. Millikan was studying the motion of very small droplets of oil suspended in air. He showed that such droplets carried a small electric charge which could be determined by measuring the change in the motion of the droplet when an electric field was applied. In this way the charges on a great many droplets were measured and were found to be always an integer multiple of a single charge, which was interpreted as the charge e on a single electron.

With separate values of the charge-to-mass ratio and the charge, the mass of the electron could be determined. From the charge of an electron and the charge required to electrolyze a mole of singly charged ions such as Ag^+ (the Faraday constant) the value of the Avogadro constant could be determined. From the molar mass of the lightest element, hydrogen, and the Avogadro constant, the mass of a single hydrogen atom could be calculated. In this way, it was shown that the mass of an electron is only about 1/1800 of the mass of a hydrogen atom. During this exciting period of science, these quantities were being measured in other experiments, and the consistency of the results of these various measurements and calculations gave confidence that the experiments were being interpreted correctly. To five significant figures, the charge of the electron is 1.6022×10^{-19} coulomb, and the mass of the electron is 9.1094×10^{-31} kg.

The phenomenon of **radioactivity** was discovered at the end of the nineteenth century, when it was shown that certain minerals emitted radiation that could blacken photographic film that was kept in the dark. Radioactivity provided several important methods of studying atoms, both through the processes of radioactive decay and by providing sources of energetic particles which could be "bounced" off atoms. The radiation was classified into three types:

α-particles are heavy and positively charged;

β-particles are light and negatively charged;

γ-particles are uncharged.

In an experiment carried out in 1911 by Hans Geiger and Ernest Marsden in collaboration with Ernest Rutherford, a beam of α-particles was directed at a very thin film of gold, and the intensity of scattering of the α-particles in various directions was measured. It had been thought that, since they are heavy and moving fast, the α-particles would be only slightly deflected by the foil. Instead, it was found that although most of the α-particles passed straight through the foil, some of the α-particles were scattered through large angles, and a few bounced back towards the source from which they had come. This result could only be interpreted as indicating that the α-particles had collided with something that was heavy, positively charged, and much smaller than the atom itself. This "something" was the **nucleus** inside each of the gold atoms in the metal foil. Refinement of the measurements and calculations allowed a determination of the charge on the nucleus and it was shown that the charge on a gold nucleus is about 100 times larger than the charge on an electron, and of opposite sign.

In due course, experiments showed that α-particles are the nuclei of helium atoms, β-particles are electrons, and γ-particles are electromagnetic waves like light but of much higher energy.

These three experiments provided the basis for our knowledge of the particles of which atoms are made. A very small positively charged nucleus carries almost all of the mass of the atom, and is surrounded by a number of much lighter negatively charged electrons. The charge of the nucleus is an integer multiple of the fundamental charge e, and the number of electrons is equal to that multiple so that the atom as a whole is electrically neutral. The nuclear charge determines the chemical properties of an atom, and all atoms of a given element have the same charge.

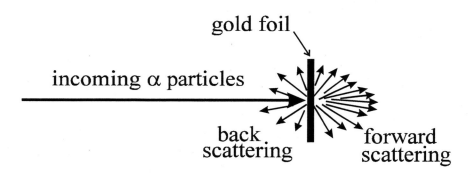

Figure 10-2 The scattering of α-particles by a gold foil. The incoming α-particles are indicated by the horizontal arrow coming from the left and striking the foil indicated by the thick vertical line, and the paths of various scattered α-particles are indicated by the arrows radiating out from the foil.

Nuclei consist of an assembly of **protons** and **neutrons** held together by strong nuclear forces; these particles are known collectively as **nucleons**. A proton is the nucleus of an hydrogen atom and has an electric charge of +1, and the electron has a charge of –1, in units of the fundamental charge e. The neutron has no electric charge and a mass which is about 0.1 per cent larger than the mass of the proton. The atomic number Z of an atom is the number of protons in the nucleus, while the mass number A is the total number of nucleons. A nucleus with particular values of A and Z is called a **nuclide**. In most nuclei there are more neutrons than protons and the mass number is slightly more than twice the atomic number. At the heavy end of the periodic table, bismuth has $Z = 83$ and $A = 209$, so the number of neutrons = $A–Z$ = 209–83 = 126 and $A/Z \approx 2.5$. It is possible to have several different nuclides with different mass numbers A for a given atomic number Z, and such nuclides are called **isotopes**. For a given element, the chemical reactions and other chemical properties of isotopes are almost identical. Separation of isotopes is nearly always done by physical rather than chemical means, except in the case of the isotopes of hydrogen. Nearly pure stable isotopes of many elements are available commercially. Perhaps the most important isotope in chemistry is the heavy isotope of hydrogen, ^{2}H, which has a special name, deuterium, and is often represented by a special chemical symbol, D.

Some nuclides are unstable and decay by radioactive processes; most of the radioactive elements are the heaviest elements, at the end of the periodic table, but there are a few lighter elements which are radioactive, such as technetium, with atomic number $Z = 43$.

10-3 The nature of light

Light, which we receive and interpret with our eyes, is our most effective source of information, both personally and in science. Light can be classified qualitatively by means of its intensity and its colour, and can be broken into its component colours by means of a prism. Light that has been analyzed in this way forms a **spectrum**. In every spectrum the colours always appear in the same sequence, red, yellow, green, blue and violet, regardless of whether the spectrum is generated in a prism or appears in the sky as a rainbow.

Accepted ideas about the nature of light have changed over the centuries. In the seventeenth century Newton believed light to be a stream of particles (despite having studied a common interference effect now called Newton's rings), but a little later the theory proposed by the Dutch physicist Christiaan Huygens that light is a wave motion became widely accepted. In this theory, the various colours of light correspond to different wavelengths, which can be measured very accurately by means of the interference effects generated by a diffraction grating, which is a mirror ruled with very closely spaced parallel lines. The wavelength of red light is about 700 nanometres, and that of violet light is about 400 nanometres. **White light** has roughly equal intensity at all visible wavelengths, while coloured light has more intensity at some wavelengths than at others. Most of the colour that we see around us is due to absorption of light of particular wavelengths by specific chemical compounds; we see the coloured light that survives after absorption of other wavelengths from white light.

A wave moves with a characteristic speed c. The distance from one peak of the wave to the next is the wavelength λ (Greek *lambda*), and at a fixed position, the number of cycles of oscillation per second is the frequency ν (Greek *nu*). The unit of frequency is the hertz, named for Heinrich Hertz who first detected radio waves; the abbreviation for hertz is Hz.

Each complete cycle of the wave occupies a length λ, and the number of cycles passing a fixed point per second is equal to the frequency ν, so the speed c of the wave moving through space is the product of the wavelength and the frequency:

$$c = \lambda \nu \qquad\qquad (10\text{-}1)$$

The speed of light is 3.00×10^8 m/s, so the frequency corresponding to blue light of wavelength 400 nm is:

$$v = \frac{3.00\times10^8 \text{ m/s}}{400\times10^{-9} \text{ m}} = 7.5\times10^{14} \text{ s}^{-1} \text{ or hertz} .$$

Red light, with a wavelenth of about 700 nm, has a frequency of about 4.3×10^{14} Hz.

The wave theory received support from Maxwell's theory of electromagnetic waves put forward around 1873 and from early experiments with radio waves by Hertz in 1888. These developments showed that what we call light is only part of a much wider spectrum of electromagnetic radiation. Light beyond the red end of the visible spectrum was called **infrared** light (with a frequency below that of red light), and light beyond the violet was called **ultraviolet** light (with a frequency higher than that of violet light). These forms of light, often abbreviated to IR and UV, are invisible to the eye but can be detected by photographic film (in the case of UV) or a suitable electronic detector (for the IR). There are other categories of electromagnetic radiation beyond even these and the full spectrum classified according to wavelength is shown in Figure 10-3.

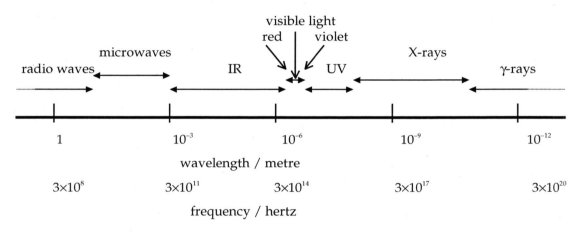

Figure 10-3 The electromagnetic spectrum plotted on a scale of wavelength and frequency, showing the various regions of the spectrum with their conventional names and ranges of wavelength. The boundaries between the regions are not precise, and it is now possible technically to generate and detect waves of any wavelength in the spectrum. The wavelength scale used is a *logarithmic* scale in which powers of 10 are equally spaced along the axis.

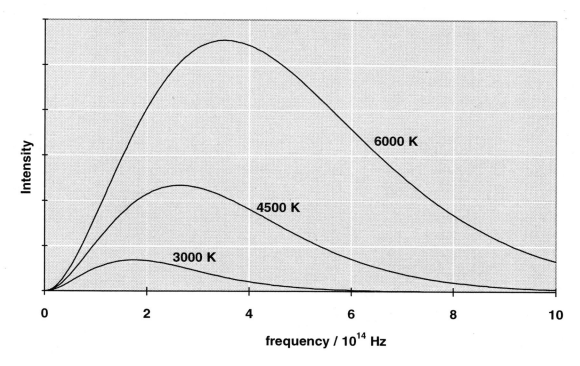

Figure 10-4 The distribution of energy in thermal radiation plotted as a function of frequency for several different temperatures. The frequency scale, in units of 10^{14} hertz, should be compared with that in Figure 10-3. Red light has a frequency of about 4×10^{14} hertz, and blue light has a frequency of about 7×10^{14} hertz.

An instrument capable of separating light according to wavelength is called a *spectroscope*; if it is able to measure wavelengths precisely it is called a *spectrometer*, and if it can in addition measure the intensity of the light at each wavelength it is called a *spectrophotometer*. Spectrophotometers are used routinely in the modern chemical laboratory.

At the end of the nineteenth century, the wave nature of light came to be questioned, and within a few years the idea of light as a flow of particles found acceptance again. The wave theory was very well established, however, and for some time there was confusion over the idea that light could behave sometimes as a wave, sometimes as a particle, a conundrum known as wave-particle duality. The origin of the confusion was the colour of a "red-hot" object. The classical wave theory of light predicts that the light emitted from a hot object should contain more blue light than red light, which conflicts with the fact that a red-hot object emits mostly red light.

The light emitted from a hot object is called "thermal radiation". Figure 10-4 shows the measured intensity of thermal radiation as a function of frequency for several different temperatures; the highest temperature shown, 6000 K, is approximately the temperature of the surface of the sun. The distribution has a maximum and the intensity of the radiation drops at high frequencies, contrary to classical theory. For sunlight, the intensity of red light (with a frequency of about 4.3×10^{14} Hz) is higher than of blue light (with a frequency of about 7.5×10^{14} Hz). As the temperature increases, the maximum intensity shifts to higher frequency and the total intensity of light emitted increases rapidly.

In 1900, Max Planck proposed a new theory of thermal radiation which successfully explained the distribution of colours in thermal radiation. The theory was based upon the assumption that light is emitted and absorbed, not as a wave motion, but as a stream of particles. These particles are called **photons**. It was shown that in order to obtain the correct distribution of light intensity in thermal radiation as depicted in Figure 10-4, each photon had to carry an amount of energy proportional to its frequency. In a famous equation, the energy of a photon of frequency ν is:

$$E = h\nu \tag{10-2}$$

where h is a fundamental constant called Planck's constant. By comparing his theory with experiment, Planck determined the value of h; the modern value of h is 6.626075×10^{-34} joule seconds.

The second phenomenon which helped establish the photon theory of light was the *photoelectric effect* in which ultraviolet light shining on a clean metal surface causes the emission of electrons from the metal. In careful studies of the effect using monochromatic light (i.e. light of only one colour or wavelength), the number of electrons emitted, and their kinetic energy, were measured. It was found that no electrons were emitted unless the frequency of the light was higher than a certain threshold value, even if the light was very intense. But if the frequency of the light was high enough, then electrons were emitted with kinetic energy which was a linear function of the frequency of the light, but independent of the intensity of the light. The constant of proportionality between frequency and energy was found to be equal to Planck's constant h:

$$\text{kinetic energy} = \tfrac{1}{2}mv^2 = h\nu - \phi \tag{10-3}$$

This equation is hard to understand on the basis of the electromagnetic theory of light, but in 1905 Albert Einstein provided a simple explanation by applying the quantum theory of light. He suggested that when light is absorbed at the surface of the metal, the photons are destroyed and the energy $h\nu$ is transferred to an electron. If the energy transferred to an electron is larger than the energy required to remove it from the metal, then the electron is able to leave the metal. According to this theory, the energy ϕ in equation (10-3) is the minimum energy needed to remove an electron from the metal, sometimes called the *work function* of the metal. Equation (10-3) is interpreted to mean that the kinetic energy of the emitted electron is the photon energy minus the energy ϕ.

Einstein's equation for the photoelectric effect can be expressed in a diagram, Figure 10-6, showing the energy of the photon and the kinetic and potential energy of the electron as differences between **energy levels**. The quantum theory leads naturally to energy level diagrams, and we will meet them again in considering the quantum nature of electrons in atoms.

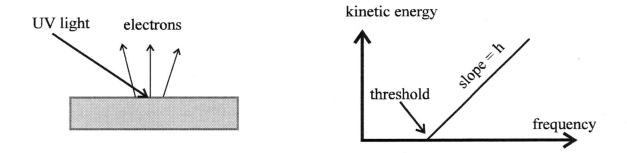

Figure 10-5 The photoelectric effect, in which electrons are ejected from a metal surface by absorption of monochromatic ultraviolet light. The graph at the right shows the linear relationship between the kinetic energy of the electron and the frequency of the light.

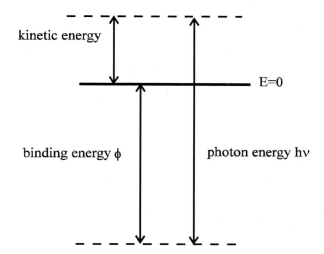

Figure 10-6   The energy relationships in the photoelectric effect. Energy levels are plotted on a vertical energy scale. The dashed line at the bottom shows the potential energy of the electron inside the metal, which "binds" the electron to the metal. The photon transfers energy $h\nu$ to the electron; if this energy is greater than ϕ the electron is able to leave the metal with kinetic energy $h\nu-\phi$. The dashed line at the top shows the kinetic energy of the electron after it leaves the metal. The full line in the middle labelled "E=0" is the energy of an electron at rest outside the metal.

10-4 The hydrogen atom spectrum

The spectrum of the light emitted by atoms provided yet another puzzle that was solved by the quantum theory. When a high voltage is applied between electrodes in a gas at low pressure, an electric discharge is formed and light is emitted. The colour of the light emitted depends on the chemical composition of the gas: each substance has its own **spectrum**, which is the distribution of intensity as a function of frequency. The spectrum of the light emitted by atoms in an electric discharge consists of many extremely narrow peaks or "lines" of sharply defined wavelength. By comparison, the spectrum of thermal radiation from a hot solid object, shown in Figure 10-4, is a continuous distribution of energy across a broad range of wavelengths. Hydrogen being the lightest and simplest atom, its spectrum is of particular importance. Figure 10-7 shows a representation of part of the spectrum of atomic hydrogen.

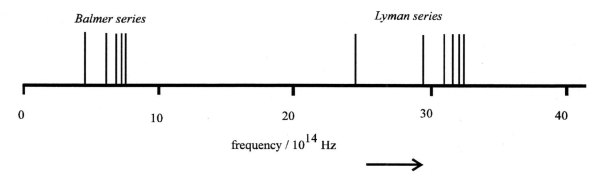

Figure 10-7   The spectrum of the hydrogen atom, plotted on a frequency scale. The vertical lines show the discrete frequencies of the light emitted by hydrogen atoms. Two series, or groups, of lines are shown, the Balmer series in the visible region, and the Lyman series in the ultraviolet. Other series are to be found in the infrared.

Chapter 10

To early workers, the sharp lines at specific frequencies in the spectrum seemed to indicate the presence of "oscillators" inside the atoms, but no theory could explain why there are so many different oscillators or why the frequencies were related by a simple formula. The accepted view of an atom was a kind of solar system with the electrons held in the atom by electrostatic forces, perhaps like planets in orbits around the sun under gravitational forces, but close examination showed that this concept was at best incomplete if not entirely wrong. The solution came from application of the quantum theory.

The spectrum of the hydrogen atom consists of several groups or "series" of spectral lines, one in the visible part of the spectrum, one in the ultraviolet, and more in the infrared. Two such series are shown in Figure 10-7. Johannes Rydberg and others showed that the measured wavelengths could all be fitted to a single simple equation to very high precision:

$$\frac{1}{\lambda} = R_H \left[\frac{1}{n_1^2} - \frac{1}{n_2^2} \right] \tag{10-4}$$

where R_H is the Rydberg constant equal to 1.09678×10^7 m^{-1} and n_1 and n_2 are positive integers. Each series of lines is characterized by a particular value of n_1 and each line within a series corresponds to a value of n_2, which must be greater than the value of n_1 for that particular series. For the *Lyman series* in the ultraviolet, $n_1 = 1$ and $n_2 = 2,3,4,...$; for the *Balmer series* in the visible region, $n_1 = 2$ and $n_2 = 3,4,...$; and so on.

The accuracy of fit of the Rydberg formula to experiment is very high. The following example shows that the discrepancy is smaller than 1 part in 200 000, far better than the accuracy of fit to most empirical formulae. The simplicity and accuracy of the formula suggests that it reflects an underlying fundamental theory, and this is indeed the case.

Example 10-1 The wavelength of the longest wavelength member of the Balmer series was found by measurement to be 656.460 nm. Calculate the wavelength from the Rydberg formula.

The Balmer series consists of lines for which $n_1 = 2$, and the longest wavelength line is the one with the smallest value of n_2 within this series, i.e. $n_2 = 3$. From the formula with $n_1 = 2$ and $n_2 = 3$, the calculated inverse wavelength is:

$$\frac{1}{\lambda} = 1.09678 \times 10^7 \left[\frac{1}{2^2} - \frac{1}{3^2} \right] = 1.52333 \times 10^6 \text{ m}^{-1}$$

From this equation, the wavelength is found to be $\lambda = 656.47$ nm.

Example 10-2 Calculate the wavelength of the transition $n = 33$ to $n = 34$ in the hydrogen atom spectrum. In what part of the electromagnetic spectrum does this transition lie?

From the Rydberg formula,

$$\frac{1}{\lambda} = 1.09678 \times 10^7 \left[\frac{1}{33^2} - \frac{1}{34^2} \right] = 5.837 \times 10^2 \text{ m}^{-1}$$

Hence the wavelength is $\lambda = 1.713$ mm and the transition falls in the microwave region of the spectrum.

The hydrogen atom is the simplest possible atom, and any theoretical model for the structure of atoms must be able to give a satisfactory account of the properties of the hydrogen atom before dealing with more complex atoms. Attempts to do this based upon classical mechanics and electromagnetic theory failed, for a variety of reasons, until Niels Bohr in 1913 combined the nuclear model of the atom with the quantum theory of the light. In the nuclear model, the energy of a hydrogen atom is determined by the electrostatic attraction between the nucleus and the electron. The essence of Bohr's theory can be summarized in three hypotheses:

First hypothesis: Certain discrete quantum states of the atom are stable and have fixed energies.

Second hypothesis: Light is emitted or absorbed when an atom passes from one quantum state to another, and the frequency (and wavelength) of the light is determined by the energies E_1 and E_2 of the two states involved, according to the Planck formula:

$$hv = \frac{hc}{\lambda} = E_2 - E_1 \tag{10-5}$$

Third hypothesis: The quantum states of the atom are selected by the requirement that only certain values are permitted for the *angular momentum* of the electron in its motion around the nucleus.

The first hypothesis states without proof an explicit assumption that energy levels in the atom are quantized. The second hypothesis shows how the energies of the quantum states are related to the observed spectrum of the hydrogen atom. In the third postulate, the "angular momentum" is a quantity related to the motion of the electron in its orbit around the nucleus.

Combining the Rydberg formula, equation (10-4), with the second hypothesis as summarized in equation (10-5), we get:

$$\frac{1}{\lambda} = \frac{R_H}{n_1^2} - \frac{R_H}{n_2^2} = \frac{E_2}{hc} - \frac{E_1}{hc}$$

and from the second equality the permitted energies of a quantum state must correspond to an integer n according to the following equation:

$$E_n = -\frac{hcR_H}{n^2} \qquad \text{for } n = 1,2,3,4,... \tag{10-6}$$

The integer n is called the **principal quantum number** and can be used to catalogue the energy levels. Figure 10-8 shows the energy level diagram for a hydrogen atom corresponding to equation (10-6) with the various series of lines in the spectrum shown as **transitions** between the energy levels. The spectrum does not fix the zero of the energy level scale, since every line in the spectrum corresponds to a difference between two energies. In the diagram the zero of energy is placed at the $n = \infty$ limit, which corresponds to the energy when the electron is removed from the atom and is at rest. This is the same as the zero of the energy scale used in Figure 10-6.

The concept of an energy level diagram was a great simplification of atomic spectroscopy for it meant that the thousands of lines in a spectrum could be described in terms of a much smaller number of energy levels. The energy levels are of more fundamental importance than the transitions, and as a diagram is constructed, the wavelengths of spectral lines not yet seen could be predicted with great accuracy. The energy level concept is valid for all atoms, molecules and other quantum systems, and has its origins in Bohr's theory of the hydrogen atom.

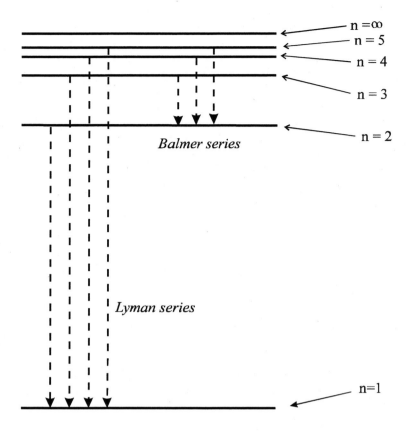

Figure 10-8 The energy levels of the hydrogen atom, with several transitions of the Lyman and Balmer series of lines indicated by vertical arrows.

Example 10-3 Calculate $N_A hcR_H$.

Using the accepted values of these constants,

$$hcR_H = 6.626075\times10^{-34}\ \text{J s}\times2.99792458\times10^8\ \text{m s}^{-1}\times1.09678\times10^7\ \text{m}^{-1} = 2.17870\times10^{-18}\ \text{J}$$

Hence $N_A hcR_H = 6.022136\times10^{23}\ \text{mol}^{-1}\times2.17870\times10^{-18}\ \text{J} = 1312.04\ \text{kJ mol}^{-1}$

Example 10-4 Calculate the energy difference between the $n = 1$ and $n = 2$ levels of the hydrogen atom.

Using the value of hcR_H calculated in the last example, and the Rydberg formula for the wavelength of the transition between the $n = 1$ and $n = 2$ levels, the energy difference is:

$$E_2 - E_1 = 2.17870\times10^{-18}\times\left[\frac{1}{1^2} - \frac{1}{2^2}\right] = 1.63402\times10^{-18}\ \text{J}$$

The third hypothesis of Bohr refers to the angular momentum of the electron. In classical mechanics, the linear momentum of a particle is the product of mass and velocity, mv. The angular momentum of a particle is the analogous quantity for motion in an orbit. For a particle moving in a circular orbit the angular momentum is the product of the linear momentum and the radius of the orbit. Bohr assumed that the angular momentum can only have certain "quantized" values. In this way he explained the observed spectrum and energy levels of the hydrogen atom, and calculated the Rydberg constant in terms of fundamental constants:

$$R_H = \frac{m_e e^4}{8\varepsilon_0^2 h^3 c(1 + m_e / m_p)} \tag{10-7}$$

where m_e is the mass of an electron, m_p is the mass of a proton, ε_0 is the permittivity of free space (used in the theory of electrostatics), and the other symbols have their usual values. The value of the Rydberg constant R_H given by equation (10-7), $1.0967758(1) \times 10^7$ m^{-1}, agrees with the experimental value of R_H quoted under equation (10-4) to high accuracy.

We will not discuss in any further detail Bohr's analysis of the orbits of the electron in a hydrogen atom. The concept of sharply defined orbits is inconsistent with the uncertainty principle and has been replaced by the wave theory of quantum mechanics. Further, the values of the angular momentum predicted by his theory are wrong. However several features of Bohr's theory are still important in modern quantum theory: the interpretation of spectra in terms of quantized energy levels, the stability of quantized energy levels, and the importance of angular momentum in quantum mechanics.

In the quantum description of the hydrogen atom a new quantum number appears, called the **orbital quantum number** λ, which takes the values 0,1,2,3,...up to $n-1$ (i.e. one less than the principal quantum number). Quantum mechanics shows that angular momentum is a multiple of $h/2\pi$, Planck's constant divided by 2π; the units of h are joule second, which is equivalent to the units for angular momentum, kilogram metre^2 second^{-1}. The angular momentum L for a given orbital quantum number λ is:

$$L = \sqrt{\lambda(\lambda+1)} \, \frac{h}{2\pi} \tag{10-8}$$

Although it is not needed in classifying the energy levels of the hydrogen atom, the angular momentum quantum number is of importance in classifying the energy levels of atoms other than hydrogen.

10-5 The spectra and energy levels of other atoms

The spectra of atoms other than hydrogen are complex and there is no simple formula that can be used to calculate wavelengths with high precision, such as the Rydberg formula, which works so well for hydrogen. However there are many regularities in the spectra of the elements. For instance, the spectra of atoms of elements in the same column of the periodic table show similarities, from which it follows that the electronic structures of these atoms are similar.

The alkali metals of group 1 of the periodic table have the simplest spectra of the elements other than hydrogen, and a study of the energy level diagrams deduced from the spectra allows us to understand certain features of the periodic table and the structure of atoms. The energy level diagram of the sodium atom is typical and will be discussed in some detail. Light emitted by excited sodium atoms is familiar as the yellow light of modern street lighting; and the same yellow colour can be seen by sprinkling common salt into a Bunsen burner flame. The yellow colour is due to very strong emission of two closely spaced spectral lines in the yellow part of the spectrum.

The energy level diagram of sodium is shown in Figure 10-9. The energy levels are arranged in several groups arranged in columns, instead of the single column used in the case of hydrogen. The energy levels depend upon the orbital quantum number λ as well as the principal quantum number n. Several series of spectral lines are observed in the spectrum of the sodium atom, and in the early days of spectroscopy these were given the names *principal, sharp, diffuse and fundamental*. Each series of lines corresponds to transitions between levels in adjacent columns of energy levels in Figure 10-9. As quantum theory developed, it became apparent that energy levels in different columns corresponded to different values of the orbital quantum number. The initial letters s, p, d and f of the sharp, principal, diffuse and fundamental series were then used to refer to both the energy levels and the values of the orbital quantum number, as shown in Table 10-1.

Table 10-1 The classification of energy levels by the orbital quantum number λ

symbol	λ value	name of spectral series
s	0	sharp
p	1	principal
d	2	diffuse
f	3	fundamental
g, h, ...	4, 5, ...	

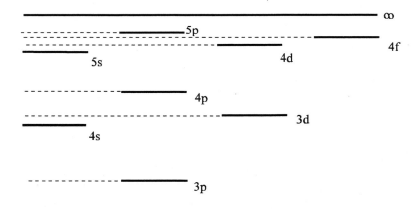

Figure 10-9 The energy levels of the sodium atom, labelled with the principal and orbital quantum numbers. The energy levels are placed in columns, each column corresponding to a particular value of the orbital quantum number; the horizontal dotted lines show the relationship between the various energy levels. Note the relationship between levels with the same n but different λ, such as the 4s, 4p, 4d and 4f levels.

The number that labels the energy levels in Figure 10-9 is the principal quantum number for the outermost valence electron. These numbers start at 3 in the case of the s, p and d columns, because the quantum states with $n = 1$ and 2 play no part in the optical spectrum of the atom. In the case of the f levels, the lowest level is the 4f level because, according to the rules of quantum mechanics of atoms, λ cannot be bigger than $n-1$, so for f electrons with $\lambda = 3$, the lowest possible value of n is 4. More will be said about this in the next section.

The higher energy levels for each λ value come closer together as the principal quantum number n increases, and the spacing of the energy levels is similar to that of the energy levels of the hydrogen atom. In high quantum states, the outermost electron is only loosely bound to the remainder of the atom, which is a singly charged positive ion.

As the energy levels become closer together for large values of the principal quantum number n, they approach a limiting energy. This energy can be measured from the corresponding series limit in the spectrum, and is the energy required to remove an electron from the atom (with zero kinetic energy), which is called the **ionization energy**.

Close examination of the spectrum of sodium shows that each level (except for the s levels) shown in Figure 10-9 is actually split into two closely spaced levels, which are too close in energy to show separately on the diagram. This small splitting is due to the effects of an internal angular momentum of electrons called **spin**; spin angular momentum is separate from the orbital angular momentum that arises from the motion of the electron around the nucleus. For a classical analogy, think of the earth moving in its orbit around the sun once a year, and at the same time spinning on its polar axis once a day; both motions carry angular momentum. The classical analogy should not be pushed too far however, since the spin angular momentum quantum number is $\pm\frac{1}{2}$, rather than the integer quantum numbers derived from classical rotational motion. The most important aspect of spin at this stage is its effect on the way in which electrons are allowed to fill the energy levels of an atom.

10-6 X-ray spectra of the elements

X-rays have much shorter wavelengths than visible light, often less than 1 nanometre, and (according to the quantum theory) have much higher energies. They have the important property of being able to penetrate solid substances that are opaque to visible light. For this reason, X-rays are used frequently in medical practice, dentistry, and for inspection of baggage at airports. X-rays can be excited by bombarding a substance with high energy electrons. The bombarding electrons knock out an inner shell electron so that an electron from one of the outer shells can drop in energy, causing the emission of high energy photons. The process is illustrated in Figure 10-10. The spectrum of X-rays emitted by an element can be analyzed using crystals as diffraction gratings.

The characteristic spectrum of X-rays emitted by an element is simpler than the optical spectrum of the atom because, as shown in Figure 10-10, transitions can only come from levels that are occupied by electrons. The X-ray spectrum consists of only a few lines rather than thousands of lines. The English physicist Henry Moseley showed that the X-ray spectrum of an element is simply related to its atomic number. For a series of elements with neighbouring values of Z, the spectra are very similar except for being shifted to shorter wavelengths as Z increases. To a good approximation, the characteristic wavelength of a particular line in the spectrum varies with atomic number Z according to the following equation:

$$\lambda = \frac{1}{(aZ + b)^2}$$

where *a* and *b* are constants. This relationship provided a means of demonstrating that the correct order of atomic number in the periodic table is not necessarily the order of increasing molar mass. For instance, cobalt and nickel appear in the periodic table in the reverse order of molar mass. This assignment is based upon the X-ray spectra, and is consistent with the chemistry of these elements. Further, Moseley showed that the number of elements is finite, and that (at that time) only a few elements remained to be discovered in order to complete Mendeleev's periodic table.

X-ray spectroscopy is important historically for establishing experimentally the correct order of atomic number of the elements. It is also the basis for a method of chemical analysis called **X-ray fluorescence**.

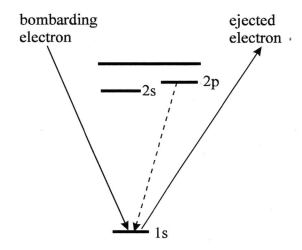

Figure 10-10   The mechanism for emission of X-rays. An energetic electron (shown coming from the left) has enough energy to eject a 1s electron from the atom. This leaves only one electron in the 1s level, and an electron from an upper level (in this case 2p) makes the transition to the 1s level. The 2p→1s transition causes the emission of an X-ray photon which has an energy equal to the difference between the 1s and 2p levels for atoms of that particular element.

10-7 The four quantum numbers for the electrons in an atom

The electrons in an atom occupy quantum states, and we turn now to discuss the four quantum numbers that characterize these states.

The principal quantum number, *n*, corresponds to the quantum number used to identify the energy levels of the hydrogen atom, and is the most important quantum number in determining the energy of the quantum state. In a hydrogen atom the energy is exactly proportional to $1/n^2$, but in other atoms the energy depends in a complicated way upon both *n* and the orbital quantum number λ. There is no *simple* way of calculating the energy levels from theory except in an approximate way; advanced computing techniques have been used to calculate the properties of atoms (and molecules) to very high accuracy, but the calculations are complex.

The orbital quantum number λ determines the angular momentum of the electron in its motion under the electrostatic attraction of the nucleus. It plays a role in determining the energy of a state, but has less influence than the principal quantum number. Both *n* and λ must be specified in order to specify the energy of a quantum state.

Both n and λ take integer values, $n = 1,2,3,...$ and $\lambda = 0,1,2,..,n-1$, the upper limit to λ being one less than the principal quantum number for that state; the theoretical justification of these rules is based upon quantum mechanics beyond the level of this book. Apart from this restriction, n and λ are independent quantities. It is usual to use spectroscopic notation for λ: s for $\lambda = 0$, p for $\lambda = 1$, and so on. Thus the 3p state has a principal quantum number of 3 and an orbital quantum number of 1.

The angular momentum of an electron is a vector quantity (like the linear momentum). The magnitude of the angular momentum is $\sqrt{\lambda(\lambda+1)}(h/2\pi)$ but to specify the direction of this vector requires two more pieces of information, such as two components of the vector. However, as a result of the uncertainty principle mentioned earlier, it is only possible to specify one component of the angular momentum vector with respect to an axis fixed in space. Measuring a second component of angular momentum alters the value of the first component unpredictably. The quantum number associated with one component of angular momentum is called the **magnetic quantum number** and given the symbol m_λ. The corresponding component of angular momentum is $m_\lambda(h/2\pi)$. The magnetic quantum number m_λ takes integer values running from $-\lambda$ through zero to $+\lambda$, a total of $2\lambda+1$ values. This range of values reflects the fact that a component of a vector can be positive or negative, but cannot be longer than the vector itself. The energy of a quantum state does not depend on the magnetic quantum number, unless the atom is in a magnetic field, a situation that we do not consider here. The permitted values of m_λ are summarized in Table 10-2.

Table 10-2 The orbital and magnetic quantum numbers.

symbol	λ	m_λ values	no. of values
s	0	0	1
p	1	$-1, 0, +1$	3
d	2	$-2, -1, 0, +1, +2$	5
f	3	$-3, -2, -1, 0, +1, +2, +3$	7
in general:	λ	$-\lambda, ...-1, 0, +1,...,+\lambda$	$2\lambda+1$

Electrons have an internal spin angular momentum, and the quantum number that determines the magnitude of this angular momentum is always ½ for electrons. But by analogy to the magnetic quantum number there is a quantum number to specify one component of the spin angular momentum. This quantum number is called the **spin quantum number** and given the symbol m_s, which can take one of two values, $+\frac{1}{2}$ and $-\frac{1}{2}$. These two possible spin states are often described as the "spin-up" and "spin-down" states of the electron and may be given special symbols such as α and β, or $\uparrow$ and $\downarrow$.

The spin quantum number has only a very small effect on the energy of a quantum state. If energy were the only consideration, this quantum number would hardly be worth considering for the purposes of chemistry. Yet electron spin has a profound effect on the properties of atoms. The reason for this is that electrons in an atom are indistinguishable in quantum mechanics, and the quantum states of an atom containing more than one electron must reflect this property.

It follows from fundamental symmetry arguments that, because electrons have spin ½, no two electrons in an atom or molecule can have the same set of four quantum numbers. This is called the **Pauli exclusion principle** and applies to all particles with half-integer spin. The exclusion principle is a result of the existence of the spin of the electron.

We will see how the exclusion principle affects the electronic structure of atoms in the next section.

10-8 The electronic configurations of the elements

The quantum state of an individual electron in an atom is usually referred to in the chemical literature as an **atomic orbital**. An orbital is a **wavefunction** which describes the distribution of an electron in space for that quantum state, and is named by analogy with the classical orbit of a particle around a centre of attraction. An atomic orbital is specified by the three quantum numbers n, λ and m_λ described in the last section.

The **electronic configuration** of an atom is a list of the occupied orbitals with the number of electrons in each. The configuration is usually given in abbreviated form with the number of electrons in each orbital indicated by a superscript, and the magnetic quantum number omitted; Table 10-1 lists the ground state configurations for all the elements. In the following we consider the configurations of the elements in order of atomic number: hydrogen, helium, lithium, beryllium, and so on. In this "thought process" an atom of each element is constructed from an atom of the preceding element by addition of a proton to the nucleus and an electron in the space surrounding the nucleus. This procedure is called the **aufbau process** based upon the German word for "building up". The energy of an atom is, in the first approximation, a sum of the energies of all the orbitals that are occupied by electrons. We consider here only the *ground state* of each atom, which is the state with the lowest energy. The ground state is obtained by placing electrons into the lowest energy orbitals, subject to the various restrictions we have discussed.

Orbitals with the same value of the principal quantum number together form a **shell** of electrons. The shells may labelled with a letter based upon X-ray spectroscopy, K-shell for $n = 1$, L for $n = 2$, and so on. Within a shell, orbitals having the same value of the orbital quantum number form a **sub-shell**. A shell or sub-shell that contains the maximum number of electrons permitted by the exclusion principle is called a **full shell** or a **closed shell**.

We begin by listing in detail the quantum numbers for the ground state of hydrogen:

	n	λ	m_λ	m_s
H 1s:	1	0	0	$\pm\frac{1}{2}$

Helium has two electrons, and they are both accommodated in the 1s orbital, but the spins must be opposed, or "paired" because otherwise the two electrons would have the same set of quantum numbers:

		n	λ	m_λ	m_s
He	$1s^2$	1	0	0	$+\frac{1}{2}$
		1	0	0	$-\frac{1}{2}$

Lithium has three electrons, but the 1s shell can accommodate only two electrons. Hence one of the electrons must go into the second shell, and the configuration is as follows:

		n	λ	m_λ	m_s
Li	$1s^2 2s$	1	0	0	$+\frac{1}{2}$
		1	0	0	$-\frac{1}{2}$
		2	0	0	$\pm\frac{1}{2}$

The first shell, with $n = 1$, lies much lower in energy than the second shell, with n = 2, and so is filled first. The third electron, being excluded from the first shell, is placed in the lowest energy sub-shell of the second shell. In this shell, there are two sub-shells, the 2s and the 2p sub-shells, and of these two, the 2s sub-shell has the lower energy. In every shell, the s levels have lower energy than the p levels with the same principal quantum number. This can be seen in the energy level diagram for the sodium atom shown in Figure 10-9.

Although we cannot easily calculate the exact energy levels of the various orbitals, two principles govern the order of the energy levels in most cases. The first principle is that energy increases with the principal quantum number. The second principle is that the size of the spherical space occupied by electrons in a given shell increases with the principal quantum number, n, for that shell; the "inner" shells with low n are very compact and shield the electrons in the "outer" shells from the full nuclear charge. In the hydrogen atom, the 1s level lies much lower than the 2s level. In the lithium atom, the difference in energy is even larger. The electrons in the first shell are closest to the nucleus, and feel the full electrostatic attraction of the nucleus with charge Z = 3. The nucleus and the two tightly bound 1s electrons together have a net charge of +1, and hence the 2s electron behaves similarly to an electron in a hydrogen atom.

The chemical properties of lithium differ very markedly from those of helium. In helium, both electrons are tightly bound to the nucleus, forming a closed shell. Helium is a gas, and forms no stable chemical compounds. Lithium is a metal in which the atoms are bonded together by the interaction of the 2s electrons; the outermost electron can be removed from the atom to form a Li^+ ion with relative ease, so that lithium forms many ionic compounds. The difference in properties between helium and lithium are the result of the exclusion principle, which requires the third electron to go into a 2s orbital rather than the lower energy 1s shell.

The procedure of listing all four quantum numbers for every electron is too clumsy for continuing the discussion up to heavy elements, and an abbreviated notation is needed. It is sufficient for many purposes to list the number of electrons in each shell or sub-shell. In writing down a configuration the sub-shell is specified by the n and λ values and the number of electrons is written as a superscript. Hydrogen has the configuration $1s^1$, helium $1s^2$, and lithium $1s^2 2s^1$. In all atoms (except the first two) there is a core of inner shell electrons, which have lower energy and are more tightly bound than the outer or **valence** electrons. There is usually no need to give the detailed configuration of the inner shells, which can be represented by the chemical symbol of the corresponding noble gas (helium, neon, argon, krypton or xenon), placed in brackets. In this notation, the configuration of lithium is written $(He)2s^1$.

Table 10-3 The Electronic Configurations of the Elements

Z		configuration	Z		configuration	Z		configuration
1	H	$1s^1$	35	Br	$(Ar)4s^23d^{10}4p^5$	69	Tm	$(Xe)6s^24f^{13}$
2	He	$1s^2$	36	Kr	$(Ar)4s^23d^{10}4p^6$	70	Yb	$(Xe)6s^24f^{14}$
3	Li	$(He)2s^1$	37	Rb	$(Kr)5s^1$	71	Lu	$(Xe)6s^24f^{14}5d^1$
4	Be	$(He)2s^2$	38	Sr	$(Kr)5s^2$	72	Hf	$(Xe)6s^24f^{14}5d^2$
5	B	$(He)2s^22p^1$	39	Y	$(Kr)5s^24d^1$	73	Ta	$(Xe)6s^24f^{14}5d^3$
6	C	$(He)2s^22p^2$	40	Zr	$(Kr)5s^24d^2$	74	W	$(Xe)6s^24f^{14}5d^4$
7	N	$(He)2s^22p^3$	41	Nb	$(Kr)5s^14d^4$	75	Re	$(Xe)6s^24f^{14}5d^5$
8	O	$(He)2s^22p^4$	42	Mo	$(Kr)5s^14d^5$	76	Os	$(Xe)6s^24f^{14}5d^6$
9	F	$(He)2s^22p^5$	43	Tc	$(Kr)5s^24d^5$	77	Ir	$(Xe)6s^24f^{14}5d^7$
10	Ne	$(He)2s^22p^6$	44	Ru	$(Kr)5s^14d^7$	78	Pt	$(Xe)6s^14f^{14}5d^9$
11	Na	$(Ne)3s^1$	45	Rh	$(Kr)5s^14d^8$	79	Au	$(Xe)6s^14f^{14}5d^{10}$
12	Mg	$(Ne)3s^2$	46	Pd	$(Kr)4d^{10}$	80	Hg	$(Xe)6s^24f^{14}5d^{10}$
13	Al	$(Ne)3s^23p^1$	47	Ag	$(Kr)5s^14d^{10}$	81	Tl	$(Xe)6s^24f^{14}5d^{10}6p^1$
14	Si	$(Ne)3s^23p^2$	48	Cd	$(Kr)5s^24d^{10}$	82	Pb	$(Xe)6s^24f^{14}5d^{10}6p^2$
15	P	$(Ne)3s^23p^3$	49	In	$(Kr)5s^24d^{10}5p^1$	83	Bi	$(Xe)6s^24f^{14}5d^{10}6p^3$
16	S	$(Ne)3s^23p^4$	50	Sn	$(Kr)5s^24d^{10}5p^2$	84	Po	$(Xe)6s^24f^{14}5d^{10}6p^4$
17	Cl	$(Ne)3s^23p^5$	51	Sb	$(Kr)5s^24d^{10}5p^3$	85	At	$(Xe)6s^24f^{14}5d^{10}6p^5$
18	Ar	$(Ne)3s^23p^6$	52	Te	$(Kr)5s^24d^{10}5p^4$	86	Rn	$(Xe)6s^24f^{14}5d^{10}6p^6$
19	K	$(Ar)4s^1$	53	I	$(Kr)5s^24d^{10}5p^5$	87	Fr	$(Rn)7s^1$
20	Ca	$(Ar)4s^2$	54	Xe	$(Kr)5s^24d^{10}5p^6$	88	Ra	$(Rn)7s^2$
21	Sc	$(Ar)4s^23d^1$	55	Cs	$(Xe)6s^1$	89	Ac	$(Rn)7s^26d^1$
22	Ti	$(Ar)4s^23d^2$	56	Ba	$(Xe)6s^2$	90	Th	$(Rn)7s^26d^2$
23	V	$(Ar)4s^23d^3$	57	La	$(Xe)6s^25d^1$	91	Pa	$(Rn)7s^25f^26d^1$
24	Cr	$(Ar)4s^13d^5$	58	Ce	$(Xe)6s^25d^14f^1$	92	U	$(Rn)7s^25f^36d^1$
25	Mn	$(Ar)4s^23d^5$	59	Pr	$(Xe)6s^24f^3$	93	Np	$(Rn)7s^25f^46d^1$
26	Fe	$(Ar)4s^23d^6$	60	Nd	$(Xe)6s^24f^4$	94	Pu	$(Rn)7s^25f^6$
27	Co	$(Ar)4s^23d^7$	61	Pm	$(Xe)6s^24f^5$	95	A	$(Rn)7s^25f^7$
28	Ni	$(Ar)4s^23d^8$	62	Sm	$(Xe)6s^24f^6$	96	Cm	$(Rn)7s^25f^76d^1$
29	Cu	$(Ar)4s^13d^{10}$	63	Eu	$(Xe)6s^24f^7$	97	Bk	$(Rn)7s^25f^9$
30	Zn	$(Ar)4s^23d^{10}$	64	Gd	$(Xe)6s^24f^75d^1$	98	Cf	$(Rn)7s^25f^{10}$
31	Ga	$(Ar)4s^23d^{10}4p^1$	65	Tb	$(Xe)6s^24f^9$	99	Es	$(Rn)7s^25f^{11}$
32	Ge	$(Ar)4s^23d^{10}4p^2$	66	Dy	$(Xe)6s^24f^{10}$	100	Fm	$(Rn)7s^25f^{12}$
33	As	$(Ar)4s^23d^{10}4p^3$	67	Ho	$(Xe)6s^24f^{11}$	101	Md	$(Rn)7s^25f^{13}$
34	Se	$(Ar)4s^23d^{10}4p^4$	68	Er	$(Xe)6s^24f^{12}$	102	No	$(Rn)7s^25f^{14}$
						103	Lw	$(Rn)7s^25f^{14}6d^1$

Reprinted with permission from CRC Handbook of Chemistry and Physics, 77th edition. Copyright CRC Press, Boca Raton Florida.

Beryllium has a total of four electrons, with the configuration (He)$2s^2$. The two electrons in the closed 2s sub-shell must have their spins paired. Boron, with one more electron, has the configuration (He)$2s^2 2p$ since the extra electron must go into the 2p sub-shell. The 2p orbital has higher energy than the 2s since it is more effectively shielded from the full nuclear charge. For a given principal quantum number n the energy increases with the orbital quantum number λ; this effect can be seen in the energy level diagram for sodium in Figure 10-9. Boron typically shows a valence of 3 in its compounds, which indicates that all the valence electrons are involved in forming chemical compounds. But the element thallium, which lies below boron in the periodic table and has a similar configuration, shows valences of both 1 and 3.

Following boron, the 2p sub-shell is progressively filled. Carbon, (He)$2s^2 2p^2$ shows a characteristic valence of 4 in its compounds, as might be expected from the presence of four valence electrons. The next four elements are nitrogen, (He)$2s^2 2p^3$, oxygen (He)$2s^2 2p^4$, fluorine (He)$2s^2 2p^5$ and neon (He)$2s^2 2p^6$. At this point the 2p shell is full, containing the six electrons allowed by the three possible values of the magnetic quantum number (–1, 0, +1) and the two possible values of the spin quantum number (–½, +½). In the 2p elements, the characteristic valence starts to drop: the usual valence of nitrogen is 3, of oxygen 2, of fluorine 1, and neon zero. The valence is related to the number of **vacancies** or **holes** in the valence shell: if x is the number of electrons in the 2s and 2p sub-shells, the number of holes is equal to $8-x$.

The 2p elements are typical non-metals, and tend to form negative ions or covalent bonds by gaining electrons rather than losing electrons to form positive ions. The number of holes in the 2p sub-shell is equal to the normal valence, which was discussed in Chapter 3. The last element in the second row, neon, has a closed n=2 shell. Neon does not form any stable compounds, and has a valence of zero.

After neon, the next element is sodium for which one electron must be placed in the 3s sub-shell. The arrangement of the energy levels in sodium has already been discussed. The configurations of the elements from sodium up to argon follow exactly the same pattern set as for the elements following lithium, except that the core corresponds to neon rather than helium and the principal quantum number of the valence shell is 3 instead of 2.

Table 10-3 lists the electronic configurations of all the elements, and should be studied in connection with the periodic table.

At this stage the periodicity of the properties of the elements can be understood in terms of the quantum theory of atoms. The properties of the quantum numbers, and the Pauli exclusion principle, lead to the periodic repetition of similar electronic configurations as successive elements are considered. The periodicity in the configurations exactly matches the periodicity in the properties of the elements: it takes 2 electrons to fill an s sub-shell, 6 to fill a p sub-shell, 10 to fill a d sub-shell, and 14 to fill an f sub-shell. These numbers correspond to the widths of the corresponding blocks of the periodic table, shown in Figure 10-11. The trends in the chemical properties of the elements, represented broadly by the structure of the periodic table, reflect the different configurations of the valence shell electrons of the atoms in different parts of the table.

Bohr's theory of the hydrogen atom predicts that the radius of the orbit of the electron is proportional to n^2 and so increases rapidly as n increases. The theory also predicts that, if the nuclear charge were increased from 1 up to Z, the radius of an orbit for a particular value of n is decreased by the factor $1/Z^2$. These predictions are confirmed by modern quantum theory. When combined with the Pauli exclusion principle, the two opposing trends explain in a qualitative way the periodicity in the molar volumes of the elements, which has been noted in Figure 3-3. The molar volume of an element in the solid or liquid state is approximately proportional to the cube of the radius of the atoms.

To summarize, the chemical properties of an element are determined by the number of electrons in the valence shell. Similarities between elements in the same column of the periodic table are the result of closely related configurations of the valence electrons in the atoms. The width of a block of the periodic table corresponding to orbital quantum number λ is equal to $2(2\lambda+1)$, which is the number of possible combinations of the spin and magnetic quantum numbers: the width is 2 for the s-block, 6 for the p-block and so on.

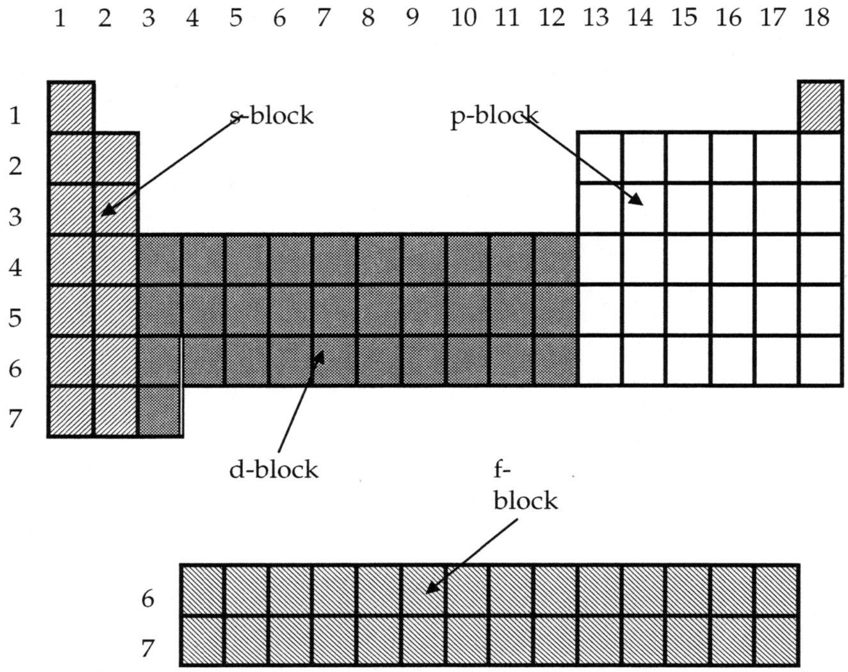

Figure 10-11 The periodic table with blocks shaded corresponding to the sub-shell (s, p, d or f) which is most important in determining chemical properties of the elements in that block. Usually these are the last electrons added in the *aufbau* process. Notice that the group 12 elements Zn, Cd and Hg are d-block elements but not transition elements (see Table3-3)

Within a given shell the principal quantum number is the same, and the energies of the sub shells increase with λ, i.e. in the order s, p, d, f. In agreement with this, the p-block elements follow the s-block elements in the second and third rows of the table. It might be expected that in the third row, the elements of the d-block would follow those of the p-block but this is not the case. The element following argon is not a d-block element. Instead, potassium has the configuration (Ar)4s instead of (Ar)3d, making potassium an alkali metal.

This can be understood on the basis of the relative positions of the energy levels. Examination of the energy levels of the sodium atom in Figure 10-9 shows how these two trends lead to overlapping of the levels in different shells. The energies of the orbitals increase with increasing n and λ, in such a way that the 3d level lies above the 4s level, and hence in the aufbau process the 4s elements precede the 3d elements. In the next row of the periodic table, the 5s elements precede the 4d elements, and in the following row a similar reversal of the 4f and 5d levels occurs.

For almost every element, the order of filling the energy levels in the aufbau process is described by the following sequence:

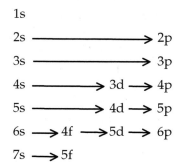

The order of filling follows the pattern of the blocks of the periodic table of the periodic table shown in Figure 10-11. The periodic table can therefore be used to recall the order of filling of the orbitals, keeping in mind that the f-block elements of the bottom two rows belong between the s-block and the d-block. The periodic table is almost always available to students, and it is not necessary to memorize anything more than the locations of the blocks corresponding to each type of orbital.

Following potassium and calcium are the first row of the d-block elements, also called transition metals, which correspond to the filling of the 3d orbitals. Examination of the configurations listed in Table 10-3 shows that there are several irregularities in the order of filling. These occur at chromium and copper, where an electron is transferred from 4s to 3d, resulting in respectively a half-filled and a filled d sub-shell, which leads to a lower energy state for the atom as a whole; similar irregularities are also found in subsequent rows of the table.

Much of the chemistry of the d-block elements involves ions rather than atoms. In forming ions of the d-block elements, the first electrons removed are the s electrons, after which the d electrons are removed; the following list of the configurations of the +2 ions shows that the number of d electrons increases regularly across the row for these ions.

21	Sc^{2+}	(does not occur)	26	Fe^{2+}	$(Ar)3d^6$
22	Ti^{2+}	$(Ar)3d^2$	27	Co^{2+}	$(Ar)3d^7$
23	V^{2+}	$(Ar)3d^3$	28	Ni^{2+}	$(Ar)3d^8$
24	Cr^{2+}	$(Ar)3d^4$	29	Cu^{2+}	$(Ar)3d^9$
25	Mn^{2+}	$(Ar)3d^5$	30	Zn^{2+}	$(Ar)3d^{10}$

Most of the ions of d-block elements do not have closed shells, whereas s-block elements always form closed shell ions such as Na^+ and Ca^{2+}. Ions that do not have closed shells often have interesting magnetic properties and absorb visible light which results in brightly coloured solutions or crystals of compounds of these ions. Many magnetic materials contain transition metals.

Following the filling of the 3d orbitals, the 4p levels are filled, and the right hand end of the row consists of non-metals. The next row of the table, row 5, follows a very similar pattern, which is notable because the 4f levels are not filled until row 6. In row 6, the f-block elements, called the lanthanides, precede the transition metals; there are several irregularities in the order of filling of the levels, which can be seen in Table 10-1. The lanthanide elements commonly form ions of charge +3 and +4, and in forming these ions, the 6s and 5d electrons are removed before the 4f electrons, and the configurations of the ions form a regular sequence. The lanthanide elements are very similar in their chemical properties. The main difference between the ions of different elements is the number of 4f electrons, and because the 4f electrons lie inside the 5p and 5s electrons, they are largely shielded from outside influences. Hence the lanthanide ions resemble each other chemically. Many lanthanide ions have unfilled shells, and are coloured and highly magnetic.

The final row of the periodic table begins with the filling of the 7s shell, and then the 5f shell. The f-block elements are the **actinides.** The actinides are all radioactive, because their nuclei are unstable. The last naturally occurring element in the periodic table is uranium, no. 92, but more than 10 more elements have been manufactured by nuclear processes. Plutonium has been manufactured on an industrial scale for half a century, for the use in nuclear weapons and reactors.

10-9 A closer look at configurations

For some purposes it is necessary to consider the magnetic and spin quantum numbers, because there is more than one way to assign the electrons. For a given value of the orbital quantum number λ there are $2\lambda+1$ possible values of the magnetic quantum number m_λ. For s, p and d orbitals there are respectively 1, 3 and 5 possible values of m_λ which can be represented by "boxes" into which electrons can be classified:

Electrons can be assigned to the orbital boxes using arrows to indicate the spin quantum number, and the exclusion principle is obeyed as long as no box contains more than two electrons and the two electrons in each box have opposite spins. Opposite arrows in the same box represent **paired spins**, and parallel arrows (which must be in different boxes) represent **unpaired spins**. For example, the valence shell configuration of the carbon atom, $2s^2 2p^2$, requires two electrons with paired spins in the s box, and two electrons distributed among the three p boxes. This can be done in a number of ways, of which three are shown:

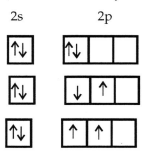

In the first configuration, the two 2p electrons are in the same orbital and must have opposite spins. In the second and third configurations, the 2p electrons are in different boxes and may have opposite or parallel spins without violating the exclusion principle. The three configurations shown are different states of the carbon atom, with different energies; the state represented by the third diagram has the lowest energy. This conforms to a general rule of spectroscopy called **Hund's rule**, that where there is a choice, the state with the lowest energy is the one with the maximum number of unpaired (or parallel) spins.

Some of the irregularities in the configurations of the transition metals can be understood on the basis of Hund's rule. For chromium, for instance, we can compare the following two possible configurations:

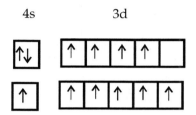

Both configurations contain six valence electrons, but the second has more electrons with unpaired spins. The 4s and 3d orbitals are close enough in energy that it is worthwhile to transfer an electron from the 4s orbital to the 3d orbital in order to increase the number of unpaired spins. It is the second of these two configurations which has the lowest energy, and is listed as the ground state configuration in Table 10-3.

10-10 Ionization energy and electron affinity

If an electron is removed from an atom, a positive ion is formed, and many atoms can also form negative ions by attachment of an electron. In this section we discuss the energies involved in these ionization processes for atoms and ions in the gas phase.

Atoms or ions of different elements which have the same number of electrons are said to be **isoelectronic**. For example, the fluoride ion F^- has 10 electrons, and is isoelectronic with the neon atom Ne. The calcium ion Ca^{2+} has 18 electrons, and is isoelectronic with the argon atom Ar. The N^+ ion has 6 electrons and is isoelectronic with the carbon atom C. For the s- and p-block elements, ions have the same electronic configuration as the isoelectronic neutral atoms, but this is not the case for the d-block elements, as we saw earlier.

The smallest amount of energy required to remove an electron from an atom is called the **ionization energy** E_i of the atom. In the conventional notation of chemical reactions, this process can be written:

$$A(g) \rightarrow A^+(g) + e^-$$

The second ionization energy of an atom is the ionization energy of the ion A^+, i.e. the energy for the process:

$$A^+(g) \rightarrow A^{2+}(g) + e^-$$

The ionization energy of an atom is closely related to its electronic configuration and hence is a strongly periodic property of the elements. Ionization energy is sometimes called ionization potential and quoted in units of electron volts. The conversion factor is 96.4856 kJ/mol per electron volt.

There are several methods of measuring ionization energies. In the spectroscopic method, the limit of a series of spectral lines is identified and the wavelength measured; the ionization energy is the energy of photons of light with the wavelength at the series limit. In another method, the atoms are be bombarded with either electrons of known and controlled energy, or photons of known wavelength, and the onset of ion formation is detected with a mass spectrometer. The latter method can also be used to measure the ionization energy of molecules.

There is no simple way to calculate ionization energies, but sophisticated computing methods now permit calculation of ionization energies with an accuracy comparable to that of experimental data.

Example 10-5   The principal series of lines in the spectrum of the sodium atom is due to transitions between the 3s ground state and the 3p, 4p, 5p, ... excited states. The lines converge to a series limit at a wavelength of 241.3 nm. Calculate the ionization energy of a sodium atom.

At the series limit, the wavelength corresponds to a transition of the valence electron between the 3s ground state and states of infinite principal quantum number. The energy of the photon emitted in this transition is the ionization energy:

$$E_i = h\nu = \frac{hc}{\lambda} = \frac{6.626\times10^{-34}\ \text{J s}\times2.998\times10^{8}\ \text{m s}^{-1}}{241.3\times10^{-9}\ \text{m}} = 8.232\times10^{-19}\ \text{J}$$

Expressed as an energy per mole of atoms, this is:

$$E_i = 8.232\times10^{-19}\ \text{J}\ \times6.022\times10^{23}\ \text{mol}^{-1} = 495.8\ \text{kJ mol}^{-1}$$

The series limit corresponds to excitation of an electron from the 3s ground state to a state of infinite principal quantum number, in which the electron is able to leave the atom. The ionization energy is therefore 49.58 kJ/mol

---

The ionization energies of the elements are plotted as a function of atomic number in Figure 10-12, in which the periodic nature of E_i is apparent. The alkali metals of Group 1 have the lowest value of E_i , and the rare gases of group 18 have the highest value, in each row of the periodic table. E_i decreases in successive rows going down the periodic table, and there is a general trend upwards across each row.

These trends are readily interpreted for the light elements. As the nuclear charge increases across each row, orbitals of a given type (e.g. 2p) become more tightly bound , their energy decreases, and the ionization energy increases. When the limit of 6 electrons in the p orbitals is reached, at the noble gases, the next electron must be placed in an s orbital of the next higher quantum number with higher energy, and so the ionization energy for the next element is much smaller.

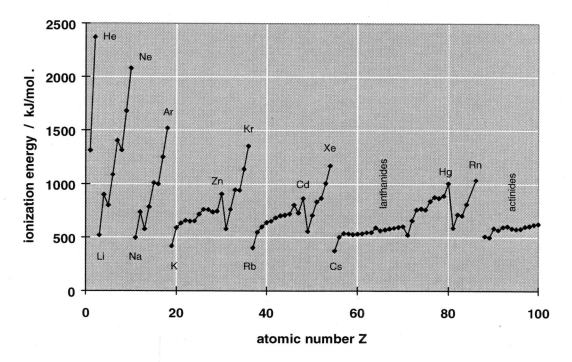

Figure 10-12 The ionization energies of the elements plotted as a function of atomic number. The elements at the beginning and end of each row of the periodic table, plus the elements at the end of the d-blocks and the lanthanide and actinide elements are marked to help with identification.

Closer examination of the sequences Li–Ne and Na–Ar shows that within the general increasing trend there are two small decreases. E_i for boron is slightly lower than for beryllium because in boron the 2s sub-shell is full and the outermost valence electron must go into the 2p sub-shell, of higher energy. A similar effect is seen for aluminum in the third row, and at the end of each row of the d-block elements, when passing from the d-block into the p-block at Group 13.

In the middle of each row of the p-block elements there is another drop in E_i for a different reason. In the second row, for example, the ionization energy of oxygen is slightly less than of nitrogen. The reason is related to Hund's rule. In the nitrogen atom there are three 2p electrons with unpaired spins. In the oxygen atom there are four 2p electrons, so there can only be two electrons with unpaired spins. The effect of the number of unpaired electron spins on the energy, though small, is sufficient to affect the ionization energies measurably. This effect is seen in atoms containing a half-filled sub-shell.

Many atoms form stable negative ions in the gas phase by combining with an electron. The process can be represented by the equation:

$$A(g) + e^- \rightarrow A^-(g).$$

The energy which binds the additional electron is called the **electron affinity**, E_{ea} and may be regarded as the ionization energy of the negative ion, i.e. the energy required for the reverse of the process given above:

$$A^-(g) \rightarrow A(g) + e^-$$

A positive value of E_{ea} indicates that the negative ion is stable. For every element, the electron affinity is smaller than ionization energy because the additional electron in the negative ion is loosely bound and can be removed easily. Figure 10-13 shows electron affinity values for the elements plotted as a function of atomic number. The electron affinity is strongly correlated with electronic structure, and hence is a periodic property of the elements, like the ionization energy. Electron affinities generally increase across each row of the periodic table, like the ionization energies and for the same reason. For the rare gases and some of the group 2 elements, the additional electron would have to go into a new sub-shell, so the negative ion is not stable. Elements with a half-filled shell show lower electron affinity values because addition of another electron reduces the number of unpaired electrons, and the Hund's rule stabilization of the energy is less effective. The halogens have the largest electron affinities, but there is also a pronounced peak in the electron affinity at $Z = 78$ and 79 (platinum and gold) showing that these elements can readily accept an extra electron like the halogens.

Metallic elements characteristically form positive ions, whereas the non-metals form negative ions or covalent molecules. Metals have low ionization energies and low electron affinities, so the loss of an electron is a low energy process while an additional electron in a negative ion is only loosely bound, although negative ions of alkali metals have been observed in some circumstances. In contrast, the non-metallic elements have high ionization energies and high electron affinity: positive ions are hard to form but negative ions are easily formed and stable. The trend from metallic to non-metallic character of the elements across each row of the periodic table can therefore be explained in terms of the trends in ionization energy and electron affinity of the atoms, which in turn is related to the electronic structure of the atoms.

There is also a trend in metallic/non-metallic character of the elements running down a column of the periodic table. Consider for instance the elements of group 14, starting with carbon. Carbon is a non-metal that forms compounds by formation of covalent bonds. Silicon and germanium are semi-metals or semiconductors, while tin and lead are metals which conduct electricity well and form positive ions. This change in metallic character can be correlated primarily to the reduction in the ionization energy in successive rows of the periodic table. The result of these trends is that the most metallic elements are those at the bottom left corner of the periodic table, and the most non-metallic elements are those at the upper right corner. These trends can also be expressed in terms of the **electronegativity** of the elements, to be discussed in the next chapter.

Key concepts

An atom consists of a heavy positively charged nucleus, surrounded by a number of light negatively charged electrons. The charge on the nucleus is equal to the magnitude of the electronic charge multiplied by an integer, which is the atomic number for that particular element.

Planck's analysis of the light emitted by red-hot objects led to the concept of a quantum of light energy, and this proposal was supported by experiments on the photoelectric effect and by experiments on spectroscopy.

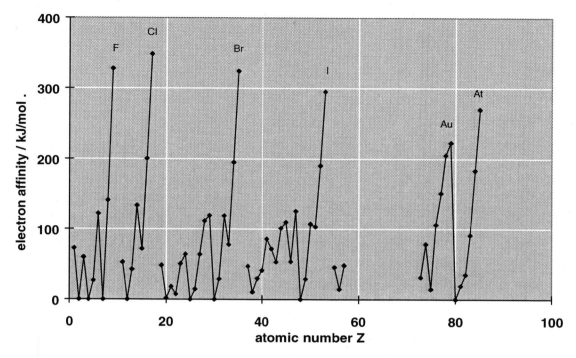

Figure 10-13 The electron affinities of the elements plotted as a function of atomic number.

Atoms can emit and absorb light only at specific sharply defined wavelengths or frequencies, due to the existence of quantized energy levels. The simplest spectrum is that of the hydrogen atom. The energy levels of atoms can be classified using the principal quantum number and the orbital quantum number. There are two more quantum numbers for electrons, the magnetic quantum number and the spin quantum number.

The electrons in an atom are arranged in shells, corresponding to the quantum numbers of the electrons. The quantum numbers not independent, but must satisfy the Pauli exclusion principle. The electronic configuration of an atom is a list of the occupied quantum states of the atom, and the number of electrons occupying each state. The aufbau process of building the atoms of successive elements leads to a natural explanation for the periodic table of the elements.

The ionization energy is the energy required to remove an electron from an atom, and the electron affinity is the energy required to remove an electron from a negative ion. These quantities are strongly correlated with the electronic configuration, and so are periodic properties of the elements.

Review Questions

1. What was the first evidence that atoms contain a heavy nucleus?

2. Who first proposed the existence of quantized energy levels in atoms?

3. Describe the nature of α, β and γ particles.

4. If a set of spectral lines belong to a "series", what do they have in common?

5. Why does hydrogen have the simplest spectrum of any atom?

6. What are the names of the four named series of spectral lines of the alkali metal atoms?

7. What are the names of the four quantum numbers of electrons in atoms?

8. What is an electronic configuration of an atom?

9. What is special about the numbers 2, 8, 18, 36 for atomic structure?

10. What experiment was used to count the elements and assign atomic numbers?

11. What is Hund's rule? In what situation is Hund's rule important?

12. What is the difference between the ionization energy and the electron affinity of an atom?

Problems

1. How many electrons can be accommodated in each of the following sub-shells of an atom?

     (a) 3p sub-shell   (b) 4s sub-shell   (c) 3d sub-shell   (d) 4f sub-shell

2. How many electrons does it take to fill the $n = 3$ shell of an atom?

3. Which of the following atoms has five valence electrons: Na P Mn O Br

4. Hydrogen occurs in the forms H, H^+ and H^- but not H^{2+}. Explain why the last ion does not exist.

5. Which of the following have the same electronic configuration as a noble gas?

$$Cl^-   Mn^{2+}   Fe^{3+}   Na^+   Al^{3+}$$

6. Without consulting the periodic table, calculate the atomic number of the third noble gas (argon) using only the properties of the quantum numbers and the fact that the noble gases have filled shells of electrons.

7. How many electrons are there in the outermost p sub-shell of the group 16 elements, the chalcogens?

8. What is the total number of p electrons in a selenium atom, which belongs in group 16?

9. Using only a periodic table, calculate how many s electrons there are in mercury atom.

10. Using only a periodic table, calculate how many d electrons there are in lead atom.

11. If an element has the electronic configuration $(Xe)4f^{14}5d^{7}6s^{2}$, which one of the following categories does the element belong to?

     (a) halogen   (b) alkaline earth   (c) transition element   (d) rare earth   (e) noble gas

12. Draw a box diagram for the ground state of each of the following atoms, using the configurations given in Table 10-3. In some cases it is possible to draw more than one diagram.

      N   Ti   Cu   Cr   Ne   S

13. Which doubly charged negative ion X^{2-} has the same electronic configuration as argon Ar?

14. Which doubly charged positive ion X^{2+} has the same electronic configuration as Ne?

15. Which positive ion X^{+} has the same electronic configuration as Cl^{-}?

16. What is the characteristic valence shell configuration for the chalcogens, or group 16 elements?

     (a) $ns^{2}np^{2}$ (b) $ns^{2}np^{3}$ (c) $ns^{2}np^{4}$ (d) $ns^{2}np^{5}$ (e) $ns^{2}np^{6}$

17. What is the characteristic valence shell configuration for the group 14 elements?

18. Draw a box diagram for the ground state of each of the following ions, starting from the configurations for the neutral atoms given in Table 10-3. In some cases it is possible to draw more than one diagram.

     Na^{+} Cl^{-} O^{2-} V^{2+} Cu^{+} Cu^{2+} Fe^{3+} In^{+}

19. State which of the following atomic orbital descriptions is impossible. For each case that is impossible, explain which rule about quantum numbers would be broken.

     4s   2d   3f   4d   99s   1p   2p

20. State which of the following atomic configurations is impossible. For each case that is impossible, explain which rule about quantum numbers would be broken.

     (a) $1s^{2}2s^{3}$ (b) $1s^{2}2s^{2}2p^{2}$ (c) $1s^{2}2s^{2}2p^{6}3s^{2}3p^{6}$ (d) $1s^{2}2s^{2}2p^{6}3s^{2}3p^{6}3f^{3}$

     (e) $(Kr)4s^{2}$ (f) $(Kr)5s^{1}$ (g) $(Kr)4d^{12}$ (h) $(Kr)5p^{1}$

21. Which of the following combinations of quantum numbers is not possible for an electron in an atom? For each case that is impossible, explain which rule about quantum numbers would be broken.

	n	λ	m_{λ}	m_{s}
(a)	1	0	0	½
(b)	3	2	−1	−½
(c)	3	3	−2	½
(d)	3	1	2	−½
(e)	6	1	−1	½

22. Calculate the energy of a mole of photons of:

    (a) infrared photons of wavelength 10. micrometres.   [12 kJ]

    (b) red light of wavelength 700. nanometres.   [171 kJ]

    (c) violet light of wavelength 400. nanometres.   [299 kJ]

    (d) ultraviolet light of wavelength 180. nanometres.   [665 kJ]

    (e) X-rays of wavelength 0.154 nanometres.   [777 MJ]

23. A laser produces pulse of light of wavelength 337.1 nanometres. If the energy contained in each pulse of the laser is 10.0 millijoules, how many photons are contained in each pulse?

    [1.70×10^{16}]

24. The ionization energy of a neon atom is 2081 kJ/mol. What is the longest wavelength light that is capable of removing an electron from a neon atom?   [57.5 nm]

25. From equation (10-4), calculate the wavelength of the line of the Balmer series in the spectrum of the hydrogen atom having the *second* longest wavelength.   [486.27 nm]

26. How much energy (in joule) is required to ionize an electron in the $n = 3$ state of a single hydrogen atom?   [2.42×10^{-19} J]

27. The first ionization energy of potassium is 419 kJ mol^{-1}. What is the maximum wavelength of light that can ionize an atom of this element?   [286 nm]

28. Take a good look at the graph of ionization energy versus atomic number shown in Figure 10-12, and memorize the way in which ionization energy varies across each of the first four rows of the periodic table. Using this mental image and a periodic table for reference, choose from each of the following pairs of elements the one which has the higher ionization energy:

    (a) O and Li   (b) Mg and Cl   (c) Kr and Fe   (d) H and He   (e) K and Fe

29. Take a good look at the graph of ionization energy versus atomic number shown in Figure 10-12, and memorize the way in which ionization energy varies going down a column of the periodic table, for the elements of the last six columns, i.e. groups 13 to 18. Using this mental image and a periodic table for reference, choose from each of the following pairs of elements the one which has the higher ionization energy:

    (a) F and Cl   (b) Se and S   (c) Ne and He   (d) C and Si   (e) N and As

30. Which of the following has the smallest ionization energy?

    Na   F   Mg   S   Li$^+$ Al^{3+}

31. The ionization energy of a sodium atom is 496 kJ/mol, and the electron affinity of a chlorine atom is 349 kJ/mol. Calculate the energy of the following electron transfer process:

    $$Na(g) + Cl(g) \rightarrow Na^+(g) + Cl^-(g)$$ [+147 kJ/mol]

32. The ionization energy of a cesium atom is 376 kJ/mol, and the electron affinity of a fluorine atom is 328 kJ/mol. Calculate the energy of the following electron transfer process:

    $$Cs(g) + F(g) \rightarrow Cs^+(g) + F^-(g)$$ [+48 kJ/mol]

33. For each of the following ions, name isoelectronic neutral atom: Li$^+$, C$^+$, P$^+$, O$^-$, Br$^-$, Br$^+$.

11 Molecular Structure

Objectives

After reading this chapter, the student should be able to do the following:

♦ Describe the shapes of simple molecules.

♦ Use bond energies to estimate enthalpy change of reactions.

♦ Define Pauling and Mulliken electronegativity.

♦ Draw Lewis structures for molecules.

♦ Determine oxidation numbers and formal charges from Lewis structures.

♦ Use Lewis structures and VSEPR theory to predict and account for the shapes of molecules.

♦ Describe the effect of lone pairs of electrons on the shapes and chemical properties of molecules.

♦ Define resonance in connection with Lewis structures.

♦ Discuss hydrogen bonding in terms of electronic structure of molecules.

Related topics to review:

Thermochemistry in Chapter 6. Structure of atoms in Chapter 10.

Related topics to look forward to:

Quantum theory in Chapter 12. Acid-base equilibrium in Chapter 14.

11-1 Introduction

A molecule is the smallest unit of a substance that retains all the chemical properties of that substance. If the molecules of a substance are broken down into their constituent atoms, the unique chemical properties of the substance itself are lost.

A molecule consisting of only one atom is called **monatomic**. In this chapter we are concerned with molecules containing more than one atom. Simple molecules contain only a few atoms; **diatomic** molecules contain two atoms, **triatomic** molecules contain three atoms. **Polyatomic** molecules contain more than two atoms. Large molecules may contain tens of atoms, and very large molecules hundreds, thousands or millions of atoms. Polyatomic ions are included in the discussion, since they are simply molecules that are electrically charged.

Molecules are made of atoms, but only a few simple properties of a molecule, such as mass, can be directly related to the properties of the constituent atoms; most chemical properties of a molecule are totally different from those of the separate atoms of the elements. On a more fundamental level, molecules consist of nuclei and electrons, and this is the approach taken in modern quantum chemistry. Through the use of sophisticated software and fast computers quantum chemistry is now able to give a good quantitative account of the properties of some small molecules and their chemical reactions, but this is too fundamental an approach to take at this stage of the discussion.

Both experimental evidence and theoretical calculations show that the inner shell electrons of the atoms are hardly affected by chemical bonding, and that only the outer, or **valence shell,** electrons are involved in the formation of chemical bonds. This is the basis for the concepts of valence and periodicity which have been accepted by generations of chemists.

In this chapter our approach will be to describe molecules in terms of chemical bonds formed by valence shell electrons of the atoms bonded together. In addition to the **bonding electrons**, there may be other valence electrons, called **non-bonding electrons**, which do not form bonds but nevertheless play an important role in determining the properties of the molecule. In the next chapter we will study the quantum description of electrons in molecules.

11-2 The Shapes of Simple Molecules

The shape of a molecule is defined by the relative positions of the atoms that form the molecule. The position of each atom is specified by the position of its nucleus. This is because nucleus of an atom contains almost all of the mass of the atom, and within each atom the electrons are distributed around the nucleus.

We consider first the typical shapes of small molecules consisting of a central atom bonded to several outer atoms of a different element. Figure 11-1 shows the most common shapes of simple molecules, together with typical examples and the names used to describe the shapes.

Diatomic molecules contain two atoms. If the two atoms in a diatomic molecule are of the same element, the molecule is described as **homonuclear**; examples are oxygen O_2 and nitrogen N_2. If the two atoms are different the molecule is described as **heteronuclear**; examples are carbon monoxide CO, hydrogen halides such as hydrogen fluoride HF, and the hydroxide ion OH^-.

Triatomic molecules with two outer atoms form one of two different structures. In the **CO_2 structure**, the three atoms lie in a straight line. The molecule is described as **linear** and the bond angle is 180°. In the **H_2O structure**, the three atoms do not lie in a straight line. The molecule is described as either **angular** or **bent**, and the bond angle is less than 180°. Other examples of bent molecules are sulfur dioxide SO_2, and the nitrite ion NO_2^-.

Molecules with three outer atoms are described as **trigonal**. There are two different structures. In the **BF_3 structure**, the central atom lies in the plane defined by the three outer atoms, and the molecule is described as **trigonal planar**. The bond angles are 1/3 of a circle or 120°, and the entire molecule lies in a single plane. Sulfur trioxide SO_3 , and nitrate ion NO_3^- are other examples of trigonal planar molecules.

In the **NH_3 structure** the central atom lies outside the plane of the three outer atoms, the molecule is described as **trigonal pyramidal**, since it forms a three-sided pyramid; the H–N–H bond angles are less than 120°. Other examples of the NH_3 structure are the hydrides and halides of Group 15 elements, such as phosphine PH_3 and arsenic trichloride $AsCl_3$, and the hydronium ion H_3O^+.

Most molecules with four outer atoms are found to form one of two structures. The most common structure is the **CH_4 structure**, which is a regular tetrahedron and is described as **tetrahedral**. A regular tetrahedron is a three-dimensional figure with four identical faces, each of which is an equilateral triangle. The other structure is the **XeF_4** structure, which is **square planar**; the four outer atoms form a square, and the central atom is located at the centre of the square.

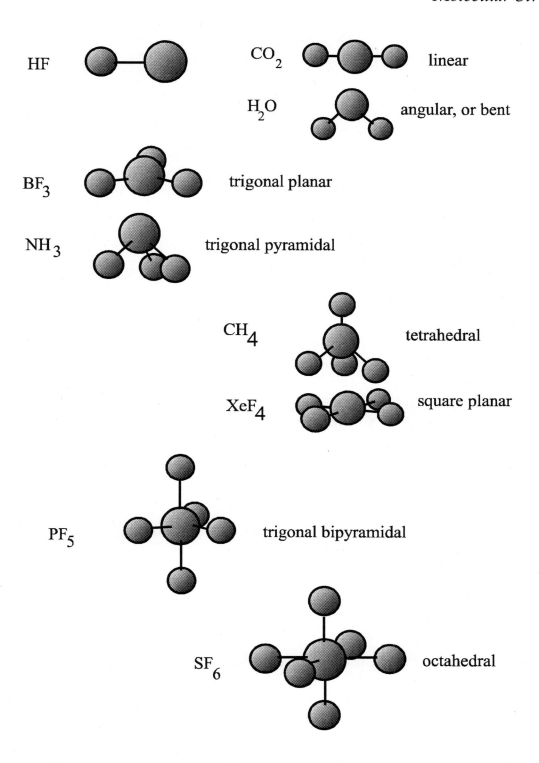

HF

CO_2 linear

H_2O angular, or bent

BF_3 trigonal planar

NH_3 trigonal pyramidal

CH_4 tetrahedral

XeF_4 square planar

PF_5 trigonal bipyramidal

SF_6 octahedral

Figure 11-1 The shapes of simple molecules with a central atom and up to six outer atoms. Spheres of different sizes are used to show the two different types of atom present; the sizes of these spheres are not intended to represent the sizes of the atoms. Straight lines drawn between the spheres represent the chemical bonds between the atoms.

Figure 11-2 shows how a tetrahedral molecule can be drawn in relationship to a cube. The central atom is placed at the centre of the cube, and the outer atoms are placed at the alternate corners of the cube. This diagram is very useful when making calculations on the geometry of a tetrahedral molecule. In a regular tetrahedral molecule, the bond angles are 109.5°, which is called the **tetrahedral angle.** The tetrahedral shape is found throughout structural chemistry, particularly in the structures of organic molecules. Examples are the hydrides and halides of Group 14 elements such as methane CH_4 and carbon tetrachloride CCl_4.

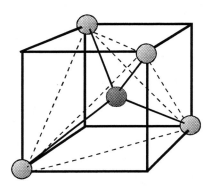

Figure 11-2 A tetrahedral molecule inscribed in a cube. The central atom is at the centre of the cube and the outer atoms are at alternate corners of the cube. The four faces of the tetrahedron are equilateral triangles defined by three of the outer atoms, and are indicated by the dotted lines.

Molecules with five outer atoms typically form the **PF_5 structure**, which is described as **trigonal bipyramidal**. This structure is similar to two triangular pyramids joined with a common triangular face. The structure is related to the trigonal planar structure by the addition of two atoms on each side of the plane, on a line perpendicular to the plane. The three atoms forming the equilateral triangle occupy **equatorial** positions, and the two atoms above and below the triangle occupy **axial** positions. The equatorial bond length is different from the axial bond length. Molecules of the pentahalides of the Group 15 elements such as phosphorus pentachloride PCl_5 have this structure.

Most molecules with six outer atoms form the **SF_6 structure** and are **octahedral** in shape. An octahedron is a figure with six corners and eight triangular faces. Figure 11-3 shows how an octahedron can be drawn in relationship to a cube. The central sulfur atom is located at the centre of the cube, and the outer fluorine atoms are located at the centres of the six faces of the cube. The S–F bond lengths are all equal, and the bond angles are all right angles. Examples of octahedral molecules are other hexafluorides of Group 16 elements, and the hexafluorides of transition metals, such as molybdenum hexafluoride MoF_6.

A few molecules and ions with seven outer atoms are known. The structure is a pentagonal bipyramid, with a planar pentagon of five outer atoms and two axial atoms situated above and below the plane, and so is similar to the trigonal bipyramid structure. An example is iodine heptafluoride, IF_7.

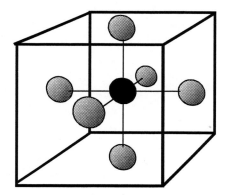

Figure 11-3 A molecule AX$_6$ in the shape of a regular octahedron inscribed in a cube. The atom A is at the centre of the cube and the outer atoms X are at the centres of each square face of the cube. The eight faces of the octahedron are equilateral triangles defined by three of the outer atoms.

11-3 The shapes of organic molecules

The structures of many organic molecules consist of combinations of the AX$_4$, AX$_3$ and AX$_2$ shapes discussed in the previous section. Figure 11-4 shows some of the basic structures.

Methane, CH$_4$, has the tetrahedral structure shown in Figure 11-1. Ethane, C$_2$H$_6$, consists of two methyl groups, –CH$_3$, joined by a carbon-carbon bond, H$_3$C–CH$_3$. The geometry at each carbon atom is tetrahedral, but the bond angles are slightly different from the regular tetrahedral bond angle of 109.47° because the C–C bond is not the same as the C–H bond. Figure 11-4 shows two views of the ethane molecule. The CH$_3$ groups are able to rotate relative to each other about the carbon-carbon single bond; the most stable arrangement is that shown in the view along the C–C bond, in which the hydrogen atoms of each methyl group lie between the hydrogen atoms of the other. This is called the **staggered conformation** of the molecule.

Ethene (or ethylene), C$_2$H$_4$, differs from ethane in having a double bond between the carbon atoms, as indicated by the formula H$_2$C=CH$_2$. The presence of the double bond has two important consequences for the shape of the ethene molecule. First, the placement of the atoms around each carbon atom is trigonal planar and the H–C–H and H–C–C bond angles are both close to the regular trigonal planar angle of 120°. Second, the entire molecule is planar, and one end of the molecule does not rotate with respect to the other end around the C=C double bond. This is perhaps the most important difference between a C–C single bond and a C=C double bond: rotation is possible around a single bond but not around a double bond, under normal circumstances.

Ethyne (or acetylene), C$_2$H$_2$, contains a triple bond between the carbon atoms, HC≡CH. Each end of the molecule is linear and all the atoms lie on a single straight line.

Benzene, C$_6$H$_6$, has a hexagonal structure. The carbon atoms form a hexagonal ring, and there is one hydrogen atom bonded to each carbon atom. The carbon-carbon bonds are of equal lengths, despite the conventional formula showing alternating double and single bonds around the ring; we will have more to say about this later in this chapter. The entire molecule is planar and has a hexagonal shape. The geometry around each carbon atom is trigonal planar and all the bond angles are 120°.

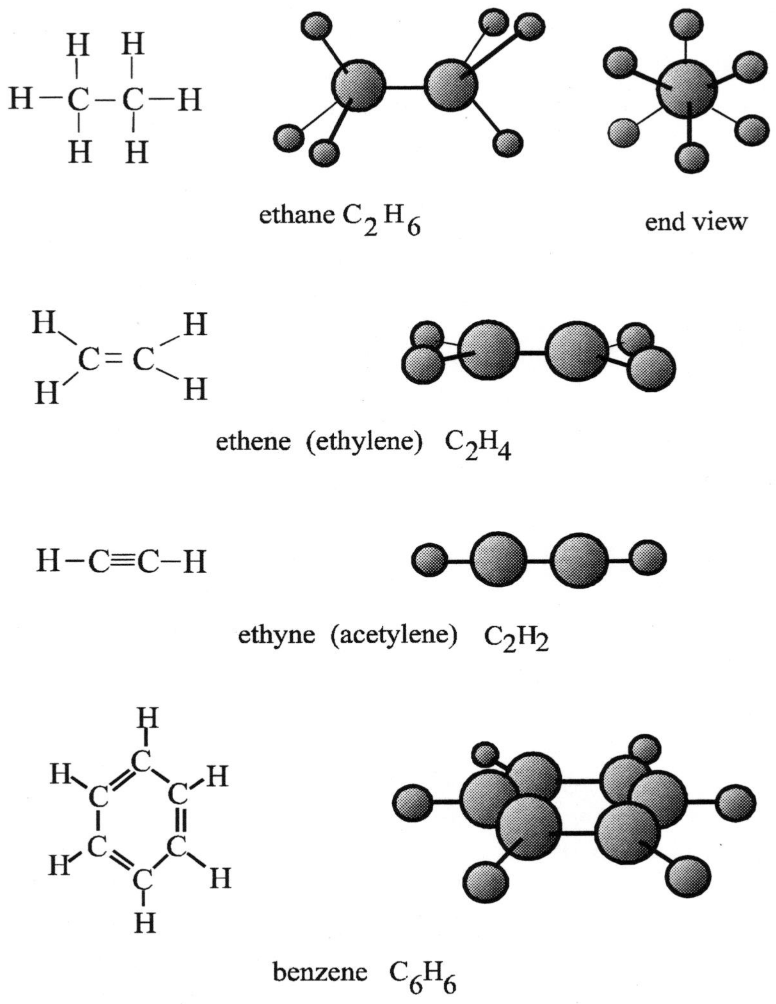

ethane C_2H_6 end view

ethene (ethylene) C_2H_4

ethyne (acetylene) C_2H_2

benzene C_6H_6

Figure 11-4 The characteristic shapes of simple organic molecules.

11-4 Bond lengths and bond angles

The distance between two atoms joined by a chemical bond is called the **bond length**, and the angle between two bonds is the **bond angle**. Various techniques are available for measuring bond lengths and bond angles. Molecular structures in crystals are determined by diffraction experiments using X-rays or neutrons, and a variety of spectroscopic experiments give the structures of molecules in gases and liquids. The most convenient unit for measuring distance on the atomic or molecular scale is the Ångstrom unit, abbreviated Å and equal to 10^{-10} metre or 0.1 nanometre.

For a given type of bond in similar bonding situations, bond lengths and bond angles do not vary greatly between molecules. For example, the C–H bond length varies by less than 2 per cent from 1.09 Å in the molecules of many hydrocarbons and their derivatives. In molecules containing carbon atoms bonded to four other atoms, the bond angles in most cases deviate by at most a few degrees from the tetrahedral angle of 109.5°. In the absence of other information, these values may be taken as good estimates of the likely bond lengths and angles when considering the geometry of other molecules containing similar bonds.

Table 11-1 Typical bond lengths

Bond lengths are given in Ångstrom units.

Bond type	Bond length/Å	Bond type	Bond length/Å
C–H	1.09	C–N	1.47
C–C	1.53	C–F	1.38
C=C	1.34	C–Cl	1.77
C≡C	1.20	O–H	0.96
C–O	1.42	N–H	1.02
C=O	1.21	P–H	1.42

Table 11-1 lists typical bond lengths for some common types of chemical bond, which can be used in making models or drawings of many molecules if the bond lengths in a particular molecule are not known. Models with fixed bond lengths and bond angles are often helpful in visualizing the three dimensional shapes and other features of organic molecules, and commercial model-building kits are used for this purpose.

The differences between single, double and triple bonds should be noted carefully. Double bonds are shorter than single bonds, and triple bonds are shorter still, as shown by the data for carbon-carbon and carbon-oxygen bonds.

The bond angles around a carbon atom bonded to four other atoms usually fall within a few degrees of 109.5°, the angle in a regular tetrahedron. Where there is a double bond to a carbon atom, as in ethene, the geometry is normally trigonal planar, with bond angles close to 120°. Where there is a triple bond to a carbon atom, as in ethyne, the geometry is linear with a bond angle of 180°.

11-5 Bond energy

In Section 6-6 we divided the energy of a chemical system into two parts: the thermal energy and the chemical energy. For molecular substances, the chemical energy is the energy associated with chemical bonds, and the energy change in a chemical reaction is due to the breaking of chemical bonds in the reactant molecules and the formation of new bonds in the product molecules.

We now consider whether there is a specific energy associated with a particular type of chemical bond. If true, then the thermochemistry of molecular compounds would be greatly simplified. Analysis of thermochemical data shows that this is in fact the case, to within reasonable limits of error. The chemical energy of a particular type of bond is approximately the same in different molecules.

The energy required to break the chemical bond in a diatomic molecule can be calculated readily from enthalpies of formation from the list of thermochemical data in Appendix 1. Consider the hypothetical **atomization reaction** in which a hydrogen molecule is decomposed into atoms:

$$H_2(g) \rightarrow 2\,H(g)$$

The enthalpy change of atomization is $\Delta H^o = -(0.0) + 2 \times (217.965) = 435.930\ kJ/mol$. This enthalpy change will be referred to as the **exact bond energy** of the H–H bond, since the difference between enthalpy change and energy change is smaller than other uncertainties in the calculations. This energy is the exact energy of the H–H bond, and is not applicable to any other molecule. Table 11-2 lists the exact bond energies for a number of diatomic molecules calculated in this way.

Table 11-2 Exact bond energies in diatomic molecules

Bond energies are in kilojoules per mole of bonds.

Bond	Bond energy	Bond	Bond energy	Bond	Bond energy
H–H	436.0	H–F	569.9	F–F	158.8
O=O	498.4	H–Cl	431.6	Cl–Cl	242.6
N≡N	945.3	H–Br	366.4	Br–Br	192.8
C≡O	1076.5	H–I	298.4	I–I	151.1
C=C	607	Si–Si	326.8	C-Si	451.5

Reprinted with permission from CRC Handbook of Chemistry and Physics, 77th edition. Copyright CRC Press, Boca Raton, Florida, U.S.A.

The situation in polyatomic molecules is more complicated because they are so many and varied in their properties. One approach is to consider the enrgy required to break specific bonds. For example, the exact bond energy of a single $H_3C–H$ bond in the methane molecule is 438.5 kilojoules per mole of bonds. This information is useful in considering reactions of methane, but does not, by itself, give any information about C–H bonds in other molecules. The exact bond energy of a single $H–C_2H_5$ bond in ethane is 422.8 kJ/mol, which is different from the value in methane. This shows that the C–H bond energy varies somewhat from one molecule to another. This approach is often used in courses on organic and inorganic chemistry.

Instead of pursuing this approach, we focus on **average bond energies** which can be used for approximate calculations for a wide range of molecules. This approach gives a simple but effective way to summarize a large amount of data on many different molecules. Consider the atomization reaction in which a methane molecule is decomposed completely into atoms:

$$CH_4(g) \rightarrow C(g)\ +\ 4\,H(g)$$

$$\Delta H^o = -(-74.81) + (+716.682) + 4 \times (217.965) = +1663.35\ kJ/mol$$

In this atomization process, four C–H bonds are broken and so the average bond energy for a C–H bond is a quarter of this, or 415.8 kJ/mol.

It should be noted that the average bond energy of a C–H bond differs from the exact bond energy for a $H_3C–H$ bond in the methane molecule, 438.5 kJ/mol. This is because if the hydrogen atoms are removed one by one, the structure of the remaining fragment of the molecule changes with the loss of each hydrogen atom.

The corresponding process of breaking a molecule of ethane up into atoms is:

$$C_2H_6(g) \rightarrow 2\,C(g) + 6\,H(g)$$

$$\Delta H^o = -(-84.68) + 2 \times (+716.682) + 6 \times (217.965) = +2825.83 \text{ kJ / mol}$$

The atomization process involves breaking six C–H bonds, and one C–C bond. If the energy of the C–H bonds in ethane is the same as in methane, the energy required to break six of them is 6×415.8 kJ/mol, Hence the energy of atomization is $+6 \times 415.8 + E_b(C-C)$, where $E_b(C-C)$ is the energy required to break the C–C bond. This must be equal to the energy of atomization calculated above, $+2825.83$ kJ/mol. Solving for the C–C bond energy, we find that $E_b(C-C) = 331.0$ kJ/mol.

Working in this way, bond energies can be calculated by combining thermochemical data for different molecules. While it is not possible to calculate unique values that fit all cases exactly, average bond energies have been estimated which fit a wide range of molecules. These average values are of necessity approximate, and the error involved has to be judged by comparison with thermochemical data, which is based firmly on experiment.

Table 11-3 lists average bond energies for some common types of bond. The C=O bond energy in CO_2 is sufficiently different from that in organic molecules that a special value is given. Average bond energies can be used for approximate thermochemical calculations if data based on experiment is not available for some of the molecules involved in a reaction. Such calculations do not include latent heats of vaporization, so if condensed phases are involved the appropriate latent heats of vaporization must be included separately.

Table 11-3 Average bond energies in polyatomic molecules

Energies are in kilojoules per mole of bonds.

Bond	Bond energy	Bond	Bond energy	Bond	Bond energy
C–H	414	C–F	441	O–H	464
C–C	347	C–Cl	326	O–O	146
C=C	599	C–Br	276	N–H	389
C≡C	829	C–I	240	N–N	263
C–N	285	Si–H	393	N–Cl	201
C≡N	866	Si–Si	340	P–H	318
C–O	335	Si–O	450	P–Cl	318
C=O in CO_2	804	Si–Cl	380	S–S	264
C=O (organic)	700			S–H	340

Average bond energies can often be used to estimate the enthalpy change of a reaction, even if ΔH_f° is not known for one or more of the substances taking part. In doing this calculation, the enthalpy change of reaction ΔH contains two kinds of contributions:

(a) Contributions for all the bonds in the reactant molecules which are broken. These are positive since energy must be put into the system to break the bonds.

(b) Contributions for all the bonds formed in the product molecules. These are negative since energy is released upon bond formation.

The calculation can be summarized in the following formula:

$$\Delta H \approx \sum_{\substack{\text{bonds} \\ \text{broken}}} \text{bond energies} - \sum_{\substack{\text{bonds} \\ \text{formed}}} \text{bond energies} \qquad \text{(11-1)}$$

Example 11-1 Estimate the enthalpy of combustion of gaseous n-pentane to give carbon dioxide and water vapour using bond energies and compare with the value calculated from thermochemical data.

The equation for the reaction is $C_5H_{12}(g) + 8\ O_2(g) \rightarrow 5\ CO_2(g) + 6\ H_2O(g).$

A molecule of n-pentane, shown below, has four C–C bonds and twelve C–H bonds.

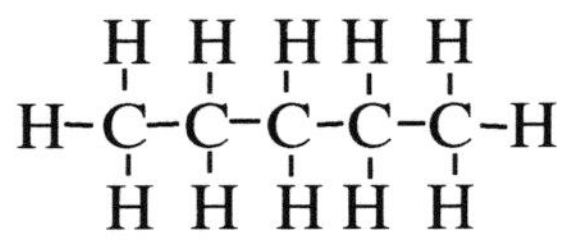

$$\begin{array}{c} \text{H H H H H} \\ | \ | \ | \ | \ | \\ \text{H--C--C--C--C--C--H} \\ | \ | \ | \ | \ | \\ \text{H H H H H} \end{array}$$

Hence the reaction can be summarized in the following operations on the chemical bonds, with the corresponding bond energies taken from Tables 11-3 and 11-4.

Bonds broken:	8 O=O	$+8 \times 498.4 =$	+3987 kJ/mol
	4 C–C	$+4 \times 347\ \ =$	+1388 kJ/mol
	12 C–H	$+12 \times 414 =$	+4968 kJ/mol
Bonds formed:	10 C=O	$-10 \times 804 =$	−8040 kJ/mol
	12 O–H	$-12 \times 464 =$	−5568 kJ/mol

The estimated total enthalpy change is the sum of these contributions: $\Delta H° \approx -3265$ kJ/mol.

For comparison, the enthalpy change calculated from enthalpy of formation data is:

$$\Delta H^o = -\Delta H_f^o\,(C_5H_{12}\,(g)) + 5\Delta H_f^o\,(CO_2\,(g)) + 6\Delta H_f^o\,(H_2O(g)) = -3272 \text{ kJ / mol}$$

The two answers to this question are in reasonable agreement. Of the two answers, the second one based on enthalpy changes of formation is the more reliable since it is based upon experimental data for the specific substances involved in the reaction. However, the calculation using average bond energies gives a result which is good enough for many purposes, and could be carried out even if the enthalpy change of formation of n-pentane were not known.

A measure of the likely errors in calculations based on average bond energies is the comparison of structural isomers of hydrocarbons. The result of the bond energy calculation in Example 11-2 would be the same if n-pentane were replaced by one of the other two isomers of pentane, namely 2-methylbutane and 2,2-dimethyl propane, since these isomeric molecules have equal numbers of the same types of bond. However data in Appendix 1 shows that the enthalpy change of formation for these three hydrocarbons cover a range of about 20 kJ/mol, and this indicates that uncertainties in calculations based on average bond energies are at least as large as this.

The two alternative methods of calculation can be compared by means of the diagram in Figure 11-5. In both methods the overall reaction is carried out by way of an intermediate stage in which reactants are converted to elements. In the calculation using enthalpy change of formation, the elements in the intermediate stage are in their standard state, which may be a solid, liquid or gas consisting of diatomic or larger molecules. In the bond energy method, which is limited to reactants and products in the gas phase, the elements in the intermediate stage are in the form of separate atoms in the gas phase.

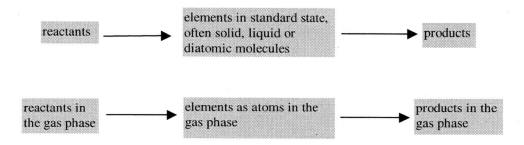

Figure 11-5   The upper diagram shows the calculation of the enthalpy change of reaction by means of standard enthalpy change of formation data for reactants and products, and is similar to Figure 6-8; in the intermediate stage, the elements are in their standard states. The lower diagram shows the calculation by means of the average bond energy data, involving conversion of the reactants to atoms in the gas phase, which is not the standard state for any elements except the noble gases.

11-6 Electronegativity

A covalent bond consists of electron pairs shared between two atoms. If the two atoms in a diatomic molecule are identical, then the bonding electrons are shared equally, but if the atoms are of different elements, then the bonding electrons are not shared equally, and some electric charge is transferred from one atom to the other. The extent to which charge is transferred depends on the nature of the atoms bonded together.

If the amount of charge transferred within a diatomic molecule is comparable to the charge on an electron, then it is reasonable to regard the molecule as a pair of ions held together by electrostatic energy. This is the case in a molecule of sodium chloride in the gas phase, which is best represented by the formula Na^+Cl^-.

The extent of charge transfer in diatomic molecules can be determined by measuring the **dipole moment** of the molecule, which is the product of the charge transferred Q and the distance l between the atoms:

$$\mu = Ql \qquad \qquad (11\text{-}2)$$

The dipole moment can be measured spectroscopically and is expressed in the S.I. unit of coulomb metre. For example in the Na^+Cl^- molecule the bond length l is 2.3609 Å, or 2.3609×10^{-10} m, and the dipole moment is equal to 3.00×10^{-29} C m. It follows that the amount of charge transferred is:

$$Q = \frac{3.00 \times 10^{-29} \text{ C m}}{2.3609 \times 10^{-10} \text{ m}} = 1.27 \times 10^{-19} \text{ C} = 0.79e$$

where e is the charge of an electron.

For most molecules the extent of charge transfer from one atom to another is less than one electron, and can be indicated in a chemical formula by placing partial charges δ+ and δ– on the atoms. The hydrogen chloride molecule for instance can be represented by the formula $^{\delta+}H–Cl^{\delta-}$ to show unequal sharing of the bonding electrons by the H and Cl atoms.

The dipole moment is a vector quantity, as shown in Figure 11-18, and in more complicated molecules the overall dipole moment of the molecule is the vector sum of contributions from all the bonds in the molecule. For example in the water molecule, which is angular, there is a net dipole moment, whereas in the linear carbon dioxide molecule the bond contributions are equal and opposite and there is no net dipole moment.

The dipole moment of the water molecule is important in the modern kitchen. A microwave oven works by coupling a strong oscillating electric field to the dipole moments of the water molecules. As the water molecules in the food rotate, they absorb electromagnetic energy and convert it into thermal energy, which raises the temperature of the food.

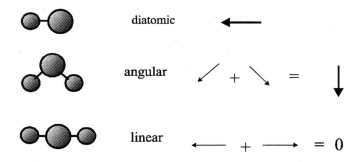

Figure 11-6 The vector addition of bond contributions to the overall molecular dipole moment. The dipole moment of an angular molecule such as water is non-zero, whereas in a linear molecule like carbon dioxide (lowest diagram) there is exact cancellation and the dipole moment is zero.

The extent of charge transfer between two atoms bonded together allows us to estimate the relative ability of each atom to attract electrons. For this purpose, the American chemist Linus Pauling introduced the concept of **electronegativity**. There is more than one way to define and calculate electronegativity, but despite some ambiguity it remains an important concept.

Pauling based his measure of electronegativity on bond energies. Consider two atoms A and B that form homonuclear diatomic molecules A_2 and B_2 as well as the heteronuclear molecule AB. Consider the following reaction in which the heteronuclear molecule is broken up into two homonuclear molecules:

$$AB(g) \rightarrow \tfrac{1}{2} A_2(g) + \tfrac{1}{2} B_2(g)$$

The enthalpy change of the reaction can be written in terms of bond energies E_b:

$$\Delta H = E_b(A-B) - \tfrac{1}{2}E_b(A-A) - \tfrac{1}{2}E_b(B-B)$$

If the atoms A and B are of equal "electron attracting power", then it should make no difference to the energy whether the atoms bonded together are like or unlike, and so the enthalpy change ΔH should be zero. Hence for atoms of equal electronegativity, the enthalpy change should be zero: $\Delta H = 0$. If this is the case, then the A–B bond energy is the arithmetic mean of the A–A and B–B bond energies:

$$E_b(A-B) = \tfrac{1}{2}\{E_b(A-A) + E_b(B-B)\}$$

For nearly all pairs of elements, the enthalpy change ΔH for the above reaction is positive, and the A–B bond energy is larger than the arithmetic mean of the A–A and B–B bond energies. The excess bond energy is ascribed to partial electron transfer from one atom to the other, which makes the A–B bond stronger than it would otherwise be.

In refining this concept, it was found that the best measure of electronegativity was given by comparing the A–B bond energy to the geometric mean, rather than the arithmetic mean, of the A–A and B–B bond energies. The difference x_A-x_B between the Pauling electronegativities x_A and x_B of elements A and B can be estimated from bond energies using the following equation:

$$k(x_A - x_B)^2 = E_b(A-B) - \sqrt{E_b(A-A)E_b(B-B)} \tag{11-3}$$

where k is a constant with the value $k = 125$ kJ/mol. Electronegativity is dimensionless and has no units.

Calculations based on this formula yield only the difference between the electronegativities of the two elements concerned, and comparisons of many different pairs of elements must be made to determine the electronegativities of all the elements.

Example 11-2 Calculate the difference in electronegativities for hydrogen and chlorine from exact bond energy data in Table 11-2.

From Table 11-2, $E_b(H-H) = 436.0$ kJ/mol, $E_b(Cl-Cl) = 242.6$ kJ/mol and $E_b(H-Cl) = 431.6$ kJ/mol. Substituting these values in formula (11-3),

$$431.6 = \sqrt{436.0 \times 242.6} + 125(x_H - x_{Cl})^2$$

from which the magnitude of the difference is $|x_H - x_{Cl}| = 0.92$.

The American chemist Robert S. Mulliken proposed a different method of determining electronegativities based upon the properties of the individual atoms involved in the bond. Consider the transfer of an electron from one atom to the other in the gas phase by ionizing one atom and attaching the electron to the other. The enthalpy change can be calculated from the ionization energy E_i of atom A and the electron affinity E_{ea} of atom B:

$$A(g) \rightarrow A^+(g) + e^- \qquad \Delta H = E_i(A)$$

$$e^- + B(g) \rightarrow B^-(g) \qquad \Delta H = -E_{ea}(B)$$

so that for the electron transfer,

$$A(g) \; + \; B(g) \; \rightarrow A^+(g) \; + B^-(g) \qquad \qquad \Delta H = E_i(A) - E_{ea}(B).$$

If the electron were transferred in the other direction, the process would be:

$$A(g) \; + \; B(g) \; \rightarrow A^-(g) \; + B^+(g) \qquad \qquad \Delta H = E_i(B) - E_{ea}(A).$$

If the electronegativities of the two atoms are equal, then the energies of these two processes would be the same, so we could write:

$$\Delta H = E_i(A) - E_{ea}(B) = E_i(B) - E_{ea}(A).$$

Collecting the terms for each atom together, this leads to the equation:

$$E_i(A) + E_{ea}(A) = E_i(B) + E_{ea}(B).$$

We conclude that, if ΔH for transfer of an electron between two atoms A and B is the same regardless of the direction of transfer of the electron, then $E_i + E_{ea}$ is the same for both atoms. This suggests that $E_i + E_{ea}$ should give a measure of the electronengativity of an atom. The Mulliken electronegativity is equal to this energy divided by a constant:

$$x = \frac{E_i + E_{ea}}{k'} \qquad \qquad (11\text{-}4)$$

where $k' = 500$ kJ/mol. The advantage of this scale is that it can be calculated for each element from the properties of that element alone, without reference to other elements. Mulliken electronegativities agree reasonably well with the Pauling values for most elements, even though the two calculations are based on entirely independent data. This supports the validity of the concept of electronegativity.

Example 11-3   Calculate the Mulliken electronegativity of carbon given that the ionization energy is 1087 kJ/mol and the electron affinity is 122 kJ/mol.

Substituting the ionization energy and electron affinity into equation (11-4), the electronegativity is:

$$x = \frac{1087 + 122}{500} = 2.4$$

Notice that the energy units cancel. This result may be compared with the Pauling value of 2.5 for carbon given in Table 11-4.

Table 11-4 Pauling electronegativities of the main group elements

	1	2		13	14	15	16	17	18
	1A	2A		3A	4A	5A	6A	7A	8A
1	H 2.1								He
2	Li 1.0	Be 1.5		B 2.0	C 2.5	N 3.0	O 3.5	F 4.0	Ne
3	Na 0.9	Mg 1.2		Al 1.5	Si 1.8	P 2.1	S 2.5	Cl 3.0	Ar
4	K 0.8	Ca 1.0		Ga 1.6	Ge 1.8	As 2.0	Se 2.4	Br 2.8	Kr
5	Rb 0.8	Sr 1.0		In 1.7	Sn 1.8	Sb 1.9	Te 2.1	I 2.5	Xe
6	Cs 0.7	Ba 0.9		Tl 1.8	Pb 1.8	Bi 1.9	Po 2.0	At 2.2	Rn

Table 11-4 lists Pauling electronegativities for the s and p block elements. Electronegativities are strongly correlated with position in the periodic table. The most electronegative elements are the non-metals in the upper right hand corner of the periodic table, and these are the ones which form negative ions most easily. Electronegativities decrease from element to element down each column, and to the left along each row. The metals have low electronegativities and characteristically form positive ions.

When a chemical bond is formed between elements of different electronegativities, the bonding electrons are not shared equally between the two atoms. The amount of charge transferred from one atom to the other increases as the difference between the electronegativities of the atoms increases. If the difference in electronegativities is greater than about 2.0, then the bond is largely ionic and an electron is transferred from the less electronegative atom to the more electronegative atom. The resulting ions are held together by electrostatic attraction to form a molecule or (more commonly) an ionic solid.

For example, the fluorides of most metals are ionic, since the electronegativity differences between fluorine and the metals are larger than 2.0. Bonds between the other halogens and metals are partially covalent, with the ionic character of the bonds decreasing from chlorine to bromine to iodine, because of the decreasing electronegativity of the halogens.

If the difference between the electronegativities of two atoms is about 1.0, then the bond between them is primarily covalent, with a shared pair of electrons, although there is still appreciable ionic character. If the electronegativity difference is less than 0.5, then the ionic character of the bond is small, and the electron pair forming the bond is shared about equally between the atoms.

11-7 Lewis structures

The theory of chemical bonding in molecules based on electronic configurations began with the work of the American chemist Gilbert N. Lewis in 1916. Naturally some modifications and developments of the theory have taken place over the years, but after more the 80 years, the Lewis theory of molecular structure remains an important part of the language of chemistry.

The Lewis theory is crude in comparison with the modern quantum theory of bonding, but it provides a powerful connection between the concept of valence, and the electronic structure of atoms. It provides a simple explanation for the periodicity of the normal valences of the elements, and provides a picture of how single, double and triple bonds are formed. With some extensions, it can be used to predict the shapes of molecules and their chemical properties. All of this is achieved with a model that requires nothing beyond pencil and paper and a knowledge of the periodic table.

The essence of the theory is that a covalent bond consists of a shared pair of electrons, or several pairs of electrons in the case of double or triple bonds. While exceptions to this statement are known, the study of chemical bonds begins with bonds formed from shared pairs of electrons.

The outer shell of electrons in an atom is called the **valence shell**. In the s- and p-block elements, the valence shell is the one with the highest principal quantum number. The number of electrons in the valence shell of a p-block atom is equal to the total number of s and p electrons. For instance, sulfur has six valence electrons: two s electrons and four p electrons; this can be determined quickly from the place of sulfur in the periodic table. The elements of the first two rows with their valence electrons indicated as dots are shown below.

$$H \cdot \quad He:$$

$$Li \cdot \quad \cdot Be \cdot \quad \cdot \dot{B} \cdot \quad \cdot \dot{C} \cdot \quad \cdot \dot{N}: \quad \cdot \ddot{O}: \quad \cdot \ddot{F}: \quad :\ddot{N}e:$$

For the first four elements of the second row, the electrons are shown as being unpaired, and no distinction is made between the s and p electrons because, in most compounds of these elements, all valence electrons are involved in the formation of chemical bonds. For the fifth element, N, there are five valence electrons but only four orbitals to hold them (one 2s and three 2p orbitals) so two of the electrons must occupy the same orbital and (according to the exclusion principle) have paired spins. Hence the diagram shows one pair of electrons and three unpaired electrons. Obviously, the number of unpaired electrons is equal to the number of holes in the valence shell. The normal valence of nitrogen is three, which is equal to the number of unpaired electrons in the atom. The subsequent elements (O, F and Ne) have respectively two, one and zero unpaired electrons, in agreement with their normal valences.

A molecular structure drawn with dots to represent the valence shell electrons is called a **Lewis structure**. The essential feature of a covalent bond is the sharing of pairs of valence electrons between atoms. If the shared electrons are counted together with the other valence shell electrons, the formation of chemical bonds results in an increase in the number of electrons associated with each atom. The known common valences of the elements suggest that enough bonds are formed to bring each atom up to a full valence shell. This implies that, for elements at the right hand side of the periodic table, the number of single bonds formed by sharing electron pairs is equal to the number of holes in the valence shell of the atom concerned.

The hydrogen molecule H_2 is formed out of two hydrogen atoms, which have one electron each. The two shared electrons are represented by a pair of dots placed between the symbols for the atoms:

$$H:H$$

The valence shell of the hydrogen atom, with a principal quantum number $n = 1$, can accommodate a maximum of two electrons, and since both electrons are counted for each atom, each hydrogen atom in the H_2 molecule achieves a full valence shell by forming a single bond. Atoms of the next element, helium, have a full valence shell themselves, and so helium is chemically inert and does not form chemical bonds.

For atoms of the second row of the periodic table, the maximum number of s and p electrons in any shell is eight, made up of two 2s electrons and six 2p electrons and these elements form enough chemical bonds to share the unpaired electrons in the valence shell. This results in an "octet" of eight electrons around each atom. The application of the theory is best illustrated by starting at the right hand end of the second row of the periodic table, and working to the left. Neon has eight electrons in its valence shell and does not form chemical bonds. Fluorine has seven electrons in the valence shell, of which one is unpaired. By sharing the unpaired electron with another atom, a single bond is formed and an octet of electrons around the fluorine atom is reached. This can be seen in the structures of hydrogen fluoride HF and fluorine F_2:

$$H \!:\! \ddot{\underset{..}{F}} \!: \qquad\qquad :\!\ddot{\underset{..}{F}}\!:\!\ddot{\underset{..}{F}}\!:$$

Oxygen, with six valence electrons and two holes in the valence shell, can form two single bonds. An example is the water molecule H_2O in which two bonds join the two hydrogen atoms to the oxygen atom. Nitrogen has five valence electrons, and with three holes in the valence shell, has a valence of three, as in ammonia, NH_3. Carbon has four electrons and four holes in the valence shell and can form four single bonds, as in methane, CH_4. Lewis structures for these molecules are as follows:

$$H\!:\!\overset{\displaystyle H}{\underset{\displaystyle H}{\ddot{C}}}\!:\!H \qquad H\!:\!\overset{\displaystyle H}{\underset{\displaystyle H}{\ddot{N}}}\!: \qquad H\!:\!\overset{..}{\underset{\displaystyle H}{\ddot{O}}}\!:$$

In these Lewis structures there are two types of electron pairs. Electron pairs shared between atoms are called **bonding pairs**, and those not shared are called **non-bonding pairs** or **lone pairs**. The bonding pairs form the bonds between the atoms, and the lone pairs, although not directly involved in the bonding, nevertheless influence the shape and chemical reactivity of some molecules.

Multiple bonds are represented by multiple pairs of shared bonding electrons. In the oxygen molecule O_2, the normal valence of two for oxygen suggests that two pairs of electrons be assigned to form a double bond, leaving two non-bonding pairs on each atom. In the nitrogen molecule N_2, the normal valence of three for nitrogen suggests three pairs of bonding electrons, leaving one non-bonding pair on each atom. The Lewis structures for F_2, O_2 and N_2 are as follows:

$$:\!\ddot{\underset{..}{F}}\!:\!\ddot{\underset{..}{F}}\!: \qquad\qquad \ddot{\underset{..}{O}}\!::\!\ddot{\underset{..}{O}} \qquad\qquad :\!N\!:::\!N\!:$$

When we discuss the electronic structures of these three molecules in terms of molecular orbital theory, we will see that this Lewis structure of the oxygen molecule is inconsistent with some of the properties of the molecule. But for our present purposes Lewis structures are adequate to explain why oxygen has a normal valence of two.

The Lewis structures of ethane, which has a C–C single bond, ethene, with a C=C double bond, and ethyne, with a C≡C triple bond, are as follows:

$$H:\overset{\displaystyle H}{\underset{\displaystyle H}{C}}:\overset{\displaystyle H}{\underset{\displaystyle H}{C}}:H \qquad \overset{\displaystyle H}{\underset{\displaystyle H}{C}}::\overset{\displaystyle H}{\underset{\displaystyle H}{C}} \qquad H:C:::C:H$$

For main group elements to the left of carbon in the periodic table (including the group 12 elements Zn, Cd and Hg), the normal valence is equal to the number of electrons in the valence shell, and not the number of holes. Most of these elements are metals, and form ionic compounds with high melting points. However there are some molecular compounds for which Lewis structures can be drawn. Two examples are the fluorides of beryllium and of boron.

The beryllium atom has two valence electrons and has a normal valence of two. Beryllium difluoride, BeF_2, is a high melting point solid, but at high temperatures it forms a vapour of BeF_2 molecules. In the BeF_2 molecule each fluorine atom is bonded to the beryllium atom by a single bond that is at least partially covalent, in which the valence shell of the beryllium atom contains four bonding electrons. The boron atom has three valence electrons and has a normal valence of three. Boron trifluoride, BF_3, is a gas at room temperature. In the BF_3 molecule each fluorine atom is bonded to the boron atom by a single covalent bond, so the valence shell of the boron atom contains six bonding electrons.

The Lewis structures of BeF_2 and BF_3 are shown below.

$$:\overset{..}{\underset{..}{F}}\ :Be:\ \overset{..}{\underset{..}{F}}\ : \qquad\qquad :\overset{..}{\underset{..}{F}}:B\overset{\overset{\displaystyle :F:}{}}{\underset{\displaystyle :F:}{}}$$

These are sometimes called **electron-deficient molecules** because they do not have a full octet in the valence shell around the central atom. A similar situation is found in the halides of the group 12 metals such as cadmium. The cadmium atom has the configuration $(Kr)5s^2 4d^{10}$; the valence shell of the cadmium atom (consisting of the 5s and 5p sub-shells outside the filled 4d sub-shell) contains only two electrons. The two valence electrons can be used to form two covalent bonds in molecules such as $CdCl_2$.

For molecules with a large number of electrons, the Lewis structures can be rather cluttered and hard to read, but the structures may be simplified by replacing each pair of electrons by a short line. Each line between atoms represents a pair of bonding electrons, either a single bond or part of a double or triple bond. A lone pair of electrons is indicated by a line drawn as a tangent to the atom. Examples of Lewis structures for H_2O, CF_4 and BeF_2 drawn according to this convention are shown below:

$$H-\overline{\underset{\displaystyle |}{\underset{\displaystyle H}{O}}|} \qquad\qquad |\overline{F}-\overset{\overset{\displaystyle |\overline{F}|}{\displaystyle |}}{\underset{\underset{\displaystyle |\overline{F}|}{\displaystyle |}}{C}}-\overline{F}| \qquad\qquad |\overline{F}-Be-\overline{F}|$$

As a further simplification, the lone pairs on the outer atoms (such as the fluorine atoms in the above structures) are often omitted if there is no danger of ambiguity. However the lone pairs on a central atom, such as the oxygen atom in the water molecule, should not be omitted from Lewis structures since they play an important role in determining the shape of the molecule, as we shall see shortly.

The elements of the third and subsequent rows of the periodic table follow similar patterns of valence to the second row elements, as would be expected from their similar valence shells, but there are some differences. Firstly, multiple bonding is unusual unless these atoms are bonded to an atom of a second row element. Secondly, in some of their compounds, the valence of these elements is greater than the normal valence.

For example, phosphorus forms two fluorides, phosphorus trifluoride PF_3 and phosphorus pentafluoride PF_5, with the Lewis structures shown below.

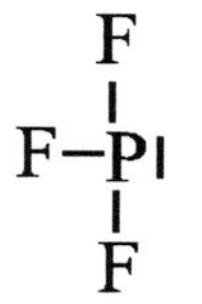

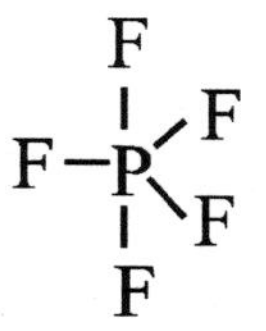

F   F
| | F
F−P| F−P
| | F
F   F

In phosphorus pentafluoride PF_5 the phosphorus atom has a valence of five, and is an example of **hypervalent** compound, in which the phosphorus atom has a valence greater than the normal valence. For hypervalent phosphorus, the Lewis structure has ten electrons in the valence shell, whereas for the normal valence (for example PF_3) there are eight electrons in the valence shell of the phosphorus atom. A valence shell containing more than eight electrons is described as an **expanded valence shell.**

In atoms of the second row elements, the 2s sub-shell can hold two electrons, and the 2p sub-shell can hold six electrons, making a total of eight. For these elements, the octet "rule" can be relied on. But for third row elements, the 3d sub-shell is available in addition to the 3s and 3p sub-shells; involvement of the 3d sub-shell in chemical bonding leads to hypervalency and an expanded valence shell. A similar situation is found for elements of subsequent rows as well.

In its hypervalent state, the valence of phosphorus is increased by 2 over its normal valence of 3. This is because a pair of electrons with opposite spins is split into two unpaired electrons, each of which takes part in a covalent bond. This can only be done by placing one of the electrons in a 3d orbital.

The following diagram shows the five valence electrons in a phosphorus atom, first in the normal trivalent state and then in the hypervalent state in which one electron is promoted to the 3d orbital, making five unpaired electrons which can form bonds.

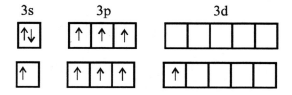

The splitting of a pair of electrons leads to two unpaired electrons, and so in hypervalent compounds, the valence is larger than the normal valence by an even number, in this case 2.

The valence of an element in a hypervalent compound will be referred to as the **hypervalence** of that element. A **normal hypervalence** is equal to the normal valence plus an even number (2, 4 or 6). The maximum value possible for the hypervalence is the number of valence electrons in the atom. A normal hypervalence results from splitting up pairs of electrons. The maximum hypervalence is found when all pairs of valence electrons have been split up.

As we saw above, phosphorus (group 15) shows a normal valence of 3 and a hypervalence of 5. The normal valence of sulfur (group 16) is 2, but it also shows hypervalences of 4 and 6, in the compounds SF_4 and SF_6. The normal valence of iodine (group 17) is 1, but it also shows hypervalences of 3, 5 and 7, in the compounds IF_3, IF_5 and IF_7, respectively.

It was thought for a long time that the noble gases of group 18 were inert chemically and did not form any chemical compounds. This thinking was probably induced by a too-high regard for the octet rule: since the group 18 atoms already have an octet of valence electrons, formation of chemical bonds was thought to be impossible. However, in 1962 the first compound of xenon was prepared by the Canadian chemist Neil Bartlett at the University of British Columbia, and subsequently a number of componds of xenon and krypton have been identified.

The Lewis structures for three different hypervalent fluorides of xenon, XeF_2, XeF_4 and XeF_6 are shown below. These are all cases of expanded valence shells of the xenon atom.

Notice that the normal valence of Xe is zero, but that in these compounds the hypervalence of Xe is respectively 2, 4 and 6, and is due to successive splitting of pairs of electrons into two unpaired electrons.

It is difficult to formulate rules for writing Lewis structures that will work in all cases, but the following procedure can be used to write the **normal Lewis structure** for molecules and ions. The normal Lewis structure is based upon the normal valences of the elements, listed in Table 3-4.

(1) *Write a structural formula for the molecule showing how the atoms are connected together by single, double bond or a triple bonds. Attempt to satisfy the normal valences or hypervalences of all the atoms, as far as possible.*

(2) *For each atom, determine the number of valence electrons for that atom; this is based on the position of the element in the periodic table.*

(3) *For each atom, assign one valence electron to each single bond, two to each double bond, and three to each triple bond originating on the atom chosen. Then group the remaining valence electrons into lone pairs on that atom. If there is an odd number of electrons, one electron will remain unpaired.*

(4) *Check that atoms of second row elements do not have more than 8 electrons around them. If necessary reposition a lone pair so as to conform to the octet rule.*

All the examples shown above can be generated by this procedure, and the following examples give further illustrations.

Example 11-4 Draw the Lewis structure for ammonia NH_3 using the above rules.

Nitrogen has a normal valence of 3, and so the structure consists of three hydrogen atoms joined by single bonds to the nitrogen atom. Nitrogen belongs in group 15 and has five valence electrons. Assigning three of these to the three single bonds leaves two electrons left over; these two electrons form a lone pair on the nitrogen atom. Thus we reach the structure shown earlier in this section.

Example 11-5 Draw a Lewis structure for hydrogen peroxide H_2O_2.

Hydrogen peroxide has a single bond between the two oxygen atoms, and a single bond from each oxygen atom to a hydrogen atom. Hence the structure can be written H–O–O–H.

Start by considering an oxygen atom, which has six valence electrons. Of the six valence electrons, one takes part in the O–O single bond, and one takes part in the O–H single bond; the remaining four electrons then form two lone pairs on the oxygen atom. Each hydrogen atom has only one valence electron, which takes part in the O–H single bond. The Lewis structure is:

$$\text{H–}\underline{\overline{\text{O}}}\text{–}\underline{\overline{\text{O}}}\text{–H}$$

Example 11-6 Draw a Lewis structure for hydrogen cyanide HCN.

Nitrogen has a normal valence of three, carbon a normal valence of four. Hence the structure can be written H–C≡N.

Nitrogen has 5 valence electrons, of which 3 take part in the C≡N triple bond. Hence there is a single lone pair on nitrogen. Carbon has four valence electrons, of which three take part in the C≡N triple bond and one takes part in the C–H single bond. Hydrogen has a single valence electron, which takes part in the C–H single bond. Hence the Lewis structure is:

$$\text{H–C≡N}\mathrm{\textbf{I}}$$

Example 11-7 Draw a Lewis structure for sulfur tetrafluoride, SF_4.

Fluorine has a normal valence of one, so there are four S–F single bonds in the molecule. Sulfur has a normal valence of two, but in this molecule it is clear that sulfur has a hypervalence of four. The sulfur atom has six valence electrons, of which four take part in the four S–F bonds leaving two electrons as a lone pair on the sulfur atom. The fluorine atoms each have seven valence electrons, of which 1 takes part in the single bond to the sulfur atom, leaving three lone pairs on each fluorine atom. The Lewis structure (without the three lone pairs on each of the fluorine atoms) is:

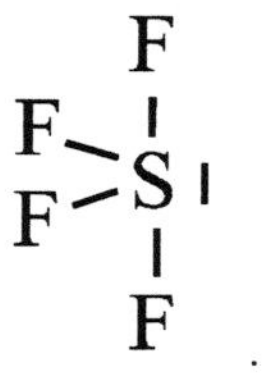

$$\begin{array}{c} \text{F} \\ | \\ \text{F}{\sim}\text{S}{-}| \\ \text{F}{^{\nearrow}} | \\ | \\ \text{F} \end{array}$$

Example 11-8 Draw a Lewis structure for nitrogen dioxide NO_2.

First we note that this molecule has an odd number of electrons, since nitrogen has five valence electrons and each oxygen has six. Nitrogen has a normal valence of three, and oxygen a normal valence of two. It is impossible to satisfy both of these, so we assume double bonds between nitrogen and each oxygen. This leaves one unpaired electron on nitrogen, and two lone pairs on each oxygen:

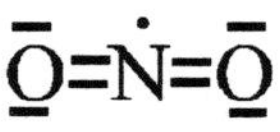

$$\overline{\text{O}}{=}\dot{\text{N}}{=}\overline{\text{O}}$$

To draw a Lewis structure for an ion, we add or subtract the appropriate number of electrons needed to get the correct charge on the ion. Monatomic ions are straightforward to deal with. Metals form positively charged cations by loss of the valence electrons. Usually all the valence electrons are lost: alkali metals form monovalent cations such as Na^+, and alkaline earth metals form divalent cations such as Ca^{2+}. Group 13 metals form trivalent cations with charge +3, though the heavier metals indium and thallium also form monovalent cations in some compounds.

The non-metals form anions with negative charge by gain of electrons. Halogens (group 17) form monovalent anions such as Cl^-, and chalcogens (group 16) form divalent anions such as S^{2-}. The group 15 elements form trivalent anions with charge –3 in some compounds, though covalent compounds of these elements are more common.

Lewis structures for polyatomic ions can be written by adding or subtracting the electrons from the central atom. For instance, in the ammonium ion NH_4^+, an electron is missing from the nitrogen atom, giving it four valence electrons. The Lewis structure is then drawn in the ordinary way. There are four N–H bonds which make use of the four valence electrons on the nitrogen atom, and the Lewis structure is as follows. The overall charge on the ion is indicated by the superscript outside the brackets.

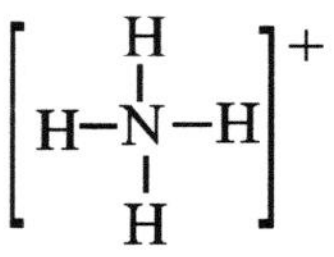

$$\left[\begin{array}{c} \text{H} \\ | \\ \text{H}{-}\text{N}{-}\text{H} \\ | \\ \text{H} \end{array} \right]^+$$

As an example of an anion, consider the tetrafluoroborate anion BF_4^-. A number of tetrafluoroborate slats are known. In this ion, the boron atom has gained an electron in addition to the three valence electrons in the neutral atom. Hence the boron atom has four valence electrons, and there are four single bonds to the fluorine atoms. The Lewis structure is therefore as follows:

$$\left[\begin{array}{c} F \\ | \\ F-B-F \\ | \\ F \end{array}\right]^{-}$$

11-8 Molecular shapes and Lewis structures: VSEPR

It might be thought that the shapes of the AX_n molecules discussed in section 11-2 are determined by the interactions between the atoms bonded to the central atom. Atoms take up a certain amount of space, and, in the absence of a chemical bond between them, two atoms can be expected to repel each other if they get too close together. Two outer atoms bonded to the central atom but not to each other are likely to avoid each other by increasing the bond angle XAX as much as possible. This effect is called **steric repulsion.**

The problem of molecular shapes is therefore related to the problem of choosing positions on the surface of a sphere which are as far apart as possible. The solution to this problem is shown in Figure 11-7: two points are located on opposite sides of the sphere, three points form a trigonal planar configuration, four points form a tetrahedron, five points form a trigonal bipyramid and six points form an octahedron.

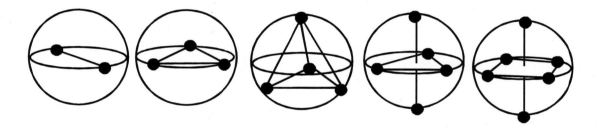

Figure 11-7 The arrangements of 2, 3, 4, 5 and 6 points on the surface of a sphere which places them as far apart as possible. Each arrangement is named by analogy with the description of the molecular shapes shown in Figure 11-1.

The tetrahedral arrangement of the four hydrogen atoms in methane, CH_4, can be explained simply on this basis. But consider a molecule of ammonia, NH_3: if repulsions between the three hydrogen atoms alone determined the geometry, the ammonia molecule would be trigonal planar instead of pyramidal. This shows that inter-atomic repulsions are not the only influence on molecular shape. The lone pairs of electrons on the central atom also play a role and must be considered.

Ultimately, calculations of molecular shape must be based on quantum theory, but without carrying out the complicated calculations necessary to obtain reliable results, valuable chemistry can be learned from the relationship between the shape of a molecule and its Lewis structure. The theory that connects Lewis structure to molecular shape is called the **valence shell electron pair repulsion** theory, or **VSEPR** theory for short. The theory was developed and popularized by Ronald J. Gillespie of McMaster University and co-workers.

The VSEPR model depends upon a quantum effect. Electrons are negatively charged, and repel each other electrostatically. But in addition electrons have a spin of $\frac{1}{2}$ and can exist in the spin-up (α or $\uparrow$) state or the spin-down (β or $\downarrow$) state. Quantum theory shows that electrons with parallel spins (both α or both β) tend to avoid each other, whereas electrons with paired spins have no such restriction except for their electrostatic repulsion. This effect is called **electron correlation**.

We have already seen some effects of electron correlation on atoms in Section 10-9. The lowest energy of an atom is achieved by having as many electrons with parallel spin as possible, other things being equal or almost equal. Electron correlation acts like an additional repulsion that keeps parallel-spin electrons apart, thus reducing electrostatic repulsion between the electrons and giving a lower energy.

Valence shell electrons with parallel spins favour the spatial arrangements that keep them as far apart as possible. The commonest case is that of an octet of electrons in the valence shell of the central atom; no distinction is made between the s and p electrons. Of the eight electrons in an octet, four must have α spin and four must have β spin. The repulsion between four electrons of parallel spin leads to a tetrahedral distribution of the electrons. Hence the four α-spin electrons tend to be arranged in a tetrahedron, and the same is true for the β-spin electrons. This is shown in Figure 11-8.

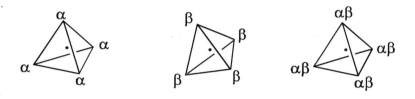

Figure 11-8   The most likely arrangement of four electrons with parallel spins is tetrahedral as shown in the left hand and centre diagrams. In a noble gas atom without chemical bonds, the tetrahedron of β spin electrons (centre diagram) is not necessarily oriented the same way as the tetrahedron of α-spin electrons (left hand diagram). In an atom such as carbon or oxygen, which forms chemical bonds consisting of pairs of electrons with opposite spins, the two tetrahedra take up similar orientations as shown in the right hand diagram.

Figure 11-8 depicts the electrons as occupying definite positions at the corners of tetrahedra, this should not be interpreted too literally. Electrons in an atom or molecule do not occupy fixed positions in space, but are distributed in space according to quantum theory. The locations indicated by the corners of the tetrahedra shown in the figure indicate only the relative positions of regions of space where the repulsion between electrons with parallel spins is minimized.

In the neon atom, the tetrahedron of α-spin electrons is not correlated with the tetrahedron of β-spin electrons, so the whole atom is spherical on average. But where there are chemical bonds to other atoms, each bond consists of a pair of electrons with opposite spin, which draws electrons with opposite spins into the approximately the same bonding region. Hence the α- and β-tetrahedra adopt the same orientation and this places the electrons of opposite spin in the same region of space, as shown in the third of the diagrams in Figure 11-8.

In a molecule, each pair of bonding electrons is restricted to the region of the chemical bond between the central atom and the outer atom, and so the tetrahedron of electron pairs becomes fixed in the molecular framework. In molecules containing lone pairs of electrons, these lone pairs are just as real as the bonding pairs, and occupy domains that influence the arrangement of the atoms in space. To show the distribution of valence electrons in a molecule, the space around the central atom is divided into regions or **domains**. Each pair of electrons forming a single covalent bond occupies one domain. Each lone pair of electrons occupies one domain. In a double or triple bond, the two or three pairs of electrons that form the bond are located in a single domain.

The number of domains around an atom is called the **steric number** for that atom. Bearing in mind electron-deficient molecules, molecules with an expanded valence shell, and the existence of multiple bonds, the steric number be anything from two up to seven. The arrangement of the domains around the central atom is called the **domain geometry**. The predicted domain geometry around a given atom is determined by the steric number, and the requirement that the domains be as far from each other as possible. For a given number of domains, the predicted domain geometry is the same as the distribution of points on the surface of a sphere shown in Figure 11-14 and the predicted domain geometries are listed in Table 11-5.

Table 11-5 The domain geometry for various steric numbers

Steric number	Domain geometry
2	linear
3	trigonal planar
4	tetrahedral
5	trigonal bipyramid
6	octahedral

The prediction of molecular shape from its Lewis structure requires an extension of the usual chemical formula by introducing a symbol to show lone pairs on the central atom. Consider molecules consisting of a central atom of an element A and outer atoms of another element X. Lone pairs of electrons on the central atom A are designated by the symbol E. Including the lone pairs of electrons, the formula is written AX_nE_m where n is the number of outer atoms and m is the number of lone pairs on the central atom. This type of formula can be described as the **steric formula**.

We can now distinguish between the domain geometry, which describes the arrangement of the domains around the central atom, and the molecular shape, which describes the arrangement of the outer atoms around the central atom. A domain may contain a pair of bonding electrons forming a single bond, a lone pair of electrons, two pairs of bonding electrons forming a double bond, or three pairs of bonding electrons forming a triple bond.

For example, in molecules with an octet of valence electrons around the central atom there are four electron pairs. If these four pairs occupy four domains, then the domain geometry is tetrahedral. There are four different steric formulae and molecular shapes derived from this domain geometry:

AX_4 has no lone pairs on the atom A and the molecule is tetrahedral.   Example: CH_4

AX_3E has one lone pair on A and the molecule is trigonal pyramidal.   Example: NH_3

AX_2E_2 has two lone pairs on A and the molecular is bent.   Example: H_2O

AXE_3 has three lone pairs on A and the molecular is linear.   Example: HF

These shapes, including lone pairs, are illustrated in Figure 11-16. The lone pairs, though not shown in Figure 11-1, are just as important as the bonding pairs in determining how the bonded atoms are arranged around the central atom. In fact, the lone pairs occupy more space than the bonding pairs, since they do not have a second nucleus that serves to contract the electron cloud. This influences molecular geometry in situations where several molecular shapes are possible.

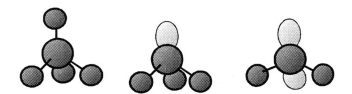

Figure 11-17   Three molecules with steric number of four, and hence tetrahedral domain geometry. The molecular shapes are as follows: the AX_4 molecule is tetrahedral, the AX_3E molecule is trigonal pyramidal, and the AX_2E_2 molecule is bent. The atoms are shaded dark, and the lighter shading indicates the lone pairs.

Double bonds are formed from two pairs of bonding electrons. In VSEPR theory the two pairs of electrons that form a double bond between two atoms belong in the same domain since both pairs lie in the region between the atoms. For example, the Lewis structure for carbon dioxide, CO_2, is:

$$\overline{\underline{O}} = C = \overline{\underline{O}}$$

The four bonding pairs of electrons form two double bonds from the carbon atom to the two oxygen atoms and hence occupy two domains around the carbon atom. Hence the domain geometry is linear, and the molecular shape is linear.

A molecule of ethene, $H_2C=CH_2$, is planar, as shown in Figure 11-4 and has a double bond between the two carbon atoms. The Lewis structure was shown in the previous section. The two electron pairs of the double bond occupy a single domain and there are three domains around each carbon atom. The domain geometry for each carbon atom is therefore trigonal planar, and each carbon atom and the three atoms bonded to it are coplanar. The angles between the bonds are close to 120°. Furthermore, the entire molecule is planar, which means that there is a fixed relationship between the two planes containing the atoms at each end of the molecule. The explanation for this lies outside VSEPR theory, but is to be found in the quantum theory of molecular structure, discussed in Chapter 12.

A molecule of ethyne, $H_2C\equiv CH_2$, is linear, as shown in Figure 11-4 and has a triple bond between the two carbon atoms. The Lewis structure was shown in the previous section. The three electron pairs of the triple bond occupy a single domain and there are two domains around each carbon atom. The domain geometry for each carbon atom is therefore linear, and each carbon atom and the two atoms bonded to it are collinear. The angles between the bonds are 180°; it follows that the entire molecule is collinear.

In Section 11-7, we encountered molecules with expanded valence shells of five or six pairs of electrons. The domain geometry of these molecules is trigonal bipyramidal and octahedral respectively.

There are a number of interesting molecules with a steric number of five and hence trigonal bipyramidal domain geometry. Lone pairs in this domain shape are found always in equatorial positions, since this gives them more space than the axial positions. Some typical shapes are shown in Figure 11-10.

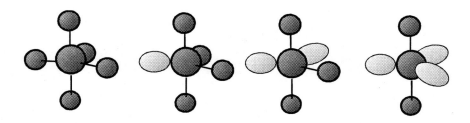

Figure 11-18 The shapes of molecules with a steric number of five. From left to right, phosphorus pentafluoride PF_5, sulfur tetrafluoride SF_4, chlorine trifluoride ClF_3, and xenon difluoride XeF_2. The atoms are shaded dark, and lighter shading indicates the lone pairs.

The pentahalides of the group 15 elements phosphorus, arsenic, antimony and bismuth, such as PCl_5, have five pairs of bonding electrons and the molecule is trigonal pyramidal, the same as the domain geometry.

Sulfur tetrafluoride SF_4 with six valence electrons on sulfur and one each contributed from the four fluorine atoms has the steric formula AX_4E, with one lone pair. The lone pair occupies an equatorial position since that gives it more room than the axial positions. The structure is described formally as **disphenoidal**, but a more picturesque name is **see-saw shaped**. (To see the see-saw, turn the molecule on its side.) The two axial S–F bonds are not quite collinear, and are bent slightly away from the equatorial lone pair.

Chlorine trifluoride ClF_3 has the steric formula AX_3E_2. The two lone pairs both occupy equatorial positions and the molecule is **T-shaped**.

The Lewis structure of the noble gas compound XeF_2 was shown in the previous section, and corresponds to the steric formula AX_2E_3. All three lone pairs occupy equatorial positions in the trigonal bipyramidal domain shape and the molecule is linear.

The hexahalides such as sulfur hexafluoride SF_6 have six bonding electron pairs and the domain geometry is therefore octahedral. The shape of AX_5E molecules is **square pyramidal**, which is formed from an octahedron (Figures 11-1 and 11-3) by removing one atom; examples are ClF_5 and TeF_5^-. In molecules with octahedral domain geometry but two lone pairs, the lone pairs are found to occupy positions on opposite sides of a square planar arrangement of bonds. This is almost the only situation in which molecules of chemical formula AX_4 are found in the square planar shape, and an example is the molecular ion ICl_4^-.

Example 11-9   Use VSEPR theory to predict the shape of arsenic trichloride $AsCl_3$.

Arsenic belongs in group 15 of the periodic table and so the atom has five electrons in its valence shell. The three chlorine atoms contribute one electron each to the valence shell of the arsenic atom in the molecule. Hence $AsCl_3$ is similar to ammonia in its Lewis structure, with three single As–Cl bonds and a lone pair on the arsenic atom. There are four electron domains, the domain geometry is tetrahedral, and the molecular shape is trigonal pyramidal.

Example 11-10   Use VSEPR theory to predict the shape of formaldehyde CH_2O.

There is a double bond from carbon to oxygen, to satisfy the valences of both carbon and oxygen, so the formula can be written $H_2C=O$. The Lewis structure of formaldehyde is shown below. There are three domains around the carbon atom, so the domain geometry is trigonal planar. There are no lone pairs and the molecular shape is trigonal planar.

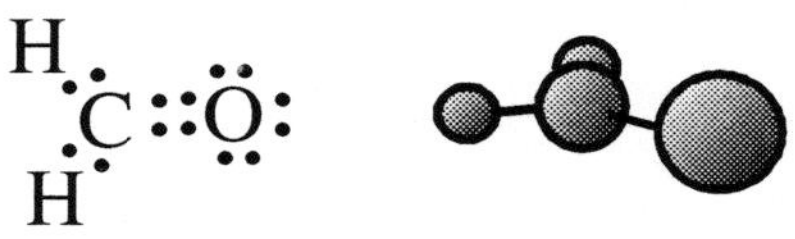

Example 11-11   Use VSEPR theory to predict the shape of the SbF_5^{2-} ion.

The element antimony, Sb, belonging to group 15, has five valence shell electrons. With the two extra electrons due to the ionic charge of –2, there are seven valence electrons in the valence shell of the antimony atom. Five of electrons take part in the five Sb–F bonds, leaving one lone pair of electrons on the Sb atom. Hence there are six pairs of electrons around Sb, the steric number is six and the domain geometry is octahedral. One of the six locations is occupied by a lone pair, and the molecular shape is square pyramidal. The Lewis structure and molecular shape are as follows; the lone pairs on the fluorine atoms have been omitted from the Lewis structure.

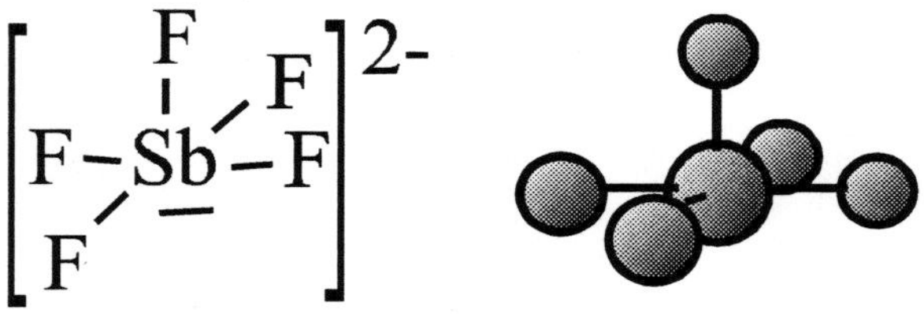

11-9   Oxidation number and formal charge

Empirical rules for determination of oxidation number of an element in a compound were stated in Section 2-9, without any justification in terms of the structure of atoms. Those empirical rules are based on the following definition.

The **oxidation number** of an atom in a molecule is the charge that would be found on that atom if all the electrons in each bonding pair between atoms were assigned to the atom with the higher electronegativity. For bonding pairs between atoms of the same element, the bonding electrons are shared equally.

Fluorine is the most electronegative element and always forms single bonds, so if the pair of bonding electrons are assigned completely to fluorine, it acquires eight electrons, a charge of –1 and hence an oxidation number of –1. This is true regardless of which atom it is bonded to. For example, if all the bonding electrons in the Lewis structure for BF_3 are assigned to the fluorine atoms, each fluorine atom has a charge of –1 and hence an oxidation number of –1. The boron atom has a charge of +3 and hence an oxidation number of +3.

Oxygen is the next most electronegative element and forms bonds to most other atoms. Oxygen has two holes in its valence shell, so if two extra bonding electrons are assigned to oxygen, it has a charge and an oxidation number of –2. In peroxides such as hydrogen peroxide H_2O_2, there is an O–O bond, and since the two oxygen atoms have the same electronegativity, the two electrons of that bond are shared equally and there is no transfer of electrons within this bond. However the two electrons in each O–H bond are assigned to the more electronegative oxygen atom, which gives the oxygen atom one extra electron and hence an oxidation number of –1. The Lewis structure of hydrogen peroxide is shown in Example 11-5.

In a neutral molecule the sum of the oxidation numbers of all the atoms is equal to zero. This is because the assignment of a bonding electron to one atom or the other increases the charge on one atom and reduces the charge on the other. For an ion, the sum of the oxidation numbers is equal to the net charge on the ion.

Clearly the assignment of electrons in this way is very artificial. It is a completely ionic model of chemcal bonding in which all the bonding electrons are transferred completely to the more electronegative atom, except where a chemical bond joins two atoms of the same element. Such a picture is valid only if there is a large difference between the electronegativities of the two elements involved. But in calculating the oxidation number, it is assumed that bonding electrons are completely transferred to the more electronegative element, even if the difference in electronegativities is small. Hence the oxidation number is not a good indicator of the actual charge on an atom in a molecule. Despite its limitations, oxidation number is useful in classifying compounds of elements with variable valence, and in balancing redox equations.

Another indicator of the distribution of valence electrons in a molecule is the **formal charge** on each atom in a molecule. The formal charge of an atom in a molecule is the charge it would have if the two electrons in each bonding pair are shared equally between the two atoms joined by the bond, regardless of a difference in electronegativities. This is reasonable where the electronegativity differences are not too large. Formal charges are zero if the bonding pair consists of one electron from each atom. This is the case if each atom in a molecule has its normal valence or normal hypervalence, but formal charges can be non-zero in several interesting situations.

For a neutral molecule, the sum of the formal charges over all atoms is zero. For an ion, the sum of the formal charges is equal to the total charge on the ion.

Example 11-12 Calculate the oxidation number and formal charge for each atom in the ammonium ion, NH_4^+.

The ammonium ion contains four N–H bonds; the Lewis structure is shown in Section 11-7. The electronegativity of nitrogen is 3.0, and that of hydrogen is 2.1, so in calculating oxidation number all eight bonding electrons are assigned to nitrogen. A nitrogen atom has five valence electrons, and the three additional electrons give nitrogen a negative charge of –3. Hence the oxidation number of nitrogen is –3. The hydrogen atoms each lose their one electron, giving them an oxidation number of +1. The sum of the oxidation numbers is +1, which is the total charge on the ion.

In calculating formal charges, the bonding electrons in each bond are shared equally between nitrogen and hydrogen regardless of electronegativity. This gives nitrogen a total of four valence electrons, one from each N–H bond, and hence nitrogen has a formal charge of +1. Each hydrogen atom is assigned one electron from the N–H bond, and so the formal charge on each hydrogen atom is zero. The sum of the formal charges is +1, which is the total charge on the ion.

Example 11-13 Draw a Lewis structure for carbon monoxide, CO, and calculate the oxidation number and formal charge for each atom.

The Lewis structure for the carbon monoxide molecule seems at first a puzzle, since carbon has a normal valence of 4 and oxygen a normal valence of 2. One way to approach this is to recognize that CO is isoelectronic with the nitrogen molecule, N_2. In other words, CO has the same number of electrons as the nitrogen molecule, N_2. In the N_2 molecule there is a triple bond between the nitrogen atoms, so we can draw a Lewis structure for CO with a triple bond between the two atoms: In fact no other Lewis structure satiusfies the octet rule.

$$:C\!:\!:\!:O:$$

Trial and error shows that no other Lewis structure satisfies the octet rule. Oxygen is more electronegative than carbon, so in calculating the oxidation number all six bonding electrons are assigned to oxygen, giving it eight electrons and a net negative charge of –2 relative to the neutral atom which has six valence electrons, and hence an oxidation number of –2. The carbon atom is left with only two electrons, giving it an oxidation number of +2. The sum of the oxidation numbers is zero.

If the six bonding electrons are equally divided between the atoms, then each atom has five electrons, which gives oxygen a formal charge of +1 and carbon a formal charge of –1. The sum of the formal charges is zero.

In Table 11-2, a triple bond C≡O is indicated for the carbon monoxide molecule, and this is supported by experimental evidence. The bond energy of 1076.4 kJ/mol is significantly larger than the average C=O bond energy listed in Table 11-3. Further, the bond length of 1.13 Å in CO is significantly shorter than the C=O bond length in CO_2, 1.16 Å, and in other organic molecules, 1.21 Å (see Table 11-1). It is notable that carbon monoxide has a very small dipole moment despite the difference in electronegativities of carbon and oxygen.

There is another way to think about formal charge. Consider the ammonium ion, in which nitrogen has a formal charge of +1 and is bonded to four other atoms by single bonds. In the ammonium ion, the nitrogen atom has a valence of four, like a carbon atom in methane, instead of its normal valence of three. A nitrogen atom could have a valence of four if it were isoelectronic with carbon, i.e. have the same number of electrons as carbon. To achieve this, the nitrogen atom would have to lose an electron, forming the N^+ ion. In a sense, we could regard the ammonium ion as four hydrogen atoms bonded to an N^+ ion. This is what the formal charge of +1 on N indicates.

The rules for determining formal charge by this approach are as follows.

1. The formal charge is zero for any atom with its normal valence, or normal hypervalence.

2. If an atom has an abnormal valence in a Lewis structure, the formal charge is not zero.

3. To determine the formal charge on an atom with an abnormal valence, consider which of the adjacent elements in the periodic table has the same normal valence as the abnormal valence of the atom in question. In other words, which adjacent element does the abnormal atom resemble?

4. The formal charge on the abnormal atom is the charge which that atom would carry if it were made isoelectronic with the nearby element of equal valence.

To return once again to the ammonium ion: nitrogen has a valence of 4, which is abnormal for nitrogen. But 4 is the normal valence for the adjacent element carbon. To make a nitrogen atom isoelectronic with a carbon atom, one electron must be removed, producing the N^+ ion. Hence the formal charge on N in NH_4^+ is +1.

In the Lewis structure for the carbon monoxide molecule, which was discussed in Example 11-13, both the carbon and oxygen atoms are trivalent, which is abnormal for both atoms. Both atoms resemble nitrogen atoms. To make the carbon atom isoelectronic with a nitrogen atom, an electron must be added, turning it into a C^- ion and giving a formal charge of –1. To make the oxygen atom isoelectronic with a nitrogen atom, an electron must be removed, turning it into an O^+ ion and giving a formal charge of +1.

We will see more examples of this idea when considering resonance structures in the next section.

11-10 Resonance

For some molecules it is possible to draw more than one Lewis structure by moving electrons from one location to another in the molecule, without breaking the rules and guidelines for drawing Lewis structures. Such structures are called **resonance structures**. This word suggests that the molecule oscillates or "resonates" between the various possible structures, but the modern view based on quantum mechanics is that the actual structure is intermediate between the resonance structures so that no single Lewis structure is satisfactory by itself. In many cases, the existence of resonance structures indicates unusual chemical properties.

The main feature of the benzene molecule, C_6H_6, is a ring of carbon atoms. In drawing Lewis structures, the normal valence of carbon (four) and the octet rule are satisfied by a structure with alternating double and single bonds between the carbon atoms. However, this can be achieved in either of two equivalent ways, which are shown in the following Lewis structures:

Both these Lewis structures predict that there should be two different bond lengths which alternate around the ring, one corresponding to the C–C single bonds (about 1.53 Å) and the other to the C=C double bonds (1.34 Å). However, experimental studies show that all the carbon-carbon bond lengths in benzene are equal in length, and that the actual bond length is 1.40 Å, in between the single and double bond lengths. Thus simple Lewis theory gives the wrong structure for benzene.

The solution to this problem is to assume that the actual structure of benzene is a combination or average of both resonance structures with equal weights. These two resonance forms are equivalent in the sense that they both contain three double and three single carbon-carbon bonds, and so they may be called **equivalent resonance structures**.

In a single Lewis structure, every electron pair is localized either as a bonding pair or a lone pair. Resonance involving two or more Lewis structures is an indication of the **delocalization of electrons**. Where an electron is able to occupy a larger region of space, quantum mechanics indicates that the energy of the electron will be lowered, other things being equal. In benzene, the delocalization extends over all six carbon atoms.

The existence of two equivalent resonance forms for benzene, and the delocalization of some of the electrons, is reflected in its chemical properties and in its thermodynamic stability. The enthalpy change of formation of benzene is lower than would be expected on the basis of bond energies, by about 200 kJ/mol. This energy difference is called the **resonance energy** and can be estimated by calculating the enthalpy change of formation of benzene vapour using bond energies, and comparing the result with thermodynamic data.

Example 11-14 Calculate the resonance energy for benzene from its enthalpy change of formation and average bond energies.

The enthalpy of formation of a single resonance form of benzene can be calculated from the following two (conceptual) chemical reactions. First we form atoms of carbon and hydrogen in the gaseous state:

$$6\ C(s) + 3\ H_2(g) \rightarrow 6\ C(g) + 6\ H(g)$$

This reaction starts from elements in their standard state, so enthalpy change is:

$$\Delta H = +6 \times \Delta H_f(C(g)) + 6 \times \Delta H_f(H(g)) = +6 \times (+716.682) + 6 \times (+217.965) = 5607.9\ \text{kJ/mol}$$

In the second reaction, these atoms are assembled to form one of the resonance forms of benzene:

$$6\ C(g) + 6\ H(g) \rightarrow \text{one resonance form of } C_6H_6(g)$$

The enthalpy change is estimated from average bond energies. Starting from atoms, we form 3 C–C single bonds, 3 C=C double bonds and 6 C–H single bonds:

$$\Delta H \approx -3 \times 347 - 3 \times 599 - 6 \times 414 = -5322\ \text{kJ/mol}$$

Hence the enthalpy change of formation of one resonance form of $C_6H_6(g)$ is estimated to be;

$$\Delta H_f \approx +5607.9 - 5322 = +286\ \text{kJ/mol}$$

From Appendix I, however, the enthalpy change of formation of $C_6H_6(g)$ is +82.927 kJ/mol. This is about 200 kJ/mol lower than the enthalpy change of formation of one resonance structure, so the resonance energy is estimated to be 200 kJ/mol in this case.

Resonance plays an important role in the structure of oxygen-containing molecules. As an example, consider sulfur dioxide, SO_2. Both sulfur and oxygen have six valence electrons, and both have a normal valence of 2; in addition, sulfur has normal hyervalences of 4 and 6. The following structure with double bonds between sulfur and oxygen satisfy these normal valences. Since both oxygen atoms have their normal valence, and sulfur has one of its normal hypervalences, the formal charges on all atoms are zero. The sulfur has an expanded valence shell of ten electrons.

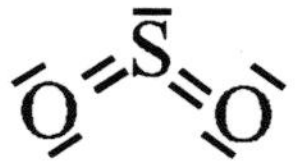

But the following two resonance structures are also acceptable, and should be considered because the octet rule is obeyed for all atoms:

These two structures are equivalent to each other. It is known from experiment that the two sulfur-oxygen bond-lengths are equal, and hence these two resonance structures must contribute equally. In both structures, the formal charge on the singly bonded oxygen atom is –1, since it resembles a fluorine atom with a normal valence of one. The sulfur atom has an abnormal valence of 3, it resembles an atom of the adjacent element phosphorus, for which the normal valence is 3. To make the sulfur atom isoelectronic with phosphorus, an electron must be removed, and hence the formal charge on sulfur is +1.

The actual structure of an SO_2 molecule can be regarded as a combination of all three structures, with equal contributions from the second and third. In all three structures, the oxidation numbers are –2 for oxygen and +4 for sulfur.

The structures of ozone, O_3, and the nitrite ion, NO_2^-, are related to that of SO_2, and involve similar resonance structures. However, the first resonance structure with two double bonds is not permitted since all the atoms are of second row elements, and obey the octet rule.

An important case of non-equivalent resonance structures concerns the carbon-nitrogen bond in organic compounds called **amides**. An amide contains a C=O group adjacent to an N–H group. This group of atoms, –CONH–, is sometimes called a **peptide bond**, and is found in protein molecules.

The simplest amide is formamide, $HCONH_2$, which has the structure shown below on the left:

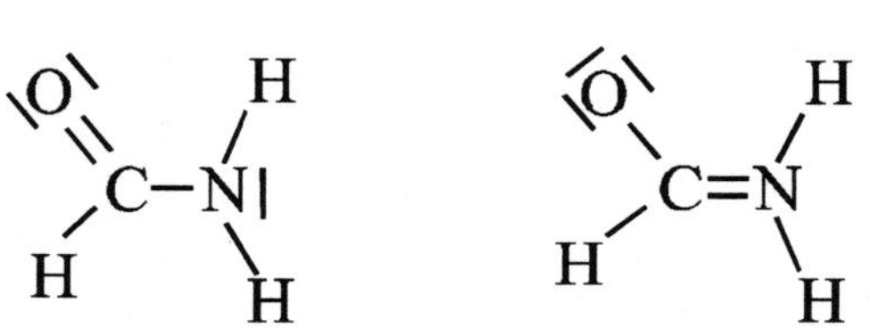

The right-hand structure is an alternative Lewis structure for formamide, which also satisfies the octet rule but has a double bond between carbon and nitrogen and a univalent oxygen atom. In the second structure, the formal charges are –1 on oxygen (with an abnormal valence of 1) and +1 on nitrogen (with an abnormal valence of 4). The second structure is not equivalent to the first, and does not contribute equally to the actual structure, but the double bond in the second structure suggests that the carbon-nitrogen bond has some of the characteristics of a double bond.

Hence the atoms adjacent to the carbon-nitrogen bond are expected to be coplanar (as in ethene), and rotation around this bond is expected to be hindered, whereas rotation about a single bond would take place easily and rapidly. These predictions are confirmed by experimental evidence.

11-11 Electron pair donors and acceptors

A covalent bond exists whenever a pair of electrons is shared between two atoms. In the cases considered so far, one electron is contributed from each of the two atoms bonded together, but this need not be the case. A covalent bond consisting of a pair of electrons contributed by one atom is called a **coordinate bond** between an **electron pair donor** and an **electron pair acceptor**. Of course, the electrons cannot be distinguished from one another after the bond is formed, but the source of the electrons can be identified before the bond is formed.

Positive metal ions have lost electrons and can accept electron pairs in their valence shell. The water molecule has two lone pairs of electron, and in aqueous solution metal ions are usually bonded to six water molecules to form the **hexaquo** complex; for example the cupric ion in aqueous solution, $Cu^{2+}(aq)$, can be represented more explicitly by the structure $Cu(H_2O)_6^{2+}$. The water molecules are electron pair donors and the copper ion is an electron pair acceptor. The water molecules are called **ligands**. Other ligands are molecules and ions rich in lone pairs of electrons such as ammonia NH_3, chloride ion Cl^-, and anions of weak acids such as the oxalate ion $C_2O_4^{2-}$.

There is a close relationship between the acid-base reactions and the formation of coordinate bonds. The simplest reaction between an acid and a base is that between a hydrogen ion and a hydroxide ion:

$$H^+ + OH^- \rightarrow H_2O$$

The result of the reaction is the formation of a covalent bond between the oxygen atom and the hydrogen ion in which both electrons are contributed by the base. In the reaction between a hydrogen ion and ammonia,

$$H^+ + NH_3 \rightarrow NH_4^+$$

the new N–H bond is formed from the lone pair of electrons on the ammonia molecule. Bases are electron pair donors and acids are electron pair acceptors.

Electron pair donors are called **Lewis bases** and electron pair acceptors are called **Lewis acids** even in situations where no proton transfer is involved. This definition is general enough to include the ordinary definition of acids and bases in Section 2-8 and in Chapter 14.

11-12 Hydrogen bonding

Hydrogen has an electronegativity of 2.1, and there are several elements with higher electronegativity. When hydrogen is bonded to an element X with high electronegativity such as fluorine, oxygen or nitrogen, the hydrogen atom becomes positively charged and the other atom becomes negatively charged:

$$^{\delta-}X–H^{\delta+}$$

where the partial transfer of an electron is indicated by the partial charges $\delta+$ and $\delta-$. In the presence of another electronegative atom Y which carries a lone pair of electrons, there is an electrostatic attraction between the positively charged hydrogen atom and the negatively charged lone pair of electrons, which is called a **hydrogen bond**. A hydrogen bond is usually represented by a dotted line between the hydrogen atom and the atom Y:

$$X–H\cdots Y$$

The atoms X and Y can be of the same element or different elements, and may be either in the same molecule or in different molecules. The energy of a hydrogen bond varies from one case to another, but is generally in the range 10 to 30 kJ/mol, which is much less than ordinary bond energies listed in Tables 11-2 and 11-3.

In Section 7-3 we discussed the anomalously high boiling points of the hydrides of the second row non-metals, HF, H_2O and NH_3. The most important of these cases is liquid water because it plays such a large role in biological and environmental processes. The water molecule has two covalent O–H bonds and two lone pairs of electrons. In liquid water and solid ice, each O–H bond takes part in a hydrogen bond to another molecule through the lone pairs on the other oxygen atom.

The following structure indicates how water molecules in water or ice form a network of hydrogen bonds. The diagram shows only a two-dimensional array of water molecules, but the actual arrangement of water molecules in ice is three-dimensional, with a tetrahedral arrangement of covalent bonds and hydrogen bonds around each oxygen atom.

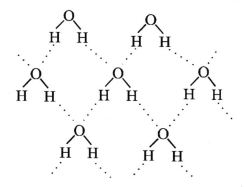

Ice has a low density because each oxygen atom has only four nearest neighbours, which means that ice has a very open structure and hence a low density. When ice melts to water, some of the regular tetrahedral arrangement of the hydrogen bonds becomes disordered, and this allows the molecules to pack more closely in the liquid state, and so the density of water at 0°C is higher than that of ice at the same temperature. This is easy to remember since ice floats on the surface of water. Many of the interesting properties of water are due to clusters of water molecules joined by hydrogen bonds.

The hydrogen-bonded structure of liquid water makes water a very good solvent for substances that can also take part in hydrogen bonding. Alcohols, carboxylic acids, and amines are highly soluble in water, due to the formation of hydrogen bonds between solute and solvent. Water is also a good solvent for ionic materials such as salts.

Substances that cannot form hydrogen bonds, such as hydrocarbons, are generally not very soluble in water, even though the enthalpy change of solution is negative and therefore favourable to formation of a solution. The reason is that the presence of such molecules in water would disrupt the tetrahedral network of hydrogen bonds between water molecules. This leads to what is called the **hydrophobic effect**, which is discussed in Chapter 16.

Further reading

R.J.Gillespie and E.A.Robinson have recently published a review of the valence shell electron pair repulsion theory in the journal Angewandte Chemie, International Edition, volume 35, pages 495-514 (1996) . The article contains much information on molecular geometry and VSEPR theory, which will be of interest to some students.

The Nature of the Chemical Bond by L.Pauling (3rd edition, Cornell University Press, Ithaca, N.Y. 1960) is a classic book which has influenced thinking about structural chemistry over a long period.

Key concepts

Each molecule has a characteristic shape that reflects the spatial arrangement of the atoms. The common molecular shapes are linear, bent, trigonal planar, trigonal pyramidal, tetrahedral, square planar, trigonal bipyramidal, and octahedral. Organic molecules have characteristic shapes that are related to the bonds involving the carbon atoms.

The chemical energy of molecules is associated mostly with the bonds between the atoms, and each type of bond has a bond energy, which is roughly the same in different molecules.

The power of atoms to attract electrons within a molecule is indicated by its electronegativity. The electronegativity difference between the atoms involved determines the distribution within a chemical bond: the more electronegative atom is negatively charged, the other atom is positively charged.

Lewis structures are a simple model for covalent bonds between atoms in molecules. Each single bond consists of a pair of electrons that is shared between the atoms. Double and triple bonds consist of two and three shared pairs of electrons respectively. Some molecules contain pairs of non-bonding electrons that are not shared between atoms. From Lewis structures and electronegativities, oxidation numbers and formal charges can be assigned to atoms in a molecule.

The shape of a molecule can be predicted from the Lewis structure of the molecule using the valence shell electron pair repulsion theory. The bonding and non-bonding electrons around an atom are assumed to be grouped into domains, and the shape of the molecule is determined by the requirement that the domains be as far apart as possible.

For some molecules, more than one Lewis structure must be considered in order to give a satisfactory account of the known molecular geometry and chemical properties. Such structures are called resonance structures.

Review questions

1. Give an example of a tetrahedral organic molecule.

2. Give an example of a trigonal bipyramidal inorganic molecule.

3. Give an example of a trigonal planar inorganic molecule.

4. What is the relationship between the normal valence and the number of valence electrons?

5. What is the relationship between the number of valence electrons and group number of an element?

6. What is electronegativity?

7. Describe two different methods of estimating electronegativity.

8. What do you understand by the phrase "average bond energy"?

9. How would you describe a Lewis structure?

10. What is the difference between a bonding pair and a lone pair?

11. What do the letters VSEPR stand for?

12. How do you calculate an oxidation number given a Lewis structure?

13. How do you calculate a formal charge given a Lewis structure?

14. What is a hydrogen bond?

15. What is a Lewis base?

Problems

1. Draw structures for the following molecules, which are structural isomers with the formula C_5H_{12}: n-pentane, methylbutane, and dimethylpropane. For each molecule, count the number of C–C bonds and C–H bonds.

2. Draw Lewis structures for the following molecules and ions and use VSEPR to predict their shapes: H_3O^+, OH^-, CH_3OH, CH_2F_2, HOCl, CH_2O, PH_3, H_2S.

3. Draw a Lewis structure for the sulfate ion SO_4^{2-} and the nitrate ion NO_3^-, including resonance structures. Use VSEPR to predict their shapes.

4. Phosphorus pentachloride is found in several different crystalline forms. One form consists of PCl_5 molecules, while another form is ionc and consists of PCl_4^+ and PCl_6^- ions. Draw Lewis structures for the molecule and each of the ions, and use VSEPR to predict their shapes. Determine the formal charges on the phosphorus atom in each case.

5. Draw Lewis structures for the following ions: hypochlorite ClO^-, chlorite ClO_2^-, chlorate ClO_3^- and perchlorate ClO_4^-. Use VSEPR to predict their shapes.

6. Draw Lewis structures for chlorine dioxide ClO_2, and nitric oxide NO. Use VSEPR to predict the shape of the first molecule. Note that these molecules contain an odd number of electrons so the octet rule must be broken.

7. Draw Lewis structures and predict shapes for the ions Br_3^+, $AlCl_4^-$, $FClF^-$, $FClF^+$, BrF_4^+.

8. VSEPR can be used to speculate about the shapes of molecules which are met only in specialized research laboratories. Draw a Lewis structure for, and predict the shape of, thiazyl fluoride, NSF. (Preparation of this compound was a challenge to American chemists since its formula consists of the initials of the National Science Foundation, an important granting agency.)

9. Draw Lewis structures and use VSEPR theory to predict the shapes of the following ions:

$$ClF_4^+, AsF_6^-, NO_3^-, SO_3^{2-}.$$

10. Write an appropriate Lewis structure for ozone, O_3, and predict the shape of the molecule. (Hint: compare it with the structure of SO_2)

11. The compound CF_3NO is a blue gas. Draw a Lewis structure for the molecule and predict the shape of the molecule.

12. Use average bond energies to estimate ΔH for the reaction

$$CH_4(g) + 2\,Cl_2 \rightarrow CH_2Cl_2(g) + 2\,HCl(g) \qquad\qquad [-200\ kJ/mol]$$

13. Use average bond energies to estimate ΔH for the pyrolysis of ethane (see Section 4-7):

$$H_3C-CH_3 \rightarrow H_2C=CH_2 + H_2 \qquad\qquad [+140\ kJ/mol]$$

14. Use average bond energies to estimate ΔH for the following two possible reactions in the pyrolysis of propane (see section 4-7):

$$H_3C-CH_2-CH_3 \rightarrow H_3C-CH=CH_2 + H_2 \qquad\qquad [+140\ kJ/mol]$$

$$H_3C-CH_2-CH_3 \rightarrow H_2C=CH_2 + CH_4 \qquad\qquad [+95\ kJ/mol]$$

15. Phosphorus vapour contains P_4 molecules in which the phosphorus atoms are at the corners of a regular tetrahedron.

(a) Draw a sketch of the P_4 molecule. What is the P–P–P bond angle in this molecule?

(b) Calculate ΔH for the following reaction from thermodynamic data:

$$P_4(g) + 6\,H_2(g) \rightarrow 4\,PH_3(g). \qquad\qquad [-37.3\ kJ/mol]$$

(c) Hence calculate the P–P bond energy in P_4 using data from Tables 11-4 and 5. [194 kJ/mol]

16. Estimate $ΔH_f$ for trichloromethane in the gas phase using bond energies and any other necessary thermochemical data. [–92 kJ/mol]

17. Calculate $ΔH$ per monomer unit for the polymerization of ethylene, discussed in Section 4-7, using average bond energies. [–95 kJ/mol]

18. (a) Calculate $ΔH$ for the atomization of sulfur tetrafluoride SF_4. [1370 kJ/mol]

(b) Calculate $ΔH$ for the atomization of sulfur hexafluoride SF_6. [1962 kJ/mol]

(c) Hence calculate and compare the average bond energies in these two molecules.

[342 and 327 kJ/mol]

19. XeF_4 is a white solid, which melts at 117°C and sublimes easily. From the enthalpy of formation in Appendix 1, and a reasonable estimate of the enthalpy of sublimation (see table 7-3), estimate the Xe–F bond energy in this molecule. Hence estimate the Pauling electronegativity of Xe, assuming that the Xe–Xe bond energy is zero. [137 kJ/mol, 3.0]

20. Discuss the enthalpy of combustion of a general hydrocarbon C_nH_{2n+2} using bond energies and assuming that both the hydrocarbon and the product water are in the gas phase. Show that the enthalpy of combustion is a linear function of the number of carbon atoms, n, and that the enthalpy of combustion per unit mass is approximately -47 kJ/g. Discuss how your result is affected when the latent heats of vaporization are taken into account. Compare your calculations with the data in Table 8-1.

21. Estimate the resonance energy of benzene by considering the following (hypothetical) reaction in which benzene vapour reacts with hydrogen gas to form cyclohexane vapour:

$$C_6H_6(g) + 3\,H_2(g) \rightarrow C_6H_{12}(g)$$

    Hint: First use enthalpy of formation data to calculate the enthalpy change of the reaction. Then estimate the enthalpy change for the same reaction using average bond energy data, assuming that the benzene ring consists of alternating C=C double bonds and C–C single bonds. The difference between your two values is an estimate of the resonance energy of benzene. [214 kJ/mol]

22. The crystal structure of urea, $O=C(NH_2)_2$, has been determined by neutron diffraction, and shows that all the atoms in the urea molecule are coplanar. The bonding at each nitrogen atom is trigonal planar, and not pyramidal as in ammonia. The C=O bond length is 1.26 Ångstoms, and the C–N bond length is 1.35 Ångstoms. Compare these bond lengths with the typical bond lengths given in Table 11-1. Draw the "normal" Lewis structure, and appropriate resonance structures that help to understand these facts. Hint: refer to the discussion of the amide bond in Section 11-10.

23. Iodine has a normal valence of 1 and normal hypervalences of 3, 5 and 7. Draw box diagrams for the iodine atom in its normal valence state, and the three hypervalent states.

12 The Theory of Chemical Bonding

Objectives

After reading this chapter, the student should be able to do the following:

♦ Describe the duality between wave and particle properties of electrons and other "particles".

♦ Describe the relationship between a wave function and the motion of a particle.

♦ Identify atomic and molecular orbitals as wave functions.

♦ State the relationship between a wave function and electron density.

♦ Describe the shapes of s and p atomic orbitals.

♦ Describe the shapes of σ and π molecular orbitals.

♦ Distinguish between bonding and anti-bonding orbitals.

♦ Describe the electronic configurations of homonuclear diatomic molecules.

♦ Define bond order in relation to electronic configurations of diatomic molecules.

♦ Describe hybrid atomic orbitals and their relationship to s and p orbitals.

Related topics to review:

Structure of atoms in Chapter 10. Structure of molecules in Chapter 11.

Related topics to look forward to:

Organic chemistry in Chapter 19.

12-1 The Quantum Theory

In the last chapter we examined the Lewis theory of covalent bonds, and the valence shell electron pair repulsion (VSEPR) theory of molecular shapes. Together these two theories provide a valuable picture of the role of the valence electrons in binding atoms together in molecules, and allow useful predictions to be made about the valence of atoms, number and order of chemical bonds and the shapes of molecules. However these theories are incomplete and do not provide a reliable method of calculating bond energies or bond lengths. A full understanding of chemical bonding comes only through study of the quantum theory of electrons.

The quantum theory is based on mathematics. To understand it adequately requires a level of mathematical sophistication that is beyond the training or experience of most readers of this book, and so the present discussion of this topic must be limited in scope. However an introduction to the basics of quantum chemistry does not require the full mathematical treatment.

Physicists and mathematicians developed quantum theory in its modern form in the 1920's, in order to explain a number of new and puzzling experimental facts about spectroscopy and the structure of atoms. Louis de Broglie proposed the existence of waves associated with moving particles. Erwin Schrödinger proposed a mathematical equation that describes how those waves behave, and solved his equation for several important applications. Max Born gave an interpretation of the waves in terms of the probability for the finding the electron at various places. Werner Heisenberg developed an equivalent theory using a different mathematical formalism, and demonstrated the uncertainty principle stating that there are limits to the precision of simultaneous knowledge of position and momentum of electrons. Eugene Wigner showed the importance of symmetry in determining the outcome of quantum calculations. In the few years following 1926 most of the fundamentals of the new theory were established, and the theory was applied to electrons in atoms, molecules and solids.

In applying quantum theory to the problem of chemical bonding, mathematical difficulties defeated early efforts to solve the mathematical equations exactly. However mathematical approximations and simplified pictorial models soon gave an understanding of the main features of chemical bonds. The concepts of quantum chemistry developed in the early days are still used when discussing chemical bonding. Since the development and application of computers in the 1950's and 1960's, mathematical methods and computing technology have improved so much that as we enter the new millenium, the energies and structures of molecules can be calculated at modest cost with accuracy comparable to experiment. This position has been reached only after seventy years of intense study by many chemists, physicists and mathematicians.

12-2 Waves

The hypothesis proposed by de Broglie was that what we know as an electron may, under certain circumstances, behave like a wave instead of a particle. A wave is an oscillation which varies in a periodic way both in time and space. Waves are familiar in everyday life. Waves on the surface of water are found wherever there is water. Sound is carried by waves of compression through the air, and light consists of electromagnetic waves travelling through space. Special features of wave motion are **interference** effects when two wave trains cross, **diffraction** effects when a wave passes near an obstacle or a change in the properties of the medium, and **stationary waves** when a wave is reflected from boundaries.

de Broglie waves are represented mathematically by **wave functions**, and exhibit interference and diffraction phenomena just like other waves.

In a wave there are positive and negative displacements, and at any instant, the displacements at two points in space may be of opposite sign, one positive and the other negative. de Broglie waves are no exception, and the wave function may take values of opposite sign at different points in space. The relative signs of the wave function at different places are an important characteristic of the wave function.

The wavelength of the de Broglie wave for an electron (or other very small particle) is determined by the speed of the electron. By a calculation based upon the theory of relativity, de Broglie showed that the wavelength λ of the wave associated with a particle of mass m moving with speed v is:

$$\lambda = \frac{h}{mv} \tag{12-1}$$

where h is Planck's constant, which we met in Chapter 10 when discussing the nature of light. For ordinary "particles" the de Broglie wavelength is so short that the wave is not observable, but for electrons moving at high speed the wavelength becomes comparable with the size of an atom or molecule, and then the wave motion dominates the behaviour of the electron. The calculations are shown in the following examples.

Example 12-1 Calculate the de Broglie wavelength for a pebble of mass 10. grams thrown at a speed of 10. metre/second.

The value of Planck's constant is $h = 6.626 \times 10^{-34}$ J s. Substituting in the above formula (12-1), the de Broglie wavelength is $\lambda = \dfrac{6.626 \times 10^{-34} \text{ J s}}{0.010 \text{ kg} \times 10. \text{ m s}^{-1}} = 6.6 \times 10^{-33}$ metre .

This is an unimaginably small distance which can have no consequences for the way the pebble moves.

Example 12-2 Calculate the speed of an electron for which the de Broglie wavelength is 0.10 nanometre, which is approximately the size of a hydrogen atom.

The value of Planck's constant is $h = 6.626 \times 10^{-34}$ J s and the mass of an electron is 9.109×10^{-31} kg.

Substituting in the above formula (12-1), $v = \dfrac{6.626 \times 10^{-34} \text{ J s}}{9.109 \times 10^{-31} \text{ kg} \times 0.10 \times 10^{-9} \text{ m}} = 7.3 \times 10^{6}$ m/s

The speed calculated in the last example is of the same order of magnitude as the speed of an electron in a hydrogen atom calculated according to the Bohr theory, and hence it is no surprise that quantum effects in atoms are prominent and easily observable.

The wave-particle duality of atomic "particles" can be used for very practical purposes. Neutrons are uncharged nuclear particles with approximately the same mass as a proton, and are produced profusely in the nuclear fission processes inside a nuclear reactor. Neutrons from a nuclear reactor have almost the same kinetic energy as a molecule in a gas at room temperature, and have a root mean square speed of approximately 2200 m/s. The average de Broglie wavelength for neutrons from a nuclear reactor is comparable to the length of a chemical bond, and so neutrons can be used to study the properties of crystals and molecules. Figure 12-1 shows an instrument used for this purpose, which is operated by the National Research Council at the NRU reactor at Chalk River, Ontario.

Chapter 12

Figure 12-1 In this apparatus, called a diffractometer, the wave-like properties of neutrons are used to study the structures of crystals. The neutrons from a nuclear reactor in the background enter the chamber labelled "DUALSPEC". A diffraction device selects neutrons that all have the same wavelength, and these neutrons then pass through the crystalline sample and into the detector chamber on the right, where the neutrons are detected by making use of their particle-like properties. From the various angles through which the neutrons are scattered, the structure of crystals is determined. *Photo courtesy of National Research Council of Canada, Chalk River Laboratories.*

Example 12-3 Calculate the de Broglie wavelength for a neutron of mass 1.67×10^{-27} kg travelling at a speed of 2200. metre/second.

The value of Planck's constant is $h = 6.626 \times 10^{-34}$ J s. Substituting in the above formula (12-1), the de Broglie wavelength is $\lambda = \dfrac{6.626 \times 10^{-34} \text{ J s}}{1.67 \times 10^{-27} \text{ kg} \times 2200. \text{ m s}^{-1}} = 1.80 \times 10^{-10}$ metre.

The wavelength is 1.80×10^{-10} m, or 1.80 Ångstrom, which is approximately the length of a chemical bond.

To represent the motion of a particle through space, wave mechanics uses the concept of a **wave packet**, which is a localized set of waves. To help visualize a wave packet, imagine yourself fishing in a small boat at anchor on a calm lake, when a group of waves from some far-off disturbance travels across the lake towards you. The waves take a while to arrive but you can see them coming. As they approach, the surface of the water starts to move up and down a little, then a little more, reaching a maximum amplitude and then dying away as the group or "packet" of waves passes. When the waves have passed, you can still see them as they continue to travel across the lake, although at your particular position there is no longer any motion. The amplitude of the wave is large only within a certain range of the centre of the packet, and dies away on each side of the centre. Figure 12-1 shows such a wave packet.

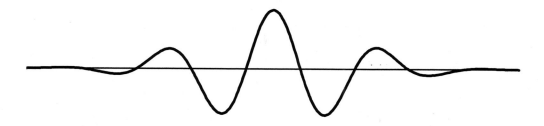

Figure 12-2 A localized wave packet that is moving through space and oscillating in time. The amplitude of the wave is only large near the centre of the wave packet. The diagram can be interpreted either as a snapshot showing how the wave varies with position in space, or a graph of the wave as a function of time at a fixed position, as in the example of an anchored fishing boat in the text.

In quantum theory, a packet of de Broglie waves moves in the same way that the particle itself would move according to Newton's laws of motion. However the position of the particle cannot be determined to any greater accuracy than the width of the wave packet, and as this is narrowed, the wavelength and hence the momentum of the particle becomes less clearly defined. This is the origin of the **Heisenberg uncertainty principle**, which states that as the uncertainty of the position of an electron is made smaller, the uncertainty in the momentum of the electron increases.

Quantum chemistry is more concerned with electrons bound in atoms and molecules than with electrons moving freely through space. Quantum effects become important whenever an electron is confined in a small space. When an electron is localized by forces such as the electrostatic attraction to the nuclei in an atom or molecule, the de Broglie wave for the electron is reflected from the potential energy barrier holding the electron and **stationary wave** patterns are set up. A stationary wave is formed if the electron is in a quantized energy state of an atom. The electron remains in the vicinity of the nucleus; correspondingly, the stationary wave for the electron stays with its centre at the nucleus of the atom. The quantum properties of bound electrons reflect the nature of the stationary wave patterns.

The nature and shape of the stationary wave pattern can be calculated from an equation called the **Schrödinger equation**. The wave associated with an electron or other quantum particle is described by the wave function. The wave function must be a solution to the Schrödinger equation and must satisfy certain conditions which control the shape of the wave function at the boundaries of the system. The boundary conditions and symmetry considerations turn out to be almost as important as the details of the Schrödinger equation itself. Except in very simple cases, the Schrödinger equation is a differential equation involving many co-ordinates, and solving the equation is a major mathematical challenge. However it is helpful to know a little bit about the nature of the stationary waves which are solutions of the Schrödinger equation, even if a full discussion is not possible at this stage.

The connection between the wave function and the properties of the electrons is that, although the position of an electron at any instant is a random quantity, the distribution of the electron in space follows a probability distribution function, which is equal to the square of the wave function. Where the wave function is large, there is a high probability of finding the electron in that neighbourhood. For a stationary wave corresponding to a quantized state, the square of the wave function at a particular point within an atom or molecule is independent of time, and is proportional to the **electron density** at that point.

To help visualize what is meant by electron density, again imagine yourself in a small boat at anchor on a calm lake, at the height of the mosquito season. It is likely that the boat will be surrounded by a cloud of mosquitoes, like the electrons in an atom or molecule. The mosquito density at a place near you is the number of mosquitoes per unit volume at that place. To measure the mosquito density you can take a small volume at a particular place, count the number of mosquitoes in that volume, and divide the number of mosquitoes by the volume. The density of mosquitoes probably varies from one place to another, and is likely to be a maximum somewhere near you. The position of a particular mosquito at a particular time may be difficult to determine and impossible to predict, but the total density of mosquitoes in the space around the boat is fairly constant. In an atom or molecule, the electron density is high at places where the magnitude of the wave function is large, and in turn the magnitude of the wave function is determined by the Schrödinger equation for that particular atom or molecule.

A recent advance in theory has been the development of a method of calculating the electronic properties of atoms and molecules from the electron density alone, without dealing with the wave function. However the wave function remains of central importance in quantum theory.

The quantized energy levels in an atom can be deduced from the sharp lines in the spectrum of that atom, as discussed in Chapter 10. In quantum theory, the quantization of the energy and the existence of the various quantum numbers is a consequence of the boundary conditions which the wave function must satisfy. The permitted values of the principal quantum number n, the orbital quantum number λ, and the magnetic quantum number m in an atom are determined by boundary conditions on the wave functions for the various states of the atom.

Can wave functions ever be observed? In the conventional view of quantum mechanics, the wave function can not be observed except through the results of measurements of quantities such as energy, angular momentum, or electron density. Such a view is probably too restrictive, and direct observation of some aspects of the wave function has been achieved in certain experiments, even if filtered through a maze of experimental techniques and theoretical interpretation.

Are wave functions "real"? This question leads us to philosophical questions about what is "real" and what is "unreal", and discussion of these questions is beyond our immediate purpose here. What is definite is that wave functions have been invented for the purpose of describing quantum effects in atoms and molecules, and that there are mathematical rules that must be followed when talking about them or manipulating them. It is misleading to say that because "we" invented them, "we" can do whatever we like with them, for that can lead to serious misunderstanding and error in later work. Wave functions are as real as other theoretical concepts such as potential energy or electric fields, because the predictions of quantum theory based upon wave functions have been verified by experiment. Quantum theory may be superseded one day, but any new theory must include many of the concepts of quantum theory.

12-3 Atomic orbitals

The wave function for an electron in a particular atomic state is called an **atomic orbital**. For atoms and molecules, the words "wave function" and "orbital" are interchangeable in most circumstances. The word orbital is a reference to the classical orbit of a particle, such as the orbit of the earth around the sun. However, according to quantum theory, an electron in an atom does not follow a single path or orbit around the nucleus, but is distributed statistically throughout the space occupied by the atom. In a particular state, the electron is most likely to be found at places where the wave function for that state is numerically large. More precisely, the probability of finding the electron near a particular point is proportional to the square of the value of the wave function at that point.

In some books, the word "orbital" is used to refer to the square of the wave function, or the electron density. This is not consistent with the definition used by quantum chemists.

For the s states of an atom, the orbitals are spherically symmetrical around the nucleus. That is, the value of the orbital at a point is a function only of the distance from the nucleus and does not depend on the direction of the line from the point to the nucleus. Hence the s orbitals can be represented by a graph of the orbital as a function of radius, r.

The 1s, 2s and 3s orbitals for the electron in a hydrogen atom are plotted in Figure 12-3 as a function of position along a line passing through the nucleus of the atom. Only one half of each graph is necessary to specify the whole function, but both sides have been drawn to show the similarity of these functions to the wave packet shown in Figure 12-2.

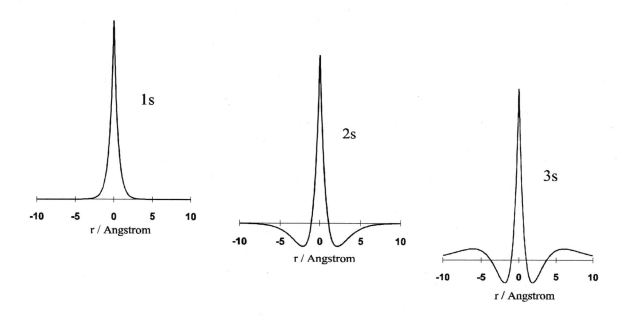

Figure 12-3 The 1s, 2s and 3s orbitals for the electron in a hydrogen atom. The orbital is plotted as a function of electron co-ordinate along a line passing through the nucleus of the atom.

Every s orbital has its largest value at the nucleus, and oscillates with decreasing amplitude as the distance from the nucleus increases. The 1s orbital has the same sign everywhere, the 2s orbital changes sign once, and the 3s orbital changes sign twice, as a function of distance from the nucleus.

All atomic orbitals approach zero at large distances from the nucleus, but (at least in principle) there is no specific place where they reach exactly zero. Comparison of the graphs in Figure 12-3 shows that the 1s, 2s and 3s orbitals extend to larger distances as the principal quantum number increases. The outer parts of the 2s and 3s orbitals are numerically smaller than the peak near the nucleus, but the electron is more likely to be found in those regions than near the nucleus because there is more volume at larger distances from the nucleus. The most likely distance from the nucleus to the electron in a hydrogen atom is 0.53 Ångstrom in the 1s orbital, about 2.6 Ångstrom units in the 2s orbital, and about 7.4 Ångstrom units in the 3s orbital.

The most important feature of an s orbital is its spherical shape, rather than its size or the details of the oscillations shown in Figure 12-3. Figure 12-4 shows a spherical surface to represent an s orbital, and indicates that the orbital has equal values at equal distances from the nucleus.

Figure 12-4 A sphere indicating the spherical shape of an s orbital.

In Chapter 10, we learned that electrons in atoms can occupy p quantum states as well as s states. The p states have characteristic wave functions, or orbitals. The mathematical form of a p orbital differs from that of an s orbital, and the difference can be explained in several ways.

The numerical value of a p orbital at a point varies with the direction of that point from the nucleus, as well as its distance from the nucelus. This may be compared with an s orbital, which has the same value in all directions, as indicated by the spherical surface shown in Figure 12-4. A p orbital is positive on one side of the nucleus, negative on the other side, and zero right at the nucleus. This is shown in Figure 12-5, showing the 2p atomic orbital for the electron in hydrogen is plotted as a function of position along a line passing through the nucleus.

The angular dependence gives p orbitals a characteristic shape, which is shown in Figure 12-6. The light and dark shading differentiates between regions in which the orbital has opposite signs. The figure shows three p orbitals, which are identical in shape but differ in their orientation in space. Each of the p orbitals points along one of the three axes of a Cartesian frame of reference shown at the left of the diagram, and the name of the axis (x, y, or z) is used as a subscript to label the orbitals.

Notice that there are three p orbitals, since the value of the orbital quantum number is $\lambda = 1$, and there are three values of the magnetic quantum number m, namely −1, 0 and +1. However, the three orbitals p_x, p_y and p_z shown in Figure 12-6 do not correspond directly to the three values of m.

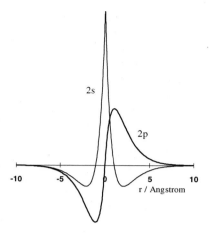

Figure 12-5 The heavy line is a graph of the 2p orbital for an electron in a hydrogen atom plotted as a function of position along the main axis of the orbital. The light line shows the 2s orbital for comparison. The 2s orbital has its maximum value at the nucleus, and has the same sign on opposite sides of the nucleus. The 2p orbital is zero at the nucleus, and has opposite signs on opposite sides of the nucleus.

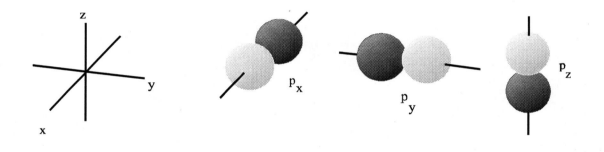

Figure 12-6 The shapes of the p orbitals. There are three p orbitals, which have the same shape but differ in their orientation relative to an external axis system. Each orbital is identified by the axis along which the orbital is oriented. The centre of each orbital is located at the nucleus of the atom. The light and dark shading indicates distinct regions of the orbital; in the light region, the sign of the orbital is opposite to that in the dark region. In each orbital, these regions are separated by a plane where the orbital is zero.

The surfaces in Figure 12-6 indicate qualitatively the regions of space where the numerical value of each orbital is significantly different from zero. The light and dark shading of the two regions of each orbital indicates that the orbital is of opposite sign in the two regions. The sign is an important feature of the orbital, and should be shown in any diagram representing an orbital. At a particular point in the orbital, the sign of the orbital, either positive or negative, is called the **phase** at that point. The light and dark shading of the two regions indicate that the phases are opposite in those regions. At the boundary between the two regions, the orbital must be zero, since it must change smoothly from a positive to a negative value at that boundary. A surface where the orbital is zero is called a **node** or a **nodal surface**. The nodal surface of a p orbital is a plane passing through the nucleus of the atom.

12-4 Electrons – the "glue" of chemical bonds

Electrons are very much lighter than atomic nuclei, and are bound to the nuclei by strong electrostatic forces. Wherever the nuclei go, the electrons follow. But when two atoms interact with each other, the valence electrons play a dominant role in determining whether or not a chemical bond is formed, as we have seen in Chapter 11. We therefore ask, do the electrons follow the motion of the nuclei, or is it the other way round, with the nuclei moving under the influence of forces determined by the electrons? The answer to both parts of the question is yes, though this may seem contradictory.

Because they are so much lighter than the nucleus, the electrons in an atom move much faster than the nucleus and so are easily able to follow the nucleus as it moves. The atomic orbitals that determine the distribution of the electrons in an atom therefore remain centred on the nucleus regardless of motion of the latter.

When two atoms come close together, the electrons in each atom adjust their motion and distribution in space to take account of the approach of the other atom. The adjustment takes place continuously as the atoms approach each other, because the electrons move so much faster than the nuclei. The total energy of the two atoms changes as the electrons redistribute themselves. If the total energy goes down, then there is an attractive force drawing the two atoms together and a chemical bond will be formed. If the total energy goes up, then there will be a repulsive force pushing the two atoms apart. When atoms interact, the electrons, particularly the valence electrons, determine the relative motion of the nuclei.

Whether a chemical bond is formed or not depends upon how the total energy of the electrons and nuclei change as the atoms come close together. An interaction that lowers the total energy significantly will result in formation of a chemical bond; this is called a **bonding** interaction. An increase of total energy prevents formation of a chemical bond, and this is called an **anti-bonding** interaction.

All nuclei are positively charged and so there is an electrostatic repulsion between nuclei. A chemical bond is formed between two atoms if the distribution in space of the valence electrons changes so as to "screen" the electrostatic repulsion between the nuclei by moving electron density into the space between the two nuclei. This region is called the **bonding region**. In an anti-bonding interaction, electron density is moved out of the bonding region, and the atoms are driven apart by electrostatic repulsion between the nuclei. The formation of bonds is the result of overlap of atomic orbitals in such a way as to give positive reinforcement of the overlapping parts of the orbitals with the same phase.

12-5 Molecular orbitals in diatomic molecules

When atoms come together to form a chemical bond, the electrons move under the influence of two or more nuclei, instead of the one nucleus at the centre of each atom. The orbitals, which describe the electron distribution in a molecule, are called **molecular orbitals**. A molecular orbital belongs to the molecule as a whole and is determined by solving the Schrödinger equation for the whole molecule including the interaction of every electron with every nucleus.

Molecular orbitals are even more complex to calculate than atomic orbitals. Because of the complexity of the mathematical problem, molecular orbitals are often described qualitatively by relating them to atomic orbitals centred on the atoms in the molecule. The formation of a chemical bond results from the overlap and combination of valence shell atomic orbitals on the two atoms involved. The atomic orbitals combine to form molecular orbitals, which can then accommodate the valence electrons of the atoms bonded together.

The number of molecular orbitals formed is equal to the number of atomic orbitals which are combined: two atomic orbitals form two molecular orbitals, four atomic orbitals form four molecular orbitals, and so on.

The allowed combinations can be described approximately in terms of algebraic sum or difference of the atomic orbitals on the different atoms. In the case of two identical atoms, the allowed combinations of atomic orbitals are particularly simple. From two atomic orbitals, two molecular orbitals are formed: in one molecular orbital the two atomic orbitals are added, and in the other the atomic orbitals are subtracted. These two molecular orbitals differ sharply in their properties, for one of them results in formation of a chemical bond, and the other does not.

When considering the sum and difference of atomic orbitals, it is important to pay attention to the phase or sign of the orbitals. Opposite shading (light or dark) indicates opposite sign, or phase. The sum of orbitals with the same shading at a point leads to reinforcement of the wave function, whereas the sum of orbitals with opposite shading leads to cancellation. The difference of orbitals with the same shading at a point leads to cancellation of the wave function, whereas the difference of orbitals with opposite shading leads to reinforcement.

Another way to think about these interactions is in terms of constructive interference (reinforcement), or destructive interference (cancellation) between waves.

We start by considering the overlap of s orbitals. The two possible ways of combining the orbitals is shown in Figure 12-7. The sum of the atomic s orbitals shows reinforcement of the orbital between the nuclei. This orbital results in a build-up of electron density in the bonding region of the molecule, which shields the electrostatic repulsion between the nuclei. The result is that the energy of the molecule is lower than the energy of the separate atoms. In the language of chemistry, a chemical bond is formed. This molecular orbital is therefore called a **bonding orbital**.

The difference of the atomic s orbitals leads to a molecular orbital which is zero in the plane bisecting the molecule between the nuclei, since on this plane the two atomic orbitals have the same value. Hence electron density between the nuclei is zero in this plane. Since this plane is in the middle of the bonding region, the electron density is small throughout the bonding region. This reduces the electronic shielding of the inter-nuclear repulsion, and increases the energy of the molecule. Because of the unshielded repulsion between the atoms, no chemical bond is formed and the molecular orbital is called an **anti-bonding orbital**. In Figure 12-7, light and dark shading indicates the regions of opposite phase, in the same way as in Figure 12-6. The orbital is zero at the boundary between the light and dark parts of the molecular orbital.

The bonding molecular orbital is called a σ (the Greek letter "sigma") orbital, and the anti-bonding orbital is called σ*, (pronounced "sigma star"). These are sσ and sσ* molecular orbitals because they are formed from s atomic orbitals on the two atoms. The principal quantum number may also be added to the label: for instance, 2sσ means a bonding molecular orbital formed by overlap of two 2s atomic orbitals.

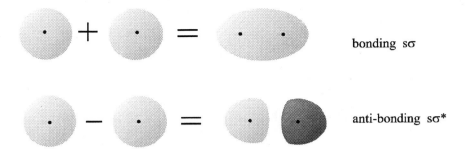

Figure 12-7 The sum and difference combinations of s orbitals on adjacent atoms leads to a bonding molecular orbital in the case of a sum, and an anti-bonding orbital in the case of the difference. The positions of the nuclei of the atoms are indicated by the black dots. The designations sσ and sσ* are explained in the text.

The formation of molecular orbitals from atomic p orbitals is more complex because it depends on the orientation of the p orbitals relative to the line between the two atoms (called the molecular axis). Figure 12-8 shows the situation for two p orbitals parallel to the molecular axis is shown in Figure 12-8. Addition of the two p orbitals leads to cancellation between the nuclei, and hence to an anti-bonding molecular orbital. Subtraction, on the other hand leads to reinforcement in the region between the nuclei and hence to a bonding molecular orbital. The result is an orbital similar to the bonding orbital formed from s atomic orbitals. These are the pσ and pσ* molecular orbitals, because they are formed from p atomic orbitals, and are cylindrically symmetrical about the molecular axis like the molecular orbitals formed from s atomic orbitals.

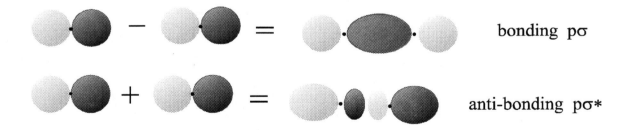

Figure 12-8 The sum and difference combinations of p orbitals oriented parallel to the line between the two adjacent atoms leads to an anti-bonding molecular orbital in the case of a sum, and a bonding orbital in the case of the difference. The positions of the nuclei are indicated by the black dots.

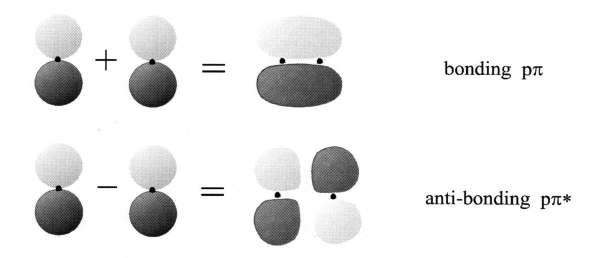

bonding pπ

anti-bonding pπ*

Figure 12-9 The sum and difference combinations of p orbitals oriented perpendicular to the line between the two adjacent atoms leads to a bonding molecular orbital in the case of a sum, and an anti-bonding orbital in the case of the difference.

When the two p orbitals are oriented parallel to each other but at right angles to the molecular axis, we find a new kind of molecular orbital. The two orbitals fit together side by side, to form a molecular orbital that varies with angle around the axis of the molecule, like the p orbitals themselves. The sum of the two p atomic orbitals gives a molecular orbital which is bonding in character, and is called a pπ orbital. The difference of the two atomic orbitals gives an anti-bonding orbital called a pπ* orbital; the anti-bonding orbital is zero on the plane through the middle of the molecule perpendicular to the molecular axis. The label π indicates that the molecular orbital is similar in shape to a p atomic orbital, with regions of opposite phase on opposite sides of the molecular axis.

There are six p atomic orbitals (three p orbitals on each of two atoms) and they form a total of six molecular orbitals. If the molecular axis is taken as the z axis, then the p_z atomic orbitals form the pσ and pσ* molecular orbitals, as shown in Figure 12-9. The two p_x atomic orbitals form $p_x\pi$ and $p_x\pi^*$ molecular orbitals, as shown in Figure 12-9; these orbitals are often referred to simply as pπ and pπ*. The two p_y atomic orbitals also form pπ and pπ* molecular orbitals which are equivalent to those formed from p_x atomic orbitals but are rotated by 90 degrees around the molecular axis.

12-6 Electronic configurations of diatomic molecules

The energies of the sσ and sσ* molecular orbitals are related to those of the s atomic orbitals from which they are formed. The energy of the sσ molecular orbital is lower, and the energy of the sσ* molecular orbital is higher, than the energy of the s atomic orbitals. The difference between the sσ and sσ* energies depends on the degree of overlap between the atomic orbitals, and varies with the distance between the nuclei. These energy levels are shown in Figure 12-10.

The electronic configurations of the diatomic molecules of the first row elements are found by using the aufbau process described in Chapter 10 in connection with the configurations of the atoms. For each successive molecule, the electrons are assigned to the lowest available energy levels, consistent with the Pauli exclusion principle. The exclusion principle states that each orbital can "hold" two electrons, as long as the spins of the two electrons are paired. The electrons in a molecule are therefore distributed among the orbitals in a kind of shell structure, in much the same way as the electrons in an individual atom.

Electrons in bonding orbitals tend to hold the atoms together, and form a covalent chemical bond; they are called bonding electrons. Electrons in anti-bonding orbitals tend to drive the atoms apart, and so reduce the strength of a covalent chemical bond; they are called anti-bonding electrons.

The **bond order** in a diatomic molecule depends on how many valence electrons are in bonding molecular orbitals, and how many are in anti-bonding molecular orbitals. If there are n_b electrons in bonding orbitals, and n_a electrons in anti-bonding orbitals, then the net number of bonding electrons is the difference $n_b - n_a$. Since a single covalent bond consists of a pair of electrons, the bond order is defined as half the net number of bonding electrons:

$$\text{bond order} = (n_b - n_a)/2 \tag{12-2}$$

A bond order of 1 indicates a covalent single bond, 2 indicates a double bond, and 3 indicates a triple bond. If the bond order is zero, there are equal numbers of bonding and anti-bonding electrons, and no covalent bond is formed. This concept is illustrated in the following examples.

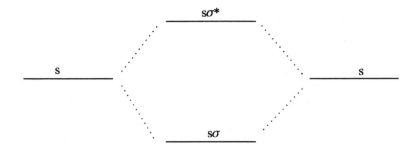

Figure 12-10 The energies of the molecular orbitals formed from two equivalent s atomic orbitals on adjacent atoms. The sσ bonding orbital is lower in energy because of the electron density that is located between the nuclei, as shown in Figure 12-6.

In a hydrogen molecule, H_2, there are two molecular orbitals formed by overlap of the 1s orbitals of the separate H atoms, the 1sσ and 1sσ* orbitals. The molecule contains two electrons, which can both occupy the sσ level provided that their spins are opposite or "paired", and the anti-bonding 1sσ* orbital is not occupied. The electronic configuration is written $(1s\sigma)^2$ by analogy with atomic configurations. There are two electrons in the bonding orbital and no electrons in the anti-bonding orbital, so the bond order is (2-0)/2 = 1. This is the prototype single bond formed from a pair of spin-paired electrons.

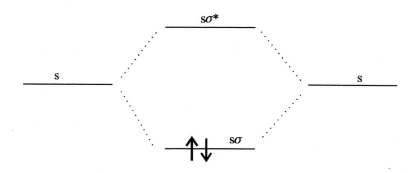

Figure 12-11 A diagrammatic representation of the $(1s\sigma)^2$ electronic configuration of the electrons in an H_2 molecule, showing the electrons with paired spins.

Helium atoms do not form chemical bonds, and this can be explained using molecular orbital theory. If a He_2 molecule were to form, then it would contain four electrons. In the lowest energy state, two electrons would occupy the $1s\sigma$ bonding orbital, and the other two would have to occupy the $1s\sigma^*$ anti-bonding orbital because of the exclusion principle. The configuration would be $(1s\sigma)^2(1s\sigma^*)^2$ and the expected bond order is zero. The increase in energy of the anti-bonding electrons cancels the decrease in energy of the bonding electrons, and no chemical bond is formed.

The molecule Li_2 exists in the gas phase, with a bond energy of 110 kJ/mol. The derivation of the molecular orbital electronic configuration is as follows. The valence shell of the lithium atom is the 2s shell, and each lithium atom contains one valence electron. In the molecule, the two valence electrons occupy a molecular orbital formed by overlap of two 2s atomic orbitals, and the electronic configuration of the molecule is written $(2s\sigma)^2$. The bond order is 1, indicating a single bond, so the formula can be written Li–Li.

Beryllium atoms do not form a diatomic molecule, which would have the formula Be_2. This is consistent with prediction: each atom has two el;ectrons in the 2s valence shell, so the electronic configuration of the molecule would be $(2s\sigma)^2(2s\sigma^*)^2$. There are two bonding electrons and two anti-bonding electrons, so the expected bond order is zero.

The configurations of the p-block diatomic molecules are more complicated to deal with. The six p atomic orbitals (three p orbitals on each of two atoms) form a total of six molecular orbitals, a $p\sigma$ orbital, a $p\sigma^*$ orbital, two $p\pi$ orbitals, and two $p\pi^*$ orbitals. There are however only four energy levels because the two $p\pi$ molecular orbitals are equivalent except for orientation and hence have equal energies. Similarly the two $p\pi^*$ orbitals have equal energy and have equal energies. Orbitals that have equal energies are described as **degenerate**.

Figure 12-12 shows the four energy levels corresponding to the six molecular orbitals formed from p atomic orbitals. The relative positions of the four energy levels vary from one molecule to another, but the diagram shows the correct order of the energy levels in the molecules B_2, C_2 and N_2.

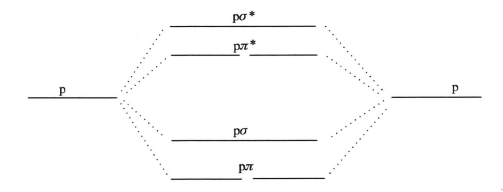

Figure 12-12 The energies of the six molecular orbitals formed from the three p atomic orbitals on two adjacent atoms in the homonuclear molecules of the lighter elements of the second row of the periodic table. The pσ and pσ* orbitals are formed from p_z atomic orbitals oriented parallel to the molecular axis. The two pπ orbitals and the two pπ* orbitals are formed from the p_x and p_y atomic orbitals on each atom oriented perpendicular to the molecular axis.

Boron atoms form diatomic molecules B_2, and the bond energy is 297 kJ/mol. The boron atom has configuration $1s^2 2s^2 2p^1$. The eight electrons from the 1s and 2s orbitals in the separate atoms occupy the 1sσ, 1sσ*, 2sσ and 2sσ* molecular orbitals. The two remaining electrons, one from the 2p orbital on each boron atom, occupy the next lowest energy level, which corresponds to the two 2pπ bonding molecular orbitals. Since there are two 2pπ orbitals with the same energy, there are various ways to accommodate the electrons in the available orbitals. In this situation, Hund's rule applies, just as in atoms, and tells us that in the lowest energy configuration one bonding electron is placed in each 2pπ orbital with parallel spins. Hence the valence shell configuration of the B_2 molecule is $(2s\sigma)^2 (2s\sigma^*)^2 (2p_x\pi)^1 (2p_y\pi)^1$. Subscripts have been added to show that there are two distinct 2pπ orbitals, which differ only in their orientation.

The calculation of the bond order in the molecule B_2 is as follows. There are 6 valence electrons altogether; 4 electrons are in bonding orbitals (2sσ and 2pπ), and 2 electrons in anti-bonding orbitals (2sσ*), so the bond order is $(4-2)/2 = 1$. Hence the bond in B_2 is a single bond, though it is not the same as the single bond in H_2 of Li_2.

The carbon diatomic molecule C_2 exists, and the bond energy is 607 kJ/mol. This is not the normal form for carbon, but the C_2 molecule has been detected in high temperature flames and furnaces, in the atmospheres of stars (including the sun) and in the tails of comets. The electronic configuration of the molecule is derived as follows. The four electrons from the 2s sub-shell of the carbon atoms are accommodated in the 2sσ and 2sσ* orbitals, and the four electrons from the p sub-shell are accommodated in the two 2pπ orbitals. Hence the molecule has the configuration

$$(2s\sigma)^2 (2s\sigma^*)^2 (2p_x\pi)^2 (2p_y\pi)^2,$$

or more concisely $(2s\sigma)^2 (2s\sigma^*)^2 (2p\pi)^4$. There are six electrons in the 2sσ and 2pπ bonding orbitals, and two in the anti-bonding 2sσ* orbital, so the bond order is $(6-2)/2 = 2$. Hence the bond is a double bond, and the structural formula should be written C=C. The valence of carbon in this molecule is 2 instead of the usual value of 4.

The nitrogen molecule N_2 has two more electrons than C_2, and these can be accommodated in the $2p\sigma$ orbital. The valence shell electronic configuration of the molecule is $(2s\sigma)^2(2s\sigma^*)^2(2p\pi)^4(2p\sigma)^2$. There are 8 electrons in bonding orbitals and 2 in an antibonding orbital, so the bond order is $(8-2)/2 = 3$. Hence we show a triple bond between the nitrogen atoms, $N\equiv N$. This is consistent with the normal valence of three for the nitrogen atom. Of the three bonds, one is formed from a σ orbital and two are π bonds.

The oxygen molecule O_2 has two more electrons than N_2, and these can be accommodated in the next highest molecular orbital, which is the anti-bonding $2p\pi^*$ molecular orbital. There are two such orbitals with the same energy and, by Hund's rule, one electron is placed in each of the $2p\pi^*$ orbitals with parallel spins. The electronic configuration is:

$$(2s\sigma)^2(2s\sigma^*)^2(2p\sigma)^2(2p\pi)^4(2p_x\pi^*)^1(2p_y\pi^*)^1$$

As in B_2, the two electrons with the highest energy are in separate $2p\pi^*$ orbitals, which have the same energy but differ in orientation. In the valence shell, there are 8 electrons in bonding orbitals and 4 in anti-bonding orbitals, so the bond order is $(8-4)/2 = 2$. This is consistent with the double bond usually shown between the oxygen atoms: $O=O$.

In both O_2 and B_2, there are two electrons with unpaired spins, and these give these molecules special magnetic properties. Oxygen is a **paramagnetic** substance because it has unpaired spins, while nitrogen is **diamagnetic** because all the electron spins are paired.

Note that in the electronic configuration of the oxygen molecule, the order of the $2p\sigma$ and $2p\pi$ orbitals has been reversed. This is done because in the heavier molecules of the second row elements (O_2 and F_2) the $2p\sigma$ energy is lower than the $2p\pi$ energy level, contrary to what is shown in Figure 12-12. This is however a minor point since both levels are fully occupied, and the order of the occupied levels does not matter for our present purposes.

The fluorine molecule F_2, has two more electrons than O_2, and these go into the $2p\pi^*$ anti-bonding orbital, to make the configuration:

$$(2s\sigma)^2(2s\sigma^*)^2(2p\sigma)^2(2p\pi)^4(2p\pi^*)^4$$

There are 8 electrons in bonding orbitals, and 6 in anti-bonding orbitals, so the bond order is $(8-6)/2 = 1$. This is consistent with the single bond usually shown between the fluorine atoms: $F-F$.

Neon does not form chemical bonds. This is because, in a hypothetical Ne_2 molecule, there would be an equal number of bonding and anti-bonding pairs of electrons, which lead to a bond order of zero.

In this way, the molecular orbital theory explains the properties of the diatomic molecules of the second row elements, and relates the known valences of these elements to their position in the periodic table. The success of the molecular orbital picture in accounting for the paramagnetism of oxygen so simply is an indication of the usefulness of this approach.

The molecular orbital picture of bonding is quite different from that given by Lewis structures, but the conclusions about valence and bond order are similar in most cases. The molecular orbital picture is an enormous advance over Lewis structures, though, because with the application of the Schrödinger equation it is possible to calculate the energy, the bond-length and other properties from first principles. Such calculations are referred to as *ab initio* calculations.

Example 12-3 Write the electronic configuration for the molecular ion O_2^+ and calculate the bond order.

The molecular ion O_2^+ is related to the O_2 molecule by the removal of one electron from the highest occupied molecular orbital of the neutral molecule, and so the electron configuration is: $(2s\sigma)^2(2s\sigma^*)^2(2p\sigma)^2 (2p\pi)^4 (2p\pi^*)^1$. There are 8 electrons in bonding orbitals and 3 electrons in anti-bonding orbitals, so the bond order is (8-3)/2 = 2.5.

According to this calculation, there are "two and a half" bonds between the oxygen atoms in the O_2^+ molecule, and so we would expect the bond to be shorter and stronger than that in the neutral O_2 molecule. This is confirmed by experiment: the bond length is 1.12 Ångstroms, which is shorter than the bond length of 1.22 Ångstroms in O_2; the bond energy in O_2^+ is 650 kJ/mol, which is larger than the bond energy of 498.3 kJ/mol in O_2 (see Table 11-2). This is one of those surprizing cases in which removing a valence electron from a molecule increases the strength of the bond.

12-7 Chemical bonds in polyatomic molecules

Molecular orbitals can be defined, calculated and studied for molecules with more than two atoms. Molecular orbitals extend over the whole molecule, and so are suitable for describing delocalized electrons. Delocalization of electrons in benzene, and in other molecules for which different resonance forms can be drawn, was discussed in Section 11-10.

However, for molecules in which delocalization is not important, molecular orbital theory is often replaced by a simpler approach. We saw in Chapter 11 that individual bonds in a molecule have well-defined properties, such as bond length, bond angles and bond energy, and it is an advantage to be able to identify each chemical bond with a feature of the molecular orbital. This is not easy to do with molecular orbitals.

It is common therefore to use a different theory in which each individual bond in a molecule is formed by overlap of orbitals on the two atoms that are bonded together. This approach to chemical bonding is called the **valence bond method**, and historically it dates back to the earliest days of the application of quantum theory to chemistry. Through the concept of **hybridization**, atomic orbitals can be formed which match the geometry of a molecule, which is known from experiment, or predicted by VSEPR theory.

In describing the chemical bonding of the second row elements, the 2s and 2p atomic orbitals play the most important part. The 2s orbital is spherically symmetrical, and the three 2p orbitals are oriented at right angles to each other in space. These orbitals therefore do not match any of the common shapes of polyatomic molecules. But if certain mathematical combinations of the 2s and 2p orbitals on the central atom are taken, new sets of orbitals are formed which do match the observed shapes. These new atomic orbitals are, in a sense, equivalent to the 2s and 2p atomic orbitals from which they are formed, but favour specific directions along which bonding pairs or lone pairs of electrons are expected to be located. The new orbitals are called **hybrid orbitals.**

Consider a linear AX_2 molecule, such as beryllium difluoride BeF_2. Choose the molecular axis to be the x axis of the co-ordinate system. The bonding between the Be atom and the F atoms involves both s and p_x orbitals on the central atom, as well as orbitals on the outer atoms. It is possible to form orbitals on the central atom which are equivalent to each other in shape, but point in opposite directions along the x axis. The new orbitals are linear combinations of orbitals on the central atom:

$$h_1 = s + p_x$$

$$h_2 = s - p_x \tag{12-3}$$

These orbitals h_1 and h_2 are called **sp hybrid orbitals** because they are a mixture of an s and a single p atomic orbital on the same atom. Figure 12-13 shows a representation of the two sp hybrid orbitals.

The hybrid orbitals are functions of position, just like the original orbitals s and p_x. Because the s orbital has the same phase in all directions, while the p_x orbital has opposite phases on opposite sides of the atom, the s and p_x orbitals reinforce each other on one side, and to some extent cancel on the other side, of the atom. This can be seen in Figure 12-5, which shows that at distances greater than about 1.5 Ångstroms, the s and p orbitals reinforce each other on the left of the graph, but have opposite signs and cancel each other on the right. This makes each of the hybrid orbitals h_1 and h_2 lopsided.

One of the sp hybrid orbitals points in the positive x direction, and the other points in the negative x direction, so the angle between the orbitals is 180°. It should be noted that the cosine of 180° is –1, which is the coefficient of the p_x orbital in the second of equations (12-3). An angle of 180° between the orbitals is just what we need to form the two A–X single bonds in a linear AX$_2$ molecule.

The overlap of an sp hybrid orbital with an s atomic orbital to form a σ bond is shown in Figure 12-14. The sp hybrid orbitals are cylindrically symmetrical around the bond axis and can overlap with other cylindrically symmetrical orbitals on other atoms to form σ bonds. The other two p orbitals are oriented at right angles to the axis of the σ bond and are not involved in the formation of the bond.

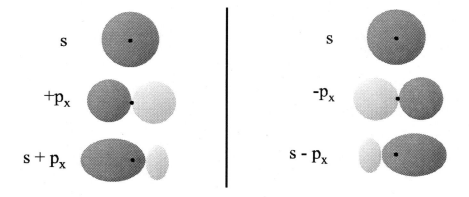

Figure 12-13 The sp hybrid orbitals are made by combining s and p_x orbitals *on the same atom* according to equation (12-3). On the left, the s and p_x orbitals are added together, and reinforce each other to the left of the nucleus. The resulting sum hybrid orbital s+p_x "points" to the left. On the right, the s and –p_x orbitals are combined to form the difference hybrid orbital s–p_x, which points to the right. Notice that changing the sign of the p_x orbital exchanges the light and dark shaded regions.

Figure 12-14 The overlap of an s orbital on the left hand atom with an sp hybrid orbital on the right hand atom to form a σ bond between the two atoms. The positions of the two nuclei are shown by the black dots.

Trigonal planar geometry requires the use of two p orbitals in addition to the s orbital. Choose the z axis of the co-ordinate system to be perpendicular to the plane of the molecule, so the molecule lies in the (x,y) plane. With this definition of axes, the bonding involves the s, the p_x and the p_y orbitals. Mathematical expressions for the three hybrid orbitals are as follows:

$$h_1 = s + \sqrt{2}\,p_x$$

$$h_2 = s + \sqrt{2}\left(-\tfrac{1}{2}p_x + \tfrac{\sqrt{3}}{2}p_y\right) \qquad (12\text{-}4)$$

$$h_3 = s + \sqrt{2}\left(-\tfrac{1}{2}p_x - \tfrac{\sqrt{3}}{2}p_y\right)$$

These are called **sp² hybrid orbitals** because they are a mixture of an s and two p atomic orbitals on the same atom. Figure 12-15 shows a representation of the three sp² hybrid orbitals. The curious coefficients that multiply each orbital inside the square brackets are chosen to give three equivalent orbitals that differ only in their orientation in the x-y plane, with equal angles of 120° between them. The coefficients –1/2 and ±√3/2 inside the parentheses of the second and third hybrid orbitals are the cosine and sine of angles of 120° and 240°. The first hybrid orbital described by equation (12-4) points along the x axis, and the other two hybrid orbitals lie in the x,y plane and point at angles of 120° and 240° to the first orbital.

The p_z orbital is at right angles to the plane of the molecule and is not involved in the formation of the bonds in the plane of the molecule.

Each of these sp² hybrid orbitals is cylindrically symmetrical around its axis and hence can overlap with s or a properly oriented p orbital on an outer atom to form σ bonding orbitals.

The bonds in trigonal planar molecules such as boron trifluoride, BF_3, are conveniently described in terms of sp² hybridization. In ethene, C_2H_4, there is a double bond between the carbon atoms. Part of this bond is formed by overlap of carbon sp² hybrid orbitals to form a σ bonding orbital. The p_z orbitals on the two carbon atoms are perpendicular to the plane of the molecule, and overlap each other to form a π bonding orbital between the carbon atoms, in the manner shown in Figure 12-9. Thus the double bond in ethene consists of one σ bonding orbital and one π bonding orbital.

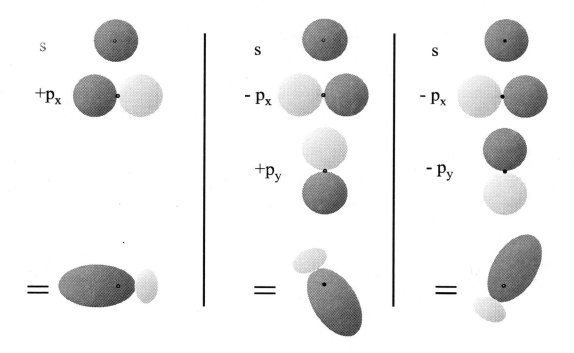

Figure 12-15 The formation of sp^2 hybrid orbitals on an atom. The combination of the s, the p_x and the p_y orbitals on a single atom according to equation (12-4) gives the three hybrid orbitals shown at the bottom. The three hybrid orbitals are equivalent except for a rotation through 120 degrees. The coefficients shown in equation (12-4) have been omitted for clarity.

Tetrahedral geometry requires the involvement of an s orbital and all three p orbitals. Mathematical expressions for the four equivalent hybrid orbitals are as follows:

$$h_1 = s + p_x + p_y + p_z$$

$$h_2 = s - p_x - p_y + p_z$$

$$h_3 = s - p_x + p_y - p_z \qquad (12\text{-}5)$$

$$h_4 = s + p_x - p_y - p_z$$

These are called **sp^3 hybrid orbitals**, and point in the four tetrahedral directions at angles of 109.47° to each other. These four hybrid orbitals are similar in shape to the sp and sp^2 hybrid orbitals and are oriented so as to point along the four tetrahedral bond directions. It is helpful to refer back to Figure 11-2 showing the relationship between a tetrahedral molecule and a cube. In that diagram, imagine x, y and z axes from the origin at the centre of the cube, passing through the centre of each face of the cube. Then each sp^3 hybrid orbital points towards the corner of the cube in Figure 11-2 that corresponds to the coefficients of the p orbitals in equations (12-5).

For example, the coefficients of the three p orbitals in the first hybrid orbital h_1 are (+1,+1,+1), and this hybrid orbital points in the direction of the corner of the cube that has co-ordinates (+1,+1,+1). The coefficients of the three p orbitals in the second hybrid orbital h_2 are (−1,−1,+1), and this orbital points in the direction of the corner of the cube that has co-ordinates (−1,−1,+1). The orientations of the two remaining orbitals are similarly related to the coefficients. There is therefore a simple relationship between the coefficients of the atomic orbitals and the geometry of the hybrid orbitals, just as there was for the sp and sp^2 hybrid orbitals. The angle between any two sp^3 hybrid orbitals is 109.47°.

The sp^3 hybrid orbitals are cylindrically symmetrical around their axis and hence can overlap with s or a properly oriented p orbital on an outer atom to form σ bonding orbitals. The tetrahedral arrangement of four bonds from carbon atoms to four other atoms, which is found in methane and thousands of other organic compounds, is usually described in terms of sp^3 hybridization of the atomic orbitals on the carbon atom.

Molecules in which there are lone pairs on the central atom can be accommodated within the hybridization picture. In the ammonia molecule, NH_3, the nitrogen atom is often described as sp^3 hybridized, with three of the hybrid orbitals forming σ bonding orbitals by overlapping with the 1s atomic orbitals on the hydrogen atoms, and the lone pair occupying the fourth hybrid orbital on the carbon atom. This is consistent with the trigonal pyramidal shape of the molecule, and the VSEPR picture for an AX_3E molecule, shown in Figure 11-9. Ammonia reacts as a base or proton acceptor because of the lone pair on the nitrogen atom. Many other organic bases have similar geometry at the nitrogen atom, with a lone pair occupying the fourth sp^3 hybrid orbital.

In the water molecule, H_2O, the oxygen atom is usually considered to be sp^3 hybridized, with two of the hybrid orbitals forming σ bonds to the hydrogen atoms, and the other two holding the lone pairs. This is consistent with the bent geometry of the molecule, and the tetrahedral arrangement of the hydrogen bonds in ice.

The hybridization of s and p atomic orbitals thus provides an adequate framework for understanding the bonding of the second row elements. For elements of the third and subsequent rows, the 3d orbitals can be involved in hybrid orbitals with trigonal bipyramidal or octahedral geometry.

Key concepts

The behaviour of electrons in atoms and molecules is governed by quantum theory. The motion of the electrons is described in terms of waves, and the nature of the waves is determined by the Schrödinger equation. For electrons that are bound to an atom or molecule, the waves form stationary wave patterns called orbitals, and the distribution of the electrons is determined by the square of the orbital.

In an atom, the orbitals are classified by the orbital quantum number. The s orbitals are spherical and have the same sign all around the atom, while p orbitals are positive on one side of the atom and negative on the other side.

In a molecule, the electrons hold the atoms together and form the chemical bonds. Molecular orbitals that describe the bonds can be thought of as being formed from atomic orbitals on the atoms bonded together. From two atomic orbitals, two molecular orbitals are formed, of which one is bonding and the other is anti-bonding. Chemical bonding in diatomic molecules can be understood in terms of these molecular orbitals, by assigning the valence electrons from the atoms to the molecular orbitals.

In polyatomic molecules, the atomic orbitals on a single atom can be combined to form hybridized orbitals that match the shape of the molecule. Hybrid orbitals formed from s and p orbitals can match tetrahedral, trigonal planar and linear molecular shapes. Hybrid orbitals provide an explanation of the effects of multiple bonding on the shapes of organic molecules.

Review questions

1. What is a wave packet?

2. What determines the de Broglie wavelength of a particle?

3. What is an atomic orbital?

4. What is a molecular orbital?

5. What is a bonding molecular orbital?

6. What is an anti-bonding molecular orbital?

7. What is a σ molecular orbital?

8. What is a π molecular orbital?

9. Define bond order in a diatomic molecule.

10. What is a hybrid orbital?

11. What is the characteristic hybridization for planar trigonal geometry?

12. What is the characteristic hybridization for tetrahedral geometry?

Problems

1. Show that the four vectors with components $(+1,+1,+1)$, $(-1,-1,+1)$, $(-1,+1,-1)$ and $(+1,-1,-1)$ point from the origin to the four corners of a regular tetrahedron. Compare these vectors with the coefficients of the p orbitals in the sp^3 hybrid orbitals in equation (12-5), and with the diagram in Figure 11-2.

2. Calculate the bond order in the following molecules: H_2, N_2, C_2, He_2^+, N_2^+, O_2^-.

3. Describe the hybridization of all the atoms except hydrogen in each of the following molecules:

$$C_2H_6, \ CH_3NH_2, \ CH_3OH, \ CH_3CH=CH_2, \ CH_3C\equiv CH, \ CH_2O.$$

4. Calculate the de Broglie wavelength for each of the following "particles".

   (a) a steel ball with a mass of 1.0 g moving at a speed of 1.0 cm/s;

   (b) an electron which has been accelerated from rest through a potential difference of 1.0 volt;

   (c) an electron which has been ejected from a sodium atom in the gas phase by light of wavelength 200. nanometres, given that the ionization energy of sodium is 495 kJ mol^{-1}.

   $[6.6\times10^{-29} \text{ m}; 1.22 \text{ nanometres}; 1.19 \text{ nanometres}]$

5. Of the first ten elements, which do not form diatomic molecules?

6. Draw energy level diagrams with arrows to represent the configurations of all the second row diatomic molecules from Li_2 to F_2.

7. When a proton leaves a water molecule, the hydroxide ion OH^- remains. When a proton leaves an ammonia molecule, the amide ion NH_2^- remains. Draw a Lewis structure for the amide ion and predict its shape. Describe the hybrization of the nitrogen atom. What chemical property would you expect the amide ion to have in common with the hydroxide ion?

8. When a water molecule accepts a proton, the hydronium ion H_3O^+ is formed. Draw a Lewis structure for the hydronium ion, and predict its shape. Describe the hybridization of the oxygen atom in this ion.

9. Draw a sketch of the ethene (ethylene) molecule, C_2H_4, similar to that in Figure 11-4. Indicate the locations of the sp^2 hybrid orbitals. Sketch the π molecular orbital formed from the carbon p orbitals which are perpendicular to the plane of the molecule, and indicate the phases of the various parts of the orbital. Use this diagram to explain why the whole molecule is planar, and why rotation of one end of the molecule relative to the other end around the C=C bond does not occur.

10. Draw a sketch of the ethyne (acetylene) molecule, C_2H_2. similar to that in Figure 11-4. What is the hybridization of the carbon atomic orbitals? Indicate in your sketch the locations of the hybrid orbitals. Sketch the π molecular orbitals formed from the carbon p orbitals that are perpendicular to the axis of the molecule, and indicate the phases of the various parts of each orbital. How would you describe the triple bond between the two carbon atoms?

13 Chemical Equilibrium in Gases

Objectives

After reading this chapter, the student should be able to do the following:

♦ Describe the general nature of chemical equilibrium.

♦ Define relative activity for gases in terms of partial pressure.

♦ Define relative activity for pure solids and liquids.

♦ Write an expression for the equilibrium constant for a chemical equation.

♦ Write an expression for the reaction quotient for a chemical equation.

♦ Calculate partial pressures and mole fractions for reactions at equilibrium in the gas phase using the equilibrium constant.

♦ Calculate the equilibrium constant as a function of temperature using the enthalpy change of reaction.

Related topics to review:

Chemical reactions in Chapter 2. Industrial processes involving gases, in Chapter 4. Properties of gases in Chapter 5. Thermochemistry in Chapter 6.

Related topics to look forward to:

Thermodynamics of chemical equilibrium in Chapter 16. Chemical kinetics in Chapter 18.

13-1 Chemical equilibrium and Le Chatelier's principle

In many chemical reactions, the reactants are not completely used up, and less of each product is formed than would be permitted by the laws of stoichiometry. In other words, these reactions do not go to completion. This is true even for reactions which take place quickly: after the reactants are mixed, concentrations become constant within a few seconds or less, and no matter how long one waits the reaction does not go to completion.

It is important to understand why this is so, and to be able to predict how far a reaction will proceed under given circumstances. Both in industry and in the laboratory, the usefulness of a chemical reaction depends upon how much of the product is formed, and it is important to know how to change the conditions of the reaction so as to improve the yield. This problem has been studied for more than a century, and remains central to a great deal of practical chemistry.

Consider, for example, the reaction in which sulfur dioxide reacts with oxygen to form sulfur trioxide:

$$2\,SO_2(g) + O_2(g) \rightarrow 2\,SO_3(g)$$

When the reactants are mixed, they start to react and the composition of the mixture starts to change. The amount of SO_2 decreases, the amount of O_2 decreases, and the amount of SO_3 increases. As time goes on, the amounts of each substance tend towards constant values, and after sufficient time has elapsed, no further change in the composition of the mixture can be detected. This is illustrated in Figure 13-1, in which the amount of each substance present is measured by its partial pressure.

In Figure 13-1, the time-scale of the reaction is not of importance, so no numbers or units are shown on the horizontal axis. The important point is that eventually the reaction reaches a condition in which no further changes in the partial pressures take place. This condition is called **chemical equilibrium**.

The stoichiometric relationships between the reactants and products, and the gas laws, must be obeyed at every stage of the reaction. Note that the decrease in the partial pressure of SO_2 is equal to the increase in partial pressure of SO_3, and equal to twice the decrease in the partial pressure of oxygen.

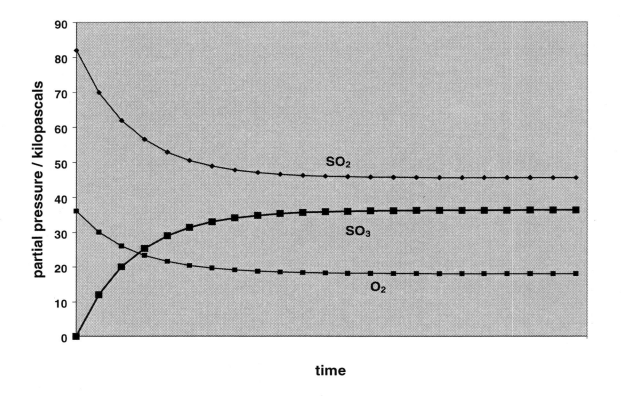

Figure 13-1 Changes in the partial pressures of SO_2, O_2 and SO_3 in a mixture, as functions of time. The amount of each substance present is measured by its partial pressure. The reactants are indicated by the lighter lines, and the product by the heavier line. In the case shown, the initial mixture contained no SO_3, and the temperature was 1000. K.

Suppose that after the mixture has reached chemical equilibrium, more oxygen is added to the mixture. Obviously, the partial pressure of oxygen would increase, but this is not the only change to take place. Some of the added O_2 would react with the SO_2 to produce SO_3, and so the partial pressure of SO_2 would decrease and the partial pressure of SO_3 would increase. The partial pressure of oxygen would increase, but not by as much as you would expect from the gas laws. After a suitable period of time, the mixture would reach chemical equilibrium again, with different partial pressures for all substances. This shows that when there is a chemical equilibrium, the partial pressures are not independent: a change in one results in a change in all the others as the chemical reaction comes back to equilibrium.

In other words, the existence of a chemical equilibrium means that the partial pressures of all substances taking part in the equilibrium reaction are interdependent. This interdependence can be expressed mathematically by an equation involving the partial pressures of the substances taking part in the chemical equilibrium. The equation is obeyed whenever the mixture reaches chemical equilibrium, regardless of the initial composition of the reacting mixture.

The original name for the equations describing chemical equilibrium was the **law of mass action**. The law was badly named, for it is partial pressures or molar concentrations that are important in determining the nature of a chemical equilibrium. Both pressures and concentrations are related fundamentally to amounts in moles, rather than masses in grams, but the original name remains in use and is worth remembering.

A reaction at equilibrium has certain characteristics:

♦ every substance involved in the reaction is present, even if in only a tiny amount;

♦ the composition of the equilibrium mixture is affected by the initial composition of the mixture of reacting substances;

♦ the same equilibrium condition may be reached either by the forward or the reverse reaction;

♦ the equilibrium is dynamic, and the partial pressures and concentrations are constant because the rates of the forward and reverse reactions are equal;

♦ the composition of the equilibrium mixture changes in response to a change of external conditions according to Le Chatelier's principle;

♦ the concentrations (in solution) or partial pressures (of gases) of the substances taking part in the reaction at equilibrium are not independent of each other but are related by a mathematical equation;

♦ the presence of a catalyst may increase the rate of reaction but does not affect the composition of the mixture at equilibrium.

Le Chatelier's principle, which was introduced in Section 2-3, states that if a system at equilibrium is subjected to a "stress", then the equilibrium shifts in a direction so as to reduce the effect of the stress. "Stress" can be applied in several different ways, which can be summarized as follows.

♦ If a mixture of gases at equilibrium is compressed to a smaller volume, the equilibrium moves in the direction that reduces the total amount of gas, if possible.

♦ If more of one of the reactants is added to the system, the position of equilibrium changes so as to convert some of the added reactant to products. Conversely, if more of one of the products is added to the system, the position of equilibrium changes so as to convert some of the added product to reactants.

♦ If one of the products of the reaction is removed from the equilibrium mixture, or is allowed to escape, the equilibrium shifts to produce more of the products.

♦ If the temperature is increased, the position of equilibrium moves in whichever direction is endothermic, so as to absorb heat.

These four aspects of Le Chatelier's principle will be made quantitative in the next few chapters, so that the consequences of a particular change in conditions can be predicted precisely. Even without doing any calculations, the principle is often useful in practical chemistry by helping to decide what direction to make a change in order to achieve a desired result.

13-2 The equilibrium constant for gas-phase reactions

For chemical equilibrium involving gases, the conditions in a system which is in chemical equilibrium can be described in terms of either the partial pressures, or the concentrations, of all the gases involved.

Partial pressures in a mixture of gases were defined in Section 5-8. For a substance A with a mole fraction of $y(A)$ in the gas-phase at a total pressure P, the partial pressure $p(A)$ is the product of the mole fraction and the total pressure:

$$p(A) = y(A)P \qquad (13\text{-}1)$$

In a mixture of reacting gases at equilibrium, the amounts of each gas present are mathematically related through a quantity called the equilibrium constant. The equilibrium constant for a gas phase reaction can be defined in terms of either partial pressures or concentrations of the gases present and taking part in the chemical equilibrium. We will make use of partial pressures for most of the work in this chapter, but will use concentrations when dealing with reactions in solution in the next several chapters.

It is possible to write the equilibrium constant directly in terms of partial pressures, and indeed this is how the idea of the equilibrium constant was discovered experimentally. We take a more general approach, which simplifies things in some cases, and helps in connecting the idea of chemical equilibrium with thermodynamics. Our initial definition of the equilibrium constant is stated in terms of a quantity called the relative activity of each substance taking part in the reaction.

 The **activity** of a substance measures the effectiveness of that substance in influencing the position of equilibrium. In a reacting mixture of gases, a substance with a high partial pressure is more "active" in driving the reaction than it would be if the partial pressure were low. The activity of a gas therefore increases with increasing partial pressure. In fact, the activity of a substance in a mixture of gases is proportional to its partial pressure, as long as the pressure is not too high.

The **relative activity** of a substance is its activity relative to its activity if it were present in its standard state. The standard state of any substance is the pure substance at the standard pressure $P° = 100.$ kilopascals.

The relative activity of a gaseous substance in a mixture is proportional to its partial pressure, and is equal to 1 when the partial pressure is $P°$. Hence the relative activity is equal to its partial pressure divided by the standard state pressure $P° = 100$ kPa. Putting this into the form of an equation, the relative activity $a(A)$ of a gas A at a partial pressure $p(A)$ is given by the equation:

$$a(A) = \frac{p(A)}{P^o} \qquad (13\text{-}2)$$

Since the relative activity is a ratio of pressures, it is has no units. If the partial pressure of the gas is equal to the standard pressure $P°$, then the relative activity is one.

For a pure liquid or solid, the relative activity hardly varies at all with pressure, and the relative activity is equal to 1.000 to very good approximation at all ordinary pressures. Thus gases differ from liquids and solids in the way their relative activity varies with pressure. This is because gases are relatively easy to compress, whereas liquids and solids are almost incompressible (see Section 1-6).

The relative activity of a solute in a solution is related to the concentration of the solute; this concept will be developed and used extensively in the next few chapters.

Example 13-1 The partial pressure of oxygen in air is 20.9 kPa. What is the relative activity of oxygen in air?

Since standard pressure is 100. kPa, the relative activity is $a(O_2) = 20.9 \text{ kPa}/100. \text{ kPa} = 0.209$.

The **equilibrium constant** K for any chemical reaction is defined in terms of the relative activities of reactants and products when the reaction is at equilibrium. In a mixture of reacting gases, the relative activities can then be expressed in terms of the partial pressures.

Consider the equilibrium between sulfur dioxide, oxygen and sulfur trioxide, which was discussed in Section 4-2. The reaction and the corresponding expression for the equilibrium constant are:

$$2 SO_2(g) + O_2(g) \rightleftharpoons 2 SO_3(g)$$

$$K = \frac{a(SO_3)^2}{a(SO_2)^2 \, a(O_2)} = \frac{\left(\dfrac{p(SO_3)}{P^o} \right)^2}{\left(\dfrac{p(SO_2)}{P^o} \right)^2 \left(\dfrac{p(O_2)}{P^o} \right)} .$$

The right hand side is written with the product of the reaction in the numerator, and the reactants in the denominator. The exponents are equal to the stoichiometric coefficients in the balanced chemical equation for the reaction.

The law of mass action states that, when the reacting mixture of O_2, SO_2 and SO_3 has come to equilibrium, the particular combination of partial pressures on the right hand side of the last equation always has the same numerical value, at a particular temperature. This is true regardless of the total pressure of the gas mixture, or the initial composition of the mixture when the gases were first mixed.

The constant value of the right hand side of the above equation is called the **equilibrium constant** and is designated by the symbol K. The equilibrium constant for the above reaction is found by experiment to be $K = 3.4$ at a temperature of 1000. K.

The equilibrium "constant" changes if the temperature changes. In other words, for a particular reaction, K is a function of the temperature; this will be discussed further later in this chapter.

For a general chemical equilibrium,

$$w A + x B \rightleftharpoons y C + z D$$

the equilibrium constant is

$$K = \frac{a(C)^y \, a(D)^z}{a(A)^w \, a(B)^x} \tag{13-3}$$

The products of the reaction appear as factors in the numerator, and the reactants in the denominator of the quotient. For each factor the exponent is the stoichiometric coefficient in the balanced chemical equation.

It is always a good idea to write the chemical equation when writing the expression for the equilibrium constant. Obviously it is important that the chemical equation be properly balanced.

It is convenient to define another closely related quantity called the **reaction quotient**. The expression for the reaction quotient is the same as for the equilibrium constant:

$$Q = \frac{a(C)^y a(D)^z}{a(A)^w a(B)^x}$$
(13-4)

The expressions for K and Q are same but there is a crucial difference between them. The equilibrium constant expression (13-3) is valid only after the reaction has come to equilibrium, whereas the reaction quotient expression (13-4) can be calculated for the mixture whether it is at equilibrium or not. While Q can have a wide range of values when the system is not at equilibrium, it can only have one value at equilibrium, which is the equilibrium constant K.

When a chemical reaction takes place, the value of Q changes as the various partial pressures change. As the reaction proceeds, the reaction quotient Q changes smoothly, continuously and monotonically (i.e. without reversing the direction of change) until it is equal to the equilibrium constant K. If Q is less than K initially, then Q increases towards K and the reaction proceeds in the forward direction. If Q is greater than K initially, then Q decreases and the reaction proceeds in the reverse direction.

The reaction quotient will be used in we discuss chemical thermodynamics in Chapter 16 and electrochemistry in Chapter 17.

When quoting an equilibrium constant, the chemical equation to which it refers should always be made clear. For example, if the reaction between O_2 and SO_2 were described using the equation

$$SO_2(g) + \tfrac{1}{2} O_2(g) \;\rightleftharpoons\; SO_3(g),$$

the equilibrium constant would have a different value, which we may designate as K'.

Example 13-2 For the following reactions, find the relationship between the equilibrium constants K' and K:

$$2\,SO_2(g) + O_2(g) \;\rightleftharpoons\; 2\,SO_3(g) \qquad K$$

$$SO_2(g) + \tfrac{1}{2} O_2(g) \;\rightleftharpoons\; SO_3(g) \qquad K'$$

For the first chemical equation, the equilibrium constant expression is:

$$K = \frac{a(SO_3)^2}{a(SO_2)^2 a(O_2)}$$

For the second chemical equation, the equilibrium constant expression is:

$$K' = \frac{a(SO_3)}{a(SO_2) a(O_2)^{1/2}}$$

Comparing these two expressions, we see that K' is the square root of K: $K' = \sqrt{K}$

Similarly, if the chemical equation used to describe the same chemical equilibrium were written in the reverse direction,

$$2\,SO_2(g) + O_2(g) \;\rightleftharpoons\; 2\,SO_3(g) \qquad K''$$

the equilibrium constant would be $K'' = 1/K$.

When two chemical reactions are combined, the equilibrium constant for the combined reaction is the product of the equilibrium constants for the individual reactions. Consider the following two reactions for the two-stage oxidation of nitrogen, with equilibrium constants K_1 and K_2:

$$N_2(g) + O_2(g) \rightleftharpoons 2\,NO(g) \qquad K_1$$

$$2\,NO(g) + O_2(g) \rightleftharpoons 2\,NO_2(g) \qquad K_2$$

The overall reaction is:

$$N_2(g) + 2\,O_2(g) \rightleftharpoons 2\,NO_2(g) \qquad K_3$$

The product of the first two equilibrium constants is:

$$K_1 K_2 = \frac{a(NO)^2}{a(N_2)a(O_2)} \times \frac{a(NO_2)^2}{a(NO)^2 a(O_2)} = \frac{a(NO_2)^2}{a(N_2)a(O_2)^2} = K_3$$

Hence, when chemical reactions are added in this way, the equilibrium constants are multiplied together. This rule is most useful when the chemical equations are written so that the amount of product of one equation exactly matches the amount of a reactant in the other equation. Then that substance can be "cancelled" and does not appear in the combined reaction; this the case for NO in the equations above.

Many reactions of gases also involve liquids or solids. Liquids and solids are not part of the gas phase, and so partial pressure has no meaning. However, liquids and solids can certainly react with gases, and their influence on the equilibrium must be recognized in some other way when writing the equilibrium constant. When dealing with chemical equilibria that involve pure solids or pure liquids, the relative activity of these substances is equal to exactly one, since these substances are in their the standard states. This affects how the expression for the equilibrium constant is written, as illustrated in the following example.

Example 13-3 Write an expression for the equilibrium constant for the following equilibrium in terms of partial pressures:

$$CaCO_3(s) \rightleftharpoons CaO(s) + CO_2(g)$$

In terms of relative activities, $\qquad K = \dfrac{a(CaO(s)) \times a(CO_2(g))}{a(CaCO_3(s))}$

For the two solids, $a(CaO(s)) = 1$ and $a(CaCO_3(s)) = 1$, and for the gas, $a(CO_2(g)) = p(CO_2)/P^o$. Hence:

$$K = \frac{1 \times \left(\dfrac{p(CO_2)}{P^o}\right)}{1} = \frac{p(CO_2)}{P^o}$$

You can see how important it is to take note of the physical state of each substance.

In many books it is common practice to define equilibrium constants directly in terms of partial pressures or concentrations rather than relative activities. For a chemical equation

$$w\,A + x\,B \rightleftharpoons y\,C + z\,D$$

the equilibrium constant in terms of pressures is:

$$K_p = \frac{p(C)^y \, p(D)^z}{p(A)^w \, p(B)^x}$$
(13-5)

It is not difficult to show that $K = K_p \times (P^o)^{w+z-x-y}$. An equilibrium constant K_c written in terms of concentrations can be defined similarly.

For any chemical reaction in which sum of the stoichiometric coefficients $w+x$ is not equal to $y+z$, the units of pressure do not cancel in the expression for K_p. For example, consider the following reaction, which we have already discussed:

$$2\,SO_2(g) + O_2(g) \; \rightleftharpoons \; 2\,SO_3(g).$$

At a temperature of 1000 K, the equilibrium constant expressed in terms of partial pressures is K_p = 0.034 kPa^{-1}, when the partial pressures are expressed in kilopascals.

Calculations based upon equilibrium constants defined in this way have been used for over a century, but there are good reasons for using relative activities instead. In this book we will not make use of K_p or K_c in our calculations.

13-3 Determination of equilibrium constants

Equilibrium constants are determined experimentally in many different ways, usually by determining the composition of the equilibrium mixture. It is necessary to determine the composition without disturbing the position of equilibrium. Common methods of doing this are by measuring the absorption of light, or by using electrochemistry, but each chemical equilibrium presents its own problems of chemical analysis and there is no standard technique that applies in all cases. In this section we see several examples of calculations of equilibrium constants from experimental data. The relationship between equilibrium constants and thermodynamic data is discussed in Chapter 16.

The general procedure is to prepare an initial mixture of the substances involved in the reaction, and to follow the progress of the reaction, until equilibrium is reached. The partial pressures of the gases in the equilibrium mixture are then measured or calculated, and the equilibrium constant for the reaction is calculated.

The analysis of a reaction is best analyzed using a systematic procedure, with the calculations laid out in a table which summarizes the initial conditions, the changes in those conditions, and the conditions in the equilibrium mixture. The changes must conform to the stoichiometry required by the balanced chemical equation for the reaction. The table is called the ICE table, from the first letters of the three lines in the table: Initial, Change and Equilibrium.

The ICE table can be calculated using partial pressures, amounts in moles, concentrations or mole fractions. In order to avoid error, it is wise to label the ICE table according to which quantity is being tabulated.

Example 13-4 A mixture of hydrogen and nitrogen initially containing 3.10 moles of $H_2(g)$ and 1.00 moles of $N_2(g)$ is brought to equilibrium at a pressure of 9800. kPa. The equilibrium mixture is found to contain 10.0 % NH_3 by mole. Calculate K for the reaction $N_2(g) + 3\,H_2(g) \; \rightleftharpoons \; 2\,NH_3(g)$.

The initial mixture contained 3.10 mole of H_2 and 1.00 moles of N_2. The changes which occur as a result of the chemical reaction must be consistent with the stoichiometry of the reaction and are summarized in the ICE table based upon the amount (in moles) of each substance:

amount/moles	N_2	+	$3 H_2$	$\rightleftharpoons$	$2 NH_3$	total
initial	1.00		3.10		0	4.10
change	$-x$		$-3x$		$+2x$	$-2x$
equilibrium	$1.00-x$		$3.10-3x$		$2x$	$4.10-2x$

The initial amount in moles, the change and the final amount are written under each substance taking part in the reaction. The change is written as an algebraic variable x, which will be determined from the information given in the question. The heading "moles" is useful since other quantities, such as partial pressures, are sometimes used to do this accounting work. The last column gives the total amount of substance for each line, and is simply the sum of the amount of each substance.

It is stated in the question that NH_3 forms 10.0% by mole of the equilibrium mixture, which means that the mole fraction of NH_3 is 0.100. According to the calculations above, the mole fraction of NH_3 is:

$$y(NH_3) = \frac{2x}{4.10 - 2x}$$

and hence we can equate the right hand side of this equation to the experimental value of 0.100:

$$\frac{2x}{4.10 - 2x} = 0.100$$

This equation can be simplified and solved, yielding the value $x = 0.1863$. The total amount of gas at equilibrium is $n_T = 4.10 - 2 \times 0.186 = 3.728$ moles, and so the partial pressures are:

$$p(NH_3) = \frac{n(NH_3)}{n_T} P_T = \frac{2 \times 0.186}{3.728} \times 9800. \, kPa = 978 \, kPa$$

$$p(N_2) = \frac{n(N_2)}{n_T} P_T = \frac{1.0 - 0.186}{3.728} \times 9800. \, kPa = 2140 \, kPa$$

$$p(H_2) = \frac{n(H_2)}{n_T} P_T = \frac{3.1 - 3 \times 0.186}{3.728} \times 9800 \, kPa = 6680 \, kPa$$

The relative activities are obtained by dividing by the standard state pressure of 100 kPa:

$$a(NH_3) = 9.78 \qquad a(N_2) = 21.4 \qquad a(H_2) = 66.8$$

and hence the equilibrium constant is:

$$K = \frac{9.78^2}{21.4 \times 66.8^3} = 1.50 \times 10^{-5}$$

Example 13-5 Carbon dioxide $CO_2(g)$ is passed through a bed of heated carbon to produce carbon monoxide $CO(g)$ according to the reaction

$$CO_2(g) + C(s) \rightleftharpoons 2 \, CO(g)$$

At equilibrium when the total pressure is 100.0 kPa, 99.0% of the $CO_2(g)$ is found to be converted to $CO(g)$. Calculate K.

Consider 1.000 mole of CO_2 passed into the bed of heated carbon. The ICE table describing the initial and final situations can be described as follows:

amount/moles	$CO_2(g) + C(s)$ $\rightleftharpoons$	$2\ CO(g)$	total
initial	1.000	0	1.000
change	–0.990	+1.980	+0.990
equilibrium	0.010	1.980	1.990

Notice that the relative activity of solid carbon is equal to 1.000, regardless of changes in the amount of carbon present. Since the total pressure is 100.0 kPa the partial pressures of CO_2 is:

$$p(CO_2) = \frac{0.010}{1.990} \times 100\ kPa = 0.50\ kPa$$

The partial pressure of CO is therefore $(100.0 - 0.50) = 99.5\ kPa$.

Hence the relative activities of all substances involved in the equilibrium are:

$$a(CO_2) = \frac{0.50}{100.0} = 5.0 \times 10^{-3} \qquad a(CO) = \frac{99.5}{100.0} = 0.995 \qquad a(C(s)) = 1.000$$

The equilibrium constant is: $\qquad K = \dfrac{0.995^2}{1 \times 5.02 \times 10^{-3}} = 1.97 \times 10^2$

Note how the presence of a pure solid reactant or product is treated: as long as at least some of the solid is present, then its relative activity is 1.000 regardless of how much is present and how much has reacted.

The formalism of chemical equilibrium can be applied to vaporization and sublimation processes, since they come to equilibrium under the same thermodynamic constraints as a chemical equilibrium.

Example 13-6 The vapour pressure of liquid methanol is 55.5 kPa at 50°C. What is the equilibrium constant for the process $CH_3OH(\lambda) \rightleftharpoons CH_3OH(g)$ at that temperature?

This problem casts a simple vapour equilibrium in the form of a chemical equilibrium. Since the vapour pressure is $p = 55.5\ kPa$, the relative activity of the vapour is $a(g) = 55.5\ kPa/100\ kPa = 0.555$. The relative activity of the liquid is 1 since it is a pure condensed phase. Hence the equilibrium constant is:

$$K = \frac{a(\text{vapour})}{a(\text{liquid})} = a(\text{vapour}) = \frac{p}{p^o} = \frac{0.555}{1} = 0.555$$

13-4 Calculations using equilibrium constants

When the equilibrium constant for a chemical equation is known, then it is possible to calculate the composition of an equilibrium mixture if certain information is available. The calculations often involve solving algebraic equations, usually a quadratic equation, and we begin with a summary of how to do this.

The quadratic equation for a variable x is usually written in a standard form with numerical coefficients a, b and c:

$$ax^2 + bx + c = 0$$

If a problem in chemical equilibrium requires solving a quadratic equation, the equation should be rearranged into this standard form before solving it. There are two solutions, or roots, to this equation:

$$x = \frac{-b \pm \sqrt{b^2 - 4ac}}{2a}$$

In solving problems of chemical equilibrium, only one of the solutions is meaningful. The other solution does not make sense in the context of the chemical situation, and can be ignored. For example, a solution to the quadratic which predicts a negative partial pressure, or a partial pressure larger than the total pressure can be ignored.

Example 13-7 The equilibrium constant for the dissociation reaction

$$N_2O_4(g) \rightleftharpoons 2\,NO_2(g)$$

is $K = 0.15$ at a temperature of 300. K. If the partial pressure of $NO_2(g)$ is 35.0 kPa in an equilibrium mixture at this temperature, calculate the partial pressure of $N_2O_4(g)$.

The equilibrium constant for the reaction is:

$$K = \frac{(p(NO_2)/P^o)^2}{p(N_2O_4)/P^o} = \frac{p(NO_2)^2}{P^o\,p(N_2O_4)} = 0.15$$

Since $p(NO_2) = 35.0$ kPa, and $P^\circ = 100.$ kPa, we can solve for $p(N_2O_4)$:

$$p(N_2O_4) = \frac{(35.0 \times 10^3)^2}{(100. \times 10^3) \times 0.15} = 8.2 \times 10^4 \text{ Pa} = 82 \text{ kPa}$$

Example 13-8 A mixture containing mole fractions of 0.800 of carbon monoxide CO(g) and 0.200 of steam, $H_2O(g)$, is brought to equilibrium according to the equation

$$CO(g) + H_2O(g) \rightleftharpoons CO_2(g) + H_2(g)$$

at a temperature of 690 K. At this temperature the equilibrium constant is $K = 8.30$. Calculate the mole fractions of all substances at equilibrium.

Consider one mole of the incoming gas mixture. The ICE table expressed in terms of moles is as follows:

amount/moles	$CO(g)$ +	$H_2O(g)$	$\rightleftharpoons$	$CO_2(g)$ +	$H_2(g)$	total
initial	0.800	0.200		0	0	1.000
change	$-x$	$-x$		$+x$	$+x$	0.000
equilibrium	0.800–x	0.200–x		x	x	1.000

The mole fractions in the equilibrium mixture are equal to the numbers of moles of each substance listed in the last line, since the total number of moles does not change in the reaction. Hence if the total pressure is P, then the relative activities are:

$$a(CO) = (0.800 - x)\frac{P}{P^o} \qquad a(H_2O) = (0.200 - x)\frac{P}{P^o} \qquad a(CO_2) = a(H_2) = x\frac{P}{P^o}$$

and so the equilibrium constant expression is:

$$K = \frac{a(CO_2)a(H_2)}{a(CO)a(H_2O)} = \frac{(xP/P^o)^2}{(0.800 - x)(P/P^o)(0.200 - x)(P/P^o)} = \frac{x^2}{(0.800 - x)(0.200 - x)} = 8.30$$

The factor (P/P^o) cancels from the quotient. Multiplying out the last equality, a quadratic equation is obtained:

$$7.30x^2 - 8.30x + 1.328 = 0$$

The two solutions of the quadratic equation are $\quad x = \dfrac{8.30 \pm \sqrt{8.30^2 - 4 \times 7.30 \times 1.328}}{2 \times 7.30} = 0.94$ or 0.193

The first solution is rejected since it exceeds the initial amounts of steam and carbon monoxide. The mole fractions of all substances calculated from the second solution are:

$$y(CO_2) = 0.193 \qquad\qquad\qquad y(H_2) = 0.193$$

$$y(H_2O) = 0.200 - 0.193 = 0.007 \qquad\qquad\qquad y(CO) = 0.800 - 0.193 = 0.607$$

Example 13-9 Steam is passed over hot carbon and the following reaction comes to equilibrium:

$$C(s) + H_2O(g) \rightleftharpoons CO(g) + H_2(g)$$

At the temperature of the reaction, the equilibrium constant is $K = 1.34$, and the total pressure of the equilibrium mixture is 200. kPa. What are the mole fractions of all substances in the final mixture?

Consider the reaction in which 1.000 mole of steam is passed into the reactor. The ICE table expressed in terms of moles is as follows:

amount/moles	$C(s)$ +	$H_2O(g)$	$\rightleftharpoons$	$CO(g)$ +	$H_2(g)$	total
initial	1.000			0	0	1.000
change	$-x$			$+x$	$+x$	$+x$
equilibrium	1.000–x			x	x	1.000+x

Hence the mole fractions of all substances in the gas phase are:

$$y(CO) = y(H_2) = \frac{x}{1.000 + x} \qquad y(H_2O) = \frac{1.000 - x}{1.000 + x}$$

The partial pressure of each gas is the product of its mole fraction y and the total pressure of 200. kPa, and the relative activity is the partial pressure divided by the standard state pressure of 100. kPa. Hence the relative activities of the gases are as follows:

$$a(CO) = a(H_2) = \frac{x}{1.000 + x} \times \frac{200.\,kPa}{100.\,kPa} = \frac{2.00x}{1.000 + x}$$

$$a(H_2O) = \frac{1.000 - x}{1.000 + x} \times \frac{200.\,kPa}{100.\,kPa} = \frac{2.00(1.000 - x)}{1.000 + x}$$

The relative activity of solid carbon is 1. Hence the equilibrium constant is:

$$K = \frac{a(CO)a(H_2)}{a(C)a(H_2O)} = \frac{\left(\dfrac{2.00x}{1.000 + x}\right)\left(\dfrac{2.00x}{1.000 + x}\right)}{1 \times \left(\dfrac{2.00(1 - x)}{1.000 + x}\right)}$$

Simplifying this expression and setting it equal to the numerical value of the equilibrium constant, we get:

$$\frac{2.00x^2}{1.000 - x^2} = 1.34$$

This appears to be a quadratic equation, but is in fact a linear equation in x^2 which can be solved to give $x^2 = 0.401$ from which we calculate the positive square root: $x = 0.633$. Hence the mole fractions of the three gases are:

$$y(CO) = y(H_2) = \frac{0.633}{1.633} = 0.388 \qquad y(H_2O) = \frac{0.367}{1.633} = 0.224$$

There is an alternative solution to Example 13-9 using mole fractions instead of actual amounts of substances. From the equation, the equal amounts of CO and H_2 must be produced. Hence the mole fractions of these gases must be equal, and can be denoted by a single variable z. Since the sum of the mole fractions of all substances in the gas phase must be unity by definition, the mole fraction of H_2O at equilibrium must be $1-2z$.

The ICE table expressed in terms of mole fractions rather than moles is as follows. Note that

mole fractions	C(s) +	H_2O(g)	$\rightleftharpoons$	CO(g) +	H_2(g)	total
initial	1			0	0	1
change		$-2z$		z	z	0
equilibrium		$1-2z$		z	z	1

Notice that the sum of the mole fractions must always be unity, so the sum of the changes in the mole fractions is zero. In terms of the variable z, the relative activities are:

$$a(CO(g)) = a(H_2(g)) = \frac{z \times 200.\ kPa}{100.\ kPa} = 2.00z$$

$$a(H_2O(g)) = \frac{(1-2z) \times 200.\ kPa}{100.\ kPa} = 2.00(1-2z)$$

Hence $K = \dfrac{4.00z^2}{2.00(1-2z)} = 1.34$. The meaningful positive solution to this quadratic equation is $z = 0.388$, and hence the mole fractions are $y(CO) = y(H_2) = 0.388$ and $y(H_2O) = 1-2 \times 0.388 = 0.224$, as in the previous solution.

Example 13-10 Limestone, quicklime and coke (which can be treated as pure carbon) are heated to a temperature of 1000 K in a closed container, and the following two reactions come to equilibrium with the indicated equilibrium constants:

$$CaCO_3(s) \rightleftharpoons CaO(s) + CO_2(g) \qquad K_1 = 0.039$$

$$C(s) + CO_2(g) \rightleftharpoons 2\,CO(g) \qquad K_2 = 1.9$$

Calculate the partial pressures of CO and CO_2 in the vessel.

The first equilibrium fixes the relative activity and partial pressure of CO_2, since the relative activities of solid CaO and solid $CaCO_3$ are both exactly 1:

$$K_1 = \frac{a(CaO)a(CO_2)}{a(CaCO_3)} = a(CO_2) = \frac{p(CO_2)}{P^o} = 0.039$$

Since $P^o = 100.\ kPa$, the partial pressure of CO_2 is $p(CO_2) = 0.039 \times 100\ kPa = 3.9\ kPa$

The relative activity of solid carbon is exactly 1, and we have relative activity of CO_2 is fixed by the first equilibrium, so the equilibrium constant for the second reaction can be written:

$$K_2 = \frac{a(CO)^2}{a(C)a(CO_2)} = \frac{a(CO)^2}{1 \times 0.039} = 1.9$$

From this equation we find $a(CO) = \sqrt{0.039 \times 1.9} = 0.27$ and so the partial pressure of CO is:

$$p(CO) = 0.27 \times 100\ kPa = 27.\ kPa.$$

Example 13-11 Ethane, C_2H_6, decomposes when it is heated to a high temperature, to give ethene, C_2H_4, and hydrogen, H_2:

$$C_2H_6(g) \rightleftharpoons C_2H_4(g) + H_2(g).$$

At a temperature of 900 K, the equilibrium constant is $K = 0.054$. Calculate the mole fractions of all gases in the equilibrium mixture if ethane is heated to this temperature and brought to equilibrium with its decomposition products at a total pressure of 60.0 kPa.

We are not given an initial pressure. But the two product gases are produced in equimolar amounts, and so must be present at the same partial pressure, which we denote by x kPa.

Further, the total pressure of 60.0 kPa is the sum of all the partial pressures, and so the partial pressure of ethane must be $(60.0 - 2x)$ kPa.

It is convenient to express the ICE table terms of pressures, and we only need the equilibrium line:

pressure/kPa	$C_2H_6(g)$	$\rightleftharpoons$	$C_2H_4(g) + H_2(g)$		total
equilibrium	$60.0-2x$		x	x	60.0

The relative activities of the various gases are:

$$a(C_2H_4(g)) = a(H_2(g)) = \frac{x}{100.} \qquad a(C_2H_6(g)) = \frac{60.0 - 2x}{100.}$$

Hence the equilibrium constant expression is:

$$K = \frac{\left(\dfrac{x}{100.}\right)^2}{\left(\dfrac{60.0 - 2x}{100.}\right)} = \frac{x^2}{100. \times (60.0 - 2x)} = 0.054$$

Multiplying out the quadratic we get $x^2 + 10.8x - 324. = 0$ and the positive solution is $x = 13.4$. Hence the partial pressures of the product gases are both 13.4 kPa, and the mole fractions are:

$$y(C_2H_4(g)) = y(H_2(g)) = \frac{13.4}{60.0} = 0.223 \qquad y(C_2H_6(g)) = 1 - (2 \times 0.223) = 0.554$$

Example 13-12 3.50 gram of a mixture of $NO_2(g)$ and $N_2O_4(g)$ is placed in a closed vessel of volume 1.00 dm^3 at 25.0°C, and the following reaction comes to equilibrium:

$$N_2O_4(g) \rightleftharpoons 2\,NO_2(g)$$

At this temperature, the equilibrium constant is K = 0.090. Calculate the total pressure at equilibrium.

Initially we do not know the proportion of the total mass that is in each form, and this will have to be determined from the equilibrium constant expression. Let x grams be the mass of NO_2 so that the mass of N_2O_4 is $(3.50-x)$ grams. The molar mass of NO_2 is 46.005 g/mol and that of N_2O_4 is 92.010 g/mol. Hence the amount (in moles) of each substance is:

$$n(NO_2) = \frac{x}{46.005} \text{ mol} \quad \text{and} \quad n(N_2O_4) = \frac{3.50 - x}{92.010} \text{ mol}$$

Treating each gas as an ideal gas, we can use the known volume of 1.00×10^{-3} m^3 and temperature of 298.2 K in the ideal gas equation:

$$p(NO_2) = \frac{n(NO_2)RT}{V} = \frac{x}{46.005} \times \frac{8.3145 \times 298.2}{1.00 \times 10^{-3}} = 5.39 \times 10^4 x \text{ Pa}$$

$$p(N_2O_4) = \frac{n(N_2O_4)RT}{V} = \frac{3.50 - x}{92.010} \times \frac{8.3145 \times 298.2}{1.00 \times 10^{-3}} = 2.69 \times 10^4 \times (3.50 - x) \text{ Pa}$$

From these partial pressures the relative activities can be calculated by dividing by $P° = 1.00 \times 10^5 \, \text{Pa}$:

$$a(NO_2) = \frac{p(NO_2)}{P^o} = 0.539x \qquad\qquad a(N_2O_4) = \frac{p(N_2O_4)}{P^o} = 0.269 \times (3.50 - x)$$

Hence the equilibrium constant is:

$$K = \frac{(0.539x)^2}{0.269(3.50 - x)} = 0.090$$

Upon multiplying out the quadratic, we get: $0.290x^2 + 0.0242x - 0.0847 = 0$

to which the positive solution is $x = \dfrac{-0.0242 + \sqrt{0.0242^2 + 4 \times 0.290 \times 0.0847}}{2 \times 0.290} = 0.500$

Hence the mixture contains 0.50 g of NO_2 and 3.00 g of N_2O_4. Knowing x, the partial pressures can be calculated directly from the equations above:

$$p(NO_2) = 5.39 \times 10^4 \times 0.50 = 27. \text{ kPa}$$

$$p(N_2O_4) = 2.69 \times 10^4 \times (3.50 - 0.50) = 81. \text{ kPa}$$

The total pressure is the sum of the partial pressures: $P = 27. + 81. = 108. \text{ kPa}$

13-5 The temperature dependence of equilibrium constants

Equilibrium "constants" are only constant if the temperature is constant. The temperature dependence of the equilibrium constant for a reaction is determined qualitatively by Le Chatelier's principle. An increase in temperature causes a shift of the position of equilibrium so as to absorb heat, i.e. the equilibrium shifts in the endothermic direction.

The mathematical form of the dependence on temperature of an equilibrium constant is similar to that of vapour pressure, which was discussed in Section 7-9, except that the enthalpy change of a reaction may be either positive or negative. A graph of the natural logarithm of the equilibrium constant as a function of the inverse absolute temperature is a straight line, with a slope proportional to the negative of the enthalpy change of the reaction.

A graph of the natural logarithm of the equilibrium constant as a function of the inverse absolute temperature is called a **van't Hoff** plot. For most reactions, the graph is very nearly a straight line with constant slope. To a good approximation, ln K is a linear function of $1/T$ and can be represented satisfactorily by the equation:

$$\ln K = -\frac{\Delta H^o}{R}\left(\frac{1}{T}\right) + b \tag{13-6}$$

In this equation, b is a constant. The slope of the graph is $-\Delta H°/R$, where $\Delta H°$ is the standard enthalpy change of the reaction and R is the gas constant.

At two temperatures identified by the subscripts 1 and 2, the two equilibrium constants are therefore related by the **van't Hoff equation:**

$$\ln\left(\frac{K_2}{K_1}\right) = -\frac{\Delta H^o}{R}\left(\frac{1}{T_2} - \frac{1}{T_1}\right) \tag{13-7}$$

The van't Hoff equation can be used to evaluate the standard enthalpy change of a reaction by measuring the equilibrium constant over a range of temperatures, or to calculate the variation of the equilibrium constant with temperature.

In a van't Hoff plot, $1/T$ is plotted increasing to the right on the horizontal axis, and so the right hand end of the horizontal corresponds to low temperatures, and the left hand end to high temperatures. In addition, the inverse of the absolute temperature is a rather small number, and it is convenient to use the dimensionless ratio $(1000 \text{ K})/T$ for the horizontal axis.

For exothermic reactions with negative $\Delta H°$, the slope of the van't Hoff graph is positive and the equilibrium constant is smaller at higher temperatures. For endothermic reactions with positive $\Delta H°$, the slope of the van't Hoff graph is negative and the equilibrium constant is larger at higher temperatures.

For any reaction, one direction of reaction is exothermic and the other direction of reaction is endothermic. The position of equilibrium moves in the endothermic direction if the temperature increases. This consistent with Le Chatelier's Principle.

Figure 13-2 shows a van't Hoff plot for the ammonia synthesis reaction:

$$1/2 \, N_2(g) + 3/2 \, H_2(g) \rightleftharpoons NH_3(g).$$

The reaction is exothermic, so the slope is positive. The graph is almost a straight line. However, the graph covers a very wide range of temperatures, and by squinting along the paper it is possible to see that the graph is slightly curved. The curvature is due to variation of the enthalpy change of the reaction with temperature.

─────────────────────────────

Example 13-13   The equilibrium constant for the equilibrium

$$1/2 \, N_2(g) + 3/2 \, H_2(g) \rightleftharpoons NH_3(g)$$

is 668 at 300. K, and 6.04 at 400. K. Calculate the enthalpy change of the reaction.

─────────────────────────────

The data can be substituted directly into equation (13-7):

$$\ln\left(\frac{668.}{6.04}\right) = -\frac{\Delta H^o}{8.314}\left(\frac{1}{300.} - \frac{1}{400.}\right)$$

From this equation, the enthalpy change can be calculated: $\Delta H° = -47.0 \text{ kJ/mol}.$

This result is an average over the temperature range from 300 K to 400 K, and agrees satisfactorily with the enthalpy of formation of ammonia at 298.15 K given in Appendix 1, −46.11 kJ/mol.

─────────────────────────────

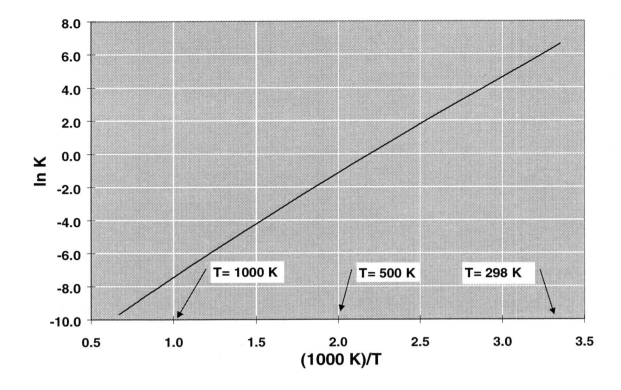

Figure 13-2 The natural logarithm of the equilibrium constant for the synthesis of ammonia plotted as a function of the quantity (1000 K)/T. The high temperature end of the scale is at the left. The graph covers the range of temperatures from 300 K (on the right) to 1500 K (on the left), and several actual temperatures are shown. This is an exothermic reaction and so *K* decreases with increasing temperature.

13-6 Some important gas–phase reactions

Most of the chemical experiments that are familiar to students are carried out in solution, and only a few involve reactions in the gas phase. But in industry some gas-phase reactions are carried out on a very large scale, as we saw in Chapter 4. We finish the chapter by listing in Table 13-1 some gas-phase reactions that are important in industry, together with some relevant information.

The second column in the table lists the equilibrium constant for each reaction at 25°C. The third column lists the enthalpy change for the reaction, from which the effect of temperature on the equilibrium constant may be predicted. For example, if $\Delta H°$ is positive, then high temperature increases the value of *K*. The fourth column lists the change in the amount of gas for the reaction as written, from which the effect of pressure on the position of equilibrium may be predicted. For example, if Δn_g is negative, then high pressure shifts the equilibrium to the right.

Most chemical reactions are faster at high temperatures, and so unless the reaction is strongly exothermic, a high temperature is usually favourable because the higher rate of reaction outweighs the disadvantage of a smaller equilibrium constant (in the case of a moderately exothermic reaction). The choice of conditions for a particular industrial process is always the result of balancing conflicting requirements in order to optimize the economics of the process.

Temperature control is of greater importance for exothermic gas-phase reactions than for reactions in liquid solutions, because the heat capacity of the reacting mixture is much smaller than the heat capacity of water or other solvent. In mixtures of reacting gases, the temperature may change by hundreds of degrees if arrangements are not made to remove the heat produced in the reaction. The high temperature reaction products produced in flames are familiar examples of this observation. The consequence of a rise in temperature of the reacting mixture is a reduction in the equilibrium constant and hence in the yield of the reaction, as we noted in discussing the oxidation of SO_2 in Section 4-2.

The examples of the Fischer-Tropsch and methanol reactions in Table 13-1 show that, in some cases, more than one product can be produced from the same reactants. The choice of conditions and the use of an appropriate catalyst can selectively improve the yield of one of the possible products.

Table 13-1 Data for some important gas-phase reactions

The equilibrium constant K and the enthalpy change of reaction ΔH° are quoted at 25°C. Δn_g is the change in the amount of gas in the chemical equation.

Reaction	K (25°C)	ΔH° (25°C) kJ/mol	Δn_g moles	Typical conditions
Sulfur trioxide				
$SO_2 + \frac{1}{2}O_2 \rightleftharpoons SO_3$	2.7×10^{12}	−98.9	−0.5	500°C
Ammonia				
$N_2 + 3H_2 \rightleftharpoons 2NH_3$	7.6×10^{2}	−46.1	−2	450°C, 100 MPa
Synthesis gas				
Steam reforming:				
$\quad CH_4 + H_2O \rightleftharpoons CO + 3H_2$	1.3×10^{-25}	+206.1	+2	900°C
Shift conversion:				
$\quad CO + H_2O \rightleftharpoons CO_2 + H_2$	1.0×10^{5}	−41.2	0	300°C
Partial oxidation of methane:				
$\quad CH_4 + \frac{1}{2}O_2 \rightleftharpoons CO + 2H_2$	1.4×10^{15}	−35.7	+1.5	1400°C, 2 MPa
Water gas				
$\quad C(s) + H_2O \rightleftharpoons CO + H_2$	9.8×10^{-17}	+131.3	+1	1000°C
Fischer-Tropsch				
$\quad CO + 3H_2 \rightleftharpoons CH_4 + H_2O$	7.7×10^{24}	−206.1	−2	
Methanol				
$CO + 2H_2 \rightleftharpoons CH_3OH$	2.2×10^{4}	−90.1	−2	300°C, 30 MPa
Ethylene				
$\quad H_3C{-}CH_3 \rightleftharpoons H_2C{=}CH_2 + H_2$	2.1×10^{-18}	+136.9	+1	750–900°C

Key concepts

A chemical reaction reaches chemical equilibrium when the concentrations of the reactants and products are no longer changing. The same condition of equilibrium can be reached either by the forward or the reverse reaction, and at equilibrium both forward and reverse reactions are going on at equal rates.

Le Chatelier's principle states that a system at chemical equilibrium that is subjected to a stress responds by shifting in whichever direction will relieve the stress. Examples of stresses are a change of temperature, a change of pressure, and the addition or removal of a substance taking part in the reaction.

The condition of equilibrium is described using the equilibrium constant. The equilibrium constant is defined in terms of the relative activities of the substances involved. For gases, the relative activity is the partial pressure divided by a standard pressure of 100 kPa. For pure liquids and solids, the relative activity is 1. The equilibrium constant is a ratio of products of the equilibrium values of the relative activities, raised to a power equal to the stoichiometric coefficient of that substance in the chemical equation.

The reaction quotient is defined in the same way, but can be used to refer to mixtures which are not at equilibrium; when the reaction reaches equilibrium, the reaction quotient is equal to the equilibrium constant.

The equilibrium constant for a gas phase reaction can be determined by measurements of the partial pressures of the substances involved. Conversely, given the value of the equilibrium constant and the initial conditions for a reaction, the partial pressures at equilibrium can be calculated by combining the stoichiometry of the reaction with the equilibrium constant expression.

The temperature dependence of an equilibrium constant is described by the van't Hoff equation, which makes use of the standard enthalpy change of the reaction.

Review questions

1. Define partial pressure of a gas in a mixture of gases.

2. Define relative activity of a gas.

3. What is the relative activity of a pure solid or liquid?

4. Define the reaction quotient.

5. Define the equilibrium constant.

6. What is the difference between the reaction quotient and the equilibrium constant for a reaction?

7. Does the equilibrium constant vary with the total pressure?

8. Describe how to write an "ICE" table.

9. Does the equilibrium constant vary with temperature?

Problems

1. For each of the following reactions, write an expression for the equilibrium constant K:

   (a) $3/2\ O_2(g) \rightleftharpoons O_3(g)$ (formation of ozone in the air)

   (b) $NH_3(g) + 5/4\ O_2(g) \rightleftharpoons NO(g) + 3/2\ H_2O(g)$.   (manufacture of nitric acid)

   (c) $CH_4(g) + 2\ O_2(g) \rightleftharpoons CO_2(g) + 2\ H_2O(g)$ (combustion of natural gas)

   (d) $CO(g) + 1/2\ O_2(g) \rightleftharpoons CO_2(g)$ (combustion of carbon monoxide)

   (e) $1/2\ N_2(g) + 1/2\ O_2(g) \rightleftharpoons NO$ (formation of nitric oxide)

(f) $CH_4(g) + 4 Cl_2(g) \rightleftharpoons CCl_4(l) + 4 HCl(g)$ (chlorination of methane)

(g) $2 NaHCO_3(s) \rightleftharpoons Na_2CO_3(s) + CO_2(g) + H_2O(g)$ (soda ash production)

(h) $2 H_2S(g) + SO_2(g) \rightleftharpoons 3 S(s) + 2 H_2O(\lambda)$ (purification of sour natural gas)

2. For the production of methanol by the reaction $CO(g) + 2 H_2(g) \rightleftharpoons CH_3OH(g)$, the enthalpy change of reaction is $\Delta H° = -25$ kJ/mol. Which of the following conditions favours the production of methanol?

   (a) High pressure and high temperature   (b) High pressure and low temperature

   (c) Low pressure and high temperature   (d) Low pressure and low temperature

3. Name two "heavy chemicals" which are produced in Canada by gas-phase reactions on a very large scale, one of which is an acid and the other a base.

4. Calculate the relative activity of each of the following at a temperature of 25.0°C. (a) Pure solid carbon (graphite) at a pressure of 100. kPa (b) oxygen gas O_2 at a partial pressure of 23.0 kPa. (c) methane gas CH_4 at a partial pressure of 221. kPa (d) pure liquid water H_2O at a pressure of 100. kPa.

   [1.000, 0.230, 2.21, 1.000]

5. Calculate the relative activity of each of the following at a temperature of 50.0°C. (a) Pure solid zinc metal at a pressure of 100. kPa (b) nitrogen gas N_2 at a partial pressure of 7.54 kPa. (c) sulfur trioxide gas SO_3 at a partial pressure of 72.3 kPa (d) pure liquid benzene C_6H_6 at apressure of 100. kPa.

   [1.000, 0.0754, 0.723, 1.000]

6. Calculate the relative activity of each of the following at a temperature of 300.°C. (a) Pure solid iron metal at a pressure of 100. kPa (b) water vapour H_2O at a partial pressure of 310. kPa. (c) sulfur dioxide gas SO_2 at a partial pressure of 101.3 kPa (d) pure liquid lead metal Pb at a pressure of 100. kPa.

   [1.000, 3.10, 1.013, 1.000]

7. In an equilibrium mixture of SO_2, SO_3 and O_2 at a particular temperature, the partial pressure of SO_2 is half of the partial pressure of SO_3, and the partial pressure of oxygen is 15.5 kPa. What is the equilibrium constant for the following reaction?

$$SO_2(g) + \tfrac{1}{2} O_2(g) \rightleftharpoons SO_3(g)$$ [5.08]

8. A bulb contains an equilibrium mixture of SO_2, SO_3 and O_2 at a fixed temperature, and enough argon is pumped into the bulb to double the total pressure in the bulb. What effect will this have on the partial pressure of SO_3?

9. The equilibrium constant for the reaction $N_2(g) + 3 H_2(g) \rightleftharpoons 2 NH_3(g)$ is 6.90×10^{-4} at 500°C. If the volume of a vessel containing some of the equilibrium mixture is halved but the temperature is kept constant, what is the new value of the equilibrium constant?

10. The following table summarizes some experimental measurements on the equilibrium

$$2 SO_2(g) + O_2(g) \rightleftharpoons 2 SO_3(g)$$

at a temperature of 1000. K in a series of experiments starting with different initial amounts of the three substances involved. The partial pressures of the gases are expressed in units of atmospheres.

(a) For each experiment calculate K_p with the pressures in units of atmospheres, and then calculate the average value of K_p over the whole series of experiments.

(b) From the average K_p, calculate the equilibrium constant K. Recall that 1 atmosphere = 101.325 kPa, and $P° = 100.000$ kPa. [3.40 atm^{-1}, 3.36]

p(SO$_2$)/atmosphere	p(O$_2$)/atmosphere	p(SO$_3$)/atmosphere
0.279	0.399	0.322
0.309	0.353	0.338
0.456	0.180	0.364
0.470	0.167	0.365
0.481	0.164	0.355
0.564	0.102	0.334
0.566	0.101	0.333
0.775	0.022	0.203
0.248	0.080	0.128
0.283	0.068	0.136
0.273	0.402	0.325

11. Nitric oxide NO can be formed from atmospheric oxygen and nitrogen in the following reaction, for which $K = 7.\times10^{-16}$ at 25°C:

$$½\,N_2(g) + ½\,O_2(g) \rightleftharpoons NO(g).$$

(a) Estimate the partial pressure of NO in the atmosphere given the partial pressures $p(O_2) =$ 20. kPa and $p(N_2) = 80.$ kPa. [3.×10^{-11} Pa]

(b) The heat of formation of NO is $\Delta H_f° = +90.25$ kJ/mol. Would you expect the partial pressure of NO in the air passing through a flame to be larger, the same or smaller than in air at room temperature?

12. When ammonia gas, NH$_3$, is heated at a pressure of 1000. kPa and a temperature of 673 K in the presence of a catalyst, it decomposes: $2NH_3(g) \rightleftharpoons N_2(g) + 3H_2(g)$. It is found that the mole fraction of NH$_3$ in the equilibrium mixture is 0.0385. Calculate K. [6.07×10^3]

13. From the data in Table 13-1, calculate the equilibrium constant K for the following reactions at 25°C:

$$CH_4(g) + 2\,H_2O(g) \rightleftharpoons CO_2(g) + 4\,H_2(g) \qquad [1.3×10^{-20}]$$

$$CH_4(g) + H_2O(g) \rightleftharpoons CH_3OH(g) + H_2(g) \qquad [2.9×10^{-21}]$$

14. The equilibrium constant for the reaction $H_2(g) + I_2(g) \rightleftharpoons 2HI(g)$ is 6.4 at a temperature of 800 K.

(a) What is the equilibrium constant for the reaction $HI(g) \rightleftharpoons ½\,H_2(g) + ½\,I_2(g)$ at the same temperature? [0.40]

(b) In a mixture of H_2, I_2 and HI at 800 K, the partial pressures are $p(H_2) = 2.0$ kPa, $p(I_2) = 2.0$ kPa, $p(HI) = 96.$ kPa. Evaluate the reaction quotient Q for the reaction

$$H_2(g) + I_2(g) \rightleftharpoons 2HI(g).$$

As the reaction mixture comes to equilibrium, will the partial pressure of hydrogen iodide HI increase or decrease?
[2.3×10^3, decrease]

15. The equilibrium constant for the dissociation reaction $N_2O_4(g) \rightleftharpoons 2 NO_2(g)$ is K = 0.140 at a temperature of 300. K.

(a) If N_2O_4 did not dissociate at all, calculate the density in g/cm^3 of pure N_2O_4 at a pressure of 200. kPa and a temperature of 300. K.
[7.38×10^{-3} g cm^{-3}]

(b) If N_2O_4 comes to equilibrium as described above, calculate the density in g/cm^3 of the equilibrium mixture if the total pressure is 200. kPa.
[6.52×10^{-3} g cm^{-3}]

(c) If N_2O_4 comes to equilibrium as described above, calculate the density in g/cm^3 of the equilibrium mixture if the partial pressure of N_2O_4 is 200. kPa.
[8.35×10^{-3} g cm^{-3}]

16. A sealed tube initially contains 9.84×10^{-4} mol of $H_2(g)$ and 1.380×10^{-3} mol of $I_2(s)$. The tube is heated to 350. °C, at which temperature iodine becomes a vapour and the following equilibrium is established: $H_2(g) + I_2(g) \rightleftharpoons 2HI(g)$. At equilibrium it is found that there is 4.73×10^{-4} mol of I_2 present.

(a) Calculate the amounts of each of H_2 and HI present in the tube.

[0.77×10^{-4} mol, 1.81×10^{-3} mol]

(b) Calculate K for the reaction at this temperature.
[90.]

17. A bulb contains 7.5 g of carbon, and a gaseous mixture containing only carbon dioxide, CO_2, and carbon monoxide, CO, at equilibrium partial pressures of 29. kPa and 85. kPa respectively.

(a) Calculate K at this temperature for the following reaction:

$$C(s) + CO_2(g) \rightleftharpoons 2CO(g)$$
[2.5]

(b) Some more CO_2 is pumped into the bulb so that the total pressure increases to 200. kPa. The temperature remains constant. What are the partial pressures of CO_2 and CO in the new mixture?
[69. kPa, 131 kPa]

18. A sample of nitrosyl bromide NOBr at a pressure of 5.218 kPa and a temperature of 298.2 K has a density of 0.1861 g/L. This density is lower than expected for pure NOBr because of the dissociation equilibrium $NOBr(g) \rightleftharpoons NO(g) + \frac{1}{2} Br_2(g)$. What fraction of NOBr has dissociated?
[0.486]

19. Methanol is produced industrially by the reaction

$$CO(g) + 2 H_2(g) \rightleftharpoons CH_3OH(g)$$

for which $K = 0.0088$ at a temperature of 225°C. A mixture of CO and H_2 in the ratio 1:2 by mole is compressed and brought to equilibrium at this temperature. Calculate the total pressure required if 10.0 % of the CO in the original gas mixture is to be converted to methanol.
[560 kPa]

20. The equilibrium constant for the reaction $N_2O_4(g) \rightleftharpoons 2 NO_2(g)$ is $K = 0.150$ at 25°C. Consider a mixture of NO_2 and N_2O_4 at equilibrium at this temperature at a total pressure of 100. kPa in a sealed bulb of fixed volume.

(a) What are the partial pressures of NO_2 and N_2O_4 in the mixture?   [31.9 kPa, 68.1 kPa]

(b) Using the enthalpy change of reaction (from data in Appendix 1) calculate K at 40°C. [0.453]

(c) (For an extra challenge!) If the temperature is raised from 25°C to 40 °C, calculate the total pressure in the bulb at this temperature.   [114.7 kPa]

21. Methane reacts with steam at high temperature as follows:

$$CH_4(g) + H_2O(g) \rightleftharpoons CO(g) + 3 H_2(g)$$

At a temperature of 600 K the equilibrium constant for the reaction is $K = 1.8 \times 10^{-7}$. A mixture of steam at an initial partial pressure of 150. kPa, and methane at an initial partial pressure of 100. kPa, is placed in a fixed volume vessel at 600 K and brought to equilibrium. What is the partial pressure of hydrogen at equilibrium?   [3.0 kPa]

22. The equilibrium constant for the process $FeO(s) + CO(g) \rightleftharpoons Fe(s) + CO_2(g)$ is $K = 0.403$ at 1000. K A stream of pure $CO(g)$ is passed over powdered $FeO(s)$ at this temperature. What is the mole fraction of $CO(g)$ in the gas stream assuming that the reaction has come to equilibrium?   [0.713]

23. At high temperature salicylic acid $C_6H_4(OH)(COOH)$ vapour decomposes to carbon dioxide and phenol C_6H_5OH vapour:

$$C_6H_4(OH)(COOH)(g) \rightleftharpoons CO_2(g) + C_6H_5OH(g)$$

A 0.300 g sample of salicylic acid was placed in an evacuated bulb of volume 50.0 cm^3 and heated to a temperature of 200. °C.

(a) What would be the pressure in the bulb if no dissociation took place?   [170.9 kPa]

(b) When the system had come to equilibrium at 200. °C, the total pressure in the bulb was measured and found to be 323. kPa. What was the partial pressure of salicylic acid at equilibrium?

[18.8 kPa]

(c) What is the equilibrium constant for the reaction at this temperature?   [12.3]

24. At a temperature of 1325 K, phosphorus vapour exists in the form of the molecules P_4 and P_2 which are in equilibrium, $P_4(g) \rightleftharpoons 2P_2(g)$. The equilibrium constant at this temperature is $K = 0.100$. If a sample of phosphorus vapour is maintained at a total pressure of 100 kPa at this temperature, what is the mole fraction of P_4?   [0.730]

14 Acids and Bases in Aqueous Solution

Objectives

After reading this chapter, the student should be able to do the following:

♦ Describe reactions between acids and bases.

♦ Define relative activity for solutes in solution.

♦ Write expressions for the equilibrium constant for acid-base reactions.

♦ Define conjugate acids and bases.

♦ Define K_a and K_b for acid-base equilibria.

♦ Calculate concentrations at equilibrium using equilbrium constants.

♦ Define and recognize monoprotic and polyprotic acids.

♦ Define and recognize buffer solutions, and describe how to prepare them.

♦ Define and calculate pH of solutions.

♦ Define and sketch distribution diagrams for acid-base equilibria.

♦ Use distribution diagrams to interpret acid base equilibria.

♦ Describe and calculate titration curves for acid-base reactions.

♦ Describe how indicators work, and choose the correct indicator for each titration.

Related topics to review:

Acid-base reactions in Chapter 2.

Related topics to look forward to:

Precipitation reactions in Chapter 15.

14-1 Introduction

Water and aqueous solutions form an important part of our environment. Water is everywhere around us, in rain, rivers, lakes and oceans. Our bodies are largely made of water. Many chemical reactions take place in aqueous solution, and of these the most important are those involving the transfer of hydrogen ions in acid-base reactions.

Although acid-base reactions do not involve any new principles of chemical equilibrium, the equilibrium calculations are complicated somewhat by the fact that the solvent, water, always takes part in acid-base reactions, and is not simply an inert medium in which the reaction takes place.

The hydrogen atom has only one electron, and so the hydrogen ion H^+ consists of just the nucleus, which is a proton. Acid-base reactions are therefore referred to as **proton-transfer reactions**. In aqueous solution, the proton is attached to one or more water molecules, to form the **hydronium ion,** which is often represented by the formula H_3O^+, but during the actual reaction process, it is a proton itself which is transferred between the reacting molecules or ions. In most equations for acid-base equilibria in this chapter, the hydrogen ion in aqueous solution will be represented by the symbol $H^+(aq)$, rather than H_3O^+ because it reduces the need to include unnecessary water molecules in the equations.

In the theory of proposed independently by Johannes Brønsted and Thomas Lowry, the reaction between an acid and a base is regarded as the transfer of a proton from one molecule, the **proton donor**, to another molecule, the **proton acceptor**. The proton donor is called an **acid** and the proton acceptor is called a **base**.

The molecule or ion that remains after a proton has left an acid can, of course, accept a proton to form the original acid again, and hence is a base. The acid and base that are related by loss or addition of a proton are described as **conjugate** to each other. This reciprocal relationship between an acid and its conjugate base lies at the centre of the Brønsted-Lowry theory of the chemistry of acids and bases.

14-2 Water as the solvent

Most acids and bases are soluble in water, and form ions in solution. The solutions conduct electricity because of the presence of electrically charged ions, which can move in an electric field. In other words, acids and bases in aqueous solutions are electrolytes.

Water is not a good conductor of electricity unless it contains some dissolved electrolyte. When carefully purified, water is a very poor conductor of electricity but even at the highest levels of purity, when dissolved electrolytes are eliminated as a source of ions, the electrical conductivity is not zero, because ions are formed from water molecules themselves by a proton transfer equilibrium:

$$H_2O(\ell) \rightleftharpoons H^+(aq) + OH^-(aq)$$

The equilibrium constant for this process is called the **auto-ionization constant**, and, in terms of relative activities, is written:

$$K_w = \frac{a(H^+)a(OH^-)}{a(H_2O)}$$

The relative activity measures the driving force or activity of the specified species (i.e. ion or molecule), relative to its activity in the standard state. For the solvent, the standard state is taken to be the pure liquid, and as long as we limit ourselves to solutions which are not too concentrated, the relative activity of the solvent, $a(H_2O)$, remains close to 1, so we write:

$$a(H_2O) \approx 1$$

For solutes, the activity is proportional to the concentration c, as long as the solution is not too concentrated. The standard state concentration c^o is 1 mol/L; and hence the activity of each solute relative to the standard state is, to a good approximation, equal to the ratio c/c^o.

The relative activities of the hydrogen and hydroxide ions are therefore:

$$a(H^+) \approx \frac{c(H^+)}{c^o} \qquad a(OH^-) \approx \frac{c(OH^-)}{c^o}$$

The standard state concentration for solutes in solution is taken as 1 mol/L, and so the ratio c/c^o is equal to the numerical value of the molar concentration c expressed in mol/L, or M, but without the units. We will use the traditional square brackets to denote this quantity, and so the last two equations can be extended:

$$a(H^+) \approx \frac{c(H^+)}{c^o} = [H^+] \qquad a(OH^-) \approx \frac{c(OH^-)}{c^o} = [OH^-]$$

Square brackets will be used in formulae to indicate the numerical value of the molar concentration (without units). However they can also be used to mean the molar concentration including the units of mol/L, as is done in many other books.

Making these substitutions, we can write the auto-ionization constant of water as follows:

$$K_w = [H^+][OH^-] \qquad (14\text{-}1)$$

In pure water the ionization process produces equal concentrations of hydrogen and hydroxide ions. At 25°C, $[H^+] = [OH^-] = 1.0 \times 10^{-7}$, so the value of K_w is:

$$K_w = 1.0 \times 10^{-7} \times 1.0 \times 10^{-7} = 1.0 \times 10^{-14} \quad \text{at } 25°C$$

The auto-ionization constant K_w varies considerably with temperature, from 0.11×10^{-14} at 0°C to $50. \times 10^{-14}$ at 100°C. In most of the discussion in this chapter we assume a temperature of 25°C, which is close to room temperature. However, if dealing with water at a different temperature, the appropriate value of K_w should be used.

The acidity of a solution is measured by the concentration of hydrogen ions in solution. If the solution is acidic, then $[H^+]$ is high and $[OH^-]$ is low. If the solution is basic, then $[OH^-]$ is high and $[H^+]$ is low. Regardless of whether the solution is acidic or basic, equation (14-1) must be obeyed and the product of $[H^+]$ and $[OH^-]$ is equal to K_w.

14-3 Dissociation of acids and bases

A weak acid in aqueous solution is only partially dissociated into ions. An example is acetic acid, CH_3COOH, the acid found in ordinary vinegar. In aqueous solution, acetic acid dissociates into hydrogen ions and acetate ions by transfer of a proton to a water molecule:

$$CH_3COOH(aq) + H_2O(\ell) \rightleftharpoons H_3O^+(aq) + CH_3COO^-(aq)$$

In this process the acetic acid molecule acts as an acid, donating a proton to the water molecule, which acts as a base or proton acceptor. Reading the chemical equation from right to left, which is legitimate since the process is reversible, acetate ion acts as a base when it accepts a proton from the hydronium ion.

In writing a symbolic formula for a general acid, therefore, we will write HB for the acid and B^- for the conjugate base of that acid. (The student should be careful not to confuse this usage of B with the symbol for the element boron.) An acid such as acetic acid with one acidic hydrogen atom per molecule is called **monoprotic**; in a later section we will discuss acids with more than one acidic hydrogen atom.

The dissociation of a general weak acid HB is written:

$$HB(aq) + H_2O(\ell) \rightleftharpoons H_3O^+(aq) + B^-(aq)$$

or in simplified form,

$$HB(aq) \rightleftharpoons H^+(aq) + B^-(aq),$$

and the equilibrium constant for the process is called the **acid dissociation constant:**

$$K_a = \frac{[H^+][B^-]}{[HB]} \qquad (14\text{-}2)$$

The strength of an acid is measured by the value of K_a. A weak acid has a small value of K_a while a strong acid has a large value of K_a. A strong acid is almost completely dissociated into ions at all concentrations, while a weak acid is only partially dissociated into ions, and the degree of dissociation depends upon concentration.

A weak base in aqueous solution is also partially dissociated into ions. For example ammonia, NH_3, is a gas at ordinary temperatures and pressures, but dissolves readily in water to form an aqueous solution that is basic; household cleaning solutions often contain ammonia. In aqueous solution, the ammonia molecule accepts a proton from a water molecule to form the ammonium ion NH_4^+ and the hydroxide ion OH^-, and the following equilibrium is set up:

$$NH_3(aq) + H_2O(\ell) \rightleftharpoons NH_4^+(aq) + OH^-(aq)$$

Recalling that the relative activity of the solvent water is 1, the equilibrium constant for this process is:

$$K_b = \frac{[NH_4^+][OH^-]}{[NH_3]}$$

In general, the reaction of a weak base B with water can be written:

$$B(aq) + H_2O(\ell) \rightleftharpoons HB^+(aq) + OH^-(aq)$$

The equilibrium constant for this reaction is called the **base dissociation constant**, K_b:

$$K_b = \frac{[HB^+][OH^-]}{[B]} \qquad (14\text{-}3)$$

The dissociation constants for an acid and its conjugate base are closely related to each other. Consider again the dissociation of an acid:

$$HB(aq) + H_2O(\ell) \rightleftharpoons H_3O^+(aq) + B^-(aq)$$

The dissociation constant for the acid HB is:

$$K_a(HB) = \frac{[H^+][B^-]}{[HB]}$$

Consider a solution of the sodium salt NaB of the weak acid HB. When dissolved in water, the salt is completely dissociated into Na^+ and B^- ions:

$$NaB(aq) \rightarrow Na^+(aq) + B^-(aq)$$

The sodium ions Na^+ do not take part in any acid-base equilibria, but the anions B^- react with the water as a base by accepting protons:

$$B^-(aq) + H_2O(\ell) \rightleftharpoons HB(aq) + OH^-(aq)$$

The equilibrium constant for this reaction is the base dissociation constant for the base B^-.

$$K_b(B^-) = \frac{[HB][OH^-]}{[B^-]}$$

If the two equilibrium constants are multiplied together, we find:

$$K_a(HB)K_b(B^-) = \frac{[H^+][B^-]}{[HB]} \times \frac{[HB][OH^-]}{[B^-]} = [H^+][OH^-] = K_w \qquad (14\text{-}4)$$

Therefore the acid dissociation constant and the base dissociation constant for a conjugate acid-base pair are not independent quantities: the product of the two is equal to the auto-ionization constant for water.

Equation (14-4) is true for any conjugate acid/base pair, such as the acetic acid/acetate ion system or the ammonium ion/ammonia system. Therefore it is only necessary to specify one dissociation constant, either for the acid or for the base.

Example 14-1 For acetic acid at 25°C, K_a = 1.74 x 10^{-5}. What is K_b for acetate ion at this temperature?

For acetic acid K_a = 1. 74 x 10^{-5}, so for acetate ion, $K_b = \dfrac{K_w}{K_a} = \dfrac{1.0 \times 10^{-14}}{1.74 \times 10^{-5}} = 5.7 \times 10^{-10}$

Table 14-1 lists the acid and base dissociation constants for a number of weak monoprotic acids and bases, and shows the relationship between each acid and its conjugate base. It is worth spending a little time looking at the contents of the table. The columns labelled pK_a and pK_b will be explained later, in Section 14-7.

In Table 14-1, the acids are listed in order of decreasing K_a values, with the stronger acids at the top of the table, and weaker acids at the bottom. The conjugate bases are in the reverse order, with the weaker bases at the top and the stronger ones at the bottom. "Strong" acids, such as hydrochloric acid, are not included in the table; their K_a values are large enough that for practical purposes they are completely dissociated in aqueous solution.

The acids can be divided into two broad categories, inorganic and organic. Examples of inorganic acids are hydrofluoric acid HF and nitrous acid HNO_2. The organic acids are compounds of carbon containing the carboxyl group, –COOH. The various organic acids listed show that the acid dissociation constant K_a of a carboxylic acid depends on the structure of the rest of the molecule.

Weak bases can be classified into two groups, the conjugate anions of molecular acids (either organic or inorganic), and molecular bases containing a nitrogen atom. Ammonia is the simplest of the nitrogen-containing bases, and many organic bases called **amines** are related to ammonia by the replacement of one or more of the hydrogen atoms by organic groups of atoms, an example being methylamine, CH_3NH_2.

Table 14-1 Equilibrium constants for ionization of weak monoprotic acids and bases

Acid		K_a	pK_a	Base		K_b	pK_b
$CH_2ClCOOH$	chloroacetic	1.4×10^{-3}	2.85	CH_2ClCOO^-	chloroacetate	7.1×10^{-12}	11.15
HF	hydrofluoric	6.3×10^{-4}	3.20	F^-	fluoride	1.6×10^{-11}	10.80
HNO_2	nitrous	5.6×10^{-4}	3.25	NO_2^-	nitrite	1.8×10^{-11}	10.75
$HCOOH$	formic	1.8×10^{-4}	3.75	$HCOO^-$	formate	5.6×10^{-11}	10.25
C_6H_5COOH	benzoic	6.5×10^{-5}	4.19	$C_6H_5COO^-$	benzoate	1.5×10^{-10}	9.81
$C_6H_5NH_3^+$	anilininium	2.3×10^{-5}	4.63	$C_6H_5NH_2$	aniline	4.3×10^{-10}	9.37
CH_3COOH	acetic	1.7×10^{-5}	4.76	CH_3COO^-	acetate	5.8×10^{-10}	9.24
C_2H_5COOH	propanoic	1.4×10^{-5}	4.86	$C_2H_5COO^-$	propanoate	7.2×10^{-10}	9.14
$HOCl$	hypochlorous	4.0×10^{-8}	7.40	ClO^-	hypochlorite	2.5×10^{-7}	6.60
HCN	hydrocyanic	6.2×10^{-10}	9.21	CN^-	cyanide	1.6×10^{-5}	4.79
NH_4^+	ammonium	5.6×10^{-10}	9.25	NH_3	ammonia	1.8×10^{-5}	4.75
$(CH_3)_3NH^+$ trimethylammonium		1.6×10^{-10}	9.80	$(CH_3)_3N$	trimethylamine	6.3×10^{-5}	4.20
$CH_3NH_3^+$	methylammonium	2.3×10^{-11}	10.63	CH_3NH_2	methylamine	4.3×10^{-4}	3.37

14-4 Aqueous solutions of acids

An acid dissolved in pure water increases the hydrogen ion concentration, because hydrogen ions are formed when the acid ionizes. In this section we develop the techniques needed to calculate the concentrations of various ions and molecules in a solution of an acid in water.

Suppose that a solution is formed by dissolving C_a moles of an acid HB per litre of pure water, to form a solution in which the total concentration of acid is C_a mol/L. The acid ionizes according to the equation

$$HB(aq) \rightleftharpoons H^+(aq) + B^-(aq)$$

The concentrations of H^+ and B^- must be equal, and we denote their value by a variable x which is yet to be calculated. Hence we set $[H^+] = [B^-] = x$, and $[HB] = C_a - x$.

The ionization process can be represented in an "initial-change-equilibrium", or ICE, table. For reactions in solution, the ICE table is nearly always written in terms of concentrations.

	$HB(aq)$	$\rightleftharpoons$	$H^+(aq)$	$+$	$B^-(aq)$
initial:	C_a		0		0
change:	$-x$		$+x$		$+x$
equilibrium:	$C_a - x$		x		x

The equilibrium constant is: $$K_a = \frac{[H^+][B^-]}{[HB]} = \frac{x^2}{C_a - x}$$

This equation can be multiplied out to give a quadratic equation in the unknown x, which in standard form is

$$x^2 + K_a x - K_a C_a = 0$$

Solving this for x, we find $$x = [H^+] = \tfrac{1}{2}\left\{ -K_a + \sqrt{K_a^2 + 4K_a C_a} \right\} \qquad (14\text{-}5)$$

The other solution, with a negative sign in front of the square root, is ignored since a concentration cannot be negative. This formula is a satisfactory solution to the problem for all except exceedingly dilute solutions, for which it is necessary to take into account the ionization of the water itself by means of a more complex formula. As a check, the hydrogen ion concentration in a solution of an acid should be greater than 10^{-7} M.

Example 14-2   Calculate the concentrations of acetic acid and acetate ion in a 0.050 M solution of acetic acid.

We begin by writing ICE table for the dissociation process:

$$CH_3COOH(aq) \rightleftharpoons H^+(aq) + CH_3COO^-(aq)$$

initial:	0.050	0 0
change:	$-x$	$+x$ $+x$
equilibrium:	$0.050 - x$	x x

From Table 19-2, the dissociation constant for acetic acid is $K_a = 1.7\times10^{-5}$, so we can write:

$$1.7\times10^{-5} = \frac{x^2}{0.050 - x}$$

Multiplying out the quadratic, we get: $x^2 + 1.7\times10^{-5}x - 8.5\times10^{-7} = 0$, and the solution is:

$$x = \tfrac{1}{2}\left\{ -1.7\times10^{-5} + \sqrt{(1.7\times10^{-5})^2 + 4\times8.5\times10^{-7}} \right\} = 9.13\times10^{-4}$$

Hence $[H^+] = [CH_3COO^-] = 9.1\times10^{-4}$ M, and $[CH_3COOH] = 0.050 - 9.1\times10^{-4} = 0.049$ M.

Solving the quadratic equation is an exact solution to the problem, but in many cases there is a simpler calculation which is sufficiently accurate. It will be noticed in the calculation in Example 14-2 that only a small fraction of the acetic acid is ionized. We use this fact to simplify the calculation in the following procedure, which is simple and sufficiently accurate in many cases.

We start by writing the ICE table and the expression for the equilibrium constant as above. But then we assume that $[H^+] = x$ is much less than the initial concentration of acid C_a. With this assumption we can ignore x in the denominator of the equilibrium constant expression and make the following approximation:

$$K_a = \frac{[H^+][B^-]}{[HB]} = \frac{x^2}{C_a - x} \approx \frac{x^2}{C_a}$$

Hence $x^2 \approx K_a C_a$ and we can solve for x simply by taking the square root:

$$x = [H^+] \approx \sqrt{K_a C_a} \qquad (14\text{-}6)$$

We then check to see whether our assumption is correct. If the calculated value of x is less than 5% of C_a then no further calculation is needed. A result that is accurate within 5 per cent is acceptable in most circumstances in these calculations because of other approximations, which we are ignoring.

On the other hand, if x is greater than 5% of C_a, then it is best to return and use the full solution to the quadratic as described above.

Table 14-2 summarizes the general formula for calculation of $[H^+]$ in a solution of an acid, and the simplified forms that are valid for special cases.

Example 14-3 Calculate the hydrogen ion concentration in the previous example using the approximate method.

The ICE table is as follows:

$$CH_3COOH(aq) \rightleftharpoons H^+(aq) + CH_3COO^-(aq)$$

initial:	0.050	0	0
change:	$-x$	$+x$	$+x$
equilibrium:	$0.050 - x$	x	x

From Table 19-2, the dissociation constant for acetic acid is $K_a = 1.7 \times 10^{-5}$, so we can write:

$$1.7 \times 10^{-5} = \frac{x^2}{0.050 - x}$$

Assuming that $x \ll 0.050$, we can at once calculate $[H^+] = \sqrt{1.7 \times 10^{-5} \times 0.050} = 9.2 \times 10^{-4}$

This result is less than 5% of $Ca = 0.050$, and agrees satisfactorily with the result of the full calculation, which is 9.1×10^{-4} (see Example 14-2).

Example 14-4 Calculate $[H^+]$, $[CH_3COO^-]$ and $[CH_3COOH]$ in a 2.0×10^{-4} M solution of acetic acid.

The ICE table for the dissociation equilibrium is:

$$CH_3COOH(aq) \rightleftharpoons H^+(aq) + CH_3COO^-(aq)$$

initial:	2.0×10^{-4}	0	0
change:	$-x$	$+x$	$+x$
equilibrium:	$2.0\times10^{-4} - x$	x	x

Substituting the equilibrium concentrations in the expression for the equilibrium constant, we get:

$$1.7\times10^{-5} = \frac{x^2}{2.0\times10^{-4} - x}$$

The approximate solution is $x \approx \sqrt{1.7\times10^{-5} \times 2.0\times10^{-4}} = 5.8\times10^{-5}$

This result is more than 5% of 2.0×10^{-4}, and so we have to solve the full quadratic equation. The equilibrium constant expression gives the following standard quadratic form:

$$x^2 + 1.7\times10^{-5}x - 3.4\times10^{-9} = 0$$

The solution is: $\quad x = \frac{1}{2}\left\{-1.7\times10^{-5} + \sqrt{(1.7\times10^{-5})^2 + 4\times3.4\times10^{-9}}\right\} = 5.0\times10^{-5}$

Hence $[H^+] = [CH_3COO^-] = 5.0\times10^{-5}$ M and $[CH_3COOH] = 2.0\times10^{-4} - 5.0\times10^{-5} = 1.5\times10^{-4}$ M.

Table 14-2 Summary of formulae for calculating [H⁺] in a solution of an acid.

Range of concentration	Equation for [H⁺]
All concentrations:	$[H^+] = \frac{1}{2}\left\{-K_a + \sqrt{K_a^2 + 4K_aC_a}\right\}$
Approximations for special cases:	
High concentrations $(C_a > 100K_a)$:	$[H^+] \approx \sqrt{K_aC_a}$
Low concentrations $(C_a < K_a/10)$:	$[H^+] \approx C_a$
Strong acids (at any concentration):	$[H^+] \approx C_a$

There is a limit to the applicability of these calculations to extremely dilute solutions. To see this, consider a solution of acetic acid so dilute that the total concentration C_a is less than 1×10^{-7}. Calculation predicts that [H⁺] is less than 10^{-7}, which is less than in pure water. This is unrealistic. To deal with such extremely dilute solutions, the auto-ionization of water must be taken into account in a more complicated calculation, which we will not consider.

For strong acids in which $K_a > 10$, the acid is almost 100 per cent ionized in ordinary solutions with concentrations less than 1 M. This makes calculations of [H⁺] particularly simple since $[H^+] \approx C_a$.

Example 14-5 Calculate [H⁺] in a solution of 0.050 M hydrochloric acid.

_____

Since hydrochloric acid is a strong acid, it is completely ionized. We show this by using a single arrow in the chemical equation:

$$HCl(aq) \rightarrow H^+(aq) + Cl^-(aq)$$

Since dissociation is complete, $[H^+] = 0.050$ M.

_____

As a final example of acid dissociation, we consider a solution of an ammonium salt in which the ammonium ion, the conjugate acid to ammonia, acts as a weak acid and makes the solution acidic.

_____

Example 14-6 Calculate the hydrogen ion concentration in a 0.15 M solution of NH_4Cl.

_____

Ammonium chloride is a salt, and dissociates completely into ions in solution:

$$NH_4Cl(aq) \rightarrow NH_4^+(aq) + Cl^-(aq)$$

The chloride ion Cl^- does not take part in any acid-base equilibria, but the ammonium ion is a weak acid, which is the conjugate acid to ammonia NH_3. The ICE table is as follows:

	$NH_4^+(aq)$	$\rightleftharpoons$	$H^+(aq)$ +	$NH_3(aq)$
initial:	0.15		0	0
change:	$-x$		$+x$	$+x$
equilibrium:	$0.15 - x$		x	x

Table 14-1 shows that $K_a = 5.6 \times 10^{-10}$ for the ammonium ion, so that it is a very weak acid. Using the approximate method:

$$[H^+] = \sqrt{5.6 \times 10^{-10} \times 0.15} = 9.2 \times 10^{-6}$$

this is much less than 5% of 0.15, and so the assumption is justified.

_____

In a solution of an acid, the fraction of the acid that is ionized can be calculated by dividing the hydrogen ion concentration by the total concentration of the acid, C_a. Using equation (14-5), with some rearrangement, we find:

$$\text{fraction ionized} = \frac{x}{C_a} = \frac{1}{2}\left\{ -\frac{K_a}{C_a} + \sqrt{\left(\frac{K_a}{C_a}\right)^2 + 4\left(\frac{K_a}{C_a}\right)} \right\} \tag{14-7}$$

The most important feature of this equation is that the fraction ionized depends only on the ratio K_a/C_a. When the solution of a weak acid is sufficiently dilute that $C_a = K_a$ (a very dilute solution if the acid is weak), equation (14-7) shows that the fraction ionized is 0.62, and the acid is more than half ionized. For a more dilute solution in which $C_a = Ka/10$, the fraction ionized is 0.92. In even more dilute solutions, the acid is almost completely ionized and $[H^+] \approx C_a$ to a good approximation.

The fraction ionized is plotted as a function of the ratio C_a/K_a in Figure 14-1. The graph indicates that, as we have already seen, the fraction ionized is small in concentrated solutions, but approaches unity in very dilute solutions (with small C_a) or in solutions of strong acids (with large K_a). Care should be taken in interpreting this graph for very dilute solutions, because of auto-ionization of the water, as discussed above.

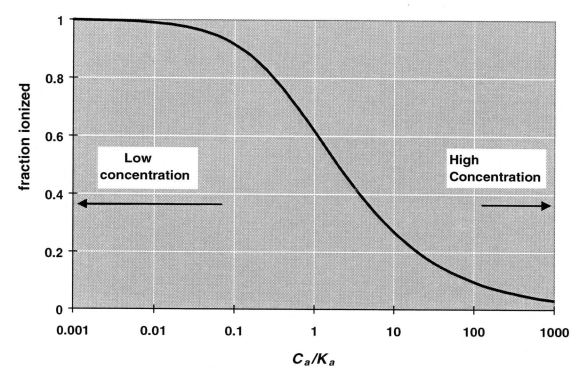

Figure 14-1 The fraction of a weak acid that is ionized, plotted as a function of the ratio C_a/K_a. The horizontal scale is plotted logarithmically, so that each division corresponds to a factor of 10. In the low concentration range, the fraction ionized is almost 1, so the acid is almost completely ionized and $[H^+] \approx C_a$. In the high concentration range, the fraction ionized is small, and hence very little of the acid is ionized and $[H^+] \approx \sqrt{(K_a C_a)}$. (see Table 14-2).

14-5 Aqueous solutions of bases

Solutions of weak bases are dealt with in a manner similar to that described in the last section, except that the focus is on the hydroxide ion rather than the hydrogen ion. The dissociation equilibrium for our typical weak base, ammonia NH_3, is:

$$NH_3(aq) + H_2O(\ell) \rightleftharpoons NH_4^+(aq) + OH^-(aq)$$

The formula for a general base will be denoted by the symbol B. In some cases the base B is a negatively charged ion; in that case the charges in the rest of the chemical equation must be adjusted, but this does not change the principle of the calculation. The ICE table for dissociation of a general base B with a total concentration of C_b is as follows:

$$B(aq) + H_2O(\ell) \rightleftharpoons BH^+(aq) + OH^-(aq)$$

initial:	C_b	0	0
change:	$-x$	$+x$	$+x$
equilibrium:	$C_b - x$	x	x

The equilibrium constant expression is: $\quad K_b = \dfrac{[BH^+][OH^-]}{[B]} = \dfrac{x^2}{C_b - x}$

and the solution is: $\qquad [OH^-] = x = \frac{1}{2}\left\{ -K_b + \sqrt{K_b^2 + 4K_bC_b} \right\}$ $\hfill$ (14-8)

For sufficiently concentrated solutions, the following approximate solution may be used:

$$[OH^-] \approx \sqrt{K_bC_b} \hfill (14\text{-}9)$$

At the other extreme, ionization is almost complete at very low concentrations, so that $[OH^-] \approx C_b$.

Table 14-3 summarizes the general formula for calculation of $[OH^-]$ in a solution of a base, and the two simplified forms that are valid for special cases. It is helpful to compare the formulae this table with those in Table 14-2.

Table 14-3 Summary of formulae for calculating [OH⁻] in a solution of a base.

Range of concentration	Equation for [OH⁻]
All concentrations:	$[OH^-] = \frac{1}{2}\left\{ -K_b + \sqrt{K_b^2 + 4K_bC_b} \right\}$
Approximations for special cases:	
High concentrations $(C_b > 100K_b)$:	$[OH^-] \approx \sqrt{K_bC_b}$
Low concentrations $(C_b < K_b/10)$:	$[OH^-] \approx C_b$
Strong bases (all concentrations)	$[OH^-] \approx C_b$

Example 14-7 Calculate the hydroxide ion concentration [OH⁻] in a 0.30 M solution of ammonia, NH_3.

The ICE table for the dissociation equation is:

$$NH_3(aq) + H_2O(\ell) \rightleftharpoons NH_4^+(aq) + OH^-(aq)$$

initial:	0.30	0	0
change:	$-x$	$+x$	$+x$
equilibrium:	$0.30 - x$	x	x

For NH_3, Table 14-1 gives the value $K_b = 1.8\times10^{-5}$, and hence:

$$1.8\times10^{-5} = \frac{x^2}{0.30 - x}$$

Assuming that $x \ll 0.30$, we can use the approximate solution:

$$x = \sqrt{1.8\times10^{-5} \times 0.30} = 2.3\times10^{-3}$$

The assumption is justified and hence $[OH^-] = 2.3\times10^{-3}$ M.

Example 14-8 Calculate the hydroxide ion concentration in a 0.13 M solution of sodium acetate.

Sodium acetate is a salt, and dissociates completely into ions in solution:

$$CH_3COONa(aq) \rightarrow CH_3COO^-(aq) + Na^+(aq).$$

The sodium ion Na^+ does not take part in any acid-base equilibria, but the acetate ion is a weak base. The ICE table is as follows:

$$CH_3COO^-(aq) + H_2O \rightleftharpoons CH_3COOH(aq) + OH^-(aq).$$

initial:	0.13	0	0
change:	$-x$	$+x$	$+x$
equilibrium:	$0.13 - x$	x	x

For the acetate ion, Table 14-1 indicates $K_b = 5.8\times10^{-10}$. The equilibrium constant expression is:

$$5.8\times10^{-10} = \frac{x^2}{0.13 - x}$$

Assuming that $x \ll 0.13$, we use the approximate solution:

$$x = \sqrt{5.8\times10^{-10} \times 0.13} = 8.7\times10^{-6}$$

The assumption is justified and hence $[OH^-] = 8.7\times10^{-6}$ M.

The alkali metal hydroxides, such as sodium hydroxide, NaOH, dissociate directly and completely into metal ions and hydroxide ions OH^- when dissolved in water:

$$NaOH(s) \rightarrow Na^+(aq) + OH^-(aq)$$

In a solution of an alkali metal hydroxide, such as sodium hydroxide, [OH⁻] is equal to the total concentration of base dissolved, C_b, as indicated in Table 14-3. These are therefore described as strong bases.

14-6 Mixtures of acids and bases: buffer solutions

A solution containing substantial and roughly equal concentrations of both a weak acid and its conjugate base is called a **buffer solution**. In a buffer solution, the hydrogen ion concentration is controlled primarily by the presence of the conjugate acid/base pair in solution, and is hardly affected by addition of small amounts of acid or base. A buffer solution can absorb added H⁺ or OH⁻ ions with little change in [H⁺] because the added ions can react with either the base or the acid of the buffer system. Buffer solutions are often used in biological experiments. In this section we discuss the preparation and properties of buffer solutions.

If a strong base such as sodium hydroxide NaOH is added to a solution of acetic acid, some of the acetic acid is converted to acetate ion by loss of a proton. The reaction is described by the following equation:

$$CH_3COOH(aq) + OH^-(aq) \rightarrow CH_3COO^-(aq) + H_2O$$

Because hydroxide ion is a strong base, almost every hydroxide added reacts, and is replaced by an acetate ion. If the amount (in moles) of hydroxide ion added is less than the initial amount of acetic acid present, the resulting solution contains a mixture of acetic acid, and its conjugate base, acetate ion. The same (or a similar) situation can be reached by adding a salt of acetic acid, such as sodium acetate CH_3COONa, to a solution of acetic acid.

When acetic acid and acetate ion are both present in substantial and roughly equal concentrations, the hydrogen ion concentration is determined by the acid dissociation constant and the ratio of the concentrations of the acid and its anion present in the solution.

Suppose that a solution is prepared by dissolving C_a mol/L of a general acid HB, and C_b mol/L of the conjugate base B⁻. The dissociation equilibrium is:

$$HB(aq) \rightleftharpoons H^+(aq) + B^-(aq)$$

If the acid is weak and the concentration C_a is not too low, then the extent of dissociation is small. The addition of conjugate base B⁻ drives the equilibrium to the left, by Le Chatelier's principle, and the extent of dissociation is reduced even further. Suppose that the initial concentrations of the acid and conjugate bases are C_a and C_b respectively. The ICE table is as follows:

	HB(aq)	$\rightleftharpoons$	H⁺(aq)	+ B⁻(aq)
initial:	C_a		0	C_b
change:	$-x$		$+x$	$+x$
equilibrium:	$C_a - x$		x	$C_b + x$

Hence the equilibrium constant expression is :

$$K_a = \frac{x(C_b + x)}{(C_a - x)}$$

This quadratic equation in the unknown x can be solved exactly. But as long as the concentrations of acid and base are large compared with K_a, then the change x is much smaller than C_a and C_b. This is not difficult to achieve this condition when preparing a buffer solution.

Then the change x can be ignored in the parentheses on the right hand side of this expression, without making serious error, and hence, to a good approximation,

$$K_a \approx \frac{xC_b}{C_a}$$

From this it follows that:

$$[\text{H}^+] = x = K_a \frac{C_a}{C_b} \tag{14-10}$$

The hydrogen ion concentration is therefore determined by the acid dissociation constant K_a, and the ratio C_a/C_b of the concentrations of the acid and conjugate base.

If, in the above calculation, it turns out that x is not much smaller than the initial concentrations of acid and base so that the assumption is not justified, then the equation can be multiplied out to give a quadratic equation. This can then be solved as usual. This is not usually the case.

Example 14-9 Calculate the hydrogen ion concentration $[\text{H}^+]$ in a solution containing 0.15 mol/L acetic acid and 0.20 mol/L sodium acetate.

The solution contains both an acid and its conjugate base at comparable concentrations and therefore is a buffer solution. The concentrations are $C_a = 0.15$ and $C_b = 0.20$. Since $K_a = 1.7 \times 10^{-5}$,

$$[\text{H}^+] = 1.7 \times 10^{-5} \times \frac{0.15}{0.20} = 1.3 \times 10^{-5}$$

Example 14-10 Calculate $[\text{H}^+]$ in a solution containing 0.050 mol of ammonia and 0.090 mol of ammonium chloride in a volume of approximately 100 mL.

Ammonium chloride has the formula NH_4Cl and dissociates completely into ammonium ions NH_4^+ and chloride ions Cl^- in aqueous solution.

$$\text{NH}_4\text{Cl(aq)} \rightarrow \text{NH}_4^+\text{(aq)} + \text{Cl}^-\text{(aq)}$$

Hence the solution contains both ammonia NH_3 and ammonium ions NH_4^+ and so is a buffer solution.

Since the volume V of the solution is known only approximately it is not possible to calculate the actual concentrations, but the ratio of concentrations is exactly equal to the ratio of the amounts:

$$\frac{C_a}{C_b} = \frac{0.090/V}{0.050/V} = \frac{0.090}{0.050} = 1.8$$

For the ammonium ion, $K_a = 5.6 \times 10^{-10}$, from Table 14-1, and so:

$$[\text{H}^+] = 5.6 \times 10^{-10} \times 1.8 = 1.0 \times 10^{-9}$$

Example 14-11 Calculate $[\text{H}^+]$ in a solution containing 0.100 mol of acetic acid to which 0.030 mol of sodium hydroxide is added. The total volume of the solution is approximately 150 mL.

The effect of adding sodium hydroxide, NaOH, to the acetic acid is to convert some of the acetic acid to an equivalent amount of acetate ion:

$$CH_3COOH(aq) + OH^-(aq) \rightarrow CH_3COO^-(aq) + H_2O(\ell)$$

Essentially all of the hydroxide ion reacts, so the amount of CH_3COOH left is (0.100–0.030) = 0.070 mol, and the amount of acetate present is 0.030 mol. As in the previous example, the exact volume of the solution does not matter. Hence $[H^+]$ is:

$$[H^+] = 1.7 \times 10^{-5} \times \frac{0.070}{0.030} = 4.0 \times 10^{-5}$$

Example 14-12 Calculate $[H^+]$ in a solution of volume 0.2 L containing 0.100 mol of sodium acetate to which has been added 0.040 mol of hydrochloric acid.

Hydrochloric acid is a strong acid which reacts with the acetate ion to produce 0.040 mol of acetic acid, and leaving (0.100–0.040) = 0.060 mol of acetate ion. The actual volume of the solution is not needed for the calculation. Hence $[H^+]$ is:

$$[H^+] = 1.7 \times 10^{-5} \times \frac{0.040}{0.060} = 1.1 \times 10^{-5}$$

It will be noticed that in all of the four examples just given, $[H^+]$ is not very much different from the dissociation constant K_a for the acid. For a buffer solution to be effective, the ratio $[HB]/[B^-]$ should be between 10 and 1/10, so $[H^+]$ is of the same order of magnitude as K_a. If this is not the case, then the approximations used to derive equation (14-10) are not valid.

The criterion for choosing a suitable conjugate acid/base pair in order to produce a buffer of a specific pH is that the acid dissociation constant K_a for the acid HB should be close to the desired value of $[H^+]$. A suitable acid can often be found by examining a table of K_a values such as Table 14-1.

Example 14-13 Choose an acid/base system from Table 14-1 which could be used to prepare a buffer with $[H^+]$ close to 1×10^{-4}.

Inspection of Table 14-1 shows that that a solution containing formic acid, with $K_a = 1.8 \times 10^{-4}$, together with the formate ion could be used to make a buffer in which $[H^+]$ is about 1×10^{-4}.

A buffer solution has the useful property that $[H^+]$ is not changed very much by moderate additions of acid or base, or by dilution. In a word, the hydrogen ion concentration is "buffered" against changes caused by addition of acid or base or water. Buffering of the hydrogen ion concentration can be understood as follows.

If a small amount of a strong acid such as hydrochloric acid is added to a buffer solution, the H^+ added reacts with the an equivalent amount of the base B^-:

$$H^+(aq) + B^-(aq) \rightarrow HB(aq)$$

The effect of this process is to convert a small amount of the base B^- to the acid HB, and hence to reduce $[B^-]$ and increase $[HB]$. Consequently the ratio $[HB]/[B^-]$ increases. The hydrogen ion concentration [H⁺] therefore increases, but the change is small as long as the amount of acid added is not enough to change the ratio [HB]/[B⁻] by very much.

On the other hand, if a small amount of a strong base such as sodium hydroxide is added to a buffer solution, the OH⁻ added reacts with the an equivalent amount of the acid HB:

$$OH^-(aq) + HB(aq) \rightarrow B^-(aq) + H_2O$$

This leads to a small decrease in the hydrogen ion concentration, but the change is small as long as the amount of base added is not enough to change the ratio [HB]/[B⁻] by very much.

This discussion can be summarized as follows. A buffer solution maintains the hydrogen ion concentration nearly constant because it contains reservoirs of both an acid HB and its conjugate base B⁻, which are available to react with moderate amounts of added acid or base, preventing a large change in [H⁺].

Finally, addition of solvent to a buffer solution changes [HB] and [B⁻] by the same factor and so their ratio is not changed. Hence the hydrogen ion concentration [H⁺] does not change if a buffer solution is diluted.

Example 14-14 Calculate the change in [H⁺] of the buffer solution specified in Example 14-12 if 1.0 mL of 1.0 M hydrochloric acid is added.

The solution initially contained 0.040 mol of acetic acid and 0.060 mol of acetate ion. The addition of 1.0 mL of 1.0 M HCl adds 0.001 mol of hydrogen ion, which converts the same amount of acetate ion to acetic acid. Hence after the addition, the solution contains 0.041 mol of acetic acid and 0.059 mol of acetate ion. After the addition, [H⁺] is:

$$[H^+] = 1.7 \times 10^{-5} \times \frac{0.041}{0.059} = 1.2 \times 10^{-5}.$$

The original [H⁺] (from Example 14-12) was 1.1×10^{-5}, so the change is very small.

14-7 The pH scale

The range of variation in the magnitude of the concentrations of hydrogen and hydroxide ions is enormous. In a solution of 1 M hydrochloric acid, [H⁺] is 1, and [OH⁻] is 10^{-14}. In a solution of 1 M sodium hydroxide [OH⁻] is 1, and [H⁺] is 10^{-14}. These are both common reagents and so very large changes of these concentrations take place in ordinary laboratory experiments. When faced with such a large range of values, it is convenient to use a logarithmic scale to base 10.

In 1909, S.P.L.Sørensen, a Danish biochemist working at a research institute related to the Carlsberg breweries, defined the pH of a solution as the negative of the logarithm to base 10 of the hydrogen ion concentration [H⁺]:

$$pH = -\log[H^+] \tag{14-11a}$$

The name is an abbreviation for *puissance d'hydrogène* or "power of hydrogen". Nowadays the pH of a solution is defined in terms of the relative activity of the hydrogen ion:

$$pH = -\log a(H^+) \tag{14-11b}$$

The pH of a solution, as defined by this equation, can be measured electrochemically by means of an electrode that is sensitive to hydrogen ions. The potential of this electrode relative to a reference electrode is a linear function of the logarithm of the activity of hydrogen ions in solution, and hence can be used to measure pH directly and accurately. However for equilibrium calculations at the beginning level it is sufficiently accurate to use the approximation that the relative activity of the hydrogen ion is $a(H^+) \approx [H^+]$. Equation (14-11b) is the strict definition of pH, but equation (11a) is used as a practical approximation in many equilibrium calculations.

The same notation can be used to represent other concentrations on a logarithmic scale:

$$pOH = -\log a(OH^-) \approx -\log[OH^-]$$

This convention is also used for equilibrium constants:

$$pK_w = -\log K_w$$

$$pK_a = -\log K_a$$

$$pK_b = -\log K_b$$

In Table 14-1, the acid and base dissociation constants are listed in this logarithmic form as well as in normal form.

From these definitions and the value of the auto-dissociation constant for water at 25°C, it follows that

$$pH + pOH = pK_w = 14.0$$

In pure water, or a neutral solution, the concentrations of hydrogen and hydroxide ions are equal, and so at 25°C the pH is 7.0 and pOH is also 7.0. In an acidic solution, the pH is less than 7.0 and pOH is greater than 7.0; in a basic solution the pH is greater than 7.0 and pOH is less than 7.0. These various conditions are represented in Table 14-4 and Figure 14-2. The very small numbers in Table 14-4 makes clear the advantage of a logarithmic scale, such as pH, when dealing with very small concentrations.

For many solutions the pH lies between 0 and 14, but pH values less than zero or greater than 14 are possible when dealing with high concentrations of strong acids and bases.

Table 14-4 The pH scale

pH	pOH	[H⁺]	[OH⁻]
0	14	1.0	0.000 000 000 000 01
2	12	0.01	0.000 000 000 001
4	10	0.000 1	0.000 000 000 1
6	8	0.000 001	0.000 000 01
8	6	0.000 000 01	0.000 001
10	4	0.000 000 000 1	0.000 1
12	2	0.000 000 000 001	0.01
14	0	0.000 000 000 000 01	1

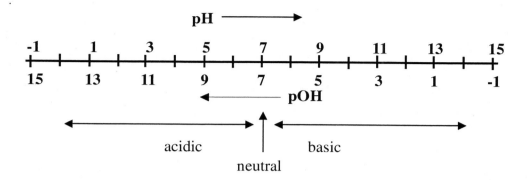

Figure 14-2 The pH scale at 25°C. The scale has been extended at both ends to show that pH is not limited to the range from 0 to 14. The pOH scale is defined by pOH = 14 – pH, and so runs in the opposite direction, from right to left.

Many of the equations derived in the previous sections can be expressed in logarithmic form. For example, equation (14-4) relates the dissociation constants for an acid and its conjugate base:

$$K_a(\text{HB})K_b(\text{B}^-) = K_w.$$

Taking the negative logarithm (to base 10) of each side of this equation, we obtain:

$$-\log K_a(\text{HB}) - \log K_b(\text{B}^-) = -\log K_w$$

so

$$pK_a(\text{HB}) + pK_b(\text{B}^-) = pK_w = 14.0 \tag{14-12}$$

This equation relates the pK_a and pK_b values for a conjugate acid-base pair. For example,

$$pK_a(\text{CH}_3\text{COOH}) + pK_b(\text{CH}_3\text{COO}^-) = 14.0$$

and

$$pK_a(\text{NH}_4^+) + pK_b(\text{NH}_3) = 14.0$$

The hydrogen ion concentration in a solution of a weak acid at sufficiently high concentration is given by equation (14-6):

$$[\text{H}^+] \approx \sqrt{K_a C_a}\ .$$

Taking the negative logarithm of both sides, and using the properties of the logarithm of a square root, we find:

$$\text{pH} \approx \tfrac{1}{2}(pK_a + pC_a) \tag{14-13a}$$

The hydroxide ion concentration in a solution of a weak base at sufficiently high concentration is given by equation (14-9):

$$[\text{OH}^-] \approx \sqrt{K_b C_b}\ .$$

Taking the negative logarithm of both sides, as before, and using the properties of the logarithm of a square root, we find:

$$pOH \approx \tfrac{1}{2}(pK_b + pC_b) \qquad\qquad (14\text{-}13b)$$

Finally, the hydrogen ion concentration in a solution of a buffer solution is given by equation (14-10):

$$[H^+] = K_a \frac{C_a}{C_b}$$

Taking the negative logarithm of both sides of this equation,

$$pH = pK_a - \log\frac{C_a}{C_b} \qquad\qquad (14\text{-}14)$$

This equation is often called the **Henderson-Hasselbalch** equation and can be used to calculate the pH of a buffer solution directly. For a buffer to be most effective, the ratio C_a/C_b should lie between 10 and 1/10, and so the pH must lie between pK_a+1 and pK_a-1.

14-8 Distribution diagrams

We turn now to a method of representing acid/base equilibrium by means of graphs or diagrams. Using diagrams does not replace any of the calculations of the previous sections, but helps to build a mental image of the acid-base equilibrium in aqueous solution.

We start by considering a particular acid HB and its conjugate base B$^-$. Suppose that we dissolve some of the acid and/or its salt in a buffer solution. As an example, suppose that a small amount of acetic acid is added to a buffer solution consisting of a different acid and its conjugate base. The buffer system controls the hydrogen ion concentration [H$^+$], or pH, of the solution. The added acetic acid has no significant effect on the pH, and instead, the buffer solution controls the equilibrium between the acetic acid and acetate ion. By using a series of buffer solutions, therefore, we can study how the state of the acetic acid/acetate dissociation equilibrium varies with pH, when the pH is controlled as an independent variable.

The concentrations of the acid [HB] and its anion [B$^-$] vary with pH but their sum must be a constant, since a molecule HB which loses a proton becomes an anion B$^-$, and vice versa. Let the sum of the concentrations [HB] and [B$^-$] be denoted by C:

$$C = [HB] + [B^-].$$

Of the total amount of "B" in the solution, the fraction in the acidic form HB is $f_a = [HB]/C$, and the fraction f_b of the total amount of "B" in the basic form B$^-$ is $[B^-]/C$. Dividing one by the other and using the expression for the equilibrium constant, $K_a = [H^+][B^-]/[HB]$., we find:

$$\frac{f_b}{f_a} = \frac{[B^-]/C}{[HB]/C} = \frac{[B^-]}{[HB]} = \frac{K_a}{[H^+]}$$

We also know that the sum of the fractions must be one: $f_a + f_b = 1$. Knowing the ratio and the sum of the two fractions, we can solve to find their values:

$$f_a = \frac{1}{1 + K_a/[H^+]} \qquad\qquad f_b = \frac{K_a/[H^+]}{1 + k_a/[H^+]}$$

Students familiar with the use of computer spreadsheets can use these two formulae to reproduce the graphs of f_a and f_b as functions of pH for a given value of pK_a.

It is useful to consider several special cases. At low pH where $[H^+] \gg K_a$, then $f_a \approx 1$ and $f_b \approx 0$; in other words the fraction ionized is small. If $[H^+] = K_a$, then pH = pK_a, and the fractions are equal: $f_a = f_b = 0.50$. Hence the two graphs always cross at the pH value equal to the pK_a value for the particular value. At higher pH where $[H^+] \ll K_a$, then $f_a \approx 0$ and $f_b \approx 1$, and the fraction ionized approaches unity.

The equations above show that the fractions f_a and f_b are functions only of the single number $Ka/[H^+]$. The functions are the same for all monoprotic acids, and all that changes from one acid to another is the value of the ionization constant K_a. The logarithm of $Ka/[H^+]$ is equal to pH–pK_a and so f_a and f_b can be expressed as functions of pH–pK_a. This means that the graphs of these fractions are the same shape for all acids, and are merely shifted along the pH axis for different acids with different pKa values.

A **distribution diagram** contains two graphs showing the two fractions f_a and f_b as function of the pH. Figure 14-3 shows the distribution diagram for the acetic acid/acetate system, for which pK_a is 4.76. At low pH, the concentration of hydrogen ions is high, and the acetic acid is hardly dissociated at all. The fraction in the acidic form CH_3COOH is close to unity, and the fraction in the basic form (the acetate ion CH_3COO^-) is very small. At high pH, the concentration of hydrogen ions is very low, so the basic form CH_3COO^- predominates and the acetic acid is almost completely dissociated, and. The two curves cross at the value 0.5 where the pH is equal to the pKa value, 4.76; at that pH, $[H^+] = K_a$, and $[CH_3COOH] = [CH_3COO^-]$. The curves are symmetrical in shape about the crossing point.

If a different acid/base system, with a different pK_a value, is considered, the distribution diagram is changed, but in a very simple way. The graphs of f_a and f_b are shifted along the pH axis without any change in shape. The pH at which the two graphs cross is equal to the pK_a value of the acid under consideration. For example, Figure 14-5 shows the distribution diagram for the ammonia/ammonium ion equilibrium. The two curves cross at the pK_a of the acid (the ammonium ion in this case), which is 9.25, but are identical in shape to the corresponding curves for acetic acid in Figure 14-3.

14-9 Using Distribution Diagrams

In the previous sections we have analyzed acid/base equilibria by algebraic analysis of the expression for the equilibrium constant. In this section the results of those calculations are interpreted in terms of distribution diagrams.

(a) Solution of a Weak Acid in Water

Consider first a solution containing only a weak acid. If the total concentration of the acid, C_a, is not too low, then $[H^+] = \sqrt{K_a C_a}$, or in logarithmic form, pH $\approx \frac{1}{2}$(pK_a + pC_a). This formula has a simple interpretation on the distribution diagram. If we mark the number p$C_a = -\log C_a$ on the horizontal axis in Figure 14-3, then the pH of the solution is halfway between this mark and the crossing of the two curves. This is shown in the following example and the accompanying Figure 14-4.

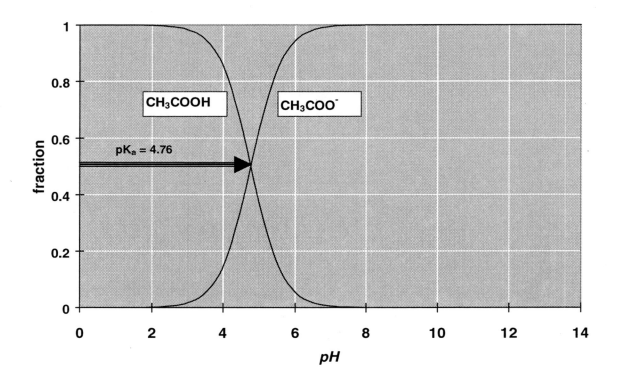

Figure 14-3 Distribution diagram for the acetic acid / acetate system, for which $pK_a = 4.76$. The curve labelled CH_3COOH is a graph of f_a, and the curve labelled CH_3COO^- is a graph of f_b. The horizontal axis is the pH of the solution, taken as an independent variable.

Example 14-15 Consider the 0.050 M solution of acetic acid discussed in Examples 14-2 and 14-3. Identify the points representing pK_a, pC_a and the pH of the solution on the distribution diagram, Figure 14-3.

For acetic acid $pK_a = 4.76$, and for the solution specified $pC_a = 1.30$. The pH of the solution is half way between these at pH = 3.03. These points are indicated on the horizontal axis in Figure 14-4. It should be noted that at the pH of the solution, the fraction of acetic acid ionized is less than 5 %. It follows that the approximation pH $\approx \frac{1}{2}(pK_a + pC_a)$ is justified.

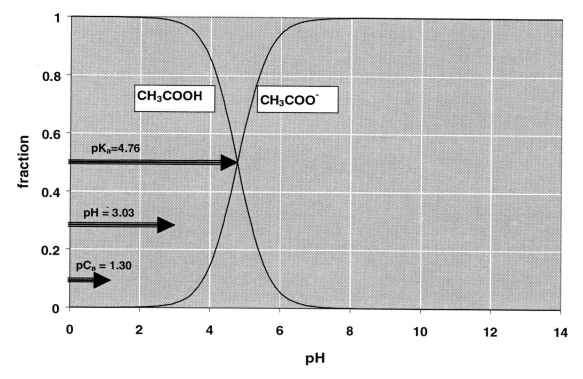

Figure 14-4 The relationship between pC_a, pK_a and the pH for a solution of 0.050 M acetic acid. The bottom arrow indicates pC_a, corresponding to the total concentration of acid; the top arrow indicates pK_a, corresponding to the dissociation constant of the acid; the middle arrow indicates the actual pH of the solution. The length of the middle arrow is the average of the lengths of the other two, in accordance with equation (14-13a). Notice that at pH =3.03, only a small fraction of the acetic acid is ionized.

The distribution diagram helps to understand why the fraction ionized increases when a solution of an acid is diluted. In a series of solutions of decreasing concentration, pC_a increases, and the approximate formula pH $\approx$ ½$(pK_a + pC_a)$ shows that pH of the solutions increases. The rising curve for f_b is a reminder that the fraction ionized increases as the crossing point is approached. If the solution is dilute and pC_a is less than two units to the left of the crossing, then the degree of dissociation may be appreciable. Then the full solution to the quadratic equation (the first line in Table 14-2) must be used to calculate the pH, and the simple geometrical construction described above becomes less useful.

For a very dilute solution of an acid in which pC_a lies to the right of the crossing, the acid is almost completely ionized. For such solutions, it should be kept in mind that the pH cannot be greater than 7, because of auto-ionization of the water: adding an acid to pure water cannot increase the pH.

(b) Solution of a Weak Base in Water

Consider next a solution containing only a weak base. We showed in section 14-5 that if the total concentration of the base is not too low, then:

$$pOH \approx \tfrac{1}{2}(pK_b + pC_b).$$

This formula has a simple interpretation on the distribution diagram, very similar to that for acid solutions except that attention is focused on the right hand side of the distribution diagram. The crossing of the curves on the distribution diagram is located pK_b units from the right hand side of the diagram. The pOH of the solution is therefore represented by a point half-way between the crossing and a point pC_b units from the right-hand side of the diagram.

The pH of the solution is calculated by subtracting pOH from 14:

$$pH = 14 - pOH = 14 - \tfrac{1}{2}(pK_b + pC_b) \tag{14-15}$$

In dilute solutions of a base, the degree of dissociation may be appreciable, so that this approximate calculation is inaccurate and the full solution to the quadratic equation must be used. In this case, this simple geometrical construction becomes less useful.

Example 14-16 Consider the solution of ammonia which we considered in Example 14-7. In the distribution diagram shown in Figure 14-5, identify the three points on the pH scale representing respectively (a) the pK_a of the ammonium ion, (b) pC_b , and (c) the pH of the solution.

For ammonia, pK_b = 4.75. For a concentration of 0.3 M, pC_b = 0.5. The solution is sufficiently concentrated that the approximate calculation is valid, hence the pOH is the average of these values, pOH = (4.75+0.5)/2 = 2.6.

The corresponding pH lies 2.6 units from the right-hand end of the scale, at pH = 14.0 − 2.6 = 11.4. These points are plotted on the diagram in Figure 14-5.

(c) Buffer Solutions

A buffer solution contains comparable amounts of both acid and conjugate base. Hence the fractions f_a and f_b of the total concentration [HB] + [B$^-$] must be comparable in magnitude. It is clear from the distribution diagram that, for this to be true, the pH of the solution must lie close to the crossing at pH = pK_a. If the pH is more than one pH unit away from the crossing, then the solution will not be very effective in maintaining a constant pH. A buffer solution is most effective when it contains substantial and equal concentrations of the acid and conjugate base, so that pH = pK_a and the two curves have their largest slopes.

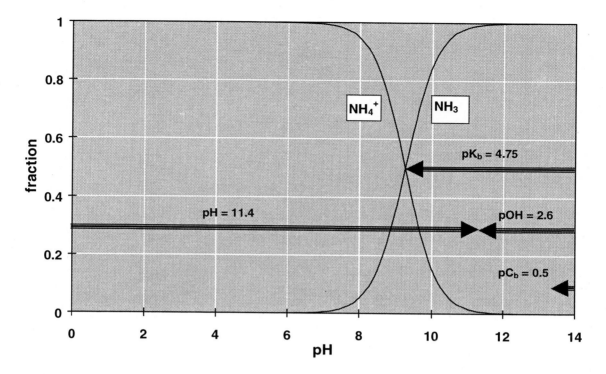

Figure 14-5 Distribution diagram for the ammonium ion/ammonia system. The curve labelled NH_4^+ is a graph of f_a , and the curve labelled NH_3 is a graph of f_b , as functions of pH. The arrows refer to the solution of ammonia discussed in Example 14-16. The bottom arrow indicates pC_b, corresponding to the total concentration of ammonia; the top arrow indicates pK_b, corresponding to the dissociation constant of ammonia. The middle arrow on the right indicates the actual pOH of the solution. The length of the middle arrow is the average of the lengths of the other two, in accordance with equation (14-13b). The arrow on the left indicates the pH of the solution, according to equation (14-15). Notice that at pH =11.4, only a small fraction of the ammonia is ionized.

14-10 Polyprotic acids

The acids discussed so far are monoprotic acids with only one acidic hydrogen atom per molecule. Some acids have more than one acidic hydrogen atom and ionize in several stages with distinct equilibria; these acids are called **polyprotic acids**. Acids containing two acidic hydrogen atoms are called **diprotic acids** and some examples are sulphuric acid, H_2SO_4, carbonic acid, H_2CO_3, and oxalic acid, $(COOH)_2$. An example of a **triprotic acid** containing three acidic hydrogen atoms is phosphoric acid, H_3PO_4. Table 14-5 lists some polyprotic acids and their dissociation constants.

A diprotic acid can be represented by the general formula H_2B, where B represents the rest of the molecule apart from the acidic hydrogen atoms; loss of one proton leads to the ion HB^- and loss of two protons leads to B^{2-}.

For a diprotic acid there are two dissociation equilibria with their associated equilibrium constants:

$$H_2B(aq) \rightleftharpoons H^+(aq) + HB^-(aq) \qquad K_{a1} = \frac{[H^+][HB^-]}{[H_2B]} \qquad (14\text{-}16a)$$

and

$$HB^-(aq) \rightleftharpoons H^+(aq) + B^{2-}(aq) \qquad K_{a2} = \frac{[H^+][B^{2-}]}{[HB^-]} \qquad (14\text{-}16b)$$

The anion HB^- which is common to these two equilibria is called **amphiprotic**, for it can react both as an acid, as shown in the second of the above equilibria, and as a base:

$$HB^-(aq) + H_2O \rightleftharpoons H_2B(aq) + OH^-(aq) \qquad K_{b1} = \frac{[H_2B][OH^-]}{[HB^-]}$$

It follows that the product of K_{a1} for the acid H_2B and K_{b1} for the conjugate base HB^- is equal to K_w, just as for monoprotic acids:

$$K_{a1}K_{b1} = K_w$$

The anion B^{2-} is also a base which is conjugate to the acid HB^-:

$$B^{2-}(aq) + H_2O \rightleftharpoons HB^-(aq) + OH^-(aq) \qquad K_{b2} = \frac{[HB^-][OH^-]}{[B^{2-}]}$$

so that

$$K_{a2}K_{b2} = K_w$$

Table 14-5 lists the dissociation constants for a number of polyprotic acids. The names of the acids and of their fully dissociated anions are given. The amphiprotic ions are named by adding the word "hydrogen", as in potassium hydrogen phthalate, with the formula $1,2\text{-}C_6H_4(COOH)COOK$. For inorganic acids, the prefix "bi-" is also used, as in the bisulfite ion, HSO_3^- and the bicarbonate ion HCO_3^-.

For most diprotic acids, the second dissociation constant is much smaller than the first, and so the amphiprotic anion HB^- is a weaker acid than H_2B. Correspondingly, the base B^{2-} is a stronger base than HB^-. As an example, for oxalic acid, $(COOH)_2$, the acid dissociation constants are $pK_{a1} = 1.23$ and $pK_{a2} = 4.19$; the second dissociation constant is smaller than the first by a factor of about 1000. The difference is even greater for sulfurous acid H_2SO_3, for which $pK_{a1} = 1.8$ and $pK_{a2} = 7.2$.

Table 14-5 Dissociation Constants for Di- and Triprotic Acids and Bases

Acid		K_a	pK_a	Base		K_b	pK_b
H_2SO_4	sulfuric	$\gg 1$	<0	HSO_4^-	bisulfate	$\ll 10^{-14}$	>14
HSO_4^-	bisulfate	1.0×10^{-2}	1.98	SO_4^{2-}	sulfate	1.0×10^{-12}	12.02
$HOOC–COOH$	oxalic	5.9×10^{-2}	1.23	$HOOC–COO^-$		1.7×10^{-13}	12.77
$HOOC–COO^-$		6.5×10^{-5}	4.19	$^-OOC–COO^-$	oxalate	1.5×10^{-10}	9.81
H_2SO_3	sulfurous	1.4×10^{-2}	1.85	HSO_3^-	bisulfite	7.1×10^{-13}	12.15
HSO_3^-	bisulfite	$6. \times 10^{-8}$	7.2	SO_3^{2-}	sulfite	1.6×10^{-7}	6.8
H_3PO_4	phosphoric	6.9×10^{-3}	2.16	$H_2PO_4^-$		1.4×10^{-12}	11.84
$H_2PO_4^-$		6.2×10^{-8}	7.21	HPO_4^{2-}		1.6×10^{-7}	6.79
HPO_4^{2-}		4.8×10^{-13}	12.32	PO_4^{3-}	phosphate	2.1×10^{-2}	1.68
$HOOCCH_2NH_3^+$		4.5×10^{-3}	2.35	$^-OOCCH_2NH_3^+$	glycine	2.2×10^{-12}	11.65
$^-OOCCH_2NH_3^+$	glycine	1.7×10^{-7}	9.78	$^-OOCCH_2NH_2$		6.0×10^{-5}	4.22
$1,2–C_6H_4(COOH)_2$	phthalic	1.3×10^{-3}	2.89	$1,2–C_6H_4COOHCOO^-$		7.8×10^{-12}	11.11
$1,2–C_6H_4COOHCOO^-$		3.1×10^{-6}	5.51	$1,2–C_6H_4(COO)_2^{2-}$	phthalate	3.2×10^{-9}	8.49
H_2CO_3	carbonic	4.5×10^{-7}	6.35	HCO_3^-	bicarbonate	2.2×10^{-8}	7.65
HCO_3^-	bicarbonate	4.7×10^{-11}	10.33	CO_3^{2-}	carbonate	2.1×10^{-4}	3.67
H_2S	hydrogen sulfide	8.9×10^{-8}	7.05	HS^-	bisulfide	1.1×10^{-7}	6.95
HS^-	bisulfide	10^{-19}	19 ± 2	S^{2-}	sulfide	$1 \times 10^{+5}$	-5 ± 2

Reprinted with permission from CRC Handbook of Chemistry and Physics, 77th edition. Copyright CRC Press, Boca Raton, Florida.

The state of dissociation of a diprotic acid can be represented on a distribution diagram. The diagram consists of three curves which represent respectively the fraction of the total concentration of the acid and its ionized forms present in solution as H_2B, HB^- and B^{2-}, as functions of the pH of the solution. If C is the sum of the concentrations of each of these forms, then

$$C = [H_2B] + [HB^-] + [B^{2-}]$$

The fractions of the total amount of "B" in the three forms H_2B, HB^- and B^{2-} will be denoted by f_1, f_2 and f_3 respectively. They can be calculated in a manner similar to that that used for monoprotic acids, and the results are as follows:

$$f_1 = \frac{1}{1 + K_{a1}/[H^+] + K_{a1}K_{a2}/[H^+]^2} \qquad f_2 = \frac{K_{a1}/[H^+]}{1 + K_{a1}/[H^+] + K_{a1}K_{a2}/[H^+]^2} \qquad f_3 = \frac{K_{a1}K_{a2}/[H^+]^2}{1 + K_{a1}/[H^+] + K_{a1}K_{a2}/[H^+]^2}$$

The fractions f_1, f_2 and f_3 can be calculated as functions of pH if the two equilibrium constants are known. Unlike the monoprotic acids, the shape of the curves depend on the relationship between the values of the two ionization constants, as we see in the following two examples.

The distribution diagram for sulfurous acid H_2SO_3, with pK_a values of 1.85 and 7.2, is shown in Figure 14-6. For this acid, the crossings, and the buffer regions associated with each crossing, are well separated. The curve representing the ion HB^- rises almost to unity between the two crossings, and the two dissociation equilibria can be considered independently. This is the case when the two pK_a values differ by at least 3 units or more.

For instance, in considering the properties of a solution of sulfurous acid, or of a sulfurous acid/bisulfite buffer, the second dissociation can be ignored. The distribution diagram shows that when the pH is less than 4.5, the concentration of sulphite ion, SO_3^{2-}, is very small and can be neglected in comparison with the concentrations of H_2SO_3 and HSO_3^-. This means that the pH of a solution of H_2SO_3 can be calculated by the techniques described in Section 14-4.

Similarly, the pH of a solution of sodium sulphite can be calculated by ignoring the concentration of H_2SO_3 and using the techniques described in Section 14-5.

There are two buffer systems, the H_2SO_3/HSO_3^- system and the HSO_3^-/SO_3^{2-} system, and both can be dealt with by the methods of Section 14-6.

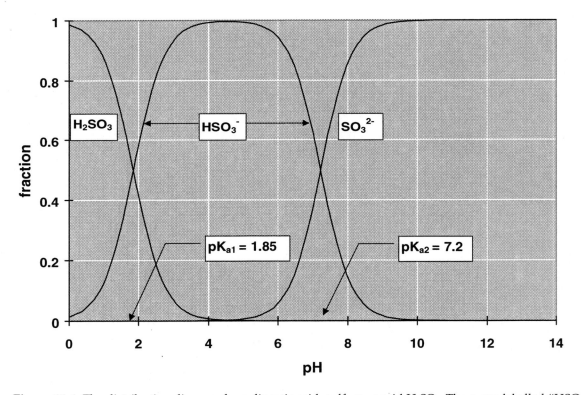

Figure 14-6 The distribution diagram for a diprotic acid, sulfurous acid H_2SO_3. The curve labelled "HSO_3^-" represents the fraction f_2 in the form of the bisulfite ion HSO_3^-.

Example 14-17 Calculate the pH and the concentrations of SO_3^{2-}, HSO_3^-, and H_2SO_3 in a solution of sodium sulphite, Na_2SO_3, of concentration 0.20 mol/L.

The sulfite ion is a base and reacts with water to give a basic solution. The basic properties of the sulfite ion control the pH of the solution. For the sulphite ion, $pK_b = 6.80$, and for this solution $pC_b = -\log 0.20 = 0.70$. Hence by the approximate calculation,

$$pOH = (6.80 + 0.70)/2 = 3.75$$

and so
$$pH = 14 - 3.75 = 10.25 \quad \text{and} \quad [OH^-] = 10^{-3.75} = 1.8 \times 10^{-4}$$

From the dissociation equilibrium, $SO_3^{2-} + H_2O \rightleftharpoons HSO_3^- + OH^-$, it follows that
$$[HSO_3^-] = [OH^-] = 1.8 \times 10^{-4} \text{ M}.$$

Hence by subtraction,
$$[SO_3^{2-}] = 0.20 - 1.9 \times 10^{-4} \approx 0.20 \text{ M}.$$

The distribution diagram in Figure 14-6 shows that at pH higher than the sulphite/bisulphite crossing, the concentration of sulphurous acid present is extremely small. Knowing the value of $[H^+]$ from the first part of the calculation, the concentration of H_2SO_3 can be calculated from the first equilibrium constant K_{a1}:

$$K_{a1} = \frac{[H^+][HSO_3^-]}{[H_2SO_3]}$$

Rearranging this equation,
$$[H_2SO_3] = \frac{[H^+][HSO_3^-]}{K_{a1}} = \frac{K_w[HSO_3^-]}{[OH^-]K_{a1}}$$

Since $[HSO_3^-] = [OH^-]$, this becomes:

$$[H_2SO_3] = \frac{K_w}{K_{a1}} = K_{b1} = 6 \times 10^{-13}$$

We see that this concentration is indeed negligible compared with the other concentrations, as was assumed above.

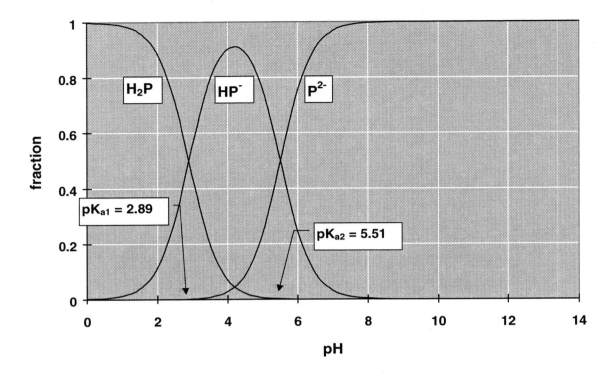

Figure 14-7 Distribution diagram for phthalic acid, which is diprotic; in labelling the graphs, the symbol H_2P is used as an abbreviation for the phthalic acid molecule. The two ionization constants are pK_{a1} = 2.89 and pK_{a2} = 5.51. These values are sufficiently close together that the faction of HP⁻ ion does not rise above about 0.9, and the two buffer regions overlap.

The distribution diagram for phthalic acid, or 1,2-benzenedicarboxylic acid, is shown in Figure 14-7. For this acid the two pK_a values are 2.89 and 5.51, which differ by 2.6. The diagram shows that in the pH range between the two crossings, all three species are present in appreciable amounts, and the buffer regions associated with the two dissociation equilibria overlap to some extent. If the two pK_a values are much closer than this, then the two equilibria cannot be considered independently. We will not concern ourselves further with that more complex situation.

There is one new calculation that is needed in considering diprotic systems, namely solutions of amphiprotic salts. An example is a solution of sodium bisulphite, $NaHSO_3$. The salt dissolves to yield sodium ions and bisulphite ions, HSO_3^-, and the pH is determined by the proton transfer equilibria of this latter ion. The following analysis is approximate and makes use of the distribution diagram for a diprotic acid. The result is simple, and is accurate enough for most purposes as long as the solution of the salt is not too dilute.

Consider a general amphiprotic salt of the diprotic acid H_2B. When dissolved in water, the salt ionizes to produce the ion $HB^-(aq)$. This amphiprotic ion takes part in two proton transfer equilibria:

$$HB^-(aq) \rightleftharpoons H^+(aq) + B^{2-}(aq)$$

$$HB^-(aq) + H_2O \rightleftharpoons H_2B(aq) + OH^-(aq)$$

One of these reactions produces hydrogen ions and the other produces hydroxide ions. The hydrogen ions combine with the hydroxide ions to form water:

$$H^+(aq) + OH^-(aq) \rightleftharpoons H_2O$$

The net reaction is obtained by adding together the above three reactions:

$$2HB^- \rightleftharpoons H_2B + B^{2-}$$

The net reaction is the transfer of a hydrogen ion from one HB^- ion to another, and this is the main equilibrium which controls the pH of the solution. The products of the reaction H_2B and B^{2-} are produced in equal amounts, and so their concentrations must be equal. This means that the fraction of the acid in the form H_2B, f_1, is equal to the fraction in the form B^{2-}, f_3. Since $f_1 = f_3$, the pH of the solution must be that pH for which the f_1 curve crosses the f_3 curve. Examination of the distribution diagrams shown in Figures 14-6 and 14-7 shows that the two graphs are symmetrical about this point. Hence the crossing of f_1 and f_3 lies half-way between the crossing of f_1 and f_2 and the crossing of f_2 and f_3. It follows that the pH of the solution is the average of pK_{a1} and pK_{a2}:

$$pH = \tfrac{1}{2}(pK_{a1} + pK_{a2}) \tag{14-17}$$

This formula can also be derived from algebraic analysis of the chemical equilibria. The pH of a solution of an amphiprotic salt is therefore independent of the concentration of the salt, and depends only on the two acid dissociation constants. Detailed algebraic analysis shows that this result is accurate as long as the solution is not too dilute.

Example 14-18 Calculate the pH of a 0.10 M solution of sodium bisulphite.

Since $pK_{a1} = 1.85$ and $pK_{a2} = 7.2$,   pH = (1.85 + 7.2)/2 = 4.5

A similar situation is met when considering a solution of a salt of a weak acid and a weak base. For example, consider a solution of ammonium acetate. The salt dissociates fully into ions:

$$CH_3COONH_4(aq) \rightarrow CH_3COO^-(aq) + NH_4^+(aq)$$

The main reactions of the ions are as follows:

$$CH_3COO^-(aq) + H_2O(\ell) \rightleftharpoons CH_3COOH(aq) + OH^-(aq)$$

$$NH_4^+(aq) \rightleftharpoons NH_3(aq) + H^+(aq)$$

$$H^+(aq) + OH^-(aq) \rightleftharpoons H_2O(\ell)$$

Adding these together gives the overall reaction:

$$CH_3COO^-(aq) + NH_4^+(aq) \rightleftharpoons CH_3COOH(aq) + NH_3(aq)$$

These reactions should be compared with those for an amphiprotic salt. Since the concentrations of acetic acid and ammonia are equal (within our approximations), the pH of the solution must be the average of the pK_a values for acetic acid and ammonium ion. It is left as an exercise for the student to sketch the distribution diagram showing both the acetic acid and ammonia equilibria, and to show that the pH of a solution of ammonium acetate is 7.0.

14-11 Amino acids

Some organic substances are at the same time acids and bases, and so are amphiprotic. For instance, an **amino acid** contains both an acidic carboxyl group –COOH and a basic amino group –NH$_2$. The simplest example is glycine, H$_2$NCH$_2$COOH, which has the following molecular structure:

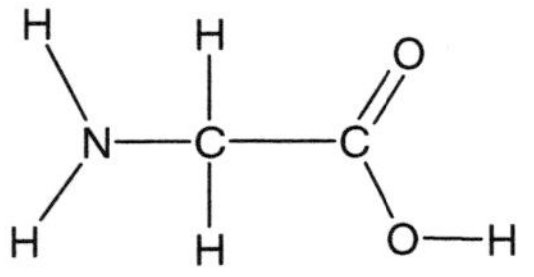

In other amino acids, one of the hydrogen atoms on the central carbon atom is replaced by another group of atoms. If this group of atoms is designated by the symbol R, the formula can be written H$_2$NCHRCOOH.

The acidic carboxyl group of glycine, –COOH, tends to transfer a proton to the basic amino group, –NH$_2$, as shown in the following equation:

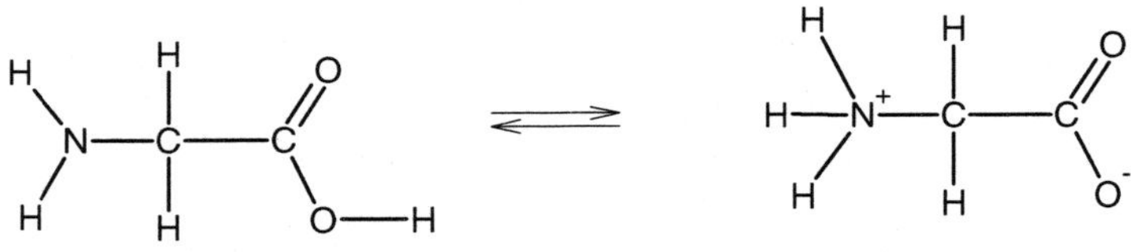

The equilibrium lies far to the right, and in aqueous solution the glycine molecule itself is present only in small concentrations. The molecule on the right, $^+$H$_3$NCH$_2$COO$^-$, is electrically neutral overall, but one end of the molecule is positively and the other end is negatively charged. This molecule is called a **dipolar ion** or **zwitterion** (from the German word *zwitter* meaning a hybrid).

The zwitterion is amphiprotic, since the –COO$^-$ group is basic, and the –NH$_3^+$ group is acidic. The proton transfer equilibria for glycine can therefore be represented by the following equations:

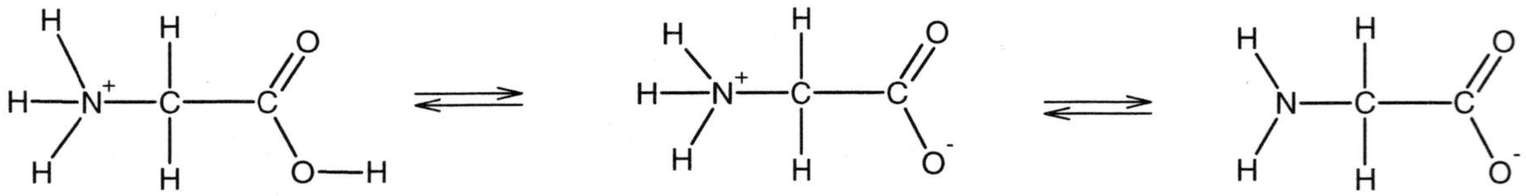

There are two proton transfer equilibria, which are very similar to those of a diprotic acid. In writing these equations, the hydrogen ions have been omitted, for clarity. The pK_a values for the two equilibria are 2.35 and 9.78 respectively, and a distribution diagram can be drawn as for a diprotic acid with these two dissociation constant values. The distribution diagram is similar to that for sulfurous acid, shown in Figure 14-6.

The relative amounts of the three predominant forms of glycine depend upon pH, naturally. When the pH lies halfway between the two crossings, pH = ½(pK_{a1} + pK_{a2}), the fraction in the form of the zwitterion, f_2, is a maximum, and the concentrations of the other two ions are equal.

This pH is called the **isoelectric point**; at this pH the concentrations of the anion and cation are equal and the concentration of the dipolar ion is a maximum. The pH at the isoelectric point for glycine is 6.1.

14-12 Titrations

Titrations are used to determine the relationship between the concentrations of acids and bases in solution. A solution of one reactant (the base, for instance) is added from a buret to a known amount of the other reactant (the acid). The point in the titration where the amount of base added equals the initial amount of acid is called the **equivalence point** of the titration. When the equivalence point has been determined, the concentration of one solution can be calculated from the concentration of the other solution.

An accurate titration depends upon being able to determine the equivalence point accurately. In planning and carrying out a titration, it is essential to understand how the *p*H changes as the titration proceeds. In addition, the pK_a of a weak acid can be determined by following a titration with a pH meter.

The calculations involved are examples of the application of what has been learned earlier in this chapter. The analysis of a titration problem involves no new theory, since every formula given in this section has been met before. No new formulae need be memorized.

(i) Titration of a strong acid with a strong base

We consider first the titration of a strong acid, HCl, with a strong base, NaOH. Suppose, for instance, a volume V_a of HCl of concentration C_a is taken in an Erlenmeyer flask, and NaOH of concentration C_b is added from a buret.

Initially, before any base has been added, $[H^+] = C_a$. As base is added, the amount of hydrogen ion present is reduced by the amount of base added. After a volume V_b of base has been added, but before the equivalence point, the amount of H^+ remaining unreacted is $C_aV_a - C_bV_b$. The concentration $[H^+]$ is this amount divided by the total volume of the solution in the Erlenmeyer flask, which is $V_a + V_b$:

$$[H^+] = \frac{C_aV_a - C_bV_b}{V_a + V_b} \quad \text{before the equivalence point.}$$

At the equivalence point, the acid is completely reacted with base, and the amounts of acid and of base taking part are equal, $C_aV_b = C_bV_b$. Since there is neither an excess of H^+ ions nor an excess of OH^- ions,

$$[H^+] = 10^{-7} \text{ M and pH} = 7.0 \quad \text{at the equivalence point.}$$

Table 14-6 Titration of HCl with NaOH

$H^+ + OH^- \rightarrow H_2O$ $C_a = 0.20$ M $C_b = 0.20$ M

$V_a = 25.00$ mL   Volume is in mL, amount is in mmol, concentration is in mol/L

V_b	$V_a + V_b$	$C_aV_a - C_bV_b$	$[H^+]$	pH	
0	25	5.00	0.200	0.70	start
5	30	4.00	0.133	0.88	
10	35	3.00	0.0857	1.07	
15	40	2.00	0.0500	1.30	
20	45	1.00	0.0222	1.65	
25	50	0.00	"0.0"	7	equivalence
		$C_bV_b - C_aV_a$	$[OH^-]$	pH	
30	55	1.00	0.0182	12.26	
35	60	2.00	0.0333	12.52	

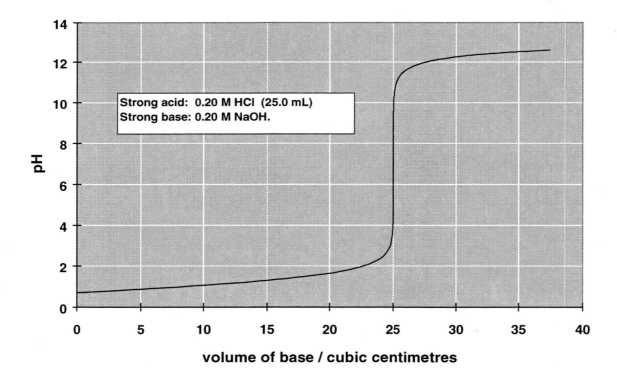

Figure 14-8 Graph of pH *versus* volume of base added for a titration of 25.00 mL of 0.200 M hydrochloric acid HCl with 0.200 M sodium hydroxide NaOH. See Table 14-6.

When excess base is added beyond the equivalence point, there is an excess of hydroxide ions. The total amount of OH⁻ added is $C_b V_b$, and of this amount, $C_a V_a$ moles was needed to reach the equivalence point. The amount of OH⁻ present is equal to the amount of base added *after* the equivalence point, which is $C_b V_b - C_a V_a$. The concentration [OH⁻] is this amount of hydroxide ion, divided by the total volume:

$$[OH^-] = \frac{C_b V_b - C_a V_a}{V_a + V_b} \quad \text{after the equivalence point.}$$

These calculations are summarized in Table 14-6 for a titration of 25.00 mL of 0.200 M HCl with 0.200 M NaOH. Figure 14-8 shows a graph of pH as a function of the volume of base added in this titration. The pH remains low until the equivalence point is almost reached. As the equivalence point is reached and then passed, the pH changes sharply from a low value through 7 to a value near the *pH* of the NaOH solution. The sharp change of pH makes it easy to determine the equivalence point accurately.

(ii) Titration of a weak acid with a strong base

The stages in a titration of a weak acid with a strong base are rather different from those of a titration of a strong acid. Consider a titration in which a volume V_a of acetic acid of concentration C_a, is taken in an Erlenmeyer flask, and sodium hydroxide of concentration C_b, is added from a buret.

Initially, the Erlenmeyer flask contains only a solution of acetic acid and by Equation (14-13a) the pH is:

$$pH = \tfrac{1}{2}(pC_a + pK_a) \quad \text{initially}$$

Addition of the solution of NaOH converts some of the acetic acid to acetate ion, because of the reaction:

$$CH_3COOH(aq) + OH^-(aq) \rightarrow CH_3COO^-(aq) + H_2O(\ell)$$

After the addition of a volume V_b of base (but before the equivalence point), the amount of acetic acid in solution is reduced to $C_a V_a - C_b V_b$ and the amount of acetate ion is increased from a very low value to $C_b V_b$. Because the solution now contains significant amounts of both acetic acid and acetate ion, it is a buffer solution. At this stage of the titration, the pH is given by the Henderson-Hasselbalch equation (14-14):

$$pH = pK_a - \log\left\{\frac{C_a V_a - C_b V_b}{C_b V_b}\right\} \quad \text{before the equivalence point}$$

Half way through the titration, $C_b V_b = \tfrac{1}{2} C_a V_a$ and the amount of acid present is equal to the amount of conjugate base. This corresponds to the crossing of the two curves in the distribution diagram for the acid. It follows, either from the digram or from the last equation, that at this point the pH of the solution is equal to the pK_a of the acid:

$$pH = pK_a \quad \text{half-way to the equivalence point}$$

At the equivalence point, amount of base added equals the amount of acid present initially, and the solution in the Erlenmeyer flask can be regarded as a solution of the salt of the acid and base, namely sodium acetate. Such a solution was considered in Example 14-8. The concentration of acetate ion present at the equivalence point is equal to the amount of acid present initially ($C_a V_a$), divided by the total volume of the solution ($V_a + V_b$). The pH is calculated from the concentration of the acetate ion, using Equation (14-13b):

$$pH = 14 - pOH = 14 - \frac{1}{2}\left\{ pK_b - \log\left(\frac{C_a V_a}{V_a + V_b}\right) \right\} \quad \text{at the equivalence point.}$$

Table 14-7 Titration of CH$_3$COOH with NaOH

$$CH_3COOH + OH^- \rightarrow CH_3COO^- + H_2O \quad pK_a = 4.7$$

$V_a = 25.00$ mL $C_a = 0.20$ M $C_b = 0.20$ M

Volume is in mL, amount is in mmol, concentration is in mol/L. The third and fourth columns give the actual amounts of acetic acid and acetate present.

V_b	$V_a + V_b$	$n(CH_3COOH)$	$n(CH_3COO^-)$	$[H^+]$	pH	
0	25	5.00	"0"	1.8×10^{-3}	2.73	start
5	30	4.00	1.00	1.8×10^{-4}	4.17	
10	35	3.00	2.00	7.9×10^{-5}	4.59	
15	40	2.00	3.00	4.7×10^{-5}	4.95	
20	45	1.00	4.00	3.0×10^{-5}	5.37	
25	50	"0.0"	5.00	2.0×10^{-5}	9.88	equivalence
			$C_b V_b - C_a V_a$	$[OH^-]$	pH	
30	21	0.0	1.00	1.8×10^{-2}	12.38	
35	22	0.0	2.00	43.3×10^{-2}	12.66	

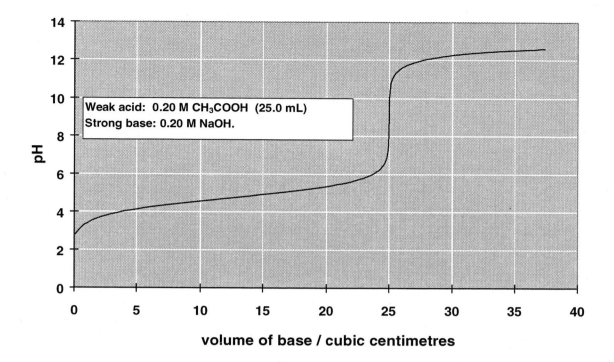

Figure 14-9 Graph of pH *versus* volume of base added for a titration of 25.00 mL of 0.2 M acetic acid with 0.2 M sodium hydroxide. See Table 14-7. The left hand end of the curve gives the pH of the acid, the gently sloping middle section is the buffer region, and the sudden rise in pH marks the equivalence point.

Beyond the equivalence point, the acetic acid has been converted entirely to acetate, and the pH is determined by the amount of excess hydroxide ion, just as for the titration of a strong acid:

$$[OH^-] = \frac{C_b V_b - C_a V_a}{V_a + V_b} \quad \text{after the equivalence point.}$$

The results of the pH calculations for a titration of 25.00 mL of 0.20 M acetic acid with 0.20 M NaOH are summarized in Table 14-7 and plotted in Figure 14-9.

After an initial small rise in pH, the solution enters the buffer region in which the pH is close to pK_a for acetic acid. As the equivalence point is approached, the pH rises sharply towards the pH of a solution of the sodium acetate. Beyond the equivalence point, the pH continues to increase as the amount of excess hydroxide ion increases; the curve at this stage is the same as the curve for the titration of a strong acid.

An **indicator** is a weak acid for which the solution of the acid has a different colour from that of a solution of the conjugate base. At least one form of an indicator must be strongly coloured so that only a very small amount of indicator is needed to detect the equivalence point. The molecular structure of the indicator known as methyl orange is shown below in its protonated (acidic) and unprotonated (basic) forms. The acidic form of the indicator gives the solution a red colour, while the basic form is yellow. The colour change is related to the rearrangement of the double bonds.

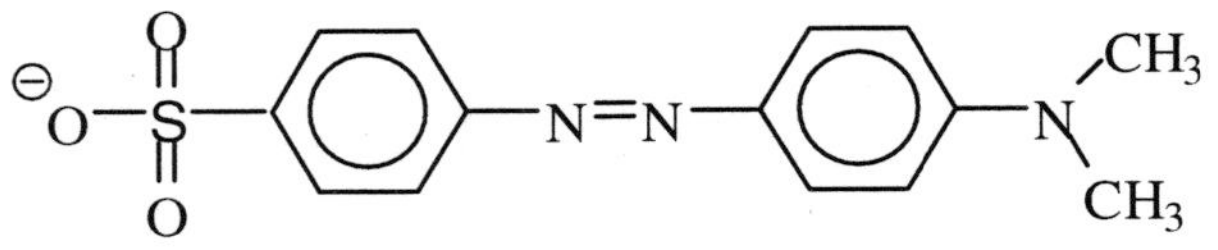

basic   yellow

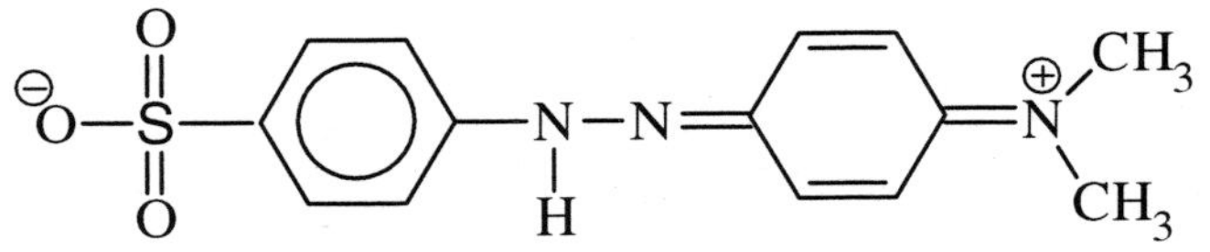

acidic   red

The protonated form of an indicator can be designated by the symbol HIn, and the conjugate base by In⁻. The equilibrium constant for proton transfer between the indicator and water can be represented by the following equations:

$$HIn(aq) \rightleftharpoons H^+(aq) + In^-(aq) \qquad K_{in} = \frac{[H^+][In^-]}{[HIn]} \qquad (14\text{-}18)$$

There is a distribution diagram for each indicator, just like the distribution diagram for any acid/base system. If the pH is lower than pK_{in}, the acidic form of the indicator predominates, while if the pH is greater than pK_{in}, the basic form predominates. Hence the colour of a solution containing a small concentration of indicator changes over about two pH units centred at pH = pK_{in}. As the equivalence point of a titration is passed, the addition of just a few drops of base cause the pH to change by several units (see Figure 14-9). If the indicator has a pK_{in} value close to the pH at the equivalence point of the titration it will change colour sharply at the equivalence point.

For a titration of a weak acid with strong base, an indicator with pK_{in} in the range 9 to 11 is likely to be suitable. Figure 14-10 shows the distribution diagram for phenolphthalein, an indicator commonly used for titrations of weak acids. On the other hand, for a titration of a weak base with a strong acid, an indicator with pK_{in} in the range 3 to 5 would be used. For a titration of a strong acid with a strong base, the change in pH as the equivalence point is passed is so large that any indicator with a pK_{in} in the range 4 to 10 will be satisfactory.

Table 14-8   **Indicators for Acid/Base Titrations**

Indicator	Acidic colour	Basic colour	pH range	pK_{in}
thymol blue	red	Yellow	1.2 – 2.8	2.0
methyl orange	red	yellow	3.2 – 4.4	3.8
Bromcresol green	yellow	blue	3.9 – 5.5	4.7
methyl red	red	yellow	4.7 – 6.0	5.3
Litmus	red	blue	5.0 – 8.0	6.5
Bromthymol blue	yellow	blue	6.1 – 7.6	6.9
thymol blue	yellow	blue	8.0 – 9.6	8.8
Phenolphthalein	colourless	red	8.3 – 10.0	9.1
alazarin yellow	yellow	red	10.1 – 12.0	11.1

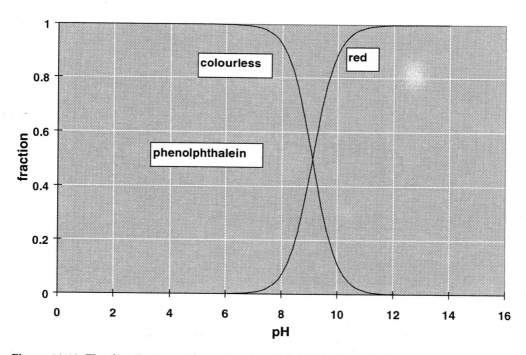

Figure 14-10 The distribution diagram for phenolphthalein, for which pK_{in} = 9.1. The acidic form of the indicator is colourless, and the basic form is red.

When a diprotic acid is titrated with a base, there are two distinct stages to the titration and two well-defined equivalence points, unless the two pK_a values are too close together. The first equivalence point is reached when one mole of base per mole of diprotic acid has been added; at this stage, the solution is in effect a solution of the amphiprotic salt, and the pH = (pK_{a1} + pK_{a2})/2. Before this stage is reached, the solution passes through the buffer region centred at pH = pK_{a1}. If more base is added after the first equivalence point is reached, then the solution passes through the buffer region centred at pH = pK_{a2}. The second equivalence point is reached when two moles of base per mole of diprotic acid have been added. The two equivalence points can be detected separately by using appropriate indicators. The titration curve is shown in Figure 14-11.

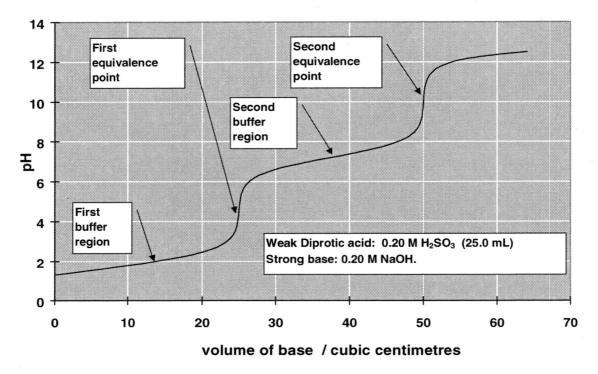

Figure 14-11 Titration curve for 25.00 mL of 0.20 M sulfurous acid with 0.20 M sodium hydroxide. There are two equivalence points for this diprotic acid.

Key concepts

In an acid-base reaction, a hydrogen ion (or proton) is transferred from an acid to a base. In aqueous solution, acids are ionized by transfer of hydrogen ions to the water molecules. A strong acid is completely ionized. A weak acid is partially ionized, and the strength of the acid is measured by the equilibrium constant for this equilibrium. The conjugate base of a weak acid is the base formed by loss of a hydrogen ion from the acid.

In writing the equilibrium constant for a reaction in solution, the relative activities of the solute ions and molecules are assumed to be equal to the numerical value of the relevant molar concentrations expressed in mole/litre.

A strong base is completely ionized in solution. Common strong bases are the alkali metal hydroxides, which release hydroxide ions into solution. Weak bases ionize by transfer of hydrogen ions from the water molecules to the weak base, and the strength of the base is measured by the equilibrium constant for this equilibrium. The conjugate acid of a weak base is the acid formed by gain of a hydrogen ion.

Water itself ionizes by transfer of a hydrogen ion from one water molecule to another.

The concentrations of the ions and molecules in a solution of a weak acid or base can be calculated from the dissociation constant and the concentration. The extent of ionization increases as the concentration decreases.

A buffer solution contains substantial and roughly equal concentrations of both an acid and its conjugate base. The hydrogen ion concentration in a buffer solution is approximately equal to the ionization constant of the acid, and is hardly affected by addition of small amounts of a strong acid or a strong base.

The hydrogen ion concentration is often expressed as the pH, which is the negative logarithm (to base 10) of the hydrogen ion concentration. The pH is 7 in neutral solution at room temperature, and varies from near 0 in strongly acidic solution, to near 14 in strongly basic solution.

The position of an acid-base equilibrium can be visualized using a distribution diagram, which shows the degree of ionization of an acid or base as a function of the pH. All distribution diagrams have the same shape, except that the curves are displaced along the pH axis for different acids. The conditions in a solution of a weak acid, or a weak base, or in a buffer solution, can be estimated by eye from the diagram.

Diprotic acids have two acid hydrogen atoms, and two ionization equilibria. The two ionization processes are conveniently represented on a distribution diagram, and can be treated as independent as long as the corresponding equilibrium constants are sufficiently different.

In an acid-base titration, the acid and base are mixed in a controlled way, and an indicator is used to determine the point in the reaction at which equal amounts of acid and base have been added to the reaction mixture.

Review questions

1. What is an acid?
2. What is a base?
3. Write an expression for the auto-ionization constant for water.
4. Write an expression for the ionization constant for acetic acid.
5. Write an expression for the ionization constant for ammonia.
6. What is the difference between a strong acid and a weak acid?
7. What is a buffer solution?
8. What does the pH of a solution indicate?
9. How does the degree of ionization of a weak base vary with its concentration?
10. What is a polyprotic acid? Name an example.
11. What is an amphoteric salt?
12. Describe a distribution diagram.
13. What is an indicator? At what pH does an indicator change colour?
14. What is a titration?

Chapter 14

Problems

1. Calculate [OH⁻] in a solution in which $[H^+] = 3.5 \times 10^{-4}$, assuming the $K_w = 1.0 \times 10^{-14}$.

    $[2.8 \times 10^{-11} \text{ M}]$

2. The acid dissociation constant for butanoic acid, C_3H_7COOH, is $K_a = 1.5 \times 10^{-5}$ at 25°C. Calculate the base dissociation constant K_b for the butanoate ion $C_3H_7COO^-$. $[6.7 \times 10^{-10}]$

3. The base dissociation constant for propylamine, $C_3H_7NH_2$, is $K_b = 4.0 \times 10^{-4}$ at 25°C. Calculate the acid dissociation constant K_a for the propylammonium ion $C_3H_7NH_3^+$.

    $[2.5 \times 10^{-11}]$

4. Calculate $[H^+]$, $[CH_3COO^-]$, $[CH_3COOH]$ and $[OH^-]$ in a 0.0015 M solution of acetic acid, CH_3COOH. $[1.5 \times 10^{-4} \text{ M}, 1.5 \times 10^{-4} \text{ M}, 0.0014 \text{ M}, 6.7 \times 10^{-11}]$

5. Calculate $[OH^-]$, $[NH_4^+]$, $[NH_3]$, and $[H^+]$ and in a 0.0070 M solution of ammonia.

    $[3.5 \times 10^{-4} \text{ M}, 3.5 \times 10^{-4} \text{ M}, 0.0066 \text{ M}, 2.9 \times 10^{-11} \text{ M}]$

6. In each of the following solutions, which molecule or ion has the largest concentration, apart from H_2O? (a) Solution containing 0.25 M CH_3COOH (b) Solution containing 0.5 M NH_3 (c) Solution containing 0.2 M HCl   (d) Solution containing 0.25 M HCl and 0.3 M CH_3COOH.

7. If some ammonia NH_3 is added to a 0.15 M solution of acetic acid does $[CH_3COOH]$ increase, decrease, or stay the same?

8. What is the pH of a 0.45 M solution of benzoic acid?   [2.3]

9. A 0.10 M solution of a certain acid has a pH = 3.5. What is the pK_a of the acid?   [6.0]

10. Make a sketch of the distribution diagram for methylamine, CH_3NH_2, in aqueous solution and label your diagram appropriately.

11. Calculate the pH of each of the following solutions:

    (a) 0.025 M acetic acid   [3.2]

    (b) 0.080 M nitrous acid   [2.2]

    (c) 0.015 M ammonia   [10.7]

    (d) 0.015 M ammonium chloride   [5.5]

    (e) 0.035 M sodium nitrite   [7.9]

    (f) 0.0012 M nitrous acid   [3.2]

12. Sketch a distribution diagram for nitrous acid HNO_2 using the pK_a value from Table 14-1. Mark on it the approximate pH you would expect for each of the following solutions:

    (a) a solution of approximately 0.1 M nitrous acid;

    (b) solution of approximately 0.1 M sodium nitrite;

    (c) buffer solution containing approximately equal amounts of nitrous acid and sodium nitrite.

13. Sketch a distribution diagram for oxalic acid, $(COOH)_2$. Mark on it the approximate pH you would expect for each of the following solutions:

    (a) a solution of approximately 0.5 M oxalic acid;

    (b) a solution containing approximately 2 g of $K_2C_2O_4.H_2O$ dissolved in 100 mL of water;

    (c) a solution containing equal amounts of potassium oxalate $K_2C_2O_4$ and potassium hydrogen oxalate KHC_2O_4.

    (d) a solution containing oxalic acid $H_2C_2O_4$ and potassium hydrogen oxalate KHC_2O_4 in which there is about twice as much of the former as of the latter.

    (e) a saturated solution of potassium hydrogen oxalate KHC_2O_4.

14. Calculate the pH of each the following solutions:

    (a) 0.080 M HCl: (b) 0.15 M acetic acid;   (c) 0.050 M HCN;

    (d) 0.45 M ammonia: (e) 0.15 M sodium acetate;   (f) 0.20 M sodium oxalate. $Na_2C_2O_4$.

    [1.1, 2.8, 5.2, 11.4, 9.0, 8.7]

15. Calculate the pH of the following solutions: (a) 1.5×10^{-4} M formic acid; (b) 0.05 M ammonium chloride: (c) 0.20 M potassium hydrogen phthalate; (d) 0.50 M potassium dihydrogen phosphate.

    [4.0, 5.3, 4.2, 4.7]

16. What concentration of an aqueous solution of acetic acid which would have a pH of 3.00?

    [0.060 M]

17. A sample of a monoprotic acid is dissolved in water to make a solution of concentration 0.080 M. and it is found that 10.0% of the acid is ionized. What percentage of the acid would be ionized in a 0.40 M solution?   [4.7%]

18. Calculate the pH of each of the solutions made by mixing the following pairs of solutions:

    (a) 30.0 mL of 0.10 M HCl and 20.0 mL of 0.50 M CH_3COONa.   [5.1]

    (b) 30.0 mL of 0.10 M CH_3COOH and 20.0 mL of 0.50 M CH_3COONa;   [5.3]

    (c) 20.0 mL of 0.050 M NH_4Cl and 30.0 mL of 0.20 M NH_3.   [10.0]

    (d) 20.0 mL of 0. 10 M $NaHCO_3$, and 40.0 mL of 0.10 M Na_2CO_3;   [10.6]

    (e) 20.0 mL of 0. 10 M $NaHC_2O_4$ and 40.0 mL of 0.10 M $Na_2C_2O_4$;   [4.5]

    (f) 20.0 mL of 0.50 M HCl and 30.0 mL of 0.10 M CH_3COONa.   [0.8]

19. What range of pH can be covered by buffer solutions containing ammonia and ammonium chloride? Assume that for effective buffer action. the ratio of the amount of acid to that of the conjugate base must lie between 4 and 1/4.   [8.6 to 9.8]

20. Calculate the change in the pH which results when each of the following are separately added to 1.00 L of a buffer solution containing 1.00 M NH_3 and 0.90 M NH_4Cl: (a) 100. mL of water; (b) 100. mL of 0.20 M KOH; (c) 100. mL of 0.15 M HCl.   [0, +0.01, − 0.02]

21. For a solution containing 0.45 M acetic acid CH_3COOH and 0.85 M chloroacetic acid $CH_2ClCOOH$, calculate $[H^+]$, $[CH_2ClCOOH]$, $[CH_2ClCOO^-]$, $[CH_3COOH]$, and $[CH_3COO^-]$.

    [0.034 M, 0.82 M, 0.034 M, 0.45 M, 2.2×10^{-4} M]

22. A student takes 25.00 mL of 0.25 M HCl, and titrates it with a solution of 0.15 M NaOH. What volume of NaOH solution is required to reach the equivalence point? What is the *p*H of the solution after 15.35 mL of NaOH solution are added? What is the *p*H after 48.50 mL are added?   [41.7 mL, 1.01, 12.14]

23. A student takes 25.00 mL of 0.25 M formic acid HCOOH, and titrates it with a solution of 0.15 M NaOH. What volume of NaOH solution is required to reach the equivalence point? What is the *p*H of the solution after 15.35 mL of NaOH solution are added? What is the *p*H after 48.50 mL are added? What volume of NaOH would be required to bring the *p*H to 4.20?   [41.7 mL, 3.52, 12.14, 30.9 mL]

24. A student takes an unknown amount of an unknown acid and dissolves it in an unknown amount of water. She makes an exploratory titration of a sample of this solution with base of unknown concentration, measuring the pH with a pH meter, and concludes from the shape of the titration curve that the acid is monoprotic. She then takes another sample of the solution of the acid and repeats the titration more carefully. After adding 13.7 mL of base the pH is found to be 4.7. To reach the equivalence point, judged to be defined by the centre of the rapid rise in pH after leaving the buffer region, 35.2 mL of base were required. Calculate pK_a for the acid, estimate the pH of the solution at the equivalence point, and sketch the graph of pH versus volume of base added.   [4.9, about 9]

25. A student takes a sample of an acid which is known to be diprotic, and dissolves it in water. He titrates a sample of the solution with base, using a pH meter. He finds that the first equivalence point is reached after 22.4 mL of base have been added, and that the pH at that stage of the titration is 7.0. He continues the titration and finds that the pH is 9.8 after a total of 32.4 mL of base have been added. Calculate pK_{a1} and pK_{a2} for the acid, estimate the pH of the solution at the second equivalence point, and sketch the graph of pH versus volume of base added.   [4.1, 9.9, about 11]

26. Ammonium acetate is an amphiprotic salt, for NH_4^+ is an acid and CH_3COO^- is a base. Draw a distribution diagram showing the fractions of NH_3, NH_4^+, CH_3COOH and CH_3COO^- present as functions of the pH. Calculate the pH of a solution of CH_3COONH_4 with a concentration of 0.15 M.   [7.0]

27. A 0.8342 g sample of potassium hydrogen phthalate, 1,2-C_6H_4COOHCOOK, is dissolved in 65.00 mL of water.

    (a) Calculate the pH of this solution.   [4.2]

    (b) The above solution is titrated with a 0.147 M solution of NaOH. What is the pH at the equivalence point?   [9.1]

    (c) After sufficient NaOH has been added to reach the equivalence point, 12.00 mL of a 0.500 M solution of nitric acid is added. Calculate the *p*H of the resulting solution.   [2.94]

28. 0.50 mole of potassium hydrogen phosphate, K_2HPO_4, is dissolved in 1.0 litre of water.

    (a) Sketch a distribution diagram for the phosphoric acid (H_3PO_4) system;

    (b) Calculate the pH and [PO_4^{3-}] in the above solution.   [9.8, 1.5×10^{-3} M]

    (c) Calculate the pH after 0.65 mole of HCl is added to the solution.   [2.5]

29. (a) Calculate [Cl^-] in 0.20 M HCl.   [0.20 M]

    (b) Calculate [F^-] in 0.20 M HF.   [0.011 M]

    (c) Equal volumes of the above two solutions are mixed. Calculate [Cl^-] and [F^-] in the resulting solution.   [0.10, 6.3×10^{-4}]

30. (a) Natural water containing dissolved CO_2 (in the form of carbonic acid) and carbonate minerals is found to have a pH of 8.0. What are the relative amounts of H_2CO_3, HCO_3^- and CO_3^{2-} present in the water, expressed as percentages of the total amount?

    (b) The waste water from a lime works has a pH of 10.0 and a total carbonate content (CO_3^{2-}, HCO_3^- and H_2CO_3) of 1.00×10^{-3} mol/L. The amounts of other acids and bases present are negligible. How many moles of strong acid (e.g. HNO_3) must be added per litre to bring the pH to 8.0 before discharge into the natural water described in part (a)?

    $$[0.32 \times 10^{-3}\, mol/L]$$

31. Draw a distribution diagram for glycine, and use the diagram to show why the zwitterion form is predominant in the pH range 7 to 9.

32. Calculate the pH of each of the following solutions:

    (a) 0.015 M propanoic acid C_3H_7COOH [3.3]

    (b) 0.20 M ammonium chloride NH_4Cl [5.0]

    (c) 0.14 M ammonia NH_3 [11.2]

    (d) 0.075 M sodium acetate CH_3COONa [8.8]

    (e) 0.0080 M chloroacetic acid $CH_2ClCOOH$ [2.6]

    (f) 0.0080 M nitrous acid HNO_2 [2.7]

    (g) 0.0095 M sodium hypochlorite $NaOCl$ [9.7]

33. Calculate the pH of each of the following solutions, made by adding to water the indicated concentrations of each of the two solutes indicated:

    (a) 0.15 M acetic acid CH_3COOH and 0.50 M sodium acetate CH_3COONa [5.3]

    (b) 0.15 M acetic acid CH_3COOH and 0.050 M sodium hydroxide $NaOH$ [4.4]

    (c) 0.15 M acetic acid CH_3COOH and 0.20 M chloroacetic acid   [1.8]

    (d) 0.10 M ammonia NH_3 and 0.20 M ammonium chloride   [8.9]

34. (a) What volume of 0.35 M sodium hydroxide must be added to 100. mL of 0.45 M acetic acid to bring the solution to a pH of 5.0?   [82 mL]

    (b) If an additional 1.0 mL of the sodium hydroxide solution were added to this buffer solution, what would be the change in the pH?   [+0.02]

    (c) If 1.0 mL of 0.35 M hydrochloric acid were added to the original buffer, instead of sodium hydroxide, what would be the change in pH?   [−0.01]

35. A student titrated a sample of potassium hydrogen phthalate, $C_6H_4(COOH)(COOK)$, with a solution of 0.3 M sodium hydroxide $NaOH$. The equivalence point was reached after 44.0 mL of the base solution had been added. Make a careful sketch of the titration curve of pH as a function of volume of base added, and indicate the pH at the beginning, the midpoint and the end of the titration. Indicate the shape of the curve for addition of base beyond the equivalence point.

36. What is the pH of a 0.25 M solution of potassium dihydrogen phosphate KH_2PO_4?   [4.7]

Chapter 14

15 Precipitation and Solubility

Objectives

After reading this chapter, the student should be able to do the following:

♦ Define solubility product.

♦ Calculate solubility using the solubility product.

♦ Describe the common ion effect.

♦ Describe effect of acid-base and complex ion equilibria on solubility.

Related topics to review:

Precipitation reactions in Chapter 2. Acid-base reactions in Chapters 2 and 14.

Related topics to look forward to:

Thermodynamics of chemical equilibrium in Chapter 16.

15-1 Solubility product

In this chapter we discuss the equilibria between sparingly soluble salts in the solid phase and ions in aqueous solution. Such equilibria are important in analytical chemistry, and in many large-scale reactions in industrial and environmental chemistry. Equilibrium may be reached by mixing ionic reactants in solution, from which a solid precipitate forms, or by placing the pure, dry salt in contact with some water, so that the salt dissolves up to the solubility limit. The final state of the system is the same in both cases.

We are concerned here primarily with salts whose solubility is considerably less than 0.01 mol/L, since more concentrated solutions deviate from ideal behaviour and substantial corrections must be made to the simple calculations outlined in the present discussion.

Consider for example the precipitation of silver chloride, AgCl. Silver nitrate, $AgNO_3$, and potassium chloride, KCl, are both very soluble salts, and the solutions contain the ions Ag^+ and NO_3^-, and K^+ and Cl^- respectively. When the two solutions are mixed, a white precipitate of AgCl(s) is immediately formed. The Ag^+ and Cl^- ions cannot coexist in solution at the substantial concentrations at which they exist in the separate solutions, and instead form a precipitate of AgCl which removes some ions of both kinds from solution and reduces both concentrations. The process can be described by the net ionic chemical equation:

$$Ag^+(aq) + Cl^-(aq) \rightarrow AgCl(s)$$

How far does this process go? Does precipitation proceed until one or other of the ions is completely removed from solution? No, but it does come to an equilibrium condition such as we have been discussing in the previous two chapters.

The other approach is to consider what happens when solid AgCl is placed in contact with pure water. When sparingly soluble silver chloride is placed in contact with pure water, some of the salt dissolves even though the solubility, as measured by the concentration of the salt in solution, is very small. The dissolved silver chloride is present in solution in the form of ions, and so the equilibrium between ions in solution and the solid salt can be expressed by the equilibrium equation:

$$AgCl(s) \rightleftharpoons Ag^+(aq) + Cl^-(aq).$$

The process described by the previous equation represents the approach to equilibrium from the right hand side of the present equation.

In Chapter 13 the concept of relative activity was introduced. One of the important applications of this formalism is to heterogeneous equilibria in which a chemical reaction involves more than one phase. This was discussed in Chapter 13 for reactions involving both gases and a condensed phase (either a solid or a liquid). A pure condensed phase is in its standard state and so the relative activity is unity regardless of what other substances may be present. Condensed phases do not appear in the expressions for equilibrium constants, not because these substances do not take part in equilibria, but because their relative activities are fixed at 1.000 as long as some of the phase is present.

A similar situation was met in Chapter 14 in the case of acid-base equilibria in aqueous solutions. The solvent, water, does not appear explicitly in the equilibrium constant expression, because its relative activity is very close to 1.000.

For the equation $AgCl(s) \rightleftharpoons Ag^+(aq) + Cl^-(aq)$ the equilibrium constant written in terms of relative activities is:

$$K = \frac{a(Ag^+(aq))a(Cl^-(aq))}{a(AgCl(s))}$$

For the ions in dilute solution, the relative activities of $Ag^+(aq)$ and $Cl^-(aq)$ can be approximated by the numerical values of the molar concentrations, as was done in the case of acid-base equilibria:

$$a(Ag^+(aq)) = [Ag^+] \qquad a(Cl^-(aq)) = [Cl^-]$$

The square brackets indicate the numerical value of the molar concentration in units of moles per litre, as in the previous chapter. The relative activity of $AgCl(s)$ is unity since this is a pure substance at standard state pressure:

$$a(AgCl(s)) = 1$$

Hence the equilibrium constant becomes:

$$K_{sp} = [Ag^+][Cl^-] \tag{15-1}$$

The equilibrium constant for this type of solubility equilibrium is called the **solubility product** since it consists only of the product of concentrations of the ions that take part in the solubility equilibrium. This name is reflected in the special symbol used for the equilibrium constant, K_{sp}.

It cannot be emphasized too firmly that the solid salt does not appear in the equilibrium expression. It would be quite wrong to put [AgCl] in the denominator to represent the concentration of the solid. Such a concentration has no meaning. The solid AgCl is a separate phase from the liquid solution, and cannot be ascribed a concentration. The solid is omitted from the solubility product because its relative activity is 1.000 regardless of how much solid salt is present, as long as *some* solid is present. The omission of AgCl(s) from the solubility product does not mean that the solid plays no role in the equilibrium; indeed the solid plays a central role, as long as some solid is present in contact with the solution so as to be able to exchange ions with the solution.

The form of the solubility product depends on the stoichiometry of the equation for the solubility equilibrium, as for all equilibrium constants. Some examples of other solubility products are:

$$Ag_2SO_4(s) \rightleftharpoons 2\,Ag^+(aq) + SO_4^{2-}(aq) \qquad K_{sp} = [Ag^+]^2[SO_4^{2-}]$$

$$BaCO_3(s) \rightleftharpoons Ba^{2+}(aq) + CO_3^{2-}(aq) \qquad K_{sp} = [Ba^{2+}][CO_3^{2-}]$$

$$Sr_3(AsO_4)_2(s) \rightleftharpoons 3\,Sr^{2+}(aq) + 2\,AsO_4^{3-}(aq) \qquad K_{sp} = [Sr^{2+}]^3[AsO_4^{3-}]^2$$

It is necessary to know the ions involved in the equilibrium of course, and this cannot always be guessed from the composition of the salt. For instance, the sparingly soluble salt mercurous chloride, Hg_2Cl_2, ionizes in aqueous solution to form the diatomic mercurous ion $Hg_2^{2+}(aq)$ and chloride ions $Cl^-(aq)$:

$$Hg_2Cl_2(s) \rightleftharpoons Hg_2^{2+}(aq) + 2\,Cl^-(aq) \qquad K_{sp} = [Hg_2^{2+}][Cl^-]^2$$

Some salts crystallize with "water of crystallization" in the crystal structure. When the salt dissolves in water, the water from the crystal is indistinguishable from the water that forms the solvent. As in the case of solutions of acids and bases, we assume here that the solutions involved are not very concentrated, and that the relative activity of the solvent water does not differ significantly from its value in pure water, which is unity. Hence the water is not included in the solubility product expression. An example is the following:

$$Ba(OH)_2.8H_2O(s) \rightleftharpoons Ba^{2+}(aq) + 2\,OH^-(aq) + 8\,H_2O(\ell)$$

$$K_{sp} = \frac{a(Ba^{2+})\,a(OH^-)\,a(H_2O)^8}{a(Ba(OH)_2.8H_2O)} = [Ba^{2+}][OH^-]^2$$

In this equation, $a(H_2O) = 1$ since water is the solvent, and $a(Ba(OH)_2.8H_2O) = 1$ since the solid hydrated hydroxide is a pure phase.

Table 15-1 lists solubility product values for a number of sparingly soluble salts at a temperature of 25°C; like all equilibrium constants solubility products vary with temperature. The table does not include any very soluble salts, since the concentrations of the solutions would be too high for the calculations to be accurate; such salts are often dealt with graphically as in Figure 8-9. Metal sulfides will be discussed in Section 15-4.

Comparison of the data in Table 15-1 with other tabulations may show discrepancies. Solubility equilibria are complicated and interpretation of experimental results in terms of a K_{sp} value is often not straightforward, for reasons that will become clear after studying later sections of this chapter. The results of calculations based on solubility equilibria are therefore subject to some uncertainty in many cases.

Table 15-1 Solubility products of sparingly soluble salts at 25 °C

Salt	K_{sp}	Salt	K_{sp}	salt	K_{sp}
AgCl	1.77×10^{-10}	CaF_2	3.45×10^{-11}	$NiCO_3$	1.42×10^{-7}
AgBr	5.35×10^{-13}	$CaSO_4$	4.93×10^{-5}	$PbCl_2$	1.70×10^{-5}
AgI	8.52×10^{-17}	$Ca(OH)_2$	5.02×10^{-6}	$PbBr_2$	6.60×10^{-6}
$Ag_2C_2O_4$	3.5×10^{-11}	$CdCO_3$	1.8×10^{-14}	$PbCrO_4$	1.8×10^{-14}
Ag_2CO_3	8.46×10^{-12}	$Cd(OH)_2$	7.2×10^{-15}	$PbCO_3$	7.40×10^{-14}
Ag_2SO_4	1.20×10^{-5}	$Cu(OH)_2$	4.8×10^{-20}	$Pb(IO_3)_2$	3.69×10^{-13}
Ag_2CrO_4	1.12×10^{-12}	$Cu_3(PO_4)_2$	1.40×10^{-37}	$Pb(OH)_2$	1.43×10^{-20}
$AlPO_4$	9.84×10^{-21}	$Fe(OH)_2$	4.87×10^{-17}	$PbSO_4$	2.53×10^{-8}
$Ba(IO_3)_2$	4.01×10^{-9}	$Fe(OH)_3$	2.79×10^{-39}	$Sn(OH)_2$	5.45×10^{-27}
$BaCO_3$	2.58×10^{-9}	Hg_2Cl_2	1.43×10^{-18}	$SrCO_3$	5.60×10^{-10}
$BaSO_4$	1.08×10^{-10}	Hg_2Br_2	6.2×10^{-20}	$Sr_3(AsO_4)_2$	4.29×10^{-19}
$BaCrO_4$	1.17×10^{-10}	Hg_2I_2	2.9×10^{-29}	SrF_2	4.33×10^{-9}
$Ba(OH)_2 \cdot 8H_2O$	2.55×10^{-4}	$MgCO_3$	6.82×10^{-6}	$SrSO_4$	3.44×10^{-7}
$CaCO_3$	3.36×10^{-9}	$Mg(OH)_2$	5.61×10^{-12}	$Y(OH)_3$	1.00×10^{-22}
$CaC_2O_4 \cdot H_2O$	2.32×10^{-9}	$Ni(OH)_2$	5.48×10^{-16}	$Zn(OH)_2$	3×10^{-17}

Reprinted with permission from CRC Handbook of Chemistry and Physics, 77th edition. Copyright CRC Press, Boca Raton, Florida. In this table one value only has been selected for each salt, although in some cases, more than one form of the precipitate may exist.

15-2 Solubility calculations

The solubility product for an electrolyte can be used to calculate its solubility when it is dissolved in pure water. The details of the calculation depend on the stoichiometry of the equilibrium, and the following two examples illustrate typical calculations.

Example 15-1 Calculate the solubility of silver chloride AgCl in pure water from the solubility product.

Suppose the solubility of AgCl in pure water is s moles/litre. Then the process of dissolving is described by the following ICE table:

concentrations AgCl(s)	$\rightleftharpoons$	Ag^+(aq) +	Cl^-(aq).
initial		0	0
changes		$+s$	$+s$
equilibrium		s	s

Hence the solubility product is (with data from Table 15-1):

$$K_{sp} = [Ag^+][Cl^-] = s^2 = 1.77 \times 10^{-10}$$

This equation can be readily solved for the solubility:

$$s = \sqrt{1.77 \times 10^{-10}} = 1.3 \times 10^{-5}$$

Hence the solubility of AgCl in pure water is 1.3×10^{-5} M.

Example 15-2 Calculate the solubility of silver chromate Ag_2CrO_4 in pure water from the solubility product.

Suppose the solubility of Ag_2CrO_4 in pure water is s moles/litre. Then the process of dissolving and the situation at equilibrium is described by the following ICE table:

concentrations Ag_2CrO_4(s)	$\rightleftharpoons$	2 Ag^+(aq) +	CrO_4^{2-}(aq).
initial		0	0
changes		$+2s$	$+s$
equilibrium		$2s$	s

Hence the solubility product is (with data from Table 15-1):

$$K_{sp} = [Ag^+]^2[CrO_4^{2-}] = (2s)^2 \times s = 4s^3 = 1.12 \times 10^{-12}$$

which can be readily solved for the solubility:

$$s = \left(\frac{1.12 \times 10^{-12}}{4} \right)^{1/3} = 6.5 \times 10^{-5}$$

Hence the solubility of Ag_2CrO_4 in pure water is 6.5×10^{-5} M.

It should be noted that the silver ion concentration is both doubled and squared in this calculation. The final step involves taking a cube root of a number, and it is important to be able to carry out such calculations with confidence using a hand calculator.

15-3 Common ion effect

The solubility of a sparingly soluble electrolyte can be greatly influenced by the presence in solution of another electrolyte that shares a common ion. An example is silver chloride in the presence of a soluble silver salt such as silver nitrate. The silver ion concentration is larger than the chloride ion concentration because of the silver nitrate in the solution. Since $[Ag^+]$ is increased by the presence of the $AgNO_3$, the chloride ion concentration $[Cl^-]$ is decreased. This can be seen as an application of Le Chatelier's principle. The quantitative calculation is shown in the following example.

Example 15-3 Calculate the solubility of silver chloride, AgCl, in a solution of 0.005 M $AgNO_3$.

Suppose the solubility of AgCl in 0.005 M $AgNO_3$ is s moles/litre. Then the process of dissolving can be described by the following ICE table:

concentrations	AgCl(s) ⇌	Ag^+(aq) +	Cl^-(aq).
initial		0.005	0
changes		+s	+s
equilibrium		0.005+s	s

Hence the solubility product is (with data from table 15-1):

$$K_{sp} = [Ag^+][Cl^-] = (0.005+s)s = 1.77 \times 10^{-10}$$

The solubility can be determined by solving this quadratic equation for the positive root:

$$s^2 + 0.005s - 1.77 \times 10^{-10} = 0$$

$$s = \tfrac{1}{2}\left(-0.005 + \sqrt{0.005^2 + 4 \times 1.77 \times 10^{-10}}\right) = 3.5 \times 10^{-8}$$

Hence the solubility of AgCl in 0.005 M $AgNO_3$ is 4×10^{-8} M (to one significant figure).

In this calculation, the answer is found by subtracting two numbers that are very nearly equal, and so round-off errors can creep in. In most cases of common ion calculations it is better to use an approximate solution.

In the case discussed in Example 15-3, the solubility in pure water (which was calculated in Example 15-1 above) is considerably smaller than the concentration of the common ion, 0.005 M. The reduction in solubility due to the common ion leads us to expect that the solubility in the $AgNO_3$ solution will be even less. Hence in the solubility product expression $(0.005+s)s = 1.77 \times 10^{-10}$, we expect to find $s \ll 0.005$; if we assume that this is true, the equation becomes:

$$0.005s \approx 1.77 \times 10^{-10}$$

This equation is linear, rather than quadratic, and so can be solved easily to give $s = 3.5 \times 10^{-8}$, the same value as the full solution of the quadratic.

Example 15-4 Calculate the solubility of lead iodate, $Pb(IO_3)_2$, in a solution of 0.005 M potassium iodate KIO_3.

Suppose the solubility of $Pb(IO_3)_2$ in 0.005 M KIO_3 is s moles/litre. Then the process of dissolving is described by the following ICE table:

$$concentrations \quad Pb(IO_3)_2(s) \rightleftharpoons Pb^{2+}(aq) + 2\ IO_3^-(aq).$$

		Pb^{2+}	IO_3^-
initial		0	0.005
changes		$+s$	$+2s$
equilibrium		s	$0.005+2s$

Hence the solubility product is (with data from table 15-1):

$$K_{sp} = [Pb^{2+}][IO_3^-]^2 = (0.005+2s)s^2 = 3.69 \times 10^{-13}$$

This equation is cubic in the solubility s and the exact calculation is not familiar to most students. However it is expected that s will be considerably less than 0.005, and so the approximate method should be used. Assuming that $s << 0.005$, the equation becomes:

$$0.005 \times s^2 \approx 3.68 \times 10^{-13}$$

This equation can be solved easily for s:

$$s = \sqrt{\frac{3.69 \times 10^{-13}}{0.005}} = 8.6 \times 10^{-6}.$$

This result is indeed smaller than 0.005, and so the assumption is justified. Hence the solubility of $Pb(IO_3)_2$ in 0.005 M KIO_3 is 9×10^{-6} M.

Differences in solubility are often used to separate ions in solution. Silver ions can be separated from sodium ions by adding dilute hydrochloric acid HCl. This procedure precipitates almost all of the silver ions as AgCl(s) leaving the sodium ions in solution. This case is easy to understand since one salt (NaCl) is very soluble and the other (AgCl) is not.

Separations are still possible even if both salts are sparingly soluble, as long as the solubilities are sufficiently different. This is illustrated by the following calculation for the addition of a soluble chromate salt to a solution containing lead ions Pb^{2+} and silver ions Ag^+.

Example 15-5 A solution contains Pb^{2+} at a concentration of 0.010 M and Ag^+ at a concentration of 0.005 M. A solution of potassium chromate K_2CrO_4 is added slowly to the stirred solution. Which precipitates first, yellow lead chromate $PbCrO_4$, or red silver chromate Ag_2CrO_4? What fraction of the first metal ion to precipitate as chromate remains in solution when the other chromate precipitate first appears?

Both $PbCrO_4$ and Ag_2CrO_4 are sparingly soluble. Their K_{sp} values are 1.8×10^{-14} and 1.12×10^{-12}, so precipitation of one or the other will begin with the first drop or two of the chromate solution.

Precipitation of $PbCrO_4$ begins when $[CrO_4^{2-}] = \dfrac{K_{sp}}{[Pb^{2+}]} = \dfrac{1.8 \times 10^{-14}}{0.010} = 1.8 \times 10^{-12}$ M.

Precipitation of Ag_2CrO_4 begins when $[CrO_4^{2-}] = \dfrac{K_{sp}}{[Ag^+]^2} = \dfrac{1.12 \times 10^{-12}}{0.005^2} = 4.5 \times 10^{-8}$ M.

The lower value is reached first, as the chromate ion is added. Hence $PbCrO_4$ will precipitate before Ag_2CrO_4, and as more chromate is added, precipitation of $PbCrO_4$ continues until the concentration of chromate ion reaches 4.5×10^{-8} M. At that point, Ag_2CrO_4 begins to precipitate. At this point in the process, the concentration of Pb^{2+} ion is:

$$[Pb^{2+}] = \frac{1.8 \times 10^{-12}}{4.5 \times 10^{-8}} = 4.0 \times 10^{-5} \text{ M}.$$

The concentration of Pb^{2+} is reduced from 0.010 M to 4×10^{-5} M when the first Ag_2CrO_4 begins to precipitate, and so only 0.4 % of the Pb^{2+} remains in solution. Further addition of chromate ion will of course lead to precipitation of more Ag_2CrO_4. Almost complete separation of the two salts is therefore possible.

———————————————————————

Although the hydroxides of the alkali metals (group 1 of the Periodic Table) are very soluble in water, a number of hydroxides of alkaline earth (group 2) and other metals are sparingly soluble, and their solubility is directly related to the pH of the solution. A sparingly soluble hydroxide dissolved in pure water releases OH^- ions into solution, thus raising the pH. If the pH of the solution is controlled by another acid-base equilibrium, such as a buffer system, then the pH controls the solubility. These situations are illustrated in the following examples.

———————————————————————

Example 15-6 What is the pH of the solution formed by adding excess solid calcium hydroxide, $Ca(OH)_2$, to pure water?

———————————————————————

Suppose the solubility of $Ca(OH)_2$ in pure water is s moles/litre. Then the process of dissolving is described by the following ICE table:

concentrations	$Ca(OH)_2(s)$	$\rightleftharpoons$	$Ca^{2+}(aq)$	$+ 2\,OH^-(aq)$.
initial			0	0
changes			$+s$	$+2s$
equilibrium			s	$2s$

Hence the solubility product is:

$$K_{sp} = [Ca^{2+}][OH^-]^2 = s \times (2s)^2 = 4s^3 = 5.02 \times 10^{-6}$$

which can be readily solved for the solubility:

$$s = \sqrt[3]{\frac{5.02 \times 10^{-6}}{4}} = 0.011$$

Hence $[OH^-] = 2 \times 0.011 = 0.022$ M, $pOH = 1.7$ and so $pH = 14.0 - 1.7 = 12.3$.

———————————————————————

Example 15-7 What is the solubility of cadmium hydroxide $Cd(OH)_2$ in a buffer of pH = 8.0?

———————————————————————

At pH = 8.0, pOH = 6.0, and $[OH^-] = 1.0 \times 10^{-6}$ M. Since the solution is a buffer solution, the hydroxide ion concentration remains at this value regardless of the amount of $Cd(OH)_2$ which dissolves, within reason. Hence the solubility is measured by the concentration at equilibrium of cadmium ion. Taking the solubility product from Table 15-1,

$$[Cd^{2+}] = \frac{K_{sp}}{[OH^-]^2} = \frac{7.2 \times 10^{-15}}{(1.0 \times 10^{-6})^2} = 7.2 \times 10^{-3} \text{ M}$$

The solubility in the buffer at pH = 8.0 is therefore 7.2×10^{-3} M, which is greater than the solubility in pure water, which would be 1.2×10^{-5} M. The solubility would increase if the pH of the buffer were decreased.

15-4 Effect of acid-base equilibrium on solubility

The solubility equilibrium for electrolytes often interacts with other equilibria in solution, which may cause a large change in the solubility.

We first consider the acid-base equilibrium involving (usually) the anions. Anions of weak acids are weak bases, and so can be protonated at low pH. This situation is most easily described by means of distribution diagrams, which were discussed in Chapter 14. Consider the solubility of calcium fluoride, CaF_2, in water. The solubility equilibrium is:

$$CaF_2(s) \rightleftharpoons Ca^{2+}(aq) + 2\,F^-(aq) \qquad K_{sp} = [Ca^{2+}][F^-]^2 = 3.45 \times 10^{-11}$$

A simple calculation of the solubility considering only the solubility product leads to:

$$s = \left(\frac{3.45 \times 10^{-11}}{4} \right)^{1/3} = 2.0 \times 10^{-4} \text{ M}.$$

But fluoride ion is a weak base, and the following equilibrium must also be considered:

$$F^-(aq) + H_2O \rightleftharpoons HF(aq) + OH^-(aq).$$

For hydrofluoric acid, HF, $pK_a = 3.20$, and the distribution diagram for this acid is shown in the Figure 15-1. For pH above about 5, the fluoride ion predominates, and the above calculation can be expected to be reasonably accurate. However, at lower pH, some fluoride ion is converted to hydrofluoric acid, HF, and the concentration of fluoride ion, $[F^-]$, is reduced. Hence $[Ca^{2+}]$ must increase to maintain the solubility product equilibrium. Thus the solubility of CaF_2 is increased in acidic solution. The following example illustrates how the solubility can be calculated at low pH.

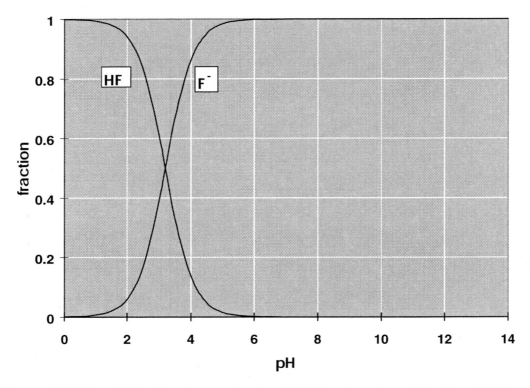

Figure 15-1 The distribution diagram for the HF/F⁻ system, for which pKa = 3.2. For pH larger than about 5, the concentration of HF present in solution is negligible compared to the concentration of F⁻.

Example 15-8 Calculate the solubility of CaF_2 in a solution buffered at pH = 3.0.

We will assume that the pH of the solution is controlled by the buffer equilibrium, and is not affected by the dissolved CaF_2. Hence we can set $[H^+] = 1 \times 10^{-3}$. The fraction of F⁻ that is protonated at this pH can be calculated directly from the acid dissociation constant for HF:

$$HF(aq) \rightleftharpoons H^+(aq) + F^-(aq)$$

$$K_a = 6.3 \times 10^{-4} = \frac{1 \times 10^{-3} \times [F^-]}{[HF]}$$

From this equation, we calculate that $[HF] = (1 \times 10^{-3}/6.3 \times 10^{-3})[F^-] = 1.58 \times [F^-]$. The total number of fluorine atoms in solution must be twice the number of calcium atoms in solution, from the solubility equilibrium, so:

$$[HF] + [F^-] = 2 \times [Ca^{2+}]$$

and so $\qquad (1.58 + 1) \times [F^-] = 2 \times [Ca^{2+}]$, and hence $[F^-] = 0.775 \times [Ca^{2+}]$.

If $[Ca^{2+}] = s$, then $[F^-] = 0.775 \times s$ and the solubility product becomes:

$$s \times (0.775s)^2 = 3.45 \times 10^{-11}$$

From this equation, we calculate $s = 3.8 \times 10^{-4}$ M. Hence the solubility of CaF_2 is increased by a factor of about two, as compared with its solubility in a solution of pH of 5 or higher.

The acid-base equilibrium of the anion is particularly important in the case of sulfides. The simple solubility product equilibrium for zinc sulfide ZnS, for instance, would be written:

$$ZnS(s) \rightleftharpoons Zn^{2+}(aq) + S^{2-}(aq) \qquad K_{sp} = [Zn^{2+}][S^{2-}]$$

However, Table 14-5 shows that the pK_{a2} for HS^- is about 19, and so sulfide ion S^{2-} is a strong base. In the ordinary pH range of 14 and less, sulfide ion would be converted almost entirely to HS^-:

$$S^{2-}(aq) + H_2O \rightleftharpoons HS^-(aq) + OH^-(aq)$$

Adding together these two equilibria, we get:

$$ZnS(s) + H_2O \rightleftharpoons Zn^{2+}(aq) + HS^-(aq) + OH^-(aq)$$

The equilibrium constant for this reaction is taken to be the solubility product of ZnS:

$$K_{sp} = \frac{a(Zn^{2+})a(HS^-)a(OH^-)}{a(ZnS(s))a(H_2O)} = [Zn^{2+}][HS^-][OH^-]$$

In solutions of pH below 7, the HS^- ion is further protonated to $H_2S(aq)$ since $pK_{a1} = 7.05$ for $H_2S(aq)$, as shown in Table 14-5. Under these conditions, we work with the equilibrium:

$$ZnS(s) + 2 H^+(aq) \rightleftharpoons Zn^{2+}(aq) + H_2S(aq)$$

The equilibrium constant for this equation is denoted K_{spa}. The subscript "spa" indicates the solubility product in acid solution:

$$K_{spa} = \frac{a(Zn^{2+})a(H_2S)}{a(ZnS(s))a(H^+)} = \frac{[Zn^{2+}][H_2S]}{[H^+]^2}$$

This formula can also be used for solutions with pH greater than 7.

It is clear that the solubility of sulfides depends on the pH of the solution. Table 15-2 lists some K_{spa} values for some sulfides. It should be noticed that in several cases there are two different crystal forms of the solid metal sulfide with different values of K_{spa}.

Example 15-9   What is the solubility of ZnS(sphalerite) in a solution of pH = 4.0?

Let s be the required solubility. Then $[Zn^{2+}] = [H_2S] = s$, and $[H^+] = 1.0 \times 10^{-4}$. Hence the equilibrium constant expression becomes:

$$K_{spa} = \frac{[Zn^{2+}][H_2S]}{[H^+]^2} = \frac{s^2}{(1.0 \times 10^{-4})^2} = 2 \times 10^{-4}$$

The value of K_{spa} has been taken from Table 15-2. The last equality is easily solved to yield $s = [Zn^{2+}] = 1.4 \times 10^{-6}$.

It is clear from Example 15-9 that ZnS is highly insoluble. The solubility of all sulfides increases as the pH is lowered. There is a great range of values of K_{spa} in Table 15-2, showing that at low pH some sulfides remain sparingly soluble, while others become soluble to an appreciable extent. At high pH, almost all sulfides are extremely insoluble, and hence separation of metal ions can be achieved by precipitation at controlled pH. Sulfide precipitation can be achieved by addition of a solution of sodium sulfide, Na_2S, which contains HS^- ions rather than sulfide ions S^{2-}. There are further considerations in the solubility equilibria for metal sulfides, but the strongly basic character of the sulfide ion plays a major role in determining solubilities.

Table 15-2 Solubility products of sulfides in acid solution at 25 °C

The solubility product is expressed as the equilibrium constant K_{spa} for the reaction

$$MS(s) + 2H^+(aq) \rightleftharpoons M^{2+}(aq) + H_2S(aq).$$

Salt	K_{spa}	Salt	K_{spa}	Salt	K_{spa}
Ag_2S	6×10^{-30}	HgS (red)	4×10^{-33}	SnS	1×10^{-5}
CdS	8×10^{-7}	HgS (black)	2×10^{-32}	ZnS (sphalerite)	2×10^{-4}
CuS	6×10^{-16}	MnS	3×10^{7}	ZnS (wurtzite)	3×10^{-2}
FeS	6×10^{2}	PbS	3×10^{-7}		

Reprinted with permission from CRC Handbook of Chemistry and Physics, 77th edition. Copyright CRC Press, Boca Raton, Florida.

15-5 Complex ion formation

The second complication in solubility equilibria of electrolytes is the formation of **complex ions** by attachment of anions or neutral molecules to the cations. Simple evidence for formation of complex ions is that the presence of another solute increases solubility. For instance, the solubility of silver chloride in a solution containing ammonia is increased by the formation of **ammine** complexes:

$$Ag^+(aq) + NH_3(aq) \rightleftharpoons Ag(NH_3)^+ \qquad K_1 = 2.0\times10^3$$

$$Ag(NH_3)^+ + NH_3(aq) \rightleftharpoons Ag(NH_3)_2^+ \qquad K_2 = 8.1\times10^3$$

The equilibrium constants K_1 and K_2 are called the **stepwise** equilibrium constants for formation of the two complexes. The overall equilibrium for the formation of the diammine complex, and the **overall** equilibrium constant are:

$$Ag^+(aq) + 2\,NH_3(aq) \rightleftharpoons Ag(NH_3)_2^+ \qquad \beta_2 = K_1K_2 = 1.6\times10^7.$$

These are large equilibrium constants, and in the presence of ammonia, a large fraction of Ag^+ ions in solution are converted to the diammine complex $Ag(NH_3)_2^+$. This reduces $[Ag^+]$ and hence the solubility of a salt such as silver chloride, AgCl, is increased.

Stepwise formation equilibria can be described by means of distribution diagrams similar to those used for polyprotic acids, and a full discussion of the calculations is discussed in more advanced books. If the concentration of the ligands is not too small, then the overall equilibria, with their equilibrium constants β_n for formation of the complex with n ligands, can be used.

In these and similar equilibria, the ion or molecule bonded to the metal ion is called a **ligand**. The ligand is nearly always a molecule or ion carrying a lone pair of electrons, and hence can act as a Lewis base, while the metal ion acts as a Lewis acid by accepting a pair of electrons. The bond between metal ion and the ligand consists of the lone pair of electrons provided by the ligand. Other ligands are nitrogen containing bases such as ethylenediamine $H_2N–CH_2CH_2–NH_2$, and the anions of weak acids such as acetate CH_3COO^-, oxalate $C_2O_4^{2-}$, and cyanide CN^-. Cyanide complexes are used in the extraction and analysis of gold in the mining industry. Metallic gold is highly resistant to oxidation, but reacts with aerated cyanide solutions to form a complex in which gold is in the +1 oxidation state:

$$4\,Au(s) + 8\,CN^-(aq) + O_2(aq) + 2\,H_2O \rightarrow 4\,Au(CN)_2^-\,(aq) + 4\,OH^-(aq)$$

The solubility equilibrium can be expressed by combining the solubility product equilibrium with the complex formation equilibrium. Consider the solubility of silver chloride in ammonia solution. The two equilibria involved and their equilibrium constants are:

$$AgCl(s) \;\rightleftharpoons\; Ag^+(aq) + Cl^-(aq) \qquad\qquad K_{sp} = 1.77 \times 10^{-10}$$

$$Ag^+(aq) + 2\,NH_3(aq) \;\rightleftharpoons\; Ag(NH_3)_2^+ \qquad\qquad \beta_2 = 1.6 \times 10^7$$

These chemical equations can be added together to give an overall equation:

$$AgCl(s) + 2\,NH_3(aq) \;\rightleftharpoons\; Ag(NH_3)_2^+(aq) + Cl^-(aq)$$

The equilibrium constant for this equation is:

$$K = K_{sp}\beta_2 = \frac{[Ag(NH_3)_2^+][Cl^-]}{[NH_3]^2} = 1.77 \times 10^{-10} \times 1.6 \times 10^7 = 2.8 \times 10^{-3}$$

Example 15-10 Calculate the solubility of silver chloride in 0.050 M ammonia solution.

Let s be the required solubility. The equilibrium can be described by the following ICE table.

concentrations	$AgCl(s) + 2\,NH_3(aq)$	$\rightleftharpoons$	$Ag(NH_3)_2^+(aq)$	$+ Cl^-(aq)$
initial	0.050		0	0
change	$-2s$		$+s$	$+s$
equilibrium	$0.050-2s$		s	s

Hence the equilibrium constant is:

$$K = \frac{[Ag(NH_3)_2^+][Cl^-]}{[NH_3]^2} = \frac{s^2}{(0.050-2s)^2} = 2.8 \times 10^{-3}$$

Taking the square root of this equation we get $\dfrac{s}{0.05-2s} = \sqrt{2.8 \times 10^{-3}} = 0.053$. This can be rearranged into a linear equation, which is easily solved to yield $s = 2.4 \times 10^{-3}$. Hence the solubility is 2.4×10^{-3} M. Note that this is more than a hundred times greater than the solubility of AgCl in pure water, which is 1.3×10^{-5} M.

Another example is the formation of complexes of silver with the thiosulfate ion, $S_2O_3^{2-}$, which can be regarded as a sulfate ion SO_4^{2-} in which one oxygen atom has been replaced by a sulfur atom. The most important complex formation equilibria are:

$$AgCl(s) + S_2O_3^{2-}(aq) \;\rightleftharpoons\; [Ag(S_2O_3)]^-(aq) + Cl^-(aq) \qquad K_1 = 6.6 \times 10^8$$

$$[Ag(S_2O_3)]^-(aq) + S_2O_3^{2-}(aq) \;\rightleftharpoons\; [Ag(S_2O_3)_2]^{3-}(aq) \qquad K_2 = 5.1 \times 10^4$$

The overall equation can be written:

$$AgCl(s) + 2 S_2O_3^{2-}(aq) \rightleftharpoons [Ag(S_2O_3)_2]^{3-}(aq) + Cl^-(aq) \qquad \beta_2 = K_1K_2 = 3.4 \times 10^{13}$$

Because of these equilibria, a solution of sodium thiosulfate, $Na_2S_2O_3$, dissolves silver chloride readily. Sodium thiosulfate solution is known as "fixer" in processing black-and-white photographic film. After treatment with the solution, the light-sensitive solid silver halide is dissolved and further exposure to light does not affect the image which has been developed.

In Section 15-3 we discussed how the common ion effect reduces the solubility of a salt in a dilute solution containing a common ion. However, a high concentration of the common ion in some cases reverses this effect and may increase the solubility, because of the formation of complexes. Silver chloride provides an example:

$$Ag^+(aq) + 2 Cl^-(aq) \rightleftharpoons AgCl_2^-(aq) \quad \beta_2 = 1.8 \times 10^5$$

When excess chloride ion is added, the solubility at first decreases due to the common ion effect, but reaches a minimum and then increases at higher chloride ion concentrations due to the formation of the complex $AgCl_2^-$.

Further reading

Solubility product and acid-base equilibria are studied in detail in analytical chemistry. Two standard reference books are:

Quantitative Chemical Analysis by D.C.Harris. 4th edition. (W.H.Freeman and Co. 1995).

Fundamentals of Analytical Chemistry by D.A.Skoog, D.M.West and F.J.Holler. (Saunders College Publishing. 1996).

A useful discussion of the solubility of sulfides and the dissociation equibrium of H_2S in aqueous solution is to be found in an article by R.J.Myers in the Journal of Chemical Education, volume 63, pages 687-690 (1986).

Key concepts

The equilibrium constant for the solubility equilibrium of a sparingly soluble salt is called the solubility constant. From the solubility product, the solubility of a sparingly soluble salt in pure water can be calculated.

The solubility of a sparingly soluble salt in a solution which contains a soluble salt with a common ion is reduced by the presence of the common ion.

Acid-base equilibria and complex ion formation can have a large effect on the solubility of a sparingly soluble salt through the effects of the second chemical equilibrium on the solubility equilibrium. In particular, the solubilities of metal sulfides vary strongly with pH because sulfide ion is a strong base.

Review questions

1. What is the activity of a pure solid precipitate?

2. Write an expression for the solubility product of Ag_3PO_4.

3. What is the common ion affect and how does it affect solubility?

4. Why does the solubility of a metal sulfide increase as the pH of the solution is decreased?

5. Why does sparingly soluble silver chloride dissolve readily in a solution of sodium thiosulfate?

Problems

1. The solubility of silver bromide in pure water is measured to be 8.4 μg of AgBr per 100. mL of water. From this data calculate the solubility in mol/L and the solubility product of AgBr.
[4.5×10^{-7} M, 2.0×10^{-13}]

2. Calculate the solubility of $BaSO_4$ in pure water from solubility product data.   [1.0×10^{-5} M]

3. Calculate the solubility of $PbSO_4$ in pure water from solubility product data.   [1.6×10^{-4} M]

4. Calculate the solubility of $Ba(IO_3)_2$ in pure water from solubility product data.   [1.0×10^{-3} M]

5. Calculate the solubility of Hg_2Cl_2 in pure water from solubility product data.   [7.1×10^{-7} M]

6. Calculate the solubility in pure water of $CaC_2O_4 \cdot H_2O$ from solubility product data. Express your result in mol/L and g/L.   [4.8×10^{-5} M, 7.0×10^{-3} g/L]

7. Calculate the solubility in pure water of $Mg(OH)_2$ from solubility product data and find the pH of the resulting solution.   [1.1×10^{-4} M, 10.3]

8. What mass of lead bromide $PbBr_2$ can be dissolved in 150. mL of pure water?   [0.66 g]

9. Calculate the solubility in pure water of $Y(OH)_3$ from solubility product data and find the pH of the resulting solution.   [1.4×10^{-6} M, 8.6]

10. Calculate the solubility in pure water of Ag_2CrO_4 from solubility product data.   [6.5×10^{-5} M]

11. A solution initially contains Ca^{2+} ions at a concentration of 0.20 M. In what range of pH will a precipitate of $Ca(OH)_2$ form?   [pH > 11.7]

12. What is the solubility of $BaSO_4$ in a solution of 0.10 M Na_2SO_4?   [1.1×10^{-9} M]

13. Calculate the solubility of $PbSO_4$ in a solution with pH = 1.0 containing sulfate ion at a total concentration of 0.80 M, taking into account that bisulfate ion HSO_4^- is a weak acid.
[3.5×10^{-7} M]

14. A solution of potassium chromate K_2CrO_4 is added slowly to a solution containing Ag^+ at a concentration of 0.005 M, and Ba^{2+} at a concentration of 0.25 M. Which salt precipitates first? When the second salt begins to precipitate, what fraction of the cation of the first salt to precipitate remains in solution?   [$BaCrO_4$, 0.01]

15. A solution contains cupric ions Cu^{2+}, manganese ions Mn^{2+} and zinc ions Zn^{2+} at roughly equal concentrations. The solution is made basic and sodium sulfide is added, which precipitates all three metals as sulfides. A solution of sulfuric acid is added slowly, thus decreasing the pH. Which of the sulfides dissolves first, which second, and which third?
[MnS, ZnS, CuS]

16. What is the concentration of Ag^+ ions in a solution of pH = 4.0 which is in contact with solid silver sulfide?   [5×10^{-13} M]

17. The mineral galena consists of lead sulfide, PbS. If a sample of galena is in contact with a buffer solution with pH = 6.0. Calculate the concentration of lead in the solution. [5×10^{-10} M]

18. Calculate the solubility of silver bromide AgBr in a solution containing ammonia at a concentration of 0.080 M. The equilibrium constant for the equilibrium

$$Ag^+(aq) + 2\,NH_3(aq) \;\rightleftharpoons\; Ag(NH_3)_2^+(aq)$$

is $\beta_2 = 1.7 \times 10^7$. 　　　　　　　　　　　　　　　　　　　　　　　[2.4×10^{-4} M]

19. Calculate the solubility of silver bromide AgBr in a solution containing sodium chloride NaCl at a concentration of 0.080 M. The equilibrium constant for the equilibrium

$$Ag^+(aq) + 2\,Cl^-(aq) \;\rightleftharpoons\; AgCl_2^-(aq)$$

is $\beta_2 = 1.8 \times 10^5$. 　　　　　　　　　　　　　　　　　　　　　　　[2.5×10^{-5} M]

20. Calculate the solubility of silver chloride AgCl in a solution containing sodium chloride NaCl at a concentration of 0.080 M. The equilibrium constant for the equilibrium

$$Ag^+(aq) + 2\,Cl^-(aq) \;\rightleftharpoons\; AgCl_2^-(aq)$$

is $\beta_2 = 1.8 \times 10^5$. Compare your result with a calculation based only on the common ion effect.

[2.6×10^{-6} M]

16 Thermodynamics and Equilibrium

Objectives

After reading this chapter, the student should be able to do the following:

♦ Define reversible and irreversible processes.

♦ Define entropy change for a reversible process.

♦ Describe entropy change, heat and temperature.

♦ Describe the relationship between entropy and disorder.

♦ Calculate entropy changes using tabulated data.

♦ Define Gibbs energy and relate Gibbs energy change to work.

♦ Relate standard Gibbs energy change to the equilibrium constant for a chemical reaction.

Related topics to review:

Gases in Chapter 5. Thermochemistry in Chapter 6. Chemical equilibrium in Chapters 13, 14 and 15.

Related topics to look forward to:

Electrochemistry in Chapter 17.

16-1 Spontaneous chemical processes

The last three chapters have been devoted to the study of chemical equilibrium in a variety of different circumstances. In the initial stage of a chemical reaction, the concentrations or partial pressures change, and the direction of change is always towards equilibrium. Once equilibrium is reached, the concentrations and partial pressures become constant and do not change unless there is a change in the external conditions such as temperature or pressure.

A **spontaneous process** is a process that takes place without external intervention. For example, a gas flows spontaneously into a vacuum and distributes itself so that the pressure is the same throughout the volume occupied by the gas. If a metal bar is heated at one end, heat flows spontaneously from the hot end to the cold end until the temperature becomes uniform.

Many chemical reactions are spontaneous. When the reactants are mixed and the reaction begins, the products of the reaction appear without any further action on the part of the experimenter. When an acid is mixed with a base, the neutralization reaction starts at once. When a fuel starts to burn in air, the fire continues as long as some fuel remains. When a soluble salt is added to some water, the salt dissolves spontaneously, up to the limit set by the equilibrium between the solid and the dissolved solute. When exposed to damp air, metallic iron rusts spontaneously to form iron oxides and hydroxides; although the iron rusts slowly, there is no doubt about the direction of the process. If the two terminals of a flashlight battery are joined through an external circuit, the electrochemical reaction inside the battery spontaneously drives an electric current through the circuit and lights up the flashlight bulb.

In some cases, a reaction may not occur until it is initiated. For example, gasoline can be exposed to air without catching fire, but it burns vigorously once it is ignited by a match; the size of the resulting fire depends on the amount of gasoline available, and not on the size of the match. Such reactions are regarded as spontaneous, even though they may not start by themselves.

When a spontaneous chemical reaction begins, the composition of the system changes in the direction of chemical equilibrium. This can be expressed in terms of the equilibrium quotient Q, which we defined in Chapter 13. The concentrations or partial pressures change in the direction that brings the reaction quotient Q towards the equilibrium constant K. The reaction quotient Q is equal to the equilibrium constant K when equilibrium is reached.

When a chemical reaction has reached equilibrium, the concentrations or partial pressures become constant. This is not to say that nothing is happening in a system at equilibrium. At equilibrium, both the forward and the reverse reactions are taking place. But the rates of the forward and reverse reactions are equal, and hence the amounts of reactants and products in the system do not change with time.

A spontaneous process does not necessarily reduce the enthalpy of the system. If that were true, only exothermic chemical reactions would take place spontaneously. In fact, many endothermic reactions are spontaneous. Table 13-1 contains several examples of industrially important gas phase reactions which are endothermic: the steam reforming reaction, the water gas reaction and the thermal decomposition of ethane to form ethylene are all endothermic. For many soluble salts, the process of dissolving in water is endothermic; for example potassium chloride dissolves readily in water, but the enthalpy change of solution is positive. The evaporation of a liquid and the melting of a solid both require the input of the latent heat, but these endothermic processes take place spontaneously under the appropriate conditions of temperature and pressure.

Thus the spontaneous direction for a process can not predicted purely on the basis of the enthalpy change for the process. The objective of thermodynamics in the study of chemical equilibrium is to identify the principle which determines whether a given chemical process is spontaneous or not, and to establish the relationship between equilibrium constants and thermodynamic data.

16-2 Reversible processes and chemical equilibrium

In section 13-1 we stated that chemical equilibrium can be approached from either direction, and that the chemical composition of a chemical system at equilibrium does not depend on the direction from which equilibrium is approached.

Consider, for example, the reaction

$$2\,NO_2(g) \rightleftharpoons N_2O_4(g)$$

The equilibrium constant for the reaction is 6.7 at 25°C, and so both reactant and product are present in appreciable amounts at equilibrium. The reaction can proceed in either direction depending on the initial composition of the system. A mixture that is initially rich in nitrogen dioxide NO_2 would spontaneously form dinitrogen tetroxide, N_2O_4:

$$2\,NO_2(g) \rightarrow N_2O_4(g)$$

Conversely, a mixture that is initially rich in N_2O_4 would spontaneously form NO_2:

$$N_2O_4(g) \rightarrow 2\,NO_2(g)$$

With a given total mass of NO_2 and N_2O_4 in a vessel at a fixed temperature, the reaction mixture would come to the same equilibrium composition regardless of whether one starts with pure NO_2 or pure N_2O_4. Starting from the pure reactants on the left-hand side of the equation, the forward reaction is spontaneous and continues until equilibrium is reached. Starting from pure products on the right-hand side of the equation, the reverse reaction is spontaneous and continues until equilibrium is reached.

The equilibrium mixture of NO_2 and N_2O_4 can result from either the forward reaction or the reverse reaction. Chemical equilibrium is therefore associated with both the forward and reverse reactions. At equilibrium, both the forward and reverse reactions are possible, and in fact are taking place.

Each spontaneous reaction has a natural direction, which is the direction towards equilibrium. The reverse reaction, leading away from chemical equilibrium, is never seen to take place spontaneously, unless the experimenter intervenes. But spontaneous processes can be resisted, or even reversed, by external intervention. This intervention often requires the use of a mechanical force or an electrical potential. For example, consider the expansion of a compressed gas, which was our first example of a spontaneous process. For this purpose, imagine the compressed gas to be inside a cylinder fitted with a piston, as shown in Figure 16-1. An external force can be applied to the piston by means of the piston rod.

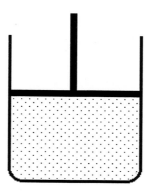

Figure 16-1 A sample of gas contained in a piston and cylinder. There is an internal force of the gas pushing on the inside of the piston. There are external forces on the outside of the piston, consisting of a mechanical force on the piston rod and the force of the atmosphere. The balance between the internal and external forces determines the movement of the piston.

Suppose that the external force on the piston is smaller than the internal force of the gas on the piston. Then the piston moves out and the gas expands spontaneously. While this expansion is taking place, the gas does work against the external force. On the other hand, if the external force on the piston is greater than the internal force of the gas, then the piston moves in and the gas is compressed. In that case, the external force does work on the gas. The gas is controlled by the piston and can be either compressed or expanded by adjusting the external force.

If the external force is adjusted so that, at every moment it is slightly smaller than the internal force of the gas, then the gas will expand gently. On the other hand, if the external force is increased slightly, the direction of the process will be reversed and the gas will be compressed gently. The process of changing the volume of the gas under these special conditions of gentle and slow change is described as a **reversible process**.

Any process can be reversed if enough effort is expended. For example, the products of a chemical reaction can usually be converted back into the reactants, by carrying out the proper sequence of chemical reactions. But a reversible process differs from a spontaneous process in an important way. A reversible process can be reversed easily by making a very small change in the external conditions. A spontaneous process can be reversed only by making a large change in the external conditions or by carrying out a complicated series of other processes. A spontaneous process is often called an **irreversible** process, even though it can usually be reversed if we try hard enough.

A chemical reaction proceeding towards equilibrium undergoes a spontaneous process. But once the reacting system reaches chemical equilibrium, the reaction becomes reversible and can be shifted slightly in either direction by small changes in external conditions, in accordance with Le Chatelier's principle. We will use the difference between reversible and spontaneous processes in thermodynamics to learn about chemical equilibrium.

16-3 Entropy

The basis for understanding the nature of irreversible processes is a quantity called the **entropy**. The definition of entropy depends on the second law of thermodynamics, which can be traced back to studies of steam engines by the French engineer Sadi Carnot in 1824. Various authors have stated the second law of thermodynamics in different ways, and full discussion of the law and its consequences is complex and beyond the level of the present book. It is sufficient to know that the second law of thermodynamics provides a firm theoretical basis for defining the entropy function and deducing its properties. Here we will summarize the important properties of the entropy, and learn how it is used to distinguish between reversible and irreversible processes.

The entropy is a function of the state of the system, like the enthalpy and the internal energy. This means that the change of the entropy of a system during a process depends only on the initial and final states of the system, and not on the path followed in that particular process. If a system consists of two parts, the entropy of the whole is the sum of the entropy of each part. The entropy is always designated by the symbol S.

The entropy change during a reversible process is related to the heat involved in the process, and the temperature. Consider a process in a system that is maintained at a constant temperature, perhaps by being immersed in a large tank of stirred water, as shown in Figure 6-3. Suppose the process is carried out very gently so it is reversible. To make this quite clear, the heat exchanged between the system and the surroundings in a reversible process is designated by the symbol q_{rev}. The change in the entropy, ΔS, in a reversible process is equal to the heat transferred to the system q_{rev} divided by the absolute temperature of the system T:

$$\Delta S = \frac{q_{rev}}{T} \qquad \text{for a reversible isothermal process.} \qquad (16\text{-}1)$$

which can also be written

$$q_{rev} = T\Delta S \qquad \text{for a reversible isothermal process.} \qquad (16\text{-}2)$$

The units of entropy are joules per kelvin.

If the process is spontaneous and irreversible, then the relationship between the entropy change ΔS, the heat q and the temperature T is an inequality rather than an equation. Consider the process of compressing a gas using the piston and cylinder shown in Figure 16-1. The work of the mechanical force required for a gentle, reversible compression is designated w'_{rev}. But if the piston is pushed in suddenly with a greater force than necessary, then more work w' is done on the gas than would be required for a gentle, reversible compression. Hence the work required for irreversible compression, w', is greater than the work required fior a reversible compression, w'_{rev}. Putting this algebraically, $w' > w'_{rev}$.

The same inequality is true for expansion of the gas, rather than compression. A gas expanding spontaneously does less work than it would if the expansion were gentle and reversible. Because the work of expansion is negative, however, the algebraic relationship is the same: $w' > w'_{rev}$.

A similar analysis can be applied to electrochemical processes, such as charging and discharging a car battery.

For a given initial state and a given final state of the system, the sum of the heat q and the mechanical or electrical work w' is always the same regardless of whether the process is reversible or not. This was the conclusion that we drew from Joule's experiments, and expressed in terms of the enthalpy function in Chapter 6. For any two processes with the same initial and final states, one of which is reversible, the enthalpy change must be the same for both processes, so we can write:

$$\Delta H = q + w' = q_{rev} + w'_{rev}$$

Since the sum of the heat and the work is the same for the two processes, it follows that if w' is larger than w'_{rev}, then q must be smaller than q_{rev}. In mathematical terms, if $w' > w'_{rev}$ then $q < q_{rev}$. From equation (16-2), $q_{rev} = T\Delta S$ and hence the last inequality can be written:

$$q < T\Delta S \qquad \text{for an irreversible isothermal process.} \qquad (16\text{-}3)$$

This can also be written: $\qquad \Delta S > \dfrac{q}{T} \qquad$ for an irreversible isothermal process. $\qquad (16\text{-}4)$

Equations (16-2) and (16-3) can be combined into a single equation:

$$q \leq T\Delta S \quad \text{or} \quad q - T\Delta S \leq 0 \qquad \text{for any isothermal process.} \qquad (16\text{-}5)$$

The equality applies if the process is reversible, and the inequality applies if the process is spontaneous or irreversible. The entropy is a state function, and so the entropy change is always the same for fixed initial and final states of the system. Equations (16-5) gives the relationship between the heat q, which varies according to how the process is carried out, and the entropy change ΔS, which has a fixed value once the initial and final states of the system are specified.

If a process is adiabatic, no heat is exchanged between the system and its surroundings, and $q = 0$. In a reversible adiabatic process, the entropy of the system does not change, and the entropy change ΔS is zero. In a spontaneous adiabatic process, the entropy change ΔS is positive and the entropy of the system increases. In no case does the entropy of the system decrease in an adiabatic process. This can be stated in mathematical terms:

$$T\Delta S \geq 0 \qquad \text{for any adiabatic process} \qquad (16\text{-}6)$$

Example 16-1 A hot piece of metal at a temperature of 50.0°C is briefly placed in a tank of water at 15.0°C and then removed. While the metal is in the water, 100. joules of heat flows from the metal to the water, but the temperatures of both metal and water hardly change as a result of the heat transfer. Calculate the entropy changes of the metal, the water and the combined system of water and metal as a result of the heat transfer.

During the brief time when the metal is immersed in the water, the temperature of the metal and the temperature of the water hardly change. Hence for the piece of metal,

$$q_{metal} = -100.0 \text{ J, and } T = 323.2 \text{ K so } \Delta S_{metal} = -\frac{100. \text{ J}}{323.2 \text{ K}} = -0.309 \text{ J K}^{-1}$$

For the water,

$$q_{water} = +100.\ \text{J, and } T = 288.2 \text{ K, so } \Delta S_{water} = +\frac{100.\ \text{J}}{288.2 \text{ K}} = +0.347 \text{ J K}^{-1}$$

For the combined system, $\Delta S_{combined} = -0.309 + 0.347 = +0.038 \text{ J K}^{-1}$

Notice that the entropy of the combined system increases because the heat flows spontaneously from the hot metal to the cooler water.

In this example the piece of metal can be regarded as the system, and the tank of water as representing the whole of the surroundings. Clearly the transfer of heat from the hot metal to the cold water is spontaneous and irreversible. Recalling now that the system and the surroundings together constitute the whole of the universe, the calculation shows that in this spontaneous process the entropy of the universe increases.

Further analysis shows that the entropy of the universe increases in every spontaneous process. One way to understand this is as follows. By definition, the universe contains everything, so heat cannot enter or leave the universe. If we regard the universe as a single system, every process in the universe is adiabatic, and as we discussed in the paragraph above Example 16-1, the entropy of the universe must therefore increase whenever a spontaneous process occurs. Arguments such as this may seem to belong more in the field of cosmology (or even philosophy) rather than chemistry, but the conclusion has important implications in many fields of science.

16-4 Entropy changes in Simple Processes

We now turn to calculations of entropy changes for various simple chemical process. Entropy changes in chemical reactions will be considered in a later section of this chapter. The way to calculate entropy changes is to imagine a reversible process by which the system changes from the specified initial state to the specified final state.

The entropy change for a change of phase, such as boiling, is easy to calculate, since the process is isothermal and reversible: adding heat evaporates some liquid and removing heat condenses some vapour. The entropy change of boiling ΔS_b is the latent heat of boiling ΔH_b divided by the boiling point temperature T_b:

$$\Delta S_b = \frac{\Delta H_b}{T_b} \tag{16-7}$$

Trouton's rule expressed in equation (7-1) can now be interpreted as a statement that the entropy change of boiling has a characteristic value of 75 to 85 J K^{-1} mol^{-1} for most liquids, and is a little higher for hydrogen bonded liquids.

Example 16-2 Calculate the entropy of vaporization per mole of water at the boiling point, from data on the latent heat given in Table 7-1.

From Table 7-1, the latent heat of vaporization at the boiling point is 40.65 kJ/mol, and the temperature is 373.15 K. Hence the entropy change is:

$$\Delta S = \frac{40650 \text{ J mol}^{-1}}{373.15 \text{ K}} = 108.9 \text{ J K}^{-1} \text{ mol}^{-1}$$

The entropy change due to a change of temperature can be calculated by considering a gradual transfer of heat. The temperature of a system can be increased reversibly by adding heat gradually to the system from a succession of water baths with slightly different temperatures, each a little warmer than the previous one. There should never be a large difference between the system and its surroundings, since heat transfer across a substantial temperature difference is irreversible, as we saw in Example 16-1.

From the definition of heat capacity in equation (6-9), a temperature change ΔT in a system at constant pressure with a heat capacity C_p requires heat $q = C_p \Delta T$, so the entropy change for a small change of temerpature is:

$$\Delta S = \frac{C_p \Delta T}{T} \tag{16-8}$$

It is necessary to specify whether the pressure or the volume is to be kept constant. If there is a significant temperature change during the process, then the entropy change must be calculated by integration, which gives the following result:

$$\Delta S = C_p \ln \frac{T_2}{T_1} \tag{16-9}$$

where T_1 and T_2 are the initial and final temperatures.

Example 16-3   Calculate the entropy change when 3.00 moles of water are heated at constant pressure from 25.°C to 45.°C.

From Appendix 1, the molar heat capacity of water at constant pressure is $C_p = 75.291 \text{ J K}^{-1} \text{ mol}^{-1}$, so the total heat capacity of the water is 3.00 times this, or 225.87 J K^{-1}. Hence the entropy change is:

$$\Delta S = 225.87 \ln \frac{318.2}{298.2} = 14.7 \text{ J K}^{-1}$$

Example 16-4   A hot piece of metal with a heat capacity of 2000. J K^{-1} at a temperature of 50.0°C is placed in an insulated tank of water with a heat capacity of 4000. J K^{-1} at 15.0°C. Calculate the final temperatures of both metal and water, and the entropy changes of the metal, the water and the combined system consisting of the metal and the water.

Let T be the final temperature of both metal and water. Since the total system is insulated, the net heat is zero. For the water the heat is $4000 \times (T - 15.0)$, and for the metal the heat is $2000 \times (T - 50.0)$ so, with temperatures expressed in Celsius for the moment,

$$2000 \times (T - 50.0) + 4000 \times (T - 15.0) = 0$$

which can be solved for the final temperature: $T = 26.7°C = 299.9$ K.

Since the temperatures of both the metal and the water have changed significantly during the process, the entropy changes are calculated by equation (16-9):

$$\Delta S_{metal} = 2000 \ln \frac{299.9}{323.2} = -149.6 \text{ J K}^{-1}$$

$$\Delta S_{water} = 4000 \ln \frac{299.9}{288.2} = +159.2 \text{ J K}^{-1}$$

$$\Delta S_{combined} = -149.6 + 159.2 = +9.6 \text{ J K}^{-1}$$

16-5 Entropy and disorder

Much effort has been put into study of the theoretical basis of the entropy function and its relationship to the properties of the atoms and molecules of which matter is made. This subject is called **statistical mechanics**, and was pioneered by Ludwig Boltzmann in Austria and Willard Gibbs in the United States. These studies have shown that entropy increases if the disorder in the system increases. The relationship is a logarithmic one. The entropy of a system in a given state is proportional to the logarithm of the number of ways W in which the molecules of the system can be assigned to molecular energy states, consistent with the state of the system:

$$S = k_B \ln W \tag{16-10}$$

where k_B is called the Boltzmann constant and is equal to R/N_a, the gas constant divided by the Avogadro constant. Interpretation and use of equation (16-10) is not straightforward, but its simplicity makes it attractive for discussion, and in fact it is engraved on Boltzmann's gravestone.

Each way of assigning the individual molecules to molecular energy levels is called a **microstate** of the system. The number of microstates that are available in a system is a measure of the disorder in the system. The tendency for entropy to increase in an adiabatic irreversible process implies that the number of microstates tends to increase. In an irreversible process the degree of disorder increases.

As an example, think of a pack of cards. If all the cards are required to be in a definite order of suits, and in numerical order within each suit, then only one arrangement of the cards is possible. If the limitation on numerical order were relaxed, so that the order of suits is specified but the cards can be in any order within each suit, then there is a huge number W of different possible arrangements of the cards which satisfies this requirement. If no limitation at all is placed on how the cards are to be ordered, there is an even larger number of possible arrangements of the cards.

If a pack of cards arranged in a specific order, (for instance, in a specific order of suits and in numerical order within suits) were thrown across the room and picked up at random, it is almost certain that the cards would be in a different order afterwards. It is possible that by accident the cards would be picked in the same order that they were in before being thrown, but it is so unlikely that the possibility can be ignored. The disorder will increase irreversibly simply because of the laws of probability. Through the Boltzmann relationship, equation (16-10), the increase in entropy in an adiabatic irreversible process is the result of increased disorder in the system. Because ordinary chemical systems contain so many molecules (of the order of 10^{23}) and each molecule has so many possible states available to it, the increase in disorder in irreversible processes becomes a certainty because the probability that the system becomes more ordered is unimaginably small.

The number of microstates available to the molecules of a gas is proportional to the volume occupied by the gas. Hence if the temperature is kept constant, the entropy of an ideal gas varies logarithmically with volume. For an isothermal expansion or compression of an ideal gas from initial volume V_1 to final volume V_2, the entropy change per mole of gas is:

$$\Delta S = R \ln \frac{V_2}{V_1} \qquad (16\text{-}11)$$

where R is the gas constant. The proof of this equation is not complicated but requires the use of calculus and is omitted here. If the gas is ideal and obeys Boyle's law, then $P_1 V_1 = P_2 V_2$ because the temperature is constant, and so

$$\frac{V_2}{V_1} = \frac{P_1}{P_2}$$

Replacing the ratio of volumes by the ratio of pressures, and remembering the properties of the logarithm function, the entropy change for an isothermal change of pressure is:

$$\Delta S = -R \ln \frac{P_2}{P_1} \qquad (16\text{-}12)$$

Example 16-5 Calculate the entropy change when 2.00 moles of an ideal gas expand isothermally so that the pressure decreases from 250.0 kPa to 100.0 kPa.

For one mole, the entropy change is calculated from equation (16-12):

$$\Delta S = -8.314 \ln \frac{100.0}{250.0} = 7.618 \text{ J K}^{-1} \text{ mol}^{-1}$$

and so the total entropy change is $\Delta S = 7.618 \times 2.00 = 15.24 \text{ J K}^{-1}$.

In the previous section we have seen that the entropy of a system increases logarithmically with temperature, as stated in equation (16-9). In the statistical interpretation of thermodynamics, an increase in temperature makes more microstates available to the system, resulting in an increase in entropy. Figure 16-2 shows the distribution of molecular speeds in a gas at two different temperatures, as an extension of Figure 5-9. At higher temperatures, the average speed increases, the distribution extends to higher velocities, and the larger range of velocities occupied by the molecules is reflected in the higher entropy.

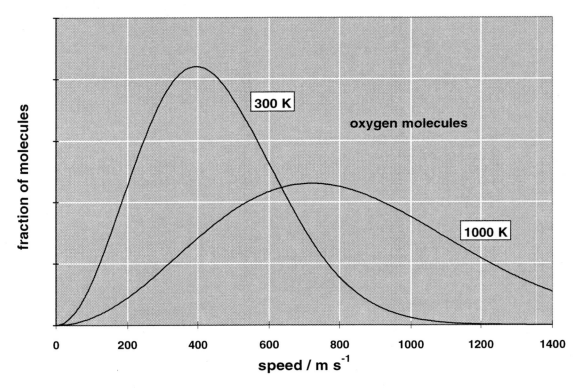

Figure 16-2 The distribution of molecular speeds in oxygen at two temperatures, 300 K and 1000 K. At the higher temperature the molecular speeds are distributed over a wider range, so that more microstates of the system are occupied.

The statement that the entropy of the universe cannot decrease, which was stated in equation (16-6), has been a source of fascination for philosophers for more than a century. The German physicist Rudolph Clausius summarized the first and second laws of thermodynamics in two succinct statements:

> *The energy of the universe is constant.*
>
> *The entropy of the universe tends to a maximum.*

If the direction of time were reversed, purely mechanical systems would simply run backwards because Newton's laws of motion would not be affected. The world would evolve like a film run backwards through the projector or a video run in reverse. But the second law gives a fundamental indication of which is the correct direction of evolution of time. Since everything that happens spontaneously increases the entropy of the universe, the positive direction of time is the direction of increased entropy of the universe. The ultimate fate of the universe therefore is the state in which the entropy has reached an absolute maximum. The universe will run down, not because of loss of energy, but because of gain of entropy.

Life processes might seem to violate the second law, since a living organism is so beautifully organized in a complex structure, formed out of water, carbon dioxide and nutrients. The Boltzmann equation (16-10) shows that the highly ordered, complex structures found in plants and animals have low entropy. But plants and animals do not live in isolation from their surroundings. A complex living organism can only be made and maintained with the constant input of *energy*, and this increases the entropy of the surroundings enough that the entropy of the universe as a whole increases.

16-6 Entropy changes in chemical reactions

Measurement of entropy changes in spontaneous chemical reactions cannot be done directly. For a chemical reaction under constant external pressure the heat q is equal to ΔH but the quotient $\Delta H/T$ does not measure the entropy change. This is because the reaction is spontaneous, not reversible, and the equality sign in equation (16-5) does not apply. This is a very important point to emphasize: only for a reversible process is the entropy change equal to q/T. For a spontaneous chemical reaction, the entropy change of reaction can only be determined by an indirect method.

The entropy of every substance decreases at low temperature, partly because of the temperature dependence expressed in equation (16-9), and partly because of the entropy decrease when gases condense and liquids freeze. At very low temperatures, the heat capacity approaches zero and the entropy approaches a constant value.

As the temperature decreases the number of microstates accessible to the system decreases, reflecting the increasing order of the molecules as gases become liquids and then solids in which the molecules have lost much of their freedom to move around. The Boltzmann equation (16-10) suggests that if a substance were to become completely ordered, so that $W = 1$ and only one microstate were possible, then the entropy would be zero.

The third law of thermodynamics states that entropy of a substance approaches zero as the temperature approaches absolute zero, unless the solid is disordered. Although the law cannot be proved, it is consistent with the Boltzmann equation and with the failure of all attempts to obtain a temperature of exactly zero kelvin. The lowest temperature reached is of order 10^{-6} kelvin, but the absolute zero has never been achieved.

Although the third law seems like an abstruse piece of physics, it is important for chemistry because it provides a method of calculating the entropy changes for chemical reactions. The absolute entropy of a substance at an ordinary temperature can be calculated if the heat capacity is measured from very low temperatures up to room temperature. Appendix 1 lists the absolute entropies S^o of elements and compounds in their standard states at 25°C in the third column of numbers, which can be used to calculate entropy changes for chemical reactions. The entropies of some ions in solution are included in the table. These values are based upon the (arbitrary) assignment that the entropy of the hydrogen ion, $H^+(aq)$ is zero.

The principle of the calculation is that since all entropies are zero at zero kelvin, the entropy change for any reaction is zero at that temperature. For the general chemical reaction at any temperature,

$$aA \quad + \quad bB \quad \rightarrow \quad cC \quad + \quad dD$$

the entropy change is $\qquad \Delta S = -aS^o(A) - bS^o(B) + cS^o(C) + dS^o(D)$ \hfill (16-13)

The principle of the calculation is illustrated in Figure 16-3. Note that the absolute entropy of an element is not zero, and must be included in the calculation.

Example 16-6 Calculate ΔS^o for the reaction $C(s) + O_2(g) \rightarrow CO_2(g)$ from standard state entropies at 298 K.

The standard state entropies from Appendix 1 are as shown:

$$C(s) + O_2(g) \rightarrow CO_2(g)$$

$$\Delta S^o = -5.740 - 205.138 + 213.74 = +2.86 \text{ J K}^{-1} \text{ mol}^{-1}.$$

Since the reaction given in Example 16-6 is the reaction in which carbon dioxide is formed from the elements, with all substances being in the standard state, the result can be referred to as the standard entropy change of formation of CO_2:

$$\Delta S_f^o (CO_2) = +2.86 \text{ J}^{-1} \text{ K}^{-1} \text{ mol}^{-1}$$

However entropies of formation are not usually tabulated since the absolute entropies are more useful.

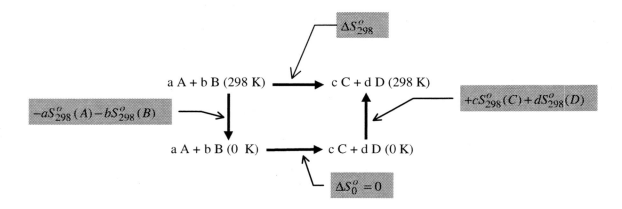

Figure 16-3 The method used to calculate the standard entropy of reaction at 298 K from the absolute entropies of the reactants and products. The entropy change is shown for the various steps which make up two pathways from reactants to products at 298 K. The entropy change of reaction is zero at absolute zero since the absolute entropy of every substance is zero at that temperature, by the third law of thermodynamics.

Reactions involving the production of gases from solid or liquid reactants tend to have positive entropy changes, while reactions in which gaseous reactants are converted to solids or liquids tend to have negative entropy changes. The entropy of vaporization calculated in Example 16-2 is an example of the former, and the following is an example of the latter.

Example 16-7 Calculate the standard entropy change at 298 K for $H_2(g) + \frac{1}{2} O_2(g) \rightarrow H_2O(\lambda)$

For the reaction $\qquad\qquad H_2(g) + \frac{1}{2} O_2(g) \rightarrow H_2O(\lambda)$

the standard entropy change is: $\quad \Delta S^o = -130.684 - 0.5 \times 205.138 + 69.91 = -163.34 \text{ J K}^{-1} \text{ mol}^{-1}.$

Reactions in solution involving ions sometimes follow a similar pattern: if the number of independent molecules or ions increases, then the entropy increases. However, this is not always the case, as the following examples show.

Example 16-8 Calculate the standard entropy change of solution per mole of sodium chloride in water at 298 K.

The process can be written $NaCl(s) \rightarrow Na^+(aq) + Cl^-(aq)$

The standard entropy is listed in Appendix 1 both for the solid salt and for the ions in aqueous solution. The standard entropy change of solution is :

$\Delta S° = -72.13 + 59.0 + 56.5 = +43.4 \, J \, K^{-1} \, mol^{-1}$.

Example 16-9 Calculate the standard entropy of ionization of one mole of acetic acid in aqueous solution at 298 K.

The process can be written: $CH_3COOH(aq) \rightarrow H^+(aq) + CH_3COO^-(aq)$

Reading data from Appendix 1, the standard entropy change of ionization is:

$\Delta S° = -178.7 + 0.0 + 86.6 = -92.1 \, J \, K^{-1} \, mol^{-1}$.

These two contrasting examples invite comment. When NaCl dissolves in water the Na^+ and Cl^- ions are released from the crystal and are able to move about in the solution; the ions in solution are more disordered in solution than in the crystal, and so the increase in entropy is not unexpected. In example 6-12, we showed that enthalpy change $\Delta H°$ for the process is small and positive, so that the process of dissolving is slightly unfavourable from the point of view of the energy. The solubility of the salt in water is high because of the favourable standard entropy change.

A similar situation might be expected when acetic acid ionizes, since two ions are formed from a single molecule, and the two ions have more freedom to move around in solution than the single molecule. In example 6-14, we showed that enthalpy change $\Delta H°$ for the process is very close to zero, so that there is no significant energy barrier to ionization. However Example 16-9, above, shows that the standard entropy of ionization of acetic acid is strongly negative, and as a result acetic acid is a weak acid and is only partly ionized in solution. The negative standard entropy change of ionization shows that the solution containing the ionized acid would be more ordered than a solution of molecular acetic acid.

There are two possible reasons why a solution is more ordered when the solute is ionized than when it is not. Water molecules have a large electric dipole moment and hence interact with the electric field generated by the ions. Around each positively charged cation, the water molecules tend to be oriented with the negatively charged oxygen atoms closest to the ion, and around each negatively charged anion the water molecules tend to be oriented with the positively charged hydrogen atoms closest to the ion. The orientational disorder of the water molecules is reduced and the entropy of the solution as a whole is smaller. Orientational ordering of the water molecules occurs in both solutions of sodium chloride and solutions of acetic acid. The case of the acid is different from that of a salt, however, because ionization of an acid results in the formation of a hydrogen ion. The "bare" hydrogen ion (or proton) becomes covalently bonded to one or more water molecules, to form the hydronium ion H_3O^+ or larger ions which can be written $H(H_2O)_n^+$. Thus one or more water molecules is involved in the ionization process, which can be written:

$$CH_3COOH(aq) + nH_2O \rightarrow H(H_2O)_n^+(aq) + CH_3COO^-(aq)$$

The strongly negative entropy of ionization suggests that n is at least as big as 2.

16-7 Gibbs energy

In order to take into account both energy and entropy considerations in determining whether a process is spontaneous or not, a thermodynamic function called the **Gibbs energy** is defined. From this function alone, the spontaneity of a process and the equilibrium situation can be determined under conditions that are of particular relevance to chemistry. The function is named for J. Willard Gibbs, the American scientist who laid the foundations of chemical thermodynamics about a century ago. This function used to be called the Gibbs free energy, or sometimes just the free energy.

The Gibbs energy is defined by the equation

$$G = H - TS. \tag{16-14}$$

Since H, T and S are state functions, the Gibbs energy is also a state function. This means that numerical values of the Gibbs energy can be tabulated for various substances and for various conditions of temperature etc. Data on the standard Gibbs energy change of formation are listed in Appendix 1, and may be used to calculate Gibbs energy changes in chemical reactions in a manner similar to that used for enthalpy change of reaction.

The Gibbs energy is particularly useful under conditions of constant temperature and constant external pressure. These are the conditions to be found in many laboratory experiments in which chemical reactions are carried out at constant temperature and the system is open to the atmosphere. For a process that takes the system from an initial state 1 to a final state 2, the change in the Gibbs energy of the system is

$$\Delta G = (H_2 - T_2 S_2) - (H_1 - T_1 S_1)$$

For an isothermal process at temperature T, the initial and final temperatures are equal to T and the entropy terms can be gathered together with a common factor:

$$\Delta G = (H_2 - H_1) - T(S_2 - S_1) = \Delta H - T\Delta S$$

But for a process at constant external pressure, the enthalpy change is the sum of the heat and the electrical or mechanical work, $\Delta H = q + w'$, and hence:

$$\Delta G = q + w' - T\Delta S$$

Earlier in this chapter, in equation (16-5), we showed that for any isothermal process, $q - T\Delta S \leq 0$. Since $q - T\Delta S$ must be zero or negative, it follows that:

$$\Delta G \leq w' \quad \text{at constant temperature and pressure} \tag{16-15}$$

In this equation, the equality sign applies only if the process is reversible, and the inequality applies if the process is irreversible. The implications of equation (16-15) for electrochemical processes will be discussed in Chapter 17.

For a chemical reaction to proceed spontaneously without electrochemical or mechanical work, equation (16-15) must be satisfied with $w' = 0$, which means that the Gibbs energy change must be zero or negative:

$$\Delta G \leq 0 \text{ at constant temperature and pressure} \qquad (16\text{-}16)$$

The equality sign applies if the process is reversible, and the inequality sign applies if the process is irreversible.

Under conditions of chemical equilibrium, the reaction is reversible and hence the Gibbs energy change ΔG for a small amount of reaction at equilibrium is zero. If the system is not at equilibrium, then ΔG for the reaction leading towards equilibrium is negative. As the extent of reaction changes spontaneously towards the equilibrium situation, the Gibbs energy decreases as a result of the changing composition of the system until a minimum value is reached. When a minimum in the Gibbs energy is reached, the system is in chemical equilibrium. Any small changes away from equilibrium then are reversible because they can go in either direction in response to very small changes in conditions, and correspondingly $\Delta G = 0$. The Gibbs energy in a chemical system plotted as a function of the extent of reaction is shown in Figure 16-4.

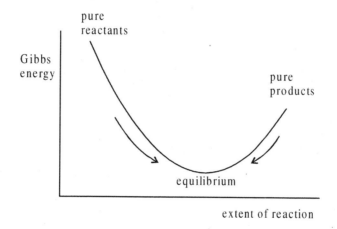

Figure 16-4 A diagram showing how the Gibbs energy comes to a minimum at equilibrium. The arrows show the spontaneous reactions that lead towards equilibrium at the minimum in the Gibbs energy. The same equilibrium is reached regardless of whether a reaction starts from the substances on the left hand side of the equation, the "reactants", or from the substances on the right hand side, the "products".

An analogy is helpful in understanding this argument. Imagine a ball rolling on a surface like the inside of a soup bowl or a skateboard bowl. If released from rest, the ball runs downhill spontaneously so that the gravitational potential energy of the ball decreases. The ball is at equilibrium on the surface only at the lowest point where the potential energy is a minimum. Starting from rest, the ball moves in whatever direction decreases its potential energy, unless it is already at a minimum in the surface. A ball at equilibrium at the bottom of the bowl can move easily a small distance in any direction; such movements are reversible, unlike the spontaneous motion down the sides of the bowl.

The Gibbs energy plays the same role for a chemical system as the gravitational potential energy plays for a purely mechanical system. For a chemical system at constant temperature and pressure, the condition under which the Gibbs energy is a minimum is the condition of chemical equilibrium. Hence the problem of calculating the equilibrium condition becomes equivalent to finding the minimum in the Gibbs energy for that particular system. This is done by finding the conditions under which ΔG for the reaction is zero. The calculation requires knowing the Gibbs energy change of reaction when the reactants and products are in their standard states and the dependence of Gibbs energy on partial pressure or concentration. These are considered in the next two sections.

16-8 Standard Gibbs energy of formation

From the definition of the Gibbs energy, $G = H - TS$, it follows that $\Delta G = \Delta H - T\Delta S$ for any process at constant temperature. Hence for a particular substance the Gibbs energy change of formation ΔG_f can be calculated from the enthalpy change of formation ΔH_f and the entropy change of formation ΔS_f, for a given state of the substance. The calculation is illustrated in Example 16-10.

Example 16-10 Calculate the Gibbs energy of formation of carbon dioxide from the enthalpy change of formation and the absolute entropy at 298.15 K.

From Appendix 1, the enthalpy change of formation of $CO_2(g)$ is $\Delta H_f^o = -393.509$ kJ mol^{-1}. From Example 16-6, the entropy change of formation of $CO_2(g)$ was calculated from the absolute entropies of $C(s)$, $O_2(g)$ and $CO_2(g)$, with the result $\Delta S_f^o = +2.86$ J K^{-1} mol^{-1}. Hence the Gibbs energy change of formation of $CO_2(g)$ is:

$$\Delta G_f^o = \Delta H_f^o - T\Delta S_f^o = -393.509 - 298.15 \times (+2.86 \times 10^{-3}) = -394.36 \text{ kJ mol}^{-1}$$

This agrees with the value listed for $CO_2(g)$ in the second column of numbers in Appendix 1.

Data on the Gibbs energy of formation of a number of compounds in their standard states are tabulated in Appendix 1. It should be noted that the Gibbs energy of formation of an element in its standard state is zero, for the same reason that the enthalpy change of formation of an element in its standard state is zero. From data on the Gibbs energy of formation for compounds given in Appendix 1, the standard Gibbs energy change of reaction can be calculated by the same process as that used for the enthalpy change of reaction. For a general chemical reaction,

$$aA \quad + \quad bB \quad \rightarrow \quad cC \quad + \quad dD$$

$$\Delta G^o = -a\Delta G_f^o(A) - b\Delta G_f^o(B) + c\Delta G_f^o(C) + d\Delta G_f^o(D) \qquad (16\text{-}17)$$

Example 16-11 Calculate ΔG° at 298 K for the reaction: $2\,NO_2(g) \rightarrow N_2O_4(g)$.

For the reaction $2\,NO_2(g) \rightarrow N_2O_4(g)$

$$\Delta G^o = -2 \times \Delta G_f^o(NO_2(g)) + \Delta G_f^o(N_2O_4(g)) = -2 \times (51.31) + (+97.89) = -4.73 \text{ kJ mol}^{-1}$$

The standard Gibbs energy change ΔG° for a reaction does not indicate the spontaneous direction of the reaction except under standard state conditions. If ΔG° is negative, it means that the reaction in which reactants in their standard state are converted to products in their standard state is spontaneous. If ΔG° is positive, it means that the reaction with all substances in their standard states is not spontaneous. However, a positive ΔG° does not mean that the reaction does not occur at all, only that the equilibrium constant is smaller than 1 and the reverse reaction is favoured.

At a particular temperature, the equilibrium constant can be calculated from the standard Gibbs energy change, as we see in the next section.

16-9 Gibbs energy and the equilibrium constant

Since entropy is a function of temperature and pressure, the Gibbs energy of a substance also varies with its temperature and pressure. In a reacting mixture, the Gibbs energy of the system changes as the reaction proceeds, because the partial pressures or concentrations of the substances involved change. We therefore need to know how the Gibbs energy of a substance varies with its pressure or concentration.

For an ideal gas the enthalpy H does not vary with pressure, and the pressure dependence of the Gibbs energy is due entirely to the pressure dependence of the entropy, which can be calculated from equation (16-12). The difference in Gibbs energy per mole of an ideal gas between two states at two pressures P_1 and P_2, but at the same temperature, is:

$$G(P_2) - G(P_1) = RT \ln \frac{P_2}{P_1} \tag{16-18}$$

We can apply this formula to show how the Gibbs energy of an ideal gas varies with its partial pressure. If we replace P_2 by the partial pressure p of the gas, and P_1 by the standard state pressure P°, then the equation reads as follows:

$$G(p) - G(P^o) = RT \ln \frac{p}{P^o}$$

or in a slightly different notation,

$$G = G^o + RT \ln \frac{p}{P^o} \tag{16-19}$$

In this equation, G is the molar Gibbs energy of this particular substance at partial pressure p and at the specified temperature, and G° is the molar Gibbs energy at the standard pressure $P^{\circ} = 100$ kPa.

In Chapter 13, equation (13-3), we introduced the concept of the **relative activity** a of a substance in a gaseous mixture, which is equal to p/P° as long as the pressure is not too high. With this identification, the Gibbs energy for a particular substance can be written:

$$G = G^o + RT \ln a \tag{16-20}$$

In solution, the relative activity of a solute is approximately equal to the ratio of concentration to the standard state concentration as discussed in Section 14-2:

$$a \approx \frac{c}{c^o}$$

The relationship between Gibbs energy and concentration of a solute in solution is still given by the equation (16-20), and so:

$$G \approx G^o + RT \ln \frac{c}{c^o} \tag{16-21}$$

Equations (16-17) and (16-20) are the basis for calculation of the equilibrium constant. Knowing how the Gibbs energy depends on partial pressure or concentration, we can now calculate the Gibbs energy change for the reaction under any general condition from the standard Gibbs energy change. Consider the following reaction:

$$aA \quad + \quad bB \quad \rightarrow \quad cC \quad + \quad dD$$

In the thermodynamic cycle shown in Figure 16-5, the Gibbs energy change ΔG under general conditions is shown by the top horizontal arrow, and the standard Gibbs energy change $\Delta G°$ corresponds to the bottom horizontal arrow, for the reaction under standard conditions.

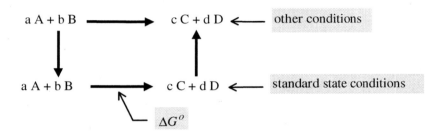

Figure 16-5 The scheme used for calculating the Gibbs energy change for a reaction under general conditions. The reaction at the top is carried out under general conditions, with relative activities other than unity. The reaction at the bottom arrow is carried out with both the reactants and products in their standard states. The two steps indicated by the vertical arrows change the states of the reactants and products by changing partial pressures or concentrations.

The Gibbs energy change of each reactant and product in the processes indicated by the two vertical arrows can be calculated by applying equation (16-20) to each substance:

$$G(A) = G°(A) + RT \ln a(A)$$

$$G(B) = G°(B) + RT \ln a(B)$$

$$G(C) = G°(C) + RT \ln a(C)$$

$$G(D) = G°(D) + RT \ln a(D)$$

Adding these equations together with coefficients of respectively $-a$, $-b$, $+c$ and $+d$ then yields the following:

$$-aG(A) - bG(B) + cG(C) + dG(D)$$
$$= -aG°(A) - bG°(B) + cG°(C) + dG°(D) + RT\{-a \ln a(A) - b \ln a(B) + c \ln a(C) + d \ln a(D)\}$$
$$= -aG°(A) - bG°(B) + cG°(C) + dG°(D) + RT \ln \frac{a(C)^c a(D)^d}{a(A)^a a(B)^b}$$

in which the terms can be gathered together to form familiar quantities:

$$\Delta G = \Delta G° + RT \ln Q \tag{16-22}$$

where Q is the reaction quotient defined in equation (13-5):

$$Q = \frac{a(C)^c \, a(D)^d}{a(A)^a \, a(B)^b}$$

This equation applies to all conditions of the system which are consistent with the laws of stoichiometry, including the condition of equilibrium. Equation (16-22) will be used in the discussion of electrochemistry in the next chapter.

For the condition of equilibrium, the reaction process is reversible, and so under these conditions, $\Delta G = 0$, and the reaction quotient Q is equal to the equilibrium constant K. Hence equation (16-22) becomes:

$$0 = \Delta G^o + RT \ln K$$

This equation can be rearranged to give:

$$\ln K = -\frac{\Delta G^o}{RT} \quad \text{or} \quad K = \exp\left(-\frac{\Delta G^0}{RT}\right) \tag{16-23}$$

This equation allows calculation of the equilibrium constant for a reaction from the standard Gibbs energy of formation data in Appendix 1, and several examples follow. The equation can be applied to reactions in the gas phase or in solution, or in more than one phase, as long as the relative activity and the standard states are properly interpreted.

It follows from equation (16-23) that a negative ΔG° corresponds to an equilibrium constant K greater than 1, while a positive ΔG° corresponds to a K value less than 1. If the stoichiometric coefficients of the chemical equation are all doubled, the standard Gibbs energy change for the reaction is doubled and the equilibrium constant is squared. This is consistent with the discussion of the properties of the equilibrium constant in Chapter 13, and follows from the exponential relationship between ΔG° and K.

Example 16-12 Calculate the equilibrium constant at 298 K for the reaction

$$2 \, NO_2(g) \; \rightleftharpoons \; N_2O_4(g).$$

In Example 16-11, we calculated $\Delta G^\circ = -4.73$ kJ mol^{-1}, and so:

$$K = \exp\left(-\frac{(-4730)}{8.3145 \times 298.2}\right) = 6.7$$

Example 16-13 Calculate the equilibrium constant at 298 K for the reaction

$$N_2(g) + 3/2 \, H_2(g) \; \rightleftharpoons \; NH_3(g)$$

The standard Gibbs energy change for the reaction is just the standard Gibbs energy of formation of ammonia, which is -16.45 kJ mol^{-1}. Hence:

$$K = \exp\left(-\frac{(-16450)}{8.3145 \times 298.2}\right) = 7.6 \times 10^2$$

Example 16-14 Calculate the equilibrium constant at 298 K for the steam reforming reaction between methane and steam (Table 13-1):

$$CH_4(g) + H_2O(g) \rightleftharpoons CO(g) + 3 H_2(g)$$

The standard Gibbs energy change for the reaction is:

$$\Delta G^o = -(-50.72) - (-228.572) + (-137.168) + 3 \times 0 = +142.12 \text{ kJ mol}^{-1}$$

and hence

$$K = \exp\left(-\frac{(+142120)}{8.3145 \times 298.2}\right) = 1.3 \times 10^{-25}$$

Example 16-15 Calculate the equilibrium constant for ionization of acetic acid in aqueous solution at 25°C.

The ionization process is: $CH_3COOH(aq) \rightleftharpoons CH_3COO^-(aq) + H^+(aq)$

The standard Gibbs energy change is:

$$\Delta G^o = -(-396.46) + (-369.31) + (0) = +27.15 \text{ kJ mol}^{-1}$$

and hence

$$K = \exp\left(-\frac{(+27150)}{8.3145 \times 298.2}\right) = 1.75 \times 10^{-5}$$

This result agrees with the value of K_a given in Table 14-2. The positive value of ΔG° reflects the fact that acetic acid is not a strong acid. Since the standard enthalpy of ionization of acetic acid in aqueous solution is very close to zero (see Example 6-14), the positive value of ΔG° is due entirely to the negative standard entropy of ionization (see Example 16-9).

Example 16-16 Calculate the vapour pressure of water at 25°C.

The equilibrium between liquid water and water vapour can be written

$$H_2O(\lambda) \rightleftharpoons H_2O(g)$$

and so the standard Gibbs energy change is :

$$\Delta G^o = -(-237.129) + (-228.572) = +8.557 \text{ kJ mol}^{-1}$$

and hence

$$K = \exp\left(-\frac{(+8557)}{8.3145 \times 298.2}\right) = 3.17 \times 10^{-2}$$

Writing the expression for the equilibrium constant,

$$K = \frac{a(g)}{a(l)} = \frac{p/P^o}{1} = \frac{p}{P^o} = 3.17 \times 10^{-2}$$

Hence the vapour pressure is $p = 3.17 \times 10^{-2} \times 100.$ kPa = 3.17 kPa.

16-10 Temperature dependence of equilibrium constants

Since many reactions, particularly gas phase reactions, are carried out at temperatures quite different from 25°C it is necessary to extend the theory to permit calculations of equilibrium constants at any temperature from the data in Appendix 1.

Appendix 1 lists the Gibbs energy of formation for many compounds at a temperature of 25°C or 298 K, which can be used to calculate equilibrium constants for many reactions at that temperature. The Gibbs energy data from Appendix 1 cannot be used directly to calculate equilibrium constants at any other temperature. This is because the Gibbs energy varies considerably with temperature. *It is a serious error to use equation (6-22), $K = exp\{-\Delta G°/RT\}$, to calculate an equilibrium constant K unless the $\Delta G°$ value used is correct at the temperature T.*

The temperature dependence of equilibrium constants is determined by the enthalpy change of reaction, as described by the **van't Hoff equation**. The van't Hoff equation has already been discussed in Sections 7-9, in connection with vapour pressures, and Section 13-5, in connection with equilibrium constants for reactions in the gas phase. The van't Hoff equation follows from equation (16-23), which can be written as follows using the definition of the Gibbs energy:

$$\ln K = -\frac{\Delta G^o}{RT} = -\frac{\Delta H^o - T\Delta S^o}{RT} = -\frac{\Delta H^o}{R}\left(\frac{1}{T}\right) + \frac{\Delta S^o}{R}$$

The final form on the right hand side is similar to equation (13-8). Since for most reactions $\Delta H°$ and $\Delta S°$ vary only slightly with temperature, they may be treated as constants to a good approximation. At two different temperatures T_1 and T_2, the last equation gives:

$$\ln K_1 = -\frac{\Delta H^o}{R}\left(\frac{1}{T_1}\right) + \frac{\Delta S^o}{R}$$

$$\ln K_2 = -\frac{\Delta H^o}{R}\left(\frac{1}{T_2}\right) + \frac{\Delta S^o}{R}$$

Subtracting the first of these equations from the second, the entropy terms cancel, and the standard enthalpy change $\Delta H°$ is a common factor of the inverse temperatures. Hence we obtain the **van't Hoff equation**, which was given before in equation (13-7):

$$\ln\frac{K_2}{K_1} = -\frac{\Delta H^o}{R}\left(\frac{1}{T_2} - \frac{1}{T_1}\right) \tag{16-24}$$

The van't Hoff equation is the quantitative expression of Le Chatelier's principle as it applies to change of temperature: if the temperature increases from T_1 to a higher temperature T_2 and $\Delta H°$ > 0, then $\ln(K_2/K_1)$ is positive and hence K_2 is larger than K_1. Putting this in words, a temperature increase shifts the equilibrium position in the endothermic direction.

Calculation of an equilibrium constant for a reaction at a temperature T other than 25°C requires the values of both $\Delta G°$ and $\Delta H°$ from Appendix 1. The simplest procedure is to calculate K from $\Delta G°$ at 25°C using equation (16-23), and then K at the temperature T from $\Delta H°$ using the van't Hoff equation (16-24). The second step has been illustrated for equilibrium constants in Section 13-5, and for vapour pressures in Section 7-9.

Calculations using the van't Hoff equation are reliable as long as the standard enthalpy change $\Delta H°$ does not change much over the temperature range from 25°C to T. Over large ranges of temperature (more than a few hundred degrees for instance), $\Delta H°$ may not be constant, and in such cases a more detailed calculation is required for accurate results.

Example 16-17 Calculate the equilibrium constant at a temperature of 200.0°C for the reaction

$$SO_2(g) + \tfrac{1}{2}\,O_2(g) \;\rightleftharpoons\; SO_3(g).$$

For the reaction $SO_2(g) + \tfrac{1}{2}\,O_2(g) \rightleftharpoons SO_3(g)$ the standard Gibbs energy change at 298.2 K is:

$$\Delta G^o = -(-300.194) - 0 + (-371.08) = -70.89 \text{ kJ mol}^{-1}$$

Hence the equilibrium constant at 298.2 K is: $\quad K = \exp\left(-\dfrac{(-70890)}{8.3145 \times 298.2}\right) = 2.6 \times 10^{12}$

The standard enthalpy change is:

$$\Delta H^o = -(-296.830) - 0 + (-395.72) = -98.89 \text{ kJ mol}^{-1}$$

Substituting these values in the van't Hoff equation for the temperatures 473.2 K and 298.2 K,

$$\ln\frac{K_{473}}{K_{298}} = \ln\frac{K_{473}}{2.6 \times 10^{12}} = -\frac{(-98890)}{8.3145}\left(\frac{1}{473.2} - \frac{1}{298.2}\right) = -14.8$$

and hence $\qquad\qquad K_{473} = 2.6 \times 10^{12} \times \exp(-14.8) = 1.0 \times 10^6$

The equilibrium constant is much less favourable at the higher temperature. It is for this reason that temperature control and the removal of the heat of reaction is so important for this reaction, as discussed in Section 4-2.

16-11 Entropy effects in chemical equilibrium

In the previous section we showed that the equilibrium constant can be expressed in terms of the standard Gibbs energy change of reaction, which has contributions from the standard enthalpy change of reaction and the standard entropy change of reaction. This can be seen in equation (16-23) which is repeated here:

$$\ln K = -\frac{\Delta G^o}{RT} = -\frac{\Delta H^o - T\Delta S^o}{RT} = -\frac{\Delta H^o}{RT} + \frac{\Delta S^o}{R}$$

For some reactions the entropy change term is small compared with the enthalpy change term. In such a case, the equilibrium constant is determined primarily by the enthalpy change term. But this is not true in general. We have seen that, for the ionization of acetic acid, the opposite is true: the enthalpy change is very small and the entropy change is the main contributor to the standard Gibbs energy change. This was discussed in connection with Examples 16-9 and 16-15.

Large compilations of thermodynamic data are available from which reliable data for many reactions may be obtained, so assumptions about the relative sizes of the $\Delta H°$ and $\Delta S°$ contributions to the Gibbs energy change are not always necessary.

As a final example, we use thermodynamics to learn about the solubility of hydrocarbons and noble gases in water. Consider the solubility of methane in water, as expressed by the equilibrium

$$CH_4(g) \;\rightleftharpoons\; CH_4(aq)$$

The standard Gibbs energy change for this process is the standard Gibbs energy of solution, and it may be calculated at 25°C using Gibbs energy of formation data from Appendix 1:

$$\Delta G° = -(-50.72) + (-34.33) = +16.39 \text{ kJ mol}^{-1}$$

The corresponding equilibrium constant is, by equation (16-23),

$$K = \frac{a(CH_4 (aq))}{a(CH_4 (g))} = \frac{[CH_4 (aq)]}{p(CH_4 (g)) / P^o} = 1.3 \times 10^{-3}$$

The solubility of gases can also be described by Henry's law, equation (8-4), which states that the partial pressure of a gas in equilibrium with the solution is proportional to the mole fraction of the gas dissolved in the liquid solution:

$$p_B = x_B K_H$$

where B refers to the solute, p_B is the partial pressure of the gas, x_B is the mole fraction of the dissolved gas, and K_H is the Henry's law constant. A gas for which K_H is large is only slightly soluble in water. This was shown for oxygen in the solution to Example 8-4. For methane dissolved in water, the Henry's law constant at 25°C is $K_H = 3.97$ GPa. If we assume a gas pressure of 100. kPa, the mole fraction of methane in solution calculated from Henry's law is:

$$x(CH_4 (aq)) = \frac{100. \times 10^3 \text{ Pa}}{3.97 \times 10^9 \text{ Pa}} = 2.52 \times 10^{-5}$$

and hence the molar concentration of methane in solution is 1.4×10^{-3} mol/L, by the method shown in Example 8-4. This is very close to the value of 1.3×10^{-3} mol/L expected from the thermodynamic calculation above.

Oil and water do not mix. Another way of saying this is that the solubility of hydrocarbons in water is low. The calculation we have just done shows that this is the case for the lightest hydrocarbon, methane, and the thermodynamic reason is that the Gibbs energy change of solution is positive. We now ask which is the bigger contributor to the standard Gibbs energy change of solution, the entropy term or the enthalpy term? The standard enthalpy and Gibbs energy changes of solution are, from data in Appendix 1:

$$\Delta H° = -(-74.81) + (-89.04) = -14.23 \text{ kJ mol}^{-1}$$

$$\Delta G° = -(-50.72) + (-34.33) = +16.39 \text{ kJ mol}^{-1}$$

The negative enthalpy change indicates that the transfer of a methane molecule from the gas phase into aqueous solution lowers the energy of the molecule, and so is energetically favourable. The entropy change of solution can be calculated from $\Delta H°$ and $\Delta G°$:

$$\Delta S° = \frac{\Delta H° - \Delta G°}{T} = \frac{(-14230) - (+16390) \text{ J mol}^{-1}}{298.2 \text{ K}} = -102.7 \text{ J K}^{-1} \text{ mol}^{-1}$$

With a strongly negative entropy change of solution, the situation is similar to that for the ionization of acetic acid: the low solubility of methane in water is caused by entropy effects, not enthalpy effects.

Why is the entropy change of solution strongly negative? The methane molecules do not move so freely in solution as they do in the gas phase. But this is only part of the story. The methane molecule does not form hydrogen bonds with neighbouring water molecules. In the neighbourhood of a dissolved methane molecule, the network of hydrogen bonds between water molecules (discussed in Section 11-11) is rearranged to form a "cage" of water molecules around each methane molecule, so as to retain as many hydrogen bonds as possible. Formation of the cage results in a decrease of the orientational freedom of the neighbouring water molecules, with a resulting decrease in the entropy of the solution. This effect is known as the **hydrophobic effect**. The word "hydrophobic" means "water-hating". We have shown by means of thermodynamics that methane and water "hate" each other because of the negative entropy change of solution, and not because methane molecules and water molecules repel each other. The hydrophobic effect is important in biological systems where hydrophobic molecules must coexist with aqueous solutions.

Key concepts

Chemical reactions always proceed towards chemical equilibrium, and so can be described as spontaneous and irreversible. When a reaction reaches equilibrium, the reaction process becomes reversible since the equilibrium condition can be reached by either the forward or reverse reaction. A reversible process is one which is carried out under conditions of equilibrium.

In thermodynamics, a quantity called the entropy can be used to distinguish between reversible and irreversible processes. The entropy is a state function, so the entropy change in a process depends only on the initial and final states of the system, not on how the process takes place. For a reversible process, heat divided by the absolute temperature is equal to the entropy change. For an irreversible process, the heat divided by the absolute temperature is less than the entropy change.

The entropy of a substance is related to the degree of molecular disorder in the substance. The entropy increases with increasing temperature. The entropy of a gas increases with increasing volume. The entropy increases when a solid melts to a liquid, and when a liquid evaporates to a gas.

By combining the entropy with the enthalpy, the Gibbs energy can be defined. For a reaction in which electrical or mechanical work is done, the amount of work done is algebraically greater than the Gibbs energy change for the reaction.

For a spontaneous reaction in which no electrical or mechanical work is done, the Gibbs energy change is negative. The Gibbs energy always decreases in such a reaction, until it reaches a minimum. At the minimum of the Gibbs energy, the reaction has reached chemical equilibrium.

Entropy and Gibbs energy values have been measured and tabulated for many substances in their standard states. The standard Gibbs energy change of a reaction can be used to calculate the equilibrium constant for the reaction. The temperature dependence of the equilibrium constant is determined by the enthalpy change of the reaction. The Gibbs energy contains a full explanation of Le Chatelier's principle.

The Gibbs energy change for a reaction has two contributions, due respectively to the enthalpy and the entropy contributions. The entropy contribution is more important than the enthalpy contribution in some chemical reactions, leading sometimes to unexpected conclusions.

Review questions

1. Give an example of a spontaneous process.

2. How would you compress a gas reversibly?

3. How would you calculate the entropy change for a reversible isothermal process?

4. What condition governs the entropy change for a spontaneous adiabatic process?

5. State Trouton's law in terms of entropy change of vaporization.

6. In general, how is entropy related to molecular disorder?

7. How would you calculate the entropy change for a chemical reaction?

8. Why is the Gibbs energy useful in dealing with chemical reactions?

9. How would you calculate the Gibbs energy change for a chemical reaction?

10. What determines the temperature dependence of an equilibrium constant?

Problems

1. Which of the following processes would result in a decrease of the entropy of the system:
   (a) boiling water to form steam;
   (b) isothermal compression of a gas from 100 kPa to 300 kPa;
   (c) mixing two gases in a container;
   (d) freezing of water to form ice
   (e) cooling ice from 0°C to –50°C.

2. Calculate the entropy change ΔS of 50.0 g of water when it is heated from 25.0°C to 35.0°C at atmospheric pressure.
   $$[6.90 \text{ J K}^{-1}]$$

3. A piece of copper metal of mass 20.0 g at a temperature of 100.0°C is dropped into 100.0 g of water at a temperature of 10.2°C contained in a dewar flask. If the heat capacity of the dewar flask is 50. J K^{-1}, calculate the final temperature of the system, and the entropy changes of the copper, the water plus dewar, and the universe.
   $$[11.6°C, -2.08 \text{ J K}^{-1}, +2.31 \text{ J K}^{-1}, +0.23 \text{ J K}^{-1}]$$

4. A sample of 2.0 dm^3 of ethane gas, C_2H_6, at 100. kPa and 30.0°C is compressed isothermally to a volume of 0.20 dm^3, and then cooled to 0.0°C at constant pressure. Calculate the final pressure and the entropy change of the whole process, assuming that ethane is an ideal gas.
   $$[901 \text{ kPa}, -1.95 \text{ J K}^{-1}]$$

5. For the decomposition of ammonium chloride, calculate $\Delta G°$ and K at 25°C, and the equilibrium constant at 100°C: $NH_4Cl(s) \rightleftharpoons NH_3(g) + HCl(g)$
   $$[+91.12 \text{ kJ mol}^{-1}, 1.1\times10^{-16}, 1.7\times10^{-10}]$$

6. Calculate $\Delta S°$ and $\Delta G°$ for the following reactions at 25°C:
   (a) $N_2(g) + O_2(g) \rightarrow 2 NO(g)$ $\quad$ [+24.77 J K^{-1} mol^{-1}, +173.10 kJ mol^{-1}]
   (b) $3O_2(g) \rightarrow 2 O_3(g)$ $\quad$ [–137.55 J K^{-1} mol^{-1}, +326.4 kJ mol^{-1}]
   (c) $SO_2(g) + \frac{1}{2} O_2(g) \rightarrow SO_3(g)$ $\quad$ [–94.03 J K^{-1} mol^{-1}, –70.89 kJ mol^{-1}]
   (d) $N_2(g) + 3 H_2(g) \rightarrow 2 NH_3(g)$ $\quad$ [–198.76 J K^{-1} mol^{-1}, –32.90 kJ mol^{-1}]
   (e) $CH_4(g) + \frac{1}{2} O_2(g) \rightarrow CH_3OH(\lambda)$ $\quad$ [–162.0 J K^{-1} mol^{-1}, –155.55 kJ mol^{-1}]

7. From the K_a of propanoic acid (see table 14-2), calculate $\Delta G°$ at 25°C for the reaction

   $$C_2H_5COOH(aq) \rightleftharpoons H^+(aq) + C_2H_5COO^-(aq) \quad\quad [+27.7 \text{ kJ/mol}]$$

8. From data in Appendix 1, calculate $\Delta G°$ at 25°C for the reaction

   $$NH_3(aq) + H_2O(\lambda) \rightleftharpoons NH_4^+(aq) + OH^-(aq)$$

   and hence K_b for ammonia at 25°C.
   $$[+27.08 \text{ kJ/mol}, 1.8\times10^{-5}]$$

9. From data in Appendix 1, calculate ΔG° and ΔH° at 25°C for the reaction

$$H_2O(\lambda) \rightleftharpoons H^+(aq) + OH^-(aq)$$

and hence K_w for water at 25°C and 100°C.

[+79.89 kJ/mol, +55.84 kJ/mol, 1.0×10^{-14}, 9.2×10^{-13}]

10. The Henry's law constants in Table 8-4 are all large, and increase as the temperature increases. What does this imply for the signs of each of the Gibbs energy change of solution, the enthalpy change of solution, and the entropy change of solution, for these gases?

11. Calculate ΔG° and ΔH° for the dissolving of O_2 gas in water at 25°C from the Henry's law constant given in Table 8-4 and its temperature dependence. Compare your answers with the data given in Appendix 1. [+16.6 kJ/mol, 12.2 kJ/mol]

12. Calculate and compare the standard molar entropy changes for the following two processes at 25°C: (a) the condensation of water vapour to form liquid water, and (b) the dissolving of oxygen gas in liquid water. [−118.91 J K^{-1} mol^{-1}, −94.2 J K^{-1} mol^{-1}]

13. From data in Appendix 1, calculate the solubility product for barium sulfate at 25°C, and compare with the data in Table 15-1: $BaSO_4(s) \rightleftharpoons Ba^{2+}(aq) + SO_4^{2-}(aq)$ [1.1×10^{-10}]

14. From data in Appendix 1 and your answer to the previous question, calculate the solubility product for barium sulfate at 80.°C. [5.7×10^{-10}]

15. From data in Appendix 1, calculate K for the water gas reaction (Table 13-1) at 25°C and 1000.°C:

$$C(s) + H_2O(g) \rightleftharpoons CO(g) + H_2(g)$$

Note that because the temperature range is so wide, the result of the calculation using the van't Hoff equation in this case has considerable uncertainty. [9.8×10^{-17}, 40.]

16. Calculate the vapour pressure of n-hexane at 25.0°C from data in Appendix 1. [19.8 kPa]

17. Calculate the boiling point of n-hexane at a pressure of 100.0 kPa from data in Appendix 1, and compare with the data in Table 7-1. [341.6 K or 68.4°C]

18. At temperatures in the neighbourhood of 25°C, the vapour pressure of solid benzoic acid has been found to follow the relationship $\ln\dfrac{p}{p^o} = a - \dfrac{b}{T}$, where a = 22.88 and b = 1.07×10^4 K.

Calculate ΔH°, ΔG° and ΔS° for the sublimation of benzoic acid at 25°C.

[89.0 kJ/mol, 32.2 kJ/mol, 190 J K^{-1} mol^{-1}]

19. It can be claimed that all the oxides of nitrogen are thermodynamically unstable with respect to decomposition into the elements. Explain why this is so by reference to Appendix 1.

20. What is the relationship between the pK_a of an acid and the standard Gibbs energy of ionization of the acid in aqueous solution?

21. Calculate ΔG° and ΔH° for the explosive decomposition of ammonium nitrate. Hence show why this substances is explosive. Can you state general conditions for a substance to be an explosive?

22. The following reaction can be used to model the process of photosynthesis of sucrose in plants by the absorption of light:

$$12\ CO_2(g) + 11\ H_2O(\lambda) \rightarrow C_{12}H_{22}O_{11}(aq) + 12\ O_2(g)$$

(a) For sucrose in aqueous solution, the following estimates have been made for a temperature of 298 K: $\Delta H_f^\circ = -2211$ kJ mol^{-1} and $\Delta G_f^\circ = -1547$ kJ mol^{-1}. Calculate ΔH° and ΔG° for the photosynthesis reaction. [+5655 kJ/mol, +5794 kJ/mol]

(b) The system is open to the atmosphere at a total pressure of 100. kPa; the mole fractions of $O_2(g)$ and CO_2 are indicated in Table 5-1. The sucrose is formed in aqueous solution at a concentration of 0.8 mol/L. Write down an expression for the reaction quotient Q for the photosynthesis reaction and evaluate it numerically for the given conditions. Hence calculate ΔG (as opposed to ΔG°) for the photosynthesis reaction under the conditions of the reaction, and show that the reaction cannot occur spontaneously. [$Q = 1.2 \times 10^{33}$, $\Delta G = +5983$ kJ/mol]

(c) The mechanism of photosynthesis is complex, and four photons are believed to be absorbed by the green leaves for every molecule of CO_2 which reacts. Taking the wavelength of the photons to be 540 nm, calculate the energy of the photons absorbed per mole of sucrose produced. [10600 kJ/mol]

(d) If the energy of the photons absorbed is interpreted thermodynamically as the work w', show that w' exceeds the ΔG, so that equation (16-15) is satisfied and the photochemical reaction can is able to take place as long as the light energy is supplied.

Chapter 16

17 Electrochemistry

Objectives

After reading this chapter, the student should be able to do the following:

♦ Describe electrochemical cells and cell diagrams.

♦ Describe several special electrodes.

♦ Define standard cell potentials, and standard reduction potentials.

♦ Calculate standard cell potentials from tabulated standard reduction potentials.

♦ Calculate equilibrium constants from standard cell potentials.

♦ Calculate dependence of cell potentials on concentrations and partial pressures.

♦ Apply thermodynamic concepts of enthalpy change and Gibbs energy change to cells.

♦ Describe some commercial galvanic and electrolytic cells.

♦ Describe corrosion in terms of electrochemistry.

Related topics to review:

Reduction-oxidation reactions in Chapter 2. Thermodynamics in Chapters 6 and 16.

17-1 Introduction

Chemical reactions involving the transfer of electrons are of great importance in the laboratory, in biological processes, and in industry. Examples of electron-transfer reactions are reduction-oxidation (redox) reactions, electrolysis, and the chemical reactions in batteries. Reduction-oxidation and electrolytic reactions were introduced in Section 2-9, and a review of that section is likely to be helpful while studying this chapter. This general area of chemistry is called **electrochemistry**.

For many redox reactions it is possible to construct electrochemical cells in which the reduction and oxidation processes occur at separate locations and the electron transfer takes place through an external metal wire. This permits electrical measurements that yield information about the redox reaction itself. Many equilibrium constants and other thermodynamic data are determined by means of electrochemical measurements.

Electrochemistry provides excellent examples of the application of the principles of thermodynamics. The distinction between spontaneous, reversible and non-spontaneous processes is readily seen in electrochemical devices such as batteries and electrolytic cells. In many cases, electrochemical processes can be carried out reversibly in practice as well as in theory. When this is possible, measurement of the potential of the cell provides a direct measure of the reversible electrical work involved in the reaction, which is equal to the Gibbs energy change of the cell reaction.

17-2 Electrochemical cells

An **electrolyte** is an electrical conductor in which electric current is carried by the movement of ions, in contrast to a metal or a semiconductor, in which current is carried by electrons. In aqueous solution, an electrolyte is a substance that forms ions when dissolved in water.

In an **electrochemical cell** the redox reaction proceeds by transferring electrons from one part of the cell to another through an external metal wire. An electrochemical cell consists of electrolytes and metal electrodes, and the detailed arrangement depends on the reaction involved. Cells in which reactions take place spontaneously are called **galvanic cells,** or **voltaic cells.** Cells in which a chemical reaction is driven by electric current from an external source are called **electrolytic cells.**

If metallic zinc powder is added to a solution containing silver ions, the ions are reduced to metallic silver:

$$Zn(s) + 2\ Ag^+(aq) \rightarrow Zn^{2+}(aq) + 2Ag(s).$$

The equilibrium constant is very large and the reaction proceeds spontaneously. In the reaction metallic zinc forms zinc ions $Zn^{2+}(aq)$, silver ions $Ag^+(aq)$ form metallic silver, and electrons are transferred directly from zinc metal to silver ions.

Figure 17-1 shows an electrochemical cell in which this reaction can proceed without the solution containing the silver ions coming into contact with zinc metal. One half of the cell consists of a solution of a zinc salt in contact with a metallic zinc electrode; the other half is a solution of a silver salt in contact with a metallic silver electrode. At the zinc electrode, zinc metal is oxidized to zinc ions in solution:

$$Zn(s) \rightarrow Zn^{2+}(aq) + 2e^-$$

The zinc metal acquires an excess of electrons as the zinc ions move away from the electrode into the solution, leaving the metal with an excess of electrons. At the silver electrode, silver ions are reduced to silver metal:

$$Ag^+(aq) + e^- \rightarrow Ag(s)$$

The electrons required for the reduction of silver ions to silver atoms at the surface of the silver electrode are supplied through the external metal wire.

An **electrode** is a piece of metal used for an electrical connection to a solution, and in every cell there are two electrodes, the anode and the cathode. The **anode** of any electrochemical cell, no matter whether electrolytic or galvanic, is defined as the electrode at which oxidation takes place, and the **cathode** is the electrode at which reduction takes place. In the galvanic cell shown in Figure 17-1, the zinc metal is the anode and the silver metal is the cathode.

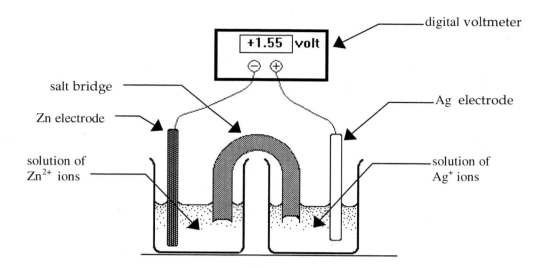

Figure 17-1 A cell for studying the reaction between silver ions and zinc metal. The reaction takes place as two half-reactions at the surfaces of the two electrodes and electrons are transferred through the metal wire. The circuit is completed by the salt bridge, which can exchange chemically inert ions with the two solutions and maintains the two solutions at the same potential. The digital voltmeter indicates that the silver electrode is at a potential of +1.55 volts relative to the zinc electrode.

The transfer of electrons from one half of the cell to the other would result in a difference of potential between the solutions in the two halves of the cell unless the circuit is completed with a **salt bridge**. The salt bridge consists of a semi-rigid gel containing a concentrated solution of salt and supported inside a glass U-tube; ions can move through the gel and into or out of the solutions, without the two solutions forming the cell coming into contact with each other. The salt bridge maintains the two solutions at the same (or very nearly the same) electrical potential. The electrical driving force of the reduction and oxidation processes causes a potential difference between the two metal electrodes, which can be measured by a voltmeter.

Galvanic cells such as that shown in Figure 17-1 are constructed for the purpose of making accurate measurements, and are not suitable for driving current through external devices. Practical cells for driving electric current through external devices will be discussed later in this chapter.

The construction of a galvanic cell is often shown by a **cell diagram**. For the cell shown in Figure 17-1, the cell diagram is:

$$Zn(s) \mid Zn^{2+}(aq) :: Ag^{+}(aq) \mid Ag(s)$$

The solid vertical lines indicate boundaries between phases, and the two dotted vertical lines indicate the salt bridge between the solutions. A description of the state of each separate phase (solid, liquid or gas) is often included and in aqueous solutions the concentrations of significant solutes may be indicated.

Given a cell diagram, we can write a cell reaction. By convention, we assume that the oxidation takes place at the left-hand electrode, and the reduction takes place at the right-hand electrode. For instance, in the zinc-silver cell, the half-reactions at each electrode are:

$$Zn(s) \mid Zn^{2+}(aq) :: Ag^+(aq) \mid Ag(s)$$

$$Zn(s) \rightarrow Zn^{2+}(aq) + 2e^- \qquad Ag^+(aq) + e^- \rightarrow Ag(s)$$

oxidation at the left-hand electrode   reduction at the right-hand

electrode

The two half-reactions can be combined to give the overall cell reaction. If the silver half-reaction is multiplied by two and added to the zinc half-reaction, the electrons can be cancelled from each side of the equation for the overall reaction:

$$Zn(s) + 2Ag^+(aq) \rightarrow Zn^{2+}(aq) + 2Ag(s)$$

The cell diagram could also be written with electrodes reversed:

$$Ag(s) \mid Ag^+(aq) :: Zn^{2+}(aq) \mid Zn(s)$$

The corresponding cell reaction is:

$$Zn^{2+}(aq) + 2Ag(s) \rightarrow Zn(s) + 2Ag^+(aq)$$

This reaction is the reverse of the spontaneous reaction, and is not spontaneous.

To summarise, a cell diagram can be written with either electrode on the left, and the convention that oxidation takes place at the left-hand electrode is only an assumption used to write the cell reaction. If the spontaneous direction for the cell reaction, when written according to the convention, is from left to right, then oxidation does in fact take place at the left-hand electrode. But it may turn out that the spontaneous direction for the cell reaction is from right to left, or in other words the reverse of the cell reaction is spontaneous; in that case oxidation takes place at the right hand electrode. The spontaneous direction for the cell reaction can be determined from the sign of the cell potential, which is discussed in the next section. If the cell potential is positive, the cell reaction is spontaneous, and if it is negative, the reverse of the cell reaction is spontaneous.

In the zinc-silver cell, the electrodes take part in the reaction. However, inert platinum electrodes are used in many cells, and the electrolyte solution contains both the oxidized and reduced forms of the reactant. An example is the following cell:

$$Zn(s) \mid Zn^{2+}(aq) :: Fe^{3+}(aq), Fe^{2+}(aq) \mid Pt(s)$$

The platinum metal electrode is inert and does not take part in the reaction except as a source of electrons. A comma is used to show that the solution contains both Fe^{2+} and Fe^{3+} ions in contact with the platinum electrode. The half-reactions at the left and right electrodes are written by convention as oxidation and reduction half-reactions respectively:

oxidation at the left-hand electrode: $\qquad\qquad Zn(s) \rightarrow Zn^{2+}(aq) + 2e^-$

reduction at the right-hand electrode: $\qquad\qquad Fe^{3+}(aq) + e^- \rightarrow Fe^{2+}(aq)$

The cell reaction is: $\qquad\qquad Zn(s) + 2Fe^{3+}(aq) \rightarrow Zn^{2+}(aq) + 2Fe^{2+}(aq)$

This particular cell reaction is spontaneous when it is carried out directly by mixing the reactants on the left hand side: if zinc powder is added to a solution containing ferric ions Fe^{3+}, the Fe^{3+} ions are reduced to ferrous ions Fe^{2+}.

Some redox processes involving gases can be carried out at platinum electrodes. The platinum electrode is placed in the solution and the gas is bubbled through the solution close to the electrode. Of particular importance is the half-reaction

$$H^+(aq) + e^- \rightarrow \tfrac{1}{2}\, H_2(g)$$

This half-reaction is carried out in a device usually called the **standard hydrogen electrode**, which is shown in Figure 17-2. The standard hydrogen electrode is used as a reference for the scale of standard potentials. The solution contains an acid at pH = 0.0, and the hydrogen is bubbled through the solution at atmospheric pressure so as to make contact with both the solution and the platinum electrode.

The following cell involves a standard hydrogen electrode:

$$Zn(s) \mid Zn^{2+}(aq) :: H^+(aq), H_2(g) \mid Pt(s)$$

The anode half-reaction is $Zn(s) \rightarrow Zn^{2+}(aq) + 2e^-$, and the cell reaction is the well-known spontaneous reaction between zinc metal and an acid, in which zinc metal is oxidized to zinc ions and hydrogen ions are reduced to hydrogen gas:

$$Zn(s) + 2H^+(aq) \rightarrow H_2(g) + Zn^{2+}(aq)$$

Yet another type of electrode involves a piece of metal in contact with a sparingly soluble salt of that metal. Such electrodes can be used to measure solubility products. An example is:

$$Pt \mid H_2(g), HCl(1\ M, aq) \mid AgCl(s) \mid Ag(s)$$

In this cell there is only one solution, and no salt bridge. The solution is in contact with the solid AgCl, and contains, in addition to the HCl, a small concentration of $Ag^+(aq)$ which is determined by the concentration of $Cl^-(aq)$ and the solubility product of AgCl(s). The left-hand electrode is a hydrogen electrode, and at the right-hand electrode, solid silver chloride is reduced to silver metal at the interface between these two phases, and a chloride ion is released into solution:

$$AgCl(s) + e^- \rightarrow Ag(s) + Cl^-(aq)$$

The cell reaction is:

$$AgCl(s) + \tfrac{1}{2}\, H_2(g) \rightarrow H^+(aq) + Cl^-(aq) + Ag(s)$$

The **calomel electrode** is another electrode that makes use of a sparingly soluble salt, mercurous chloride Hg_2Cl_2, for which the traditional name is calomel. The calomel electrode is more convenient than the hydrogen electrode as a reference electrode, and is described by the following half-cell diagram:

$$Hg(\ell) \mid Hg_2Cl_2(s) \mid KCl(aq)\ MM$$

The half-reaction is $\tfrac{1}{2}\, Hg_2Cl_2(s) + e^- \rightarrow Hg(\ell) + Cl^-.$

The concentration of KCl may be fixed (at a fixed temperature) by adding sufficient KCl crystals to saturate the solution.

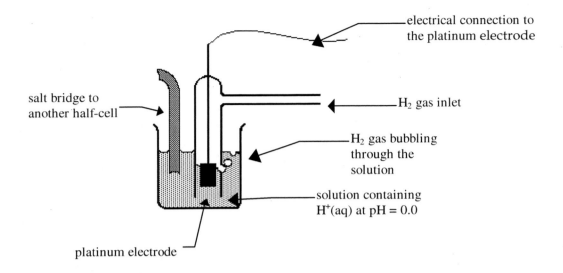

salt bridge to
another half-cell

electrical connection to
the platinum electrode

H_2 gas inlet

H_2 gas bubbling
through the
solution

solution containing
$H^+(aq)$ at pH = 0.0

platinum electrode

Figure 17-2 A hydrogen electrode, which forms half of a galvanic cell. Hydrogen gas, supplied from an external source, bubbles out of a hole in the side of the vertical tube, so that there is contact between the hydrogen gas, the hydrogen ions in solution, and the platinum metal electrode. The hydrogen electrode is connected to another half-cell by the salt bridge shown at the left.

Example 17-1 Write the half-reactions and the cell reaction for the following cell:

$$Ag(s) \mid AgNO_3(aq) :: NaBr(aq) \mid AgBr(s) \mid Ag(s)$$

At the left-hand electrode, the oxidation process is: $Ag(s) \rightarrow Ag^+(aq) + e^-$

At the right hand electrode, the reduction process is: $AgBr(s) + e^- \rightarrow Ag(s) + Br^-(aq)$

The cell reaction is obtained by adding the two half-reactions:

$$AgBr(s) \rightarrow Ag^+(aq) + Br^-(aq)$$

The cell reaction is the same chemical reaction for which the solubility product was defined in Chapter 15.

17-3 Standard cell potentials

If a galvanic cell is connected to a **voltmeter**, as shown in Figure 17-1, the **electromotive force** (e.m.f.) or **potential difference** of the cell (loosely, the potential or voltage of the cell) may be measured; the unit of potential is the **volt** (abbreviation V). In measuring the voltage of an electrochemical cell such as that shown in Figure 17-1 it is important that the voltmeter draw only a very small current. An electronic voltmeter with a very high electrical resistance is satisfactory, and often a digital voltmeter is used.

By convention, the **cell potential** is taken as the potential of the right-hand electrode in the cell diagram relative to that of the left-hand electrode, as shown in Figure 17-1. If the cell diagram is reversed, then the cell reaction is also reversed, and the cell potential changes sign. To avoid ambiguity, either a cell diagram or a cell reaction should be given when quoting a cell potential.

The potential of a galvanic cell will be denoted by the symbol E. Cell potentials vary with the concentrations and other conditions of the substances in the cell, and, if all the reactants in a cell are under standard state conditions, then the potential is the **standard potential** of the cell, $E°$. Standard potentials have been measured for a large number of electrochemical reactions, and the results are published in tables of data. Rather than publishing $E°$ values for a large number of reactions, each measured $E°$ value is broken down into two **half-cell potentials.** The justification for this procedure is as follows. Every cell consists of two electrodes, an anode and a cathode, and the cell potential is developed as a result of the combination of a reduction process and oxidation process. Electrically, the anode and cathode processes are connected in series, and so the cell potential is the sum of potentials associated with the two half-reactions taking place at the electrodes. The salt bridge, if there is one in the cell, can be assumed to generate no significant potential, although for very accurate work a small correction may be necessary.

The potential of a half-reaction is denoted by the symbol ε; if all the substances taking part in the half-reaction are at standard state, the potential is called a **standard potential** and is denoted by $\varepsilon°$. It is not possible to measure a potential for a half-reaction by itself, i.e. for a half-cell. If one electrode is connected to a voltmeter, the other terminal of the voltmeter must be connected to the solution in some way. The second connection then acts as an electrode, at which a second half-reaction takes place. Another way of saying this is that every oxidation must be accompanied by a reduction, and every cell consists of an anode and a cathode with their corresponding oxidation and reduction processes.

The cell potential is the algebraic sum of the potential for the reduction half-reaction at the cathode and the potential for the oxidation half-reaction at the anode. It is not necessary to tabulate potentials for oxidation half-reactions separately from those for reduction half-reactions, because reversing an oxidation half-reaction turns it into a reduction, and reverses the sign of the potential. By convention, standard half-cell potentials are tabulated as reduction potentials.

The reduction potential of a half-reaction or electrode process is defined as the potential of a cell in which the specified electrode forms the right-hand electrode and the left-hand electrode is a hydrogen electrode at standard state conditions. The choice of the standard hydrogen electrode as the reference electrode in defining half-cell potentials is consistent with other thermodynamic conventions.

For example, in the following cell with all substances at standard state conditions,

$$\text{Pt(s)} \mid H_2(g), H^+(aq) :: Zn^{2+}(aq) \mid Zn(s)$$

the zinc electrode is at a potential of -0.7628 volts relative to the hydrogen electrode, so the cell potential $E°$ is -0.7628 volts, and the standard reduction potential of the half-reaction at the right-hand electrode is:

$$Zn^{2+}(aq) + 2e^- \rightarrow Zn(s) \qquad \varepsilon° = -0.7628 \text{ V}$$

Since the standard hydrogen electrode is the reference electrode for the scale of reduction potentials, the standard reduction potential for the hydrogen electrode itself is exactly zero volts:

$$H^+(aq) + e^- \rightarrow \tfrac{1}{2}H_2(g) \qquad \varepsilon° = 0.0000 \text{ V}$$

Table 17-1 Standard Reduction Potentials at 25°C

Ions and molecules are in aqueous solution at the standard state unless otherwise specified, and metals are in the solid state, except for mercury which is a liquid at 25°C.

Reduction process	$\varepsilon°$/volt	Reduction process	$\varepsilon°$/volt
$Pr^{4+} + e^- \rightarrow Pr^{3+}$	+3.2	$Cu^{2+} + 2e^- \rightarrow Cu$	+0.3419
$\frac{1}{2} F_2(g) + H^+ + e^- \rightarrow HF$	+3.053	$VO^{2+} + 2H^+ + e^- \rightarrow V^{3+} + H_2O$	+0.337
$O_3(g) + 2H^+ + 2e^- \rightarrow O_2(g) + H_2O$	+2.076	$\frac{1}{2} Hg_2Cl_2(s) + e^- \rightarrow Hg(\lambda) + Cl^-$	+0.26808
$\frac{1}{2} S_2O_8^{2-} + e^- \rightarrow SO_4^{2-}$	+2.010	$AgCl(s) + e^- \rightarrow Ag + Cl^-$	+0.22233
$Co^{3+} + e^- \rightarrow Co^{2+}$	+1.92	$SO_4^{2-} + 4H^+ + 2e^- \rightarrow H_2SO_3 + H_2O$	+0.172
$\frac{1}{2} H_2O_2 + H^+ + e^- \rightarrow H_2O$	+1.776	$Cu^{2+} + e^- \rightarrow Cu^+$	+0.153
$Ce^{4+} + e^- \rightarrow Ce^{3+}$	+1.72	$Sn^{4+} + 2e^- \rightarrow Sn^{2+}$	+0.151
$PbO_2(s) + 4H^+ + SO_4^{2-} + 2e^-$ $\rightarrow PbSO_4(s) + 2H_2O$	+1.6913	$S(s) + 2H^+ + 2e^- \rightarrow H_2S(aq)$	+0.142
$MnO_4^- + 4H^+ + 3e^- \rightarrow MnO_2(s) + 2H_2O$	+1.679	$\frac{1}{2} S_4O_6^{2-} + e^- \rightarrow S_2O_3^{2-}$	+0.08
$HClO_2 + 2H^+ + 2e^- \rightarrow HClO + H_2O$	+1.645	$AgBr(s) + e^- \rightarrow Ag + Br^-$	+0.07133
$HClO + H^+ + e^- \rightarrow \frac{1}{2} Cl_2(g) + H_2O$	+1.611	$H^+ + e^- \rightarrow \frac{1}{2} H_2(g)$	0.0
$MnO_4^- + 8H^+ + 5e^- \rightarrow Mn^{2+} + 4H_2O$	+1.507	$Pb^{2+} + 2e^- \rightarrow Pb$	−0.1262
$BrO_3^- + 6H^+ + 5e^- \rightarrow \frac{1}{2} Br_2(\ell) + 3H_2O$	+1.482	$Sn^{2+} + 2e^- \rightarrow Sn$	−0.1375
$ClO_3^- + 6H^+ + 5e^- \rightarrow \frac{1}{2} Cl_2(g) + 3H_2O$	+1.47	$O_2(g) + 2H_2O + 2e^- \rightarrow H_2O_2 + 2 OH^-$	−0.146
$\frac{1}{2} Cl_2(g) + e^- \rightarrow Cl^-$	+1.35827	$AgI(s) + e^- \rightarrow Ag + I^-$	−0.15224
$ClO_2 + H^+ + e^- \rightarrow HClO_2$	+1.277	$V^{3+} + e^- \rightarrow V^{2+}$	−0.255
$Cr_2O_7^{2-} + 14H^+ + 6e^- \rightarrow 2Cr^{3+} + 7H_2O$	+1.232	$Ni^{2+} + 2e^- \rightarrow Ni$	−0.257
$O_2 + 4H^+ + 4e^- \rightarrow 2H_2O$	+1.229	$PbCl_2(s) + 2e^- \rightarrow Pb + 2 Cl^-$	−0.2675
$ClO_3^- + 3H^+ + 2e^- \rightarrow HClO_2 + H_2O$	+1.214	$Co^{2+} + 2e^- \rightarrow Co$	−0.28
$IO_3^- + 6H^+ + 5e^- \rightarrow \frac{1}{2} I_2(s) + 3H_2O$	+1.195	$PbSO_4(s) + 2e^- \rightarrow Pb + SO_4^{2-}$	−0.3588
$ClO_4^- + 2H^+ + 2e^- \rightarrow ClO_3^- + H_2O$	+1.189	$Cd^{2+} + 2e^- \rightarrow Cd$	−0.4030
$Cu^{2+} + 2CN^- + e^- \rightarrow [Cu(CN)_2]^-$	+1.103	$Cr^{3+} + e^- \rightarrow Cr^{2+}$	−0.407
$\frac{1}{2} Br_2(\ell) + e^- \rightarrow Br^-$	+1.0873	$Fe^{2+} + 2e^- \rightarrow Fe$	−0.447
$NO_3^- + 4 H^+ + 3e^- \rightarrow NO(g) + 2 H_2O$	+0.957	$CO_2(g) + H^+ + e^- \rightarrow \frac{1}{2} (COOH)_2(aq)$	−0.481
$Hg^{2+} + e^- \rightarrow \frac{1}{2} Hg_2^{2+}$	+0.920	$Zn^{2+} + 2e^- \rightarrow Zn$	−0.7628
$Hg^{2+} + 2e^- \rightarrow Hg(\ell)$	+0.851	$Ti^{3+} + e^- \rightarrow Ti^{2+}$	−0.9
$Ag^+ + e^- \rightarrow Ag$	+0.7996	$Cr^{2+} + 2e^- \rightarrow Cr$	−0.913
$\frac{1}{2} Hg_2^{2+} + e^- \rightarrow Hg(\ell)$	+0.7973	$V^{2+} + 2e^- \rightarrow V$	−1.175
$Fe^{3+} + e^- \rightarrow Fe^{2+}$	+0.771	$Mn^{2+} + 2e^- \rightarrow Mn$	−1.185
$O_2(g) + 2H^+ + 2e^- \rightarrow H_2O_2$	+0.695	$Al^{3+} + 3e^- \rightarrow Al$	−1.662
$\frac{1}{2} I_2(s) + e^- \rightarrow I^-$	+0.5355	$Mg^{2+} + 2e^- \rightarrow Mg$	−2.372
$Cu^+ + e^- \rightarrow Cu$	+0.521	$Na^+ + e^- \rightarrow Na$	−2.71
$Fe(CN)_6^{3-} + e^- \rightarrow Fe(CN)_6^{4-}$	+0.358	$Ca^{2+} + 2e^- \rightarrow Ca$	−2.868
$AgIO_3(s) + e^- \rightarrow Ag + IO_3^-$	+0.354	$K^+ + e^- \rightarrow K$	−2.931
		$Li^+ + e^- \rightarrow Li$	−3.0401

Reprinted with permission from CRC Handbook of Chemistry and Physics, 77th edition. Copyright CRC Press, Boca Raton, Florida.

This standard reduction potential is the defined zero of the potential scale at all temperatures; other standard reduction potentials vary with temperature.

Table 17-1 is a list of standard reduction potentials for some half-reactions at a temperature of 25°C. The standard reduction potentials vary from about +3 volts to about –3 volts.

It follows from the conventions linking the cell diagram with the cell reaction and the cell potential, that if the cell potential is positive, then the actual reaction proceeds spontaneously in the same direction as the cell reaction. This can be seen as follows. By convention, the direction of the cell reaction is such that reduction takes place at the right-hand electrode. If the cell potential is positive, then electrons flow through the metal wire to the right hand electrode, because it is at a positive potential relative to the left-hand electrode. Hence reduction takes place spontaneously at the right-hand electrode, and the direction of the actual reaction is the same as the direction of the cell reaction.

On the other hand, if the cell potential is negative, then the spontaneous direction for the process in the cell is opposite to that of the cell reaction.

A standard cell potential can be calculated from the table of standard reduction potentials in two ways. In the first method, the cell potential is expressed as the algebraic sum of the potentials for the oxidation and reduction half-reactions. The potential for the reduction half-reaction at the right-hand electrode (RHE) can be read directly from the table. The potential for the oxidation half-reaction at the left-hand electrode (LHE) is the negative of the reduction potential for the reversed half-reaction.

In the second method, the standard cell potential $E°$ is the difference between the standard reduction potentials of the two half-reactions:

$$E° = \varepsilon°(\text{RHE}) - \varepsilon°(\text{LHE}) \tag{17-1}$$

In this equation $\varepsilon°$ (RHE) is the reduction potential for the half-reaction at the right hand electrode, and $\varepsilon°$ (LHE) is the reduction potential for the half-reaction at the left-hand electrode. If the reduction potentials for the two half-reactions are marked on a scale calibrated in volts, then the cell potential is given by the difference between the two half-cell potentials. Figure 17-3 illustrates the situations respectively for two cell reactions, one spontaneous and the other non-spontaneous. It should be noticed that the reduction potentials appear on the potential scale in the same order as they would appear in Table 17-1.

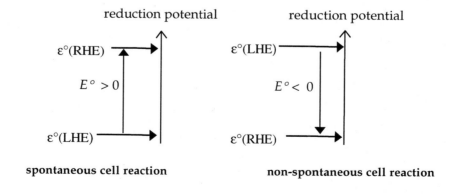

spontaneous cell reaction   **non-spontaneous cell reaction**

Figure 17-3 The standard cell potential is the algebraic difference between the two standard reduction potentials. $E° = \varepsilon°$ (RHE) $- \varepsilon°$ (LHE).   The diagram on the left is for a spontaneous reaction, and that on the right is for a non-spontaneous reaction.

Example 17-2 Determine $E°$ from data in Table 17-1 for the cell

Zn(s) | Zn^{2+}(aq) :: H^+(aq),H_2(g) | Pt(s) and state which is the positive electrode.

The reduction half-reaction at the right hand electrode , and its standard reduction potential, are:

$$H^+(aq) + e^- \rightarrow \frac{1}{2}H_2(g) \quad \varepsilon°(RHE) = 0.00 \text{ V}$$

The oxidation half-reaction at the left-hand electrode is:

$$Zn(s) \rightarrow Zn^{2+} + 2e^-$$

The reverse half-reaction is a reduction process, and its standard reduction potential is:

$$Zn^{2+} + 2e^- \rightarrow Zn(s) \quad \varepsilon°(LHE) = -0.7628 \text{ V}$$

The cell reaction is obtained by adding together the oxidation and reduction half-reactions; in this case the reduction half-reaction must be multiplied by two in order that the electrons will cancel out of the cell reaction. The cell potential is obtained by subtracting the standard reduction potential for the left-hand electrode from that for the right-hand electrode:

$$Zn(s) + 2H^+(aq) \rightarrow Zn^{2+}(aq) + H_2(g)$$

$$E° = (0.00) - (-0.7628) = +0.7628 \text{ V}$$

The cell reaction is the spontaneous reaction between zinc metal and an acid. The hydrogen electrode is the positive electrode, since electrons are transferred from the metal to the hydrogen ions.

Example 17-3 Write the separate half-reactions for the cell reaction Zn(s) + Cu^{2+} → Zn^{2+} + Cu(s), and determine $E°$ for the cell Zn(s) | Zn^{2+}(aq) :: Cu^{2+}(aq) | Cu(s) . Which is the positive electrode?

The reduction half-reaction at the right-hand electrode and its standard reduction potential are:

$$Cu^{2+}(aq) + 2e^- \rightarrow Cu(s) \quad \varepsilon°(RHE) = +0.340 \text{ V}$$

The oxidation half-reaction at the left-hand electrode is:

$$Zn(s) \rightarrow Zn^{2+}(aq) + 2e^-$$

and the reverse reaction and its standard reduction potential are:

$$Zn^{2+}(aq) + 2e^- \rightarrow Zn(s) \quad \varepsilon°(LHE) = -0.7628 \text{ V}$$

The cell reaction and cell potential are obtained by adding together the half-reactions, and subtracting the $\varepsilon°$ values, taking proper account of the signs:

$$Zn(s) + Cu^{2+}(aq) \rightarrow Zn^{2+}(aq) + Cu(s)$$

$$E° = (+0.340) - (-0.7628) = +1.103 \text{ V}$$

This result indicates that the reaction is spontaneous under standard conditions, since the standard potential is positive. The right hand (copper) electrode is positive.

Example 17-4 Calculate $E°$ for the cell $Zn(s) \mid Zn^{2+}(aq) \mathbin{\vdots\vdots} Ag^+(aq) \mid Ag(s)$.

The reduction half-reaction at the right-hand electrode and its standard reduction potential are:

$$Ag^+(aq) + e^- \rightarrow Ag(s) \quad \varepsilon°(RHE) = +0.7996 \text{ V}$$

The oxidation half-reaction at the left-hand electrode is:

$$Zn(s) \rightarrow Zn^{2+}(aq) + 2e^-$$

and the reverse reaction and its standard reduction potential are:

$$Zn^{2+}(aq) + 2e^- \rightarrow Zn(s) \quad \varepsilon°(LHE) = -0.7628 \text{ V}$$

In order to make a balanced equation, the first half-reaction must be multiplied by 2:

$$2Ag^+(aq) + 2e^- \rightarrow 2Ag(s) \quad \varepsilon°(RHE) = +0.7996 \text{ V}$$

Notice that in doubling the half-reaction the potential stays the same, because the potential measures the driving force of the reaction, not the amount of material that reacts. Adding the two half-reactions together, we get the overall reaction:

$$Cu(s) + 2Ag^+(aq) \rightarrow Cu^{2+}(aq) + 2Ag$$

$$E° = (+0.7996) - (-0.7628) = +1.5624 \text{ V}$$

This result may be compared with the potential indicated for the cell in Figure 17-1.

Example 17-5 Calculate $E°$ for the following cell reaction, and state whether or not it is spontaneous:

$$2Mn^{2+}(aq) + 5Br_2(\ell) + 8H_2O(\ell) \rightarrow 2MnO_4^-(aq) + 16H^+(aq) + 10Br^-(aq)$$

In the cell diagram corresponding to this cell reaction, the reduction half-reaction at the right-hand electrode and its potential are:

$$\tfrac{1}{2}Br_2(\ell) + e^- \rightarrow Br^-(aq) \quad \varepsilon°(RHE) = +1.0873 \text{ V}$$

The oxidation half-reaction at the left-hand electrode is:

$$Mn^{2+}(aq) + 4H_2O(\ell) \rightarrow MnO_4^-(aq) + 8H^+(aq) + 5e^-$$

and the reverse reaction and its standard reduction potential are:

$$MnO_4^-(aq) + 8H^+(aq) + 5e^- \rightarrow Mn^{2+}(aq) + 4H_2O(\ell) \quad \varepsilon°(LHE) = +1.507 \text{ V}$$

The cell potential is the difference of the standard reduction potentials:

$$E° = (+1.0873) - (+1.507) = -0.420 \text{ V}$$

Hence the reaction as written is not spontaneous, and will not proceed under standard state conditions. However the reverse reaction is spontaneous.

After studying these examples of the calculations, the structure of Table 17-1 can be seen readily. The entries in the table are arranged in order of decreasing reduction potential. The most powerful oxidizing agents are to be found on the left-hand side of the half-reactions at the top of the table with strongly positive reduction potentials: examples are fluorine, F_2, ozone, O_3, hydrogen peroxide, H_2O_2 and permanganate ion, MnO_4^-. The most powerful reducing agents are to be found on the right-hand side of the half-reactions at the bottom of the table with strongly negative reduction potentials: they are all metals, especially the alkali metals (Group 1 of the periodic table) and the alkaline earth metals (Group 2). These metals are sometimes called **active metals** or **base metals**, in contrast to the **noble metals** such as silver that are found higher in the table. As compared with the noble metals, the base metals are easily oxidized.

17-4 Dependence of cell potentials upon concentrations

The cell potential of a galvanic cell involving aqueous solutions varies with the concentrations of the solutes which are involved in the cell reaction, and if either of the electrodes involves a gas, with the pressure of the gas. The cell potential E when the reactants are not in their standard states is related to the standard cell potential $E°$ by an equation called the **Nernst equation**, after the German chemist Walther Nernst:

$$E = E^o - \frac{0.05916 \text{ volt}}{n} \log Q \qquad (17\text{-}2)$$

where Q is the reaction quotient for the cell reaction and n is the number of electrons transferred in the balanced cell reaction. The logarithm is to base 10, not to base e as in the case of the natural logarithm; this is done in order to make connection with the pH of the solution in cases where the reaction involves an acid-base process. The factor 0.05916 volt refers to a temperature of 25°C and varies slightly with temperature; the origin of this factor will be discussed further in the next section.

Example 17-6 Calculate E for the following cell.

$$Zn(s) \mid Zn^{2+} (0.030 \text{ M}) :: Ag^+ (0.0025 \text{ M}) \mid Ag(s)$$

From Example 17-4 the standard potential $E°$ for this cell is +1.5617 volt. The cell reaction is

$$Zn(s) + 2Ag^+ (aq) \rightarrow Zn^{2+} (aq) + 2Ag(s)$$

and the number of electrons transferred is $n = 2$. The expression for the reaction quotient is

$$Q = \frac{a(Zn^{2+})}{a(Ag^+)^2} \approx \frac{[Zn^{2+}]}{[Ag^+]^2}$$

where the relative activities of the two ions in solution have been approximated by their molar concentrations. Hence the cell potential is:

$$E = +1.5624 - \frac{0.05916}{2} \log \frac{0.030}{0.0025^2} = +1.5624 - 0.1089 = +1.4535 \text{ volt}$$

This example illustrates several important points. Firstly, the reaction quotient is written initially in terms of relative activities, but is evaluated numerically by replacing the relative activities of the ions by their molar concentrations.

Secondly, if the cell reaction is halved,

$$\tfrac{1}{2} \, Zn(s) + Ag^+ \, (aq) \rightarrow \tfrac{1}{2} \, Zn^{2+} \, (aq) + Ag(s)$$

then n is 1 rather than 2, and the reaction quotient for the halved reaction is the square root of the reaction quotient given in the example. In the Nernst equation, these two changes cancel because of the presence of the logarithm, and the result of the calculation is independent of how the cell reaction is written, as long as it is properly balanced.

Thirdly, the relationship between cell potential and concentrations is logarithmic, and hence cell potentials are not very sensitive to concentration. In the above example, a change of a factor of 10 in the concentration of Ag^+ causes a change of only 0.059 volts in the cell potential. Putting this the other way around, a moderate change of cell potential can be used to measure changes in concentration over many orders of magnitude.

There are many cell reactions in which hydrogen ions take part, and for these reactions the cell potential varies with pH. For such a cell, the standard state cell potential $E°$ refers to conditions in which the relative activity of H^+ (aq) is unity and hence the pH of the solution is zero. However most reactions in solution are carried out at higher pH.

Example 17-7 Calculate the potential E for the following cell reaction in which all substances are at standard state except that the pH is 4.0.

$$O_2(g) + 4Fe^{2+}(aq) + 4H^+(aq) \rightarrow 4Fe^{3+}(aq) + 2H_2O(\ell)$$

In the cell diagram corresponding to this cell reaction, the reduction half-reaction at the right-hand electrode and its potential are:

$$O_2(g) + 4H^+(aq) + 4e^- \rightarrow 2\,H_2O(\ell) \qquad \varepsilon°(RHE) = +1.229 \text{ V}$$

The oxidation half-reaction at the left-hand electrode is:

$$Fe^{2+}(aq) \rightarrow Fe^{3+}(aq) + e^-$$

and the reverse reaction and its standard reduction potential are:

$$Fe^{3+}(aq) + e^- \rightarrow Fe^{2+}(aq) \qquad \varepsilon°(LHE) = +0.771 \text{ V}$$

The cell potential is the difference of the standard reduction potentials:

$$E° = (+1.229) - (+0.771) = +0.458 \text{ V}$$

The reaction is spontaneous under standard conditions since $E°$ is positive. Under other conditions,

$$E = E^o - \frac{0.05916}{4} \log \frac{a(Fe^{3+})^4}{a(O_2)\,a(Fe^{2+})^4\,a(H^+)^4}$$

Under the conditions specified in the question, the relative activities of all species except H^+ are unity, and the relative activity of H^+ can be expressed in terms of the pH, defined as pH $= -\log_{10} a(H^+)$:

$$E = E^o - \frac{0.05916}{4} \log \frac{1}{a(H^+)^4}$$

$$= E^o - \frac{0.05916}{4} \times 4 \times (-\log a(H^+))$$

$$= E^o - 0.05916 \times pH$$

Figure 17-3 shows graphically the dependence of this cell potential on pH; the graph is a straight line with a slope of −0.05916 V per pH unit. Substituting numerical values corresponding to pH = 4.0,

$$E = +0.458 - 0.05916 \times 4.0 = +0.221 \text{ V}$$

The reaction is still spontaneous at pH = 4.0, although the potential is smaller than at pH = 0.0. The reaction is not spontaneous at pH higher than about 8.

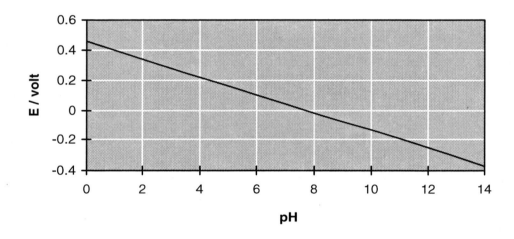

Figure 17-4 The dependence upon pH of the potential of the cell reaction $O_2(g) + 4Fe^{2+}(aq) + 4H^+(aq) \rightarrow 4Fe^{3+}(aq) + 2H_2O(\lambda)$, which is discussed in Example 17-7.

The dependence of cell potentials on pH is the basis for the electrochemical measurement of pH. The hydrogen electrode shown in Figure 17-2 can be used for pH measurement but it is not convenient or portable. Commercial pH probes contain two half-cells built into a single glass tube that is immersed in the solution to be tested. One half-cell does not involve hydrogen ions at all, and is used as a reference electrode that is in contact with the solution through a salt bridge. The other electrode and its surrounding electrolyte are contained in a glass bulb, part of which is very thin and made of special glass; the potential difference between this electrode and the test solution varies with the pH of the test solution. The operation of this so-called **glass electrode** depends upon the way in which hydrogen ions in the test solution interact with the thin glass wall. The glass electrode requires calibration using a standard buffer solution.

In Chapter 14, the pH of solutions was, as a practical matter, calculated from the molar concentration of hydrogen ions, but the true pH of a solution is related to the relative activity of the hydrogen ion, which usually differs somewhat from the magnitude of the molar concentration $[H^+]$. The potential developed by the hydrogen electrode or the glass electrode reflects the true relative activity of hydrogen ions and hence indicates the true pH rather than $-\log[H^+]$.

Example 17-8 Calculate the cell potential E for the reaction of Example 17-7 with all substances in solution at standard state except for atmospheric oxygen which is at a partial pressure of 20.3 kPa.

The reaction is:

$$O_2(g) + 4Fe^{2+}(aq) + 4H^+(aq) \rightarrow 4Fe^{3+}(aq) + 2H_2O(\ell)$$

For a gas, the relative activity is equal to the pressure divided by standard state pressure, to a very good approximation:

$$a(O_2) = \frac{p(O_2)}{p^0} = \frac{20.3}{100.0} = 0.203$$

and hence the Nernst equation becomes:

$$E = E^o - \frac{0.05916}{4}\log\frac{1}{a(O_2)}$$

$$= +0.458 - \frac{0.05916}{4} \times \log\frac{1}{0.203}$$

$$= +0.448 \text{ volt}$$

The potential is reduced slightly from the standard potential because of the reduced partial pressure of oxygen.

The Nernst equation can be applied to half-reactions as well as to complete reactions, in order to calculate a half-cell potential ε under conditions other than standard state conditions, and sometimes it is more convenient to deal with each half-reaction separately, rather than with the complete reaction. When calculating the reaction quotient Q for a half-reaction, the electrons are ignored.

Example 17-9 Calculate the reduction potential ε for the half-reaction $Cu^{2+}(aq) + e^- \rightarrow Cu^+(aq)$ when the concentration of Cu^{2+} is 0.25 M and the concentration of Cu^+ is 0.0050 M.

The standard reduction potential for this half-reaction is $\varepsilon^\circ = +0.153$ volt and the Nernst equation for the specified conditions is:

$$\varepsilon = \varepsilon^o - \frac{0.05916}{1}\log\frac{a(Cu^+)}{a(Cu^{2+})} = 0.153 - 0.05916\log\frac{0.25}{0.0050} = +0.052 \text{ volt}$$

A **concentration** cell is one in which the two half-cells involve the same half-reaction, but with a difference in the concentrations. The potential of the cell can be calculated from the Nernst equation; some care is needed to calculate the reaction quotient correctly.

Example 17-10 Calculate the potential of the following cell:

$$Zn(s) \mid Zn^{2+}(0.15\ M) :: Zn^{2+}(0.0045\ M) \mid Zn(s)$$

Since there is the same half-reaction at the two electrodes, the standard reduction potentials ε° are the same. The reduction half-reaction at the right hand electrode and its reduction potential are:

$$Zn^{2+}(0.0045\ M) + 2e^- \rightarrow Zn \qquad \varepsilon(RHE) = \varepsilon^o - \frac{0.05916}{2}\log\frac{1}{0.0045}$$

There is no need to work out a numerical value for this half-cell potential since it will be combined with the other half-cell potential after the next step. The oxidation half-reaction at the left-hand electrode is:

$$Zn \rightarrow Zn^{2+}(0.15\ M) + 2e^-$$

and the reverse reaction and its reduction potential are:

$$Zn^{2+}(0.15\ M) + 2e^- \rightarrow Zn \qquad \varepsilon(LHE) = \varepsilon^o - \frac{0.05916}{2}\log\frac{1}{0.15}$$

Hence the cell potential is the difference between the two reduction potentials. In subtracting the left hand electrode potential from the right hand electrode potential, the standard reduction potential ε° cancels, and the two logarithms can be combined:

$$E = \varepsilon(RHE) - \varepsilon(LHE) = -\frac{0.05916}{2}\log\frac{0.15}{0.0045} = -0.045\ \text{volts}$$

Thus the right hand electrode is negative, showing that the electrode in the more dilute solution is the anode. The spontaneous reaction leads to an increase in the concentration of zinc ions in the less concentrated solution, and a decrease in the concentration of zinc ions in the more concentrated solution, which is what one would expect if the solutions were placed directly in contact with each other.

17-5 Thermodynamics of cells

Galvanic cells provide excellent examples for the study of thermodynamics. For many cells, it is possible to carry out the cell reaction in both directions by making suitable arrangements in the external circuit, and the heat and work involved in the cell reaction can be measured precisely under reversible conditions.

Consider a lead-acid cell, such as those used in car batteries. The components of the fully-charged cell are summarized by the following cell diagram:

$$Pb(s) \mid H_2SO_4\ (aq) \mid PbO_2\ (s) \mid Pb(s)$$

The reduction half-reaction at the right-hand electrode is:

$$PbO_2(s) + 4\,H^+(aq) + SO_4^{2-}(aq) + 2e^- \rightarrow PbSO_4\ (s) + 2\,H_2O\ (\ell) \qquad \varepsilon^\circ(RHE) = +1.6913\ V$$

The oxidation half-reaction at the left-hand electrode is:

$$Pb(s) + SO_4^{2-}(aq) \rightarrow PbSO_4(s) + 2e^-$$

and the reverse half-reaction and its standard reduction potential are:

$$PbSO_4(s) + 2e^- \rightarrow Pb(s) + SO_4^{2-}(aq) \qquad \varepsilon°(LHE) = -0.3588 \text{ V}$$

The cell reaction and standard cell potential are:

$$Pb(s) + PbO_2(s) + 4H^+(aq) + 2SO_4^{2-}(aq) \rightarrow 2PbSO_4(s) + 2H_2O(\ell)$$

$$E° = +1.6913 - (-0.3588) = +2.0501 \text{ V}$$

The reactions have been written assuming that sulphuric acid is completely dissociated into hydrogen ions and sulfate ions.

Each cell develops about 2.0 V when fully charged, and six cells are connected in series in a 12 volt battery. As the cell is discharged, lead sulphate $PbSO_4$ is deposited on both electrodes, and the solution of sulphuric acid in the cell becomes less concentrated. Electric current can be drawn from the battery for operating the starter motor or the lights when the engine is not running. The battery can be recharged by connecting it to a generator with an output of more than 12 volts, which drives current through the cells of the battery in the reverse direction and recharges the electrochemical system by reversing the reactions at the two electrodes. The connections for the discharging and charging processes are shown in Figure 17-4.

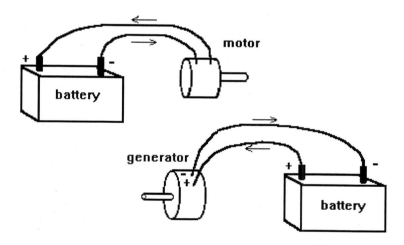

Figure 17-5 The connections between the battery, the starter motor and the generator in a car. The upper diagram shows the connections for driving the starter motor from the battery; electrical energy flows out of the battery and w' for the battery is negative. The lower diagram shows the connections for recharging the battery from the generator; electrical energy flows into the battery, and w' for the battery is positive. The arrows show the direction of electron flow in each case.

Consider a cell in the battery as a thermodynamic system, with the starter motor and the generator as part of the surroundings. Since the cell is under constant atmospheric pressure, the electrical work done can be represented by the symbol w' introduced in Chapter 6. When the cell is driving a motor or the lights, electrical energy flows out of the battery and w' is negative. When the cell is being charged by the generator, electrical energy flows into the battery and w' is positive.

The generator is able to charge the cell if it generates at its terminals a voltage somewhat greater than the potential difference of 2.0 V that exists at the terminals of the cell. If the potential generated by the external circuit is less than 2.0 V (per cell), then the cell will discharge. Therefore the cell reaction can be run in one direction or the other, depending on the potential applied to the cell by the external circuit. If the potential applied to the cell by the external circuit is exactly equal to the cell potential, no current will flow. But a small change of the external potential in either direction causes a current to flow, and the cell reaction takes place in the direction corresponding to the change. Measuring the cell potential under conditions of zero current is therefore equivalent to carrying out the cell reaction reversibly.

Suppose that a cell is connected to an external circuit and a charge passes through the external circuit. If the potential of the cell is E, the work done is the product of the charge and the potential through which the charge is carried:

$$w' = \text{charge} \times \text{potential difference}$$

This is equation (6-2) in Section 6-4. The electrical work in joules is the product of charge in coulombs and potential in volts. If the cell reaction involves transfer of one mole of electrons through the cell, then for one mole of the cell reaction the charge passing through the cell is equal to the charge of one mole of electrons, or the Faraday constant F:

$$F = 96\,485.30 \text{ coulomb/mole} \approx 96\,485 \text{ coulomb/mole (to five significant figures)}$$

If the number of electrons transferred in the cell reaction is n (*e.g.* $n = 2$ in the lead-acid cell), then for one mole of the cell reaction the charge passing through the cell is nF, and the work done is:

$$w' = -nFE \tag{17-3}$$

The negative sign is needed to make the equation consistent with the sign conventions of both electrochemistry and thermodynamics. If the cell reaction is spontaneous, then the cell potential E is positive and the electrical work w' is negative because as the cell discharges work is done by the cell on the surroundings, through the operation of the electric motor shown in Figure 17-5.

If the cell potential E is measured under reversible conditions with no current flowing, the reversible electrical work w'_{rev} is equal to the Gibbs energy change ΔG for the cell reaction, according equation (16-15) in section 16-7. Hence the Gibbs energy change for the cell reaction is:

$$\Delta G = -nFE \tag{17-4}$$

The reversible cell potential is a direct measure of the Gibbs energy change for the cell reaction. If all substances in the cell are at standard state conditions, the standard state Gibbs energy change is:

$$\Delta G^o = -nFE^o \tag{17-5}$$

Example 17-11 Calculate ΔG° for the lead-acid cell reaction from the cell potential of +2.0501 V.

The cell reaction is

$$Pb(s) + PbO_2(s) + 4H^+(aq) + 2SO_4^{2-}(aq) \rightarrow 2PbSO_4(s) + 2H_2O(\ell)$$

Since $n = 2$ and $E^\circ = +2.0501$ V,

$\Delta G° = -2$ x 96485 coulomb/mole x 2.0501 volt

$$= -3.95 \text{ x } 10^5 \text{ joule/mole}$$

$$= -395 \text{ kJ/mol}$$

Note that if the cell reaction had been written in the reverse direction, the cell potential E would change in sign, and so would $\Delta G°$. If the cell reaction had been written with all the stoichiometric coefficients doubled, n and $\Delta G°$ would be doubled, but the cell potential $E°$ would not change.

The relationship between cell potential and Gibbs energy can also be applied to half-reactions as well as to the full cell reactions. This leads to the Gibbs energies of formation of ions in aqueous solution. For instance, for the half-reaction

$$\tfrac{1}{2}H_2 \text{ (g)} \rightarrow H^+ \text{ (aq)} + e^- \qquad \varepsilon° = 0.0 \text{ V}$$

Hence the Gibbs energy change is: $\qquad \Delta G° = 1$ x F x 0.0 = 0.0 kJ.

We can write the Gibbs energy change for this reaction in terms of Gibbs energies of formation:

$$\Delta G° = \Delta G_f°(H^+ \text{ (aq)}) - \tfrac{1}{2} \Delta G_f°(H_2 \text{ (g)})$$

Note that the electron in the half-reaction is not included in this equation. Substituting the values of $\Delta G°$ and $\Delta G_f°(H_2 \text{ (g)})$, which are both zero, we get:

$$0.0 = \Delta G_f°(H^+ \text{ (aq)}) - 0.0$$

Hence the Gibbs energy of formation of the hydrogen ion in solution in the standard state is zero. Just as the hydrogen electrode is used as a reference for electrode potentials, the aqueous hydrogen ion in the standard state is used as a reference for the Gibbs energy of formation of other ions in solution. In Appendix 1, both the Gibbs energy and enthalpy of formation for the aqueous hydrogen ion are listed as zero.

The close connection between the standard reduction potentials in Table 17-1 and thermochemical data in Appendix 1 is shown in the following two examples.

Example 17-12 Calculate the Gibbs energy of formation of the bromide ion in aqueous solution from the following half-reaction:

$$AgBr(s) + e^- \rightarrow Ag(s) + Br^-(aq) \qquad \varepsilon° = +0.07133 \text{ V}$$

The Gibbs energy change is $\qquad \Delta G° = -1$ x 96485 x (+0.07133) $= -6.88$ kJ

The Gibbs energy change for the half-reaction is:

$$\Delta G° = -\Delta G_f°(AgBr(s)) + \Delta G_f°(Ag(s)) + \Delta G_f°(Br^- \text{ (aq)})$$

so that, substituting the above value and values from Appendix 1,

$$-6.88 = -(-96.90) + 0.0 + \Delta G_f°(Br^- \text{ (aq)})$$

from which we calculate $\qquad \Delta G_f°(Br^- \text{ (aq)}) = -103.78$ kJ/mol

This agrees well with the value listed in Appendix 1.

Example 17-13 Calculate the standard potential for the galvanic cell discussed in Example 17-3 from Gibbs energy of formation data in Appendix 1.

The cell diagram and cell reaction are:

$$Zn(s) \mid Zn^{2+}(aq) :: Cu^{2+}(aq) \mid Cu(s)$$

$$Zn(s) + Cu^{2+}(aq) \rightarrow Zn^{2+}(aq) + Cu(s)$$

The standard Gibbs energy of the reaction from thermochemical data is:

$$\Delta G^\circ = \Delta G_f^\circ(Zn^{2+}(aq)) - \Delta G_f^\circ(Cu^{2+}(aq))$$

$$= (-147.06) - (+65.49) = -212.55 \text{ kJ/mol}$$

Hence the standard potential of the cell is: $E^o = -\dfrac{(-212.55 \times 10^3 \text{ J/mol})}{2 \times 96485 \text{ C/mol}} = +1.101 \text{ V}$

This result agrees with the value obtained in Example 17-3 from half-cell potentials.

In Chapter 16 it was shown that the Gibbs energy change for a reaction under general conditions of concentrations and pressures is related to the standard state Gibbs energy change by the equation

$$\Delta G = \Delta G^o + RT \ln Q$$

where Q is the reaction quotient. Introducing the above relationships between Gibbs energy change and cell potential, this equation becomes:

$$-nFE = -nFE^o + RT \ln Q$$

and so

$$E = E^o - \frac{RT}{nF} \ln Q \tag{17-6}$$

For many purposes it is convenient to convert the logarithm to a base of 10; this is done by dividing the natural logarithm by 2.303.

$$E = E^o - \frac{1}{n}\left(\frac{RT}{2.303F}\right) \log Q$$

Further, since so much solution chemistry is done at or near room temperature, the temperature is often assumed to be 25°C, and then the number in brackets has the following value:

$$\frac{RT}{2.303F} = \frac{8.314 \text{ J K}^{-1} \text{ mol}^{-1} \times 298 \text{ K}}{2.303 \times 96485 \text{ C mol}^{-1}} = 0.05916 \text{ V}$$

And so we rediscover the Nernst equation, which was discussed at length in the last section:

$$E = E^o - \frac{0.05916 \text{ volt}}{n} \log Q$$

The Nernst equation is essentially a thermodynamic relation, a practical realization of the relation between ΔG and ΔG°.

A galvanic cell produces electrical work as a result of the electrochemical processes that carry the cell towards chemical equilibrium. The cell "runs down" as equilibrium is approached, and the falling cell potential reflects the reduction in the amount of work that is available from the cell. As the cell approaches equilibrium, the cell potential E approaches zero. The Gibbs energy change ΔG also approaches zero and the reaction quotient Q approaches the value of the equilibrium constant K.

17-6 Equilibrium Constants and Standard Cell Potentials

The thermodynamic relationships discussed in the previous section provide a method of calculating the equilibrium constant for the cell reaction from the standard cell potential. Applying the Nernst equation (17-6) to the equilibrium situation in which the reaction quotient Q becomes the equilibrium constant K and the cell potential E is zero, we find that the equilibrium constant is related to the standard cell potential:

$$K = \exp\left(+\frac{nFE^o}{RT}\right) \tag{17-7}$$

The use of this equation is illustrated in the following examples.

Example 17-14 Calculate the equilibrium constant for the cell reaction for the oxidation of ferrous ion by hydrogen peroxide, using standard reduction potentials. The reaction is:

$$\tfrac{1}{2}\,H_2O_2(aq) + Fe^{2+}(aq) + H^+(aq) \rightarrow Fe^{3+}(aq) + H_2O(\ell)$$

The reduction half-reaction and the standard reduction potential are:

$$\tfrac{1}{2}\,H_2O_2(aq) + H^+(aq) + e^- \rightarrow H_2O(\ell) \qquad \varepsilon^\circ = +1.776 \text{ V}$$

The oxidation half-reaction is $Fe^{2+} \rightarrow Fe^{3+} + e^-$ and the reverse half-reaction and standard reduction potential are:

$$Fe^{3+}(aq) + e^- \rightarrow Fe^{2+}(aq) \qquad \varepsilon^\circ = +0.771 \text{ V}$$

Hence $\qquad E^\circ = (+1.776) - (+0.771) = +1.005$ V.

For the cell reaction $n = 1$, and so from equation (17–8),

$$K = \exp\left(+\frac{1 \times 96485 \times (+1.005)}{8.314 \times 298.2}\right) = \exp(+39.1) = 1.0 \times 10^{17}$$

From this large equilibrium constant we see that hydrogen peroxide, H_2O_2, readily oxidises ferrous ion Fe^{2+} to ferric ion Fe^{3+}.

Example 17-15 Calculate the standard cell potential for the following cell (which was discussed in Example 17-1) and hence the solubility product of AgBr(s):

$$Ag(s) \mid AgNO_3(aq) :: NaBr(aq) \mid AgBr(s) \mid Ag(s)$$

The relevant ions in solution are Br^- at the right-hand electrode and Ag^+ at the left-hand electrode. The reduction half-reactions at the two electrodes and their standard reduction potentials are:

$$AgBr(s) + e^- \rightarrow Ag(s) + Br^-(aq) \qquad \varepsilon°(RHE) = +0.07133 \text{ V}$$

$$Ag^+(aq) + e^- \rightarrow Ag(s) \qquad \varepsilon°(LHE) = +0.7996 \text{ V}$$

and the cell reaction and standard potential are:

$$AgBr(s) \rightarrow Ag^+(aq) + Br^-(aq)$$

$$E° = (0.07133) - (+0.7996) = -0.7283 \text{ V}$$

The cell reaction is the equilibrium between solid AgBr, and Ag^+ and Br^- ions in solution, so the equilibrium constant for the cell reaction is the solubility product K_{sp}. of AgBr. From equation (17-7),

$$K_{sp} = \exp\left(+\frac{1 \times 96485 \times (-0.7283)}{8.314 \times 298.2} \right) = 5.0 \times 10^{-13}$$

This result is in good agreement with the solubility product for AgBr given in the Table 15-1.

17-7 Disproportionation reactions

It is not uncommon for an element to show more than one oxidation number. For example, iron is found in three oxidation states: metallic iron Fe, the ferrous ion Fe^{2+}, and the ferric ion Fe^{3+}. The standard reduction potentials for the reduction of the ions in aqueous solution are:

$$Fe^{3+}(aq) + e^- \rightarrow Fe^{2+}(aq) \qquad \varepsilon° = 0.771 \text{ V}$$

$$Fe^{2+}(aq) + 2e^- \rightarrow Fe(s) \qquad \varepsilon° = -0.447 \text{ V}$$

The reduction half-reaction of ferric iron, Fe^{3+}, directly to metallic iron is obtained by adding these two half-reactions:

$$Fe^{3+}(aq) + 3e^- \rightarrow Fe(s)$$

The potential for this half-reaction is obtained by adding together the Gibbs energies for the previous two half-reactions. If $\varepsilon°$ is the reduction potential of the last half-reaction, then by equation (17-5),

$$-3 \times F \times \varepsilon° = -1 \times F \times (+0.771) - 2 \times F \times (-0.447)$$

and so $\qquad \varepsilon° = (+1 \times 0.771 - 2 \times 0.447)/3 = -0.041 \text{ V}$

Notice that in this calculation the Faraday constant can be divided out from both sides of the equation.

In a series of three or more related ions (or molecules) with different oxidation numbers for an element, it is possible for two ions in an intermediate oxidation number to react together in a redox reaction, to produce different oxidation numbers, one higher and the other lower than the original. Such a reaction is described as **disproportionation.**

For instance, ferrous ions Fe^{2+} could conceivably react together to produce metallic Fe and ferric ions Fe^{3+}. The reaction obtained by combining the above two half-reactions and the potential are:

$$3 \, Fe^{2+}(aq) \rightarrow 2Fe^{3+}(aq) + Fe(s) \qquad E° = (-0.447) - (+0.771) = -1.218 \text{ V}$$

Since the cell potential is strongly negative, the reaction is not spontaneous under standard state conditions, and the equilibrium constant is very small. We conclude from this that in aqueous solution Fe^{2+} does not tend to disproportionate to form Fe^{3+} and metallic iron. Another way to say this is that Fe^{2+} is stable against disproportionation.

This system of reductions can be conveniently represented on a single line, with each half-reaction read as a reduction from left to right:

$$Fe^{3+} \underset{+0.771 \text{ V}}{\rule{2cm}{0.4pt}} Fe^{2+} \underset{-0.447 \text{ V}}{\rule{2cm}{0.4pt}} Fe(s)$$

The intermediate oxidation state Fe^{2+} is stable under standard conditions. This can be seen at a glance from the diagram because the standard reduction potential to the right of that species is (algebraically) smaller than the standard reduction potential to the left.

An example of an intermediate oxidation state which is not stable is to be found in the solution chemistry of copper, which is found in three oxidation states, +2, +1 and 0: the cupric ion Cu^{+2}, the cuprous ion Cu^{+}, and copper metal. The reduction potentials are summarized in the following diagram,

$$Cu^{2+} \underset{+0.153 \text{ V}}{\rule{2cm}{0.4pt}} Cu^{+} \underset{+0.521 \text{ V}}{\rule{2cm}{0.4pt}} Cu(s)$$

The oxidation and reduction processes starting from Cu^{+} are:

$$Cu^{+}(aq) + e^{-} \rightarrow Cu(s)$$

$$Cu^{+}(aq) \rightarrow Cu^{2+}(aq) + e^{-}$$

which can be added to give the disproportionation reaction:

$$2\,Cu^{+}(aq) \rightarrow Cu^{2+}(aq) + Cu(s)$$

The cell potential is $E^{\circ} = (+0.521)-(+0.153) = +0.368$ V. Since the potential is positive, the disproportionation reaction is spontaneous under standard conditions and the equilibrium constant for the reaction is large. Hence the cuprous ion Cu^{+} is not stable in aqueous solution. This can be seen from the above diagram since the standard reduction potential to the right of Cu^{+} is larger than the standard reduction potential to the left. It might be asked whether the +1 oxidation state of copper, Cu^{+}, exists at all, but complexes of Cu^{+} such as $Cu(CN)_{4}^{3-}$ are stable in solution and some insoluble salts such as $CuCl$ are stable in the solid state.

Example 17-16 Discuss the stability of the mercurous ion Hg_{2}^{2+} in aqueous solution given the following diagram. The species involved are the mercuric ion Hg^{2+}, the mercurous ion Hg_{2}^{2+} and liquid metallic mercury $Hg(\lambda)$, and the standard reduction potentials are as follows:

$$Hg^{2+} \underset{+0.920 \text{ V}}{\rule{2cm}{0.4pt}} Hg_{2}^{2+} \underset{+0.7973 \text{ V}}{\rule{2cm}{0.4pt}} Hg(\lambda)$$

The reduction half-reactions are:

$$\tfrac{1}{2}\,Hg_{2}^{2+}(aq) + e^{-} \rightarrow Hg(\ell) \qquad\qquad \varepsilon^{\circ} = +0.7973 \text{ volt}$$

$$Hg^{2+}(aq) + e^{-} \rightarrow \tfrac{1}{2}\,Hg_{2}^{2+}(aq) \qquad\qquad \varepsilon^{\circ} = +0.920 \text{ volt}$$

Since the potential to the right of Hg_{2}^{2+} is smaller than that to the left, the mercurous ion Hg_{2}^{2+} is stable in aqueous solution. However, the difference between the potentials is not large, and so the equilibrium constant is not greatly different from unity. The cell reaction and potential for the disproportionation reaction are:

$$Hg_2^{2+}(aq) \rightarrow Hg^{2+}(aq) + Hg(\ell) \qquad E^\circ = (+0.7973) - (+0.920) = -0.123 \text{ V}$$

and the equilibrium constant is:

$$K = \exp\left(\frac{1 \times 96485 \times (-0.123)}{8.314 \times 298.2}\right) = 8.3 \times 10^{-3}$$

Thus Hg_2^{2+} ion is marginally stable against disproportionation in solution.

17-8 Commercial galvanic cells

Cells built to produce a significant current through an external circuit are constructed differently from the galvanic cells we have considered so far, the objective being to produce electrical energy rather than to make measurements of the cell potential at zero current conditions for well-defined chemical reactions. Such cells can be bought cheaply from commercial suppliers. There are many types of cell, and the development of portable computers, telephones and other electronic equipment has created a large consumer market for high performance cells. Cells are often connected in series to generate more voltage than can be obtained from a single cell, and multiple cells packaged together in this way are called **batteries**. Batteries are used in cars and trucks to store energy for the starter motor and accessories, and another large market for rechargeable batteries will appear if electric cars are commercialized.

Primary cells generate electrical energy by chemical reactions which cannot be reversed by recharging. At the end of its life, a primary cell must be discarded. Usually these cells are "dry cells", in which the electrolyte is a paste, or is impregnated into a solid matrix. Three common primary cells are described below.

The **Leclanché cell** is the common cell used for powering flashlights and toys. It has a zinc anode which serves as a can to hold the entire cell, and a complex cathode consisting of a central graphite rod surrounded by a paste containing MnO_2, aqueous NH_4Cl and $ZnCl_2$, and graphite. The cell potential is about 1.5 volts and the electrode reactions are:

$$Zn(s) \rightarrow Zn^{2+} + 2e^-$$

$$2MnO_2(s) + 2NH_4^+(aq) + 2e^- \rightarrow Mn_2O_3(s) + 2NH_3(aq) + H_2O(\ell)$$

The zinc metal is eroded as the cell discharges, and the manganese is reduced from the +4 oxidation state to +3. The ammonia released at the cathode diffuses to the anode where it reacts with zinc ions to form a complex ion. The overall cell reaction is:

$$Zn(s) + 2MnO_2(s) + 2NH_4^+(aq) \rightarrow Mn_2O_3(s) + 2NH_3(aq) + H_2O(\ell)$$

In the **alkaline cell**, the main reactants are the same as in the Leclanché cell, but the electrolyte contains potassium hydroxide. Since the electrolyte is basic rather than acidic, the electrode reactions are somewhat different:

$$Zn(s) + 2OH^-(aq) \rightarrow Zn(OH)_2(s) + 2e^-$$

$$MnO_2(s) + H_2O(\ell) + e^- \rightarrow MnO(OH)(s) + OH^-(aq)$$

The hydroxide ion consumed at the anode is replaced by hydroxide ion produced at the cathode. These cells have improved shelf life, their capacity is larger and the cell potential does not fall off under load. The cell potential is about 1.5 volts and the cell is interchangeable with the Leclanché cell.

In the **Ruben-Mallory or mercury cell** the anode is a solution or "amalgam" of zinc mixed with mercury, and the cathode contains mercuric oxide HgO which is reduced to metallic mercury.

The electrolyte is potassium hydroxide contained in a disc of porous material. In simplified form the electrode reactions can be written:

$$Zn(s) + 2OH^-(aq) \rightarrow ZnO(s) + H_2O(\ell) + 2e^-$$

$$HgO(s) + H_2O(\ell) + 2e^- \rightarrow Hg(\ell) + 2OH^-(aq)$$

so the overall reaction is

$$Zn(s) + HgO(s) \rightarrow ZnO(s) + Hg(\ell)$$

The cell potential is 1.35 volts, and remains almost constant as the cell is discharged, a feature which makes the mercury cell useful as a source of a constant potential in scientific or medical equipment.

In a fuel cell, the reducing agent is a fuel, which could otherwise be burned in a furnace. Both fuel and oxidizer are supplied to the cell continuously while it is operating. The practical operation of fuel cells depends upon efficient contact between the gases, the electrolyte and the electrodes, and the use of a catalyst to make the electrode reactions sufficiently fast to generate a useful current. Fuel cells are used in spacecraft and are a potential power source for electric cars and buses.

One type of fuel cell runs on hydrogen (the fuel) and oxygen (the oxidizer) with a potassium hydroxide electrolyte. The electrode reactions can be written:

anode: $\quad H_2(g) + 2\ OH^-(aq) \rightarrow 2\ H_2O(\ell) + 2e^-$

cathode: $\quad \frac{1}{2}\ O_2(g) + H_2O(\ell) + 2e^- \rightarrow 2\ OH^-(aq)$

and the overall cell reaction is $\quad H_2(g) + \frac{1}{2}\ O_2(g) \rightarrow H_2O(\ell).$

The standard Gibbs energy change for the cell reaction is –237.2 kJ and the number of electrons transferred is $n = 2$, so the reversible cell potential is:

$$E^o = -\frac{\Delta G^o}{nF} = -\frac{(-237100)}{2 \times 96485} = +1.23\ V$$

Figure 17-6 shows a transit bus driven electrically by a fuel cell made by Ballard Power Systems of Burnaby B.C. The fuel is hydrogen gas, the oxidizer is oxygen gas, and the only exhaust emitted from these vehicles is warm moist air, which is a great advantage in a downtown transit service. The hydrogen gas is produced by electrolysis of water, or by methods such as reforming of natural gas, as discussed in Chapter 4. In this fuel cell the electrode reactions are:

anode: $\qquad\qquad\qquad H_2(g) \rightarrow 2\ H^+ + 2\ e^-$

cathode: $\quad 2H^+ + \frac{1}{2}\ O_2(g) + 2\ e^- \rightarrow H_2O(g)$

A sheet of polymer called a proton exchange membrane separates the anode from the cathode. The hydrogen ions (i.e. protons) generated at the anode are absorbed by the membrane and travel though it to the cathode, where they combine with oxygen molecules to form water. The electrons produced at the anode travel to the cathode through the external electrical circuit, which includes an electric motor.

Figure 17-6 A 205 kilowatt (275 horsepower) fuel cell engine installed in a transit bus. The bus has been developed by *dbb fuel cell engines*, a partnership of DaimlerChrysler, Ballard Power Systems, and Ford. The engine is powered by Ballard fuel cells operating on air and hydrogen. Fleets of these test vehicles are operating in Vancouver and Chicago. *Photograph courtesy of Ballard Power Systems, Burnaby B.C.*

Secondary cells are galvanic cells that can be recharged after discharge by connecting the cell to an electrical generator, as shown in Figure 17-5. After the original cell reactants are regenerated, current can be drawn from the cell again. Secondary cells are also called **storage cells,** or **rechargeable cells**.

Desirable characteristics for a rechargeable cell are long shelf life in both the charged and discharged conditions, a short time required for recharging, and an ability to go through a large number of charge/discharge cycles. The market for small rechargeable cells has expanded with the introduction of battery-operated computers and other electronic equipment. The commonest rechargeable cells are the lead/acid cell used in car batteries and rechargeable nickel/cadmium cells, but other high performance batteries have been developed.

The **lead/acid cell** was discussed in Section 17-5. The anode consists of lead plates and the cathode is lead dioxide PbO_2 supported on lead plates. The electrolyte is an aqueous solution of sulphuric acid, concentrated when the cell is fully charged and dilute when discharged, and solid lead sulfate, $PbSO_4$, is deposited on both electrodes as the cell discharges. The cell potential is just over 2.0 V and the half-reactions upon discharge are:

$$Pb(s) + SO_4^{2-}(aq) \rightarrow PbSO_4(s) + 2e^-$$

$$PbO_2(s) + 4H^+(aq) + SO_4^{2-}(aq) + 2e^- \rightarrow PbSO_4(s) + 2H_2O(\ell)$$

In the **nickel/cadmium cell** the electrode reactions upon discharge are:

$$Cd(s) + 2\,OH^-(aq) \rightarrow Cd(OH)_2(s) + 2e^-$$

$$NiO(OH)(s) + H_2O(\ell) + e^- \rightarrow Ni(OH)_2(s) + OH^-(aq)$$

The electrolyte is concentrated potassium hydroxide KOH, and the concentration does not change as the cell is charged and discharged. The cell potential is 1.25 volts. These cells are available in compact form for use in flashlights and portable electronic equipment.

In a **nickel / metal hydride cell**, one electrode is constructed of a metal M that can dissolve hydrogen to form a metal hydride MH. The nickel electrode is similar to that in a nickel/cadmium cell, described above. During discharge, the following oxidation half-reaction takes place at the metal hydride electrode:

$$MH(s) + OH^-(aq) \rightarrow M(s) + H_2O(\ell) + e^-$$

Such cells have larger capacity, and can be used for more charge-discharge cycles than nickel-cadmium batteries. The key to success is the development of the alloy used to dissolve the hydrogen.

17-9 Galvanic cells and thermochemistry

The discharge of a cell produces energy in the form of work, and it is interesting to see whether heat is involved as well. The application of thermodynamics to cells in Section 17-5 was concerned with reversible processes, but when current is drawn from a cell the process is always irreversible and the amount of electrical work obtainable is less than the maximum allowed by the reversible potential of the cell.

In the discharge of a cell, both heat q and electrical work w' are transferred between the cell (which is the system) and its surroundings. Nearly always, the pressure of the cell remains equal to the constant external pressure of the atmosphere, and the temperature of the cell remains equal to that of the surroundings. By the first law of thermodynamics as expressed in equation (6-10a) in Section 6-7 *check,* the heat and the electrical work must add up to the enthalpy change for the cell reaction:

$$w' + q = \Delta H.$$

When a cell is discharged, the electrical work w' is negative because the cell does work on the surroundings, and the Gibbs energy change ΔG is negative because the process is spontaneous. The amount of electrical work w' is limited by the second law of thermodynamics. From the discussion in Chapter 16, we know that:

$$w' \geq \Delta G$$

smaller Bearing in mind that both w' and ΔG are negative quantities, the magnitude of w' must be than the magnitude of ΔG. This can be seen by plotting w' and ΔG on a vertical energy scale with negative values below the origin, as shown in Figure 17-7.

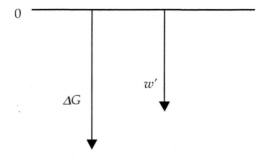

Figure 17-7 The relationship between ΔG and w' for a galvanic cell which produces energy in the form of electrical work. Both ΔG and w' are negative quantities.

The maximum amount of work is done when the process is reversible, in which case:

$$w'_{rev} = \Delta G = \Delta H - T\Delta S$$

and $$q_{rev} = T\Delta S$$

It should be kept in mind that for a specified cell reaction, ΔH, ΔG and ΔS are state functions and have fixed values regardless of whether the process is reversible or not.

Two particular cases illustrate these relationships: the hydrogen-oxygen fuel cell and the lead-acid cell. For the hydrogen-oxygen fuel cell, the cell reaction, the enthalpy change and the Gibbs energy change are:

$$H_2 + \tfrac{1}{2} O_2 \rightarrow H_2O(\ell) \qquad \Delta H^\circ = -285 \text{ kJ/mol.} \qquad \Delta G^\circ = -237 \text{ kJ/mol.}$$

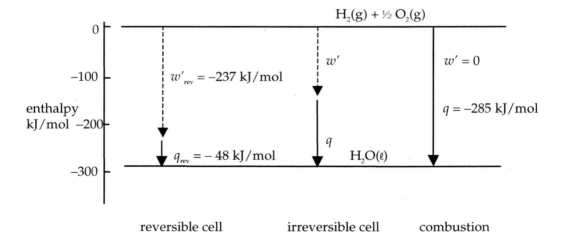

Figure 17-8 Heat and work in the reaction between hydrogen and oxygen in a fuel cell, and in a flame. The vertical scale represents the enthalpy change, made up of heat q and work w'. Three different processes are shown. On the left, the reaction in a fuel cell is assumed to be operating reversibly. In the middle part of the diagram, the reaction in a practical fuel cell is operating irreversibly and producing less than the maximum amount of work possible. On the right, the fuel is being burned in a combustion reaction, and no electrical work is done. In all cases $\Delta H^\circ = q + w' = = -285$ kJ/mol. This diagram may be compared with Figure 6-5.

If the cell were operated reversibly, then the electrical work would be $w'_{rev} = -237$ kJ/mol, and the heat would be $q_{rev} = (-285) - (-237) = -48$ kJ/mol. Hence, in reversible operation, some of the enthalpy change is transferred to the surroundings as heat, in addition to the electrical work.

In actual operation, the fuel cell would produce less electrical work and more heat than these figures indicate. For comparison, if we burn the hydrogen and oxygen in a flame, no electrical work is done and all of the enthalpy change appears as heat. The relationship between these various possible processes is shown in Figure 17-8.

The enthalpy and Gibbs energy changes for the cell reaction of the lead/acid cell (discussed in Sections 17-5 and 17-8) are $\Delta H° = -316$ kJ/mol and $\Delta G° = -395$ kJ/mol. These figures show that more energy in the form of electrical work is available from the cell than would be produced as heat if the reactants were simply mixed and allowed to react together directly. The energy relationships are shown in Figure 17-9.

In a reversible discharge of a lead/acid cell, the electrical work is –395 kJ/mol, and the heat absorbed by the cell is +79 kJ/mol. When the cell operates irreversibly, which is of course the situation when heavy current is drawn from the cell, less work is done by the cell so w' is less negative, and the heat q may be either positive or negative, as shown in the diagram. If the reaction proceeds directly without any electrical work being done, all of the enthalpy change (–316 kJ/mol) is released as heat.

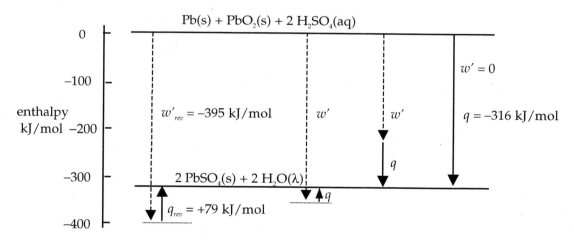

Figure 17-9 Heat and work in the discharge of a lead/acid cell. The vertical scale represents the enthalpy change, made up of heat q and work w'. Four different processes are shown. On the left, the discharge is assumed to be reversible. In the two processes in the middle part of the diagram, the discharge is irreversible and produces less than the maximum amount of work possible. On the right, the reaction takes place directly and no electrical work is done. In all cases $\Delta H° = q + w' = = -316$ kJ/mol.

Chapter 17

17-10 Industrial Electrolysis

An electrochemical process driven by current from an external electrical generator is called electrolysis. The potential required for the electrolysis to proceed must be greater than the reversible potential for the cell process. The excess potential required above the reversible potential depends on the cell reaction, the nature of the electrodes used and the concentration of the solution. A great deal of research is devoted to reducing the excess potential, since the amount of energy required increases with the potential applied to the cell.

From the cell reaction, it is possible to calculate the number of electrons transferred, n, and hence the amount of charge that must be passed through the cell to yield a given amount of product. The current required is the charge passed through the cell divided by the time during which the current flows.

In an electrolytic cell, the anode, where oxidation takes place, is connected to the positive terminal of the external current source, and the cathode, where reduction takes place, is connected to the negative terminal. The connections are shown in Figure 2-2.

The industrial production of chlorine and sodium hydroxide by electrolysis of sodium chloride solution was discussed in Chapter 4, and here we add several more examples of industrial electrolysis.

The first example is the production of sodium metal. Sodium metal is highly reactive and is one of the strongest reducing agents listed in Table 17-1; it is always found in nature as salts of the sodium ion, Na^+, rather than as sodium metal. The metal is produced by electrolytic reduction of the sodium ion in a molten mixture of sodium chloride, NaCl and calcium chloride $CaCl_2$ at a temperature of 600°C. Note that the mixture of salts melts at a lower temperature than either of the individual slats sue to fomration of a eutectic, as described in section 8-6, The cell is called the **Downs cell** and is illustrated in Figure 17-10. The electrode reactions and the overall reaction are:

cathode: $\quad Na^+ + e^- \rightarrow Na(\ell)$

anode: $\quad Cl^- \rightarrow \frac{1}{2}Cl_2\,(g) + e^-$

overall: $\quad Na^+ + Cl^- \rightarrow Na(\ell) + \frac{1}{2}Cl_2\,(g)$

Page 466

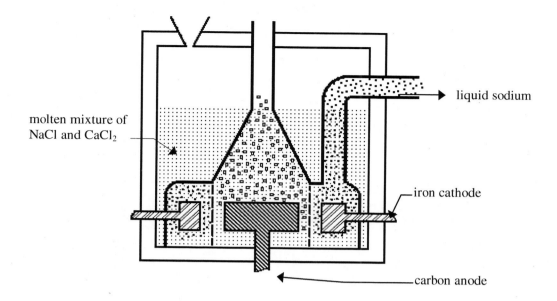

molten mixture of
NaCl and CaCl$_2$

liquid sodium

iron cathode

carbon anode

Figure 17-10 The Downs cell for electrolysis of a molten mixture of sodium chloride and calcium chloride.

Aluminum is an important metal used as a structural material and electrical conductor. It is produced by electrolytic reduction of alumina, Al$_2$O$_3$, obtained from mineral bauxite. Most Canadian aluminum smelters are located near sources of hydroelectric power because of the extremely large electrical power requirements.

Alumina, Al$_2$O$_3$, is a refractory material, which melts at about 2000°C. However, alumina dissolves in molten cryolite Na$_3$AlF$_6$ at a much lower temperature, near 1000°C, and electrolysis of the solution yields aluminum metal.

The construction of the cell is shown in Figure 17-11, and the photograph in Figure 17-12 gives an impression of the organization and the size of the plant. The following half-reactions summarize the cathode and anode processes in simplified form:

$$Al^{3+} + 3e^- \rightarrow Al(\ell)$$

$$C(s) + 2\,O^{2-} \rightarrow CO_2\,(g) + 4e^-$$

The carbon anode takes part in the reaction and is consumed in the process. The cell is maintained at a high temperature by the resistive heating of the electric current. Typically the current is 150 000 A, the applied potential is 4 to 5 V, and about 120 cells are connected in series. The production of each kilogram of metal requires about 80 000 kilojoules of energy, and involves an overall consumption of about 0.6 kg of carbon at the anode; the energy to be saved by recycling aluminum cans and other products is considerable.

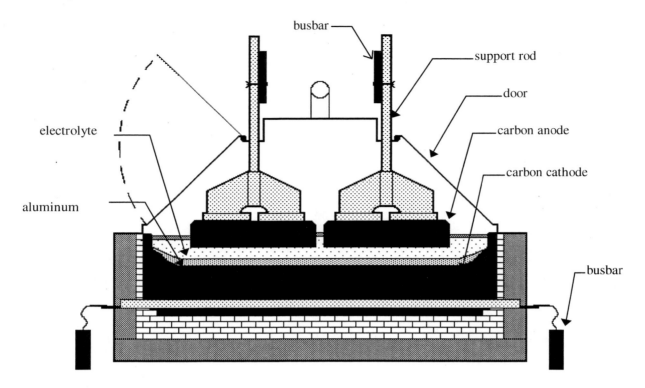

Figure 17-11 Electrolytic cell for the production of aluminum metal. The molten aluminum metal collects on top of the cathode, and the anodes are supported in the molten electrolyte. There is a crust of frozen material on top of the molten electrolyte, and fresh electrolyte is added through the doors. The cell operates at a temperature of about 1000°C. *Drawing based upon information supplied by Alcan Aluminium Limitée.*

Figure 17-12 A view of the electrolytic cells at the Alcan smelter at Laterrière, near Chicoutimi, Quebec. The main parts shown in the drawing above can be identified. Notice the size of the man standing in the aisle. *Photograph courtesy of Alcan Aluminium Limitée.*

17-11 Corrosion of Metals

Corrosion of metals is due to oxidation. In most cases, the metal is oxidized to an oxide or a hydroxide, and in the reduction process atmospheric oxygen is reduced to hydroxide ion or water. The Gibbs energy of formation of almost all metal oxides and hydroxides is negative, and so oxidation reactions are spontaneous. Hence most metals in their pure state in contact with the environment are not thermodynamically stable, and corrosion can be expected to occur spontaneously unless preventive measures are taken. Corrosion reactions are not usually fast, but their progress is certain unless steps are taken to protect the metal.

The economic costs of corrosion are enormous. Corrosion protection and replacement of corroded metal parts make up a significant part of the gross national product. For steel, it has been estimated that 25% of the steel produced is lost through corrosion.

The most serious corrosion problems are associated with the presence of water containing dissolved electrolytes. Marine structures, especially those in salt water, are constantly exposed in this way. In winter conditions in northern climates, vehicles and bridges are repeatedly exposed to slush containing salt which is spread on roads as an antifreeze. Acid rain is caused by strong acids formed from oxides of sulphur and nitrogen released into the atmosphere from factories, power plants and motor vehicles.

Any metal in contact with an electrolyte solution acts as an electrode, and corrosion is caused by an anodic oxidation reaction which converts metal atoms into ions in solution. The accompanying reduction process can take place some distance away from the oxidation process if there is a metallic connection to transport electrons, and water to transport ions between the two reaction sites. Serious corrosion is often found where two different metals are in contact, for then the more noble metal acts as a cathode to reduce oxygen and the more active metal is oxidized. The half-reaction for reduction of atmospheric oxygen is:

$$\tfrac{1}{2}O_2 \, (g) + 2H^+ \, (aq) + 2e^- \rightarrow H_2O(\ell) \qquad \varepsilon^\circ = +1.229 \text{ V}$$

Under conditions that differ from standard state conditions, the reduction potential ε depends on pH and the partial pressure of oxygen according to the Nernst equation:

$$\varepsilon = +1.229 - 0.05916 \times pH + 0.01479 \times \log\left(\frac{p(O_2)}{P^o}\right)$$

Reduction of oxygen is therefore favoured at places where the partial pressure of oxygen is high and the pH is low.

A gradient in the oxygen content of the water in contact with a metal can cause localized corrosion. Oxygen is reduced at locations where the activity of oxygen is high, while the metal is oxidized at locations where the activity of oxygen is low. The metal is therefore damaged at places that are protected from the air.

Corrosion of this sort is often seen at the inner ends of nails or bolts, which have restricted access to air. A narrow crevice in a metal structure can result in reduced activity of oxygen in stagnant water in the crevice, resulting in oxidation of the metal at the bottom of the crevice. When paint or a plastic covering is used to protect a metal part, a scratch in the covering exposes part of the metal to the atmosphere. Oxygen is reduced at the exposed metal surface, while other parts of the metal which are still covered, and hence protected from the atmosphere, become anodic and are oxidized. Metal ions formed at the anode and anions formed at the cathode diffuse towards each other and precipitate the metal oxide or hydroxide where they meet. Electrons are transported from the anode to the cathode through the metal.

Figure 17-13 shows some of practical situations in which corrosion takes place through electrochemical processes in which the anode and cathode are physically separate.

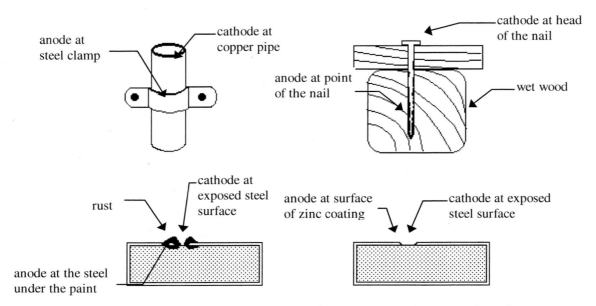

Figure 17-13 Some examples of corrosion by atmospheric oxygen in situations where there are separate anodic and cathodic sites. Corrosion occurs at the anodic site, which is the more active metal or at places where the concentration of oxygen is low. Upper left: A steel clamp on a copper cold water pipe, often covered with condensation during humid summers. The steel will corrode rapidly. Upper right: A steel nail in wet wood corrodes at the point of the nail inside the wood. Lower left: A scratch in a paint coating on steel causes corrosion under the paint. Lower right: A scratch in the zinc coating on galvanized steel causes corrosion of the zinc; the steel is protected because it forms the cathode.

In understanding corrosion, it is important to know where both the oxidation and reduction processes are taking place, and how fast. Since the two half-reactions must proceed together, the rate of corrosion can be controlled by reducing the rate of either of the half-reactions. Some corrosion control strategies work by ensuring that oxidation takes place at locations where structural strength is not affected. Galvanized steel is covered with a coating of zinc metal which is more active than iron, and hence any scratch in the zinc film causes oxidation of the zinc while the iron remains cathodic and is protected from corrosion. Galvanized steel is, in effect, an oxygen/zinc galvanic cell, in which iron forms the cathode at which oxygen is reduced.

It is sometimes possible to exclude air altogether from a metal system, and if other oxidizing agents are also excluded then the metal is said to be **immune** to corrosion. Immunity can also be achieved by applying a potential to the metal from a cell or other current source, so as to make it more negative, and therefore cathodic, relative to its surroundings.

When a film of a metal oxide or hydroxide is formed on the surface of a metal and adheres to the surface, then the metal is protected from, and perhaps electrically insulated from, the electrolyte solution, and the rate of corrosion may be reduced to a negligible amount. In effect, the product of corrosion prevents the reaction from continuing. This is called **passivation.** In the case of iron in contact with a solution of high pH, passivation is due to the formation of Fe_2O_3 on the surface. In the case of aluminum, a protective film of Al_2O_3 is formed when the pH lies between about 4 and 8. Outside this range of pH, the oxide layer is removed by one of the following acid-base reactions, and rapid corrosion may follow:

$$Al_2O_3(s) + 6H^+(aq) \rightarrow 2Al^{3+}(aq) + 3H_2O(\ell)$$

$$Al_2O_3 \text{ (s)} + 2OH^-\text{(aq)} + 3H_2O(\ell) \rightarrow 2Al(OH)_4^- \text{ (aq)}$$

In both cases, the protective film of aluminum oxide is destroyed.

Some metals can be protected by deliberately forming an oxide layer on the metal in a controlled electrolytic process called **anodizing**, a treatment which is often used for aluminum.

Key concepts

Electrochemistry is the study of reduction-oxidation reactions. The electrochemical cell is an apparatus for carrying out redox reactions so that the electrons transferred pass through an external circuit. The cell often consists of two half-cells, in which separate half-reactions take place, joined by a salt bridge to complete the circuit.

The anode of a cell is the electrode at which oxidation takes place. The cathode is the electrode at which reduction takes place. These definitions are valid whether the cell is a galvanic cell, producing electric current, or an electrolytic cell in which an electric current drives a chemical reaction.

The cell potential is the potential difference between the electrodes of a cell. The cell potential is measured using an instrument that draws almost no current from the cell. The cell potential is the algebraic sum of the potentials of the oxidation half-reaction and the reduction half-reaction. If the reactants are in their standard states, the cell potential is the standard potential for the cell reaction.

Half-cell potentials can be measured relative to a standard hydrogen electrode, which has been assigned a half-cell potential of exactly zero volts. By convention, all half-cell potentials are expressed as the potential of the reduction half-reaction. The reduction potentials of the two half-reactions can be combined to calculate the cell potential of the complete redox reaction. The cell potential is equal to the difference of the reduction potentials of the two half-reactions.

Cell potentials vary with the concentrations of the substances taking part in the reaction, as described by the Nernst equation. This is the basis for the electrochemical methods of measuring pH and the concentrations of other ions.

When a cell potential is measured for a reversible reaction, the potential gives a direct measure of the electrical work which can be done reversibly and the Gibbs energy change for the reaction. This gives a direct connection between electrochemical measurements, thermodynamics, and the equilibrium constants of redox reactions. From the standard cell potential, the standard Gibbs energy and the equilibrium constant for the cell reaction can be calculated.

Galvanic cells are commercially important as portable sources of electric power in flashlights and other domestic products. Electrolytic cells are commercially important for carrying out redox reactions with very unfavourable equilibrium constants, such as the reduction of metals, and the production of strong oxidizing or reducing agents.

The corrosion of metals by atmospheric oxygen in the presence of moisture is a redox process. The control of corrosion requires knowledge of the electrochemistry involved.

Review questions

1. What is the relationship between an electrochemical cell and a redox reaction.

2. What is an electrode?

3. Define the cathode and the anode of a cell.

4.   What is the difference between a galvanic cell and an electrolytic cell?

5.   What is a half-reaction?

6.   What does a salt bridge do?

7.   How do you write a cell reaction corresponding to a cell diagram?

8.   What is a cell potential?

9.   What is a standard reduction potential?

10. How do you calculate a standard cell potential from standard reduction potentials?

11. What is a disproportionation reaction?

12. What does the Nernst equation describe?

13. What is the relationship between cell potential and Gibbs energy change?

14. What is the relationship between standard cell potential and the equilibrium constant?

15. Name three important applications of electrochemistry in Canada.

Problems

1.   Write the cell reactions for the following cells:
(a) $Cu(s) \mid Cu^{2+}(aq) :: Zn^{2+} \mid Zn(s)$
(b) $Cd(s) \mid Cd^{2+}(aq) :: Fe^{3+}(aq), Fe^{2+}(aq) \mid Pt(s)$
(c) $Pt(s) \mid Cl^-(aq), Cl_2(g) :: HClO(aq), Cl_2(g) \mid Pt(s)$

2.   For each of the cells in Question 1, calculate the standard cell potential $E°$ at 25°C, anddetermine which is the positive electrode of the cell and which is the anode.
[−1.1047 V, +1.174 V, +0.252 V]

3.   Balance each of the following redox equations in aqueous solution, and determine the standard cell potential $E°$.
(a) $NO_3^-(aq) + Cu(s) \rightarrow Cu^{2+}(aq) + NO(g)$ [+0.615 V]
(b) $I_2(s) + S_2O_3^{2-}(aq) \rightarrow I^-(aq) + S_4O_6^{2-}(aq)$ [+0.46 V]
(c) $H_2SO_3(aq) + IO_3^-(aq) \rightarrow SO_4^{2-}(aq) + I_2(s)$ [+1.023 V]

4.   Write cell reactions for the following cells:
(a) $Pt(s) \mid Fe^{3+}(aq), Fe^{2+}(aq) :: Cl_2(g), Cl^- \mid Pt(s)$
(b) $Fe(s) \mid Fe^{2+}(aq) :: O_2(g), H^+(aq), H_2O(\ell) \mid Pt(s)$
(c) $Fe(s) \mid Fe^{2+}(aq) :: Zn^{2+}(aq) \mid Zn(s)$
(d) $Pt(s) \mid H_2(g), HCl(aq) :: AgCl(s) \mid Ag(s)$

5.   For each of the cells in Question 4, calculate the standard cell potential $E°$ at 25°C, and determine which is the positive electrode of the cell and which is the anode.

[+0.587 V, +1.676 V, −0.316 V, +0.22233 V]

6.   Calculate the cell potential for the following cell, which is not at standard state conditions:
$Pt(s) \mid H_2(g, 100 \text{ kPa}), HCl(aq, 0.01 \text{ M}) :: AgCl(s) \mid Ag(s)$ [0.4590 V]

7.   Consider the following cell: $Ag(s) \mid AgBr(s) \mid NaBr(aq, 1.0 \text{ M}) :: AgNO_3(aq, 1.0 \text{ M}) \mid Ag(s)$
The cell potential of the cell is +0.728 V, i.e. the right hand electrode is at a positive potential of 0.728 V relative to the left-hand electrode. From this information, calculate the   solubility product of silver bromide, AgBr, and compare your result with Table 15-1.   [4.9×10^{-13}]

8. From the standard potential for reduction of silver iodate, $AgIO_3(s)$, to $Ag(s)$, calculate the solubility product of $AgIO_3$. [2.9×10^{-8}]

9. Calculate $\varepsilon°$ for the following half-reaction from Gibbs energy of formation data in Appendix 1:

$$MnO_2(s) + 4 H^+(aq) + 2 e^- \rightarrow Mn^{2+}(aq) + 2 H_2O(\ell)$$ [+1.229 V]

10. Combine the following half-reactions

$$½ H_2O_2(aq) + H^+(aq) + e^- \rightarrow H_2O(\ell) \qquad \varepsilon° = +1.776 \text{ V}$$
$$O_2(g) + 4 H^+(aq) + 4e^- \rightarrow 2 H_2O(\ell) \qquad \varepsilon° = +1.229 \text{ V}$$

to obtain $\varepsilon°$ for the following half-reaction:

$$O_2(g) + 2 H^+(aq) + 2 e^- \rightarrow H_2O_2(aq)$$ [+0.682 V]

11. Use the results of the previous two questions to calculate $E°$ and K for the following reaction:

$$MnO_2(s) + H_2O_2(aq) + 2 H^+(aq) \rightarrow Mn^{2+} + O_2(g) + 2 H_2O$$

[+0.547 V, 3×10^{18}]

12. Calculate $\varepsilon°$ for the reduction of $Zn(OH)_2(s)$ to zinc metal in basic solution at pH = 14.0 using the K_{sp} value given in Table 15-1. The half-reaction is:

$$Zn(OH)_2(s) + 2 e^- \rightarrow Zn(s) + 2 OH^-(aq)$$ [−1.25 V]

13. Calculate $E°$ for the commercial mercury cell using thermodynamic data from Appendix 1, and determine which is the positive electrode. The cell can be represented by the following cell diagram:

$$Zn(s) \mid ZnO(s) \mid OH^-(aq) \mid HgO(s) \mid Hg(\ell)$$ [1.35 V]

14. (a) Determine the standard cell potential $E°$, the standard Gibbs energy change $\Delta G°$, and the equilibrium constant for the following reaction at 298 K, using standard reduction potentials:

$$Pb(s) + 2 H^+(aq) \rightarrow Pb^{2+}(aq) + H_2(g)$$ [+0.126 V, −24.3 kJ/mol, 1.8×10^4]

(b) Write an expression for the equilibrium constant for the above reaction. If a solution containing Pb^{2+} ions at a concentration of 0.05 M at pH = 2.0 is in contact with a piece of metallic lead, what pressure of hydrogen gas is required to maintain the process at equilibrium? [3.6 MPa]

15. Consider the following scheme of reduction half-reactions in the bromine system:

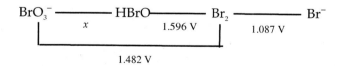

(a) Write balanced half-reactions for all four reduction processes shown.
(b) Calculate the unknown standard reduction potential x. [+1.454 V]
(c) Write a balanced equation for the disproportionation of HBrO into Br_2 and BrO_3^-, and calculate $E°$ and K for this reaction. [0.142 V, 4.0×10^9]

16. For each of the lines in the following scheme, write a balanced reduction half-reaction. From data in Table 17-1, fill in the appropriate standard reduction potential $\varepsilon°$ for each line.

Which of the ions and molecules in the reaction scheme are stable against disproportionation in acidic solution at pH = 0.0?

ClO_4^- —————— ClO_3^- —————— $HClO_2$ —————— $HClO$ —————— Cl_2 —————— Cl^-

17. Balance the following equation for a disproportionation reaction using the smallest possible integer stoichiometric coefficients, and calculate the equilibrium constant for the equation:

$$ClO_3^-(aq) \rightarrow ClO_4^-(aq) + HClO_2(aq) \qquad [7.0]$$

18. Many "oxyanions" such as nitrate NO_3^-, chlorate ClO_3^-, and permanganate MnO_4^-, are oxidizing agents in acidic solution. Show that, as a general rule, such anions become less strongly oxidizing if the pH of the solution is increased.

19. A fuel cell uses methane $CH_4(g)$ as a fuel and oxygen $O_2(g)$ as an oxidizer to produce electrical energy by means of the following reaction:

$$CH_4(g) + 2\,O_2(g) \rightarrow CO_2(g) + 2\,H_2O(\ell)$$

   (a) Write balanced equations for the half-reactions at the two electrodes.

   (b) sing data on the Gibbs energy of formation ΔG_f° of the substance involved from Appendix 1, calculate ΔG° and E° for the cell reaction at 25°C.   [-818.0 kJ/mol, +1.06 V]

   (c) In actual use, the cell potential is 1.0 V. How much electrical energy could be obtained per gram of methane?   [48.1 kJ/g]

20. From the half-reactions for the electrolytic production of aluminum, calculate the theoretical mass of carbon that is oxidized at the anode per gram of aluminum metal produced. Compare your result with the figure given in Section 17-10.   [0.33 g C/g Al]

21. Magnesium metal is produced (together with chlorine gas) by electrolysis of molten magnesium chloride, $MgCl_2$. The potential applied to the cell is 6.0 V.

   (a) If the cell carries a current of 100 000 ampères, what mass of metal is produced per second, assuming 100 per cent efficiency of the electrolysis?   [12.6 g/s]

   (b) What is the energy input per gram of metal produced?   [48 kJ/g Mg]

22. A Downs cell for electrolysis of sodium chloride NaCl produces 24.4 dm³ of chlorine per minute, when measured at 100. kPa and 25°C. What is the current through the cell?

$$[3.2×10^3\ A]$$

23. Consider the following cell: $Pt \mid H_2(g, 100\ kPa), H^+(aq,1.0\ M) :: Cu^{2+}(aq) \mid Cu(s)$. The left-hand electrode is a standard hydrogen electrode.

   (a) If E_{cell} = +0.20 volt, what is the concentration of Cu^{2+}?   [1.6×10⁻⁵ M]

   (b) If NaOH is added to the solution at the right-hand electrode, and $Cu(OH)_2(s)$ precipitates, calculate E_{cell} when [OH⁻] = 0.50 M, if the solubility product of $Cu(OH)_2$ is $1×10^{-20}$.   [-0.212 V]

24. A silver rod is immersed in an aqueous solution saturated with silver oxalate $Ag_2C_2O_4$. The solution is connected by a salt bridge to a standard hydrogen electrode to form a galvanic cell in which the silver rod is at a potential of 0.589 V relative to the hydrogen electrode.

   (a) Write a balanced half-cell reaction to describe the processes at each electrode.

   (b) Write the full cell reaction.

   (c) Calculate the solubility product for silver oxalate. $[1 \times 10^{-11}]$

25. The following electrochemical cell is set up:
   $$Cu(s) \mid Cu^{2+}(aq, 0.100 \text{ M}) \text{ MM } Cu^{2+}(aq, 0.0100 \text{ M}) \mid Cu(s)$$

   (a) Calculate the cell potential and determine which electrode is positive. $[-0.030 \text{ V}]$

   (b) 1.0 mL of a 5.0 M aqueous solution of ammonia NH_3 is added to the solution at the left hand electrode, which has a volume of 100. mL. Calculate the new cell potential.
                                                                      $[-0.028 \text{ V}]$

   (c) What is the cell potential if a total of 100. mL of the ammonia solution is added to the solution at the left-hand electrode? The equilibrium constant for the following reaction:
   $$Cu^{2+}(aq) + 4\,NH_3(aq) \rightleftharpoons Cu(NH_3)_4^{2+} \text{ is } 4.3 \times 10^{+12}.$$ $[+0.40 \text{ V}]$

18 Chemical Kinetics

Objectives

After reading this chapter, the student should be able to do the following:

♦ Define the rate of a reaction.

♦ Define the rate equation, the rate constant and the order of a reaction.

♦ Describe how concentrations change with time for zero, first and second order reactions.

♦ Define the half-life of a reaction.

♦ Describe the temperature dependence of a rate constant and define the activation energy.

♦ Describe the mechanisms of a number of reactions.

Related topics to review:

Industrial reactions in Chapter 4.

Related topics to look forward to:

Organic chemistry in Chapter 19.

18-1 Introduction

There is a lot of practical and theoretical interest in studying the progress of reactions as functions of time after the reactants are mixed. Given enough time, chemical reactions come to equilibrium. But there is a whole lot of chemistry to be learned by studying how a particular reaction system changes its composition as it moves towards equilibrium. This area of chemistry is called **chemical kinetics**.

The study of chemical kinetics has led to the discovery of the detailed processes, or **reaction mechanisms**, by which many chemical reactions take place. Knowing the reaction mechanism allows us to describe how a reaction takes place in terms of how the atoms move, and how old bonds are broken and new bonds are formed as the reactant molecules or ions are converted into the products. Studies of kinetics can reveal the path by which reactions take place, and show how new reactions can be designed.

Some reactions take place very rapidly as soon as the reactants are mixed, and are complete within a millisecond, a microsecond, or in some cases a nanosecond. Other reactions are slow and take hours or days to reach equilibrium. Most reactions become faster when the temperature is increased, and the temperature dependence of the speed of a reaction is often a key piece of information about the reaction. The introduction of a **catalyst** to a reaction system makes a chemical reaction faster, and the improvement of catalysts is an important part of pure and applied research.

Acid-base reactions in aqueous solution are usually very fast, and take place within a very short time period, while some redox reactions in solution are slow, and take minutes or hours to approach equilibrium. Combustion reactions can take place rapidly but smoothly in a flame but under some conditions are explosive; coal normally burns with a flame, but fine coal dust mixed with air can explode when ignited by a spark. Some reactions are slow and require hours of reaction time to reach equilibrium. Some reactions will not proceed unless the temperature is high and a catalyst is present, even though the equilibrium constant is favourable; an example of this is the synthesis of ammonia from nitrogen and hydrogen, which was discussed in Chapters 4 and 13.

18-2 Following the progress of a reaction

A chemical reaction can be followed as time goes on by measuring the concentrations of the reactants, or of the products, as functions of time, and plotting the results on a graph. This requires being able to measure concentrations as they change, which is not a trivial matter, particularly for fast reactions. If the concentration of a substance changes significantly during the time required to measure it, then the result of the measurement will not have much meaning. One of the familiar methods of chemical analysis, titration, usually takes at least a few minutes, so if a reaction reaches equilibrium within a minute or less, then titration is totally impractical as a way of following the progress of that reaction. For another reaction that takes hours instead of minutes, titration may be quite acceptable since changes during titration will be negligible.

There are two broad categories of measurement methods.

The first group of methods is based on taking samples from a reaction mixture at different times, and analyzing each sample. As pointed out above, it is essential that the method of analysis be fast compared with the time-scale of the reaction. If the reaction is a fast one it may be possible to slow down the reaction by one of several methods. Almost all reactions are slower at low concentration, so if the sample is diluted as soon as it is removed from the main reaction vessel, the reaction in the sample will slow down. Another way is to cool the sample, which also slows the reaction; this is called **quenching** the reaction.

The second group of methods involves taking measurements on the reaction system itself by some method that is much faster than the reaction. Many of the methods depend on optical measurements such as colour. White light contains all visible wavelengths, plus some wavelengths in the infrared and ultraviolet regions, at comparable intensity. The colour of a transparent solution is usually judged by passing white light through the solution and looking at the light which is transmitted through and emerges from the solution, as shown in Figure 18-1. If one or more of the substances involved absorbs light in a narrow range of wavelengths, the transmitted light will be depleted in that wavelength range, and so will be coloured according to the wavelengths which were not absorbed. If a reaction is occurring in a solution, the changing intensity of the colour of the solution can be used to indicate the progress of the reaction. Typical instrumentation consists of a **spectrophotometer,** which measures the absorption of light of a particular wavelength and responds immediately to the changing intensity of the colour of the solution. Spectrophotometers can also be used to determine the position of equilibrium.

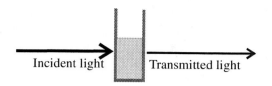

Incident light   Transmitted light

Figure 18-1 The absorption of a beam of light in a solution contained in a transparent cell. In a spectrophotometer the light has a particular wavelength, which may be anywhere in the visible, the infrared or ultraviolet part of the spectrum. Some of the light is absorbed in the solution, and the intensity of the transmitted light is less than the intensity of the incident light.

The amount of light absorbed varies with the concentration of the substance responsible for the absorption and with the thickness of the solution. If the intensity of the incident light is I_o and the intensity of the transmitted light is I, then the ratio I/I_o is the fraction of light which is transmitted through the solution and is called the **transmittance** T of the solution:

$$T = \frac{I}{I_o} \tag{18-1}$$

The transmittance is always less than one, since some of the light that went in was absorbed. Hence the logarithm of the transmittance is a negative number. The **absorbance** of the solution is defined as the negative logarithm to base 10 of the transmittance, and is a positive number:

$$A = -\log_{10} T = -\log_{10} \frac{I}{I_o} \tag{18-2}$$

On modern spectrophotometers, a switch usually allows read-out of either the transmittance or the absorbance of a solution.

The **Beer-Lambert** law states that the transmitted intensity I decreases exponentially with the length l of the path of the light through the solution, and with the molar concentration c of the solute responsible for absorbing the light. This is expressed by the following equation:

$$I = I_o e^{-2.303\varepsilon cl} = I_o 10^{-\varepsilon cl} \tag{18-3a}$$

An equivalent way of writing this is:

$$T = \frac{I}{I_o} = e^{-2.303\varepsilon cl} = 10^{-\varepsilon cl} \tag{18-3b}$$

In these equations, ε is a constant called the **molar absorption coefficient** or **extinction coefficient**. The molar absorption coefficient is a function of the wavelength, or colour, of the light and is a characteristic of each molecule and ion. The inclusion of the factor 2.303 and the expression as a power of 10 are relics from the days before hand calculators and computers made natural logarithms easy to use, but the old definitions have not been abandoned.

The Beer-Lambert law, particularly the exponential dependence of the transmitted intensity on concentration, is based on experiment and is supported by theory. The higher the concentration and the longer the path-length through the solution, the more light-absorbing species are available to absorb light of the specific wavelength.

If we substitute the Beer-Lambert law, equation (18-3b), in the definition of the absorbance of the solution, equation (18-2), we find that the absorbance is proportional to the concentration c of the molecule or ion that absorbs the light:

$$A = -\log_{10}\frac{I}{I_o} = -\log_{10}\left(10^{-\varepsilon cl}\right) = \varepsilon cl \tag{18-4}$$

By following the absorbance of a solution as a function of time, the progress of the reaction can be followed without taking samples and without any time delays. The spectrophotometer indicates the changing concentration in "real time".

Some other methods that are used in chemical kinetics are as follows:

(a) measurements of the electrical resistance of solutions containing ions;

(b) electrochemical measurements using a platinum electrode to sense changing concentrations through the Nernst equation, which was discussed in Section 17-4;

(c) measurements of the amount of gas produced, in appropriate cases;

(d) measurement of temperature change in a calorimeter.

18-3 The rate of a chemical reaction

The rates of consumption of a reactant and formation of a product are related to each other by the stoichiometry of the reaction. For example, consider the reaction in which hydrogen iodide is oxidized to iodine by hydrogen peroxide in acidic aqueous solution:

$$H_2O_2(aq) + 2\,H^+(aq) + 2\,I^-(aq) \rightarrow I_2(aq) + 2\,H_2O.$$

The changes in the molar concentrations of hydrogen peroxide H_2O_2, iodide I^- and iodine I_2 are not independent of each other. The change in the concentration of a species in solution such as I_2 over the period from time t_1 to t_2 is:

$$\Delta[I_2] = [I_2]_2 - [I_2]_1$$

In this equation, square brackets [ ] indicate molar concentrations, and the subscripts 1 and 2 outside the square brackets refer to the times at which the concentration is measured. For the equation as shown above, one mole of iodine is produced from one mole of hydrogen peroxide, two moles of iodide ion and two moles of hydrogen ion. Hence the changes in concentration in any time period are related as follows:

$$\Delta[I_2] = -\Delta[H_2O_2] = -\frac{1}{2}\Delta[I^-] = -\frac{1}{2}\Delta[H^+]$$

The average rate of change of concentration of I_2 over this period of time Δt is:

$$\text{average rate of change of concentration of } I_2 = \frac{[I_2]_2 - [I_2]_1}{t_2 - t_1} = \frac{\Delta[I_2]}{\Delta t}$$

Measuring the rate of a reaction is a typical problem of dealing with quantities which change with time, and can only be handled properly by the methods of calculus. The average rate calculated by the above equation depends on the time period Δt used for the calculation. As the period Δt is taken smaller and smaller, the average rate approaches a mathematical limit called the

derivative or **differential coefficient** of the concentration specified. This specifies the instantaneous rate of change of concentration:

$$\text{instanteous rate of change of concentration of } I_2 = \frac{d[I_2]}{dt}.$$

This is demonstrated for the graph in Figure 18-2.

Because of the stoichiometric condition discussed above, the rates of appearance or disappearance of the substances involved in a reaction are not independent. For the particular example above, these rates are related to each other by the following:

$$-\frac{d[H_2O_2]}{dt} = -\frac{1}{2}\frac{d[I^-]}{dt} = -\frac{1}{2}\frac{d[H^+]}{dt} = +\frac{d[I_2]}{dt}$$

In this set of equations, negative signs are attached to the derivatives for the reactants, and positive signs to the derivatives for the products. The negative signs are required because the concentrations of the reactants decrease with time, while the concentrations of the products increase with time.

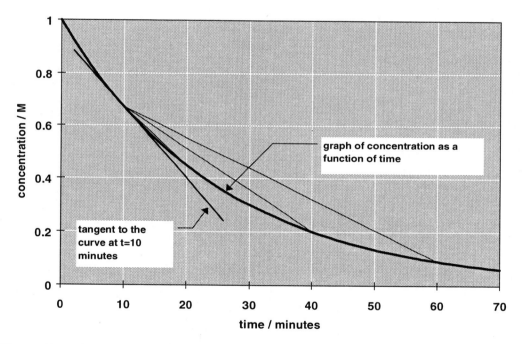

Figure 18-2 A typical curved graph showing the decrease in molar concentration of a reactant as a function of time. The average rate of change of the molar concentration over a period of time is the slope of the dotted line joining the points on the graph at the beginning and end of the period. Three such lines are drawn, covering three different time periods beginning at $t = 10$ minutes. The slope of the tangent to the curve at $t = 10$ minutes is the limit of the slopes of the other lines as the length of the time period is reduced to zero. In the notation of calculus, the slope of the tangent is the derivative d[A]/dt.

In general the **rate of reaction** for a reaction represented by the balanced equation

$$aA + bB \rightarrow cC + eE$$

is formally defined as: $\quad \text{rate} = -\dfrac{1}{a}\dfrac{d[A]}{dt} = -\dfrac{1}{b}\dfrac{d[B]}{dt} = +\dfrac{1}{c}\dfrac{d[C]}{dt} = +\dfrac{1}{e}\dfrac{d[E]}{dt}$

$\hfill$ (18-5)

With molar concentrations expressed in mol/L, the units of rate of reaction are mol L^{-1} s^{-1}. Note that the balanced equation must accompany the value of the rate, since it involves the stoichiometric coefficients with their correct signs. It is also adequate to give the rate of change of the concentration of one of the species involved in the reaction, and this is commonly done.

The **initial rate** of a reaction is the rate at the start of the reaction, when time $t = 0$. The initial rate is important because it refers to conditions when none of the concentrations have changed appreciably from their initial values, which are set by the experimenter when the reaction is started.

A case in which the initial rate can be measured by a simple and colourful method is the oxidation of iodide ion I^- by the peroxodisulfate ion $S_2O_8^{2-}$:

$$2\,I^-(aq) + S_2O_8^{2-}(aq) \rightarrow I_2(aq) + 2\,SO_4^{2-}(aq)$$

In the experiment, a small, carefully measured amount of thiosulfate ion $S_2O_3^{2-}(aq)$ and some starch are added to the solution. The iodine molecules produced in the reaction above are rapidly reduced again to iodide ions by the thiosulfate ion, which is oxidized to the tetrathionate ion $S_4O_6^{2-}$:

$$I_2(aq) + 2\,S_2O_3^{2-}(aq) \rightarrow 2\,I^-(aq) + S_4O_6^{2-}(aq)$$

The thiosulfate ion is the limiting reagent. When all the thiosulfate has been oxidized, the iodine molecules produced in the first reaction react instead with the starch indicator, forming a deep blue colour in the solution. The blue colour appears suddenly. The amount of time required for the colour to appear is measured, and the amount of iodide ion that reacts during that period is equal to amount of thiosulfate added to the solution; from these data, the initial rate of the reaction can be estimated.

The structures of the four sulfur-containing ions involved in this experiment are shown below.

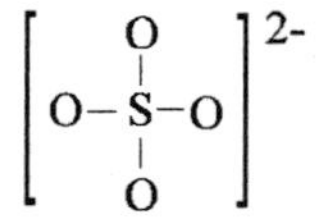

sulfate 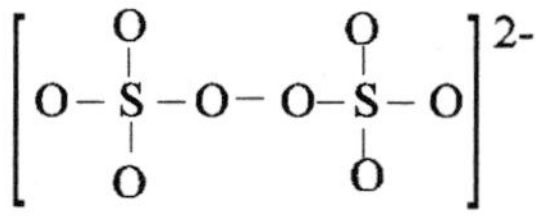   peroxodisulfate

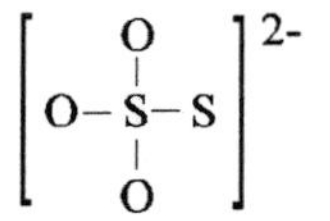

thiosulfate 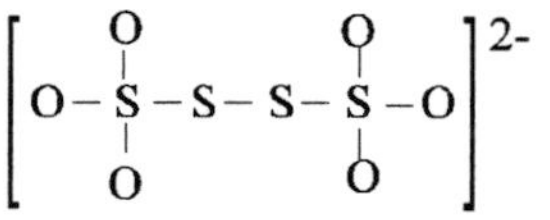   tetrathionate

18-4 The Rate Equation

Chemical reactions usually slow down as time goes on. The rate of a reaction is related to the concentrations of the reactants, so the reaction slows down because the reactants are used up. The relationship between rate and concentration can be discovered in several different ways. The simplest way is to measure the initial rate of a reaction for a series of reaction conditions in which the initial concentrations of the various substances involved are varied systematically.

Dinitrogen pentoxide, N_2O_5, is an unstable substance which can be prepared by dehydrating concentrated nitric acid with phosphorus pentoxide, which has the molecular formula P_4O_{10}, at low temperature:

$$4\ HNO_3 + P_4O_{10} \rightarrow 2\ N_2O_5 + 4\ HPO_3.$$

N_2O_5 is a solid, which sublimes readily to give a vapour. The decomposition of the vapour to give nitrogen dioxide and oxygen has been studied extensively. The decomposition reaction is:

$$N_2O_5(g) \rightarrow 2\ NO_2(g) + \tfrac{1}{2}\ O_2(g)$$

The progress of this reaction in a vessel of constant volume can be followed by measuring the pressure of the gas mixture as a function of time.

Example 18-1   Determine the rate equation for the decomposition of N_2O_5 in the following reaction given the data on the initial rate of the reaction:

$$N_2O_5(g) \rightarrow 2\ NO_2(g) + \tfrac{1}{2}\ O_2(g)$$

$[N_2O_5]$ / mol L^{-1}	$[NO_2]$ / mol L^{-1}	$[O_2]$ / mol L^{-1}	initial rate / mol L^{-1} s^{-1}
0.0050	0	0	1.0×10^{-7}
0.0025	0	0	0.50×10^{-7}
0.0010	0	0	0.20×10^{-7}
0.0025	0.0010	0	0.50×10^{-7}
0.0025	0	0.0030	0.50×10^{-7}

The first three lines in the table show that the rate of reaction is proportional to the first power of $[N_2O_5]$, and the last two lines show that the rate is independent of how much nitrogen dioxide and oxygen are present. This can be expressed algebraically as follows:

$$\frac{d[N_2O_5]}{dt} = -k[N_2O_5]$$

The negative sign on the right hand side is necessary because the concentration of N_2O_5 decreases with time, and so the derivative of the concentration is negative.

For many reactions, the rate of reaction is proportional to the concentration of one reactant raised to the first or second power, or to the product of two concentrations. The order of a reaction is the sum of the exponents of the concentrations. The reaction discussed in Example 18-1 is an example of a **first order reaction** in which the rate is proportional to the first power of the concentration of the reactant.

The equation that expresses the rate of a reaction as a function of the concentrations of the relevant substances is called the **rate equation**. The rate equation usually has a single term containing a number of concentrations, preceded by a constant factor k. The constant k is called the **rate constant** for the reaction, and allows calculation of the rate of the reaction given the relevant concentrations. The rate constant remains constant throughout the reaction, provided the temperature remains constant. The temperature dependence of the rate constant will be discussed in a later section of this chapter.

There are many reactions which do not obey a first order rate equation. An example is the disproportionation of the hypochlorite ion ClO^- into chlorate ClO_3^- and chloride Cl^- ions in aqueous solution:

$$3\ ClO^-(aq) \rightarrow ClO_3^-(aq) + 2\ Cl^-(aq)$$

The rate of the reaction is proportional to the square of the concentration of the hypochlorite ion, $[ClO^-]^2$:

$$\frac{d[ClO^-]}{dt} = -k[ClO^-]^2$$

Hence the reaction is called a **second order reaction.**

This example makes the point that the kinetic order of a reaction cannot be determined by looking at the stoichiometric coefficients in the chemical equation for the reaction. The rate equation and the order of a reaction must, in the first place, be determined by experiment, and are not necessarily related to the stoichiometric coefficients in the balanced equation.

The reaction between hypochlorite ion ClO^- and iodide ion I^- in aqueous solution is a second order reaction of a different form:

$$ClO^-(aq) + I^-(aq) \rightarrow Cl^-(aq) + IO^-(aq)$$

The rate of the reaction is proportional to the first power of the concentration of hypochlorite ion and the first power of the concentration of iodide ion:

$$\frac{d[ClO^-]}{dt} = -k[ClO^-][I^-]$$

The reaction is described as first order in hypochlorite ion, first order in iodide ion, and second order overall, since the sum of the exponents of the concentration factors is 2.

As the reaction proceeds, the changes in the concentrations of hypochlorite ion and iodide ion are related by the stoichiometry of the reaction, so the rate equation can be expressed in terms of the concentration of either species once the concentrations are fixed at the start of the reaction.

Example 18-2 If in the reaction $ClO^- + I^- \rightarrow Cl^- + IO^-$ the initial concentrations are $[I^-]_o = 0.075$ M and $[ClO^-]_o = 0.125$ M, express the rate equation in terms of the concentration of ClO^- alone.

Since one mole of I^- reacts for every mole of ClO^-, then at any time after the reaction begins the changes in the iodide ion concentration and the hypochlorite ion concentration are:

$$\Delta[I^-] = [I^-] - 0.075$$

$$\Delta[ClO^-] = [ClO^-] - 0.125$$

From the stoichiometry of the reaction, these changes must be equal, and so:

$$[I^-] - 0.075 = [ClO^-] - 0.125$$

Hence $[I^-] = [ClO^-] - 0.050$, and the rate equation can be written:

$$\frac{d[ClO^-]}{dt} = -k[ClO^-]\left(0.050 - [ClO^-]\right)$$

For some reactions the rate is constant throughout the reaction. An example is the oxidation of ethanol C_2H_5OH to acetaldehyde CH_3CHO in the body, a reaction which is catalyzed by an **enzyme** in the liver called liver alcohol dehydrogenase. The reaction can be represented by the (incomplete) equation:

$$CH_3CH_2OH \longrightarrow CH_3C\overset{\displaystyle O}{\underset{\displaystyle H}{\diagup}}$$

ethanol   acetaldehyde

The rate of the reaction is constant and independent of the concentration of ethanol, and so is described by the rate equation:

$$\frac{d[C_2H_5OH]}{dt} = -k$$

Although the rate does not vary as the concentration of ethanol decreases, it does depend on the concentrations of other substances that are not consumed or produced in the reaction. This reaction is called a **zero order reaction** since the sum of the exponents of the concentrations in the rate equation is zero. If the rate of a reaction is limited by some factor that does not change as the reaction progresses, then the reaction is of zero order. This is the case if the reaction depends on a catalyst that is present in short supply relative to the amount of reactant present. The amount of catalyst is not altered by the reaction, and so keeps the rate of reaction constant even though the reactants themselves are being depleted by the reaction.

From the various forms of the rate equation, it can be seen that the units of the rate constant vary with the order of the reaction, as shown in Table 18-1.

Table 18-1 The units of the rate constant

Reaction order	Units of rate constant*
0	$mol\ L^{-1}\ s^{-1}$
1	s^{-1}
2	$mol^{-1}\ L\ s^{-1}$

* if the concentrations are expressed in $mol\ L^{-1}$, and time in seconds.

18-5 The integrated rate equation

The rate of a reaction cannot be measured directly. In most kinetic experiments, the concentration of a reactant or product is measured as a function of time. The measured concentrations are then compared with concentrations calculated from an assumed rate equation. The rate equation is a differential equation and must be integrated in order to perform the calculations. The integrated rate equations are well known for the various cases encountered in chemical kinetics, and the simpler cases are discussed here.

(a) First order reactions

The rate equation for a first order reaction, A $\rightarrow$ products, is:

$$\frac{d[A]}{dt} = -k[A]$$

(18-6)

In any short time interval Δt, the change in concentration $\Delta[A]$ is proportional to the concentration $[A]_t$ at time t and to the length of the time interval, to a good approximation, so that $\Delta[A] \approx -k \times [A]_t \times \Delta t$. This is characteristic of an exponential decay of $[A]$, and the integrated rate equation is:

$$[A]_t = [A]_o e^{-kt}$$

(18-7)

where $[A]_o$ is the initial concentration at the beginning of the reaction. Figure 18-3 shows a typical graph of concentration as a function of time for a first order reaction.

This solution can be confirmed by differentiation:

$$\frac{d[A]_t}{dt} = [A]_o \frac{d}{dt} e^{-kt} = [A]_o (-k) e^{-kt} = -k[A]_t$$

The rate constant of a first order reaction can be determined experimentally by plotting the logarithm of the concentration *versus* time. Taking the natural logarithm of both sides of equation (18-7),

$$\ln \frac{[A]_t}{[A]_o} = -kt$$

(18-8)

This graph should therefore be a straight line of negative slope. From the slope of a line of best fit to the experimental data, the rate constant k can be determined, as shown in Figure 18-4.

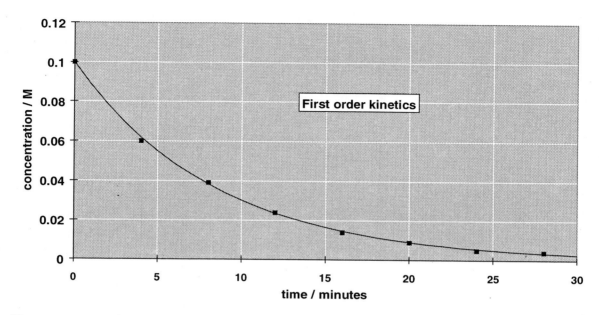

Figure 18-3 A plot of molar concentration versus time for a first order reaction with an initial concentration of 0.10 M and a rate constant of 0.12 minutes^{-1}. The squares indicate typical experimental concentration data.

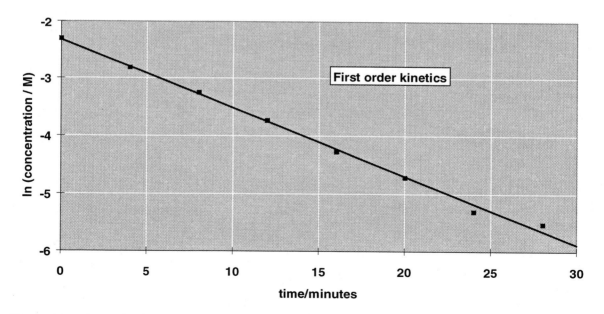

Figure 18-4 A graph of the natural logarithm of the molar concentration for the "experimental" points shown in Figure 18-3, as a function of time. The straight line is a line of best fit to the data points.

Example 18-3 The hydrolysis of t-butyl bromide in a solvent consisting of a mixture of water and acetone is described by the equation:

$$(CH_3)_3CBr + H_2O \rightarrow (CH_3)_3COH + H^+ + Br^-$$

The reaction is first order in $(CH_3)_3CBr$, and the rate constant is 8.7×10^{-4} minutes^{-1}. If the initial concentrations are $[(CH_3)_3CBr]_0 = 0.090$ M and $[Br^-] = 0.000$ M, what are the concentrations of $(CH_3)_3CBr$ and Br^- after a period of 720 minutes?

After 720 minutes, the concentration of $(CH_3)_3CBr$ is, by equation (18-7),

$$[(CH_3)_3CBr] = 0.090 \, M \times exp(-8.7 \times 10^{-4} \times 720.) = 0.048 \, M$$

Hence the concentration of t-butyl bromide has decreased by $(0.090–0.048) = 0.42$ M. Each molecule of $(CH_3)_3CBr$ which reacts produces one Br^- ion, so the concentration of Br^- is 0.048 M.

(b) Second order reactions

There are two cases of second order reactions to consider. If the rate of a reaction of the form

$$A \rightarrow products$$

is proportional to the square of the concentration of one of the reactants, the rate equation is:

$$\frac{d[A]}{dt} = -k[A]^2 \tag{18-9}$$

The solution of the equation obtained by integrating this equation is:

$$\frac{1}{[A]_t} = \frac{1}{[A]_o} + kt \tag{18-10}$$

This solution can be confirmed by differentiation of both sides with respect to time, using the chain rule to evaluate the left hand side:

$$\frac{d}{dt}\frac{1}{[A]_t} = -\frac{1}{[A]_t^2}\frac{d[A]_t}{dt} = k$$

The second of these equalities is the same as the rate equation, (18-9).

Figure 18-5 shows a typical graph of the dependence of concentration on time for a second order reaction. In this graph, the parameters have been chosen so that the initial rate of reaction is the same as for the first order reaction in Figure 18-3. This allows comparison of the different behaviour of first and second order reactions at long times. Second order reactions have characteristically long tails compared with first order reactions.

For a reaction following second order kinetics, the inverse of concentration is proportional to the time elapsed, as can be seen from Equation (18-10). If the inverse of concentration, $1/[A]_t$, is plotted as a function of time, a straight line plot is obtained, as shown in Figure 18-6, and from such a plot the rate constant can be determined from experimental data.

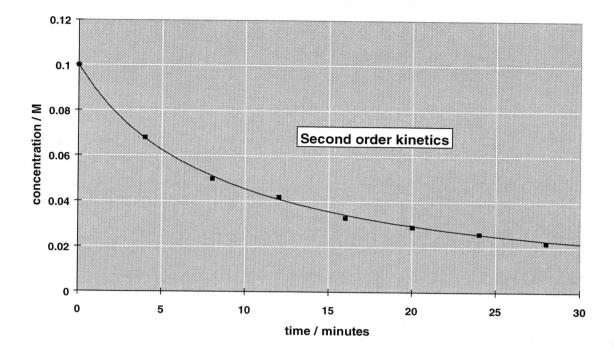

Figure 18-5 A plot of molar concentration *versus* time for a second order reaction with an initial concentration of 0.10 M and a rate constant of 1.2 mol^{-1} L $minutes^{-1}$. For the purposes of comparison, conditions have been chosen so that the initial rate of this reaction is the same as that in the first order reaction shown in Figure 18-3. The characteristically long tail of the second order reaction is clear.

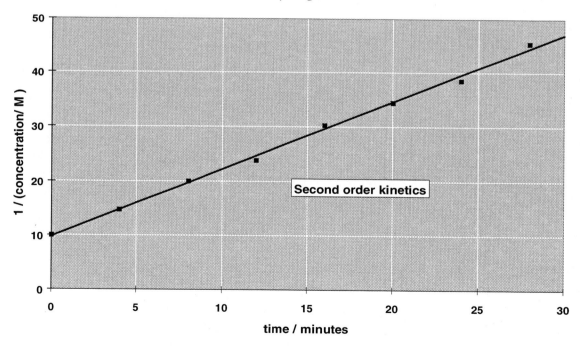

Figure 18-6 A plot of the inverse of the molar concentration versus time for the experimental points from Figure 18-5. The straight line is a line of best fit to the data points.

Suppose the rate equation for the reaction A + B → products is:

$$\frac{d[A]}{dt} = -k[A][B]$$

The reaction is first order in reactant A, first order in reactant B, and second order overall. The integrated rate equation in this case is more complex to deal with than in the previous cases, and will not be discussed here. However, modern practice in dealing with second order reactions is to make one concentration initially much larger than the other, if this is possible. If the initial concentration of one reactant, B say, is much larger than the initial concentration of the other reactant, then $[B]_o \gg [A]_o$. Then the [B] hardly changes throughout the whole of the reaction, so $k[B] \approx k[B]_o$ and remains nearly constant throughout the reaction. Hence under these conditions, $k[B]_o$ is like a rate constant k' in the first **pseudo-first order** rate equation:

$$\frac{d[A]}{dt} \approx -k[A][B]_o = -k'[A] \qquad\qquad \text{where } k' = k[B] \qquad (18\text{-}11)$$

By this technique, mixed second order reactions can be treated as first order reactions, with a characteristic exponential decrease of the concentration [A]. The pseudo-first order rate constant is a function of the concentration of one of the reactants.

(c) Zero order reactions.

If the rate of reaction is constant throughout the reaction, as described by the rate equation

$$\frac{d[A]}{dt} = -k$$

$$(18\text{-}12)$$

In this case, the reaction is said to be of zero order since the rate is constant and is independent of concentration.

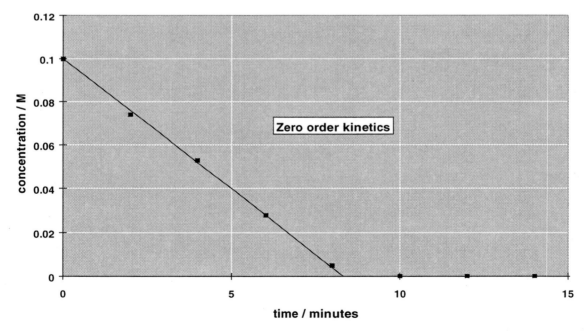

Figure 18-7 A plot of molar concentration *versus* time for a zero order reaction with an initial concentration of 0.10 M and a rate constant of 0.012 minutes^{-1}. For comparison the initial rate has been chosen to be the same as the initial rates for the first and second order reactions shown in Figure 18-3 and 18-5. The concentration decreases linearly with time until it reaches zero.

In a zero order reaction, the concentration $[A]_t$ decreases linearly with time until it reaches zero:

$$[A]_t = [A]_o - kt$$

(18-13)

This is shown in Figure 18-7. At low concentrations, some rounding off of the sudden change of slope is usually observed.

18-6 The half-life

The time required for the concentration of the reactant to be reduced to half of its initial value is called the half-life of the reaction. For a first order reaction the half-life is related simply to the rate constant. After one half-life when $t = t_{1/2}$, the ratio of concentrations is $[A]/[A]_o = \frac{1}{2}$. Substituting in equation (18-8),

$$\ln \frac{1}{2} = -0.693 = -kt_{1/2}$$

and so the half-life is

$$t_{1/2} = \frac{0.693}{k}.$$

(18-14)

The half-life of a first order reaction is another way to specify the rate constant, and remains constant as the reaction progresses. The half-life is used in nuclear physics as a way of specifying the rate of radioactive decay, which is a first order kinetic process. The half-lives of radioactive nuclides vary from nanoseconds all the way to millions of years.

Example 18-4 The half-life of a first order reaction is 5.0 minutes. How long will it take for the concentration to be reduced to 10% of its initial value?

Since $t_{1/2} = 5.0$ minutes, by equation (18-12) the rate constant is $k = 0.693/5 = 0.139$ minutes^{-1}. The time required for the concentration to be reduced to 10% = 0.10 of its initial value is given by:

$$\ln 0.10 = -kt$$

from which we calculate

$$t = -\frac{\ln 0.10}{k} = -\frac{\ln 0.10}{0.139 \text{ minutes}^{-1}} = 16.6 \text{ minutes}$$

The concept of a half-life is not as useful for a second order reaction as for a first order reaction, because it is not constant as the reaction goes on. In equation (18-10), setting $[A]_t = \frac{1}{2} [A]_o$ at $t = t_{1/2}$ gives the equation:

$$\frac{1}{\frac{1}{2}[A]_o} = \frac{1}{[A]_o} + kt_{1/2}$$

from which we get

$$t_{1/2} = \frac{1}{k[A]_o}$$

(18-15)

Thus starting at any time, the half-life depends on the concentration at the beginning of the period. The second half-life is twice as long as the first half-life, since the concentration at the beginning of the second half-life has been reduced to half of what it was at the beginning of the first half-life.

18-7 The rate equation and the equilibrium constant

When substances are mixed and start to react, the "forward" reaction begins. As the products begin to be formed, the "reverse" or "back" reaction begins to take place, converting the products back into reactants. After sufficient time has passed, the reaction reaches equilibrium, and there is no further net change in the concentrations. For example, when hydrogen and iodine vapour are brought together at high temperature, they react to form hydrogen iodide, HI:

$$H_2(g) + I_2(g) \rightarrow 2\,HI(g) \qquad\qquad \text{forward reaction}$$

As the concentration of HI increases the reverse reaction becomes faster:

$$2\,HI(g) \rightarrow H_2(g) + I_2(g). \qquad\qquad \text{reverse reaction}$$

At equilibrium we can combine these two reactions into a single equation with the familiar double arrow:

$$H_2(g) + I_2(g) \;\rightleftharpoons\; 2\,HI(g)$$

There are two interpretations of the equilibrium situation. In Chapter 13 we investigated the use of equilibrium constants to describe the situation, and in Chapter 16 we showed that equilibrium is the result of the Gibbs energy of the system taking the minimum value.

We can now contrast that interpretation with the kinetic view. On approaching equilibrium, the forward reaction slows down but does not stop, and the reverse reaction speeds up, until the two rates are equal when the concentrations reach their equilibrium values. At that point the net rate of change of concentrations is zero because the rates of the two opposing reactions are equal.

In the case of the reaction quoted above, both the forward and reverse reactions are second order, and the rate equations are:

$$\text{forward reaction:} \qquad \frac{d[H_2]}{dt} = -k_f\,[H_2][I_2]$$

$$\text{reverse reaction:} \qquad \frac{d[H_2]}{dt} = +k_b[HI]^2$$

In these equations, k_f and k_b are the rate constants of the forward and reverse reactions. The net rate of change of concentration of H_2 is:

$$\frac{d[H_2]}{dt} = -k_f[H_2][I_2] + k_b[HI]^2$$

At equilibrium, the rates of the forward and reverse reactions are equal and the net rate of change of $[H_2]$ is zero:

$$\frac{d[H_2]}{dt} = -k_f[H_2]_e[I_2]_e + k_b[HI]_e^2 = 0$$

Hence: $\qquad\qquad k_f[H_2]_e[I_2]_e = k_b[HI]_e^2$

where the subscript e on each concentration factor indicates that the system is at equilibrium. Rearranging this equation, we find:

$$\frac{[HI]_e^{\ 2}}{[H_2]_e[I_2]_e} = \frac{k_f}{k_b},$$

The left hand side of this equation is the equilibrium constant K, and so for this reaction,

$$K = \frac{k_f}{k_b}$$

This equation relates the equilibrium constant to the rate constants for the forward and reverse reactions.

There must always be a relationship between the equilibrium constant and the rates of the forward and reverse reactions, but it is not always as simple as in this case. It is prudent, when beginning the study of kinetics, to restrict ourselves to reactions far from equilibrium, or reactions with very large equilibrium constants, so that the reverse reaction can be ignored.

In some systems, there is more than one possible reaction for a given set of initial conditions, and it is important to be able to predict which of several possible products will be formed:

reactants → product C

reactants → product D.

If one of these reactions has a larger equilibrium constant and is faster than the other reaction, then the outcome is not in doubt: the product of the faster reaction will be predominate over the product of the other at all times.

But if the reaction with the larger equilibrium constant is slower than the other reaction, then different products predominate during different periods of time. Initially the product of the faster reaction predominates, despite the less favourable equilibrium constant, and during this period of time the reaction is said to be under **kinetic control**. However after sufficient time has elapsed, the product of the slower reaction with the larger equilibrium constant predominates, and at that stage the reaction is said to be under **thermodynamic control**. Usually, one of the two possible products is the desired product while the other is of little interest, so it is important to be able to predict the outcome in such situations.

Finally, some reactions that have very large equilibrium constants do not occur because of kinetic factors. A familiar example is the oxidation of fuels such as hydrogen, methane or liquid hydrocarbons. The standard Gibbs energy change for oxidation is strongly negative, and yet at room temperature combustion begins only when it is initiated by a spark or a flame. Gasoline does not catch fire spontaneously when exposed to air, and methane mixed with air does not immediately begin to form carbon dioxide and water. This is because the energy required for breaking chemical bonds is very large, making the reaction so slow that in effect it does not occur at room temperature. However, a spark or contact with a flame ignites the fuel/oxygen mixture leading to a self-sustaining fire, or an explosion. Thus favourable thermodynamics does not guarantee that a process will actually take place, unless the rate of reaction is also favourable.

18-8 The temperature dependence of rate constants

Rate constants vary with temperature. For most reactions, the rate constant increases as the temperature increases, though this is not always the case. The rate constant increases at higher temperature because of the greater average thermal energy available to the molecules. In many reactions there is an **energy barrier** to be overcome as the bonds in the reactant molecules distort, break or rearrange as the reactants become the products. The rate of the reaction is controlled by the supply of molecules that have enough energy to overcome this barrier. The average thermal kinetic energy of translation per mole of molecules is 3/2 RT, as shown in Section 5-9, which is about 4 kilojoules per mole at room temperature. Many energy barriers to reaction are much higher than this, so the rate of the reaction depends on the number of molecules in the high-speed, high-energy tail of the distribution curve shown in Figure 5-9. The number of molecules with energies exceeding a fixed value defined by the energy barrier for the reaction increases very quickly as the temperature increases, and so the rate constant for the reaction usually increases rapidly with temperature too.

Most rate constants vary with temperature according the **Arrhenius equation**:

$$k = Ae^{-E_a/RT}$$

(18-16a)

or, upon taking the natural logarithm of both sides,

$$\ln k = \ln A - \frac{E_a}{RT}$$

(18-16b)

In these equations, A is called the **pre-exponential factor** and E_a is the **activation energy**. The parameters A and E_a for a given reaction are determined by measuring the rate constant for the reaction at several different temperatures. The data are plotted as a graph of $\ln k$ as a function of $1/T$, the inverse of the absolute temperature. Such a graph is called an **Arrhenius plot**. For most reactions, the graph is found to be a straight line with negative slope, which is equal to $-E_a/R$.

Figure 18-8 shows an Arrhenius plot for the rate constant of the first order decomposition of benzenediazonium chloride:

$$C_6H_5N_2Cl \rightarrow C_6H_5Cl + N_2(g)$$

The experimental points fit accurately on a straight line graph.

From the Arrhenius equation, the relationship between rate constants at two different temperatures can be written:

$$\ln\left(\frac{k_2}{k_1}\right) = -\frac{E_a}{R}\left(\frac{1}{T_2} - \frac{1}{T_1}\right)$$

(18-17)

A large activation energy means that the rate constant is strongly temperature-dependent, while a small activation energy means that the temperature dependence of the rate constant is small.

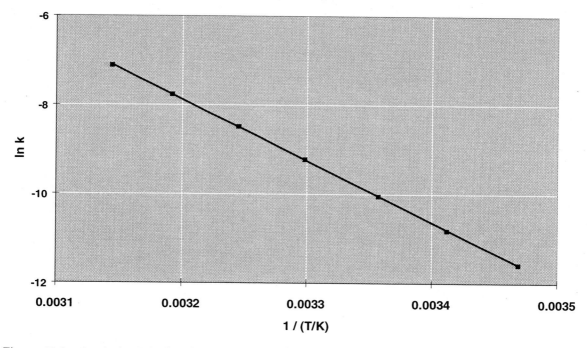

Figure 18-8 An Arrhenius plot for the decomposition of benzenediazonium chloride. The logarithm of the rate constant in (seconds)$^{-1}$ is plotted as a function of inverse temperature. The line is a straight line fitted to the experimental points.

Example 18-5 A certain rate constant is found to double when the temperature is increased from 20.0°C to 30.0°C. What is the activation energy for the reaction?

For the two temperatures $T_1 = 293.2$ K and $T_2 = 303.2$ K the ratio of rate constants is $\dfrac{k_2}{k_1} = 2$.

Hence:

$$\ln 2 = -\frac{E_a}{R}\left(\frac{1}{303.2} - \frac{1}{293.2}\right) = +\frac{E_a}{R}1.12\times10^{-4}$$

and so

$$E_a = R \times \frac{\ln 2}{1.12\times10^{-4}} = 6.16\times10^3\,R = 51.2 \text{ kJ mol}^{-1}$$

The activation energy is a measure of the energy barrier that must be overcome for the reaction to take place. Where a reaction requires breaking a chemical bond, the activation energy is large and comparable with the bond energies listed in Tables 11-4 and 11-5. Conceptually, the reaction can be thought of as proceeding along a **reaction coordinate** describing the process of converting the reactants into products, which may involve breaking a bond, or transferring an atom, or some other internal rearrangement of the molecule.

Figure 18-9 shows diagrammatically how the energy changes as a function of reaction coordinate. The energy minimum on the left-hand side of the diagram corresponds to the reactant molecules, and that on the right hand side to the product molecules. The difference in energy between the two minima is the difference in energy between the products and reactants, and is measured by the enthalpy change of the reaction (having regard to the allowance for measurements at constant pressure). In the chemical reaction, product molecules must cross the energy barrier shown by the maximum in the centre of the diagram. The activation energy for the forward reaction is the height of the barrier viewed from the left, and the activation energy for the reverse reaction is the height of the barrier viewed from the right. By inspection of the diagram, it follows that the activation energies are related to the enthalpy change of reaction as follows:

$$\Delta H = E_a(\text{forward}) - E_a(\text{reverse})$$

(18-18)

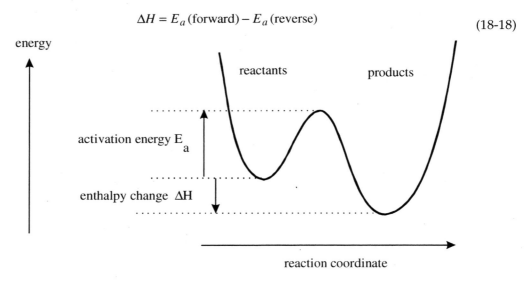

Figure 18-9 A graph of energy as a function of reaction coordinate, showing the passage from reactants on the left hand side to the products on the right hand side. The height of the energy barrier for the forward reaction is the activation energy E_a for that reaction, and the difference between the energies at the two minima is the enthalpy change of reaction, ΔH. The diagram shows an exothermic reaction with a negative enthalpy change.

18-9 Reaction mechanisms

The rate equations discussed in sections 18-4 and 18-5 describe the overall progress of chemical reactions and do not give any information about the details of how the reaction takes place. The process of determining the mechanism of a reaction from study of the kinetics is not a simple process, and requires extensive use of calculus and the analysis of systems of differential equations. At this point we will confine our discussion of the accepted mechanisms for some reactions of interest.

A **reaction mechanism** is a model for the detailed pathway by which a chemical reaction takes place. Once the rate equation for a reaction has been established experimentally, as outlined in the previous sections, a mechanism can be proposed for the reaction. Mathematical analysis of the proposed mechanism then leads to a rate equation, which can be compared with the experimental rate equation. If there is agreement between the calculated and observed rate equations, then the proposed mechanism is acceptable, but other acceptable mechanisms may be discovered subsequently. Thus a proposed mechanism for a particular reaction, even when well established and widely accepted, should not be regarded as the only possible mechanism. New experimental or theoretical studies may suggest a new mechanism or may lead to rejection of the previous mechanism.

A mechanism is often expressed in terms of **elementary reactions** to show what is happening at the molecular or atomic level. The elementary reactions often involve an ion or molecule called an **intermediate**. An intermediate does not appear as a reactant or product in the overall reaction, and is usually present in only very small concentration. The intermediate defines the pathway by which the reactants are converted to products.

Many reactions take place by means of the following general reaction mechanism:

$$\text{reactants} \rightleftharpoons \text{intermediate}$$

$$\text{intermediate} \rightarrow \text{products}$$

In this mechanism there is an equilibrium between the reactants and the intermediate, for which the equilibrium constant may be very small. The final product is formed from the intermediate in the second reaction. The rate of the overall reaction is usually controlled by the slowest of the elementary reactions, and that step in the mechanism is called the **rate-determining step**.

The first example is the hydrolysis of t-butyl bromide, which was the subject of Example (18-3):

$$(CH_3)_3CBr + H_2O \rightarrow (CH_3)_3COH + H^+ + Br^-$$

The intermediate is the cation $(CH_3)_3C^+$ formed by ionization of the reactant to a very small extent:

$$(CH_3)_3CBr \rightleftharpoons (CH_3)_3C^+ + Br^-$$

The intermediate then reacts with water to form the product:

$$(CH_3)_3C^+ + H_2O \rightarrow (CH_3)_3COH + H^+$$

The intermediate is present in only very small concentration, but it is the means by which the products are formed. The rate-determining step is the formation of the intermediate cation.

High temperature gas phase reactions often take place by vibrational excitation of the molecules in very energetic collisions between fast-moving molecules. For example, cyclopropane C_3H_6 undergoes a first order isomerization reaction at high temperature to form propene:

cyclopropane   propene

The cyclopropane molecule is rather unstable because the C–C–C bond angle of 60° in the triangular ring is much less than the usual tetrahedral angle of 109.5°. The intermediate in the reaction mechanism is a molecule of cyclopropane that is vibrating violently as a result of collisions between fast molecules. The vibrational energy of the "excited" molecules is enough to allow these molecules to rearrange into the more stable propene molecules.

The reaction mechanism can be written formally as follows. Very energetic collisions maintain a small equilibrium concentration of "vibrationally excited" cyclopropane molecules:

$$\Delta + \Delta \rightleftharpoons \Delta + \Delta^*$$

In this equation, the symbol Δ indicates a molecule of cyclopropane, and the star indicates a molecule that has been vibrationally excited in collisions with other molecules. If the energy in the excited cyclopropane molecule is sufficient, the molecule re-arranges into propene:

$$\Delta^* \ \rightarrow \ H_3C\text{–}CH{=}CH_2$$

This last step is the rate-determining step, and is called a **unimolecular** process because it involves only one molecule.

For the second order reaction between H_2 and I_2 discussed in Section 18-7, the mechanism is still under discussion, but the traditionally accepted mechanism involves an intermediate H_2I_2 from which the product is formed:

$$H_2(g) \ + \ I_2(g) \ \rightleftharpoons \ H_2I_2(g)$$

$$H_2I_2(g) \ \rightarrow \ 2\,HI(g)$$

The first step is called a **bimolecular step** because two molecules must collide for the reaction to take place.

On the other hand the reaction between H_2 and Br_2 is quite different kinetically, which is surprizing because bromine and iodine are both halogens.

For the reaction between hydrogen and bromine,

$$H_2(g) \ + \ Br_2(g) \rightarrow \ 2\,HBr(g)$$

the rate equation has been shown by experiment to be:

$$\text{rate} = \frac{k[H_2][Br_2]^{1/2}}{1 + k'\dfrac{[HBr]}{[Br_2]}}$$

where k and k' are constants. This rate equation is quite different from the second order rate equation for the $H_2 + I_2$ reaction, and indicates that the reaction proceeds by a different mechanism.

The reaction is initiated by dissociation of a small fraction of the bromine molecules into atoms,

$$Br_2 \ \rightleftharpoons \ 2\,Br{\bullet}$$

followed by reactions involving bromine atoms and hydrogen atoms. The bromine atoms contain seven valence electrons, of which one is unpaired. The dot next to the bromine atom indicates an unpaired electron that is not involved in a chemical bond. An atom or molecule containing an unpaired electron is called a **free radical**. Many free radicals are very reactive and attack other molecules rapidly to form new chemical bonds.

In the reaction between bromine and hydrogen, the bromine atoms formed initially by dissociation of bromine molecules attack hydrogen molecules:

$$Br{\bullet} \ + \ H_2 \rightarrow \ HBr \ + \ H{\bullet}$$

The hydrogen atom released in this reaction then attacks a bromine molecule, which regenerates another bromine atom:

$$H{\bullet} \ + \ Br_2 \ \rightarrow \ HBr \ + Br{\bullet}$$

Thus the bromine atoms formed initially are not depleted as HBr is formed. The last two reactions form a cycle in which a small number of bromine and hydrogen atoms can convert large amounts of H_2 and Br_2 into HBr without being used up themselves.

As the concentration of the product HBr increases, another reaction becomes important. Hydrogen atoms attack HBr molecules, to produce H_2:

$$H\bullet + HBr \rightarrow H_2 + Br\bullet$$

This elementary reaction converts some of the product of the overall reaction, HBr, back into reactant, H_2. The result is to reduce the rate of the reaction. In the rate equation, the reduction in the rate is due to the presence of the term $[HBr]/[Br_2]$ in the denominator, which decreases the rate as the ratio of product HBr to reactant Br_2 increases.

This type of reaction is called a **chain reaction**. The initial dissociation of Br_2 molecules into atoms can be caused by ultraviolet light, and so this system is sensitive to light.

There are many complicated reactions in the atmosphere. In the upper atmosphere, the pressure is low, and during the daytime the atmosphere is bathed in intense sunlight, including ultraviolet light. The energy of photons of light of wavelength 200 nm corresponds to 590 kJ/mol, and such photons are able to break any chemical bond of smaller bond energy (see table 11-4 and 11-5). The ultraviolet light from the sun therefore releases a constant supply of reactive atoms, such as oxygen atoms:

$$O_2 + light \rightarrow 2O\bullet$$

The oxygen atoms react with oxygen molecules to form ozone molecules:

$$O\bullet + O_2 \rightarrow O_3$$

The ozone molecules absorb ultraviolet light and dissociate into atoms in the reverse reaction:

$$O_3 + light \rightarrow O\bullet + O_2$$

These three processes maintain a steady concentration of ozone high in the atmosphere, in a region called the "ozone layer". Ozone absorbs light of wavelength less than 310 nm with high efficiency, and hence reduces the intensity of the so-called "UV-B" ultraviolet radiation, defined as light in the wavelength range 290-320 nm.

In recent years, measurements have shown a reduction in the concentration of ozone in the upper atmosphere, and an increase in the intensity of UV-B radiation reaching the surface of the earth. Increased intensity of UV light and an increased risk of skin cancer has become an annual feature of summer in the higher latitudes of both the northern and southern hemispheres. A major contributor to the reduction of the ozone concentration is thought to be the formation of chlorine atoms by photochemical dissociation of chlorofluorocarbons (CFC's):

$$CF_2Cl_2 + light \rightarrow \bullet CF_2Cl + Cl\bullet$$

The Cl$\bullet$ atoms then react with O_3 molecules to form $\bullet$ClO molecules, which react with O$\bullet$ atoms to regenerate the Cl$\bullet$ atoms. The process is described by the following reaction scheme:

$$Cl\bullet + O_3 \rightarrow \bullet ClO + O_2$$

$$\bullet ClO + O \rightarrow Cl\bullet + O_2$$

The net result of this cycle is the recombination of ozone molecules and oxygen atoms to form oxygen molecules. We can see this if we add the two equations together, and cancel atoms (Cl$\bullet$) and molecules ($\bullet$ClO) that occur on both sides of the equation:

$$O_3(g) + O\bullet \rightarrow 2O_2$$

Chlorine atoms are not the only intermediate by which this reaction takes place, but there is evidence that the process described is an important one and that chlorofluorocarbons in the upper atmosphere are an important factor in the reduction of the ozone concentration.

Strenuous efforts have been made to reduce the use of these substances in refrigerators and air conditioners.

18-10   Catalysis

A **catalyst** is a substance that increases the rate of a reaction without itself being consumed or produced. Catalysts can be classified into two broad groups. A catalyst that is in the same phase as the reaction is called **homogeneous**. For example, for a reaction in solution, a homogeneous catalyst would also be dissolved in solution. A catalyst that is in a different phase from the reaction is called **heterogeneous**, the commonest examples being solids that catalyze reactions in solution or in the gas phase. A catalyst provides a new path or reaction mechanism which has a smaller activation energy than the mechanism followed in the absence of the catalyst.

The decomposition of hydrogen peroxide H_2O_2 ,

$$H_2O_2(aq) \rightarrow H_2O + \tfrac{1}{2}O_2(g)$$

is slow in the absence of any catalyst, and aqueous solutions of hydrogen peroxide are fairly stable. However the decomposition is much faster in the presence of $H^+(aq)$ ions and $Br^-(aq)$ ions, which act as homogeneous catalysts. The $H^+(aq)$ ions protonate the hydrogen peroxide in the following acid/base equilibrium:

$$H^+(aq) + H_2O_2(aq) \rightleftharpoons H_3O_2^+(aq)$$

The next reactions are:

$$H_3O_2^+(aq) + Br^-(aq) \rightarrow HOBr(aq) + H_2O$$

$$HOBr(aq) + H_2O_2(aq) \rightarrow H^+(aq) + Br^-(aq) + H_2O + O_2(g).$$

Both $H^+(aq)$ and $Br^-(aq)$ are regenerated in this cycle, and their concentrations do not change as the reaction proceeds. The catalytic cycle is similar to that in a chain reaction, discussed in the previous section. The cyclic nature of the catalytic process was represented diagrammatically in Section 4-8.

An enzyme is a protein molecule that acts as a highly selective catalyst, and can increase the rate of a specific reaction by a very large factor. Enzyme catalysis depends on the formation of a complex between the enzyme and the substance undergoing reaction, called the **substrate**. The enzyme E and the substrate S form an intermediate complex, which can be designed ES. The substrate undergoes a rearrangement while bound to the enzyme, which allows it to react to form the product P. The mechanism is written as follows:

$$S + E \rightleftharpoons ES$$

$$ES \rightarrow E + P$$

The rate equation derived from this mechanism is:

$$\frac{d[P]}{dt} = \frac{k[E]_0[S]}{K+[S]}$$

where $[E]_0$ is the total amount of enzyme present in the reaction system and k and K are constants. For concentrations of the substrate sufficiently large that $[S] \gg K$, the rate equation is of zero order. This is the situation in the oxidation of ethanol in the body, as discussed in Section 18-4.

Enzyme catalysis is very selective, so each enzyme catalyses only a limited class of reaction in the body. The selectivity comes about because of the complicated structure of the reaction site in the enzyme, which matches only a limited range of substrate molecules to form the complex ES.

Key concepts

As a reaction proceeds, the concentrations of the reactants and products change as a function of time. The progress of the reaction can often be followed by a spectrophotometer, or by a similar method of chemical analysis.

The rate of a reaction is measured by the time derivative of the concentrations of the reactants or products. The rate is related to the concentrations of the reactants (and sometimes the products) through an equation called the rate equation. For many reactions, the rate is proportional to the concentrations raised to a power of the concentration of a reactant, and the order of the reaction is the exponent or power of the concentration in the rate equation. The rate constant is the constant of proportionality between the rate and the concentration (with its exponent) in the rate equation.

Many reactions follow either zero order, first order or second order rate equations. In each of these cases, the concentration of reactant with time in according to an equation derived from the rate equation by integration. By plotting the concentration appropriately as a function of time, the assumed rate law can be confirmed or rejected, and the rate constant can be calculated.

The half-life of a reaction is the time required for half of the reactant to react. For a first order reaction, the half-life is independent of concentration.

Chemical reactions are faster at higher temperature because rate constants increase with increasing temperature. The variation of the rate constant with temperature is described by the Arrhenius equation. The activation energy determined from the Arrhenius equation measures the energy barrier that controls the rate of the reaction.

Study of chemical kinetics is the main method used to discover the detailed mechanism by which chemical reactions take place. In some cases the mechanism of a reaction is very complicated, and involves one or more intermediate molecules, ions or free radicals which control the rate of the reaction.

Many reactions can be accelerated by adding a catalyst, which takes part in the reaction mechanism but is not consumed in the reaction.

Review questions

1. Define the rate of a chemical reaction.

2. What is a rate equation?

3. Define the order of a chemical reaction.

4. What is a first order reaction?

5. What is a rate constant?

6. How does a rate constant vary with temperature?

7. What are the essentials of a reaction mechanism?

8. What is a free radical?

9. What is a chain reaction?

Chapter 18

Problems

1. During the progress of the synthesis reaction $N_2(g) + 3 H_2(g) \rightarrow 2 NH_3(g)$, the rate of disappearance of nitrogen at a particular instant is:

$$\frac{d[N_2]}{dt} = -1.7 \times 10^{-5} \text{ mol L}^{-1} \text{s}^{-1}$$

Calculate the rate of rates of change of $[H_2]$ and $[NH_3]$ at the same instant.

$$[-5.1 \times 10^{-5} \text{ mol L}^{-1} \text{s}^{-1}, +3.4 \times 10^{-5} \text{ mol L}^{-1} \text{s}^{-1}]$$

2. The reaction between n-propyl bromide C_3H_7Br reacts with thiosulfate ion $S_2O_3^{2-}$ to form n-propyl thiosulfate according to the following reaction. The reaction takes place in a solvent consisting of a mixture of water and ethanol.

$$C_3H_7Br + S_2O_3^{2-} \rightarrow C_3H_7SSO_3^- + Br^-.$$

The dependence of the initial rate of the reaction on the initial concentrations of the reactants is listed in the following table. What is the order of the reaction with respect to each reactant? What is the overall order of the reaction? What is the rate constant for the reaction?

$$[1, 1, 2, 1.7 \times 10^{-3} \text{ mol}^{-1} \text{ L s}^{-1}]$$

$[C_3H_7Br] / \text{mol L}^{-1}$	$[S_2O_3^{2-}] / \text{mol L}^{-1}$	Initial rate $/ \text{mol L}^{-1} \text{s}^{-1}$
0.060	0.100	10.0×10^{-6}
0.060	0.050	5.0×10^{-6}
0.040	0.030	2.0×10^{-6}
0.040	0.050	3.3×10^{-6}
0.050	0.030	2.5×10^{-6}

3. The decomposition of sulfuryl chloride $SO_2Cl_2(g)$ is a first order reaction:

$$SO_2Cl_2(g) \rightarrow SO_2(g) + Cl_2(g)$$

In a particular experiment at a temperature of 593 K, the rate constant was found to be $2.2 \times 10^{-5} \text{ s}^{-1}$. If the initial concentration of SO_2Cl_2 was 0.020 mol/L, calculate:
(a) the initial rate of the reaction; $\qquad [4.4 \times 10^{-7} \text{ mol L}^{-1} \text{s}^{-1}]$
(b) $[SO_2Cl_2]$ after 1.0×10^5 seconds; $\qquad [2.2 \times 10^{-3} \text{ mol L}^{-1}]$
(c) the rate of the reaction after 1.0×10^5 seconds. $\qquad [4.9 \times 10^{-8} \text{ mol L}^{-1} \text{s}^{-1}]$

4. What is the half-life for the decomposition of sulfuryl chloride under the conditions described in Problem 3? $\qquad [3.2 \times 10^4 \text{ s}]$

5. Dinitrogen pentoxide N_2O_5 decomposes into nitrogen dioxide and oxygen in a first order reaction:

$$N_2O_5(g) \rightarrow 2 NO_2(g) + \tfrac{1}{2} O_2(g)$$

Suppose that initially, the concentration of $N_2O_5(g)$ is 0.010 mol/L. On a single diagram, sketch graphs showing how the concentrations of $N_2O_5(g)$, $NO_2(g)$ and $O_2(g)$ vary with time as the reaction proceeds. Show the ultimate values of these concentrations when $t = \infty$.

6. Consider the decomposition of $N_2O_5(g)$ described in the previous question at a temperature of 45°C, at which the rate constant for the reaction is $2.50 \times 10^{-4} \, s^{-1}$. If the initial concentration of N_2O_5 is 0.0100 mol/L, calculate the concentrations of $N_2O_5(g)$, $NO_2(g)$ and $O_2(g)$ after 6.0×10^3 seconds.

$$[2.2 \times 10^{-3} \, mol/L, \, 1.6 \times 10^{-2} \, mol/L, \, 3.9 \times 10^{-3} \, mol/L]$$

7. The radioactive decay of ^{14}C is a first order process with a half-life of 5700 years. What is the rate constant for the decay expressed in units of s^{-1}? $[3.9 \times 10^{-12} \, s^{-1}]$

8. Gaseous tetrafluoroethylene C_2F_4 slowly dimerizes at high temperature according to the following equation: $2 \, C_2F_4(g) \rightarrow C_4F_8(g)$
The reaction is second order in C_2F_4, and at 600 K the rate constant is 0.052 $mol^{-1} \, L \, s^{-1}$. If the initial concentration of C_2F_4 is $[C_2F_4]$ = 0.0100 mol/L, calculate $[C_2F_4]$ and $[C_4F_8]$ after 400. s, and after 2000 s.

$$[(a) \, 8.28 \times 10^{-3} \, mol/L, \, 8.60 \times 10^{-4} \, mol/L \, (b) \, 4.90 \times 10^{-3} \, mol/L, \, 2.55 \times 10^{-3} \, mol/L]$$

9. For the dimerization of gaseous tetrafluoroethylene C_2F_4 under the conditions described in the previous question, how long will it take for 95 % of the C_2F_4 to have reacted? $[3.6 \times 10^4 \, s]$

10. For the second order reaction $H_2(g) + I_2(g) \rightarrow 2 \, HI(g)$ the rate constant at a temperature of 400.°C is $2.34 \times 10^{-2} \, mol^{-1} \, L \, s^{-1}$. The activation energy is 150. kJ mol^{-1}. Calculate the pre-exponential factor, and the rate constant for the reaction at a temperature of 450.°C.

$$[1.0 \times 10^{10} \, mol^{-1} \, L \, s^{-1}, \, 0.148 \, mol^{-1} \, L \, s^{-1}]$$

11. Ethyl bromide C_2H_5Br, when heated in the gas phase, decomposes in a first order reaction to produce ethylene C_2H_4 and hydrogen bromide HBr.

   (a) Write a balanced equation for the reaction.
   (b) The activation energy for this reaction is 92.3 kJ mol^{-1} and the pre-exponential factor is $6.8 \times 10^{11} \, s^{-1}$. What is the value of the rate constant at 450. K? $[13 \, s^{-1}]$
   (c) If 0.0100 mol/L of ethyl bromide is introduced into a flask at 450. K, how long will it be before 75% of it has decomposed? $[0.11 \, s]$

12. The conversion of ethanol to acetaldehyde in the body is a zero order reaction, with a typical rate constant of $4 \times 10^{-3} \, mol \, L^{-1} \, hour^{-1}$. If the volume of fluids in the body is about 40 L, estimate the initial molar concentration and mass fraction of ethanol in the body fluids caused by rapidly ingesting 50. grams of pure ethanol, if the ethanol is dissolved uniformly. Calculate the time required for the concentration of ethanol to become zero.

$$[0.027 \, mol/L, \, 1.2 \times 10^{-3}, \, 7 \, hours]$$

13. A reaction has an activation energy of 40. kJ/mol and the enthalpy change in the reaction is −100. kJ/mol. Draw a sketch of energy as a function of reaction coordinate showing the relationship between the energy of the reactants and the products. Estimate the activation energy for the reverse reaction.   [140 kJ/mol]

14. The half-life was measured for a reaction A $\rightarrow$ products   for various different initial concentrations of the reactant A at the same temperature, with the following results:

[A] / mol L^{-1}	t$_{1/2}$ / minutes
0.50	25.
1.00	50.
2.00	100

Is this reaction second order, first order or zero order? Write the rate equation and calculate the value of the rate constant.   [0.010 mol L^{-1} min^{-1}]

15. The oxidation of I$^-$ by peroxodisulfate S$_2$O$_8^{2-}$ is a slow reaction described by the reaction

$$2 I^-(aq) + S_2O_8^{2-}(aq) \rightarrow I_2(aq) + 2 SO_4^{2-}(aq)$$

Thiosulfate ion S$_2$O$_3^{2-}$(aq) and some starch are added to the solution. As fast as it is produced, the iodine reacts with the thiosulfate ion:

$$I_2(aq) + 2 S_2O_3^{2-}(aq) \rightarrow 2 I^-(aq) + S_4O_6^{2-}(aq)$$

and when the thiosulfate is completely used up, the iodine forms a blue-coloured complex with the starch. In a particular experiment, the solution at the beginning of the reaction is prepared by mixing the following:

20.0 mL of 0.125 M (NH$_4$)$_2$S$_2$O$_8$ solution

20.0 mL of 0.22 M KI solution

1.0 mL of 0.060 M Na$_2$S$_2$O$_3$ solution

starch indicator

The solution turned blue 65 seconds after mixing. Estimate the initial value of $d[S_2O_8^{2-}]/dt$ in the first reaction by calculating the value of $\Delta[S_2O_8^{2-}]/\Delta t$ over the first 65 seconds.

[1.1×10^{-5} mol L^{-1} s^{-1}]

16. The standard reduction potentials for the half-reactions in the experiment described in Problem 14 are as follows:

$$S_2O_8^{2-} + 2e^- \rightarrow 2 SO_4^{2-} \qquad \varepsilon^\circ = +2.010 \text{ volt}$$

$$S_4O_6^{2-} + 2e^- \rightarrow 2 S_2O_3^{2-} \qquad \varepsilon^\circ = +0.08 \text{ volt}$$

$$I_2(s) + 2e^- \rightarrow 2 I^- \qquad \varepsilon^\circ = 0.5355 \text{ volt}$$

Show that it is more favourable thermodynamically for peroxodisulfate S$_2$O$_8^{2-}$ to oxidize thiosulfate S$_2$O$_3^{2-}$ than to oxidize iodide I$^-$, and hence the course of the reaction that actually takes place is kinetically controlled rather than thermodynamically controlled. How would you prove this last statement in the laboratory?   You may ignore the distinction between I$_2$(aq) and I$_2$(s) for the purpose of this problem.

17. For the isomerization of cyclopropane to propene, discussed in section 18-9, the activation energy is 272 kJ/mol. Use thermochemical data from Appendix 1 to calculate ΔH° and the equilibrium constant at 25°C for the reaction. Draw an energy diagram to scale indicating the relationship between the activation energy and the enthalpy change for the reaction.

19 Organic chemistry

By the end of this chapter the student should be able to:

♦ Describe the shapes of organic molecules.

♦ Describe some of the characteristic organic reactions.

♦ Describe the properties of amino acids.

♦ Describe polymerization reactions and the structures of organic polymers.

Related topics to review:

Nomenclature in Chapter 2. Petroleum-based industries in Chapter 4. Hydrocarbon fuels in Chapter 9. Molecular structure in Chapter 11. Weak acids and bases in Chapter 14. Entropy effects in chemical equilibrium in Chapter 16. Reaction mechanisms in Chapter 18.

19-1 Introduction

Organic chemistry is the chemistry of compounds of carbon. Organic chemistry occupies a special place in chemistry for several reasons. The number of organic compounds known is enormous, far larger than the number of compounds of all the other ninety-odd elements put together. The origin of organic chemistry was the study of compounds derived from living matter and some knowledge of organic chemistry is essential for understanding biochemistry and other basic medical sciences. Organic compounds are involved in almost every biological process in plants and animals, and so provide the links between chemistry, biology and the medical sciences. The pharmaceutical industry depends upon organic chemistry for the synthesis and purification of drugs used in medicine.

Organic chemistry has many subdivisions. One part consists of the extraction, isolation and identification of natural products derived from plants and animals. Synthetic organic chemistry is the science of making complicated new molecules from simpler reagents by carefully controlled reactions. Pharmaceutical chemistry and medicinal chemistry are concerned with the development of drugs for medical purposes and the study of how they work in the body. Figure 19-1 shows organic chemists employed in the Canadian pharmaceutical industry.

Mechanistic organic chemistry is concerned with how organic reactions take place, and makes extensive use of thermodynamics, kinetics and spectroscopy. Biochemistry is an extension of chemistry, mostly organic chemistry, into the realm of processes within humans and animals. Polymer chemistry is the study of large molecules formed from a large number of smaller molecules.

The characteristics of carbon compounds are these. Carbon falls in group 14 of the periodic table and has a normal valence of four. The electronic configuration of the carbon atom is $1s^2 2s^2 2p^2$. Carbon atoms readily form covalent bonds to other carbon atoms, to atoms of non-metals such as oxygen and nitrogen, and to metal atoms. In addition to forming covalent single bonds, carbon can also form double bonds and triple bonds. Carbon has an electronegativity of 2.5 (Table 11-6), which is close to that of hydrogen and several other non-metals, and the bonds from carbon to these other elements are not strongly polar in nature. However, bonds from carbon to oxygen, fluorine and chlorine are regarded as polar bonds.

Figure 19-1 Synthetic organic chemists from the Merck Frosst Centre for Therapeutic Research in Pointe-Claire P.Q. working to optimize and scale up processes for the preparation of potential new drug molecules. *Photo courtesy of Merck Frosst Centre for Therapeutic Research.*

Isomerism is an important feature of organic chemistry. When two molecules have the same molecular formula, but differ in the sequence of atoms bonded together, or in their spatial arrangement, they are said to be **isomers**. There are several types of isomerism. **Structural isomers** have the same number of atoms of the same elements in the two molecules, but different structural formulae. In other words, the atoms are bonded together in a different sequence.

There are other more subtle forms of isomerism called **stereoisomerism**, which is based upon the three-dimensional characteristics of molecules. **Rotational isomerism** or **conformational isomerism** occurs as a result of rotation about C–C single bonds. **Geometrical isomerism** occurs as a result of the lack of rotation about double bonds. **Optical isomerism** occurs when a molecule and its mirror image are not identical. These types of stereoisomerism will be discussed later in this chapter.

The characteristic geometry of the chemical bonds formed by carbon atoms was discussed and illustrated in Chapter 11. Carbon forms tetrahedral, trigonal planar and linear arrangements of bonds. The three-dimensional character of carbon-containing molecules plays an important role in the properties and reactions of organic compounds. The study of the relationship between the three-dimensional shape of molecules and their chemical properties is called **stereochemistry**. Carbon atoms readily bond together to form molecules containing chains and networks of carbon atoms. In Chapter 2, we described the system of naming some organic compounds. The student should review all of section 2-2 as an introduction to the work of this chapter.

19-2 The alkanes

The prototype organic compounds are the compounds of carbon and hydrogen, called **hydrocarbons**. In Chapter 2, we saw that there are various types of hydrocarbons, the most important of which are the alkanes, the alkenes, the alkynes and aromatic hydrocarbons.

Alkanes are hydrocarbons in which the carbon atoms are bonded to each other and to hydrogen atoms by covalent single bonds. Some alkanes have unbranched or "straight" chains of carbon atoms, others have branched chains. Both straight chain and branched alkanes have the general formula C_nH_{2n+2}. Alkanes are also called **saturated hydrocarbons**, because they contain the largest possible number of hydrogen atoms per carbon atom.

The alkanes with different arrangements of the chain of carbon atoms are **structural isomers.** For example, butane and methylpropane both have the molecular formula C_4H_{10} but differ in the way the carbon atoms are bonded together. Butane has a straight chain of carbon atoms, but methylpropane has a branched chain.

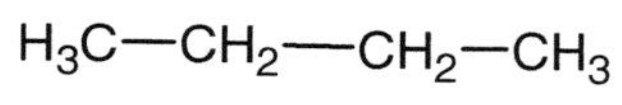

$$H_3C-CH_2-CH_2-CH_3 \qquad\qquad H_3C-\underset{\underset{CH_3}{|}}{HC}-CH_3$$

butane 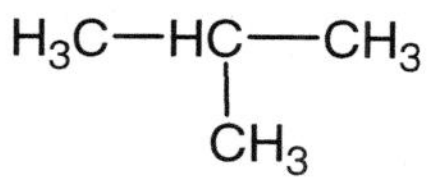   methylpropane

Each of these molecules is derived from propane by substituting a methyl group, CH_3, in place of a hydrogen atom H. The difference between them is that in butane the methyl group replaces a hydrogen atom on an end carbon atom of propane, but in methylpropane, the replacement takes place on the middle carbon atom. Another distinction is that in butane, no carbon atom is bonded to more than two other carbon atoms, but in methylpropane, one carbon atom is bonded to three other carbon atoms.

In an alkane, each carbon atom is bonded to four other atoms, and adopts a tetrahedral geometry. The usual picture of bonding is sp^3 hybridization involving the s orbital and all three p orbitals on the carbon atom. The single bond between each pair of carbon atoms is formed by overlap of sp^3 hybrid orbitals on each atom.

The geometry of alkanes is complicated by the fact that the parts of the molecule attached at each end of a C–C single bond are allowed to rotate with respect to each other about that bond. For example, the ethane molecule, C_2H_6 consists of two methyl groups CH_3 attached to each other by a C–C single bond. The different arrangements of the atoms resulting from rotation about a C–C bond are called conformations. The lowest energy conformation for the ethane molecule is the **staggered** conformation:

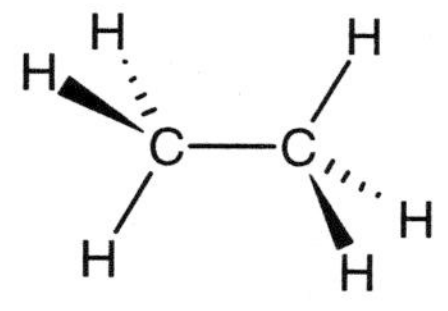

In this representation of the structure, bonds lying in the plane of the paper are drawn with ordinary lines. Bonds coming out of the paper towards the viewer are shown by solid lines getting wider towards the viewer. Bonds going into the paper are drawn with dashed lines getting narrower as they recede from the viewer. The drawing is a stylized perspective drawing intended to show the three dimensional arrangements of the atoms. If the molecule is viewed along the C–C bond, the C–H bonds at one end of the molecule lie in between the C–H bonds at the other end. The following diagram shows **Newman projections** of the ethane molecule, which are diagrams of the molecule when viewed along the C–C bond.

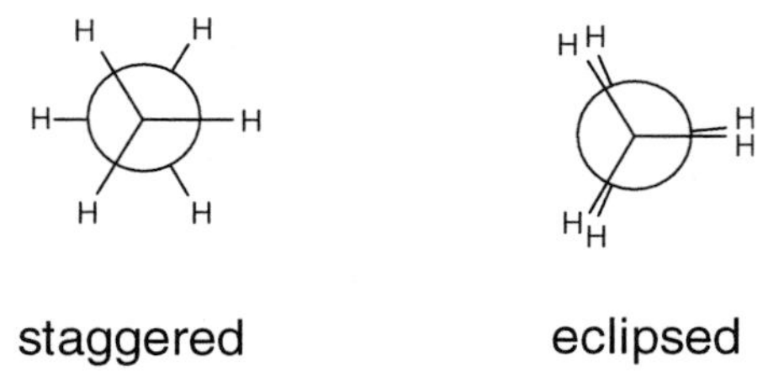

staggered   eclipsed

The left hand part of the diagram shows an ethane molecule in the **staggered conformation** in which the hydrogen atoms are as far from each other as possible. This is the lowest energy conformation of the molecule, but the two methyl groups can rotate relative to each other about the C–C bond. At room temperature, the methyl groups in an ethane molecule rotate relative to each other many millions of times per second.

The right hand part of the diagram shows the **eclipsed conformation** in which the hydrogen atoms are at their closest approach during the rotation. The difference in energy between the eclipsed and staggered conformations is about 12 kJ/mol. The reason for this barrier is that, when one methyl group rotates relative to the other, the hydrogen atoms of one methyl group come close to the hydrogen atoms of the other methyl group, and repulsive forces between the hydrogen atoms increase the energy of the molecule.

Because of the tetrahedral nature of the bonds around each carbon atom, the C–H bonds are all identical. It should not be inferred from the usual two-dimensional representation of alkane molecules that there is any difference between C–H bonds.

Example 19-1 Draw structural formulae for all the structural isomers of dichloroethane.

Dichloroethane has the formula $C_2H_4Cl_2$. The two chlorine atoms may be attached to the same carbon atom, or to different carbon atoms, as shown in the following two structural formulae:

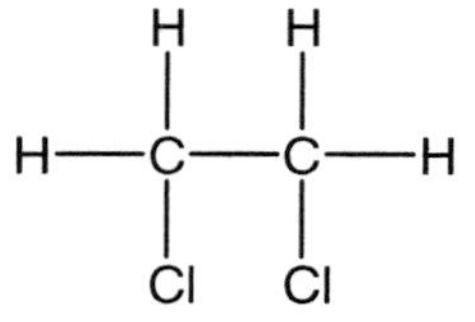

1,2-dichloroethane 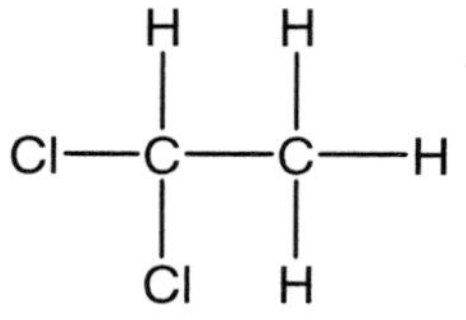   1,1-dichloroethane

These two isomers are distinguished by using prefix numbers to identify the carbon atoms to which the chlorine atoms are bonded. There are other ways of placing the chlorine atoms around these two-dimensional formulae, but they do not correspond to new isomers. This is because firstly, the bonds around each carbon atom form a tetrahedron in three dimensions, and secondly, the rapid relative rotation of the two ends of the molecule around the C–C bond converts one distinct form of the molecule to another almost immediately. Hence there are only two structural isomers of dichloroethane.

In longer chain alkanes, the energy barrier to rotation about C–C bonds is higher than in ethane, but nevertheless rotation about C–C single bonds takes place very rapidly. Alkanes are therefore flexible molecules and in the liquid or gaseous states, the molecules do not have a fixed shape. In the crystalline state, long chain alkanes adopt a zig-zag arrangement of the C–C bonds. A molecule of octane, C_8H_{18}, is shown in this conformation:

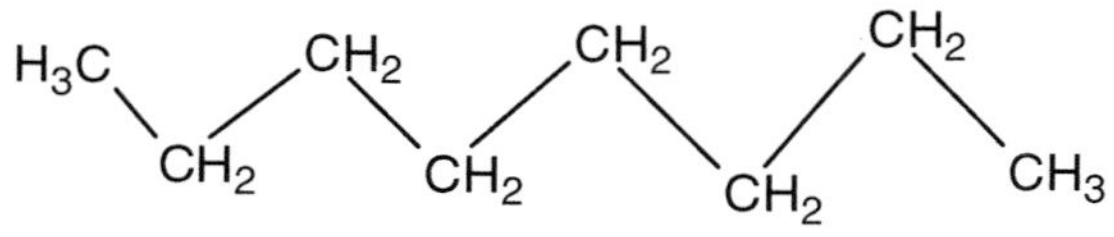

Alkanes are not very reactive compounds, but there are three important reactions. The first is combustion in air, in which the hydrocarbon reacts with oxygen to form carbon dioxide and water. The combustion of methane (natural gas) has been discussed in Chapter 9, and this is a typical reaction:

$$CH_4(g) + 2\,O_2(g) \rightarrow CO_2(g) + 2\,H_2O(g)$$

The combustion reactions of the higher alkanes are similar. Combustion reactions do not usually take place spontaneously, but once started they are highly exothermic and generate flames, which consist of gases at very high temperature. The water produced by the reaction is therefore in the form of vapour, but when it cools the water vapour condenses to a liquid.

The second characteristic reaction of alkanes is the cracking reaction induced by heating of the gas to high temperature in the absence of oxygen. This is a decomposition reaction, also described as pyrolysis or dehydrogenation. It was discussed in connection with the industrial production of ethene from ethane, in Chapter 4:

$$H_3C\text{–}CH_3 \rightarrow H_2C\text{=}CH_2 + H_2$$

This reaction replaces a C–C single bond by a C=C double bond. The product, ethene, is used for further reactions.

The third typical reaction of alkanes is with halogens, such as chlorine. The product of the reaction of methane with chlorine is chloromethane, CH_3Cl, in which a chlorine atom is substituted for a hydrogen atom:

$$CH_4 + Cl_2 \rightarrow CH_3Cl + HCl$$

The reaction is therefore called a **substitution reaction**. Further substitution reactions also take place, in which more chlorine atoms are substituted for the remaining hydrogen atoms:

$$CH_3Cl + Cl_2 \rightarrow CH_2Cl_2 + HCl$$

$$CH_2Cl_2 + Cl_2 \rightarrow CHCl_3 + HCl$$

$$CHCl_3 + Cl_2 \rightarrow CCl_4 + HCl$$

The product of the reaction between chlorine and methane is typically a mixture of the four chlorine derivatives of methane.

Combustion and substitution reactions are highly exothermic reactions, while cracking reactions are endothermic and take place only at high temperature.

Cyclic alkanes contain a ring of carbon atoms and have the general formula C_nH_{2n}. The structures of some cyclic alkanes and their names are shown below:

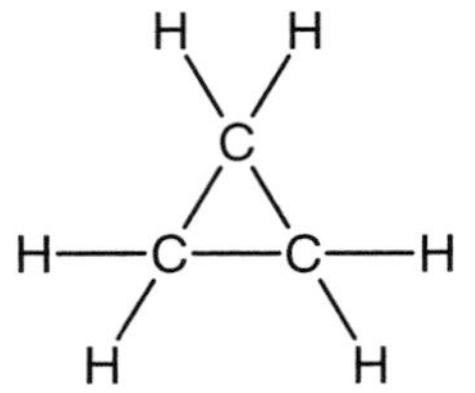

cyclopropane 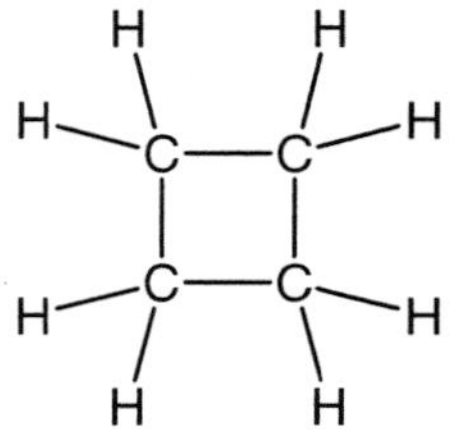   cyclobutane 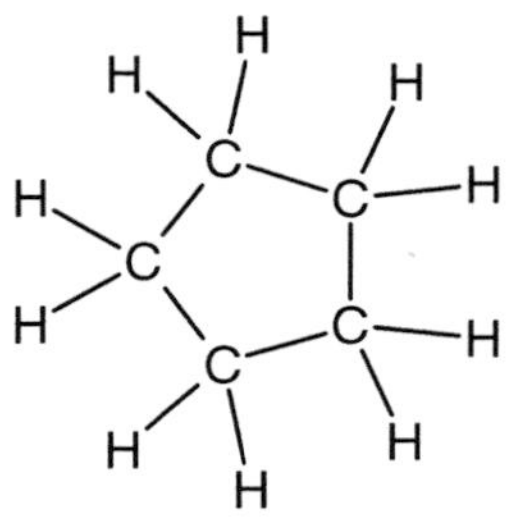   cyclopentane 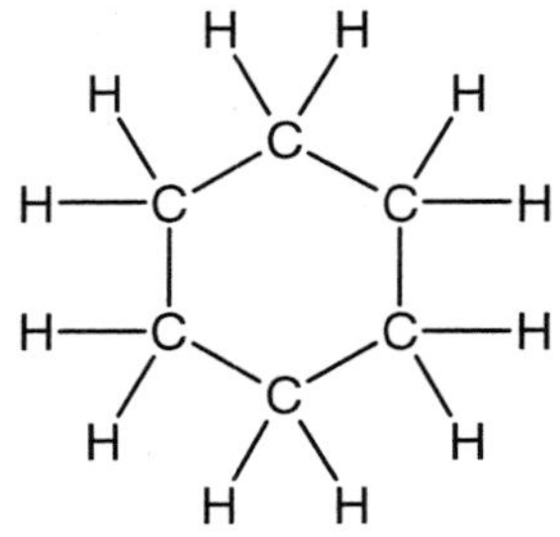   cyclohexane

Cyclopropane, C_3H_6, is triangular in shape, and the C–C–C bond angle is 60°. This is highly distorted from the angle of 109.5° normally found in sp^3 hybridized carbon bonds, so the molecule is highly **strained**. In molecules of cyclobutane, cyclopentane, and larger cyclic alkanes, the molecular geometry is determined by the need to minimize the strain energy by bringing the C–C–C angle as close as possible to the normal tetrahedral value. The result is that the ring of carbon atoms is not planar and instead is "puckered". A particularly important case is the six-membered ring in cyclohexane, which adopts a form shaped like a chair. Cyclohexane is often represented by the following structural formula:

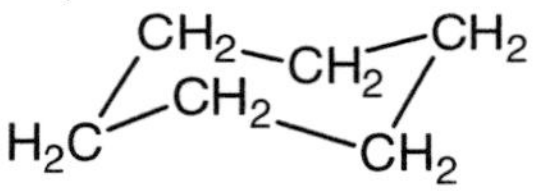

The C–C–C bond angle in cyclohexane is 111.3° which is sufficiently close to the tetrahedral value of 109.5° that the molecule is not significantly strained.

Example 19-2 Calculate the atomization energy for cyclopropane from enthalpy change of formation data, and compare it with the estimate based on average bond energies.

For the atomization reaction $C_3H_6(g) \rightarrow 3\ C(g) + 6\ H(g)$, the enthalpy change of atomization calculated from ΔH_f° data is:

$$\Delta H^\circ = -(+53.220) + 3 \times (+716.682) + 6 \times (+217.965) = 3404.6\ kJ/mol$$

In the atomization reaction, three C–C bonds and six C–H bonds are broken. Hence, if the C–C and C–H bonds were similar to those in other alkanes, the enthalpy change of atomization should be equal to the estimate based on average bond energies for the C–C and C–H bonds from Table 11-5:

$$\Delta H^\circ = (3 \times 347) + (6 \times 414) = 3525\ kJ/mol.$$

Hence the actual enthalpy change of atomization is smaller than expected by about 120 kJ/mol. The cyclopropane molecule is therefore easier to break up into its component atoms than expected. Hence the energy of the actual molecule is higher than expected by about 120 kJ/mol, which is the **strain energy**. The strain energy is due primarily to the severely distorted C–C–C bond angle, which is 60° instead of the tetrahedral value of 109.5°.

19-3 Optical isomerism

Tetrahedral geometry, which is always found when a carbon atom is bonded to four other atoms, leads to a form of stereoisomerism called **optical isomerism**. This is derived from the geometry of three-dimensional space and the symmetry of molecules.

If we look in a mirror, we see a reflection of whatever is in front of the mirror. The image of an object in front of the mirror is obviously related to the object, but is not necessarily identical to it. For instance, if you look at the image of your left hand reflected in a mirror, you will see that the image is the same as your right hand. If you compare your right hand with your left hand, they are clearly different, and cannot be turned around in any way so as to make them identical. Each of your two hands has all the qualities of a hand, but the two hands are not identical. One hand is the mirror image of the other hand.

An object that is not identical to its mirror image is described as **chiral**. A chiral molecule is closely related to the molecule that its mirror image, but is not identical to it. Highly symmetrical molecules are identical to their mirror images, and are not chiral. A molecule of methane, CH_4, is highly symmetrical, is identical to its mirror image, and is not chiral. But molecules of lower symmetry can be chiral.

An example of a chiral molecule is an ethane derivative such as 1,1-bromochloroethane, with formula $HBrClC–CH_3$. The four atoms, or groups of atoms, bonded to the first carbon atom are all different, namely a hydrogen atom, a chlorine atom, a bromine atom and a methyl group. There are two distinct molecules with this formula, which are explored in the following diagram.

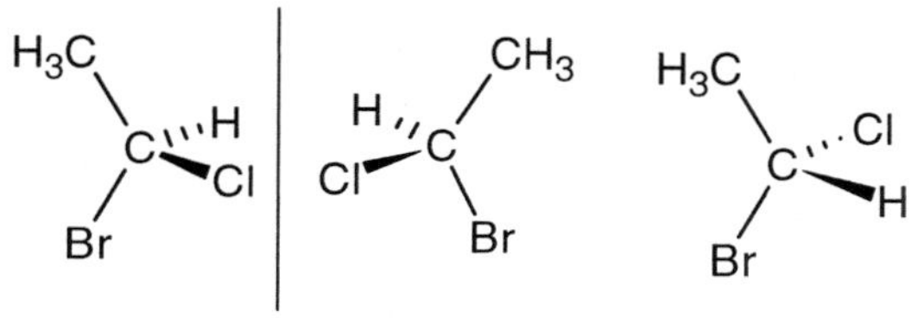

On the left, the first formula shows one molecule; the bromine atom and the two methyl groups lie in the plane of the paper, the chlorine atom lies in front of, and the hydrogen atom lies behind, the paper. The vertical line shows a mirror that is perpendicular to the plane of the paper, and immediately to the right of the mirror is a second molecule that is the mirror image of the first molecule. The third molecule, on the right of the diagram, is the second (mirror image) molecule rotated by 180° about an axis that is parallel to the mirror and lying in the plane of the paper. Comparing the first and third molecules, the bromine atom and the methyl group are in the same relationship to the central carbon atom in both molecules, but the hydrogen atom and the chlorine atom are interchanged. It is impossible to bring the mirror image molecule into coincidence with the original molecule by rotating it. The original molecule and its image are therefore different molecules. These are called **optical isomers** or **enantiomers**. The word "otical" in describing these isomers refers to the way in which a chiral molecule interacts with polarized light.

A carbon atom that is bonded to the four different atoms or groups of atoms is described as a **chiral centre**. If two of the four atoms or groups bonded to a tetrahedral carbon atom are the same, then the carbon atom is not a chiral centre. A carbon atom bonded to three other atoms or groups in trigonal planar geometry is not a chiral centre. There are many further aspects of the chemistry of chiral molecules, particularly in molecules containing two or more chiral centres.

Example 19-3 Consider the compound 2-chlorobutane. Is this molecule chiral? If your answer is yes, which carbon atom is the chiral centre?

The structural formula for the compound is:

$$H_3C-\overset{\displaystyle H}{\underset{\displaystyle Cl}{C}}-CH_2-CH_3$$

The second carbon from the left is bonded to a chlorine atom, a hydrogen atom , a methyl group and an ethyl group. Since these are all different groups, the molecule is chiral. The second carbon atom is the chiral centre.

Note that the molecule is chiral even though the second carbon atom is bonded to two carbon atoms, because these two carbon atoms are parts of different functional groups, a methyl group and an ethyl group.

Example 19-4 Consider the compound 1-chlorobutane. Is this molecule chiral? If your answer is "yes", which carbon atom is the chiral centre?

The structural formula for the compound is: $\quad Cl-CH_2-CH_2-CH_2-CH_3$

Every carbon is bonded to either two or three hydrogen atoms, and hence the molecule is not chiral.

19-4 Alkenes and alkynes

Alkenes are hydrocarbons containing a carbon-carbon double bond, C=C, such as ethene $H_2C=CH_2$ and propene $H_2C=CH-CH_3$. In an alkene molecule, the atoms around the double bond are co-planar, as discussed in Chapter 11. The double bond consists of a σ bond and a π bond, as discussed in Chapter 12. The industrial preparation of alkenes and some of their reactions were discussed in Chapter 4. **Alkynes** are hydrocarbons with a C≡C triple bond. The smallest alkyne is ethyne, H–C≡C–H, which also known as acetylene. The geometry of this molecule is linear: all four atoms lie on a straight line. The triple bond consists of a σ bond and two π bonds. The reactions of alkynes are similar to those of alkenes.

Alkenes and alkynes contain less than the maximum number of hydrogen atoms for a given number of carbon atoms, and are sometimes called **unsaturated hydrocarbons**.

The C=C double bond differs from the C–C single bond in its geometry and its chemical reactivity. The ethene molecule is planar, and rigid. The geometry at each carbon is trigonal planar, rather than tetrahedral, and the two trigonal planar groups at each carbon atom lie in the *same* plane. In sharp contrast to the methyl groups in ethane, the two CH$_2$ groups in ethene are not able to rotate relative to each other.

There are many molecules related to ethene by replacement of one or more of the hydrogen atoms by other atoms or functional groups. In these molecules, the rigid planar geometry of the double bond is retained, and this leads to a kind of stereoisomerism called **geometrical isomerism**. To illustrate this, we consider dichloroethene, with formula C$_2$H$_2$Cl$_2$. There are three isomeric compounds with this molecular formula, and their structural formulae are shown below.

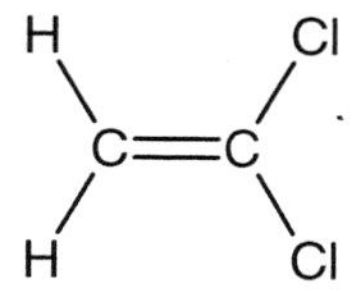

1,1-dichloroethene 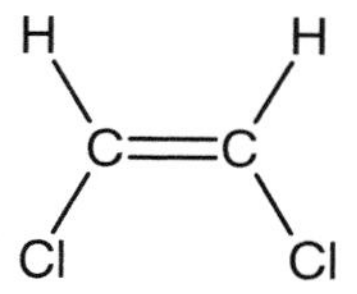   *cis*-1,2-dichloroethene 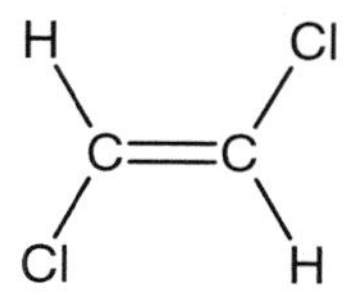   *trans*-1,2-dichloroethene

In 1,1-dichloroethene, the two chlorine atoms are bonded to the same carbon atom, while in the other two compounds, the chlorine atoms are bonded to different carbon atoms; the first molecule is a structural isomer of the other two. The difference between the second and third molecules is in the relative positions of the two chlorine atoms, and so is geometrical in nature. The relative positions of the chlorine atoms are described by the prefixes *cis* and *trans*, which mean respectively "on the same side" and "on opposite sides". Since rotation around the C=C bond does not occur, the *cis* and *trans* isomers retain their identity and are different chemical compounds, which can be isolated and do not inter-convert from one form to another.

The bonding in the C=C double bond consists of a σ bond formed by overlap of sp^2 hybrid orbitals and the third p orbital on each carbon atom which form a pπ bond, as shown in Chapter 12. In a trigonal planar group of atoms centred on a carbon atom the p orbital which is not involved in the sp^2 hybrid orbitals must be oriented perpendicular to the plane of the atoms. The p orbitals on the two adjacent carbon atoms can overlap effectively to form the pπ bond only if they are parallel to each other. This can only happen if the two trigonal planar groups of atoms lie in the same plane. Rotation about the carbon-carbon bond would therefore destroy the overlap of the p orbitals that form the pπ bond; the energy barrier to rotation is therefore so high that rotation does not occur under ordinary circumstances.

In a molecule of an alkene, the region of the double bond contains twice as many electrons as a single bond, and so is electron-rich.

The characteristic reactions of alkenes with halogens are **addition reactions**, as opposed to the substitution reactions of alkanes. In an addition reaction, two atoms (or groups of atoms) are added to the alkene, one to each carbon atom joined by the double bond. For example, bromine Br$_2$ reacts with ethene to form 1,2-dibromoethane:

$$Br_2 + H_2C=CH_2 \rightarrow BrH_2C–CH_2Br$$

The double bond is replaced by a single bond, and the geometry at each carbon atom changes from trigonal planar to tetrahedral.

The reaction between hydrogen chloride HCl and an alkene to produce an alkyl chloride is another example of an addition reaction:

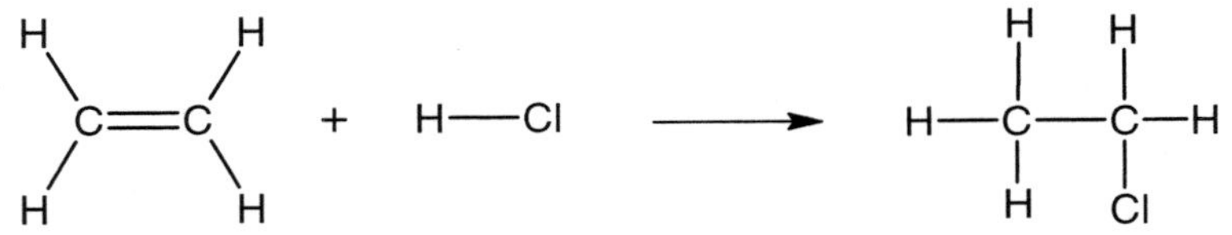

In the molecule of the reactant ethene, the carbon atoms at each end of the double bond are both bonded to two hydrogen atoms, and are equivalent. In the product molecule, the hydrogen atom from the HCl is bonded to one carbon atom, and the chlorine atom is bonded to the other. Because the two carbon atoms are equivalent, there is only one product of the reaction, namely chloroethane, regardless of whether the chlorine atom becomes bonded to the left-hand or the right-hand carbon atom.

If an alkene is unsymmetrical so that the carbon atoms at each end of the double bond are non-equivalent, then there are two possible products of an addition reaction. For example, consider the reaction between HCl and propene. In propene, $H_2C=CHCH_3$, it is easy to see that the two doubly-bonded carbon atoms are inequivalent: one is bonded to two hydrogen atoms, and the other is bonded to only one hydrogen atom. There are two possible reactions, and the products of the two reactions are distinct structural isomers, namely 1-chloropropane and 2-chloropropane:

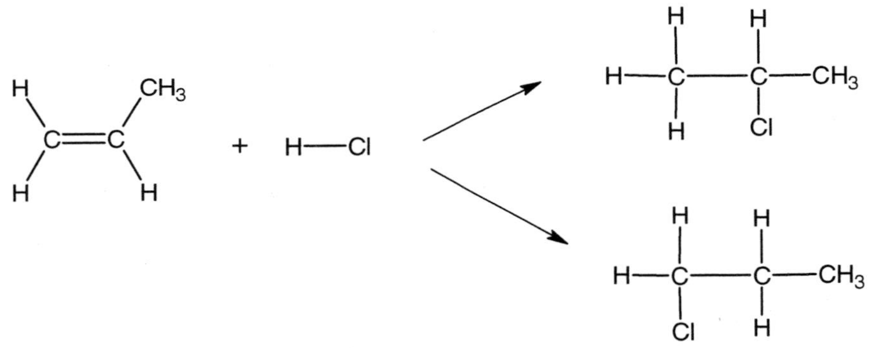

The two possible products are not formed in equal amounts. One product predominates and is formed in much greater amounts than the other, so much so that the minor product can usually be ignored. The predominant product of this reaction is 2-chloropropane, and in effect, only the upper reaction takes place.

There are many possible addition reactions between an acid HX and an unsymmetrical alkene. In 1869 the Russian chemist Vladimir Markovnikov discovered a simple rule which reliably predicts the predominant product. The hydrogen atom from HX becomes bonded to the carbon atom that, in the alkene, carries the larger number of attached hydrogen atoms. This is known as **Markovnikov's rule**. The rule correctly predicts that the major product of the reaction between hydrogen chloride and propene is 2-chloropropane, not 1-chloropropane.

The explanation for Markovnikov's rule is to be found in the mechanism of the addition reaction. The first step in the reaction is the transfer of a hydrogen ion from the acid to the alkene, and it is structure of the resulting organic cation that determines the course of the remainder of the reaction. This mechanism is discussed in detail in second year courses on organic chemistry.

19-5 Carboxylic acids and Amines

Carboxylic acids can be represented in general by the formula RCOOH, and their typical acid-base reactions have already been discussed in Chapter 2 and Chapter 14. Most carboxylic acids have pK_a values in the range from about 3 up to 6, and are moderately weak acids.

The value of pK_a is affected by the nature of the group R in the general formula. For example, substitution of chlorine atoms for hydrogen atoms in acetic acid results in a decrease in pK_a. For example, chloroacetic acid (pK_a = 2.85) is a stronger acid than acetic acid (pK_a = 4.76), and trichloroacetic acid is even stronger. These effects can be correlated with the electronic structure of the molecules of the acid, but it is also important to keep in mind the effects of the solvent water on the ionization process. The enthalpy change of ionization of carboxylic acids is small and does not vary greatly from one acid to another, and the entropy change of ionization plays an equally important role in determining trends in the strength of carboxylic acids.

Carboxylic acids react with alcohols to form **esters**, which have the general formula RCOOR'. In an ester, an alkyl group R' replaces the acidic hydrogen atom in the acid RCOOH. For example, acetic acid reacts with ethanol in acidic solution to form ethyl acetate:

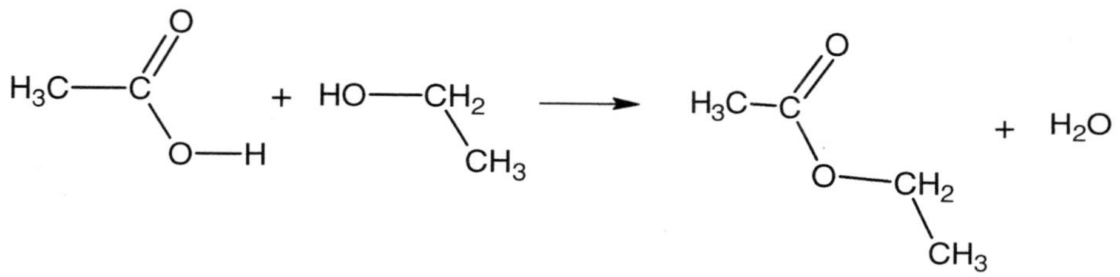

The product ester is called ethyl acetate. In a molecule of ethyl acetate, an ethyl group $-CH_2CH_3$ replaces the acidic hydrogen atom of acetic acid. The other product of the reaction is water, and for that reason this type of reaction is called a **condensation reaction**.

Esters react with bases to form a salt of the original acid and an alcohol, in what is essentially the reverse of the above reaction. For instance ethyl acetate reacts with sodium hydroxide to form sodium acetate and ethanol.

Amines, RNH_2, are typical weak bases, due to the presence of the lone pair on the nitrogen atom. Their acid-base reactions have been discussed in Chapters 2 and 14. Many amines have pK_b values in the range 3 to 5.

19-6 Amino acids

An **amino acid** contains both an acidic carboxyl group –COOH and a basic amino group –NH$_2$. For example glycine is often represented by the following structure:

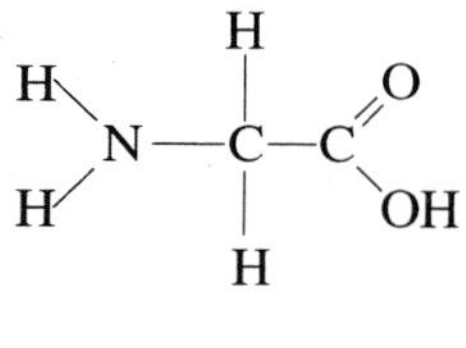

As pointed out in Chapter 14, the uncharged glycine molecule, H_2NCH_2COOH, is present in solution only in very small concentrations, and the predominant species present in neutral solution is the zwitterion $^+H_3NCH_2COO^-$. The equilibrium between the uncharged molecule and the zwitterion,

$$H_2NCH_2COOH \rightleftharpoons {}^+H_3NCH_2COO^-$$

lies far to the right. In practice the uncharged molecule can be ignored and the proton transfer equilibria in aqueous solution can be represented adequately by the following equations:

$$^+H_3NCH_2COOH \rightleftharpoons {}^+H_3NCH_2COO^- + H^+ \rightleftharpoons H_2NCH_2COO^- + 2\,H^+$$

In addition, pure crystalline glycine consists of the zwitterion, not the uncharged molecule.

In other amino acids, one of the hydrogen atoms on the central carbon atom is replaced by an alkyl group or other functional group of atoms, which may be designated by the symbol R. The structural formula can be written as follows:

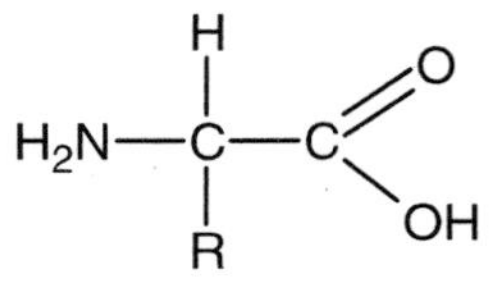

In this structure, the group R is called the **side-group** of the amino acid. Each amino acid has a different side-group, and some examples are shown below:

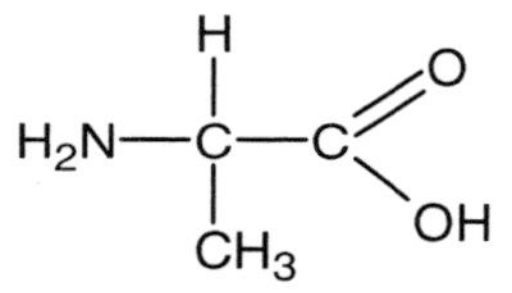

alanine

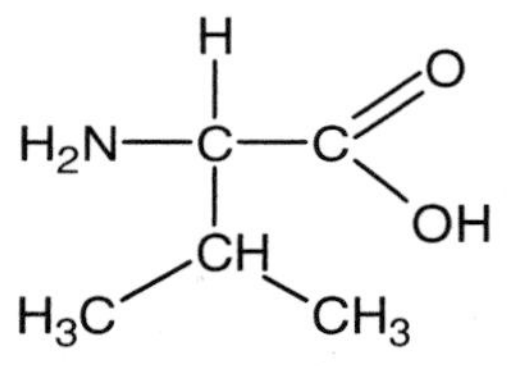

valine

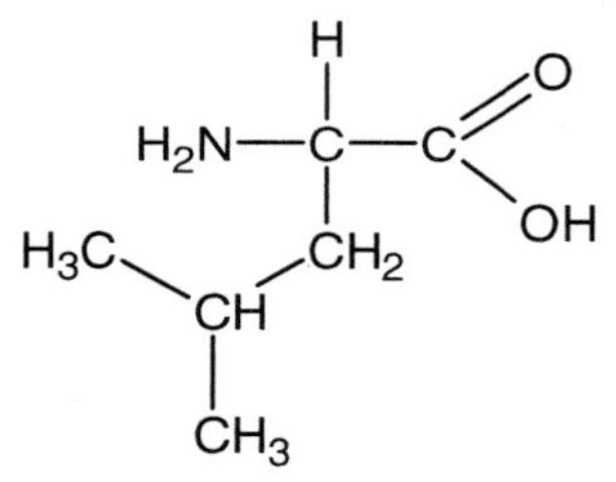

leucine

These amino acids undergo proton transfer equilibria similar to those of glycine discussed above. In all cases the amphiprotic forms of the amino acids are the zwitterions, rather than the molecules depicted above.

The amine and carboxyl groups in an amino acid are hydrophilic groups, which can form hydrogen bonds to water molecules in aqueous solution. The side-group in an amino acid may be either hydrophilic or hydrophobic. In the three amino acids shown above, the side-groups are alkyls groups, which are hydrophobic.

Amino acids undergo condensation reactions involving the carboxylic group of one molecule and the amino group of another. The condensation reaction between two amino acids can be written as follows:

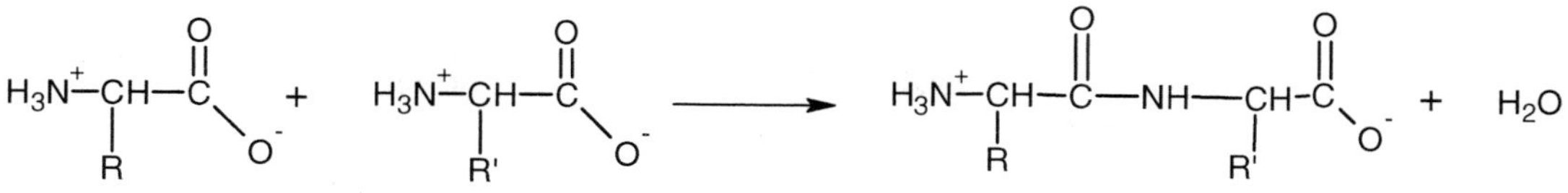

The product molecule is called a **dipeptide** or simply a **peptide**. It contains the amide group –NHCO– at the centre. This molecule can react further with other amino acids to form higher **polypeptides**.

19-7 Aromatic hydrocarbons

Benzene, C_6H_6, is the parent compound to a class of cyclic unsaturated hydrocarbons called **aromatic hydrocarbons**. The structure of the benzene molecule consists of a ring of carbon atoms with a hydrogen atom bonded to each carbon atom:

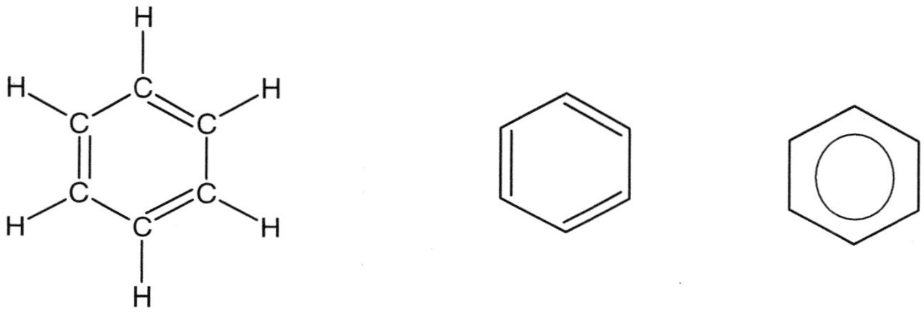

The structure on the left shows all the atoms of the molecule. The structure in the centre shows a shorthand version of the structure in which the hydrogen atoms are not shown. The shorthand structure is often used when the hydrogen atoms are not directly involved in a reaction. The structure on the right has a circle to indicate the alternating bonds of the aromatic ring, in order to show that the bonds between the carbon atoms are all the same.

If one hydrogen atom is removed from a benzene molecule, the resulting functional group has the formula $–C_6H_5$ and is called the **phenyl** group.

In order to satisfy the normal carbon valence of 4, the formula shows alternating double and single bonds around the ring. However, careful experiments have shown that the carbon-carbon bond lengths are all equal, and that the ring is planar. In Chapter 11, we discussed the concept of resonance as it applies in this case: if the positions of the double and single bonds are interchanged, an equivalent structure is obtained, which is a resonance structure of the structure shown above. The actual structure is a combination of these two structures. In section 11-10 we showed that resonance lowers the energy of the benzene molecule by an amount called the resonance energy.

In terms of quantum bonding models, the orbitals at the carbon atoms of a benzene ring are divided as follows. The carbon 2s orbital and the $2p_x$ and $2p_y$ orbitals that lie in the plane of the molecule are hybridized to form three sp^2 orbitals. These orbitals are oriented at angles of 120° to each other, and overlap to form σ single bonds from each carbon atom to its three neighbours. The third p orbital on the carbon atom is the $2p_z$ orbital, and is oriented perpendicular to the plane of the molecule. The $2p_z$ orbitals overlap to form π molecular orbitals, which extend over the whole ring of carbon atoms. The π molecular orbitals are similar to the π molecular orbital in ethene, except that they extend over six carbon atoms instead of two. Since there are six carbon atoms that contribute one $2p_z$ orbital each, there are six π molecular orbitals, of which three are bonding and three are anti-bonding.

The six carbon atoms each have four valence electrons and the six hydrogen atoms each have one valence electron. Hence there is a total of 30 valence electrons in the benzene molecule. There are six C–H bonds and six C–C bonds, each consisting of a pair of valence electrons; this accounts for a total of 24 valence electrons. The remaining 6 valence electrons are accommodated in the three bonding π molecular orbitals.

There are many derivatives of benzene in which hydrogen atoms are replaced by other atoms or functional groups. Some of these are shown below.

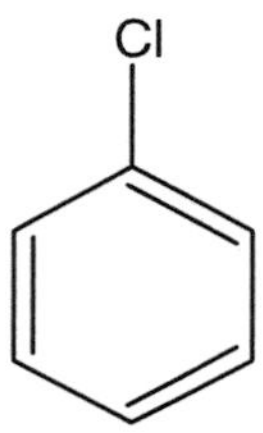

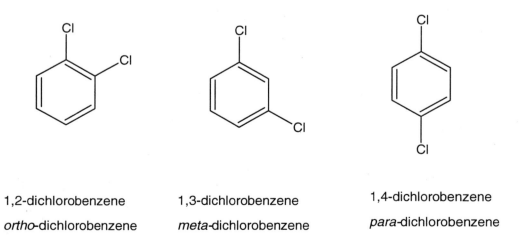

chlorobenzene	aniline	phenol	toluene	benzoic acid

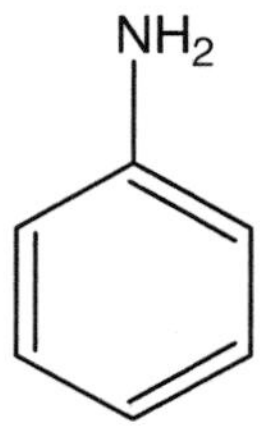

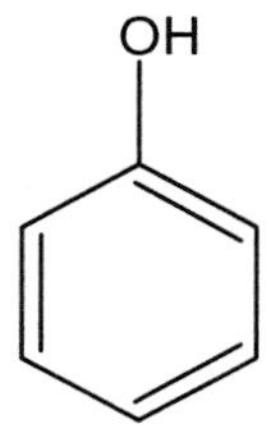

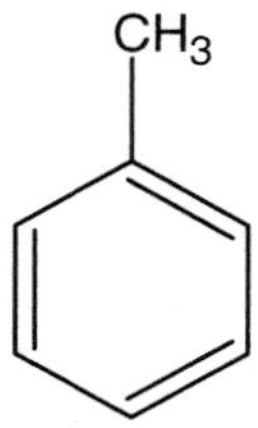

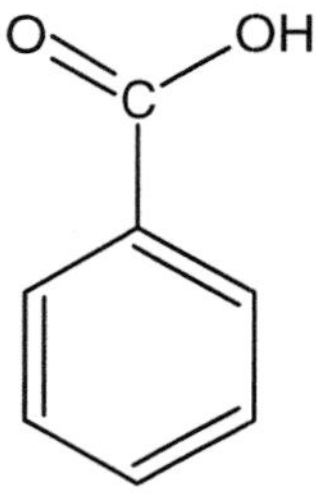

Where there is more than one substituent on a benzene ring, their relative positions around the ring are indicated either by numbers, or by the prefixes *ortho*, *meta* and *para*. This is illustrated by the following examples.

1,2-dichlorobenzene

ortho-dichlorobenzene

1,3-dichlorobenzene

meta-dichlorobenzene

1,4-dichlorobenzene

para-dichlorobenzene

There are other aromatic hydrocarbons consisting of more than one ring of carbon atoms, such as naphthalene, anthracene and phenanthrene. These compounds were mentioned in Chapter 9 under the heading of coal tar, which was the traditional source of these compounds.

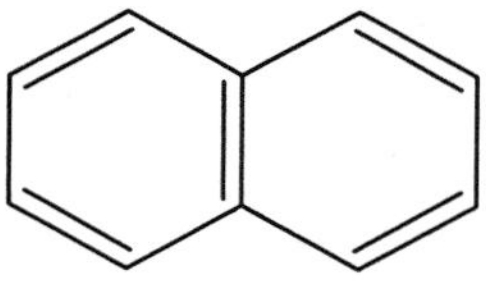

naphthalene 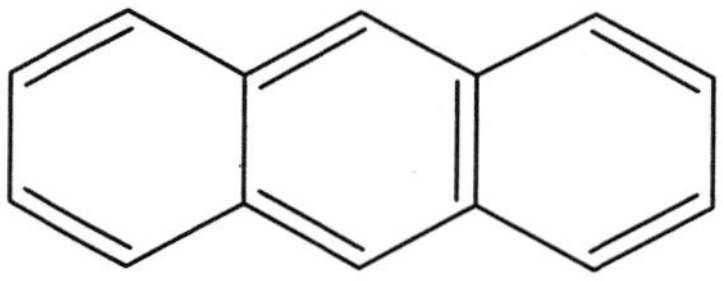   anthracene

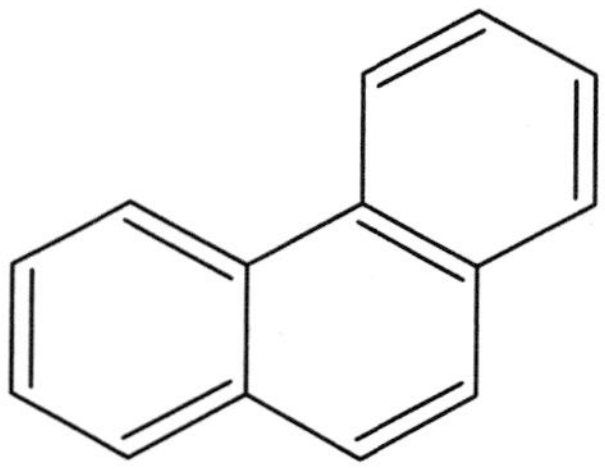

phenanthrene

The existence of the ring structure with a π bond system makes benzene more stable than would be expected on the basis of the individual single and double bond energies, due to the resonance energy. This stability influences the chemistry of benzene and other aromatic compounds. Although they are unsaturated hydrocarbons, aromatic hydrocarbons typically undergo substitution reactions, rather than addition reactions like alkenes. For example, the reaction between chlorine and benzene leads to substitution at a single carbon atom, rather than addition across a double bond:

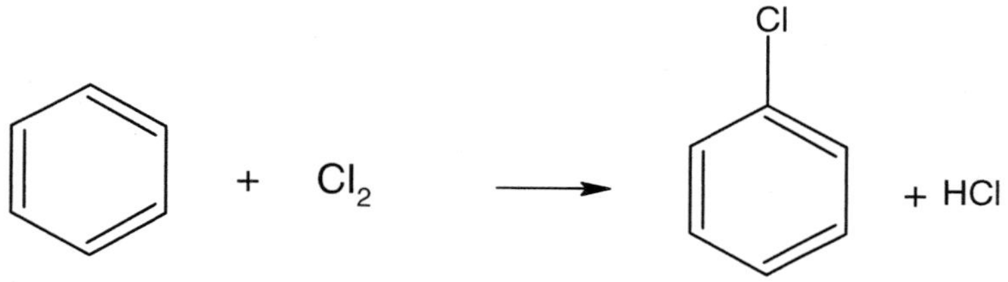

$$+ \quad Cl_2 \quad \longrightarrow \quad + \quad HCl$$

19-8 Polymers.

Polymers are large molecules formed by linking together many small molecules into chains. The small molecules from which the polymer is formed are called **monomers**, and the process of reaction is called **polymerization**. The chains in a polymer may contain many thousands of atoms. There are many polymers found in nature, but in the last half-century many synthetic polymers have been produced and manufactured for specific purposes. For many purposes, such as clothing, rope and consumer wrapping, synthetic polymers have replaced natural polymers that were used formerly. Polymers have also replaced metals and glass for many everyday objects, often with better performance, lighter weight and lower cost.

The polymerization of alkenes is one of the most important methods of preparing synthetic polymers. Alkenes have a C=C double bond which can react to form a chain of single bonds. The simplest example is that of ethylene $H_2C=CH_2$ (ethene is usually called ethylene in polymer chemistry) which polymerizes to form **polyethylene**:

$$\ldots + H_2C=CH_2 + H_2C=CH_2 + H_2C=CH_2 + \ldots \rightarrow \ldots -CH_2-CH_2-CH_2-CH_2- \ldots$$

In the polymerization reaction, a chain of single bonds in polyethylene replaces the double bonds of the ethylene molecules. The reaction can be carried out in a number of different ways, and the physical properties of the product depend strongly on the reaction conditions.

The enthalpy change involved in polymerization of ethylene and related monomers can be estimated from the bond energies given in Table 11-5. Polymerization results in the replacement of a C=C double bond by two C–C single bonds. The enthalpy change for the polymerization reaction can be estimated from bond energies, as follows.

Bonds broken: 1 C=C   +1×599 = +599 kJ/mol

Bonds formed: 2 C–C   –2×347 = –694 kJ/mol

$$\Delta H^\circ \approx +599 - 694 = -95 \text{ kJ/mol}$$

Hence the polymerization of ethylene is exothermic by approximately –95 kJ/mol. As a result, polymerization proceeds vigorously once it is initiated. Other alkenes also polymerize, and lead to many useful polymers.

Chloroethene, for which the traditional name is vinyl chloride, has the following structure:

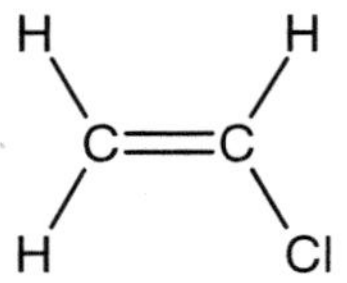

Vinyl chloride polymerizes to form **poly(vinyl chloride)**, commonly abbreviated to PVC, in which there is a chlorine atom bonded to every second carbon atom:

$$\dots-CH_2-CHCl-CH_2-CHCl-\dots$$

Tetrafluoroethylene, $F_2C=CF_2$, polymerizes to form polytetrafluorethylene, commonly known as PTFE or by the trade name of Teflon. The structure of the polymer is as follows:

$$\dots-CF_2-CF_2-CF_2-CF_2-\dots$$

Table 19-1 lists some common synthetic polymers made from ethylene and its derivatives, and their applications.

Table 19-1 Some ethylene-based polymers

Monomer	Polymer	Application
ethylene $H_2C=CH_2$	polyethylene $\ldots-CH_2-CH_2-CH_2-CH_2-\ldots$	Flexible sheeting, rigid containers
propylene $CH_3HC=CH_2$	polypropylene $..-CH_2-CHCH_3-CH_2-CHCH_3-..$	sheeting, rope, small parts
vinyl chloride $H_2C=CHCl$	poly(vinyl chloride) (PVC) $\ldots-CH_2-CHCl-CH_2-CHCl-\ldots$	electrical insulation, pipes, floor coverings
styrene $CH_2=CHC_6H_5$	polystyrene $\ldots-CH_2-CH(C_6H_5)-CH_2-CH(C_6H_5)-\ldots$	foam thermal insulation
tetrafluoroethylene $F_2C=CF_2$	polytetrafluoroethylene (PTFE) $\ldots-CF_2-CF_2-CF_2-CF_2-\ldots$	non-stick coatings, rigid containers
acrylonitrile $H_2C=CHCN$	polyacrylonitrile $\ldots-CH_2-CHCN-CH_2-CHCN-\ldots$	Clothing fibres

Another type of polymer is formed by condensation reactions. These are called **condensation polymers**. For example, **nylon** is formed by reacting hexamethylenediamine with adipic acid. The structures of these two substances are as follows:

$$H_2N-(CH_2)_6-NH_2 \qquad \text{hexamethylenediamine}$$

$$HOOC-(CH_2)_4-COOH \qquad \text{adipic acid}$$

The two reactants are mixed together in a concentrated aqueous solution. Hydrogen ions are transferred from the acid to the base, and the solution is referred to as "nylon salt". The polymerization reaction takes place when the salt solution is heated. In the acid-base equilibrium, some hydrogen ions are transferred back to the adipic acid, and the polymerization reaction involves the neutral molecules rather than ions:

$$H_2N-(CH_2)_6-NH_2 + HOOC-(CH_2)_4-COOH \rightarrow H_2N-(CH_2)_6-NH-OC-(CH_2)_4-COOH + H_2O$$

In this condensation reaction, a covalent bond is formed between the nitrogen atom of the amine and the carbon atom of the carboxyl group in the acid, and a water molecule is produced. The product has an amino group $-NH_2$ at one end that can react with another adipic acid molecule, and a carboxyl group $-COOH$ at the other end that can react with another hexamethylenediamine molecule. Thus the product of the above reaction can grow by adding more monomer molecules to form a polymer with long chains. Polymers formed by condensation reactions are called **condensation polymers**. This particular polymer is known as **nylon**. A more specific name is **nylon 66**, which indicates that the two monomers from which it is formed each contain 6 carbon atoms.

Nylon is an example of a group of polymers called **polyamides**. The nylon polymer molecule contains the amide group $-NHCO-$ spaced regularly along its length. The barrier to rotation about the C–N bond in the amide group is considerable, about 75 kJ/mol, and the group is planar, as discussed in Chapter 11. The well-defined geometry of the amide group lends some rigidity to the polymer. Hydrogen bonding between amide groups on adjacent molecules also helps to lock the molecules in place and make the polymer even more rigid.

Another type of condensation polymer is the copolymer of a glycol, or dialcohol, and a dicarboxylic acid, to form an ester. An example is the reaction between ethylene glycol, $HOCH_2$–CH_2OH, and terephthalic acid:

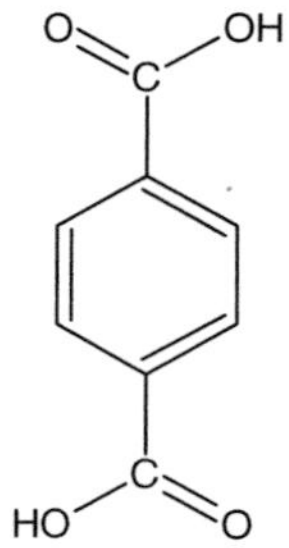

The reaction between terephthalic acid and ethylene glycol can be written:

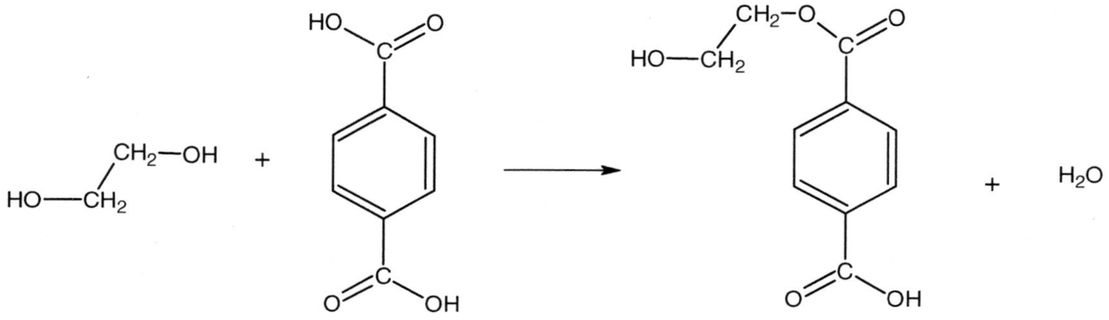

The product of the reaction is an ester. Since it contains an –OH group at one end and a –COOH group at the other, this ester can react with further monomers to form a polymer, which has the following structure:

$$...-OCH_2-CH_2OOC-C_6H_4-COOCH_2-CH_2OOC-C_6H_4-COOCH_2-CH_2OOC-C_6H_4-CO-...$$

This polymer is called **poly(ethylene terephthalate)**, and is marketed under several trade names. It is an example of a general class of copolymers called **polyesters**.

Table 19-2 Condensation Polymers

Reactants	Polymer	Application
hexamethylenediamine $N–(CH_2)_6–NH_2$ adipic acid $HOOC–(CH_2)_4–COOH$	Nylon	Fibre for rope, tyre cord, carpets
ethylene glycol $HOCH_2–CH_2OH$ terephthalic acid $1,4-HOOC–C_6H_4–COOH$	PET, poly(ethylene terephthalate)	Fibre, film, beverage containers

Many condensation polymers are found in nature. **Polysaccharides** such as starch consist of sugar molecules bonded together through ether linkages, $–O–$. **Cellulose** is a similar naturally occurring polymer which differs from starch in the stereochemistry of the linkages between the sugar molecules.

Proteins are condensation polymers formed from amino acids as monomers, and are called **polypeptides**. When bonded together in a protein, the amino acid units are sometimes called amino acid **residues**. There are many different amino acids, which differ only in their sidegroups, and in a protein the different amino acids are bonded together in the polymer in a specific order that determines the properties of the protein.

Key concepts

Organic chemistry is the chemistry of carbon compounds. Carbon atoms readily form bonds to other carbon atoms, and there are many complex organic molecules. Some of these have the same structural formulae, and are called isomers.

A carbon atom with four single bonds to other atoms has tetrahedral geometry, which is hard to depict accurately on paper. Rotation of groups of atoms around single bonds takes place rapidly in many molecules. Optical isomerism is found when four different atoms or groups of atoms are bonded to a tetrahedral carbon atom; left-handed and right-handed molecules that are mirror images of each other can be formed.

The common reactions of alkanes are combustion with oxygen, and substitution reactions with halogens, in which a single halogen atom replaces a hydrogen atom.

A carbon atom with a double bond to another atom has trigonal planar geometry. Rotation about the double bond does not take place, which leads to the existence of geometrical isomers of derivatives of alkenes. Alkenes undergo addition reactions with halogens, in which one halogen atoms is added to each carbon atom joined by the double bond.

Carboxylic acids and amines are important classes of weak acids, and amino acids contain both the carboxyl group and the amine group. Carboxylic acids react with alcohols in condensation reactions.

Aromatic hydrocarbons are planar ring molecules similar to benzene. With halogens they undergo substitution reactions rather than addition reactions, even though the ring appears to contain double bonds.

Polymers are large molecules formed by linking many small molecules to form very large molecules, usually containing long chains of carbon atoms. Some polymers are based upon the polymerization of alkenes or alkene derivatives, others are formed by condensation reactions.

Chapter 19

Review questions

1. What is the key element in organic chemistry?
2. What is the difference between alkanes, alkenes and alkynes?
3. What is the difference between saturated hydrocarbons and unsaturated hydrocarbons?
4. What are structural isomers?
5. What are geometrical isomers?
6. What are optical isomers?
7. What is an amino acid?
8. What is an aromatic hydrocarbon?
9. What is an addition reaction?
10. What is a substitution reaction?
11. What is a condensation reaction?
12. What is a polymer?

Problems

1. Draw structural formulae for all the structural isomers of dichloropropane and name them.

2. The structural isomers of dichloroethane can be distinguished by chemical conversion to trichloroethane. How many different isomers of trichloroethane could be formed by chlorination of 1,1-dichloroethane and what are their structures? How many different isomers of trichloroethane could be formed by chlorination of 1,2-dichloroethane and what are their structures?

3. Draw structural formulae for all the structural isomers of trichloropropane, and name them.

4. Draw structural formulae for all the alcohols that are structural isomers of butanol, and name them.

5. Draw structural formulae for all the structural isomers of trichlorobenzene, and name them.

6. Ethylbenzene $C_6H_5C_2H_5$ can be converted to styrene $C_6H_5C_2H_3$ by the following gas phase reaction:

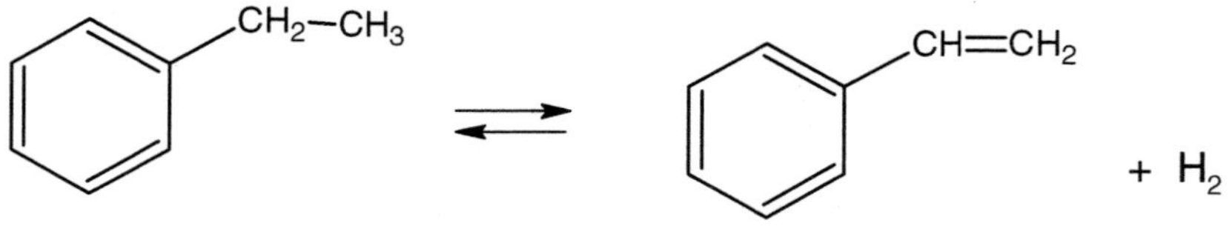

What name would you use to describe this reaction? Under what conditions of temperature and pressure would you expect the equilibrium to be favourable to the production of styrene? What is styrene used for?

7. Write structural formulae for the zwitterion forms of alanine, valine and leucine.

8. Which of the following amino acids is chiral: glycine, alanine, valine, leucine?

9. When a dipeptide is formed from glycine $H_2N–CH_2–COOH$ and alanine $H_2N–CH(CH_3)–COOH$, how many possible products are there? Draw structural formulae for all the products.

10. Predict the product of each of the following addition reactions. In each case write the structural formula and name the compound.

Appendix 1

Thermodynamic data at 298.15 K for the standard state of 100 kPa.

This Appendix contains thermodynamic data for elements and compounds at 25.00°C and standard pressure of 100. kPa. The data listed are the standard enthalpy change of formation, the standard Gibbs energy change of formation, the absolute entropy and the heat capacity at constant pressure.

The Appendix is divided into two parts: Part I lists inorganic substances, and Part II lists organic substances. In Part I, each entry is listed alphabetically by the name of the element with the strongest and most obvious association with that compound. For the compounds of carbon, inorganic compounds are listed in Part I, and organic compounds in Part II.

The standard state for thermodynamics is discussed in detail in Section 6-9. The standard state pressure for these tables is P° = 100 kPa exactly (= 1 bar), and not 101.325 kPa (= 1 atmosphere) which is used in some other tables.

The state of each substance is indicated as either (s) solid, (ℓ) liquid, (g) gas or (aq) solute in aqueous solution. For solutes in aqueous solution, the standard state is the hypothetical ideal solution with the solute specified by the formula present at a molal composition of exactly 1 mol (kg solvent)$^{-1}$. This corresponds to the designation "ao" which is defined precisely in the "NBS Tables" listed below. For very accurate work, relative activities of solutes in aqueous solution should be expressed in terms of molalities rather than molarities.

Three sources of data were used:

The NBS Tables of chemical thermodynamic properties. D.D.Wagman et al. Journal of Physical and Chemical Reference Data, volume 11, Supplement No. 2, 1982.

Thermochemical Data of Pure Substances. 2nd edition 1994 I.Barin. (VCH Verlagsgesellschaft mbH)

TRC Thermodynamic Data. Hydrocarbons, volume VIII. 1993. Thermodynamics Research Centre, The Texas A and M University, College Station, Texas.

Appendix 1

Part I Inorganic substances

Formula	ΔH_f^o kJ mol^{-1}	ΔG_f^o kJ mol^{-1}	S^o J K^{-1} mol^{-1}	C_p^o J K^{-1} mol^{-1}
Aluminum				
Al(s)	0	0	28.33	24.35
Al$_2$O$_3$(s)	−1675.7	−1582.3	50.92	79.04
AlCl$_3$(s)	−704.2	−628.8	110.67	91.84
Antimony				
Sb(s)	0	0	45.69	25.23
Sb$_4$O$_6$(s)	−1417.1	−1253.0	246.0	202.76
SbH$_3$(g)	145.105	147.75	232.78	41.05
SbCl$_3$(s)	−382.17	−323.67	184.1	107.9
(g)	−313.8 ·	−301.2	337.80	76.69
Sb$_2$S$_3$(s)	−174.9	−173.6	182.0	119.87
Argon				
Ar(g)	0	0	154.843	20.786
(aq)	−12.1	16.4	59.4	–
Arsenic				
As(s)	0	0	35.1	24.64
As$_2$O$_5$(s)	−924.87	−782.3	105.4	116.52
As$_4$O$_6$(s)	−1313.94	−1152.43	214.2	191.29
AsH$_3$(g)	66.44	68.93	222.78	38.07
AsCl$_3$(ℓ)	−305.0	−259.4	216.3	–
(g)	−261.5	−248.9	327.17	75.73
Barium				
Ba(s)	0	0	62.8	28.07
Ba^{2+}(aq)	−537.64	−560.77	9.6	–
BaO(s)	−553.5	−525.1	70.42	47.78
BaCl$_2$(s)	−858.6	−810.4	123.68	75.14
BaSO$_4$(s)	−1473.2	−1362.2	132.2	101.75
BaCO$_3$(s)	−1216.3	−1137.6	112.1	85.35
Beryllium				
Be(s)	0	0	9.50	16.44
BeO(s)	−609.6	−580.3	14.14	25.52
BeCl$_2$(s)	−490.4	−445.6	82.68	64.85
BeSO$_4$(s)	−1205.20	−1093.80	77.91	85.69
Boron				
B(s)	0	0	5.86	11.09
BF$_3$(g)	−1137.0	−1120.33	254.12	50.46
BCl$_3$(ℓ)	−427.2	−387.4	206.3	106.7
(g)	−403.76	−388.77	290.10	62.72
B$_2$O$_3$(s)	−1272.77	−1193.65	53.97	62.93
H$_3$BO$_3$(s)	−1094.33	−968.92	88.83	81.38
B$_2$H$_6$(g)	35.6	86.7	232.11	56.90

Formula	ΔH_f^o kJ mol^{-1}	ΔG_f^o kJ mol^{-1}	S^o J K^{-1} mol^{-1}	C_p^o J K^{-1} mol^{-1}
Bromine				
Br$_2$(ℓ)	0	0	152.231	75.689
(g)	30.907	3.110	245.463	36.02
Br(g)	111.884	82.396	175.022	20.786
Br$^-$(aq)	−121.55	−103.96	82.4	−
HBr(g)	−36.40	−53.45	198.695	29.142
BrF(g)	−93.85	−109.18	228.97	32.97
BrF$_3$(g)	−255.60	−229.43	292.53	66.61
BrF$_5$(g)	−428.9	−350.6	320.19	99.62
Calcium				
Ca(s)	0	0	41.42	25.31
Ca^{2+}(aq)	−542.83	−553.58	−53.1	−
CaO(s)	−635.09	−604.03	39.75	42.80
Ca(OH)$_2$(s)	−986.09	−898.49	83.39	87.49
CaF$_2$(s)	−1219.6	−1167.3	68.87	67.03
CaSO$_4$(s)	−1434.11	−1321.79	106.7	99.66
CaSO$_4$.2H$_2$O(s)	−2022.63	−1797.28	194.1	186.02
CaCO$_3$(s, calcite)	−1206.92	−1128.79	92.9	81.88
Carbon				
C(s,graphite)	0	0	5.740	8.527
C(s,diamond)	1.895	2.900	2.377	6.113
C$_{60}$(s)	2327.	−	−	−
C(g)	716.682	671.257	158.096	20.838
CO(g)	−110.525	−137.168	197.674	29.142
CO$_2$(g)	−393.509	−394.359	213.74	37.11
H$_2$CO$_3$(aq)	−699.65	−623.08	187.4	−
HCO$_3^-$(aq)	−691.99	−586.77	91.2	−
CO$_3^{2-}$(aq)	−677.14	−527.81	−56.9	−
Cesium				
Cs(s)	0	0	85.23	32.17
Cs$^+$(aq)	−258.28	−292.02	133.05	−
Chlorine				
Cl$_2$(g)	0	0	223.066	33.907
(aq)	−23.4	6.94	121.	−
Cl(g)	121.679	105.680	165.198	21.840
Cl$^-$(aq)	−167.159	−131.244	56.5	−
ClO$^-$(aq)	−107.1	−36.8	42.	−
ClO$_4^-$(aq)	−129.33	−8.52	182.0	−
HCl(g)	−92.307	−95.299	186.908	29.12
HClO(aq)	−120.9	−79.9	142.	−
ClF(g)	−54.48	−55.94	217.78	32.05
ClF$_3$(g)	−163.2	−123.0	281.61	63.85
Chromium				
Cr(s)	0	0	23.77	23.35
Cr$_2$O$_7^{2-}$(aq)	−1490.3	−1301.1	−261.9	−

Formula	ΔH_f^o kJ mol^{-1}	ΔG_f^o kJ mol^{-1}	S^o J K^{-1} mol^{-1}	C_p^o J K^{-1} mol^{-1}
Copper				
Cu(s)	0	0	33.150	24.435
Cu$^+$(aq)	71.67	49.98	40.6	–
Cu^{2+}(aq)	64.77	65.49	–99.6	–
Cu$_2$O(s)	–168.6	–146.0	93.14	63.64
CuO(s)	–157.3	–129.7	42.63	42.30
Fluorine				
F$_2$(g)	0	0	202.78	31.30
F(g)	78.99	61.91	158.754	22.744
F$^-$(aq)	–332.63	–278.79	–13.8	–
HF(g)	–271.1	–273.2	173.779	29.133
(aq)	–320.08	–296.85	–88.7	–
Helium				
He(g)	0	0	126.150	20.786
(aq)	–1.7	19.7	54.4	–
Hydrogen				
H$_2$(g)	0	0	130.684	28.824
H(g)	217.965	203.247	114.713	20.784
H$^+$(aq)	0	0	0	–
OH$^-$(aq)	–229.994	–157.244	–10.75	–
H$_2$O(ℓ)	–285.830	–237.129	69.91	75.291
(g)	–241.818	–228.572	188.825	33.577
H$_2$O$_2$(ℓ)	–187.78	–120.35	109.6	89.1
(g)	–136.31	–105.57	232.7	43.1
Iodine				
I$_2$(s)	0	0	116.135	54.438
I$_2$(g)	62.438	19.360	260.69	36.90
I(g)	106.838	70.250	180.791	20.786
I$^-$(aq)	–55.19	–51.57	111.3	–
HI(g)	26.48	1.70	206.594	29.158
Iron				
Fe(s)	0	0	27.28	25.10
Fe^{2+}(aq)	–89.1	–78.90	–137.7	–
Fe^{3+}(aq)	–48.5	–4.7	—315.9	–
Fe$_2$O$_3$(s, hematite)	–824.2	–742.2	87.40	103.85
Fe$_3$O$_4$(s, magnetite)	–1118.4	–1015.4	146.4	143.43
Lead				
Pb(s)	0	0	64.81	26.44
Pb^{2+}(aq)	–1.7	–24.43	10.5	–
PbO$_2$(s)	–277.4	–217.33	68.6	64.64
PbS(s)	–100.4	–98.7	91.2	49.50
PbSO$_4$(s)	–919.94	–813.14	148.57	103.207

Formula	ΔH_f^o kJ mol^{-1}	ΔG_f^o kJ mol^{-1}	S^o J K^{-1} mol^{-1}	C_p^o J K^{-1} mol^{-1}
Lithium				
Li(s)	0	0	29.12	24.77
Li$^+$(aq)	−278.49	−293.31	13.4	68.6
LiOH(s)	−484.93	−438.95	42.80	49.66
LiCl(s)	−408.61	−384.37	59.33	47.99
Magnesium				
Mg(s)	0	0	32.68	24.89
Mg^{2+}(aq)	−466.85	−454.8	−138.1	−
MgO(s)	−601.70	−569.45	26.94	37.15
MgCO$_3$(s)	−1095.8	−1012.1	65.7	75.52
MgSO$_4$(s)	−1284.9	−1170.7	91.6	96.48
Manganese				
Mn(s)	0	0	32.01	26.32
Mn^{2+}(aq)	−220.75	−228.1	−73.6	−
MnO$_4^-$(aq)	−541.4	−447.2	191.2	−
MnO$_2$(s)	−520.03	−465.14	53.05	54.14
Mercury				
Hg(ℓ)	0	0	76.02	27.983
(g)	61.317	31.820	174.96	20.786
Hg^{2+}(aq)	171.1	164.40	−32.2	−
Hg$_2^{2+}$(aq)	172.4	153.52	84.5	−
HgO(s)	−90.83	−58.539	70.29	44.06
HgS(s)	−58.2	−50.6	82.4	48.41
Neon				
Ne(g)	0	0	146.328	20.786
(aq)	−4.6	19.3	66.1	−
Nickel				
Ni(s)	0	0	29.87	26.07
Ni^{2+}(aq)	−54.0	−45.6	−128.9	−
NiS	−82.0	−79.5	52.97	47.11
Ni(CO)$_4$(g)	−602.91	−587.26	410.6	145.18
(ℓ)	−633.0	−588.2	313.4	204.6
Nitrogen				
N$_2$(g)	0	0	191.61	29.125
N(g)	472.704	455.563	153.298	20.786
N$_2$O(g)	82.05	104.20	219.85	38.45
NO(g)	90.25	86.55	210.761	29.844
N$_2$O$_3$(g)	83.72	139.46	312.28	65.61
NO$_2$(g)	33.18	51.31	240.06	37.20
N$_2$O$_4$(ℓ)	−19.50	97.54	209.2	142.7
(g)	9.16	97.89	304.29	77.28
N$_2$O$_5$(g)	11.3	115.1	355.7	84.5

....continued

Appendix 1

Formula	ΔH_f^o kJ mol^{-1}	ΔG_f^o kJ mol^{-1}	S^o J K^{-1} mol^{-1}	C_p^o J K^{-1} mol^{-1}
Nitrogen (cont.)				
NH$_3$(g)	−46.11	−16.45	192.45	35.06
(aq)	−80.29	−26.50	111.3	−
NH$_4^+$(aq)	−132.51	−79.31	113.4	−
NO$_3^-$(aq)	−205.0	−108.74	146.4	−
HNO$_3$(ℓ)	−174.10	−80.71	155.60	109.87
NH$_4$NO$_3$(s)	−365.56	−183.87	151.08	139.3
NH$_4$Cl(s)	−314.43	−202.87	94.6	84.1
Oxygen				
O$_2$(g)	0	0	205.138	29.355
(aq)	−11.7	16.4	110.9	−
O(g)	249.170	231.731	161.055	21.912
O$_3$(g)	142.7	163.2	238.93	39.20
Phosphorus				
P(s, white)	0	0	41.09	23.840
P(g)	314.64	278.25	163.193	20.786
P$_4$(g)	58.91	24.44	279.98	67.15
PH$_3$(g)	5.4	13.4	210.23	37.11
P$_4$O$_{10}$(s)	−2984.0	−2697.7	228.86	211.71
H$_3$PO$_4$(aq)	−1288.34	−1142.54	158.2	−
H$_2$PO$_4^-$(aq)	−1296.29	−1130.28	90.4	−
HPO$_4^{2-}$(aq)	−1292.14	−1089.23	−33.5	−
PO$_4^{3-}$(aq)	−1277.4	−1018.7	−222.	−
PF$_3$(g)	−918.8	−897.5	273.24	58.70
PCl$_3$(g)	−287.0	−267.8	311.78	71.84
PCl$_5$(g)	−374.9	−305.0	364.58	112.80
Potassium				
K(s)	0	0	64.18	29.58
K$^+$(aq)	−252.38	−283.27	102.5	−
KOH(s)	−424.764	−379.08	78.9	64.9
KCl(s)	−436.747	−409.14	82.59	51.30
Rubidium				
Rb(s)	0	0	76.78	31.062
Rb$^+$(aq)	−251.17	−283.98	121.50	−
Silicon				
Si(s)	0	0	18.83	20.00
SiO$_2$(s, quartz)	−910.94	−856.64	41.84	44.43
SiH$_4$(g)	34.3	56.9	204.62	42.84
SiF$_4$(g)	−1614.94	−1572.65	282.49	73.64

Formula	ΔH_f^o kJ mol^{-1}	ΔG_f^o kJ mol^{-1}	S^o J K^{-1} mol^{-1}	C_p^o J K^{-1} mol^{-1}
Silver				
Ag(s)	0	0	42.55	25.351
Ag$^+$(aq)	105.579	77.107	72.68	–
AgCl(s)	–127.068	–109.789	96.2	50.79
AgCl$_2^-$(aq)	–245.2	–215.4	231.4	–
AgBr(s)	–100.37	–96.90	107.1	52.38
Ag(NH$_3$)$_2^+$	–111.29	–17.12	245.2	–
AgCN(s)	146.0	156.9	107.19	66.73
Ag(CN)$_2^-$(aq)	270.3	305.5	192.	–
Sodium				
Na(s)	0	0	51.21	28.24
Na$^+$(aq)	–240.12	–261.905	59.0	–
NaCl(s)	–411.153	–384.138	72.13	50.50
NaH(s)	–56.275	–33.46	40.016	36.401
NaOH(s)	–425.609	–379.494	64.455	59.54
Na$_2$CO$_3$(s)	–1130.68	–1044.44	134.98	112.30
Sulfur				
S(s, rhombic)	0	0	31.80	22.64
S(g)	278.805	238.250	167.821	23.673
S$_2$(g)	128.37	79.30	228.18	32.47
S$_8$(g)	102.30	49.63	430.98	156.44
H$_2$S(g)	–20.63	–33.56	205.79	34.23
H$_2$S(aq)	–39.7	–27.83	121.	–
HS$^-$(aq)	–17.6	12.08	62.8	–
S^{2-}(aq)	33.1	85.8	–14.6	–
SO$_2$(g)	–296.830	–300.194	248.22	39.87
SO$_3$(g)	–395.72	–371.06	256.76	50.67
H$_2$SO$_4$(ℓ)	–813.989	–690.003	156.904	138.91
HSO$_4^-$(aq)	–887.34	–755.99	131.8	–
SO$_4^{2-}$(aq)	–909.27	–744.53	20.1	–
SF$_4$(g)	–774.9	–731.3	292.03	73.01
SF$_6$(g)	–1209	–1105.3	291.82	97.28
Tin				
Sn(s)	0	0	51.55	26.99
SnH$_4$(g)	162.8	188.3	227.68	48.95
Xenon				
Xe(g)	0	0	169.683	20.786
(aq)	–17.6	13.4	65.7	–
XeF$_4$(s)	–261.5	–	–	–
Zinc				
Zn(s)	0	0	41.63	25.40
Zn^{2+}(aq)	–153.89	–147.06	–112.1	–
ZnO(s)	–348.28	–318.30	43.64	40.25
ZnS(s)	–205.98	–201.29	57.7	46.0

Part II Organic substances

Formula		ΔH_f^o kJ mol^{-1}	ΔG_f^o kJ mol^{-1}	S^o J K^{-1} mol^{-1}	C_p^o J K^{-1} mol^{-1}
CH$_4$(g)	methane	−74.81	−50.72	186.264	35.309
(aq)		−89.04	−34.33	83.87	–
C$_2$H$_6$(g)	ethane	−84.68	−32.82	229.60	52.63
C$_3$H$_8$(g)	propane	−103.847	−23.370	270.019	73.789
C$_4$H$_{10}$(g)	n-butane	−126.148	−16.985	310.227	98.273
C$_4$H$_{10}$(g)	2-methylpropane	−134.99	−21.44	295.50	96.65
C$_5$H$_{12}$(ℓ)	n-pentane	−173.49	−9.71	263.47	167.19
(g)		−146.76	−8.65	349.56	120.04
C$_5$H$_{12}$(g)	2-methylbutane	−153.70	−13.86	343.74	118.87
C$_5$H$_{12}$(g)	2,2-dimethylpropane	−167.92	−16.82	306.00	120.88
C$_6$H$_{14}$(ℓ)	n-hexane	−198.782	−4.035	296.018	195.016
(g)		−167.193	−0.023	388.510	143.002
C$_7$H$_{16}$(ℓ)	n-heptane	−224.388	1.327	328.570	224.723
(g)		−187.778	8.290	428.007	165.918
C$_8$H$_{18}$(ℓ)	n-octane	−249.952	6.707	361.205	254.094
(g)		−208.447	16.718	466.835	193.833
C$_6$H$_{12}$(ℓ)	cyclohexane	−156.231	26.886	204.347	156.482
(g)		−123.135	31.956	298.345	105.558
C$_2$H$_4$(g)	ethene	52.26	68.15	219.56	43.56
C$_3$H$_6$(g)	propene	20.418	62.819	267.049	63.867
C$_3$H$_6$(g)	cyclopropane	53.220	104.278	238.012	90.196
C$_2$H$_2$(g)	ethyne	226.73	209.20	200.94	43.93
C$_3$H$_4$(g)	propyne	185.435	194.487	248.221	60.677
C$_6$H$_6$(ℓ)	benzene	49.036	124.534	173.259	136.106
(g)		82.927	129.789	269.308	82.530
C$_7$H$_8$(ℓ)	toluene	12.008	113.959	220.957	166.021
(g)		49.999	122.191	320.771	105.085
CH$_3$OH(ℓ)	methanol	−238.66	−166.27	126.8	81.6
(g)		−200.66	−161.96	239.81	43.89
C$_2$H$_5$OH(ℓ)	ethanol	−277.69	−174.78	160.7	111.46
(g)		−235.10	−168.49	282.70	65.44
(CH$_2$OH)$_2$(ℓ)	1,2-ethanediol	−454.80	−323.08	166.9	149.8
HCHO(g)	formaldehyde	−115.901	−109.870	218.765	35.396
CH$_3$CHO(ℓ)	acetaldehyde	−192.30	−128.12	160.2	–
(g)		−166.19	−128.86	250.3	57.3
(CH$_3$)$_2$CO(ℓ)	acetone	−248.111	−155.261	200.414	125.018
(g)		−217.568	−152.931	295.040	73.350
(CH$_3$)$_2$O(g)	dimethyl ether	−184.05	−112.59	266.38	64.39

Formula		ΔH_f^o kJ mol^{-1}	ΔG_f^o kJ mol^{-1}	S^o J K^{-1} mol^{-1}	$C_p^{\,o}$ J K^{-1} mol^{-1}
HCOOH(ℓ)	formic acid	−424.72	−361.35	128.95	99.04
(aq)		−425.43	−372.3	163.	−
HCOO$^-$ (aq)	formate	−425.55	−351.0	92.	−
CH$_3$COOH(ℓ)	acetic acid	−484.5	−389.9	159.8	124.3
(aq)		−485.76	−396.46	178.7	−
CH$_3$COO$^-$ (aq)	acetate	−486.01	−369.31	86.6	−
(COOH)$_2$(s)	oxalic acid	−827.2	−	−	117.
CH$_3$NH$_2$(ℓ)	methylamine	−47.3	35.7	150.21	−
(g)		−22.97	32.16	243.41	53.1
(CH$_3$)$_2$NH(ℓ)	dimethylamine	−43.9	70.0	182.34	137.7
(g)		−18.45	68.51	273.07	70.7
CH$_3$Cl(g)	chloromethane	−80.83	−57.37	234.58	40.75
CH$_2$Cl$_2$(ℓ)	dichloromethane	−121.46	−67.26	177.8	100.0
(g)		−92.47	−65.87	270.23	50.96
CHCl$_3$(ℓ)	trichloromethane	−134.47	−73.66	201.7	113.8
(g)		−103.14	−70.34	295.71	65.69
CCl$_4$(ℓ)	tetrachloromethane	−135.44	−65.21	216.40	131.75
(g)		−102.9	−60.59	309.85	83.30
CFCl$_3$(ℓ)	fluorotrichloromethane	−301.33	−236.79	225.35	121.55
(g)		−276	−238	309.93	78.07
CH$_3$NO$_2$(ℓ)	nitromethane	−113.09	−14.42	171.75	105.98

INDEX

ff indicates the beginning of a discussion extending
over several pages.
t indicates a table of data.

Basic SI quantities, symbols and units

Quantity and symbol	SI Unit	Abbreviation
length	metre	m
mass	kilogram	kg
time	second	s
electric current	ampere	A
temperature	kelvin	K
amount of substance	mole	mol

SI units for derived quantities

Quantity	SI unit	Abbreviation and equivalent units
velocity or speed	metre/second	$m\ s^{-1}$
acceleration	metre/second^2	$m\ s^{-2}$
force = mass×acceleration	newton	$N = kg\ m\ s^{-2}$
pressure = force/area	pascal	$Pa = N\ m^{-2} = kg\ m^{-1}\ s^{-2}$
volume = length^3	cubic metre	m^3
density = mass/volume	kilogram/metre^3	$kg\ m^{-3}$
concentration = amount/volume	mole/metre^3	$mol\ m^{-3}$
energy = work = force×distance	joule	$J \doteq N\ m = kg\ m^2\ s^{-2} = Pa\ m^3$
power = energy/time	watt	$W = J\ s^{-1}$
electric charge = current×time	coulomb	$C = A\ s$
electric potential = energy/charge	volt	$V = J\ C^{-1}$

Some commonly used non-SI units

Quantity	Unit	Abbreviation and equivalent basic units
volume	litre	$L = 10^{-3}\ m^3 = 1\ dm^3$
mass	tonne	$t = 10^3\ kg$
pressure	bar	$bar = 10^5\ Pa$
pressure	torr	$Torr = (101325\ /\ 760)\ Pa$
length	ångstrom	$Å = 10^{-10}\ m$
energy	electron volt	$eV = 1.6022 \times 10^{-19}\ J$
energy	calorie	$4.184\ J$ exactly
mass	atomic mass unit	$amu = 1.6605 \times 10^{-27}\ kg$

Where appropriate, the uncertainties are indicated in brackets and apply to the digit in the last decimal place.